D1345108

Learning, Development,
and Culture

Learning, Development, and Culture

Essays in Evolutionary Epistemology

Edited by
H. C. Plotkin
Department of Psychology, University College, London

1807 1982

JOHN WILEY & SONS
Chichester · New York · Brisbane · Toronto · Singapore

Library of Congress Cataloging in Publication Data:
Main entry under title:
Learning, Development, and Culture.

  Includes indexes.
  1. Evolution—Addresses, essays, lectures.
2. Social evolution Addresses, essays, lectures.
I. Plotkin, H. C. (Henry C.)
QH371.E77   575   82-1947

ISBN 0 471 10219 9   AACR2

British Library Cataloguing in Publication Data:
Learning, Development, and Culture.

  1. Knowledge, Theory of
I. Plotkin, H. C.
  121   BD161

ISBN 0 471 10219 9

Photosetting by Thomson Press (India) Ltd.
and printed in the United States of America

Contents

Preface ix

List of original contributors xiii

List of reprinted authors xv

SECTION 1 INTRODUCTION
1 Evolutionary epistemology and evolutionary theory 3
  H. C. Plotkin

SECTION 2 SOME ISSUES IN EVOLUTIONARY THEORY
2 Teleological and teleonomic: a new analysis 17
  Ernst Mayr

3 Natural selection, adaptation, and progress. 39
  G. C. Williams

SECTION 3 CLASSIC PIECES IN EVOLUTIONARY EPISTEMOLOGY
4 On a relationship between the theory of selection and epistemology 63
  Georg Simmel

5 Evolutionary epistemology 73
  Donald T. Campbell

6 Of clouds and clocks   109
  Karl R. Popper   .

7 Kant's doctrine of the a priori in the light of contemporary biology   121
  Konrad Lorenz

8 Functions and structures of adaptation   145
  Jean Piaget

9 Organism and environment   151
  R. C. Lewontin

SECTION 4 EVOLUTION, BEHAVIOUR AND SOCIO-CULTURE
10 Evolutionary adaptation   173
   C. H. Waddington

11 A comment on genetic assimilation   195
   G. C. Williams

12 Evolution and behavior: an iconoclastic view   205
   Jack P. Hailman

13 Behavioural antecedents of sociality   255
   Jeffrey R. Baylis and Zuleyma Tang Halpin

14 The naked meme.   273
   David L. Hull

SECTION 5 EVOLUTION, DEVELOPMENT, AND LEARNING
15 Evolution and development   331
   L. Wolpert and W. D. Stein

16 The epigenetic approach to the evolution of organisms—with notes
   on its relevance to social and cultural evolution   343
   Mae-Wan Ho and Peter T. Saunders

17 Conceptions of prenatal development: behavioral embryology   363
   Gilbert Gottlieb

18 Rules and reciprocity in behavioural development.   391
   P. P. G. Bateson

19 Learning and the evolution of developmental systems 411
   Timothy D. Johnston

20 Learning in the context of a hierarchy of knowledge gaining
   processes 443
   H. C. Plotkin and F. J. Odling-Smee

Author index 473

Subject index 481

Preface

All theories change, which is as it should be. Evolutionary theory is no exception. It has been altered in major ways at least four times in the last two hundred years, and it is constantly undergoing minor shifts and adjustments. An exceptionally vigorous and wide-ranging growth and change in evolutionary theory has occurred during the last ten years and when the history of science is written at some far-distant future date, the last quarter of the 20th century will, I think, be noted as a period of major development and importance for biology. This book is an expression of this change. I hope that it will be instrumental in bringing about further change.

Macbeth's (*Darwin Retried*: Gambit, Boston 1971) view that disciplines that do not cultivate self-criticism and iconoclasm are doomed to experience less palatable criticism and condemnation from outside is surely true. When I first thought of bringing the writings of a number of, sometimes disparate, people together between single covers, I was only just becoming aware of how deep is the discontent within contemporary evolutionary theory. My purpose then was purely constructive—to attempt to show that thinking of living systems as knowledge systems is a potentially powerful way of synthesizing theory across the widest reaches of biology. Some of the contributors to this volume have since convinced me of the need for an accompanying iconoclasm, and so I have tried in this book to strike a balance between critical re-appraisal and constructive analysis.

My reason for including in this anthology both original contributions and what I judge to be classic pieces of writing is simply that, in some cases, once said things are not again said better. Science, however, does not stand still and the things people are thinking and doing now, even if they do not themselves become classic pieces, are as important in the context of the present as what we can judge with hindsight to have been significant work in the past. As to what a 'classic' is, of course I recognize that on this there would be little agreement — certainly some (surely few would argue that G. C. Williams' 1966 book is not a classic, but that book is a rarity), but not much (Lorenz's essay on Kant's notion of the a priori is little known, much less widely judged to be significant). In the end my choice reflects my intellectual debt — those that were formative experiences for my own thinking. It was a hard task to keep the list to manageable length. To this end I concentrated on recent (post 1960) work. That made the judgement of 'classic' that much more difficult, but it also led to essays that are more closely connected to current issues. I was also guided by the conceptual structure of the book.

This structure is apparent in the five section headings. The heart of the book is the third section. Evolutionary epistemology has been developed in large part by biologists whose work has focused on behaviour, and who have therefore been acutely aware of the need for biological theory to extend to all aspects of behaviour and socio-culture. The writings of some of these are presented in this middle section, together with a critical view of the approach by a contemporary evolutionist.

The second section arises from evolutionary epistemology having to deal with cognitive and social attributes that man possesses in copious and extraordinary form. Man's exalted position in these respects gives rise to much conceptual difficulty when one is thinking about the evolution of these attributes. The second section tries to deal with these by presenting arguments in support of the teleology–teleonomy distinction and against the notion of progress in evolution. I feel that it is always important to get rid of misconceptions first, and only then to get to the heart of the matter. Hence the order of these two sections. The first, introductory, section is intended to orient the reader.

The acid test of an evolutionary theory for me is its ability to account for the evolution of culture. Recent books by Lumsden and Wilson (*Genes, mind and culture*: Harvard University Press, Cambridge 1981) and Cavalli-Sforza and Feldman (*Cultural transmission and evolution*: Princeton University Press, Princeton 1981) bear witness to the way this area has again exploded into life. David Hull remarks in his chapter in this book that socio-culture is an essential and central topic within the programme of evolutionary epistemology. The evolution of socio-culture and socio-cultural evolution are covered in the fourth section. In this section some consideration is also given to the broader issues of the evolution of behaviour and the possible role of behaviour in evolution.

Evolutionary epistemology is concerned with that nexus that is formed out of genetics, epigenetics and individual behaviour, and how these give rise to socio-culture. Development in general and learning specifically are essential to the analysis of socio-culture. Thus the final section is devoted to the relationships between epigenetics, learning and evolution.

I have provided each major section with a brief linking commentary. These comments will help the reader who is unfamiliar with the general approach taken in this book. Their advantage in this respect will, I hope, outweigh any irritation that their brevity will cause the cognoscenti. The book is intended to convert as well as to instruct.

There is one final general comment that must be stressed. This book is not about epistemology as philosophers deal with it. It is to be hoped that many of the chapters will be of interest to philosophers, but only one of the original contributors is a philosopher by training and trade and I would not like the book to be thought pretentious in this respect. I have taken the phrase evolutionary epistemology directly from the writings of Donald T. Campbell and use it in the title to this volume because I am indebted to him for directing me down this particular path; and also because, through his programme of research, the phrase is becoming increasingly used and familiar amongst evolutionists, especially those interested in socio-culture.

I must express my thanks to Maureen Cohen and Marjorie Edwards who helped with some of the typing of manuscripts, and Chris Chromerty who provided most of the illustrations. Celia Bird and Linda Burden of John Wiley & Sons assisted and supported me in all manner of ways regarding the book. It is to Mellissa Li, however, that I must address much the largest vote of thanks. She tirelessly typed and retyped large parts of the manuscript and was brave in the face of the daunting task of compiling the index. Donald T. Campbell and F. J. Odling-Smee read and commented on an early draft of chapter 1 and I am grateful to them for that and for their general encouragement. But the faults of that chapter, and of the book at large, are, of course, my responsibility.

List of original contributors

JEFFREY R. BAYLIS

Department of Zoology, University of Wisconsin, Madison, Wisconsin

JACK P. HAILMAN

Department of Zoology, University of Wisconsin, Madison, Wisconsin

ZULEYMA TANG HALPIN

Department of Biology, University of Missouri, St. Louis, Missouri

MAE-WAN HO

Department of Biology, The Open University, Milton Keynes, Bucks

DAVID L. HULL

Department of Philosophy, University of Wisconsin–Milwaukee, Wisconsin

TIMOTHY D. JOHNSTON

North Carolina Division of Mental Health, Raleigh, North Carolina

R. C. LEWONTIN

Museum of Comparative Zoology, Harvard University, Cambridge, Massachusetts

F. J. ODLING-SMEE

Departments of Psychology and Biology, Brunel University, Uxbridge, Middx

H. C. PLOTKIN

Department of Psychology, University College London, London

PETER T. SAUNDERS   *Department of Mathematics, Queen Elizabeth College, London*

W. D. STEIN   *Department of Biochemistry, The Hebrew University, Jerusalem*

G. C. WILLIAMS   *Department of Ecology and Evolution, State University of New York, Stony Brook, New York*

L. WOLPERT   *Department of Biology as Applied to Medicine, The Middlesex Hospital Medical School, London*

List of reprinted authors

P. P. G. Bateson

Donald T. Campbell

Gilbert Gottlieb

Konrad Lorenz

Ernst Mayr

Jean Piaget

Karl R. Popper

Georg Simmel

C. H. Waddington

G. C. Williams

SECTION 1

Introduction

Learning, Development, and Culture
Edited by H. C. Plotkin
© 1982, John Wiley & Sons Ltd.

CHAPTER 1

Evolutionary epistemology and evolutionary theory

H. C. Plotkin

There are two aspects to a complete account of evolutionary epistemology. They are linked and yet differentiable. The first is a cluster of issues that bears upon problems in epistemology such as pragmatism, empiricism, the validation and legitimation of knowledge; and the closely related view that man as 'knower' has certain mental or cognitive abilities that have been, and are, crucial to his survival and evolution. The notion that the ability to know has evolved and is a basic biological trait of man has implications for the philosophy of knowledge (see Quine, 1969; Rescher, 1977; and Shimony, 1971, for examples), and is central to any evolutionary approach to psychology. The second aspect of evolutionary epistemology is a way of looking at biology and it is built on two notions. The first is the idea that biological systems in general are knowledge systems, that evolution itself is a process of gaining knowledge, and (rather more contentiously) that all forms of knowledge-gain share certain features. Again a number of eminent philosophers have contributed to this view (for example Popper, 1959 and 1972; Toulmin, 1976), as, of course, have certain working biologists (Ashby, 1952; Campbell, 1959; Goodwin, 1976; and Piaget, 1971, to name but a few). The second is the idea that evolutionary theory must provide a complete account of the evolution of every aspect of any biological system; that it must encompass the phenotype as well as genes and genotypes; and hence that it must deal with development as well.

There is nothing contradictory between evolutionary epistemology as philosophy, psychology or biology, yet each can be pursued separately. Nor is there

3

anything intrinsically more fundamental to one as opposed to the other. This book, however, is about biology and so this brief chapter is concerned with the second aspect. Historically, though, there has been much cross-referencing between the philosophical, the psychological and the biological—most often, people have not even made the distinctions. The best example of an integrated approach is Campbell (1974, and his previous work referred to in that essay). He presents an incomparable historical perspective on thinking in evolutionary epistemology over the last one hundred years, and until there have been further significant advances other historical treatments will be redundant and derivative. An edited version of Campbell's essay is reprinted as Chapter 5 in this book.

EVOLUTIONARY EPISTEMOLOGY AS BIOLOGY

There is much discussion at present as to whether the adaptations that are formed in individual organisms have anything to do with speciation (see Gould, 1980; Lewin, 1980; Hailman, Chapter 12 of this book). In the absence of much supporting evidence for the gradualism of neo-Darwinian theory, it is reasonable to adopt a sceptical stance and doubt the purported coupling of micro- and macroevolutionary processes. Historically, however, evolutionary theory is not just about the origin of species. What Hailman (Chapter 12) refers to as the 'character-environment correlation' of many phenotypic attributes is a major area of evolutionary theory. This is the domain of adaptations and the ways in which phenotypes interact with their environments. It is here in particular that evolutionary epistemology has something to contribute.

Adaptations as knowledge

The notion of adaptation is very old: it was at the heart of Darwin's *Origin of Species*, and it continues to be central to evolutionary theory. There has been argument regarding definitional and semantic issues which arise whenever the word adaptation is used (see Ghiselin, 1966; Brandon, 1978; Stern, 1970) but these are trivial compared to the biological problems that attach to the concept. A composite characterization of what adaptation has come to mean, based on writings of the last thirty years or so, is (1) that adaptations are attributes of the phenotype and can only be used to refer to aspects of individual organisms (Bok and Wahlert, 1965; Williams, 1966; Bok, 1980); (2) that each adaptation must either reduce the energy costs of the phenotype (Bok, 1980), or enhance its probability of survival (Dobzhansky, 1956, 1968), or both (though see Williams 1966—Chapter 3 of this book—for reservations regarding adaptations and survival, and Stern (1970) for linkage with reproductive competence); and (3) that each adaptation constitutes a form of organization that is relative to some aspect of the environment (Pittendrigh, 1958; Lorenz, 1969; Waddington, 1969; Lewontin, 1978; Bok, 1980), the relationship between the adaptation and the environment being one of apparent goal- or end-directedness (Sommerhoff, 1950; Medawar, 1951; Pittendrigh, 1958; Waddington, 1959—see Chapter 10 of this book; Simpson, 1964; Williams, 1966).

The third point is of special interest. The seeming end-directed nature of adaptations does not require explanation within a contra-causal or Finalistic framework (see especially Sommerhoff, 1950 and 1969; Pittendrigh, 1958; and Mayr, 1974—Chapter 2 of this book) and need concern us here no further. Rather it is the organization of the adaptation and the way in which that organization is related to components or aspects of the environment that must be the focus of our attention since this is the direct point of contact between biology and evolutionary epistemology.

The origins of any adaptation are uncertain. Contemporary neo-Darwinist theory prescribes an important role for gene mutation, segregation, combination and interaction. Epigenetic theorists argue for a lesser genetic role and for the importance of complex restructurings of genotypic and epigenetic equilibria (Piaget, 1979) and for the canalization of novel developmental responses which arise from 'the intrinsic dynamical structure of the epigenetic system itself, in its interaction with the environment' (Ho and Saunders, 1979, p. 589). However they may first arise, it is clear that the final form of each and every adaptation is determined not merely by genetic factors, but also by subsequent interactions both with the environment and with other developing phenotypic attributes in the course of translation into phenotypic form. The end-product of these complexly interacting chains of chance and contingent factors is then tested by a selective filter (natural selection at the ecological level), and if the phenotypic attribute is retained (and further honed) after many phases of regeneration and repeated testing by the screen of natural selection, then it must be an effective adaptation in the sense that it is contributing to mean phenotypic fitness.

What does effectiveness actually mean in this context? Living creatures are highly improbable entities. They maintain their coherence both by exploiting energy resources in the external world and by avoiding excessively disruptive contact with a largely hostile environment. The interactions that occur between organisms and the external world may be, and usually are, very complex, especially where the active organism partly determines the degree of contact with the world; but however complex they may be, they are essentially a series of challenges to the integrity of the organism. These challenges are met by the collective effectiveness of each organism's set of adaptations. Each adaptation contributes to this effectiveness if it has the capacity to solve, directly or indirectly, a problem that is posed by the organism–environment interaction. But such a capacity is not a random characteristic. As already noted, adaptations are goal-directed, and in the broadest sense the goal is coping with some problem that is posed by the environment (or more correctly, the organism–environment interaction). In order to cope, an adaptation must incorporate within itself elements of that aspect of the environment that constitutes that particular problem. Lorenz may have overstated the case when he wrote of adaptation as a process by which the environment moulds the organism (Lorenz, 1965), or of its being the creation in the organism of a 'progressively detailed image of its environment', the latter certainly being the more accurate characterization of a process where the organism has an active part to play. Campbell (1974), for example, warns that the 'knowledge' of adaptations is expressed in an 'odd and partial language' and is 'an end product mixed with "knowledge" of other contingencies' (p. 447). Nonetheless, the Lorenzian position expresses a powerful conception of any adaptation comprising some form of organization that is congruent with the environmental order to which it is relative. Such congruence can only come about through the gaining and storing of information about the environment, including a programme for the translation of this information into appropriate phenotypic traits, and the subsequent propagation of this information and its re-expression in future organisms.

This style of thought identifies a particular approach to the study of adaptations. It is an approach that is based on understanding the way in which the information underlying any adaptation is gained; identifying where such information is stored; and understanding how it is translated into some phenotypic trait. If there is more than one way of gaining information and more than one site of storage, then there is also the need to understand how various sources of information interact in the production of an adaptation. Finally, it is necessary to know how the information subserving successful adaptations is generated and translated into the structures of future organisms.

Two cautionary notes must be entered here. The first concerns the use of the terms 'information' and 'knowledge'. Sommerhoff wrote about Quine's observation 'that the less a science is advanced, the more does its terminology tend to rest on the uncritical assumption of mutual understanding' (Sommerhoff, 1950, p. 8). Lest we be thought of as backward let us try to be explicit as to meaning, even if in doing so the conventions of information science and epistemological theory are violated. The terms 'information' and 'knowledge' are used interchangeably. They refer to coherent and conserved patterns of order in the environment and the corresponding organization of the phenotype whose end-directedness relates to those particular patterns of environmental order. Thus information or knowledge, in biological terms, describes a *relationship* between the order of the world, whatever that order is, and the answering and reciprocal organization of an organism. It is important to understand that this relationship is not solely one-way since the order of the world is only known by its reflection in the organization of the organism, and also because the order of the world may itself be modified by the organization of the organism (see below). Thus in this context information or knowledge is not absolute and can never be disembodied—it constitutes a relationship of exchange between environmental order and organismic organization that in the long term will increase the biological fitness of the organism. It is always possible that misinformation or irrelevant information may be acquired and stored and expressed in maladaptive phenotypic traits. However, wrong or unimportant knowledge will ultimately by filtered out by selection processes.

The second point of caution concerns the special status that is accorded to the notion of adaptation by theorists such as Williams (1966) and Lewontin (1978, 1979). There has been, and currently still is, much abuse of the concept of adaptation and its use as an explanatory device in biology. Despite these excesses, 'adaptation is a real phenomenon' (Lewontin, 1978) the understanding of which must be pursued using Williams' (1966) ground rule that 'adaptation is a special and onerous concept that should be used only where it is really necessary' (p. 4). The view expressed here, that adaptations are partly the products of epistemic processes, is neutral as regards the debate as to whether adaptation should always be accounted for at the lowest (i.e. genetic) level possible. Similarly, it is not at odds with the position that some or many phenotypic attributes are not adaptations; and it is entirely congruent with the view that adaptations are not necessarily optimal solutions (Lewontin, 1981).

Evolution as a knowledge process

The dominant contemporary version of evolutionary theory, most powerfully articulated by Williams (1966), is cast exclusively in terms of several selective processes resulting in the differential propagation of alternative alleles in the gene pool of a breeding population. One of the grounds for challenging this view is in terms of the adequacy and completeness of a theory that posits only a single unit that is selected (for example Ghiselin, 1981; Plotkin and Odling-Smee, 1981). The argument is that a theory that will encompass all biological phenomena, including those of a socio-cultural origin, will have to be based on multiple selection processes and multiple units that are selected. Whichever position proves to be more adequate, both are consonant with an evolutionary epistemology which maintains that the adaptive organization that exists at multiple levels, from genetic and biochemical substrates through the morphological and behavioural traits of the phenotype and on to its ecological and socio-cultural interactions, is all part-product of processes of information-gain. If a multiple-level theory does prevail, then logically this will require the postulation of information-gain and storage at more than one level (see Plotkin and Odling-Smee, 1979, 1981, for just such a model). This then leads directly to the question as to whether every level of information-gain operates on the basis of some single algorithm, or whether there are significant differences in the way in which different levels gain knowledge.

Although there are differences of view on this issue, especially as regards the possible uniqueness of man's creative thought and the way science operates, there is some agreement that at the more fundamental levels of information-gain such as the genetic, epigenetic and individual learning levels, it is descriptively possible to embrace all levels by a single algorithm. Campbell (1974) argues for a great deal more than descriptive convenience, claiming that a blind-variation-selective-retention routine is the only way by which knowledge can be gained. His position will be followed in this chapter. Campbell suggests the operation of (1) the generation of variants, (2) consistent selection on those variants, and (3) devices for propagating the selected variants. It matters not whether the variants are in the form of alternative alleles and hence ultimately different phenotypes, or whether one feels it necessary to include variant developmental pathways, variant behaviours, or variant ideas and hypotheses. The processes are the same: the underlying mechanisms subserving the processes will be different in each case.

It is worth noting that the set of processes that Campbell generalizes to all forms of knowledge gain are very similar to those presented by Lewontin (1970, for example) as embodying 'the principle of evolution by natural selection'. It is also worth noting that the elegant simplicity of Williams' argument (for evolution as being the action of natural selection on alternative alleles in Mendelian populations) is also present in a multiple-level model rooted in evolutionary epistemology. All forms of knowledge gain in any biological system, and within any level of any system, appear to be achieved in the same way. Thus, whether one chooses to consider evolution as comprising changes in gene frequencies of breeding populations, or extends the theory to include within-organism changes during development and learning (Plotkin and Odling-Smee, 1979) and the between-animal interactions that make up socio-cultural phenomena (Campbell, 1965; Durham, 1979; Plotkin and Odling-Smee, 1981), in evolutionary epistemological terms it becomes merely a matter of how many levels of a nested hierarchical information-gaining system are required for a complete account. But insofar as evolution constitutes of change above all else, and irrespective of whether this change is gradual or sudden and be it change in genes and phenotypic form and function or alterations in cultural items, since all these changes are driven by events in the external world and in the organism–environment interaction which have to be tracked over the shorter or longer term by biological systems, then evolution is clearly in part a 'knowledge process' (Campbell, 1974).

A priori and a posteriori

The consequences of a nested, hierarchical, knowledge-gaining system have been stated by Campbell (1974) and expanded upon by Plotkin and Odling-Smee (1981). Information is always gained a posteriori in biological systems. That is, it is established by the effects of selection on variant forms, and it is only after this occurs that the selected variants are projected into the future. Biological systems are never prescient. They may, however, simulate prescience by feeding information that has been gained a posteriori at a more fundamental level of a hierarchy to another less fundamental level where it then appears to be *a priori* knowledge. These effects are especially marked in the cognitive functioning of animals (see Chapters 19 and 20 of this book). They have never been adequately dealt with as biological phenomena except within the framework of evolutionary epistemology. (It might be noted that the phrase 'biological system' is used as a short-hand to encompass all forms of life—procaryote and eucaryote—and all levels of organization—from genetics to ecology—within them.)

Knowledge and activity

Piaget's genetic epistemology (see especially Piaget, 1971) consistently began with 'the fact that no form of knowledge, not even perceptual knowledge, constitutes a simple copy of reality, because it always includes a process of assimilation to previous structures' (p. 4—see also chapter 8 of this book). This means that any representation of the environment, in its broadest sense any effect of the environment as it impinges on an organism, is acted upon and changed by the structure of the biological system that it enters. This in turn means that knowledge gain is never passive. It is always active in this special sense. Furthermore, 'knowledge does not start in the subject...or in the object...but rather in interactions between subject and object' (pp. 27–28). This view obviously relates closely to the definition of knowledge given in the section above on 'adaptation and knowledge'. Knowledge is a dynamic, dialectical interaction between information entering a biological system and thus changing that system, but in turn being changed by the pre-existing structure of the system. Any biological system, as 'knower', acts upon the world that it knows and thus changes it. Knowledge is therefore never static and neither is its attainment. It is a constant interplay between a changing world and a changing knower.

This principle of the active nature of knowledge in biological systems is congruent with the repeated insistence of Waddington (e.g. 1959—chapter 10 of this book), and more recently Bateson (1980), that causality in biology is circular rather than linear. Lewontin has argued along similar lines in pointing out that 'Organisms do not experience environments passively; they create and define the environment'; and 'There is a constant interplay of the organism and the environment, so that although natural selection may be adapting the organism to a particular set of environmental circumstances, the evolution of the organism itself changes those circumstances' (Lewontin, 1978, p. 159, See also Chapter 9 of this book).

BIOLOGY AND BEHAVIOUR

Biologists have long been interested in behaviour. Lamarck had a central, a causal, role for behaviour in his view of the evolutionary scheme of things—but the obloquy in which Lamarckian theory is now held (though see Steele, 1980) is, I believe, an important reason why behaviour in this sense has been held outside of the modern synthesis of biology. And though Darwin devoted an entire chapter to instincts in *Origin of Species* and was always very open as to how evolution actually occurs, neither in the masterwork nor in later writings did he contemplate a unique and causal role for behaviour. (By causal role I mean seeing behaviour not just as an effect, a product or consequence of natural selection just as is any other phenotypic attribute, but simultaneously as cause—as one of the processes determining evolution.) The biologists most concerned with the study of behaviour in this century have, of course, been the ethologists. And they were convinced neo-Darwinists. But the comparative study of behaviour was based primarily on the notion of homology, and if behavioural study were ever seen as having a wider role in biology, it was in terms of its contribution to areas of taxonomy that were in doubt. I can think of no ethological writing that has indicated, or even hinted at the possibility, that behaviour may have a deeper role in biology beyond its being the passive outcome of the 'fundamental' forces of evolution. Most recently sociobiology has focused attention once again on behaviour, but once again behaviour is seen as hand-maid to genetics and natural selection. This is the traditional way of dealing with behaviour in biology. Behaviour is made to fit into the accepted framework of biological theory.

There is another way: this is to consider how biological theory needs to be changed in the light of the special characteristics of behaviour. In order to understand why this might be necessary, consider Piaget's (1979) definition of behaviour as 'all actions directed by organisms towards the outside world in order to change conditions therein or to change their own situation in relation to these surroundings' (p. ix). Definitions, of course, are nothing more than statements of theoretical predilections. But think of an example, say micturition in mammals. Frequently micturition is simply the end point of the process of balancing body fluids and salts. In such cases the act of urination might be faithfully recorded on an ethogram, but it really is no different as a phenotypic attribute than the structure of the kidneys themselves and scarcely warrants the label 'behaviour'. However, when micturition is used to mark territory, or directed with force at a competitor as a means of establishing dominance, or used to alter the consistency of soil such that it becomes more malleable, then these clearly are all instances of behaviour as Piaget defined it. There is no question but that animals (and plants too) act on their environments, change them and hence effect their own evolution. Yet such a theoretical position has never been formally established. Waddington hinted at it frequently (see Chapter 10 of this book, for example) and Piaget, deeply influenced by Waddington's writings, wrote extensively on the matter (see Piaget, 1979), though never lucidly and never spelling out either the logical requirements of such a theory or showing how it is compatible in terms of mechanism with neo-Darwinian theory and the central dogma of biology. It has been ecologists such as Southwood (1977) who have come closer than anyone else to the formulation of such a theory. And if the neo-Darwinian theory is wrong and epigenetic approaches to evolution prove to be more encompassing and fruitful, then it is in epigenetic theory (Ho and Saunders, 1979) that there is some room for considering a possible causal role for behaviour in evolution (see Ho and Saunders, Chapter 16 of this book).

It would seem to be self-evident that constructing theory around passive phenotypes whose only role is to propagate genes cannot be good biology because it is so limited and incomplete in scope. A formal inclusion of behaviour into the fabric of evolutionary theory, along with developmental biology, will surely lead to a true 'new synthesis'. One vehicle for such a new synthesis is evolutionary epistemology. There are two main reasons for this. First, evolutionary epistemology has, in the main, been developed by biologists whose first interest has been behaviour, and as a result much of the conceptual ground has been laid. Second, as indicated in the above section on 'knowledge and activity', the conceptual framework of evolutionary epistemology is very close to what is envisaged as the central and defining feature of some future 'new synthesis'. This conceptual framework is an account of every level of organization in any biological system in terms of interactions and information exchanges between each level and every other level, and between each level and the environment.

EVOLUTIONARY EPISTEMOLOGY AND EVOLUTIONARY THEORY

It has already been indicated that insofar as the ability of the theory to cope is concerned, evolutionary epistemology is indifferent as to the number of levels or units of selection needed for a complete account of all biological phenomena. On the other hand, evolutionary epistemology is closely concerned with learning and other forms of cognitive functioning in individual animals, as well as with the interaction between individuals in social and sociocultural settings. It is precisely these latter that stretch the evolution-as-selection-acting-between-alternative-alleles approach beyond its limits and break it. They do so by way of the evolutionary epistemological analysis of adaptations as information. Considering the behavioural consequences of perceptuo-motor development and learning as adaptations, and they can surely be seen in no other light, and considering that they are adaptations to events that occur at rates faster than the temporal resolving power of genes as an information-gaining system, then it has to be the case that the adaptive outcome of such developmental and learning processes must be explained within a framework that is larger than just the genetic one (Plotkin and Odling-Smee, 1979; 1981). Hence a complete evolutionary theory must be one which invokes multiple processes of knowledge-gain, multiple units of selection, and multiple storage sites.

It is, of course, perfectly possible to define evolutionary theory in terms only of genes and natural selection, and to call all the rest of biology something else. But I do not think that Darwin would have been impressed; besides most biologists do not deal with genes or directly with evolutionary theory, but like to think that a single unifying theory of biology will cover what they and everyone else is doing. What is being suggested is that seeing living systems as knowledge systems is one way of laying the foundations for what in the end will be a truly unified theory of evolution.

REFERENCES

Ashby, W. R. (1952). *Design for a brain*, Wiley, New York.

Bateson, G. (1980). *Mind and Nature*, Fontana, London.

Bok, W. J. (1980). The definition and recognition of biological adaptation. *American Zoologist*, **20**, 217–227.

Bok, W. J. and Wahlert, G. von. (1965). Adaptation and the form-function complex. *Evolution*, **19**, 269–299.

Brandon, R. N. (1978). Adaptation and evolutionary theory. *Studies in the History and Philosophy of Science*, **9**, 181–206.

Campbell, D. T. (1959). Methodological suggestions from a comparative psychology of knowledge processes. *Inquiry*, **2**, 152–182.

Campbell, D. T. (1965). Variation and selective retention in sociocultural evolution. In M. R. Barringer, G. I. Blanksten, and R. W. Mack (Eds), *Social change in developing areas: A reinterpretation of evolutionary theory*, Shenkman, Cambridge, Mass. pp. 19–49.

Campbell, D. T. (1974). Evolutionary epistemology. In P. A. Schilpp (Ed.), *The Philosophy of Karl Popper*, Open Court Publishers, La Salle, pp. 413–463.

Dobzhansky, T. (1956). What is an adaptive trait? *American Naturalist*, **90**, 337–347.

Dobzhansky, T. (1968). On some fundamental concepts of Darwinian Biology. In T. Dobzhansky, M. K. Hecht and W. C. Steere (Eds), *Evolutionary Biology*, Vol. 2, North-Holland Publishing Company, Amsterdam. pp. 1–34.

Durham, W. H. (1979). Toward a coevolutionary theory of human biology and culture. In N. R. Chagnon and W. Irons (Eds), *Evolutionary Biology and Human Social Behaviour*, Duxbury Press, North Scituate. pp. 39–59.

Ghiselin, M. T. (1966). On semantic pitfalls of biological adaptation. *Philosophy of Science*, **33**, 147–153.

Ghiselin, M. T. (1981). Categories, life and thinking. *The Behavioral and Brain Sciences*, **4**, 269–313.

Goodwin, B. C. (1976). *Analytical physiology of cells and developing organisms*, Academic Press, London.

Gould, S. J. (1980). Is a new and general theory of evolution emerging? *Paleobiology*, **6**, 119–130.

Ho, M. W., and Saunders, P. T. (1979). Beyond Neo-Darwinism—an epigenetic approach to evolution. *Journal of Theoretical Biology*, **78**, 573–591.

Lewin, R. (1980). Evolutionary theory under fire. *Science*, **210**, 883–887.

Lewontin, R. C. (1970). The units of selection. *Annual Review of Ecology and Systematics*, **1**, 1–18.

Lewontin, R. C. (1978). Adaptation. *Scientific American*, **239**, 156–169.

Lewontin, R. C. (1979). Sociobiology as an adaptationist program. *Behavioral Science*, **24**, 5–14.

Lewontin, R. C. (1981). On constraints and adaptation. *The Behavioural and Brain Sciences*, **4**, 244–245.

Lorenz, K. (1965). *Evolution and Modification of Behavior*, University of Chicago Press, Chicago.

Lorenz, K. (1969). Innate bases of learning. In K. H. Pribram (Ed.), *On the Biology of Learning*, Harcourt, New York. pp. 13-91.

Mayr, E. (1974). Teleological and teleonomic: a new analysis. *Boston Studies in the Philosophy of Science*, **14**, 91–117.

Medawar, P. B. (1951). Problems of adaptation. *New Biology*, **11**, 10–26.

Piaget, J. (1971). *Biology and Knowledge*, Edinburgh University Press, Edinburgh.

Piaget, J. (1979). *Behaviour and Evolution*, Routledge, Kegan and Paul, London.

Pittendrigh, C. S. (1958). Adaptation, natural selection and behavior. In A. Reo and G. G. Simpson (Eds), *Behavior and Evolution*, Yale University Press, New Haven. pp. 390–416.

Plotkin, H. C., and Odling-Smee, F. J. (1979). Learning, change and evolution. *Advances in the Study of Behaviour*, **10**, 1–41.

Plotkin, H. C., and Odling-Smee, F. J. (1981). A multiple -level model of evolution and its implications for sociobiology. *The Behavioral and Brain Sciences*, **4**, 225–268.

Popper, K. R. (1959). *The logic of scientific discovery*, Hutchinson, London.

Popper, K. R. (1972). *Objective knowledge: An evolutionary approach*, Clarendon Press, Oxford.

Quine, W. V. (1969). Natural Kinds. From *Ontological Relativity and other essays*, Columbia University Press, New York.

Rescher, N. (1977). *Methodological Pragmatism*, Basil Blackwell, Oxford.

Shimony, A. (1971). Perception from an evolutionary point of view. *The Journal of Philosophy*, **LXVIII**, 57–583.

Simpson, G. G. (1964). *This View of Life*, Harcourt, New York.

Sommerhoff, G. (1950). *Analytical Biology*, Oxford University Press, Oxford.

Sommerhoff, G. (1969). The abstract characteristics of living systems. In F. E. Emery (Ed.), *Systems Thinking*, Penguin Books, Harmondsworth. pp. 147–202.

Southwood, T. R. E. (1977). Habitat, the templet for ecological strategies? *Journal of Animal Ecology*, **46**, 337–365.

Steele, E. J. (1980). *Somatic Selection and Adaptive Evolution*, Croom Helm, London.

Stern, J. T. (1970). The meaning of adaptation and its relation to the phenomenon of natural selection. *Evolutionary Biology*, **4**, 38–66.

Toulmin, S. E. (1967). The evolutionary development of natural science. *American Scientist*, **55**, 456–471.

Waddington, C. H. (1959). Evolutionary adaptation. In Sol Tax (Ed.), *Evolution after Darwin*, University of Chicago Press, Chicago. pp. 381–402.

Waddington, C. H. (1969). Paradigm for an evolutionary process. In C. H. Waddington (Ed.), *Towards a Theoretical Biology*, Vol. 2, Edinburgh University Press, Edinburgh. pp. 106–128.

Williams, G. C. (1966). *Adaptation and Natural Selection*, Princeton University Press, Princeton.

Some issues in evolutionary theory

Evolutionary epistemology is an ambitious endeavour. It attempts to supply a framework for a general theory of biology, from the way macromolecular structures effect the storage and transmission of information as genes to how knowledge is stored and transmitted culturally. As such it faces many conceptual problems. The issues of teleology and progress in evolution have been singled out for particular attention because a successful evolutionary epistemology must deal with complex cognitive functions, and though the difficulties posed by teleology and progress may be no different in kind for cognition as for any other phenotypic attribute, they surely are present in an extreme degree when one considers traits such as learning and thought. The distinction drawn originally by Pittendrigh between teleology and teleonomy seems to hold nicely when one is considering structures such as the feathers or eyes of birds. The apparent design and goal-directed nature of these adaptations, even when very complex, can be fairly readily accounted for in terms of the history of natural selection acting upon variant forms, both phylogenetically and ontogenetically. But what of the ability to predict future events, or at least to act as if predicting future events, that many animals seem to have. In the case of man, one need not be so cautious—we obviously do predict future events and act on those predictions. Is this not teleology writ large? Is it possible, and desirable, to continue to maintain the causally acceptable framework of teleonomic explanation in the face of such strong evidence for teleology at work? I believe the answer is yes. Unless we explain man's conscious predictive capacity in terms

15

of the same *a posteriori* framework that we use for all other biological phenomena, then we have to abandon the possibility of a general theory in biology. Mayr's essay is a scholarly and subtle appraisal of the problem and highlights the way in which cybernetics helps in maintaining the distinction between a causal framework that is rooted in past events and an unacceptable form of causality that explains phenomena by having recourse to knowledge of the future.

Another persistent problem, in some ways closely similar to teleology, is the notion of progress in evolution—the idea that organic evolution as a whole is end-directed. Again it is the complex cognitive abilities and socio-culture of man that has been the principal source for maintaining the myth of evolutionary progress. To add to the confusion, the word progress is sometimes used in the context of a quite specific progression of a trait within an assumed phylogenetic lineage. Encephalization in vertebrates is a notable instance of this. There is, however, a clear distinction to be drawn between a progression and progress— the former implies no overall end-directedness and is merely an historical fact; progress, on the other hand, implies movement towards some specific and future end. That vertebrate evolution has been marked by increased brain size cannot be taken to imply that evolution has moved in a directed fashion towards man. Besides, man is excellent in only certain respects, but the fallacy continues to be implicit in the thinking of most of those who work directly on those areas of excellence. Williams' arguments against thinking in terms of progress in evolution are powerful and wide-ranging. I did have another reason for including a chapter from his 1966 book. In this particular chapter he states the position, that evolution is to be understood in terms of natural selection acting on alternative alleles, that has become famous and that is arguably the most influential piece of writing in modern biology.

Learning, Development, and Culture
Edited by H. C. Plotkin
© 1982, John wiley & Sons Ltd.

CHAPTER 2

Teleological and teleonomic:
a new analysis

Ernst Mayr*

Teleological language is frequently used in biology in order to make statements about the functions of organs, about physiological processes, and about the behavior and actions of species and individuals. Such language is characterized by the use of the words *function, purpose,* and *goal,* as well as by statements that something exists or is done 'in order to'. Typical statements of this sort are 'It is one of the functions of the kidneys to eliminate the end products of protein metabolism', or 'Birds migrate to warm climates in order to escape the low temperatures and food shortages of winter'. In spite of the long-standing misgivings of physical scientists, philosophers, and logicians, many biologists have continued to insist not only that such teleological statements are objective and free of metaphysical content, but also that they express something important which is lost when teleological language is eliminated. Recent reviews of the problem in the philosophical literature (Nagel 1961; Beckner 1969; Hull 1973; to cite only a few of a large selection of such publications) concede the legitimacy of some teleological statements but still display considerable divergence of opinion as to the actual meaning of 'teleological' and the relations between teleology and causality.

* Reprinted by permission of the author and of the publishers D. Reidel and Harvard University Press. This essay was originally published in *Boston Studies in the Philosophy of Science* (1974), **14**, 91–117. It was republished in the form reprinted here as Chapter 26 in *Evolution and the Diversity of Life* (1976), Harvard University Press, pp. 383–404. Copyright © 1976 by the President and Fellows of Harvard College.

This confusion is nothing new and goes back at least as far as Aristotle, who invoked final causes not only for individual life processes (such as development from the egg to the adult) but also for the universe as a whole. To him, as a biologist, the form-giving of the specific life process was the primary paradigm of a finalistic process, but for his epigones the order of the universe and the trend toward its perfection became completely dominant. The existence of a form-giving, finalistic principle in the universe was rightly rejected by Bacon and Descartes, but this, they thought, necessitated the eradication of any and all teleological language, even for biological processes, such as growth and behavior, or in the discussion of adaptive structures.

The history of the biological sciences from the seventeenth to the nineteeth centuries is characterized by a constant battle between extreme mechanists, who explained everything purely in terms of movements and forces, and their opponents, who often went to the opposite extreme of vitalism. After vitalism had been completely routed by the beginning of the twentieth century, biologists could afford to be less self-conscious in their language and, as Pittendrigh (1958) has expressed it, were again willing to say 'a turtle came ashore to lay her eggs', instead of saying 'she came ashore and laid her eggs'. There is now consensus among biologists that the teleological phrasing of such a statement does not imply any conflict with physicochemical causality.

Yet the very fact that teleological statements have again become respectable has helped to bring out uncertainties. The vast literature on teleology is eloquent evidence for the unusual difficulties connected with this subject. This impression is reenforced when one finds how often various authors dealing with this subject have reached opposite conclusions (e.g. Braithwaite 1954; Beckner 1969; Canfield 1966; Hull 1973; Nagel 1961). They differ from each other in multiple ways, but most importantly in answering the question: What kind of teleological statements are legitimate and what others are not? Or, what is the relation between Darwin and teleology? David Hull (1973) has recently stated, 'evolutionary theory did away with teleology, and that is that', yet, a few years earlier McLeod (1957) had pronounced, 'what is most challenging about Darwin, is his reintroduction of purpose into the natural world'. Obviously the two authors must mean very different things.

Purely logical analysis helped remarkably little to clear up the confusion. What finally produced a breakthrough in our thinking about teleology was the introduction of new concepts from the fields of cybernetics and new terminologies from the language of information theory. The result was the development of a new teleological language, which claims to be able to take advantage of the heuristic merits of teleological phraseology without being vulnerable to the traditional objections.

TRADITIONAL OBJECTIONS TO THE USE
OF TELEOLOGICAL LANGUAGE

Criticism of the use of teleological language is traditionally based on one or several of the following objections. In order to be acceptable, teleological language must be immune to these objections.

Teleological statements and explanations imply the endorsement of unverifiable theological or metaphysical doctrines in science

This criticism was indeed valid in former times, as for instance when natural theology operated extensively with a strictly metaphysical teleology. Physiological processes, adaptations to the environment, and all forms of seemingly purposive behavior tended to be interpreted as being due to nonmaterial vital forces. This interpretation was widely accepted among Greek philosophers, including Aristotle, who discerned an active soul everywhere in nature. Bergson's (1907) *élan vital* and Driesch's (1909) *Entelechie* are relatively recent examples of such metaphysical teleology. Contemporary philosophers reject such teleology almost unanimously. Likewise, the employment of teleological language among modern biologists does not imply adoption of such metaphysical concepts (see below).

The belief that acceptance of explanations for biological phenomena that are not equally applicable to inanimate nature constitutes rejection of a physicochemical explanation

Ever since the age of Galileo and Newton it has been the endeavor of the 'natural scientists' to explain everything in nature in terms of the laws of physics. To accept special explanations for teleological phenomena in living organisms implied for these critics a capitulation to mysticism and a belief in the supernatural. They ignored the fact that nothing exists in inanimate nature (except for manmade machines) which corresponds to DNA programs or to goal-directed activities. As a matter of fact, the acceptance of a teleonomic explanation (see below) is in no way in conflict with the laws of physics and chemistry. It is not in opposition to a causal interpretation, and it does not imply an acceptance of supernatural forces in any way whatsoever.

The assumption that future goals were the cause of current events seemed in complete conflict with any concept of causality

Braithwaite (1954) stated the conflict as follows: 'In a [normal] causal explanation the explicandum is explained in terms of a cause which either precedes it or is simultaneous with it; in a teleological explanation the explicandum is explained as being causally related either to a particular goal

in the future or to a biological end which is as much future as present or past.'
This is why some logicians up to the present distinguish between causal
explanations and teleological explanations.

Teleological language seemed to represent objectionable anthropomorphism

The use of words like *purposive* or *goal-directed* seemed to imply the transfer
of human qualities, such as intent, purpose, planning, deliberation, or
consciousness, to organic structures and to subhuman forms of life. Intentional,
purposeful human behavior is, almost by definition, teleological. Yet I shall
exclude it from further discussion because the words *intentional* and *consciously
premeditated,* which are usually used in connection with such behavior, may
get us involved in complex controversies over psychological theory, even though
much of human behavior does not differ in kind from animal behavior. The
latter, although usually described in terms of stimulus and response, is also
highly 'intentional', as when a predator stalks its prey or when the prey flees
from the pursuing predator. Yet seemingly 'purposive', that is, goal-directed,
behavior in animals can be discussed and analyzed in operationally definable
terms, without recourse to anthropomorphic terms like 'intentional' or
'consciously'.

As a result of these and other objections teleological explanations were widely
believed to be a form of obscurantism, an evasion of the need for a causal
explanation. Indeed some authors went so far as to make statements such as
'Teleological notions are among the main obstacles to theory formation in
biology' (Lagerspetz, 1959:65). Yet biologists insisted on continuing to use
teleological language.

The teleological dilemma, then, consists in the fact that numerous and
seemingly weighty objections to the use of teleological language have been
raised by various critics, and yet biologists have insisted that they would lose
a great deal, methodologically and heuristically, if they were prevented from
using such language. It is my endeavor to resolve this dilemma by a new analysis,
and particularly by a new classification of the various phenomena that have
traditionally been designated 'teleological'.

THE HETEROGENEITY OF TELEOLOGICAL PHENOMENA

One of the greatest shortcomings of most recent discussions of the teleology
problem has been the heterogeneity of the phenomena designated 'teleological'
by different authors. To me it would seem quite futile to arrive at rigorous
definitions until the medley of phenomena designated 'teleological' is separated
into more or less homogeneous classes. To accomplish this will be my first
task. Furthermore, mingling a discussion of teleology with consideration of such
extraneous problems as vitalism, holism, and reductionism only confuses the
issue. Teleological statements and phenomena can be analyzed without reference
to major philosophical systems.

By and large all the phenomena that have been designated in the literature as teleological can be grouped into three classes: (1) unidirectional evolutionary sequences (progressionism, orthogenesis), (2) seemingly or genuinely goal-directed processes, and the so-called (3) teleological systems. The ensuing discussion will serve to bring out the great differences between these three classes of phenomena.

Unidirectional evolutionary sequences (Progressionism, Orthogenesis)

Beginning with Artistotle and other Greek philosophers, and becoming increasingly widespread in the eighteenth century, was a belief in an upward or forward progression in the arrangement of natural objects. This was expressed most concretely in the concept of the *scala naturae,* the scale of perfection (Lovejoy, 1936). Originally conceived as something static (or even descending, owing to a process of degradation), the Ladder of Perfection was temporalized in the eighteenth century and merged almost unnoticeably into evolutionary theories such as that of Lamarck. Progressionist theories were proposed in two somewhat different forms. The steady advance toward perfection was directed either by a supernatural force (a wise creator) or, rather vaguely, by a built-in drive toward perfection. During the flowering of Natural Theology the 'interventionist' concept dominated but after 1859 it was replaced by the so-called orthogenetic theories, which were widely held by biologists and philosophers (see Lagerspetz, 1959:11–12, for a short survey). Simpson (1949) refuted the possibility of orthogenesis with particularly decisive arguments. Actually, as Weismann had said long ago (1909), the principle of natural selection solves the origin of progressive adaptation without any recourse to goal-determining forces.

It is somewhat surprising how many philosophers, physical scientists, and occasionally even biologists still flirt with the concept of a teleological determination of evolution. Teilhard de Chardin's (1955) entire dogma is built on such a teleology and so are, as Monod (1971) has stressed quite rightly, almost all of the most important ideologies of the past and present. Even some serious evolutionists play, in my opinion rather dangerously, with teleological language. For instance, Ayala (1970:11) says:

> the overall process of evolution cannot be said to be teleological in the sense of directed towards the production of specified DNA codes of information, i.e. organisms. But it is my contention that it can be said to be teleological in the sense of being directed toward the production of DNA codes of information which improve the reproductive fitness of a population in the environments where it lives. The process of evolution can also be said to be teleological in that it has the potentiality of producing end-directed DNA codes of information, and has in fact resulted in teleologically oriented structures, patterns of behavior, and regulated mechanisms.

To me this seems a serious misinterpretation. If 'teleological' means anything it means 'goal-directed'. Yet natural selection is strictly an *a posteriori* process that rewards current success but never sets up future goals. No one realized this better than Darwin, who reminded himself 'never to use the words higher or lower'. Natural selection rewards past events, that is, the production of successful recombinations of genes, but it does not plan for the future. This is precisely what gives evolution by natural selection its flexibility. With the environment changing incessantly, natural selection—in contradistinction to orthogenesis—never commits itself to a future goal. Natural selection is never goal oriented. It is misleading and quite inadmissible to designate such broadly generalized concepts as survival or reproductive success as definite and specified goals.

The same objection can be raised against certain arguments presented by Waddington (1968:55—56). Like so many other developmental biologists, he is forever looking for analogies between ontogeny and evolution. 'I have for some years been urging that quasi-finalistic types of explanations are called for in the theory of evolution as well as in that of development.' Natural selection 'in itself suffices to determine, to a certain degree, the nature of the end towards which evolution will proceed, it must result in an increase in the efficiency of the biosystem as a whole in finding ways of reproducing itself'. He refers here to completely generalized processes, rather than to specific goals. It is rather easy to demonstrate how ludicrous the conclusions are which one reaches by overextending the concept of goal direction. For instance, one might say that it is the purpose of every individual to die because this is the end of every individual, or that it is the goal of every evolutionary line to become extinct because this is what has happened to 99.9 percent of all evolutionary lines that have ever existed. Indeed, one would be forced to consider as teleological even the second law of thermodynamics.

One of Darwin's greatest contributions was to have made it clear that goal-directed processes involving only a single individual are of an entirely different nature from evolutionary changes. The latter are controlled by the interplay of the production of variants (new genotypes) and their sorting out by natural selection, a process that is quite decidedly not directed toward a specified distant end. A discussion of legitimately teleological phenomena would be futile unless evolutionary processes are eliminated from consideration.

Seemingly or genuinely goal-directed processes

Nature (organic and inanimate) abounds in processes and activities that lead to an end. Some authors seem to believe that all such terminating processes are of one kind and 'finalistic' in the same manner and to the same degree. Taylor (1950), for instance, if I understand him correctly, claims that all forms of active behavior are of the same kind and that there is no fundamental difference between one kind of movement or purposive action and any other. Waddington (1968) gives a definition of his term 'quasi-finalistic' as requiring 'that the end state of the process is determined by its properties at the beginning.' Further study indicates, however, that the class of 'end-directed processes' is composed of two entirely different kinds of phenomena. These two types of phenomena may be characterized as teleomatic processes in inanimate nature or teleonomic processes in living nature.

Teleomatic processes in inanimate nature

Many movements of inanimate objects as well as physicochemical processes are the simple consequences of natural laws. For instance, gravity provides the end state for a rock that I drop into a well. It will reach its end state when it has come to rest on the bottom. A red-hot piece of iron reaches its 'end state' when its temperature and that of its environment are equal. All objects of the physical world are endowed with the capacity to change their state and these changes follow natural laws. They are 'end-directed' only in a passive, automatic way, regulated by external forces or conditions. Since the end state of such inanimate objects is automatically achieved, such changes might be designated *teleomatic*. All teleomatic processes come to an end when the potential is used up (as in the cooling of a heated piece of iron) or when the process is stopped by encountering an external impediment (as when a falling stone hits the ground). Teleomatic processes simply follow natural laws, that is, lead to a result consequential to concomitant physical forces, and the reaching of their end state is not controlled by a built-in program. The law of gravity and the second law of thermodynamics are among the natural laws that most frequently govern teleomatic processes.

Teleonomic processes in living nature

Seemingly goal-directed behavior in organisms is of an entirely different nature from teleomatic processes. Goal-directed 'behavior' (in the widest sense of this word) is extremely widespread in the organic world; for instance, most activity connected with migration, food getting, courtship, ontogeny, and all phases of reproduction is characterized by such goal orientation.The occurrence of goal-directed processes is perhaps the most characteristic feature of the world of living organisms.

Definition of the term 'teleonomic'

For the last 15 years or so the term *teleonomic* has been used increasingly often for goal-directed processes in organisms. In 1961 I proposed the following definition for this term: 'It would seem useful to restrict the term 'teleonomic'

rigidly to systems operating on the basis of a program, a code of information'
(Mayr, 1961). Although I used the term 'system' in this definition, I have since
become convinced that it permits a better operational definition to consider
certain activities, processes (like growth), and active behaviors as the most
characteristic illustrations of teleonomic phenomena. I therefore modify my
definition as follows: *A teleonomic process or behavior is one that owes its goal
directedness to the operation of a program*. The term 'teleonomic' implies goal
direction. This, in turn, implies a dynamic process rather than a static condition,
as represented by a system. The combination of 'teleonomic' with the term
system is, thus, rather incongruent (see below).

All teleonomic behavior is characterized by two components. It is guided by
a 'program' and it depends on the existence of some end point, goal, or terminus
that is foreseen in the program that regulates the behavior. This end point
might be a structure, a physiological function, the attainment of a new
geographical position, or a 'consummatory' (Craig, 1918) act in behavior. Each
particular program is the result of natural selection, constantly adjusted by the
selective value of the achieved end point.

My definition of 'teleonomic' has been labeled by Hull (1973) a 'historical
definition'. Such a designation is rather misleading. Although the genetic
program (as well as its individually acquired components) originated in the
past, this history is completely irrelevant for the functional analysis of a given
teleonomic process. For this it is entirely sufficient to know that a 'program'
exists which is causally responsible for the teleonomic nature of a goal-directed
process. Whether this program originated through a lucky macromutation (as
Richard Goldschmidt conceived possible) or through a slow process of gradual
selection, or even through individual learning or conditioning, as in open
programs, is quite immaterial; the mere existence of a program whatever its
origin, is enough to classify a process as 'teleonomic'. However, a process that
does not have a programed end does not qualify to be designated as teleonomic
(see below for a discussion of the concept 'program').

All teleonomic processes are facilitated by specifically selected executive
structures. The fleeing of a deer from a predatory carnivore is facilitated by
the existence of superlative sense organs and the proper development of muscles
and other components of the locomotory apparatus. The proper performing
of teleonomic processes at the molecular level is made possible by highly specific
properties of complex macromolecules. It would stultify the definition of
'teleonomic' if the appropriateness of these facilitating executive structures were
made part of it. However, it is in the nature of a teleonomic program that it
does not induce a simple unfolding of some completely preformed *Gestalt*, but
that it always controls a more or less complex process which must allow for
internal and external disturbances. Teleonomic processes during ontogenetic
development, for instance, are constantly in danger of being derailed, even if
only temporarily. There exist innumerable feedback devices to prevent this or

to correct it. Waddington (1957) has quite rightly called attention to the frequency and importance of such homeostatic devices, which virtually guarantee the appropriate canalization of development.

We owe a great debt of gratitude to Rosenblueth *et al.* (1943) for their endeavor to find a new solution for the explanation of teleological phenomena in organisms. They correctly identified two aspects of such phenomena: (1) they are seemingly purposeful, being directed toward a goal; and (2) they consist of active behavior. The background of these authors was in the newly developing field of cybernetics, and it is only natural that they should have stressed the fact that goal-directed behavior is characterized by mechanisms which correct errors committed during the goal seeking. They considered the negative feedback loops of such behavior its most characteristic aspect and stated, 'teleological behavior thus becomes synonymous with behavior controlled by negative feedback.' This statement emphasizes important aspects of teleological behavior, yet it misses the crucial point: *The truly characteristic aspect of goal-seeking behavior is not that mechanisms exist which improve the precision with which a goal is reached, but rather that mechanisms exist which initiate, that is, 'cause' this goal-seeking behavior.* It is not the thermostat that determines the temperature of a house, but the person who sets the thermostat. It is not the torpedo that determines toward what ship it will be shot and at what time, but the naval officer who releases the torpedo. Negative feedbacks improve the precision of goal seeking, but they do not determine it. Feedback devices are only executive mechanisms that operate during the translation of a program. Therefore, it places the emphasis on the wrong point to define teleonomic processes in terms of the presence of feedback devices. They are mediators of the program, but as far as the basic principle of goal achievement is concerned, they are of minor consequence.

Recent usages of the term 'teleonomic'

The term 'teleonomic' was introduced into the literature by Pittendrigh (1958:394) in the following paragraphy:

> Today the concept of adaptation is beginning to enjoy an improved respectability for several reasons: it is seen as less than perfect; natural selection is better understood; and the engineer-physicist in building end-seeking automata has sanctified the use of teleological jargon. It seems unfortunate that the term 'teleology' should be resurrected and, as I think, abused in this way. The biologists' longstanding confusion would be more fully removed if all end-directed systems were described by some other term, like 'teleonomic', in order to emphasize that the recognition and description of end-directedness does not carry a commitment to Aristotelian teleology as an efficient [sic] causal principle.

It is evident that Pittendrigh had the same phenomena in mind as I do,[1] even though his definition is rather vague and his placing the term 'teleonomic' in opposition to Aristotle's 'teleology' is unfortunate. As we shall see below, most of Aristotle's references to end-directed processes refer precisely to the same things that Pittendrigh and I would call teleonomic (see also Delbrück, 1971).

Other recent usages of the term that differ from my own definition are the following. B. Davis (1961), believing that the term denotes 'the development of valuable structures and mechanisms' as a result of natural selection, considers the term virtually synonymous with adaptiveness. The same is largely true for Simpson (1949:520–521), who sees in 'teleonomic' the description for a system or structure that is the product of evolution and of selective advantage:

> The words 'finalistic' and 'teleological' have, however, had an unfortunate history in philosophy which makes them totally unsuitable for use in modern biology. They have too often been used to mean that evolution as a whole has a predetermined goal, or that the utility of organization in general is with respect to man or to some supernatural scheme of things. Thus these terms may implicitly negate rather than express the biological conclusion that organization in organisms is with respect to utility to each separate species at the time when it occurs, and not with respect to any other species or any future time. In emphasis of this point of view, Pittendrigh [above] suggests that the new coinage 'teleonomy' be substituted for the debased currency of teleology.

Monod (1971) likewise deals with teleonomy as if the word simply meant adaptation. It is not surprising, therefore, that Monod considers teleonomy 'to be a profoundly ambiguous concept.' Furthermore, says Monod, all functional adaptations are 'so many aspects or fragments of a unique primary project which is the preservation and multiplication of the species.' He finally completes the confusion by choosing 'to define the essential teleonomic project as consisting in the transmission from generation to generation of the invariance content characteristic of the species. All these structures, all the performances, all the activities contributing to the success of the essential project will hence be called teleonomic.' What Monod calls 'teleonomic' I would designate as of 'selective value'. Under these circumstances it is not surprising that Ayala (1970) claims that the term 'teleonomy' was introduced into the philosophical literature in order 'to explain adaptation in nature as the result of natural selection'. If this were indeed true, and it is true of Simpson's and Davis's cited definitions, the term would be quite unnecessary. Actually there is nothing in my 1961 account that would support this interpretation, and I know of no other term that would define a goal-directed activity of behavior that is controlled by a program. Even though Pittendrigh's discussion of 'teleonomic' rather confused the issue and has led to the subsequent mis-interpretations, he evidently had in mind the same processes and phenomena that I denoted as *teleonomic*. It would seem well worthwhile to retain the term in the more rigorous definition, which I have now given.

The meaning of the term 'program'

The key word in my definition of 'teleonomic' is the term 'program'. Someone might claim that the difficulties of an acceptable definition for teleological language in biology had simply been transferred to the term 'program'. This is not a legitimate objection, because it fails to recognize that, regardless of its particular definition, a program (1) is something material and (2) exists prior to the initiation of the teleonomic process. Hence, it is consistent with a causal explanation.

Nevertheless, it might be admitted that the concept 'program' is so new that the diversity of meanings of this term has not yet been fully explored. The term is taken from the language of information theory. A computer may act purposefully when given appropriate programed instructions. Tentatively, 'program' might be defined as *coded or pre-arranged information that controls a process (or behavior) leading it toward a given end*. As Raven (1960) has remarked correctly, the program contains not only the blueprint but also the instructions of how to use the information of the blueprint. In the case of a computer program or of the DNA of a cell nucleus, the program is completely separated from the executive machinery. In the case of most manmade automata the program is part of the total machinery.

My definition of 'program' is deliberately chosen in such a way as to avoid drawing a line between seemingly 'purposive' behavior in organisms and in manmade machines. The simplest program is perhaps the weight inserted into loaded dice or attached to a 'fixed' number wheel so that they are likely to come to rest at a given number. A clock is constructed and programed in such a way as to strike at the full hour. Any machine programed to carry out goal-directed activities is capable of doing his 'mechanically'.

The programs that control teleonomic processes in organisms are either entirely laid down in the DNA of the genotype ('closed programs') or constituted in such a way that they can incorporate additional information ('open programs') acquired through learning, conditioning, or through other experiences (Mayr, 1969). Most behavior, particularly in higher organisms, is controlled by open programs. Once the open program is filled in, it is equivalent to an originally closed program in its control of teleonomic behavior (Mayr, 1974).

Open programs are particularly suitable for demonstrating the fact that the mode of acquisition of a program is an entirely different matter from the teleonomic nature of the behavior controlled by the program. Nothing could be more purposive, more teleonomic, than much of the escape behavior in many prey species (in birds and mammals). Yet in many cases the knowledge of which animals are dangerous predators is learned by the young who have an open program for this type of information. In other words, this particular information was not acquired through selection and yet it is clearly in part responsible for teleonomic behavior. Many of the teleonomic components of the reproductive behavior (including mate selection) of species that are imprinted for mate recognition are likewise only partially the result of selection. The history of the acquisition of a program, therefore, cannot be made part of the definition of 'teleonomic'.

The origin of a program is quite irrelevant for the definition. It can be the product of evolution, as are all genetic programs, or it can be the acquired information of an open program, or it can be a manmade device. Anything that does *not* lead to what is at least in principle a predictable goal does not qualify as a program. Even though the future evolution of a species has severe limits set on it by its current gene pool, its course is largely controlled by the changing constellation of selection pressures and is therefore not predictable. It is not programed inside the contemporary gene pool.

The entire concept of a program of information is so new that it has received little attention from philosophers and logicians. My tentative analysis may, therefore, require considerable revision when subjected to further scrutiny.

How does the program operate?   The philosopher may be willing to accept the assertion of the biologist that a program directs a given teleonomic behavior, but he would also like to know how the program performs this function. Alas, all the biologist can tell him is that the study of the operation of programs is the most difficult area of biology. For instance, the translation of the genetic program into growth processes and into the differentiation of cells, tissues, and organs is at the present time the most challenging problem of developmental biology. The number of qualitatively different cells in a higher organism almost surely exceeds 1 billion. Even though all (or most) cells have the same gene complement, they differ from each other owing to differences in the repression and derepression of individual gene loci and owing to differences in their cellular environment. It hardly needs stressing how complex the genetic program must be to be able to give the appropriate signals to each cell lineage in order to provide it with the mixture of molecules that it needs in order to carry out its assigned tasks.

Similar problems arise in the analysis of goal-directed behavior. The number of ways in which a program may control a goal-directed behavior activity is legion. It differs from species to species. Sometimes the program is largely acquired by experience; in other cases it may be almost completely genetically fixed. Sometimes the behavior consists of a series of steps, each of which serves as reinforcement for the ensuing steps; in other cases the behavior, once initiated, seems to run its full course without need for any further input. Feedback loops are sometimes important, but their presence cannot be demonstrated in other kinds of behavior. Again, as in developmental biology, much of the contemporary research in behavioral biology is devoted to the nature and the operation of the programs that control behavior and more specifically teleonomic behavior sequences (Hinde and Stevenson, 1970). Almost any statement one might make is apt to be challenged by one or another school of psychologists and geneticists. It is, however, safe to state that the translation of programs into teleonomic behavior is greatly affected both by sensory inputs and by internal physiological (largely hormonal) states.

TELEOLOGICAL SYSTEMS

In the philosophical literature, the word 'teleological' is particularly often combined with the term 'system'. Is it justified to speak of 'teleological systems'? Analysis shows that this combination leads to definitional difficulties.

The Greek word *telos* means end or goal. Teleological means end-directed. To apply 'teleological' to a goal-directed behavior or process would seem quite legitimate. I am perhaps a purist, but it bothers me to apply the word *teleological*, that is *end-directed*, to a stationary system. Any phenomenon to which we can refer as teleomatic or teleonomic (discussed above) represents a movement, a behavior, or a process that is goal directed because it has a determinable end. This is the core concept of 'teleological', the presence of a *telos* (an end) toward which an object or process moves. Rosenblueth *et al.* (1943) have correctly stressed the same point.

However, extending the term 'teleological' to cover static systems leads to contradictions and illogicalities. A torpedo that has been shot off and moves toward its target is a machine showing teleonomic behavior. But what justifies calling a torpedo a teleological system when, with hundreds of others, it is stored in an ordnance depot? Why should the eye of a sleeping person be called a teleological system? It is not goal directed at anything. Part of the confusion is due to the fact that the term 'teleological system' has been applied to two only partially overlapping phenomena. One comprises systems that are potentially able to perform teleonomic actions, like a torpedo. The other comprises systems that are well adapted, like the eye. To refer to a phenomenon in this second class as 'teleological', in order to express its adaptive perfection, reflects just enough of the old idea of evolution leading to a steady progression in adaptation and perfection to make me uneasy. What is the telos toward which the teleological system moves?

The source of the conflict seems to be that 'goal directed', in a more or less straightforward literal sense, is not necessarily the same as purposive. Completely stationary systems can be functional or purposive, but they cannot be goal directed in any literal sense. A poison on the shelf has the potential of killing somebody, but this inherent property does not make it a goal-directed object. Perhaps this difficulty can be resolved by making a terminological distinction between functional properties of systems and strict goal directedness, that is, teleonomy of behavioral or other processes. However, since one will be using so-called teleological language in both cases, one might subsume both categories under teleology.

R. Munson (1971) has recently dealt with such adaptive systems. In particular, he studied all those explanations that deal with aspects of adaptation but are often called 'teleological'. He designates sentences 'adaptational sentences' when they contain the terms 'adaptation', 'adaptive', or 'adapted'. In agreement with the majority opinion of biologists he concludes that 'adaptational sentences do not need to involve reference to any purpose, final cause, or other non-empirical notion in order to be meaningful.' Adaptational sentences simply express the conclusion that a given trait, whether structural, physiological, or behavioral, is the product of the process of natural selection and thus favors the perpetuation of the genotype responsible for this trait. Furthermore, adaptation is a heuristic concept because it demands an answer to the question in what way the trait adds up to the probability of survival and does so more successfully than another conceivable trait. To me, it is misleading to call adaptational statements teleological. 'Adapted' is an *a posteriori* statement, and it is only the success (statistically speaking) of the owner of an adaptive trait that proves whether the trait is truly adaptive (=contributes to survival) or is not. Munson summarizes the utility of adaptational language in the sentence: 'To show that a trait is adaptive is to present a phenomenon requiring explanation, and to provide the explanation is to display the success of the trait as the outcome of selection' (1971:214). The biologist fully agrees with this conclusion. Adaptive means simply: being the result of natural selection.

Many adaptive systems, as for instance all components of the locomotory and of the central nervous systems, are capable of taking part in teleonomic processes or teleonomic behavior. However, it only obscures the issue to designate a system 'teleological' or 'teleonomic' because it provides the executive structures of a teleonomic process. Is an inactive, not-programed computer a teleological system? What 'goal' or 'end' is it displaying during this period of inactivity? To repeat, one runs into serious logical difficulties when one applies the term 'teleological' to static systems (regardless of their potential) instead of to processes. Nothing is lost and much is to be gained by not using the term 'teleological' too freely and for too many rather diverse phenomena.

It may be necessary to coin a new term for systems that have the potential of displaying teleonomic behavior. The problem is particularly acute for biological organs that are capable of carrying out useful functions, such as pumping by the heart or filtration by the kidney. To some extent this problem exists for any organic structure, all the way down to the macromolecules, which are capable of carrying out autonomously certain highly specific functions owing to their uniquely specific structure. It is this ability that induced Monod (1971) to call them teleonomic systems. Similar considerations have induced some authors, erroneously in my opinion, to designate a hammer as a teleological system, because it is designed to hit a nail (a rock, not having been so designed, but serving the same function, not qualifying!).

The philosophical complexity of the logical definition of 'teleological' in living systems is obvious. Let me consider a few of the proximate and ultimate causes to bring out some of the difficulties more clearly. The functioning of these systems is the subject matter of regulatory biology, which analyzes proximate causes. Biological systems are complicated steady-state systems, replete with feedback devices. There is a high premium on homeostasis, on the maintenance of the *milieu interieur*. Since most of the processes performed by these systems are programed, it is legitimate to call them teleonomic processes. They are 'end directed' even though very often the 'end' is the maintenance of the status quo. There is nothing metaphysical in any of this because, so far as these processes are accessible to analysis, they represent chains of causally interrelated stimuli and reactions, of inputs and of outputs.

The ultimate causes for the efficiency and seeming purposefulness of these living systems were explained by Darwin in 1859. The adaptiveness of these systems is the result of millions of generations of natural selection. This is the mechanistic explanation of adaptiveness, as was clearly stated by Sigwart (1881).

Proximate and ultimate causes must be carefully separated in the discussion of teleological systems (Mayr, 1961). A system is capable of performing teleological processes because it was programed to function in this manner. The origin of the program that is responsible for the adaptiveness of the system is an entirely independent matter. It obscures definitions to combine current functioning and history of origin in a single explanation.

THE HEURISTIC NATURE OF TELEONOMIC LANGUAGE

Teleological language has been employed in the past in many different senses, some of them legitimate and some of them not. When the distinctions outlined above are made, the teleological *Fragestellung* is a most powerful tool in biological analysis. Its heuristic value was appreciated by Aristotle and Galen, but neither of them fully understood why this approach is so important. Questions that begin with 'What' and 'How' are sufficient for explanation in the physical sciences. In the biological sciences no explanation is complete until a third kind of question has been asked: 'Why?' It is Darwin's evolutionary theory that necessitates this question: No feature (or behavioral program) of an organism ordinarily evolves unless it is favored by natural selection. It must play a role in the survival or in the reproductive success of its bearer. Given this premise, it is necessary for the completion of causal analysis to ask for any feature, why it exists, that is, what its function and role in the life of the particular organism is.

The philosopher Sigwart (1881) recognized this clearly:

> A teleological analysis implies the demand to follow up causations in all directions by which the purpose [of a structure or behavior] is effected. It represents a heuristic principle because when one assumes that each organism is well adapted it requires that we ask about the operation of each individual part and that we determine the meaning of its form, its structure, and its chemical characteristics. At the same time it leads to an explanation of correlated subsidiary consequences which are not necessarily part of the same purpose but which are inevitable by-products of the same goal-directed process.

The method, of course, was used successfully long before Darwin. It was Harvey's question concerning the reason for the existence of valves in the veins that made a major, if not most important, contribution to his model of the circulation of blood. The observation that during mitosis the chromatic material is arranged in a single linear thread led Roux (1883) to question why such an elaborate process had evolved rather than a simple division of the nucleus into two halves. He concluded that the elaborate process made sense only if the chromatin consisted of an enormous number of qualitatively different small particles and if their equal division could be guaranteed only by lining them up linearly. The genetic analyses of chromosomal inheritance during the next 60 years were, in a sense only footnotes to Roux's brilliant hypothesis. These cases demonstrate most convincingly the enormous heuristic value of the teleonomic approach. It is no exaggeration to claim that most of the greatest advances in biology were made possible by asking 'Why?' questions. They ask for the selective significance of every aspect of the phenotype. The former idea that many if not most characters of organisms are 'neutral', that is, that they evolved simply as accidents of evolution, has been refuted again and again by more detailed analysis. It is asking why such structures and behaviors evolved that initiates such analysis. Students of behavior have used this approach in recent years with great success. It has, for example, led to questions concerning the information content of individual vocal and visual displays (Smith, 1969; Hinde, 1972).

As soon as one accepts the simple conclusion that the totality of the genotype is the result of past selection, and that the phenotype is a product of the genotype (except for the open portions of the program that are filled in during the lifetime of the individual), it becomes one's task to ask about any and every component of the phenotype what its particular functions and selective advantages are.

It is now quite evident why all past efforts to translate teleonomic statements into purely causal ones were such a failure: a crucial portion of the message of a teleological sentence is invariably lost by the translation. Let us take, for instance, the sentence: 'The wood thrush migrates in the fall into warmer countries *in order to* escape the inclemency of the weather and the food shortages of the northern climates.' If we replace the words 'in order to' by 'and thereby', we leave the important question unanswered as to *why* the wood thrush migrates. The teleonomic form of the statement implies that the goal-directed migratory activity is governed by a program. By omitting this important message the translated sentence is greatly impoverished as far as information content is concerned, without gaining in causal strength. The majority of modern philosophers are fully aware of this and agree that 'cleaned-up' sentences are not equivalent to the teleological sentences from which they were derived (Ayala, 1970; Beckner, 1969).

One can go one step further. Teleonomic statements have often been maligned as stultifying and obscurantist. This is simply not true. Actually the non-teleological translation is invariably a meaningless platitude, while it is the teleonomic statement that leads to biologically interesting inquiries.

ARISTOTLE AND TELEOLOGY

No other ancient philosopher has been as badly misunderstood and mishandled by posterity as Aristotle. His interests were primarily those of a biologist and his philosophy is bound to be misunderstood if this fact is ignored. Neither Aristotle nor most of the other ancient philosophers made a sharp distinction between the living world and the inanimate. They saw something like life or soul even in the inorganic world. If one can discern purposiveness and goal direction in the world of organisms, why not regard the order of the Kosmos-as-a-whole also as a due to final causes, that is, as due to a built-in teleology? As Ayala (1970) said quite rightly, Aristotle's 'error was not that he used teleological explanations in biology, but that he extended the concept of teleology to the non-living world.' Unfortunately, it was this latter teleology that was first encountered during the scientific revolution of the sixteenth and seventeenth centuries (and at that in the badly distorted interpretations of the scholastics). This is one of the reasons for the violent rejection of Aristotle by Bacon, Descartes, and their followers.

Although the philosophers of the last 40 years acknowledge quite generally the inspiration that Aristotle derived from the study of living nature, they still express his philosophy in words taken from the vocabulary of Greek dictionaries that are hundreds of years old. The time would seem to have come for the translators and interpreters of Aristotle to use a language appropriate to his thinking, that is, the language of biology, and not that of the sixteenth-century humanists. Delbrück (1971) is entirely right when he insists that it is quite legitimate to employ modern terms like 'genetic program' for *eidos* where this helps to elucidate Aristotle's thoughts. One of the reasons why Aristotle has been so consistently misunderstood is that he uses the term *eidos* for his form-giving principle, and everybody took it for granted that he had something in mind similar to Plato's concept of *eidos*. Yet the context of Aristotle's discussions makes it abundantly clear that *his eidos* is something totally different from Plato's *eidos* (I myself did not understand this until recently). Aristotle saw with extraordinary clarity that it makes no more sense to describe living organisms in terms of mere matter than to describe a house as a pile of bricks and mortar. Just as the blueprint used by the builder determines the form of a house, so does the *eidos* (in its Aristotlelian definition) give the form to the developing organism, and this *eidos* reflects the terminal *telos* of the full-grown individual. There are numerous discussions in many of Aristotle's works reflecting the same ideas. They can be found the *Analytika* and in the *Physics* (Book II), and particularly in the *Parts of Animals* and in the *Generation of Animals*. Much of Aristotle's discussion becomes remarkably modern if one inserts modern terms to replace obsolete sixteenth- and seventeenth-century vocabulary. There is, of course, one major difference between Aristotle's interpretation and the modern one. Aristotle could not actually *see* the form-giving principle (which, after all, was not fully understood until 1953) and assumed therefore that it had to be something immaterial. When he said, 'Now it may be that the Form (*eidos*) of any living creature is soul, or some part of soul, or something that involves soul' (P. A. 641a 18), it must be remembered that Aristotle's psyche (soul) was something quite different from the conception of soul later developed in Christianity. Indeed, the properties of 'soul' were to Aristotle something subject to investigation. Since the modern scientist does not actually 'see' the genetic program of DNA either, it is for him just as invisible for all practical purposes as it was for Aristotle. Its existence is inferred, as it was by Aristotle.

As Delbrück (1971) points out correctly, Aristotle's principle of the *eidos* being an 'unmoved mover' is one of the greatest conceptual innovations. The physicists were particularly opposed to the existence of such a principle by

> having been blinded for 300 years by the Newtonian view of the world. So much so, that anybody who held that the mover had to be in contact with the moved and talked about an 'unmoved mover', collided head on with Newton's dictum: *action equals reaction*. Any statement in conflict with this axiom of Newtonian dynamics could only appear to be muddled nonsense, a leftover from a benighted prescientific past. And yet, 'unmoved mover' perfectly describes DNA: it acts, creates form and development, and is not changed in the process. (Delbrück, 1971:55)

As I stated above, the existence of teleonomic programs—unmoved movers—is one of the most profound differences between the living and the inanimate world, and it is Aristotle who first postulated such a causation.

KANT AND TELEOLOGY

The denial of conspicuous purposiveness in living organisms and the ascription of their adaptive properties to the blind accidental interplay of forces and matter, so popular in the eighteenth century, was not palatable to discerning philosophers. No one felt this more keenly than Immanuel Kant, who devoted the second half of his *Critique of Judgment* to the problem of teleology. It is rather surprising how completely most students of Kant ignore this work, as if they were embarrased that the great Kant had devoted so much attention to such a 'soft' subject. Yet, as in so many other cases, Kant was more perceptive than his critics. He clearly saw two points: first, that no explanation of nature is complete that cannot account for the seeming purposiveness of much of the development and behavior of living organisms and, second, that the purely mechanical explanations available at his time were quite insufficient to explain teleological phenomena. Unfortunately he subscribed to the prevailing dogma of his period that the only legitimate explanations are purely mechanical ('Newtonian') ones, which left him without any explanation for all teleological phenomena. He therefore concluded that the true explanation was out of our reach and that the most practical approach to the study of organisms was to deal with them 'as if they were designed.' Even though he was unable to free himself from the design–designed analogy, he stressed the heuristic value of such an approach: it permits us to make products and processes of nature far more intelligible than trying to express them purely in terms of mechanical laws.

Kant's interest was clearly more in the explanation of 'design' (adaptation) than in teleonomic behavior, yet he thought that an explanation of design was beyond the reach of human intellect. Just 69 years before the publication of the *Origin of Species* Kant (1790) wrote as follows:

> It is quite certain that we can never get a sufficient knowledge of organized beings and their inner possibility, much less explain them, according to mere mechanical principles of nature. So certain is it, that we may confidently assert that it is absurd for men to make any such attempt, or to hope that maybe another Newton will some day arrive to make intelligible to us even the production of a blade of grass according to natural laws which no design has ordered. Such insight we must absolutely deny to mankind. (Quoted from McFarland, 1970)

Darwin removed the roadblock of design, and modern genetics introduced the concept of the genetic program. Between these two major advances the problem of teleology has now acquired an entirely new face. A comparison of Kant's discussion with our new concepts provides a most informative insight into the role of scientific advances in the formulation of philosophical problems. Equally informative is a comparison of three treatments of Kant's teleology, roughly separated by 50-year intervals: Stadler, 1874; Ungerer, 1922; and McFarland, 1970.

CONCLUSIONS

1. The use of so-called teleological language by biologists is legitimate; it implies neither a rejection of physicochemical explanation nor a noncausal explanation.

2. The terms 'teleology' and 'teleological' have been applied to highly diverse phenomena. I have made an attempt to group these phenomena into more or less homogeneous classes.

3. It is illegitimate to describe evolutionary processes or trends as goal directed (teleological). Selection rewards past phenomena (mutation, recombination, etc.), but does not plan for the future, at least not in any specific way.

4. Processes (behavior) whose goal directedness is controlled by a program may be referred to as *teleonomic*.

5. Processes that reach an end state caused by natural laws (e.g. gravity, second law of thermodynamics) but not by a program may be designated *teleomatic*.

6. Programs are in part or entirely the product of natural selection.

7. The question of the legitimacy of applying the term 'teleological' to stationary functional or adaptive systems requires further analysis.

8. Teleonomic (i.e. programed) behavior occurs only in organisms (and manmade machines) and constitutes a clear-cut difference between the levels of complexity in living and in inanimate nature.

9. Teleonomic explanations are strictly causal and mechanistic. They give no comfort to adherents of vitalistic concepts.

10. The heuristic value of the teleological *Fragestellung* makes it a powerful tool in biological analysis, from the study of the structural configuration of macromolecules up to the study of cooperative behavior in social systems.

REFERENCES

Ayala, F. J. (1970). Teleological explanations in evolutionary biology. *Phil. Sci.*, **37**, 1–15.
Beckner, M. (1969). Function and teleology. *Jour. Hist. Biol.*, **2**, 151–164.
Bergson, H. (1907). *Evolution Créative*, Alcan, Paris.
Braithwaite, R. D. (1954). *Scientific explanation*, Cambridge University Press, Cambridge.
Canfield, J. V. (Ed.) (1966). *Purpose in nature*, Prentice-Hall, Englewood Cliffs, N. J.

Craig, W. (1918). Appetites and aversions as constituents of instincts. *Biol. Bull.*, **34**, 91–107.

Davis, B. D. (1961). The teleonomic significance of biosynthetic control mechanism. *Cold Spring Harbor Symp. Quant. Biol.*, **26**, 1–10.

Delbrück, M. (1971). Aristotle-totle-totle. In J. Monod and E. Borek (Eds), *Of microbes and life*, Columbia University Press, New York.

Driesch, H. (1909). *Philosophie des Organischen*, Quelle und Mayer, Leipzig.

Hinde, R. A. (Ed.) (1972). *Non-verbal communication*, Cambridge University Press, Cambridge.

Hinde, R. A. and Stevenson, J. G. (1970). Goals and response controls. In L. R. Aronson *et al.* (Eds), *Development and evolution of behavior*, W. H. Freeman, San Francisco.

Hull, D. (1973). *Philosophy of biological science*, Prentice-Hall, Englewood Cliffs, N. J.

Kant, I. (1790). *Kritik der Urteilskraft*, part 2.

Lagerspetz, K. (1959). Teleological explanations and terms in biology. *Ann. Zool. Soc. Vanamo*, **19**, 1–73.

Lovejoy, A. O. (1936). *The great chain of being*, Harvard University Press, Cambridge, Mass.

Mcleod, R. B. (1957). Teleology and theory of human behavior. *Science*, **125**, 477.

Mayr, E. (1961). Cause and effect in biology. *Science*, **134**, 1501–1506.

Mayr, E. (1969). The evolution of living systems. *Proc. Nat. Acad. Sci.*, **51**, 934–941.

Mayr, E. (1974). Behavior programs and evolutionary strategies. *American Scientist*, **62**, 650–659.

McFarland, J. D. (1970). *Kant's concept of teleology*, University of Edinburgh Press, Edinburgh.

Monod, J. (1971). *Chance and necessity*, Knopf, New York.

Munson, R. (1971). Biological adaptation. *Phil. Sci.*, **38**, 200–215.

Nagel, E. (1961). *The Structure of Science*, Harcourt, Brace and World, New York.

Pittendrigh, C. S. (1958). Adaptation, natural selection, and behavior. In A. Roe and G. G. Simpson (Eds), *Behavior and Evolution*, Yale University Press, New Haven.

Raven, C. P. (1960). The formalization of finality. *Folia Biotheoretica*, **5**, 1–27.

Roe, A., and Simpson, G. G. (Eds) (1958). *Behavior and evolution*. Yale University Press, New Haven.

Rosenblueth, H., Wiener, N., and Bigelow, J. (1943). Behavior, purpose, and teleology. *Phil. Sci.*, **10**, 18–24.

Roux, W. (1883). Uber die Bedeutung der Kerntheilungsfiguren. *Eine hypothetische Erörterung*, W. Engelmann, Leipzig.

Sigwart, C. (1881). 'Der Kampf gegen den Zweck.' In *Kleine Schriften*, Vol. 2, Mohr, Freiburg. pp. 24–67.

Simpson, G. G. (1949). *The meaning of evolution: a study of the history of life and of its significance for man*, Yale University Press, New Haven.

Smith, W. J. (1969). Messages of vertebrate communication. *Science*, **165**, 145–150.

Stadler, H. (1874). *Kant's Teleologie und ihre erkenntnistheoretische Bedeutung*, F. Dümmler.

Taylor, R. (1950). Comments on a mechanistic conception of purposefulness. *Phil. Sci.*, **17**, 310–317.

Teilhard de Chardin, P. (1955). *Le phénomène humain*, Editions de Seuil, Paris.

Ungerer, E. (1922). *Die Teleologie Kants und Ihre Bedeutung für die Logik der Biologie*, Borntrager, Berlin.

Waddington, C. H. (1957). *The strategy of the genes*, Allen and Unwin, London.

Waddington, C. H. (1968). *Towards a theoretical biology*, University of Edinburgh Press, Edinburgh.

Weismann, A. (1909). The selection theory. In A. C. Seward (Ed.), *Darwin and modern science*, Cambridge University Press, Cambridge.

NOTE

1.   This is quite evident from the following explanatory comment I have received from Professor Pittendrigh by letter (dated February 26, 1970): 'You ask about the word "teleonomy". You are correct that I did introduce the term into biology, and, moreover, I invented it. In the course of thinking about that paper which I wrote for the Simpson and Roe book (in which the term is introduced) I was haunted by the famous old quip of Haldane's to the effect that "Teleology is like a mistress to a biologist: he cannot live without her but he's unwilling to be seen with her in public." The more I thought about that, it occurred to me that whole thing was nonsense—that what it was the biologist couldn't live with was not the illegitimacy of the relationship, but the relationship itself. Teleology in its Aristotelian form has, of course, the end as immediate, "efficient", cause. And that is precisely what the biologist (with the whole history of science since 1500 behind him) cannot accept: it is unacceptable in a world that is always mechanistic (and of course in this I include probabilistic as well as strictly deterministic). What it was the biologist could not escape was the plain fact—or rather the fundamental fact—which he must (as scientist) explain: that the objects of biological analysis are organizations (he calls them organisms) and, as such, are end-directed. Organization is more than mere order; order lacks end-directedness; organization *is* end-directed. [I recall a wonderful conversation with John von Nevmann in which we explored the difference between "mere order" and "organization" and *his* insistence (I already believed it) that the concept organization (as contextually defined in its everyday use) always involved "purpose" or end-directedness.]

'I wanted a word that would allow me (all of us biologists) to describe, stress or simply to allude to—without offense—this end-directedness of a perfectly respectable mechanistic system. Teleology would not do, carrying with it that implication that the end is causally effective in the current operation of the machine. Teleonomic, it is hoped, escapes that plain falsity which is anyhow unnecessary. Haldane was, in this sense wrong (surely a rare event): we can live without teleology.

'The crux of the problem lies of course in unconfounding the mechanism of evolutionary change and the physiological mechanism of the organism abstracted from the evolutionary time scale. The most general of all biological "ends", or "purposes", is of course perpetuation by reproduction. *That* end [and all its subsidiary "ends" of feeding, defense and survival generally] is in some sense effective in causing natural selection; in causing evolutionary change; but not in causing itself. In brief, we have failed in the past to unconfound causation in the historical origins of a system and causation in the contemporary working of the system....

'You ask in your letter whether or not one of the "information" people didn't introduce it. They did not, unless you wish to call me an information bloke. It is, however, true that my own thinking about the whole thing was very significantly affected by a paper which was published by Wiener and Bigelow with the intriguing title "Purposeful machines." This pointed out that in the then newly-emerging computer period it was possible to design and build machines that had ends or purposes without implying that the purposes were the cause of the immediate operation of the machine.'

Learning, Development, and Culture
Edited by H. C. Plotkin
© 1982, John Wiley & Sons Ltd.

CHAPTER 3

Natural selection, adaptation, and progress

G. C. Williams*

One of the strengths of scientific inquiry is that it can progress with any mixture of empiricism, intuition, and formal theory that suits the convenience of the investigator. Many sciences develop for a time as exercises in description and empirical generalization. Only later do they acquire reasoned connections within themselves and with other branches of knowledge. Many things were scientifically known of human anatomy and the motions of the planets before they were scientifically explained.

The study of adaptation seems to show the opposite mode of development. It has already had its Newtonian synthesis, but its Galileo and Kepler have not yet appeared. The 'Newtonian synthesis' is the genetical theory of natural selection, a logical unification of Mendelism and Darwinism that was accomplished by Fisher, Haldane, and Wright more than thirty years ago. For all its formal elegance, however, this theory has provided very limited guidance in the work of biologists. Ordinarily it does little more than to give a vague aura of validity to conclusions on adaptive evolution and to enable a biologist to refer to goal-directed activities without descending into teleology. The inherent strength of the theory is restricted by the paucity of generalizations, analogous to Kepler's laws, that can serve on the one hand as summaries of large masses

---

* Reprinted from Chapter 2 of *Adaptation and Natural Selection: A Critique of Current Evolutionary Thought* (1966) (copyright © 1966 by Princeton University Press), pp. 20–55 with the permission of the author. Reprinted by permission of Princeton University Press.

of observations and, on the other hand, as logical deductions from the theory. The deficiency of course is not absolute. The kind of generalization I have in mind is well illustrated by Lack's (1954) conclusion on the selection of fecundity in animals that feed their young and Fisher's (1930) conclusion on population sex ratios. With perhaps another hundred such insights we could have a unified science of adaptation.

The current lack of such unification has some unfortunate consequences. One is that a biologist can make any evolutionary speculation seem scientifically acceptable merely by adorning his arguments with the forms and symbols of the theory of natural selection. Thus we have biologists recognizing, in the name of natural selection, mutation, isolation, etc., adaptations designed to meet the demands of geologically future events. This fallacy commonly occurs in the guise of provisions for 'evolutionary plasticity'. Other biologists speak of natural selection as ensuring that an individual or a population will have all the adaptations that are *necessary* for its survival and imply that adaptations are never expected to be more or less than *adequate* to ensure survival. Such powers might appropriately be attributed to a prescient Providence, but certainly not to natural selection, as this process is commonly described.

Another tendency that survives, despite its lack of a theoretical justification, is a belief in a deterministic succession of evolutionary stages. Simpson's book of 1944 can be taken to symbolize the end of orthogenetic interpretations of paleontological data, but long-term evolutionary determinism is still detectable in some discussions of *progress* in evolution. Huxley (1953, 1954), for example, argued that evolutionary progress was inevitable and proceeded by a series of advances to new levels until all possible levels but one had been achieved: '... by the Pliocene only one path of progress remained open—that which led to man' (1954, p. 11). Huxley admits that the details of the process of progressing to higher levels would have been unpredictable at any one point in geological time, but says, 'On the other hand, once we can look back on the facts we realize that it could have happened in no other way' (1953, p. 128). The force that drives and guides evolutionary progress is said to be natural selection. This argument is an excellent example of how one can abide by the outward forms of the theory but violate its spirit.

I doubt that many biologists subscribe to the view of evolution as a deterministic progression towards man, but there is widespread belief in some form of aesthetically acceptable progress as an inevitable outcome of organic evolution. In this chapter I will discuss some of the limitations of the process of natural selection and their bearing on some common suppositions, such as the inevitability of progress. The stress on limitations does not indicate any doubt on my part as to the importance of natural selection. Within its limited range of activity, it has a potency that may still be generally underestimated by the majority of biologists. There is a very illuminating discussion by Müller (1948) on this point.

THE ESSENCE of the genetical theory of natural selection is a statistical bias in the relative rates of survival of alternatives (genes, individuals, etc.). The effectiveness of such bias in producing adaptation is contingent on the maintenance of certain quantitative relationships among the operative factors. One necessary condition is that the selected entity must have a high degree of permanence and a low rate of endogenous change, relative to the degree of bias (differences in selection coefficients). Permanence implies reproduction with a potential geometric increase.

Acceptance of this theory necessitates the immediate rejection of the importance of certain kinds of selections. The natural selection of phenotypes cannot in itself produce cumulative change, because phenotypes are extremely temporary manifestations. They are the result of an interaction between genotype and environment that produces what we recognize as an individual. Such an individual consists of genotypic information and information recorded since conception. Socrates consisted of the genes his parents gave him, the experiences they and his environment later provided, and a growth and development mediated by numerous meals. For all I know, he may have been very successful in the evolutionary sense of leaving numerous offspring. His phenotype, nevertheless, was utterly destroyed by the hemlock and has never since been duplicated. If the hemlock had not killed him, something else soon would have. So however natural selection may have been acting on Greek phenotypes in the fourth century B. C., it did not of itself produce any cumulative effect.

The same argument also holds for genotypes. With Socrates' death, not only did his phenotype disappear, but also his genotype. Only in species that can maintain unlimited clonal reproduction is it theoretically possible for the selection of genotypes to be an important evolutionary factor. This possibility is not likely to be realized very often, because only rarely would individual clones persist for the immensities of time that are important in evolution. The loss of Socrates' genotype is not assuaged by any consideration of how prolifically he may have reproduced. Socrates' genes may be with us yet, but not his genotype, because meiosis and recombination destroy genotypes as surely as death.

It is only the meiotically dissociated fragments of the genotype that are transmitted in sexual reproduction, and these fragments are further fragmented by meiosis in the next generation. If there is an ultimate indivisible fragment it is, by definition, 'the gene' that is treated in the abstract discussions of population genetics. Various kinds of suppression of recombination may cause a major chromosomal segment or even a whole chromosome to be transmitted entire for many generations in certain lines of descent. In such cases the segment or chromosome behaves in a way that approximates the population genetics of a single gene. In this book I use the term *gene* to mean 'that which segregates and recombines with appreciable frequency.' Such genes are potentially immortal, in the sense of there being no physiological limit to their survival, because of their potentially reproducing fast enough to compensate for their destruction by external agents. They also have a high degree of qualitative stability. Estimates of mutation rates range from about 10^{-4} to 10^{-10} per generation. The rates of selection of alternative alleles can be much higher. Selection among the progeny of individuals heterozygous for recessive lethals would eliminate half the lethal genes in one generation. Aside from lethal and markedly deleterious genes in experimental populations, there is abundant evidence (e.g. Fisher and Ford, 1947; Ford, 1956; Clarke, Dickson, and Sheppard, 1963) for selection coefficients in nature that exceed mutation rates by one to many multiples of ten. There can be no doubt that the selective accumulation of genes can be effective. In evolutionary theory, a gene could be defined as any hereditary information for which there is a favorable or unfavorable selection bias equal to several or many times its rate of endogenous change. The prevalence of such stable entities in the heredity of populations is a measure of the importance of natural selection.

Natural selection would produce or maintain adaptation as a matter of definition. Whatever gene is favorably selected is better adapted than its unfavored alternatives. This is the reliable outcome of such selection, the prevalence of well-adapted genes. The selection of such genes of course is mediated by the phenotype, and to be favorably selected, a gene must augment phenotypic reproductive success as the arithmetic mean effect of its activity in the population in which it is selected.

A thorough grasp of the concept of a gene's mean phenotypic effect on fitness is essential to an understanding of natural selection. If individuals bearing gene A replace themselves by reproduction to a greater extent than those with gene A', and if the population is so large that we can rule out chance as the explanation, the individuals with A would be, as a group, more fit than those with A'. The difference in their total fitness would be measured by the extent of replacement of one by the other. By definition of mean, the mean effect on individual fitness of A would be favorable and of A' unfavorable. This maximization of mean individual fitness is the most reliable phenotypic effect of selection at the genic level, but even here there are complications and exceptions. For example, a gene might be favorably selected, not because its phenotypic expression favors an individual's reproduction, but because it favors the reproduction of close relatives of that individual. Wright (1949) and Hamilton (1964) have provided generally applicable theoretical discussions of the relationship of selection to individual fitness.

Natural selection commonly produces fitness in the vernacular sense. We ordinarily expect it to favor mechanisms leading to an increase in health and comfort and a decrease in danger to life and limb, but the theoretically important kind of fitness is that which promotes ultimate reproductive survival.

Reproduction always requires some sacrifice of resources and some jeopardy of physiological well-being, and such sacrifices may be favorably selected, even though they may reduce fitness in the vernacular sense of the term.

We ordinarily expect selection to produce only 'favorable' characters, but here again there are exceptions. In the effects of a gene there may be influences on more than one character. A given gene substitution may have one favorable effect and another unfavorable one in the same individual, often, but not necessarily, in different parts of the life cycle. The same gene may produce mainly favorable effects in one individual but mainly unfavorable effects in another, because of differences in environment or genetic background. If the mean effect is favorable, the gene will increase in frequency, and so will all its effects, both positive and negative. There are many relevant examples. An embryonic lethality is a character that has been produced in certain mouse populations by natural selection. The gene that causes this condition is favorably selected, up to an appreciable frequency, because of a favorable effect, 'meiotic drive' in the male gamete stage (Lewontin and Dunn, 1960). Senescence, certain kinds of 'normal' sterility and various hereditary diseases are other examples of unfavorable characters that owe their prevalence to natural selection. In all such examples, the favorable selection of the genetic basis for such deleterious effects must be ascribed to other effects of the same genes. Favorable selection of a gene is inevitable if it has a favorable mean effect compared to the available alternatives of the moment.

Another frequent outcome of natural selection is the promotion of the long-term survival of the population. One example, is the maintenance of fleetness in deer, and many similar examples could be given. Here again, however, there are exceptions. The constant maximization of mean fitness in some populations might bring about an increasing ecological specialization, and this might mean reduced numbers, restricted range, and vulnerability to changed conditions. Haldane (1932) mentioned flower specialization for very efficient pollination by a taxonomically small group of insects as an example of such vulnerability to extinction caused by natural selection. Haldane also mentioned the production of elaborate weapons or of conspicuous ornamentation and display, which might be favored in competition for mates, as factors that decrease population fitness by the wasteful use of resources and the damage and vulnerability to predators caused by sexual conflict. Probably most evolutionary increases in body size cause a decrease in numbers, and this might contribute to extinction. An excellent example of decrease in numbers brought about by natural selection is the evolution of the slave-making instinct in certain groups of ants (Emerson, 1960).

IN DISCUSSIONS of the role of adaptation in the survival of populations one often finds statements to the effect that selection caused certain developments because they were necessary. It is often difficult to distinguish semantic and conceptual difficulties, but I believe that there are common conceptual fallacies such as might be illustrated by this statement:

> The white coat of the polar bear is *necessary* for the stalking of game in the snowy regions in which it lives. The whiteness was favored by selection because darker individuals were unable to survive.

I would correct this argument by substituting *advantageous* for *necessary* in the first sentence, and by adding the words *as well* to the end of the second. Ecological or physiological necessity is not an evolutionary factor, and the development of an adaptation is no evidence that it was necessary to the survival of the species. We might indulge at this point in the fanciful act of rendering all present polar bears and their descendants a bright pink. We can now be sure that the species will not henceforth survive *as well*. Its numbers will suddenly decline and its geographic and ecological range rapidly contract, but we cannot be sure that this decrease will proceed all the way to extinction. Each polar bear, after meeting unaccustomed frustration in its hunting, will adapt by hunting for longer periods of time. Some may learn that they can hunt more successfully at night than by day. These and other adjustments might enable the species to continue in those regions where pinkness is, for one reason or another, less of a handicap than in others. Needless to say, there are many obviously necessary adaptations. If, instead of depriving the bear of its whiteness we deprived it of its lungs, it would immediately become extinct. Such examples, however, do not invalidate the conclusion that the mere presence of an adaptation is no argument for its necessity, either for the individual or the population. It is evidence only that during the evolutionary development of the adaptation the genes that augmented its development survived *at a greater rate* than those that did not. Usually, but not always, the presence of an adaptation causes the species to be more numerous and widespread than it would be without it. Nicholson (1956, 1960) has discussed this relationship of natural selection to population density and has concluded that improved adaptation would often have but slight effect on numbers, because even slight increases might greatly intensify the density-governed reactions that noramlly check population growth. Nicholson is the leading champion of the belief that population densities in nature represent stable equilibria.

The converse argument also holds. The fact that a certain adaptation is necessary to the survival of a species has no bearing on its likelihood of evolving. We can say of every group of organisms that is now extinct that whatever adaptations were necessary for its survival were not, in fact, evolved. This does not demonstrate that there were no tendencies in the necessary direction; it merely means that these tendencies, if there, were not adequate. However, there is no necessity for believing that they were there. The imminence of extinction does not evoke emergency measures on the part of a population. I can imagine that a sonar system would be an advantage in the nocturnal navigation of owls, just as it is for bats. I presume also that many populations of owls have become extinct and that some of these might have survived if provided with even a slight additional advantage, such as a rudimentary sonar system. Would we be more likely to see the beginnings of such a system, or of any other adaptive mechanism, in a small population declining towards extinction than in a large and expanding one? I doubt that any ornithologist would be willing to devote much time looking into such a possibility. I assume that the failure of owls to evolve sonar results from their lack of some necessary preadaptations in all their populations, regardless of size. The lack of sonar is no evidence that it is not necessary for continued existence. Perhaps a post-Recent adaptive radiation of bats will make it necessary for all owls to have an effective sonar system. If so, they will simply join the pterodactyls and hosts of other organisms that lacked necessary adaptations.

The possibility that populations can take special steps in response to the threat of imminent extinction is often implied in elementary biology texts in discussions of adaptive radiation or of the continued survival of ancient types. Certain species, we are told, were able to avoid extinction by seeking marginal habitats, thereby escaping competition from more progressive forms. The avoidance of extinction might well be a result of specialization for niches in which competition is minimal, but it cannot, historically, have been a cause of evolutionary change. Only in an endlessly recurring cycle, as is shown by the succession of generations in a population, can one class of events be both the cause and the effect of another. A mouse can retreat to a hole to avoid being killed by a cat, but a population cannot retreat to a marginal habitat to avoid being killed off by competition. Such a development can only be a secondary effect of the differences in the genetic survival of individuals in the evolving population.

This hypothetical discussion has at least one experimental parallel. Park and Lloyd (1955) showed that experimental flour-beetle populations failed to show a genetic change calculated to avoid the extinction that usually followed the introduction of a competing species. The authors, however, were reluctant to generalize and to conclude that ecological necessity never influences evolutionary change.

There is no way in which a factor of necessity-for-survival could influence natural selection, as this process is usually formulated. Selection has nothing to do with what is necessary or unnecessary, or what is adequate or inadequate, for continued survival. It deals only with an immediate better-vs.-worse within a system of alternative, and therefore competing, entities. It will act to maximize the mean reproductive performance regardless of the effect on long-term population survival. It is not a mechanism that can anticipate possible extinction and take steps to avoid it.

I have indicated above that natural selection works only among competing entities, but it is not necessary for the individuals of a species to be engaged in ecological competition for some limited resource. This requisite is often assumed, beginning with Darwin and continuing with many modern biologists. A little reflection, however, will indicate that natural selection may be most intense when competitive interactions are low. Consider a typical growth curve in an experimental population. Suppose that the genetic variation present in such a population is mainly in the ability to convert food materials, present in excess of maintenance requirements, into offspring. There will then be intense selection during the initial stages of population growth when food is present in excess. Then when competition for food becomes intense, the genetic variation will lose its expression and selection will cease. This is true of all situations in which variation in fitness has greater expressivity under conditions of lower population density. Fuller discussions of this point are provided by Haldane (1931), Birch (1957), Mather (1961), and Milne (1961).

Thus natural selection may be operative in the complete absence of competition in the usual sense. In most animal populations there is no competition for oxygen. The fact that dog A gets enough oxygen in no way influences dog B's efforts to get his share. Only very indirectly, by contributing to other functions, such as food-getting, would respiration relate to ecological competition. The elaborateness and precision of the canine respiratory system, however, leaves no room for doubt that there has been a relentless selection for respiratory efficiency. On the other hand, no organism can escape what I would call reproductive competition. Suppose dog A successfully sires three puppies this year. How can this amount of success be evaluated? Only in comparison with dog B. If neither B nor any other dog in the pack produced more than two, we would conclude that A succeeded very well in reproduction but if the pack mean were four, that A fared badly. The situation is as clear with competing alleles as with competing individuals. Suppose the gene a is present in a thousand individuals in a population in both the present generation and in the preceding one, and the rest of the population has only A. Is a being favorably selected? The answer, of course, cannot be given until 'the rest' is translated into definite numerical values. If the population is increasing, gene a is being unfavorably selected. If it is decreasing, the selection of a is favorable.

In its ultimate essence the theory of natural selection deals with a cybernetic abstraction, the gene, and a statistical abstraction, mean phenotypic fitness. Such a theory can be immensely interesting to those who have a liking and a facility for cybernetics and statistics. Fruitful applications of this theory will also require a detailed knowledge of biology. The theory certainly has little appeal to those who are not in the regular habit of using mathematical abstractions in their thinking about organisms. I doubt that the concept of mean reproductive success as applied to honey bees would have much appeal to such people. The bee population is composed of very many quite sterile individuals and a few extraordinarily fertile ones. A bee of mean fertility would be quite atypical. Yet I believe that the sterility of the workers is entirely attributable to the unrelenting efforts of Darwin's demon to maximize a mere abstraction, the mean. I see little hope of explaining the societies of the social insects in any other way.

DOES this theory, which I believe to be accurately summarized above, necessitate a belief in progress? Many biologists have stated that it does, and many more have tacitly assumed this position. I would maintain, however, that there is nothing in the basic structure of the theory of natural selection that would suggest the idea of any kind of cumulative progress. An organism can certainly improve the precision of its adaptation to current circumstances. It must often happen that a possible allele at a certain locus would be better adapted than any that actually prevail at that locus. The necessary mutation may never have occurred, or may always have been lost by drift when it did occur. Sooner or later, however, such a gene may drift to a sufficiently high frequency to be effectively selected. When this happens it will soon become the normal allele or at least one of a series of normal alleles at its locus. This gene substitution would slightly improve the precision of one or more adaptations, but as perfection is approached the opportunity for further improvement would correspondingly diminish. This is certainly not a process for which the term 'progress' would be at all appropriate.

Gene substitution may also take place because of a changing environment. A gene may at one time be in low frequency because it is unfavorably selected in the environment in which the population finds itself. After a change in environment the gene may be favorably selected and replace its alternative alleles in whole or in part. The phenotypic effect of such a substitution would be to improve one adaptation, one that has increased in importance, at the expense of another that has become less important. This again is not something that would suggest the term 'progress', but such selective gene substitution is the only expected outcome of natural selection. I suspect that no one would ever have deduced progress from the theory itself. The concept of progress must have arisen from an anthropocentric consideration of the data bearing on the history of life.

Progress has meant different things to different people. The views are not all mutually exclusive, but for convenience I will consider progress in five separate categories: as accumulation of genetic information; as increasing morphological complexity; as increasing physiological division of labor; as any evolutionary tendency in some arbitrarily designated direction; as increased effectiveness of adaptation.

The most notable contribution on progress as accumulation of information is Kimura's (1961). His discussion is an important contribution to evolutionary theory, but I believe that its value is compromised by his acceptance of some naïve preconceptions. He assumes, without any explicit evidence, that modern zygotes contain more information then Cambrian zygotes. He clearly implies that a human zygote has a higher information content than any other zygote, or at least than most other zygotes. There is no direct evidence on which this position might be contested, but there is also little evidence in its favor. Man is superlative in many ways; he is by far the most intelligent organism, and he has very recently achieved an ecological dominance of unprecedented scope. It does not follow from this that he is superlative in all important respects, such as the measure of negentropy in his genetic code. Genetic codes have changed enormously since Cambrian time, and natural selection has guided these changes, but it need not have increased the total information content.

Kimura's analysis shows that initially nonsensical DNA can be rapidly organized by natural selection so as to constitute instructions for adaptation. He estimates that 10^8 bits of information could be accumulated in a line of descent in the time elapsed since the Cambrian period by natural selection acting in opposition to randomizing forces. He notes that the amount of DNA in a cell may be ten to a hundred times the amount necessary to convey this information, and he interprets this and other evidence to indicate that the DNA message is very redundant. Evidently Kimura believes that a large proportion of the information in the genotype of a higher organism has accumulated since the Cambrian period, and been 'written' in then unspecified DNA.

Kimura's discussion is of value in indicating what natural selection can accomplish in half a billion generations. My inclination would be to accept his account of the accumulation of information but to apply it not to the Cambrian but to the period immediately after the first appearance of cellular organisms under the control of a DNA coding system. At that time genetic information would be expected to accumulate, but it is unreasonable to assume that it would accumulate indefinitely. A certain amount of information is added by selection every generation. At the same time, a certain amount is subtracted by randomizing processes. The more information is already stored, the more would mutation and other random forces reduce it in a given time interval. It is reasonable to suppose that there would be a maximum level of information content that could be maintained by selection in opposition to randomizing forces. It also seems inevitable that much of the gene substitution that is actually in progress at any one time is of a readily reversible sort. Kimura made allowances for the neutralization of some of the effect of selection by mutation pressure, and showed that some effect would remain. He assumed that all of this remainder would be available for progress in the accumulation of information, and made no allowances for the reversal of selection. If selection were to change a gene frequency from 0.2 to 0.8 in a century and then in the following century change it back to 0.2, there would have been evolution, but no net accumulation of information.

Sheppard (1954) reviewed evidence that even strong selection pressures in natural insect populations may change sign as a result of slight environmental changes. Selection of isoalleles, with very slight differences in selection coefficients, would be expected to change sign more readily than the major gene differences studied by Sheppard. Reversing selection at a gene locus would not imply a reversal of the course of evolution for the population. Reversals at different loci would be at least partly independent, and the population would have a unique set of gene frequencies at any one moment. In environments that were changing, however, much of natural selection would be directed at undoing what it had recently established. In stable environments selection would usually produce a decrease of heterozygosity (Lewontin, 1958), and this would also reduce the total genetic information. If one takes these factors into account, Kimura's calculations can be reinterpreted to mean that no genetic information is accumulating in modern organisms.

This conclusion is supported by other considerations. The accumulation of information is a function of selection pressures and numbers of generations. If man's ancestors, as Kimura suggested, have had an average generation length of one year since Cambrian time, and if much of his ancestry before that time was at the protistan stage, there might have been a thousand times as many generations before the Cambrian as since. If so, Kimura's calculations would indicate that 10^{11} bits of information might have accumulated before the Cambrian. There is not enough DNA in a human zygote to carry nearly this amount. I would suspect that long before the Cambrian most phylogenetic lineages had established an optimum amount of DNA and had fully optimized its burden of information. This conclusion is supported by Blum's (1963) reasoning on the rate of approach to perfection in adaptation in a constant environment. His thinking was quite different from Kimura's and amounts to an estimate of the proportion of untried alleles at each locus after a given period of time. The conclusion depends on estimates of mutation rate per generation, but with an average mutation rate of 10^{-6} there would be very little possible progress remaining after 10^7 generations, or perhaps a thousand years in a protist population. Only a short time should be required to establish an equilibrium between the increase of information by natural selection and its destruction by random processes. These processes should be understood to include not only mutation, but also any environmental changes that result in reversals of selection pressures.

It might seem reasonable to expect that the amount of information could be simply measured as the amount of DNA in the zygote. This would be true if we could be sure that the amount of redundancy per unit of zygotic information is constant, but I know of no basis for even indulging in guesswork on this point. Our information on DNA content is meagre and little advanced beyond the beginnings made by Mirsky and Ris (1951) and Vendrely (1955). Such simple protists as the bacteria and sporozoa have small amounts of DNA, as might be expected from the minute size of their cells. The invertebrates are highly variable but with some association between the amount of DNA and position on the phylogenetic scale. This association is largely a function of an extremely high value for the squid, greater than for any mammal. Among the vertebrates the only suggested trend is for a reduction of DNA in the lung-fish-to-bird sequence. Mammals have more than birds, but not as much as amphibians. Such inconsistencies between DNA content and the presumed level of evolutionary advance is customarily explained by assuming a high level of genetic redundancy in the lower organisms (Mirsky and Ris, 1951; Waddington, 1962, pp. 59–60). Our knowledge of phylogenetic variation in cellular DNA content is based for the most part on the grossly inadequate evidence of single values for single representatives of phyla and classes.

We have little notion of what proportion of the human zygotic information is concerned with structure at the anatomical and histological levels, and what proportion relates to cellular and biochemical mechanisms, in other words, the number of constraints imposed by selection for gross structural adaptations in comparison with those imposed by selection for cellular and biochemical characters. If we knew that three-fourths of the information in the human germ plasm were devoted to morphogenetic instructions, we might conclude that man must have about four times as much zygotic information as an amoeba. But suppose only one-tenth were concerned with morphology and the rest with biochemistry. Man would then have only a little more than an amoeba, and an alga, with its elaborate synthetic enzyme systems, might have more than either.

This is a problem that can be approached only in the most speculative manner, but some of the considerations that Kimura raised have bearing on how much information is present in the zygote. He reasoned that about 10^7 bits of information would be necessary to specify human anatomy, and that a maximum of 10^{10} bits could be carried by the DNA present in the zygote. If we assume that the DNA message is so redundant as to be utilized at only one-tenth of its maximum capacity, we could still conclude from these estimates that a hundred times as much of the information in the germ plasm is concerned with basic cellular and biochemical mechanisms as is concerned with morphogenesis. I suggest this, not as a conclusion to be seriously considered, but as one end of a spectrum of possibilities. The spectrum is so wide that it would seem premature to base any conclusions on an estimate of the difference in genetic information content of a mammal and a protist.

Presumably the amount of DNA would always be regulated at some optimum value by selection. The DNA present in the body would very seldom be a significant mechanical or nutritional burden. If increasing DNA content would permit the carrying of more information and thereby allow greater precision or versatility of adaptation, I presume that such an increase would take place. Economy and efficiency are universal characteristics of biological mechanisms, and the DNA coding system should certainly not be an exception. Its manifest purpose is the carrying of information, and it is reasonable to assume that it is in relation to this function that its quantity is optimized. The optimum would be determined by the amount of information that can be maintained by selection in the face of randomizing processes. The more micrograms of DNA are present, the less will selection be able to control the information content per microgram. Decreased control means increased noise and consequent reduction in the adaptive precision of the phenotype. Quantity of information and precision of information are somewhat opposed requirements of the genetic message. The amount of DNA in an organism would presumably reflect the optimum compromise between these opposing values. It would follow from this that genetic information is limited in amount and must be utilized as economically as possible. A number of biological phenomena suggest that some such principle of economy of information is an important evolutionary factor.

The view suggested here is that all organisms of above a certain low level of organization—perhaps that of the simpler invertebrates—and beyond a certain geological period—perhaps the Cambrian—may have much the same amounts of information in their nuclei. All such organisms have quantities of DNA capable of carrying an enormous amount of information, and all have ancestries of at least 10^9 years and an astronomical number of generations that were subject to the same information-generating force. We can interpret evolution since the Cambrian as a history of substitutions and qualitative changes in the germ plasm, not an increase in its total content. Evolution from protist to man might have been largely a matter of the substitution of morphogenetic instructions for a small proportion of the biochemical and cytological instructions in the protist DNA.

KIMURA'S conclusions on cybernetic progress arose from his acceptance of the second category of evolutionary progress, that of increasing morphological complexity. It is often stated or implied that animals of the Recent epoch are morphologically more complex than those of the Paleozoic era, but I am not aware of any objective and unbiased documentation of this point. Is man really more complex structurally than his piscine progenitor of Devonian time? We can certainly describe a more complex series of evolutionary changes in, for example, the human skull than in the Devonian fish skull, but this is at least partly attributable to our ignorance of pre-Devonian chordates. The Devonian-to-Recent lineage of man is mainly a history of changing arrangements and losses of parts, in the skull and elsewhere. Real additions are not a conspicuous part of the story. Mechanically the human skull is exceedingly simple in its workings compared to most fish skulls. Even in the Devonian period there were fishes, e.g. *Rhizodopsis*, with skulls made up of large numbers of precisely articulating bony parts that formed a complex mechanical system. I believe that it would be difficult to document objectively the general conclusion that Recent animals are structurally more complex than known Paleozoic members of the same taxa.

Man must, of course, have had morphologically simple metazoan ancestors somewhere in his history, if not in the Devonian period, then before. The question of the relative complexity of man and fish arises in connection with the popular pair of assumptions that (1) evolutionary progress from lower to higher organisms consists of increasing structural complexity; (2) the change from fish to mammal exemplifies such progress. In some respects, such as brain structure, a mammal is certainly more complex than any fish. In other respects, such as integumentary histology, the average fish is much more complex than any mammal. What the verdict after a complete and objective comparison would be is uncertain.

In considering the relative structural complexity of different organisms it is customary to limit discussion to the adults of each type. This is partly justified by the fact that the adult stage is usually the most structurally complex stage in the life cycle, but this limitation also may indicate a relatively naïve view of development. Ontogeny is often intuitively regarded as having one terminal goal, the adult-stage phenotype, but the real goal of development is the same as that of all other adaptations, the continuance of the dependent germ plasm. The visible somatic life cycle is the indispensable machinery by which this goal may be met, and every stage is as rightfully a goal as any other. Each stage has two theoretically separable tasks. First it must deal with the immediate problems of survival, a matter of ecological adjustment. Secondly it must produce the next succeeding stage. The morphogenetic instructions must provide for both jobs. The burden of ecological adaptation must inevitably be heavy in a stage that inhabits a complex and often hostile environment. In stages spent in constant and normally favorable environments, however, very little of the genetic information need be concerned with ecological adjustments, and developmental compromises can be heavily in favor of effective morphogenetic preparation at the expense of the machinery of immediate ecological adjustment. Compare, for example, the kinds of adaptation shown by human foetuses with those shown by children and adults. The foetus lives in an actively cooperative environment and has few ecological problems. It can concentrate on rapid and efficient morphogenetic preparations for later stages. The child or the man lives in a complex and frequently hostile environment. In these stages the emphasis is on precise sensory, motor, immunological, and other ecological adaptations. The morphogenetic preparations are much less fundamental in scope and much slower than those of the foetus.

But suppose the human foetus lived, not in a protective and solicitous uterus, but in an environment like that of a tadpole. Suppose that man's 'larval' development, like that of a frog, took place in an environment different from that of the adult and as complex and dangerous as that of an amphibian larva. Man's germ plasm would then undoubtedly be burdened with instructions for coping with conditions as rigorous as those on pond bottoms. Complex sensory and motor mechanisms would be developed early in life, and some of these would need drastic modification for the adult stage.

How much would the total information content of the human zygote be augmented by such additional instructions? There is no answer available at the moment, but if the question could be workably and realistically codified, perhaps a formal analysis would provide some understanding. Such an analysis might take the form of asking whether there is more developmental information in two zygotes, one of which develops into *A* and the other into *B*, than in a single zygote which develops first into *A* and then into *B*. The single zygote, while developing into *A* must, as an added duty, preserve the information necessary for producing *B*, and producing *B* may necessitate an undoing of part of *A*. Would this mean that the more complex life cycle would require more information than the two simple ones? Until sound arguments are formulated we must be wary of passing judgments on the relative complexities of organisms of very different life cycles.

There are life cycles enormously more complex than that of a frog. The lowly and 'simple' liver fluke develops from a zygote into a multicellular miracidium, which swims by means of a covering of thousands of cilia and has the neuromotor machinery necessary for locating and burrowing into a certain species of snail. Inside a snail it metamorphoses into a morphologically different sporocyst, which reproduces by internal budding. The products of this reproduction are another stage, called the redia. The rediae migrate within the snail and reproduce other rediae asexually. Eventually the rediae metamorphose into another type, the cercariae, which are equipped like the earlier miracidia for migration between hosts, but with quite different motor mechanisms. A cercaria swims by wriggling a tail, not by the action of cilia. A cercaria burrows out of the snail and swims to a blade of grass, to which it attaches, and changes into a dormant, more or less amorphous multicellular mass called a metacercaria. On ingestion by a sheep, a metacercaria hatches out as a young fluke, which develops into an adult fluke within the sheep. The adult flukes produce zygotes which then repeat the cycle. Such a complex succession of morphologically different stages must demand much more in the way of morphogenetic instructions in the germ plasm than would ever be suspected on the basis of the structural complexity visible at any one time. I can see no reliable way at present of evaluating the relative morphological complexity of such different organisms as a sheep and the fluke in its liver, and no way of determining which has the greater burden of morphological instructions or total genetic information in its zygote.

The apparent ease with which trematodes and other parasites can add and subtract distinct morphological stages in their life cycles has a bearing on the problem of the proportion of genetic information that relates to morphogenesis. Perhaps it means that the instructions for producing a cercaria, for instance, are a very trivial part of the total information that must be carried in the fluke zygote.

PROGRESS in animal evolution is sometimes assumed to mean increasing histological differentiation. Such progress, like increasing morphological complexity, must have occurred somewhere in the development of all of the Metazoa. Also, I am inclined to concede that mammalian tissues may be physiologically somewhat more specialized than those of a fish. Such tissue specialization is apparently acquired at the price of regenerative abilities. To a certain extent this implies the substitution of one adaptation for another, not merely additional adaptations. The concept of progress as tissue specialization would probably have little appeal in an application outside the vertebrates. Such cell-constant organisms as rotifers and round-worms would have to be considered higher animals than the mammals. Their tissues are so specialized that they even lack effective mechanisms for the healing of minor wounds (Needham, 1952).

Many of the concepts of evolutionary progress and the implied judgments of the degree of advancement of different organisms adhere to the forms of an earlier orthogenetic doctrine even though the doctrine is almost unanimously discredited. It would be in line with current practice to note that evolution has, in fact, produced an organism of special interest, such as man or the horse. Progress is then arbitrarily designated as any change in the direction of man or horse. As a convention most biologists would accept the judgments that *Pliohippus* is more advanced than *Mesohippus*, and that *Australopithecus* is a higher form than *Proconsul*. In groups in which there are no end products of anthropocentric importance, as in the flowering plants and the fishes, there is still a conventional recognition of lower and higher forms. It is observed in the fishes that a number of faunally important groups have independently undergone certain developments: an upward shift of the pectoral fins and a forward shift of the pelvics; the establishment of relatively low and constant numbers of vertebrae, fin rays, and other meristic parts; loss, in the adult, of the embryonic connection between the air bladder and the gut; development of defensive spines in various parts; etc. Groups that show many such developments are considered higher than those that show few or none. The mere extent of departure from primitive conditions is another important consideration. The flatfishes, with their drastic reorganization of the primitive bilateral symmetry and their many other striking modifications, are always accorded a high place by systematic ichthyologists.

Biologists who are especially zealous in avoiding such concepts as evolutionary progress will sometimes use the term *specialized* instead of *advanced*. This term, however, has value in an ecological context that is independent of phylogenetic position. Thus a pike and a bluefish are similarly and perhaps almost equally specialized for a fish diet, but one is low and the other high on the ichthyologist's conventional scale.

There is no objection to the use of such terms as *progress* and *advance* to designate conformity to common phyletic trends or approach to an arbitrarily designated final stage, but unfortunately the acceptance of the term in this sense can disguise its use in other senses. Thus mammalogists, using extensive and objective evidence, classify the primates into suborders, families, and genera, and then list these categories with tree shrews at the beginning and man at the end. The acceptance of this classification then makes it easy to imply that progress toward man is a recognized evolutionary principle that has operated throughout the history of the primates. I suspect that evolutionary progress and the inevitability of man may seem like scientific ideas only because of our heritage of such orthogenetic terms as 'higher' or 'advanced' organisms and the fact that a list of taxonomic categories has to have a beginning and an end.

PROGRESS is also commonly taken to imply improvement in the effectiveness of adaptation in a way analogous to technological improvements in man's implements. Huxley's (1954) treatment recognizes such improvement as a common result of evolution but restricts the recognition of progress to a relatively few, especially promising sorts of improvement. Brown (1958) makes a similar distinction between special adaptations and general adaptations. Brown is more liberal in his recognition of general adaptation than Huxley is in the recognition of progress. Unlike Huxley, Brown believes that there is still abundant opportunity for evolutionary progress. Waddington's (1961) concept of progress seems closely related to Brown's and emphasizes independence of environmental change as an important component. To Thoday (1953, 1958) progress means improvement in the long-term effectiveness of adaptation so as to make the population less likely to become extinct. Most of my discussion on progress as improvement of adaptation will apply to Thoday's concept.

It is certainly true that some evolutionary developments, such as the specialization of certain Devonian fishes for a marginal and often anaerobic habitat, can precipitate adaptive radiations of great importance, and that other developments have had no such consequences. Unfortunately, no one has proposed any objective criteria by which we might, *a priori*, distinguish the categories of progressive and restrictive changes. I will confine the present discussion to the treatment of the concept of adaptational improvement as synonymous with progress, or at least an aspect of it.

It may help to start with an analogy in human artifice. We would regard a modern jet-powered aircraft as more advanced than a propeller-driven craft. It should be noted that this need not imply that the improvement involves an increase in complexity. On the contrary, the jet is in basic plan much simpler, but it represents a greater achievement of engineering, and it is in many ways a better engine. The jets have rapidly replaced their ancestors in both military and commercial applications. The propeller-driven craft may not be facing complete extinction, but it has disappeared from many of the fields in which it was once dominant, and it has lost ground in many others.

There seem to be many analogies in organic evolution. The gnathostomes almost entirely replaced the agnaths, presumably because they were more effective fishes. The angiosperms largely replaced the gymnosperms, presumably because they were more effective terrestrial autotrophs. The Carnivora entirely replaced the creodonts, presumably because they were more effective mammalian carnivores; and so on. On the other hand, in the Mesozoic era the newly evolved reptilian mososaurs, plesiosaurs, and ichthyosaurs contested the seas with large carnivorous fishes, such as the ancient sharks. The sharks are still here in great abundance, while their reptilian competitors are all extinct. The Pliocene epoch saw the mass extinction of many of the higher mammalian carnivores, ungulates, and primates, but more primitive mammals and lower groups were little affected. Today the fishery biologists greatly fear such archaic fishes as the bowfin, garpikes, and lamprey, because they are such outstandingly effective competitors and predators of valued teleosts like the black basses and salmonids. I cite these examples not because I believe that the lower forms usually prevail over the supposedly more advanced, but simply to show that the game can be played both ways. The citing of selected examples of the supposed operation of a process, such as the dominance of recently evolved types over the more ancient, cannot be accepted as evidence for the process. Only an unbiased and statistically significant list of examples would be acceptable. Such evidence is conceivably obtainable, but I know of no attempt to obtain it.

I must concede that some of the traditional examples are impressive in themselves. The triumph of the placental mammals over the marsupials in South America gives every indication that the placentals are, by and large, better adapted. It is tempting to attribute the success of the placentals to such characters as their larger brains and their chorionic placentas, by which we recognize them as more progressive forms. But even here there are other possible interpretations. There is reason to believe that representatives of rich biotas, such as that of the Holarctic, are usually better able to invade new areas than representatives of poor biotas like the Neotropical, regardless of their positions on phylogenetic scales. There may also be a purely statistical factor at work. If there were many more genera and species of placentals in North America than there were marsupials in South America, we would expect many more successful north-to-south migrants through the isthmus than south-to-north ones. Even if it could be demonstrated that the placentals are adaptively superior to the marsupials, this would be only one example of the superiority of a supposedly higher form over a lower.

An even better example is the rapid, worldwide triumph of the angiosperms over all other forms of terrestrial autotrophs. Most of the more philosophical discussions of progress, however, have little to say about the plants. The botanists do make use of the concept of advancement on a phylogenetic scale, with increased specialization to the terrestrial habitat as the main criterion. Such things as the absence of dependence of the fertilization process on an aquatic medium of sperm transport receive particular emphasis. Conformity to general phylogenetic trends, especially in flower structure, is another important consideration. It would certainly be reasonable to attribute the triumph of the angiosperms to the terrestrial specializations seen in the vascular and reproductive systems.

If it should turn out that the weight of evidence favors the conclusion that what we intuitively regard as higher organisms are adaptively superior to the more primitive types, it will obviously be only a minor statistical bias, with many notable exceptions. Despite the supposed inferiority of the adaptations of amphibians—and any general zoology text can supply an impressive list—the modern anurans and urodeles seem abundantly successful. If numbers of individuals or of species is any criterion, as it is often assumed to be, we live in an age of amphibians as much as an age of mammals. The amphibians compete directly with reptiles, birds, and mammals for food and other essentials, and do not seem to be at a great disadvantage. There are many examples of ancient phyla of presumably low development that are abundant in species, individuals, and biomass even though they are often in close competition with presumably more progressive groups. The sponges and hydroids are more in evidence in coastal waters than the bryozoans and ascidians. I can think of no more important evidence on this problem than the obvious fact of the continued success of ancient and supposedly inferior types.

The most apparent explanation is that the taxonomic diversification of life has been mainly a matter of the substitution of one adaptation for another, independently in different lines of descent, rather than an accumulation of adaptation, as would be implied by the term 'progress'. The original tetrapods became better walkers at the price of becoming inferior swimmers. The original homoiotherms decreased their metabolic dependence on environmental temperatures, but thereby increased their requirements for food, and so on. There were undoubtedly some important, long-term, cumulative trends in the early evolution of life. Some may have continued even after evolution became stylized by the establishment of precise chromosomal inheritance and sexual reproduction. Some may even be in evidence today, and some may be of a kind that would suggest the term 'progress'. The demonstration and description of such trends are matters of scientific interest and deserve some attention from evolutionary biologists. On the other hand, it seems certain that within any million-year period since the Cambrian such trends were of very minor consequence. The important process in each such period was the maintenance of adaptation in every population. This required constant rectification of the damage caused by mutation, and occasionally involved gene substitutions, usually in response to environmental change. Evolution, with whatever general trends it may have entailed, was a by-product of the maintenance of adaptation. At the end of a million years an organism would almost always be somewhat different in appearance from what it was at the beginning, but in the important respect it would still be exactly the same; it would still show the uniquely biological property of adaptation, and it would still be precisely adjusted to its particular circumstances. I regard it as unfortunate that the theory of natural selection was first developed as an explanation for evolutionary change. It is much more important as an explanation for the maintenance of adaptation.

I believe that my point of view on the subject of progress and of changes in the mechanisms of adaptation is really the prevailing one in the laboratory and the field and in the technical literature of biology. It is mainly when biologists become self-consciously philosophical, as they often do when they address nontechnical audiences, that they begin to stress such concepts as evolutionary progress. This situation is unfortunate, because it implies that biology is not being accurately represented to the public.

REFERENCES

Birch, L. C. (1957). The meanings of competition. *Am. Naturalist*, **91**, 5–18.

Blum, Harold F. (1963). On the origin and evolution of human culture. *Am. Scientist*, **51**, 32–37.

Brown, William L. Jr. (1958). General adaptation and evolution. *Syst. Zool.*, **7**, 157–168.

Clarke, C. A., Dickson, C. G. C., and Sheppard, P. M. (1963). Larval color pattern in *Papilio demodocus. Evolution*, **17**, 130–137.

Emerson, Alfred E. (1960). The evolution of adaptation in population systems. In Sol Tax (Ed.), *Evolution after Darwin*, Vol. 1, University of Chicago Press, Chicago. pp. 307–348.

Fisher, Ronald A. (1930). *The Genetical Theory of Natural Selection*, Clarendon Press, Oxford; reprinted 1958, Dover, New York.

Fisher, Ronald A., and Ford, E. B. (1947). The spread of a gene in natural conditions in a colony of the moth, *Panaxia dominula* (L). *Heredity*, **1**, 143–174.

Ford, E. B. (1956). Rapid evolution and the conditions which make it possible. *Cold Spring Harbor Symp. Quant. Biol.*, **20**, 230–238.

Haldane, J. B. S. (1931). A mathematical theory of natural and artificial selection, Part VII, Selection intensity as a function of mortality rate. *Proc. Cambridge Phil. Soc.*, **27**, 131–142.

Haldane, J. B. S. (1932). *The Causes of Evolution*, Longmans, London.

Hamilton, W. D. (1964). The genetical evolution of social behaviour, I. *J. Theoret. Biol.*, **7**, 1–16.

Huxley, Julian S. (1953). *Evolution in Action*, Harper, New York.

Huxley, Julian S. (1954). The evolutionary process. In J. Huxley, A. C. Hardy, and E. B. Ford (Eds), *Evolution as a Process*, Allen and Unwin, London. pp. 1–23.

Kimura, Motoo (1961). Natural selection as the process of accumulating genetic information in adaptive evolution. *Genet. Res.*, **2**, 127–140.

Lack, David (1954). *The Natural Regulation of Animal Numbers*, Oxford University Press, Oxford.

Lewontin, R. C. (1958). Studies on heterozygosity and homeostasis, II, Loss of heterosis in constant environment. *Evolution*, **12**, 494–503.

Lewontin, R. C., and Dunn, L. C. (1960). The evolutionary dynamics of a polymorphism in the house mouse. *Genetics*, **45**, 705–722.

Mather, Kenneth (1961). Competition and cooperation. *Symp. Soc. Exp. Bio.*, **15**; 264–281.

Milne, A. (1961). Definition of competition among animals. *Symp. Soc. Exp. Bio.*, **15**, 40–61.

Mirsky, A. E., and Mis, H. (1951). The desoxyribonucleic acid content of animal cells and its evolutionary significance. *J. Gen. Physiol.*, **34**, 451–462.

Muller, H. J. (1948). Evidence of the precision of genetic adaptation. *Harvey Lectures*, **43**, 165–229.

Needham, A. E. (1952). *Regeneration and Wound Healing*, Wiley, New York.

Nicholson, J. A. (1956). Density governed reaction, the counterpart of selection in evolution. *Cold Spring Harbor Symp. Quant. Biol.*, **20**, 288–293.

Nicholson. J. A. (1960). The role of population dynamics in natural selection. In Sol Tax (Ed.), *Evolution after Darwin*, Vol. 1, University of Chicago Press, Chicago. pp. 477–521.

Park, Thomas, and Lloyd, M. (1955). Natural selection and the outcome of competition. *Am. Naturalist*, **89**, 235–240.

Sheppard, P. M. (1954). Evolution in bisexually reproducing organisms. In J. Huxley, A. C. Hardy, and E. B. Ford (Eds), *Evolution as a Process*, Allen and Unwin, London. pp. 201–218.

Simpson, George Gaylord (1944). *Tempo and Mode in Evolution*. Columbia University Press, New York.

Thoday, J. M. (1953). Components of fitness. *Symp. Soc. Exp. Biol.*, **1**, 96–113.

Thoday, J. M. (1958). Natural selection and biological progress. In S. A. Barnett (Ed.), *A Century of Darwin*, Heinemann, London. pp. 313–333.

Vendrely, R. (1955). The desoxyribonucleic acid content of the nucleus. In E. Chargaff and J. N. Davidson (Eds), *The Nucleic Acids*, Vol. 2, Academic Press, New York. pp. 155–180.

Waddington, C. H. (1961). *The Nature of Life*, Allen and Unwin, London.

Waddington, C. H. (1962). *New Patterns in Genetics and Development*, Columbia University Press, New York.

Wright, S. (1949). Adaptation and selection. In G. L. Gepson, E. Mayr, and G. G. Simpson (Eds), *Genetics, Palaeontology and Evolution*, Princeton University Press, Princeton. pp. 365–386.

SECTION 3

Classic pieces in evolutionary epistemology

Evolutionary epistemology is not yet established as a widely accepted way of thinking in biology—to use Kuhn's phrase, it has not yet become a paradigm for evolutionary biology. For around one hundred years it has maintained a presence in the literature as a series of rather separate threads such as pragmatism, empiricism, the analogy between trial-and-error learning, progress in science and evolution, genetic epistemology and epigenetic approaches to evolution, to name some. With the programme of research and writing begun by Donald T. Campbell in the 1950s, it was drawn together into a single and recognizable form. It is impossible to exclude Campbell from an anthology of essays on evolutionary epistemology, and no easy task to decide which of his works to include. The decision in the end was swayed by the 1974 paper including much historical material, and an historical perspective, that few other reviewers could make into a coherent whole. It is Campbell's unique position of providing an authoritative overview of both biological and social science that makes his work important.

It was Campbell who commissioned the translation of Simmel's essay, and through him that it was privately circulated for some years. It seems that most who read it were fascinated by it. By far the oldest piece in this book, it has a surprisingly modern ring, especially in the way it anticipates the cognition-as-action-and-interaction approach of Piaget. Both Campbell and Irene Jerison, its translator, agreed that this was an appropriate place for its first publication in English. Piaget himself, of course, wrote genetic epistemology for over fifty years. In his work are to be found certain core ideas that are important to the approach taken by this book. The most notable is that all forms of knowledge gain—genetic, epigenetic or individual animal cognition—can be described by the action of the same set of processes that define a universal knowledge-gaining algorithm, with assimilation and accomodation at its centre. '...our main

61

hypothesis (is) the supposition that cognitive mechanisms are an extension of the organic regulations from which they are derived' (Piaget, 1971, p. 346 see chapter 8 for details of reference). However difficult it is to understand his writing, Piaget's work is an essential part of evolutionary epistemology.

Campbell's 1974 essay first appeared in a book devoted to the philosophy of Karl Popper. The original contained many references and direct quotations from Popper's work. I have edited these out from the chapter reprinted here for two reasons. First, I wanted to be able to see Campbell's work in its own right. Second, I felt that Popper should have a chapter to himself. He is one of the few major modern philosophers to take an active interest in evolutionary theory, and as Campbell's original essay bore witness, he himself has contributed in no small way to the development of evolutionary epistemology. The extract from 'Of clouds and clocks' shows the philosopher's concern with an evolutionary theory that must not be too clock-like (predictable and orderly) but neither must it be too cloud-like (unpredictable and disorderly).

Lorenz's writings have always been controversial. His interest in philosophy and biological theory is much less well known than his descriptive, comparative studies of behaviour. I think that he has always been far more open in his thinking about the role of behavioural flexibility, including learning, than is usually supposed and that he was not driven to it in his later work by the criticism of psychologists. The essay on Kant's notion of the *a priori* was written about forty years ago and contains much that is of interest to present day learning theorists who are concerned with the problems of causal texture and how this relates to what animals learn. The piece also links well with Campbell's chapter which in its original form contained an extensive quotation from Lorenz. I have edited out that quotation from the Campbell and included the whole of Lorenz's paper on the doctrine of the *a priori*.

These classic pieces were written over a period of a century by philosophers, psychologists, developmentalists, an ethologist and a sociologist. What does a working evolutionist and population geneticist have to say of it all? Lewontin objects to evolutionary epistemology, at least as it is represented by the chapters in this section, for two main reasons. First, he argues that the metaphors and models of evolutionary epistemology are either incorrect or trivially generalized. Second, he rejects that hallmark of Darwinism that runs through evolutionary epistemology, namely, the passive role of the organism that merely adapts to the problems posed by the world and does not change it. My view is that Lewontin's demand for a more dynamic, dialectical approach to the relationship between living things and their worlds is absolutely correct, though I think he underestimates the extent to which Piaget has achieved this. I also think that evolutionary epistemologists can take heart from Lewontin's essay. The dialectical interaction is a universal property that extends from genes to minds. In any truly general theory of evolution, it is a basis for non-trivial generalization across the levels of life's hierarchical order.

Learning, Development, and Culture
Edited by H. C. Plotkin
© 1982, John Wiley & Sons Ltd.

CHAPTER 4

On a relationship between the theory of selection and epistemology

Georg Simmel*

It has long been assumed that human cognition has its origins in the practical needs for preserving life and providing for it. According to a generally held hypothesis, there exists an objective truth, the content of which is not influenced by the practical needs of the individual; we grasp this truth and incorporate it into our ideas because of its utility, true concepts being more useful than errors. Such a notion of truth is common to the most disparate schools of epistemology, such as realism, in which knowing is a direct assimilation and reflection of an absolute reality, and idealism, which defines knowledge in terms of *a priori* forms of thought. For even in idealism the proper content of cognition is pre-formed by means of a mutual relationship of these forms with respect to a transcendental factor. Knowledge is to its elements as the conclusion to the premises in which it is latent, so to speak. This utility principle, or any other principle which stimulates knowing, is seen to exert no formative influence on such knowing. Its only effect is that this particular content rather than some other is realized psychically. In much the same way, utility can make us perform

* Translated from 'Uber eine Beziehung der Selectionslehre zur Erkenntnistheorie', *Archiv fur systematische Philosophie*, 1895, Vol. 1 number 1, pp. 34–45 by Irene Jerison. The translation, which was requested by Donald T. Campbell, was facilitated by access to Herman Tennessen's 'Brief summary of Gerog Simmel's Evolutionary Epistemology', June 1968, being an abstract of Tennessen's 'Georg Simmel's tillemping av selecksjonslaeren pa erkjennelsesteorier', *Filosofiske Problemer*, 1955, Norwegian University Press, Oslo, pp. 23–30; and also by access to a preliminary translation by Barbara Lalljee. It is reprinted here by permission of Irene Jerison and Donald T. Campbell.

63

a computation but cannot make us obtain a result that is different from that inherent in the objective relationships among its factors whatever we may wish, and whether we regard these factors as externally empirical or as *a priori* ideals.

So it seems plausible that the objective of psychic selection should be, according to any theory of epistemology, a parallelism between thought and objective reality, for therein lies our only assurance that practice based on thought will not collide with the harsh actuality of things and thus become subject to a painful adjustment. A poet may imagine that thoughts reside within one another with ease whereas things in space clash hard. But we, being also things in space, so to speak, learn very fast from the way other things react to our own actions to restrain any such 'ease' of thought as soon as we act upon it. If inherent usefulness and purely psychic laws are the only real factors in the formation of thought, its end result must be at least to imagine and produce an objective reflection of reality. Since true thought could be the only basis for life-promoting action, the truth of an idea should be cultivated somewhat as muscle strength is.

This most plausible hypothesis brings up a question: Would it not be possible to find a unifying principle for this inherent dualism of practical vital needs on the one hand, and the objectively knowable world on the other? And could not these two elements seemingly independent of one another—external reality and subjective utility—be related on a deeper level than merely as the basis of knowing?

When we say that our concepts must be true for the actions based on them to be useful, we have no evidence for the truth of our cencepts other than the actual benefit we have obtained from these actions. If then it is really only utility which leads us to veridical thought, then the veridicality of this thought, i.e., its agreement with either an ideal reality or a materialistic one, is known only by inference from the effect to the cause. Of course, if, to start with, knowing were an independent domain with developed criteria, the truth or falsehood of a particular concept could be determined directly from these criteria in a purely theoretical manner. But whether these criteria—i.e., all of our cognition—are themselves true or false, it is impossible, according to this hypothesis, to determine theoretically. We can determine only whether actions arising from such knowledge are useful or harmful. We might say instead, therefore, that there is no theoretically valid 'truth' on which we can base appropriate actions. Rather, we call these concepts true which have proved to motivate expedient and life-promoting actions. Thus we can get rid of the dualism noted above. The truth of concepts need no longer rest on its agreement with any kind of reality. Truth becomes that quality of concepts which makes them the cause of most beneficial action. Whether the content of these concepts is similar to an objective order of things or related to them in any way remains undetermined.

The only question is whether such a notion of truth can hold when we no longer assume an objective reality corresponding to it—whether we think of that objective reality in the light of transcendental realism, or as Lotze's ideal 'validity', or in the purely empirical sense of the word, or as consistent with an idealistic conception. For such a notion of truth certainly is no longer an absolute one: truth no longer means that nature of concepts established in accordance with theoretical criteria, such concepts providing a ready-made basis for useful actions. Rather, it is those concepts which, from among innumerable emerging ideas, have subsequently proved useful that have been preserved as significant by means of natural selection. The term 'truth' denotes nothing more than those regular, practically efficacious consequences of thoughts.

If we persist in the common notion that thinking must contain some independent truth in order for the outcome of an action to be evaluated, we are inevitably bound to the preconception that cause and effect must be isomorphs. If action is based on a concept of an external reality which should, through this action, generate appropriate, definitely desirable reactions, our concept must contain an adequate image of the resultant external event and of the process leading to it. Otherwise, not just this but any other external event could transpire as a result.

At this point, let us consider the following as the first stage of such an action: the concept of stimulus which parallels what actually transpires is not a direct realization of the stimulus but rather a completely different process involving nerves and muscles, which never enters consciousness at all, and which reaches the final conceptualized goal only through additional cause-and-effect progressions. Thus an act of will never produces a result that is isomorphic to itself in content but rather one that is quite different. This result consists of a chain of various mechanical reactions, at the end of which an appropriate realization of the will becomes mainfest. Such 'realization of the will' means only that an external action has been produced which then reacts back on the individual to engender in him the concept of having grasped the content of the act of will, that is, of its having been gratified. So, if we consider a many-faceted act of will emanating from a concept as having been grounded in it, the result certainly is not to produce an image which agrees with it in content or coincides morphologically. That the will reaches its goal, that it satisfies the drives and needs of the individual, does not depend, therefore, on whether the concept from which it originates corresponds exactly in content with the reality toward which it is directed. What is more, the concept must develop an energy to move through the multifarious transitions in the mental, physical and inorganic worlds until it achieves the result that is either subjectively satisfying or objectively beneficial.

These fundamental concepts hardly need to be 'true' in the accepted sense of the word, which is also that used in idealism. Their similarity to the external empirical world is much the same as that of a Morse code message to the words printed at the receiving telegraph office. Or, to state it in another way, the concepts that determine our actions achieve their results not because of their content but rather because of the actual psychological force which they release. We might say that it is not the concept which works but the conceptualization. The concept which becomes manifest in consciousness as definite content is the final stage in the development of inner processes; the conceptualization reaches its goal in the definite conscious idea. What operates from then on is not that content but the force that carries it, the dynamic process of which that content is the conscious manifestation, acquired by as yet unknown means.

When I say, for example, that concept M has the result of summoning into consciousness concept N, associated with it, I am describing a predictable progression of inner processes, which includes stations M and N in the consciousness. The conceived content of M itself has no further effect but the conceptualization does. M as a complete conscious manifestation, attained through becoming conceptualized, is the operational cause of N, an indication that N will follow M. It simply points to the fact that N is at hand. Therefore, in order for an action which is the result of concepts to have a practically beneficial outcome, the contents of these concepts need no predetermined attributes. What is more, being actual psychological forces, these outcomes exert an influence through physiological and physical changes in the environment, the progress of which is neither continuous nor fundamental to defining the function of the relationship between their content, i.e., their logical consciousness, and that empirical environment. This relationship may or may not consist of a compatibility with the established concept of 'truth'; in neither case does it decide the course of future effects of the act of conceptualization itself. If we sever the ideal or substantive meaning of 'concept' from the dynamic, we are able to dissociate the utilitarian results of the concept from the notion of an objective reality, even in the ideal sense.

What I mean is this: Among innumerable psychogenic concepts, there are some which, on the basis of their effects on action, have proved to be useful and life-promoting for the individual. These become established in the ordinary selection process, and their totality forms the 'true' conceptual world. Kant has shown that veridical knowing of things is not due to our reflecting them directly in our minds, and that, therefore, the criterion of truth is not to be found in its metaphysical parallelism with an absolute objective reality. The question then arises as to what that criterion of truth is, what is it that determines that out of all possible concepts some are called true and other false? Some inherently limiting relationship must obtain among them, an inner agreement, a harmony between the individual concept and the total view of life. But such an agreement among individual units is not a simple mechanical identity, such as that between two congruent figures; rather it is one where certain axioms are assumed by which the compatibility can be judged. It is obviously not possible to arrive at the theoretical 'truth' of such an axiom itself from theory, since the basic assumptions of a theory are never provable within it but only from the outside, if at all.

For example, the axioms of geometry cannot be demonstrated by means of geometry, and the basic concepts of law cannot be ascertained juristically. A particular mathematical proposition is 'true' insofar as it is reducible to another; the truth of the axioms to which such reduction leads and which support the whole is not itself mathematical. Hence, we can say that mathematical truth exists only between the individual propositions of that discipline, but the discipline as a whole, insofar as its proceeds from its axioms, is not true in the same sense as its constituents. And so, demonstrable truth exists only among individual elements of knowledge, and only after certain first principles and basic facts have been assumed. As a result, the whole of knowledge is not true in the same sense as the particulars within it, since it contains no theoretical counterpart with respect to which its truth could be shown, i.e., no counterpart in relation to which it is 'true'. And in the specific situation in which concepts conforming to the criteria of truth provide the basic cause of useful action, we can assume as most probable that the fact of usefulness and its continued physiological and psychological results gave rise to that concept of special dignity which we call truth. Truth, which can no longer be said to reside in the theoretical attributes of the foundations or the totality of the conceptual world, finds the 'counterpunch' (Gegenwurf) that legitimizes it, or, rather, creates it as such, in the usefulness it possesses as the starting point of practical action.

We can carry our consideration of usefulness as the basis of truth—and not only of the acquisition of truth but also of its content and form—even farther if we look at physical and psychological systems below man. The sensory concepts with which animals respond to the influences of their environment must be different from ours in many ways. That some animals have sensations which we completely lack is beyond doubt, since it not only has been plainly observed in some of their behaviors but has also been demonstrated by the discovery of nervous systems quite unlike ours. Some animals no doubt lack certain senses which we have; still others experience sensations which are qualitatively similar to man's but to a greater or lesser degree of acuity. The reason for such differences cannot be anything other than the fact that various animals find different kinds of sensory apparatus the most useful and the most appropriate to their living conditions. It is then inevitable that quite different world-views evolve from such different raw materials.

Therefore, the concepts of 'what is' that are formed by animals always vary according to their individual life needs. Doubtless there exists for them also, within their perceptual world, a distinction between what is true and what is false. We have plenty of evidence that even animals are subject to misperceptions and rectifiable errors. But an animal's correction of an error cannot mean that a false concept was transformed into an absolute truth but rather that it was converted into what was normal for the given animal. A true concept for an animal is that which makes him behave in a way most fitting its circumstances, since it was the demand for such behavior that formed the organs that govern its knowing in the first place.

The far-reaching variety of existing sensory worlds is proof that there are many such truths. It is clear from this variety of truths, as a result of variations in practice, that man also would not tolerate holding to an independent truth inconsistent with demands of practice, a truth on which such demands would subsequently be placed in certain circumstances. Rather, in man also these demands possess the power of determining through the formation of our psychic and physiological systems what we shall call true. The fact that even those concepts which we later judge to be erroneous are useful to us, i.e., that they can lead to useful actions, makes simple sense in that our interests are often self-contradictory because of the complexity of our organism. Whatever cannot endure for long becomes a mistake, to be supplanted by concepts we take on because of their utility for our predominant lasting interests.

The point of view here presented removes the objections of those who regard the theory that a relationship exists between action and conceptualization as overly idealistic. For once we assume that conceptualization is utterly determined by the specific energies of psychological organs and does not extend to a reality of the *Ding an sich*, action and conceptualization seem to be more closely related. For it is through action that we gain the determining connection to that reality of things which, even in cognition, appears to us only in the form of individual concepts. Whether we say that we are *Dinge an sich* in will and action, or look at the distinction in question as belonging among phenomena, the distinction remains valid to the extent that our own actions help determine that reality, the reaction from which to us again becomes the subject matter of a phenomenon. In any case, the world does not appear to us the same when we act as when we conceptualize. On the one hand then, we have theoretical concepts we know to be the individual phenomenological representations of things rather than their pure objectifications; on the other hand, on the basis of such ideas, we place ourselves in a practical relationship with a reality which is not phenomenological in the same sense. And yet the progress of this relationship completely fulfils our expectations and it is favorable to the preservation and furtherance of our existence.

The obvious congruence of two factors of different nature and origin which we have here poses no less of a riddle than the dualism between mind and body posed by Descartes. Just as his dualism lies in a predetermined harmony between the substances of the inner world and the environment, so there seems to be a similar kind of harmony between the functions of conceptualization and of action. For the latter are based on the former, and, if the concepts are true, they bring certain beneficial results even though the true concepts operate within a merely phenomenological setting whereas their effects occur within at least a relative kind of reality. This astonishing fact, which, at first sight, indicates a prior stability, is explained on the basis of our previous insight that concepts become the starting point of actions not because of their content but because of their real psychological energy; that, among the actions that have thus originated, some have proved to be beneficial to the preservation of the species and others have not; that those concepts on which the beneficial actions were based have been preserved, intensified and fixed through natural selection; and that their contents have been accorded the label of truth; accordingly, the epithet of truth does not ascribe any independent theoretical quality to these concepts but merely means the quality of producing practical results that are beneficial.

Although it seems related, this theory should not be taken to mean that the most sensible and logically-thinking individuals have an advantage over their competitors in the battle for survival, that this characteristic thus became a basis for natural selection and became more enhanced until it extended over the whole species with the utmost intensity, and that, therefore, the basis for species dominance lies in the usefulness of cognition. However correct the above statement may be, it is no substitute for what we are saying, for two reasons. Firstly, it states that utility of action based on veridical thought is an accomplished fact, whereas what we wish to establish first is the relationship which exists between what is regarded as true cognition and enhanced life chances.

As long as the truth of knowing is assumed to be an autonomous quality, essentially independent of the usefulness of that knowing, the difficulty remains of how such subjectively determined knowing comes to instigate actions that are beneficial to our real existence. This becomes comprehensible only when we look at the usefulness of the action as the primary factor which gives rise to certain actions and their psychological foundations, which are then valid even for theoretical considerations as the 'true' knowing. Thus knowing is not first true and then useful, rather it first is useful and then referred to as true.

Secondly, let us assume that it were possible in principle to arrive at a purely theoretical knowledge, independent of any application, and that the acquisition of the former would become the object of the latter only subsequently. In that event we would still need particular practical experience for what actions to choose on the basis of that objective world image. For that reason there would have to be some new selection among those actions which are theoretically correct so that individual nerve-stimulating action of a more or less advantageous nature could follow. For even if the picture of the whole world lay spread out in front of me in its absolute empirical correctness, as long as I am a creature of will, my own behavior could in no way be determined in advance; and all the less so, because the coordination of the concept with the impulse of will (with which we are here concerned) usually takes place instinctively, generically, and unconsciously. Thus, even if we assume an *a priori* truth independent of application, the selection process which must establish the beneficial mode of action remains in force.

Our hypothesis, on the other hand, does away with the dualism of absolute truth versus either absolute experience or selection based on the practical actions in the known world, since experience gained as a result of action simultaneously creates truth. Even from the purely methodological standpoint of *Principia praeter necessitatem non sunt augenda*, we can put forth a theory in which a single process is sufficient to determine both practice and knowledge, and that is that the same act which establishes the stable modes of action inevitably bestows validity on the necessary psychological and intellectual conditions for the species. Once this has been established and its importance recognized on its own, then we can say that if a person who is particularly well endowed with intellectual qualities actually prevails over those less fortunate and thus contributes to the heightening of such intelligence and mental qualities in the species, it is only because practice determined in advance that these are the theoretical contents that are the most beneficial and worth keeping. That the actor is now guided by known truth and does so with good results can be understood in that originally the 'truth' was guided by the action and its results.

The problem with this theory lies in the same bias with which Kant's theory of space has always had to contend. The accepted idea of space is that of a container external to the I, in which the I has a place along with other things. This basic concept creates a paradox in idealism, in which all other things and space itself are, so to speak, packed inside the I. Once the soul has been set in space, then one cannot set space in the soul. Only when one has freed oneself of the popular bias that space is an external objective reality, does the concept of space as a form of intuition make sense at all.

Our situation is quite analogous. If we represent the truth of things, i.e., their own behavior, as logical formulations, as something that is objective in an absolute sense and which our consciousness has to copy inside itself (which is an interpretation permissible in both idealistic and realistic epistemology), then it is very odd that one would wish to deduce the psychological genesis of these formulations from the purely individual needs of the conscious being. Just as it was not possible to admit that space which is completely external to us could invade our power of intuition, so it is not feasible to admit now that absolutely objective truth could grow out of the practical needs of the individual. Moreover, just as the process of intuition, in keeping with its inherent law (the scientific expression of which consists of mathematical propositions), first gives rise to that which we term space, so certain norms governing the behavior of our thought, in keeping with the utility principle, first give rise to that which we term truth, norms which are stated in abstract form as laws of logic. If Kant resolved the dualism of conceptualization and being by treating being as a concept, then the fusion we have presented goes a step farther: the dualism of the world as it appears, as it exists for us from the theoretical and logical point of view, and of the world as the reality of that appearance, which responds to our practical actions, is resolved in that the forms of thought which create the world as concept are determined by the practical effects and counter-effects fashioned by our mental constitution—nothing other than the body—according to evolutionary needs. And if we can summarize Kant's theory in one sentence, using his own phrase, by saying that the potentiality for knowing also gives rise to the subject matter of knowing, then the theory presented here says that the usefulness of knowing also gives rise to the subject matter of knowing.

Learning, Development, and Culture
Edited by H. C. Plotkin
© 1982, John Wiley & Sons Ltd.

CHAPTER 5

Evolutionary epistemology

Donald T. Campbell*

An evolutionary epistemology would be at minimum an epistemology taking cognizance of and compatible with man's status as a product of biological and social evolution. In the present essay it is also argued that evolution—even in its biological aspects—is a knowledge process, and that the natural-selection paradigm for such knowledge increments can be generalized to other epistemic activities, such as learning, thought, and science. Such an epistemology has been neglected in the dominant philosophic traditions. It is primarily through the works of Karl Popper that a natural selection epistemology is available today.

Much of what follows may be characterized as 'descriptive epistemology', descriptive of man as knower. However, a correct descriptive epistemology must also be analytically consistent. Or, vice versa, of all of the analytically coherent epistemologies possible, we are interested in those (or that one) compatible with the description of man and of the world provided by contemporary science. Modern biology teaches us that man has evolved from some simple unicellular or virus-like ancestor and its still simpler progenitors. In the course of that evolution, there have been tremendous gains in adaptive adequacy, in stored templates modeling the useful stabilities of the environment, in memory and innate wisdom. Still more dramatic have been the great gains

* Reprinted by permission of the author and The Open Court Publishing Company, La Salle, Illinois. Originally printed in 1974 as Chapter 12 in *The Philosophy of Karl Popper* (Ed. P. A. Schilpp). Book 1, pp. 413–463. Copyright © 1974 by the Library of Living Philosophers, Inc.

in mechanisms for knowing, in visual perception, learning, imitation, language, and science. At no stage has there been any transfusion of knowledge from the outside, nor of mechanisms of knowing, nor of fundamental certainties.

An analytically coherent epistemology could perhaps be based upon a revelation to Adam of true axioms and deductive logic, from which might be derived, perhaps in conjunction with observations, man's true knowledge. Such an epistemology would not be compatible with the evolutionary model. Nor would be a direct realism, an epistemology assuming veridical visual perception, unless that epistemology were also compatible with the evolution of the eye from a series of less adequate prior stages back to a light-sensitive granule of pigment. Also incompatible would be a founding of certainty on the obviously great efficacy of ordinary language. In the evolutionary perspective, this would either commit one to a comparable faith in the evolutionary prestages to modern language, or to a discontinuity and point of special creation. Better to recognize the approximate and only pragmatic character of language at all stages, including the best. An analytic epistemology appropriate to man's evolved status must be appropriate to these evolutionary advances and to these prior stages, as well as to modern man.

We once 'saw' as through the fumblings of a blind protozoan, and no revelation has been given to us since. Vision represents an opportunistic exploitation of a coincidence which no deductive operations on a protozoan's knowledge of the world could have anticipated. This is the coincidence of locomotor impenetrability with opaqueness, for a narrow band of electro-magnetic waves. For this band, substances like water and air are transparent, in coincidental parallel with their locomotor penetrability. For other wave lengths, the coincidence, and hence the cue value, disappears. The accidental encountering and systematic cumulations around this coincidence have provided in vision a wonderful substitute for blind exploration. In this perspective, clear glass and fog are paradoxical—glass being impenetrable but transparent, fog being the reverse. Glass was certainly lacking in the ecology of evolution. Fog was rare or nonexistent in the aqueous environment of the fish where most of this evolution took place. (Modern man corrects the paradoxical opacity of fog through exploiting another coincidence in the radar wave bands.) The visual system is furthermore far from perfect, with usually overlooked inconsistencies such as double images for nonfixated objects, blind spots, optical illusions, chromatic aberration, astigmatism, venous shadows, etc.

In all of this opportunistic exploitation of coincidence in vision there is no logical necessity, no absolute ground for certainty, but instead a most back-handed indirectness. From this perspective, Hume's achievement in showing that the best of scientific laws have neither analytic truth nor any other kind of absolute truth seems quite reasonable and appropriate. Here description and analysis agree.

A. THE SELECTIVE ELIMINATION MODEL

The advances produced in the course of evolution are now seen as due to natural selection, operating upon the pool of self-perpetuating variations which the genetics of the breeding group provide, and from within this pool, differentially propagating some variations at the expense of others. The supply of variations comes both from mutations providing new semistable molecular arrangements of the genetic material and from new combinations of existing genes. Considered as improvements or solutions, none of these variations has any *a priori* validity. None has the status of revealed truth nor of analytic deduction. Whatever degree of validation emerges comes from the differential surviving of a winnowing, weeding-out, process.

Popper's first contribution to an evolutionary epistemology is to recognize the process of the succession of theories in science as a similar selective elimination process (Popper, 1959). He also adds (Popper, 1963) trial-and-error learning by man and animals to the prototypic illustrations of his basic logic of inference (logic of discovery, logic of the expansion of knowledge). They make explicit his willingness to identify the process of knowledge with the whole evolutionary sequence.

In the process, Popper has effectively rejected the model of passive induction even for animal learning, and advocated that here too the typical process involves broad generalizations from single specific initial experiences, generalizations which subsequent experiences edit. It is noteworthy that the best of modern mathematical learning theories posit just such a one-trial learning process, as opposed to older theories which implied inductive accumulation of evidence on all possible stimulus contingencies (Restle, 1962; Atkinson and Crothers, 1964; Estes, 1964).

B. LOCATING THE PROBLEM OF KNOWLEDGE

It is well to be explicit that involved in Popper's achievement is a recentering of the epistemological problem. As with Hume, the status of scientific knowledge remains important. The conscious cognitive contents of an individual thinker also remain relevant. But these no longer set the bounds of the problem. The central requirement becomes an epistemology capable of handling *expansions* of knowledge, *breakouts* from the limits of prior wisdom, *scientific discovery*.

A focus on the growth of knowledge, on acquisition of knowledge, makes it appropriate to include learning as well as perception as a knowledge process. Such an inclusion makes relevant the learning processes of animals. However primitive these may be, they too must conform to an adequate logical epistemology. Animal learning must not be ruled out as impossible by the logic of knowing.

C. A NESTED HIERARCHY OF SELECTIVE-RETENTION PROCESSES

Human knowledge processes, when examined in continuity with the evolutionary sequence, turn out to involve numerous mechanisms at various levels of substitute functioning, hierarchically related, and with some form of selective retention process at each level. Popper in *Of Clouds and Clocks* (see Chapter 6 of this volume) has expanded his evolutionary perspective along these lines. He has there spoken for that emerging position in biology and control theory which sees the natural selection paradigm as the universal non-teleological explanation of teleological achievements, of ends-guided processes, of 'fit' (see Wimsatt, 1972). Thus, crystal formation is seen as the result of a chaotic permutation of molecular adjacencies, some of which are much more difficult to dislodge than others. At temperatures warm enough to provide general change, but not so warm as to disrupt the few stable adjacencies, the number of stable adjacencies will steadily grow even if their occurrence is but a random affair. In crystal formation the material forms its own template. In the genetic control of growth, the DNA provides the initial template selectively accumulating chance fitting RNA molecules, which in turn provide the selective template selectively cumulating from among chaotic permutations of proteins. These molecules of course fit multiple selective criteria: of that finite set of semistable combinations of protein material, they are the subset fitting the template. The template guides by selecting from among the mostly unstable, mostly worthless possibilities offered by thermal noise operating on the materials in solution. Turning the model to still lower levels of organization, elements and subatomic particles are seen as but nodes of stability which at certain temperatures transiently select adjacencies among still more elementary stuff.

Turning to higher levels, the model can be applied to such dramatically teleological achievements as embryological growth and wound healing. Within each cell, genetic templates for all types of body proteins are simultaneously available, competing as it were for the raw material present. Which ones propagate most depends upon the surrounds. Transplantation of embryonic material changes the surroundings and hence the selective system. Wounds and amputations produce analogous changes in the 'natural selection' of protein possibilities. Spiegelman (1948) has specifically noted the Darwinian analogy and its advantages over vitalistic teleological pseudoexplanations which even concepts of force fields and excitatory gradients may partake of.

Regeneration provides an illustration of the nested hierarchical nature of biological selection systems. The salamander's amputated leg regrows to a length optimal for locomotion and survival. The ecological selection system does not operate directly on the leg length, however. Instead the leg length is selected to confrom to an internal control built into the developmental system which vicariously represents the ecological selective system. This control was itself selected by the trial and error of whole mutant organisms (Barr, 1964). If the ecology has recently undergone change, the vicarious selective criterion will correspondingly be in error. This larger, encompassing selection system is the organism–environment interaction. Nested in a hierarchical way within it is the selective system directly operating on leg length, the 'settings' or criteria for which are themselves subject to change by natural selection. What are criteria at one level are but 'trials' of the criteria of the next higher, more fundamental, more encompassing, less frequently invoked level.

In other writings (Campbell, 1959, 1960) the present author has advocated a systematic extrapolation of this nested hierarchy selective retention paradigm to *all* knowledge processes, in a way which, although basically compatible with Popper's orientation, may go farther than he would find reasonable in extremity, dogmatism, and claims for generality. It may on these same grounds alienate the reader. (Disagreement at this point will not rule out accepting later propositions.)

1. A blind-variation-and-selective-retention process is fundamental to all inductive achievements (the phrase is for convenience in communicating and does not imply advocacy of the Bacon–Hume–Mill explanation of these achievements), to all genuine increases in knowledge, to all increases in fit of system to environment.

2. In such a process there are three essentials: (a) Mechanisms for introducting variation; (b) Consistent selection processes; and (c) Mechanisms for preserving and/or propagating the selected variations. Note that in general the preservation and generation mechanisms are inherently at odds, and each must be compromised.

3. The many processes which shortcut a more full blind-variation-and-selective-retention process are in themselves inductive achievements, containing wisdom about the environment achieved originally by blind variation and selective retention.

4. In addition, such shortcut processes contain in their own operation a blind-variation-and-selective-retention process at some level, substituting for overt locomotor exploration or the life-and-death winnowing of organic evolution.

The word 'blind' is used rather than the more usual 'random' for a variety of reasons. It seems likely that Ashby (1952) unnecessarily limited the generality of his mechanism in Homeostat by an effort fully to represent all of the modern connotations of random. Equiprobability is not needed, and is definitely lacking in the mutations which lay the variation base for organic evolution. Statistical independence between one variation and the next, although frequently desirable, can also be spared: in particular, for the generalizations essayed here, certain processes involving systematic sweep scanning are recognized as blind, insofar as variations are produced without prior knowledge of which ones, if any, will furnish a selectworthy encounter. An essential connotation of blind is that the variations emitted be independent of the environmental conditions of the occasion of their occurrence. A second important connotation is that the occurrence of trials individually be uncorrelated with the solution, in that specific correct trials are no more likely to occur at any one point in a series of trials than another, nor than specific incorrect trials. A third essential connotation of blind is rejection of the notion that a variation subsequent to an incorrect trial is a 'correction' of the previous trial or makes use of the direction of error of the previous one. (Insofar as mechanisms do seem to operate in this fashion, there must be operating a substitute process carrying on the blind search at another level, feedback circuits selecting 'partially' adequate variations, providing information to the effect that 'you're getting warm,' etc. (Campbell, 1960).)

While most descriptions of discovery and creative processes recognize the need for variation, the present author's dogmatic insistence on the blindness of such variation seems generally unacceptable. As will be seen in what follows, particularly in the discussions of vision and thought, there is no real descriptive disagreement. The present writer agrees that overt responses of a problem-solving animal in a puzzle box are far from random, and this for several reasons: (1) Already achieved wisdom of a general sort which limits the range of trials (such wisdom due to inheritance and learning). (2) Maladaptive restriction on the range of trials. (Such biases due to structural limitations and to past habit and instinct inappropriate in a novel environment.) But these first two reasons will characterize the wrong responses as well as the correct ones, and offer no explanation of the correctness of the correct one. (3) Vicarious selection, appropriate to the immediate problem, achieved through vision. When, in considering creative thought, Poincaré is followed, allowing for unconscious variation-and-selection processes, opportunity for descriptive disagreement is further reduced. The point is not empirically empty, however, as it sets essential limits and requirements for any problem-solving computer. But the point is also analytic. In going beyond what is already known, one cannot but go blindly. If one can go wisely, this indicates already achieved wisdom of some general sort.

Expanding this orientation and applying it to the setting of biological and social evolution, a set of ten more or less discrete levels can be distinguished, and these are elaborated in the following sections.

1. *Nonmnemonic problem solving.*   At the level of Jenning's (1906) paramecium, stentor, and Ashby's (1952) Homeostat, there is a blind variation of locomotor activity until a setting that is nourishing or nonnoxious is found. Such problem-solutions are then retained as a cessation of locomotion, as a cessation of variation. There is, however, no memory, no using of old solutions over again.

In a world with only benign or neutral states, an adaptive organism might operate at this level without exteroceptors. Wherever it is, it is trying to ingest the immediate environment. When starvation approaches, blind locomotor activity is initiated, ingestion being attempted at all locations. Even at this level, however, there is needed an interoceptive sense organ which monitors nutritional level, and substitutes for the whole organism's death. In the actual case of Jennings's stentor, chemoreceptors for noxious conditions are present, vicarious representatives of the lethal character of the environment, operating on nonlethal samples or signs of that environment. It is these chemoreceptors and comparable organs which in fact provide the immediate selection of responses. Only indirectly, through selecting the selectors, does life-and-death relevance select the responses.

At this level of knowing, however, the responses may be regarded as direct rather than vicarious. And, as to presuppositions about the nature of the world (the ontology guiding epistemology), perhaps all that is assumed is spatial discontinuity somewhat greater than temporal discontinuity in the distribution of environmental substances: moving around is judged to bring changes more rapidly than staying put. At this level the species has discovered that the environment is discontinuous, consisting of penetrable regions and impenetrable ones, and that impenetrability is to some extent a stable characteristic. The animal has 'learned' that there are some solvable problems. Already the machinery of knowing is biasedly focused upon the small segment of the world which is knowable, as natural selection makes inevitable.

2. *Vicarious locomotor devices.* Substituting for spatial exploration by loco-motor trial and error are a variety of distance receptors of which a ship's radar is an example. An automated ship could explore the environment of landfalls, harbours, and other ships by a trial and error of full movements and collisions. Instead, it sends out substitute locomotions in the form of a radar beam. These are selectively reflected from nearby objects, the reflective opaqueness to this wave band vicariously representing the locomotor impenetrability of the objects. This vicarious representability is a contingent discovery, and is in fact only approximate. The knowledge received is reconfirmed as acted upon by the full ship's locomotion. The process removes the trial-and-error component from the overt locomotion, locating it instead in the blindly emitted radar beam. (The radar beam is, however, emitted in a blind exploration, albeit a systematic sweep.) Analogous to radar and to sonar are several echolocation devices in animals. Pumphrey (1950) has described the lateral-line organ of fish as a receiver for the reflected pulses of the broadcast pressure waves emitted by the fish's own swimming movements. The all-directional exploring of the wave front is selectively reflected by nearby objects, pressure wave substituting for locomotor exploration. The echolocation devices of porpoises, bats, and cave birds have a similar epistemology (Griffin, 1958; Kellog, 1958).

Assimilating vision to the blind-variation-and-selective-retention model is a more difficult task (Campbell, 1956a). It seems important, however, to make vision palpably problematic, in correction of the common sense realism or the direct realism of many contemporary philosophers which leads them to an uncritical assumption of directness and certainty for the visual process. The vividness and phenomenal directness of vision needs to be corrected in any complete epistemology, which also has to make comprehensible how such an indirect, coincidence-exploiting mechanism could work at all. Were visual percepts as vague and incoherent as the phosphors on a radar screen, many epistemological problems would be avoided. From the point of view of an evolutionary epistemology, vision is just as indirect as radar.

Consider a one-photocell substitute eye such as was once distributed for the use of the blind. To an earphone, the cell transmitted a note of varying pitch depending upon the brightness of the light received. In blind search with this photocell, one could locate some objects and some painted boundaries on flat surfaces, all boundaries being indicated by a shift in tone. One can imagine an extension of this blind search device to a multiple photocell model, each photocell of fixed direction, boundaries being located by a comparison of emitted tones or energies perhaps in some central sweep scanning of outputs. To be sure, boundaries would be doubly confirmed if the whole set were oscillated slightly, so that a boundary stood out not only as comparison across adjacent receptors at one time, but also as a comparison across times for the same receptors. (The eye has just such a physiological nystagmus, essential to its function.) Similarly, one could build a radar with multiple fixed-directional emitters and receivers. It would search just as blindly, just as openmindedly, as the single beam and sweep scanner. In such multiple receptor devices, the opportunities for excitation are blindly made available and are selectively activated.

Blind locomotor search is the more primary, the more direct exploration. A blind man's cane is a vicarious search process. The less expensive cane movements substitute for blind trials and wasted movements by the whole body, removing costly search from the full locomotor effort, making that seem smooth, purposeful, insightful (Campbell, 1956a). The single photocell device seems equally blind, although utilizing a more unlikely substitute, one still cheaper in effort and time. The multiple photocell device, or the eye, uses the multiplicity of cells instead of a multiplicity of focussings of one cell, resulting in a search process equally blind and open-minded, equally dependent upon a selection-from-variety epistemology. The substitutability of cane locomotion for body locomotion, the equivalence of opaque-to-cane and opaque-to-body, is a contingent discovery, although one which seems more nearly 'entailed', or to involve a less complex, less presumptive model of the physical world than does the substitutability of light waves or radar waves for body locomotion.

This is, of course, a skeletonized model of vision, emphasizing its kinship to blind fumbling, and its much greater indirectness than blind fumbling, phenomenal directness notwithstanding. Neglected is the presumptive achievement of the visual system in reifying stable discrete objects, stable over a heterogeneity of points of viewing; neglected is the fundamental epistemological achievement of 'identifying' new and partially different sets of sense data as 'the same' so that habit or instinct or knowledge can be appropriately applied even though there be no logically entailed identity (see also Russell's 'Structural postulate', 1948; and Lorenz, 1962a; Campbell, 1966).

3. *Habit* and 4. *Instinct.*   Habit, instinct, and visual diagnosis of objects are so interlocked and interdependent that no simple ordering of the three is possible. Much more detailed work is needed on the evolution of knowledge processes, and such an examination would no doubt describe many more stages than are outlined here. Such a study could also profitably describe the 'presumptions' about the nature of the world, or the 'knowledge' about the nature of the world, underlying each stage. Certainly, the extent of these presumptions is greater at the more advanced levels.

The visual diagnosis of reidentifiable objects is basic to most instinctive response patterns in insects and vertebrates, both for instigation of the adaptive pattern and for eliminating the trial-and-error component from the overt response elements. In a crude way, instinct development can be seen as involving a trial and error of whole mutant animals, whereas trial-and-error learning involves the much cheaper wastage of responses within the lifetime of a single animal (Baldwin, 1900; Holmes, 1916; Pringle, 1951; Ashby, 1952). The same environment is editing habit and instinct development in most cases, the editing process is analogous, and the epistemological status of the knowledge, innate or learned, no different. Thus the great resistance of the empiricists to innate knowledge is made irrelevant, but in the form of a more encompassing empiricism. It can be noted that all comprehensive learning theories, including those of Gestalt inspiration, contain a trial-and-error component, be it a trial and error of 'hypotheses' or 'recenterings' (Campbell, 1956b).

These general conclusions may be acceptable, but the evolutionary discreteness of the two processes is not as clear as implied nor should instinct necessarily be regarded as more primitive than habit. Complex adaptive instincts typically involve multiple movements and must inevitably involve a multiplicity of mutations at least as great in number as the obvious movement segments. Furthermore, it is typical that the fragmentary movement segments, or the effects of single component mutations, would represent no adaptive gain at all apart from the remainder of the total sequence. The joint likelihood of the simultaneous occurrence of the adaptive form of the many mutations involved is so infinitesimal that the blind-mutation-and-selective-retention model seems inadequate. This argument was used effectively by both Lamarckians and those arguing for an intelligently guided evolution or creation. Baldwin, Morgan, Osborn, and Poulton (see Baldwin, 1902), believing that natural selection was the adequate and only mechanism, proposed that for such instincts, learned adaptive patterns, recurrently discovered in similar form within a species by trial-and-error learning, preceded the instincts. The adaptive pattern being thus piloted by learning, any mutations that accelerated the learning, made it more certain to occur, or predisposed that animal to certain component responses, would be adaptive and selected no matter which component, or in what order affected. The habit thus provided a selective template around which the instinctive components could be assembled, Baldwin using the terms 'ortho-plasy' and 'organic selection' to cover the concept. (Stating it in other terms, learned habits make a new ecological niche available which niche then selects instinct components.) It is furthermore typical of such instincts that they involve learned components, as of nest and raw material location, etc.

This can be conceived as an evolution of increasingly specific selection-criteria, which at each level select or terminate visual search and trial-and-error learning. In what we call learning, these are very general drive states and reinforcing conditions. In the service of these general reinforcers, specific objects and situations become learned goals and subgoals, learned selectors of more specific responses. (Even for drives and reinforcers, of course, the environment's selective relevance is represented indirectly, as in the pleasureableness of sweet foods, the vicariousness of which is shown by an animal's willingness to learn for the reward of nonnutritive saccharine.) In the habit-to-instinct evolution, the once-learned goals and subgoals become innate at a more and more specific response-fragment level. For such an evolutionary development to take place, very stable environments over long evolutionary periods are required.

5. *Visually supported thought.* The dominant form of insightful problem solving in animals, e.g. as described by Kohler (1925), requires the support of a visually present environment. With the environment represented vicariously through visual search, there is a substitute trial and error of potential locomotions in thought. The 'successful' locomotions at this substitute level, with its substitute selective criteria, are then put into overt locomotion, where they appear 'intelligent', 'purposeful', 'insightful', even if still subject to further editing in the more direct contact with the environment.

6. *Mnemonically supported thought.* At this level the environment being searched is vicariously represented in memory or 'knowledge', rather than visually, the blindly emitted vicarious thought trials being selected by a vicarious criterion substituting for an external state of affairs. The net result is the 'intelligent', 'creative', and 'foresightful' product of thought, our admiration of which makes us extremely reluctant to subsume it under the blind-variation-and-selective-retention model. Yet it is in the description of this model that the trial-and-error theme, the blind permutation theme, has been most persistently invoked. When Mach in 1895 was called back to Vienna to assume the newly

created professorship in 'The History and Theory of Inductive Sciences', he chose this topic:

> 'The disclosure of new provinces of facts before unknown can only be brought about by accidental circumstances...
> ...In such (other) cases it is a psychical accident to which the person owes his discovery—a discovery which is here made "deductively" by means of mental copies of the world, instead of experimentally.' (Mach, 1896)

Poincaré's famous essay on mathematical creativity espouses such a view at length, arguing that it is mathematical beauty which provides the selective criteria for a blind permuting process, usually unconscious:

> 'one evening, contrary to my custom, I drank black coffee and could not sleep. Ideas rose in crowds: I felt them collide until pairs interlocked, so to speak, making a stable combination.
> ...What happens then? Among the great numbers of combinations blindly formed by the subliminal self, almost all are without interest and without utility; but just for that reason they are also without effect upon the esthetic sensibility. Consciousness will never know them; only certain ones are harmonious, and, consequently, at once useful and beautiful.
> ...In the subliminal self, on the contrary, reigns what I should call liberty, if we might give this name to the simple absence of discipline and to the disorder born of chance. Only this disorder itself permits unexpected combinations.' (Poincaré, 1913, pp. 387, 392, and 394)

Alexander Bain was proposing a trial-and-error model of invention and thought as early as 1855. Jevons in 1874 was advocating a similar model in the context of a rejection of Bacon's principle of induction on grounds similar to Popper's.

> 'I hold that in all cases of inductive inference we must invent hypotheses until we fall upon some hypothesis which yields deductive result in accordance with experience.
> It would be an error to suppose that the great discoverer seizes at once upon the truth or has any unerring method of divining it. In all probability the errors of the great mind exceed in number those of the less vigorous one. Fertility of imagination and abundance of guesses at truth are among the first requisites of discovery; but the erroneous guesses must be many times as numerous as those which prove well founded. The weakest analogies, the most whimsical notions, the most apparently absurd theories, may pass through the teeming brain, and

no record remain of more than the hundredth part. There is nothing really absurd except that which proves contrary to logic and experience. The truest theories involve suppositions which are inconceivable, and no limit can really be placed to the freedom of hypothesis.' (Jevons, 1892, pp. 228 and 577)

In his very modern and almost totally neglected *Theory of Invention* of 1881, Souriau effectively criticizes deduction, induction, and '*la methode*' as models for advances in thought and knowledge. His recurrent theme is '*le principe de l'invention est le hazard*':

'A problem is posed for which we must invent a solution. We know the conditions to be met by the sought idea; but we do not know what series of ideas will lead us there. In other words, we know how the series of our thoughts must end, but not how it should begin. In this case it is evident that there is no way to begin except at random. Our mind takes up the first path that it finds open before it, perceives that it is a false route, retraces its steps and takes another direction. Perhaps it will arrive immediately at the sought idea, perhaps it will arrive very belatedly: it is entirely impossible to know in advance. In these conditions we are reduced to dependence upon chance.

By a kind of artificial selection, we can in addition substantially perfect our thought and make it more and more logical. Of all the ideas which present themselves to our mind, we note only those which have some value and can be utilized in reasoning. For every single idea of a judicious and reasonable nature which offers itself to us, what hosts of frivolous, bizarre, and absurd ideas cross our mind. Those persons who, upon considering the marvellous results at which knowledge has arrived, cannot imagine that the human mind could achieve this by a simple fumbling, do not bear in mind the great number of scholars working at the same time on the same problem, and how much time even the smallest discovery costs them. Even the genius has need of patience. It is after hours and years of meditation that the sought-after idea presents itself to the inventor. He does not succeed without going astray many times; and if he thinks himself to have succeeded without effort, it is only because the joy of having succeeded has made him forget all the fatigues, all of the false leads, all of the agonies, with which he has paid for his success.

... If his memory is strong enough to retain all of the amassed details, he evokes them in turn with such rapidity that they seem to appear simultaneously; he groups them by chance in all the possible ways; his ideas, thus shaken up and agitated in his mind, form numerous unstable aggregates which destroy themselves, and finish up by stopping on the most simple and solid combination.' (Souriau, 1881, pp. 17, 43, and 114–115)

Note the similarity of the imagery in the final paragraph with that of Ashby as cited under level 1, above, and that of Poincaré, Mach, and Jevons.

In Souriau's use of the phrase 'artificial selection', he seems to refer to the analogy with Darwin's theory of natural selection, but we cannot be certain. Souriau's book is totally devoid of citations or even mentions of the works of any other. William James, however, is completely explicit on the analogy in an article published in 1880. Arguing against Spencer's model of a perfectly passive mind, he says:

'And I can easily show that throughout the whole extent of those mental departments which are highest, which are most characteristically human, Spencer's law is violated at every step; and that, as a matter of fact, the new conceptions, emotions, and active tendencies which evolve are originally *produced* in the shape of random images, fancies, accidental outbirths of spontaneous variation in the functional activity of the excessively unstable human brain, which the outer environment simply confirms or refutes, preserves or destroys—selects, in short, just as it selects morphological and social variations due to molecular accidents of an analogous sort.

... The conception of the (scientific) law is a spontaneous variation in the strictest sense of the term. It flashes out of one brain, and no other, because the instability of that brain is such as to tip and upset itself in just that particular direction. But the important thing to notice is that the good flashes and the bad flashes, the triumphant hypotheses and the absurd conceits, are on an exact equality in respect of their origin.' (James, 1880)

James departs from the more complete model presented in Poincaré, Mach, and Campbell by seemingly having the full range of mental variations selected by the external environment rather than recognizing the existence of mental selectors, which vicariously represent the external environment. (The selected products, or course, being subject to further validation in overt locomotion, etc.)

Many others have advocated such a view. (*Editor's note*: The interested reader should refer to the original essay in Schilpp where Campbell provides extensive appendices of references.) One presentation which has reached the attention of some philosophers is that of Kenneth J. W. Craik, in his fragmentary work of genius, *The Nature of Explanation* (1943), a work which in many other ways also espouses an evolutionary epistemology.

The resultant process of thought is a very effective one, and a main pillar of man's high estate. Yet it must be emphasized again that the vicarious representations involved—both environmental realities and potential loco-motions being represented in mind–brain processes—are discovered contingent relationships, achieving no logical entailment, and in fine detail incomplete and imperfect. This same vicarious, contingent, discovered, marginally imperfect representativeness holds for the highly selected formal logics and mathematics which we utilize in the processes of science.

Computer problem solving is a highly relevant topic, and is perhaps best introduced at this point. Like thinking, it requires vicarious explorations of a vicarious representation of the environment, with the exploratory trials being selected by criteria which are vicarious representatives of solution requirements or external realities. The present writer would insist here too, that if discovery or expansions of knowledge are achieved, blind variation is requisite. This being the case, it is only fair to note that Herbert Simon, both a leading computer simulator of thought and an epistemologically sophisticated scholar, rejects this point of view, at least in the extreme form advocated here. For example, he says 'The more difficult and novel the problem, the greater is likely to be the amount of trial and error required to find a solution. At the same time, the trial and error is not completely random or blind; it is, in fact, highly selective.' (Simon, 1969) Earlier statements on this have been still more rejective (Newell, Shaw, and Simon, 1958). The present writer has attempted elsewhere (Campbell, 1960) to answer in more detail than space here permits, but a brief summary is in order. The 'selectivity', insofar as it is appropriate, represents already achieved wisdom of a more general sort, and as such, selectivity does not in any sense explain an innovative solution. Insofar as the selectivity is in-appropriate, it limits areas of search in which a solution might be found, and rules out classes of possible solutions. Insofar as the selectivity represents a partial general truth, some unusual solutions are ruled out. Simon's 'heuristics' are such partial truths, and a computer which would generate its own heuristics would have to do so by a blind trial and error of heuristic principles, selection from which would represent achieved general knowledge. The principle of hierarchy in problem solving depends upon such discoveries, and once achieved, can, of course, greatly reduce the total search space, but without at all violating the requirement of blindness as here conceived. For example, one of the heuristics used in Simon's 'Logic Theorist' program (Newell *et al.*, 1958) is that any substitution or transformation which will increase the 'similarity' between a proposition and the desired outcome should be retained as a stem on which further variations are to be tried. Any transformation decreasing similarity should discarded. Similarity is crudely scored by counting the number of identical terms, with more points for similarity of location. This rule enables selection to be introduced at each transformational stage, greatly reducing the total search space. It employs an already achieved partial truth. It produces computer search similar to human problem solving in failing to discover roundabout solutions requiring initial decreases in similarity. Beyond thus applying what is already known, albeit only a partial truth, the new discoveries must be produced by a blind generation of alternatives.

7. *Socially vicarious exploration: observational learning and imitation.* The survival value of the eye is obviously related to an economy of cognition—the economy of eliminating all of the wasted locomotions which would otherwise be needed. An analogous economy of cognition helps account for the great survival advantage of the truly social forms of animal life, which in evolutionary sequences are regularly found subsequent to rather than prior to solitary forms. In this, the trial-and-error exploration of one member of a group substitutes for, renders unnecessary, trial-and-error exploration on the part of their members. The use of trial and error by scouts on the part of migrating social insects and human bands illustrates this general knowledge process. At the simplest level in social animals are procedures whereby one animal can profit from observing the consequences to another of that other's acts, even or especially when these acts are fatal to the model. The aversion which apes show to dismembered ape bodies, and their avoidance of the associated locations, illustrates such a process (Hebb, 1946). In ants and termites the back-tracking on the tracks of foragers who have come back heavy laden illustrates such a process for knowledge of attractive goal objects. The presumptions involved in this epistemology include the belief that the model, the vicar, is exploring the same world in which the observer is living an locomoting, as well as those assumptions about the lawfulness of that world which underlie all learning.

Also noted in social animals, perhaps particularly in their young, is a tendency to imitate the actions of models even when the outcomes of those actions cannot be observed. This is a much more presumptive, but still 'rational' procedure. It involves the assumptions that the model animal is capable of learning and is living in a learnable world. If this is so, then the model has probably eliminated punished responses and has increased its tendencies to make rewarded responses, resulting in net output of predominantly rewarded responses (the more so the longer the learning period and the stabler the environment). (See Asch, 1952; Campbell, 1961 and 1963; Bandura, 1969.)

But even in imitation, there is no 'direct' infusion or transference of knowledge or habit, just as there is no 'direct' acquisition of knowledge by observation or induction. As Baldwin (1906) analyzes the process, what the child acquires is a criterion image, which he learns to match by a trial and error of matchings. He hears a tune, for example, and then learns to make that sound by a trial and error of vocalizations, which he checks against the memory of the sound pattern. Recent studies of the learning of bird song confirm and elaborate the same model (Hinde, 1969).

8. *Language.* Overlapping with levels 6 and 7 above is language, in which the outcome of explorations can be related from scout to follower with neither the

illustrative locomotion nor the environment explored being present, not even visually-vicariously present. From the social-functional point of view, it is quite appropriate to speak of the 'language' of bees, even though the wagging dance by which the scout bee conveys the direction, distance and richness of his find is an innate response tendency automatically elicited without conscious intent to communicate. This bee language has the social function of economy of cognition in a way quite analogous to human language. The vicarious representabilities of geographical direction (relative to the sun and plane of polarization of sunlight), of distance, and of richness by features of the dance such as direction on a vertical wall, length of to-and-fro movements, rapidity of movements, etc., are all invented and contingent equivalences, neither entailed nor perfect, but tremendously reductive of flight lengths on the part of the observing or listening worker bees (von Frisch, 1950; Sebeok, 1968; Sebeok and Ramsay, 1969; Gould, Henerey, and MacLeod, 1970). The details of von Frisch's analysis are currently being both challenged and extended. Perhaps the dance language does not communicate as precisely as he thought. Perhaps sonic, supersonic, and odor-trail means are also involved. It seems certain, however, that there are effective means of transmitting to other bees the successful outcomes of scout bee explorations in such a manner as to greatly reduce the total wasted exploratory effort over that required of solitary bees.

Given the present controversy over 'bee language', it may be well to make the point of a functional-linguistic feature in social insects at a more primitive level. Ants and termites have independently discovered the use of pheromones for this purpose: an explorer who has encountered food exudes a special external hormone on his walk back to the nest. The other workers backtrack on this special scent. If they too are successful, if the food supply remains plentiful, they keep the pheromone track renewed. The 'knowledge' of the environment upon which the worker bases his trip is profoundly indirect. This 'knowledge' is more directly confirmed if and when the worker finds food (although the also implied information that food is more prevalent in this direction than in most others is not tested at all). But even this confirmation is profoundly indirect at the individual system level, for it involves sense-organ criteria for nourishingness rather than nourishingness itself. These criteria turn out to be approximate within limits set by the prior ecology. Nonnourishing saccharin and ant poison illustrate the indirectness and proneness to illusion in novel ecologies.

For human language too, the representability of things and actions by words is a contingent discovery, a nonentailed relationship, and only approximate. We need a Popperian model of language learning in the child and of language development in the race. Regarding the child, this would emphasize that word meanings cannot be directly transferred to the child. Rather, the child must discover these by a presumptive trial and error of meanings, which the initial instance only limits but does not determine. Rather than logically complete ostensive definitions being possible, there are instead extended, incomplete sets of ostensive instances, each instance of which equivocally leaves possible multiple interpretations, although the whole series edits out many wrong trial meanings. The 'logical' nature of children's errors in word usage amply testifies to such a process, and testifies against an inductionist version of a child's passively observing adult usage contingencies. This trial and error of meanings requires more than the communication of mentor and child. It requires a third party of objects referred to. Language cannot be taught by telephone, but requires visually or tactually present ostensive referents stimulating and editing the trial meanings.

Moving to the evolution of human language, a social trial and error of meanings and namings can be envisaged. Trial words designating referents which the other speakers in the community rarely guess 'correctly' either fail to become common coinage or are vulgarized toward commonly guessed designations. All words have to go through the teaching sieve, have to be usefully if incompletely communicable by finite sets of ostensive instances. Stable, sharp, striking object-boundaries useful in manipulating the environment have a greater likelihood of utilization in word meanings than do subtler designations, and when used, achieve a greater universality of meaning within the community of speakers. Such natural boundaries for words exists in much greater number than are actually used, and alternate boundaries for highly overlapping concepts abound. Just as certain knowledge is never achieved in science, so certain equivalence of word meanings is never achieved in the iterative trial and error meanings in language learning. This equivocality and hetero- geneity of meanings is more than trivial logical technicality; it is a practical fringe imperfection. And even were meanings uniform, the word-to-object equivalence is a corrigible contingent relationship, a product of a trial and error of metaphors of greater and greater appropriateness, but never complete perfection, never a formal nor entailed isomorphism (Campbell, 1973; see also Quine, 1969, and MacCormac, 1971).

9. *Cultural cumulation.* In sociocultural evolution there are a variety of variation and selective retention processes leading to advances or changes in technology and culture. Most direct, but probably of minor importance, is the selective survival of complete social organizations, differentially as a function of cultural features. More important is selective borrowing, a process which probably leads to increased adaptation as far as easily tested aspects of technology are concerned, but could involve adaptive irrelevance in areas of culture where reality testing is more difficult. Differential imitation of a heterogeneity of models from within the culture is also a selective system that could lead to cultural advance. The learning process, selective repetition from among a set of temporal variations in cultural practice, also produces cultural advance. Selective elevation of different persons to leadership and educational

roles is no doubt involved. Such selective criteria are highly vicarious, and could readily become disfunctional in a changing environment. For a review of this literature see Mead (1964) and Campbell (1965).

10. *Science.* With the level of science, which is but an aspect of sociocultural evolution, we return to Popper's home ground. The demarcation of science from other speculations is that the knowledge claims be testable, and that there be available mechanisms for testing or selecting which are more than social. In theology and the humanities there is certainly differential propagation among advocated beliefs, and there result sustained developmental trends, if only at the level of fads and fashions. What is characteristic of science is that the selective system which weeds out among the variety of conjectures involves deliberate contact with the environment through experiment and quantified prediction, designed so that outcomes quite independent of the preferences of the investigator are possible. It is preeminently this feature that gives science its greater objectivity and its claim to a cumulative increase in the accuracy with which it describes the world.

An emphasis on the trial-and-error nature of science is a recurrent one, perhaps more characteristic of scientists describing scientific method than of philosophers. Agassiz (1969) attributes such a view to Williams Whewell as early as 1840: 'Whewell's (is) in retrospect a Darwinian view: we must invent many hypotheses because only a few of them survive tests, and these are the ones that matter, the hard core around which research develops.' James (1880) and Huxley (1897) in the last century and Ghiselin (1969) and Monod (1971) in this are among many espousing such a view (*Editor's note*: see Appendix II in the original paper for a fuller bibliography) along with Toulmin, Kuhn, and Ackermann, to be discussed in more detail below.

There are a number of aspects of science which point in this direction. The opportunism of science, the rushing in and rapid development following new breakthroughs, are very like the rapid exploitation of a newly entered ecological niche. Science grows rapidly around laboratories, around discoveries which make the testing of hypotheses easier, which provide sharp and consistent selective systems. Thus the barometer, microscope, telescope, galvanometer, cloud chamber, and chromatograph all have stimulated rapid scientific growth. The necessity for the editing action of the experiment explains why a research tradition working with a trivial topic for which predictions can be checked advances more rapidly than research focused upon a more important problem but lacking a machinery for weeding out hypotheses.

A major empirical achievement of the sociology of science is the evidence of the ubiquity of simultaneous invention. If many scientists are trying variations on the same corpus of current scientific knowledge, and if their trials are being edited by the same stable external reality, then the selected variants are apt to the similar, the same discovery encountered independently by numerous workers. This process is no more mysterious than that all of a set of blind rats, each starting with quite different patterns of initial responses, learn the same maze pattern, under the maze's common editorship of the varied response repertoires. Their learning is actually their independent invention or discovery of the same response pattern. In doubly reflexively appropriateness, the theory of natural selection was itself multiply independently invented, not only by Wallace but by many others. Moreover, the ubiquity of independent invention in science has itself been independently discovered. (*Editor's note*: see Appendix III of original paper for a full bibliography.)

Placing science within the selective retention theme only begins the analysis that will eventually be required, for there are within science a variety of trial-and-error processes of varying degrees of vicariousness and interdependence. At one extreme is the blindly exploratory experimentalist who within a given laboratory setting introduces variations on every parameter and combination he can think of, without attention to theory. While such activity does not epitomize science, such research often provides the empirical puzzles that motivate and discipline the efforts of theoreticians. A multiple opportunism of selective systems (or 'problems') needs also to be emphasized. Whereas the mass explorations of pharmaceutical houses for new antibiotics may be single-problem oriented, 'basic' research is, like biological evolution, opportunistic not only in solutions, but also in problems. The research worker encountering a new phenomenon may change his research problem to one which is thereby solved. Serendipity as described by Cannon (1945) and Merton (1949), and the recurrent theme of 'chance' discovery, emphasize this double opportunism. Its occurrence implies that the scientist has an available agenda of problems, hypotheses, or expectations much larger than the specific problem on which he works, and that he is in some sense continually scanning or winnowing outcomes, particularly unexpected ones, with this larger set of sieves.

At the opposite extreme from this blind laboratory exploration is Popper's view of the natural selection of scientific theories, a trial and error of mathematical and logical models in competition with each other in the adequacy with which they solve empirical puzzles, that is, in the adequacy with which they fit the totality of scientific data and also meet the separate requirements of being theories or solutions. Popper has, in fact, disparaged the common belief in 'chance' discoveries in science as partaking of the inductivist belief in directly learning from experience. Although there is probably no fundamental disagreement, that issue, and the more general problem of spelling out in detail the way in which a natural selection of scientific *theories* is compatible with a dogmatic blind-variation-and-selective-retention epistemology remain high priority tasks for the future.

Intermediate perhaps, is Toulmin's (1967, 1972) evolutionary model of scientific development, which makes explicit analogue to population genetics and the concept of evolution as a shift in the composition of a gene pool shared by a population, rather than specified in an individual. In his analogy, for genes are substituted 'competing intellectual variants', concepts, beliefs, interpretations of specific fact, facts given special importance, etc. The individual scientists are the carriers. Through selective diffusion and selective retention processes some intellectual variants eventually become predominant, some completely eliminated. Some new mutants barely survive until their time is ripe.

The selective systems operating on the variations need also to be specified. As Baldwin and Peirce emphasized, the selective system of science is ultimately socially distributed in a way which any individualistic epistemology fails to describe adequately. Vicarious selectors also must be specified. Whereas the meter readings in experiments may seem to be direct selectors, this is only relatively so, and most of the proximal selection is done on the basis of vicarious criteria, including the background presumptions required to interpret the meter readings, some of which are very general in nature. In keeping with the nested hierarchy evolutionary perspective, a trial and error of such presuppositions would be expected as part of the overall process. Both Toulmin's (1961) interpretation of the history of science in terms of shifts in what does not need to be explained and Kuhn's (1962) paradigm shifts can be interpreted in this light. This is consistent with Toulmin's own evolutionary orientation. Although Kuhn also uses natural selection analogues, a natural selection of paradigms imputes to surviving paradigms a superiority over their predecessors which he explicitly questions. Ackermann has extended the evolutionary perspectives of Kuhn, Popper, and Toulmin, viewing experimental evidence as providing ecologies or niches to which theories adapt, i.e. which select theories (Ackermann, 1970).

D. HISTORICAL PERSPECTIVES ON EVOLUTIONARY EPISTEMOLOGY

What we find in Popper, and what has been elaborated so far, is but one type of evolutionary epistemology, perhaps best called a natural selection epistemology. As we have seen, there were both implicit and explicit forerunners of this in the nineteenth century, but they did not provide the dominant theme. Instead, theories of pre-Darwinian type generated the major evolutionary input into epistemology, even though their acceptance was furthered by the authority of Darwin's work. Herbert Spencer was the major spokesman for this school. Although he was an enthusiastic recipient of Darwin's theory of natural selection (and may even have coined the phrase 'survival of the fittest'), he was a vigorous evolutionist before he read Darwin, and his thinking remained dominated by two pre-Darwinian inputs. The first was the model of embryological development, and the second was a version of Lamarckian theory in which the animal mind was a passive mirror of environmental realities. Čapek (1957, 1959, 1968) has provided three excellent historical reviews of Spencer's epistemology and its influence. Among his positive contributions was his insistence that knowing had evolved along with the other aspects of life. Also valuable was his concept of the 'range of correspondences', the range becoming broader at higher evolutionary stages as manifest both in distance-receptor depth and range of environmental utilization. (His evolutionary Kantianism will be discussed below.)

What Spencer missed was the profound indirectness of knowing necessitated by the natural selection paradigm, and the inevitable imperfection and approximate character of both perceptual and scientific knowledge at any stage. Instead, believing that an infinitely refinable and sensitive human cognitive apparatus had in the course of evolution adapted perfectly to the external environment, he became a naïve realist accepting the givens of the cognitive processes as fundamentally valid. He also viewed human cognition as validly encompassing all reality, rather than just those aspects behaviourally relevant in the course of human evolution. Čapek sees the major limitations of Mach's and Poincaré's evolutionary epistemologies as stemming from their residual tendency to follow Spencer in accepting the completeness of cognitive evolution. It was against the Spencerian version of evolutionally produced cognitive perfection and completeness that Bergson rebelled. The Spencerian evolutionary epistemology had become a quite dominant view by 1890, a fact difficult to believe so absent has been any evolutionary epistemology in the major philosophical discussion of the last fifty years. William James, in 1890, speaks of the pervasive 'evolutionary empiricists'. George Simmel, in 1890, was able to write,

> 'It has been presumed for some time that human knowing has evolved from the practical needs of preserving and providing for life. The common underlying presupposition is this: there exists objective truth, the content of which is not influenced by the practical needs of the knower. This truth is grasped only because of its utility, correct conceptions being more useful than wrong ones. This view is common to various schools of epistemology, in realism where knowing is an inevitable grasping of an absolute reality, in idealism, where knowing is directed by *a priori* forms of thought.'

While accepting a natural selection epistemology, Simmel argues that, for the evolving animal, truth and usefulness are historically one. Anticipating von Uexkull and Bergson, he notes that the phenomenal worlds of animals differ from one to the other, according to the particular aspects of the world they are adapted to and the different sense organs they have.

Pragmatism's relation to natural selection and other evolutionary theories is mixed. In William James' prepragmatism writings (James, 1880, 1890), he clearly espoused a natural-selection fallibilism of thought, social evolution, and science, in explicit opposition to Spencer's passive-omniscient Lamarckianism. A vague social-evolutionary orientation appears in his writings on pragmatism, but nowhere as explicit on the issues of importance here. John Dewey's faith in experimentalism was never explicitly related to the variation-and-selective-retention epistemology, and his only reference to natural selection in his book, *The Influence of Darwin on Philosophy*, is in refutation of the argument for God's existence from the wondrous adapted complexity of organisms (Dewey, 1910). In his chapter of that book on the problem of knowledge, no mention of natural selection or trial and error occurs.

Charles Sanders Peirce (1931–1958) is profoundly ambivalent in this regard. His concept of truth as 'the opinion which is fated to be ultimately agreed to by all who investigate' partakes of the 'left-overs' or winnowing model of knowledge which is the particular achievement of the selective retention perspective.

Another Peirceian imagery that is quite sympathetic is that of a primeval chaos of chance, within which nodes of order emerged, nodes which grew but never exhausted the chaos, a background of chance and indeterminacy remaining. This imagery is preminiscent of that of Ashby (1952). But the mechanism which is used to explain the emergence is not selective retention, but a mentalistic, anthropomorphic, 'tendency to habit' on the part of physical matter.

Peirce was thoroughly conversant with the concept of natural selection and recognized it as Darwin's central contribution. Certainly he had in his creative exploration all of the ingredients for a selective retention evolutionary epistemology. Yet, the perspective if ever clearly conceived was also ambivalently rejected, and compatible statements are few and far between, overshadowed by dissimilar and incompatible elements. Wiener (1949) has carefully documented his ambivalence on the issue. In spite of all of his emphasis on evolution, and on the ontological status of chance, Peirce was not a Darwinian evolutionist. Rather he favored the views of both Lamarck and Agassiz, or at least gave them equal status. Wiener is able to quote Peirce as describing Darwin's theory as one which 'barely commands scientific respect' and 'did not appear at first at all near to being proved, and to a sober mind its case looks less hopeful now (1893) than it did twenty years ago.' While later expressing much more Darwinian positions, he hedged by regarding sports (and trial thoughts) as being initiated by lack of environmental fit, and as being formed 'not wildly but in ways having some sort of relation to the change needed.' Peirce's evolutionism was nostalgic for if not consistently committed to a God-guided evolution.

In connection with such a view, however, he had the important insight that natural laws (and perhaps even God Himself) are evolutionary products and are still evolving (see Wiener, 1949; and Vol. 1 of Peirce, para 348).

James Mark Baldwin is known to philosophers today only as the editor of the 1901–1905 *Dictionary of Philosophy* for which Peirce wrote a number of entries. Professionally a psychologist, he is perhaps today better remembered by sociologists of the Cooley tradition, or as a contender for the dubious honor of writing the first social psychology text (that by subtitle and preface) in 1897. Always a vigorous evolutionist, Darwinist–Wiesmannian and anti-Lamarckian, he turned to epistemology in his later years in his several volumes on *Thought and Things or Genetic Logic*. In 1909 he published casually a brief book on *Darwin and the Humanities* which stands in marked contrast with Dewey's contemporaneous *The Influence of Darwin on Philosophy* for its pervasive use of the natural selection and generalized selective retention theme. His distinction between pragmatism and his version of instrumentalism deserves quoting at some length:

'The theory of truth becomes either one of extreme "Pragmatism" or one merely of "Instrumentalism".

Instrumentalism holds that all truth is tentatively arrived at and experimentally verified. The method of knowledge is the now familiar Darwinian procedure of "trial and error". The thinker, whether working in the laboratory with things or among the products of his own imaginative thought, *tries our hypotheses*; and only by trying out hypotheses does he establish truth. The knowledge already possessed is used instrumentally in the form of a hypothesis or conjecture, for the discovery of further facts or truths. This reinstates in the sphere of thinking the method of Darwinian selection.

Here Darwinism gives support to the empiricism of Hume and Mill and forwards the sober British philosophical tradition. And no one illustrates better than Darwin, in his own scientific method, the soberness, caution, and soundness of this procedure. (pp. 68–69)

But a more radical point of view is possible. What is now known as Pragmatism proceeds out from this point. It is pertinent to notice it here, for it offers a link of transition to the philosophical views with which we must briefly concern ourselves.

Pragmatism turns instrumentalism into a system of metaphysics. It claims that apart from its tentative instrumental value, its value as guide to life, its value as measured by utility, seen in the consequences of its following out, truth has no further meaning. Not only is all truth selected for its utility, but apart from its utility *it is not truth*. There is no reality then to which truth is still true, whether humanly discovered or not; on the contrary, reality is only the content of the system of beliefs found useful as a guide to life.

I wish to point out that, in such a conclusion, not only is the experimental conception left behind, but the advantages of the Darwinian principle of adjustment to actual situations, physical and social, is lost; and if so interpreted, instrumentalism defeats itself. This clearly appears when we analyze a situation involving trial and error. Trial implies a problematical and alternative result: either the success of the assumption put to trial or its failure. When we ask why this is so, we hit upon the presence of some "controlling" condition or circumstance in the situation—some stable physical or social fact—whose character renders the hypothesis or suggested solution either adequate or vain, as the case may be. The instrumental idea or thought, then, has its merit in enabling us to find out or locate facts and conditions which are to be allowed for thereafter. These constitute a *control upon knowledge and action*, a system of "things".' (pp. 71–72) (Reproduced by permission of George Allen & Unwin).

E. KANT'S CATEGORIES OF PERCEPTION AND THOUGHT AS EVOLUTIONARY PRODUCTS

The evolutionary perspective is of course at odds with any view of an *ipso facto* necessarily valid synthetic *a priori*. But it provides a perspective under which Kant's categories of thought and intuition can be seen as a descriptive contribution to psychological epistemology. Though we reject Kant's claims of a necessary *a priori* validity for the categories, we can in evolutionary perspective see the categories as highly edited, much tested presumptions, 'validated' only as scientific truth is validated, synthetic *a posteriori* from the point of view of species-history, synthetic and in several ways *a priori* (but not in terms of necessary validity) from the point of view of an individual organism. Popper made this point as follows:

'. . . we are born with expectations; with "knowledge" which, although *not valid a priori*, is *psychologically or genetically a priori*, i.e. prior to all observational experience. One of the most important of these expectations is the expectation of finding a regularity. It is connected with an inborn propensity to look out for regularities, or with a *need to find* regularities. . . .

This "instinctive" expectation of finding regularities, which is psychologically *a priori*, corresponds very closely to the "law of causality" which Kant believed to be part of our mental outfit and to be *a priori* valid. One might thus be inclined to say that Kant failed to distinguish between psychologically *a priori* ways of thinking or responding and *a priori* valid beliefs. But I do not think his mistake was as crude as that. For the expectation of finding regularities is not only psychologically *a priori*, but also logically *a priori*; it is logically prior to all observational experience, for it is prior to any recognition of similarities, as we have seen; and all observation involves the recognition of similarities (or dissimilarities). But in spite of being logically *a priori* in this sense the expectation is not valid *a priori*. For it may fail: we can easily construct an environment (it would be a lethal one) which, compared with our ordinary environment, is so chaotic that we completely fail to find regularities....

Thus Kant's reply to Hume came near to being right; for the distinction between an *a priori* valid expectation and one which is both genetically and logically prior to observation, but not *a priori* valid, is really somewhat subtle.' (Popper, 1963, pp. 47–48)

This insight is the earliest and most frequently noted aspect of an evolutionary epistemology, perhaps because it can be achieved from a Lamarckian point of view, as well as from the natural selection model which is absolutely essential to the previous points. Herbert Spencer, a Lamarckian for these purposes, achieved this insight, as Höffding conveniently summarizes:

'With regard to the question of the origin of knowledge Spencer makes front on the one hand against Leibniz and Kant, on the other against Locke and Mill. He quarrels with empiricism for two reasons:–firstly, because it does not see that the matter of experience is always taken up and elaborated in a definite manner, which is determined by the original nature of the individual; secondly, because it is lacking in a criterion of truth. We must assume an original organisation if we are to understand the influence exercised by stimuli on different individuals, and the criterion by means of which alone a proposition can be established is the fact that its opposite would contain a contradiction. In the inborn nature of the individual then, and in the logical principle on which we depend every time we make an inference, we have an *a priori* element; something which cannot be deduced from experience. To this extent Spencer upholds Leibniz and Kant against Locke and Mill; but he does so only as long as he is restricting his considerations to the experience of the individual. *What is a priori for the individual is not so for the race.* For those conditions and forms of knowledge and of feeling which are original in the individual, and hence cannot be derived from his experience, have been transmitted by earlier generations. The forms of thought correspond to the collective and inherited modifications of structure which are latent in every new-born individual, and are gradually developed through his experiences. Their first origin, then, is empirical: the fixed and universal relation of things to one another must, in the course of development, form fixed and universal conjunctions in the organism; by perpetual repetition of absolutely external uniformities there arise in the race necessary forms of knowledge, indissoluble thought associations which express the net results of the experience of perhaps several millions of generations down to the present. The individual cannot sunder a conjunction thus deeply rooted in the organisation of the race; hence, he is born into the world with those psychical connections which form the substrata of "necessary truths" (see *Principles of Psychology*, pp. 208, 216; cf. *First Principles*, p. 53. "Absolute uniformities of experience generate absolute uniformities of thought"). Although Spencer is of opinion that the inductive school went too far when they attempted to arrive at everything by way of induction (for, if we adopt this method, induction itself is left hanging in the air), yet, if he had to choose between Locke and Kant, he would avow himself a disciple of the former; for, *in the long run, Spencer too thinks that all knowledge and all forms of thought spring from experience.* His admission that there is something in our mind which is not the product of our own *a posteriori* experience led Max Müller to call him a "thoroughgoing Kantian", to which Spencer replied: "The Evolution-view is completely experiential. It differs from the original view of the experimentalists by containing a great extension of that view.—*But this view of Kant is avowedly and utterly unexperiential.*"

It is of no small interest to notice that John Stuart Mill, who at first demurred at Spencer's evolutionary psychology, afterwards declared himself convinced that mental development takes place not only in the individual but also in the race by means of inherited dispositions. He expressed this modification of his view a year before his death in a letter to Carpenter, the physiologist (quoted in the latter's *Mental Physiology*).' (Höffding, 1900, pp. 457–458 and 475–476)

As Wallraff (1961) has documented, the demoting of Kant's categories to the level of descriptive rather than prescriptive epistemology began in 1807 with Jacob Fries's effort to interpret the categories as having only a psychological base, as but descriptive of human reason. While such a position was typically accompanied by a thoroughgoing dualism and was purely mentalistic, by 1866 Frederick A. Lange was able to discuss the *a priori* as aspects of a 'physico-psychological' organization of the mind (Lange, 1890), and to posit, with Mill, the possibility of 'erroneous *a priori* Knowledge'. He also wrote:

'Perhaps some day the basis of the idea of cause may be found in the mechanism of reflex action and sympathetic excitation; we should then have translated Kant's pure reason into physiology, and so made it more easily conceivable.' (Lange, 1890)

All that was lacking here was an explicit statement of the kind of validation of such physiological biases which a natural-selection evolution provides. Helmhotz's biological interpretation of the Kantian *a priori* categories is similar (Čapek, 1968).

Baldwin had the insight in 1902 and earlier:

'As Kant claimed, knowledge is a process of categorizing, and to know a thing is to say that it illustrates or stimulates, or functions as, a category. But a category is a mental habit; that is all a category can be allowed to be—a habit broadly defined as a disposition, whether congenital or acquired, to act upon or to treat, items of any sort in certain general ways. These habits or categories arise either from actual accommodations with "functional" or some other form of utility selection, or by natural endowment secured by selection from variations.' (p. 309)

In the tradition of pragmatism, the categories were seen as but pragmatically useful ways of thinking, usually products of culture history rather than biological evolution (for example, James 1907; Wartofsky, 1968), although in espousing such a viewpoint, Wright (1913) was able to say in passing:

'In a certain sense, therefore, the distinctions involved in some, at least, of the categories, viz., space, time, thing, and person, are present in the sense percepts of animals...It is clear that historically and phylogenetically perceptual elements anticipatory of some of the categories existed prior to the genesis of thought.'

Wright's position is extended explicitly by Child (1946) who posits both 'biotic categories', biological functions shared with animals and of biological survival value, and 'sociotic categories' which are cultural products. He says in passing, 'Since Kant, the term "category" has primarily referred to the presumably pervasive structures of racial mind.' (p. 320)

A great many other scholars have considered some kind of an evolutionary interpretation of Kant's categories, usually very briefly and without citing others. In approximately chronological order these include James, Morgan, Mach, Poincaré, Boltzmann, Fouillé, Cassirer, Shelton, Reichenbach, R. W. Sellars, Uexküll, Meyerson, Northrop, Magnus, Lorenz, Piaget, Waddington, Bertalanffy, Whitrow, Platt, Pepper, Merleau-Ponty, Simpson, W. S. Sellars, Hawkins, Barr, Toulmin, Wartofsky, and Watanabe. Quine, Maxwell, Shimony, Yilmaz, and Stemmer have made much the same point without explicit reference to the Kantian categories. (*Editor's note*: Appendix IV in the original presentation in Schilpp gives detailed references for all of these scholars.) Of these, many are essentially biologists generalizing into philosophy. This brief quote from Waddington epitomizes their message:

'The faculties by which we arrive at a world view have been selected so as to be, at least, efficient in dealing with other existents. They may, in Kantian terms, not give us direct contact with the thing-in-itself, but they have been moulded by things-in-themselves so as to be competent in coping with them.' (Waddington, 1954)

Most of the passages cited are very brief, noting the insight only in passing. In marked contrast is the rich exposition provided by Lorenz.

In his essay, 'Kant's Doctrine of the *A Priori* in the Light of Contemporary Biology' (reprinted as Chapter 7 in this volume), Lorenz (1962b) accepts Kant's insight as to some degree of fit between innate categories of thought and the *Ding an sich*. He accepts Kant's claim that without such prior-fitting categories, no one could achieve in his own lifetime the empirical, experiential, knowledge of the world which he does achieve. He accepts in some sense Kant's scepticism as to the form of knowledge. While to Lorenz more than Kant the *Ding an sich* is knowable, it certainly is only known in the knower's categories, not in those of the *Ding an sich* itself. Thus he accepts Kant as psychologist if not as epistemologist. As with all of those we have cited above, from Spencer on, any validity or appropriateness of the categories to the *Ding an sich* is due to their status as a product of an evolution in which the *Ding an sich* has acted in the editorial role of discarding misleading categories.

Lorenz, like Popper recognizes that it was to Kant's great disadvantage to believe Newton's physics perfectly true. When Kant then recognized the *a priori* human intuitions of space, time, and causality as fitting Newton's physics (which they do to a lesser degree than Kant thought), he had a greater puzzle on his hands than a modern epistemologist has. From our viewpoint, both Newton's laws of dynamics and the intuitive categories of space perception can be seen as but approximations to a latter more complete physics (or to the *Ding an sich*).

Lorenz portrays for the concepts of space and causality their analogues in water shrew, greylag goose, and man, arguing for each an 'objectivity', yet limitedness and imperfection. For a weak microscope, we assume that the homogeneous texture provided at its limit of resolution is a function of those limits, not an attribute of reality. We do this because through more powerful scopes this homogeneity becomes differentiated. By analogy, we extend this assumption even to the most powerful scope. Seeing our human categories of thought and intuition as but the best in such an evolutionary series, even though we might have no better scope to compare it with, generates a parallel scepticism. Actually we do have a better scope, modern physics, which today, at least, if not in Kant's time, provides a much finer grained view of reality.

There is a two-sided message in this literature: there is an 'objective' reflection of the *Ding an sich* which, however, does not achieve expression in the *Ding an sich*'s own terms. Lorenz, and many of the others, have argued that the mind has been shaped by evolution to fit those aspects of the world with which it deals, just as have other body parts. The shape of a horse's hoof certainly expresses 'knowledge' of the steppe in a very odd and partial language, and in an end product mixed with 'knowledge' of other contingencies. Our visual, tactual, and several modes of scientific knowledge of the steppe are each expressed in quite different languages, but are comparably objective. The hydrodynamics of sea water, plus the ecological value of locomotion, have independently shaped fish, whale, and walrus in a quite similar fashion. Their shapes represent independent discoveries of this same 'knowledge', expressed in this case in similar 'languages'. But the jet-propelled squid reflects the same hydrodynamic principles in a quite different, but perhaps equally 'accurate' and 'objective' shape. The *Ding an sich* is always known indirectly, always in the language of the knower's posits, be these mutations governing bodily form, or visual percepts, or scientific theories. In this sense it is unknowable. But there is an objectivity in the reflection, however indirect, an objectivity in the selection from innumerable less adequate posits.

F. PRAGMATISM, UTILITARIANISM, AND OBJECTIVITY

For both Popper and the present writer the *goal of objectivity* in science is a noble one, and dearly to be cherished. It is in true worship of this goal that we remind ourselves that our current views of reality are partial and imperfect. We recoil at a view of science which recommends we give up the search for ultimate truth and settle for practical computational recipes making no pretense at truly describing a real world. Thus our sentiment is to reject pragmatism, utilitarian nominalism, utilitarian subjectivism, utilitarian conventionalism, or instrumentalism, in favour of a critical hypothetical realism. Yet our evolutionary epistemology, with its basis in natural selection for survival relevance, may seem to commit us to pragmatism or utilitarianism. Simmel in 1895 presents the problem forcibly, as also do Mach and Poincaré.

This profound difference in sentiment deserves much more attention than can be given here, but brief comments from a variety of perspectives may be in order. These are based on the assumption that neither Popper nor the present writer intend to relinquish the goal of objectivity, and must therefore reconcile it with the natural selection epistemology to which that very quest for objective truth has led us.

Where the emphasis on utilitarian selectivity is to counter the epistemic arrogance of a naïve or phenomenal realism, we can join it unambivalently. The critical realist has no wish to identify the real with the phenomenally given. Thus the visual and tactual solidity of ordinary objects represents a phenomenal emphasis on the one physical discontinuity most usable by man and his ancestors, to the neglect of other discontinuities identifiable by the probes of modern experimental physics. Perceived solidity is not illusory for its ordinary uses: what it diagnoses is one of the 'surfaces' modern physics also describes. But when reified as exclusive, when creating expectations of opaqueness and impermeability to all types of probes, it becomes illusory. The different *Umwelten* of different animals do represent in part the differential utilities of their specific ecological niches, as well as differential limitations. But each of the separate contours diagnosed in these *Umwelten* are also diagnosable by a complete physics, which in addition provides many differentia unused and unperceived by any organism (von Bertalanffy, 1955).

Nor do we claim any firmer grounding of the scientific theory and fact of today than do the pragmatists and utilitarians. Indeed, Popper's emphasis on criticism may produce an even greater scepticism as to the realism of present-day science. There is, however, a difference in what it is that is being grounded. Consider a graph of observational points relating the volume of water to its temperature. An extreme punctiform pragmatism or definitional operationism would regard the observations themselves as the scientific truth. A more presumptive pragmatism would fit a least squares curve with minimum parameters to the data, and regard the values of the points on the fitted curve as the scientific facts, thus deviating from some of the original observations. Even at this stage, degrees of pragmatism occur. The departure may be justified purely on the grounds of computational efficiency, or the discrepant observations may be regarded as 'errorful', with the anticipation that, were the experiment repeated, the new observations would on the average fall nearer to the 'theoretical' values than to the original observations. Most scientific practice is still less pragmatic, more realistic than this: of all mathematical formulae that fit the data equally well with the same number of parameters, scientists choose that one or those whose parameters can be used in other formulae subsuming other observations. While the search for such parameters may most often be done as a search for physically interpretable parameters, it can also be justified on purely utilitarian grounds. In extending this series, were Popper's position to be classified as a pragmatism at all it would have to be as pragmatic selection from among formal theories claiming to be universally descriptive of the real world, but not identified as the real world. Even this degree of pragmatism needs to be qualified.

The extremes of pragmatism, definitional operationism, and phenomenalism would equate theory and data in a true epistemological monism. But as elaborated in actual philosophies of science, the dualism of data and theory just described is accepted. Adequately to handle the issues raised in discussions of epistemological monism and dualism (see Lovejoy, 1930; Kohler, 1938) we need to expand the framework to an epistemological trinism (trialism, triadism, trimondism) of data, theory, and real world (approximately corresponding to Popper's 'second world', 'third world', and 'first world') (Popper, 1972). The controversial issue is the conceptual inclusion of the real world, defining the problem of knowledge as the fit of data and theory to that real world.

Such a critical realism involves presumptions going beyond the data, needless to say. But since Hume we should have known that nonpresumptive knowledge is impossible. As Petrie (1969) has pointed out, most modern epistemologies recognize that scientific beliefs are radically under-justified. The question is thus a matter of which presumptions, not whether or not presumptions.

Biological theories of evolution, whether Lamarckian or Darwinian, are profoundly committed to an organism–environment dualism, which when extended into the evolution of sense organ, perceptual and learning functions, becomes a dualism of an organism's knowledge of the environment versus the environment itself. An evolutionary epistemologist is at this level doing 'epistemology of the other one' (Campbell, 1959, 1969), studying the relationship of an animal's cognitive capacities and the environment they are designed to cognize, both of which the epistemologist knows only in the hypothetical-contingent manner of science. Thus he may study the relationship between the shape of a rat's running pattern ('cognitive map') and the shape of the maze it runs in. Or he may study the polarization of sunlight (using scientific instruments since his own eyes are insensitive to such nuances) and the bee's sensitivity to plane or polarization. At this level he has no hesitancy to include a 'real world' concept, even though he may recognize that his own knowledge of that world even with instrumental augmentation is partial and limited in ways analogous to the limitations of the animal whose epistemology he studies. Having thus made the real-world assumption in this part of his evolutionary epistemology, he is not adding an unneeded assumption when he assumes the same predicament for man and science as knowers.

It is true, of course, that in an epistemology of other animals he has independent data on the 'knowledge' and 'world to be known', and thus studying the degree of fit involves no tautology. It is true that in extending this 'epistemology of the other one' to knowledge of modern physics, no separate information on the world-to-be-known is available with which to compare current physical theory. But this practical limitation does not necessitate abandoning an ontology one is already employing. (This argument is of course only compelling vis-à-vis those of such as Simmel, Mach, and Poincaré, who base their utilitarian nominalism and conventionalism on an evolutionary perspective.)

We can also examine utilitarian specificity versus realism in the evolution of knowing. Consider the spatial knowledge of some primitive locomotor animal, perhaps Konrad Lorenz's (1962b) water shrew. It may have a thirst space it uses when thirsty, a separate hunger space, a separate space for escape from each predator, a mate-finding space, etc. In its utilitarianism, there is a separate space for every utility. In a higher stage of evolution, the hypothesis has emerged that all these spaces are the same, or overlap. The realistic hypothesis of an all-purpose space has developed. There is abundant evidence that white rat, cat, dog, and chimpanzee are at or beyond this stage: that spatial learning achieved in the service of one motive is immediately available for other motives. Along with this goes spatial curiosity, the exploring of novel spaces and objects when all utilitarian motives (thirst, food, sex, safety, etc.) are sated and the exploration has no momentary usefulness. Such disinterested curiosity for 'objective', all-possible-purpose spatial knowledge-for-its-own-sake has obvious survival value, even though it may transcend the sum of all specific utilities. Scientific curiosity of course goes beyond the specifically utilitarian to a much greater extent. Survival relevant criteria are rare among the criteria actually used in deciding questions of scientific truth. The science Mach was attempting to epitomize had made most of its crucial selections from among competing theories on the basis of evidence (such as on the phases of the moons of Jupiter) of no contemporary or past utility. And in the history of science, those who took their theories as real, rather than their contemporary conventionalists, have repeatedly emerged in the main stream for future developments.

These several disparate comments scarcely begin the task of relating the critical-realist, natural-selection epistemology to the recurrent issues in the history of the theory of knowledge. Potentially it can provide a dialectic resolution to many old controversies. But spelling out the points of articulation with the main body of epistemological concerns remains for the most part yet to be done.

SUMMARY

This essay has identified Popper as the modern founder and leading advocate of a natural-selection epistemology. The characteristic focus is on the growth of knowledge. The problem of knowledge is so defined that the knowing of other animals than man is included. The variation and selective retention process of evolutionary adaptation is generalized to cover a nested hierarchy of vicarious knowledge processes, including vision, thought, imitation, linguistic instruction, and science.

Historical attention is paid not only to those employing the natural-selection paradigm, but also to the Spencerian–Lamarckian school of evolutionary epistemologists, and the ubiquitous evolutionary interpretation of the Kantian categories. It is argued that, whereas the evolutionary perspective has often led to a pragmatic, utilitarian conventionalism, it is fully compatible with an advocacy of the goals of realism and objectivity in science.

REFERENCES

Ackermann, R. (1970). *The Philosophy of Science,* Pegasus, New York.
Agassiz, J. (1969). Comment: Theoretical Entities versus Theories. *Boston Studies in the Philosophy of Science,* **5**.
Asch, S. E. (1952). *Social Psychology*, Prentice-Hall, New York.
Ashby, W. R. (1952). *Design for a Brain*, Wiley, New York.
Atkinson, R. C., and Crothers, E. J. (1964). A comparison of paired associate learning models having different acquisition and retention axioms. *Journal of Mathematical Psychology,* **1**, 285–312.
Bain, A. (1855). *The senses and the intellect*, Appleton, New York.
Baldwin, J. M. (1900). *Mental Development in the child and Race*, Macmillan, New York.
Baldwin, J. M. (1902). *Development and Evolution*, Macmillan, New York.

Baldwin, J. M. (1906). *Thought and Things. A study of the Development and Meaning of Thought, or Genetic Logic*, Volume 1, Macmillan, New York.

Baldwin, J. M. (1909). *Darwin and the Humanities*, Review Publishing Company, Baltimore.

Bandura, A. (1969). *Principles of Behavior Modification*, Holt, Rinehart, and Winston, New York.

Barr, H. J. (1964). Regeneration and Natural Selection. *American Naturalist*, **98**, 183–186.

Bertalanffy von, L. (1955). An Essay on the Relativity of Categories. *Philosophy of Science*, **22**, 243–263.

Campbell, D. T. (1956a). Perception as substitute trial and error. *Psychological Review*, **63**, 331–342.

Cambell, D. T. (1956b). Adaptive behavior from random response. *Behavioral Science*, **1**, 105–110.

Campbell, D. T. (1959). Methodological suggestions from a comparative psychology of knowledge processes. *Inquiry*, **2**, 152–182.

Campbell, D. T. (1960). Blind variation and selective retention in creative thought as in other knowledge processes. *Psychological Review*, **67**, 380–400.

Campbell, D. T. (1961). Conformity in Psychology's Theories of acquired Behavioral Dispositions. In I. A. Berg and B. M. Bass (Eds), *Conformity and Deviation*, McGraw-Hill, New York. pp. 101–142.

Campbell, D. T. (1963). Social attitudes and other Acquired Behavioral Dispositions. In S. Koch (Ed.), *Psychology: A study of a Science*, Vol. 6, McGraw-Hill, New York. pp. 94–172.

Campbell, D. T. (1965). Variation and Selective Retention in Sociocultural Evolution. In H. R. Barringer, G. I. Blanksten, and R. W. Mack (Eds), *Social Change in Developing Areas: A Reinterpretation of Evolutionary Theory*, Schenkman, Cambridge, Mass. pp. 19–49.

Campbell, D. T. (1966). Pattern matching as Essential in Distal Knowing. In K. R. Hammond (Ed.), *The Psychology of Egon Brunswick*, Holt, Rinehart, and Winston, New York. pp. 81–106.

Campbell, D. T. (1969). A Phenomenology of the Other One: Corrigible, Hypothetical and Critical'. In T. Mischel (Ed.), *Human Action*, Academic Press, New York. pp. 41–69.

Campbell, D. T. (1973). Ostensive Instances and Entitativity in Language Learning. In N.D. Rizzo (Ed.) *Unity through Diversity*, Gordon and Breach, New York.

Cannon, W. B. (1945). *The Way of an Investigator*, Norton, New York.

Čapek, M. (1957). The Development of Reichenbach's Epistemology. *Review of Metaphysics*, **11**, 42–67.

Čapek, M. (1959). La Theorie Biologique de la Connaissance chez Bergson el sa signification Actuelle. *Revue de Metaphysique et de Morale*, April–June, 194–211.

Čapek, M. (1968). Ernst Mach's Biological Theory of Knowledge. *Sythese*, **18**, 171–191.

Child, A. (1946). On the theory of the categories. *Philosophy and Phenomenological Research*, **7**, 316–335.

Craik, K. J. W. (1943). *The Nature of Explanation*, Cambridge University Press, New York.

Dewey, J. (1910). *The Influence of Darwin on Philosophy*, Henry Holt, New York.

Estes, W. K. (1964). All or none processes in Learning and Retention. *American Psychologist*, **19**, 16–25.

Frisch von, K. (1950). *Bees, Their Vision, Chemical Sense, and Language*, Cornell University Press, Ithaca.

Ghiselin, M. T. (1969). *The Triumph of the Darwinian Method*, University of California Press, Berkeley.

Gould J. L., Henerey, M., and MacLeod, M. C. (1970). Communication of Direction by the Honey Bee. *Science*, **169**, 544–554.

Griffin, D. R. (1958). *Listening in the Dark*, Yale University Press, New Haven.

Hebb, D. O. (1946). On the Nature of Fear. *Psychological Review*, **53**, 259–276.

Hinde, R. A. (1969). *Bird Vocalization*, Cambridge University Press, Cambridge.

Höffding, H. (1900). *A History of Modern Philosophy*, Macmillan, London. (Reprinted Dover, 1955.)

Holmes, S. J. (1916). *Studies in Animal Behavior*, Gorham Press, Boston.

Huxley, T. H. (1897). *Collected Essays*, Vol. 2, *Darwiniana*, Appleton, New York.

James, W. (1880). Great Men, Great Thoughts, and the environment. *Atlantic Monthly*, **46**, 441–459.

James, W. (1890). *Principles of Psychology*, Vol. 2, Henry Holt, New York.

James, W. (1907). *Pragmatism*, Longmans-Green, New York.

Jennings, H. S. (1906). *The Behavior of Lower Organisms*, Columbia University Press, New York.

Jevons, S. (1892). *The Principles of Science*, Macmillan, London.

Kellog, W. N. (1958). Echo-ranging in the Porpoise. *Science*, **128**, 982–988.

Kohler, W. (1925). *The Mentality of Apes*, Harcourt Brace, New York.

Kohler, W. (1938). *The Place of Value in a World of Facts*, Liveright, New York.

Kuhn, T. S. (1962). *The Structure of Scientific Revolutions*, University of Chicago Press, Chicago.

Lange, F. A. (1890). *The History of Materialism*. Reprinted by Humanities Press, New York, 1950.

Lorenz, K. (1962a). Gestalt perception as Fundamental to Scientific Knowledge. *General Systems*, **7**, 37–56.

Lorenz, K. (1962b). Kant's Doctrine of the *a priori* in the Light of Contemporary Biology. *General Systems*, **7**, 23–35.

Lovejoy, A. O. (1930). *The Revolt against Dualism*, Open Court, La Salle, Illinois.

Mach, E. (1896). On the part played by Accident in Invention and Discovery. *Monist*, **6**, 161–175.

MacCormac, E. R. (1971). Ostensive Instances in Language Learning. *Foundations of Language*, **7**, 199–210.

Mead, M. (1964). *Continuities in Cultural Evolution*, Yale University Press, New Haven.

Merton, R. K. (1949). *Social Theory and Social Structure*, Free Press, Glencoe.

Monod, J. (1971). *Chance and Necessity*, Alfred H. Knopf, New York.

Newell, A., Shaw, J. C., and Simon, H. A. (1958). Elements of a Theory of Human Problem Solving. *Psychological Review*, **65**, 151–166.

Peirce, C. S. (1931-1958). C. Hartshorne and P. Weiss (Eds), *Collected Papers*, Vols. 1–5, Harvard University Press, Cambridge, Mass.

Petrie, H.G. (1969). The Logical Effects of Theory on Observational Categories and Methodology. Unpublished manuscript.

Poincaré, H. (1913). *The Foundations of Science*, Science Press, New York.

Popper, K. R. (1959). *The Logic of Scientific Discovery*, Hutchinson, London.

Popper, K. R. (1963). *Conjectures and Refutations*, Routledge and Kegan Paul, London.

Popper, K. R. (1972). *Objective Knowledge,* Oxford University Press, Oxford.

Pringle, J. W. S. (1951). On the parallel between learning and evolution. *Behaviour*, **3**, 175–215.

Pumphrey, R. J. (1950). Hearing. *Symposium for the Society for Experimental Biology*, **IV**, 1–18.

Quine, W. V. (1969). *Ontological Relativity*, Columbia University Press, New York.

Restle, F. (1962). The Selection of Strategies in Cue Learning. *Psychological Review*, **69**, 329–343.

Russell, B. (1948). *Human Knowledge: Its Scope and Limits*, Simon and Schuster, New York.

Sebeok, T. A. (1968). *Animal Communication*, Indiana University Press, Bloomington.

Sebeok, T. A., and Ramsay, A. (1969). *Approaches to Animal Communication*, Mouton and Company, The Hague.

Simmel, G. (1895). Uber eine Beziehung der Selectionslehre zur Erkenntnisstheorie. *Archiv fur systematische Philosophie*, **1**, 34–45. Translated by Irene L. Jerison as 'On a Relationship between the Theory of Selection and Epistemology.

Simon, H. A. (1969). *The Sciences of the Artificial*, MIT Press, Cambridge, Mass.

Souriau, P. (1881). *Theorie de L'Invention*, Hachette, Paris.

Spiegelman, S. (1948). Differentiation as the controlled production of unique enzymatic patterns. *Symposium for the Society for Experimental Biology II: Growth in Relation to Differentiation and Morphogenesis*, Academic Press, New York.

Toulmin, S. E. (1961). *Foresight and Understanding: An inquiry into the Aims of Science*, Indiana University Press, Bloomington.

Toulmin, S. E. (1967). The Evolutionary Development of Natural Science. *American Scientist*, **55**, 456–471.

Toulmin, S. E. (1972). *Human Understanding Vol. I: The Evolution of Collective Understanding*, Princeton University Press, Princeton.

Waddington, C. H. (1954). Evolution and Epistemology. *Nature*, **173**, 880–881.

Wallraff, C. F. (1961). *Philosophical Theory and Psychological Fact*, University of Arizona Press, Tucson.

Wartofsky, M. (1968). 'Metaphysics as Heuristic for Science.' *Boston Studies in the Philosophy of Science*, **3**, 164–170.

Wiener, P.P. (1949). *Evolution and the Founders of Pragmatism*, Harvard University Press, Cambridge, Mass.

Wimsatt, W. C. (1972). Teleology and the Logical Structure of Function Statements. *Studies in History and Philosophy of Science*, **3**, No. 1.

Wright, W. K. (1913). The Genesis of the Categories. *The Journal of Philosophy, Psychology and Scientific Methods*, **10**, 645–657.

Learning, Development, and Culture
Edited by H. C. Plotkin
© 1982, John Wiley & Sons Ltd.

CHAPTER 6

Of clouds and clocks

Karl R. Popper*

XVIII

I offer my general theory with many apologies. It has taken me a long time
to think it out fully, and to make it clear to myself. Nevertheless I still feel far
from satisfied with it. This is partly due to the fact that it is an evolutionary
theory, and one which adds only a little, I fear, to existing evolutionary theories,
except perhaps a new emphasis.

My theory may be described as an attempt to apply to the whole of evolution
what we learned when we analysed the evolution from animal language to
human language. And it consists of a certain *view of evolution* as a growing
hierarchical system of plastic controls, and of a certain *view of organisms* as
incorporating—or in the case of man, evolving exosomatically—this growing
hierarchical system of plastic controls. The Neo-Darwinist theory of evolution
is assumed; but it is restated by pointing out that its 'mutations' may be
interpreted as more or less accidental trial-and-error gambits, and 'natural
selection' as one way of controlling them by error-elimination.

I shall now state the theory in the form of twelve short theses:

(1) All *organisms* are constantly, day and night, *engaged in problem-solving*;
and so are all those evolutionary *sequences of organisms*—the *phyla* which begin

* Sections XVIII–XXIV of the second Arthur Holly Compton Memorial Lecture presented at
Washington University in 1965. From *Objective Knowledge* by Karl R. Popper, © Karl R. Popper
1972. Reprinted by permission of the author and Oxford University Press.

with the most primitive forms and of which the now living organisms are the latest members.

(2) These problems are problems in an objective sense: they can be, hypothetically, reconstructed by hindsight, as it were. (I will say more about this later.) Objective problems in this sense need not have their conscious counterpart; and where they have their conscious counterpart, the conscious problem need not coincide with the objective problem.

(3) Problem-solving always proceeds by the method of trial and error: new reactions, new forms, new organs, new modes of behaviour, new hypotheses, are tentatively put forward and controlled by error-elimination.

(4) Error-elimination may proceed either by the complete elimination of unsuccessful forms (the killing-off of unsuccessful forms by natural selection) or by the (tentative) evolution of controls which modify or suppress unsuccessful organs, or forms of behaviour, or hypotheses.

(5) The single organism telescopes[1] into one body, as it were, the controls developed during the evolution of its *phylum*—just as it partly recapitulates, in its ontogenetic development, its phylogenetic evolution.

(6) The single organism is a kind of spearhead of the evolutionary sequence of organisms to which it belongs (its *phylum*): it is itself a tentative solution, probing into new environmental niches, choosing an environment and modifying it. It is thus related to its phylum almost exactly as the actions (behaviour) of the individual organism are related to this organism: the individual organism, and its behaviour, are both trials, which may be eliminated by error-elimination.

(7) Using 'P' for problems, 'TS' for tentative solutions, 'EE' for error-elimination, we can describe the fundamental evolutionary sequence of events as follows:

$$[P \rightarrow TS \rightarrow EE \rightarrow P.]$$

But this sequence is not a cycle: the second problem is, in general, different from the first: it is the result of the new situation which has arisen, in part, because of the tentative solutions which have been tried out, and the error-elimination which controls them. In order to indicate this, the above schema should be rewritten:

$$[P_1 \rightarrow TS \rightarrow EE \rightarrow P_2.]$$

(8) But even in this form an important element is still missing: the multiplicity of the tentative solutions, the multiplicity of the trials. Thus our final schema becomes something like this:

$$
\begin{array}{ccc}
 & \nearrow TS_1 \searrow & \\
P_1 \rightarrow & TS_2 \rightarrow EE & \rightarrow P_2 \\
 & \searrow \quad \nearrow & \\
 & TS_n &
\end{array}
$$

(9) In this form, our schema can be compared with that of Neo-Darwinism. According to Neo-Darwinism there is in the main one problem: the problem of survival. There is, as in our system, a multiplicity of tentative solutions—the variations or mutations. But there is only one way of error-elimination—the killing of the organism. And (partly for this reason) the fact that P_1 and P_2 will differ essentially is overlooked, or else its fundamental importance is not sufficiently clearly realized.

(10) In our system, not all problems are survival problems: there are many very specific problems and subproblems (even though the earliest problems may have been sheer survival problems). For example an early problem P_1 may be reproduction. Its solution may lead to a new problem, P_2: the problem of getting rid of, or of spreading, the offspring—the children which threaten to suffocate not only the parent organism but each other.[2]

(11) The theory here proposed distinguishes between P_1 and P_2 and it shows that the problems (or the problem situations) which the organism is trying to deal with are often *new*, and arise themselves as products of the evolution. The theory thereby gives implicitly a rational account of what has usually been called by the somewhat dubious names of '*creative evolution*' or '*emergent evolution*'.

(12) Our schema allows for the development of error-eliminating controls (warning organs like the eye; feed-back mechanisms); that is, controls which can eliminate errors without killing the organism; and it makes it possible, ultimately, for our hypotheses to die in our stead.

XIX

Each organism can be regarded as a hierarchical system of *plastic controls*—as a system of clouds controlled by clouds. The controlled subsystems make trial-and-error movements which are partly suppressed and partly restrained by the controlling system.

We have already met an example of this in the relation between the lower and higher functions of language. The lower ones continue to exist and to play their part; but they are constrained and controlled by the higher ones.

Another characteristic example is this. If I am standing quietly, without making any movement, then (according to the physiologists) my muscles are constantly at work, contracting and relaxing in an almost random fashion (see TS_1 to TS_n is thesis (8) of the preceding section), but controlled, without my being aware of it, by error-elimination (EE) so that every little deviation from my posture is almost at once corrected. So I am kept standing, quietly, by more or less the same method by which an automatic pilot keeps an aircraft steadily on its course.

This example also illustrates the thesis (1) of the preceding section—that each organism is all the time engaged in problem-solving by trial and error; that it reacts to new and old problems by more or less chance-like,[3] or cloud-like, trials which are eliminated if unsuccessful. (If successful, they increase the probability of the survival of mutations which 'simulate' the solutions so reached, and tend to make the solution hereditary,[4] by incorporating it into the spatial structure or form of the new organism.)

XX

This is a very brief outline of the theory. It needs, of course, much elaboration. But I wish to explain *one* point a little more fully—the use I have made (in theses (1) to (3) of Section XVIII) of the terms '*problem*' and '*problem-solving*' and, more particularly, my assertion that *we can speak of problems in an objective, or non-psychological sense.*

The point is important, for evolution is clearly not a conscious process. Many biologists say that the evolution of certain organs solves certain problems; for example, that the evolution of the eye solves the problem of giving a moving animal a timely warning to change its direction before bumping into something hard. Nobody suggests that this kind of solution to this kind of problem is consciously sought. Is it not, then, just a metaphor if we speak of problem-solving?

I do not think so; rather, the situation is this: when we speak of a problem, we do so almost always from hindsight. A man who works on a problem can seldom say clearly what his problem is (unless he has found a solution); and even if he can explain his problem, he may mistake it. And this may even hold of scientists—though scientists are among those few who consciously try to be fully aware of their problems. For example, Kepler's conscious problem was to discover the harmony of the world order; but we may say that the problem he solved was the mathematical description of motion in a set of two-body planetary systems. Similarly, Schrödinger was mistaken about the problem he had solved by finding the (time-independent) Schrödinger equation: he thought his waves were charge-density waves, of a changing continuous field of electric charge. Later Max Born gave a statistical interpretation of the Schrödinger wave amplitude; an interpretation which shocked Schrödinger and which he disliked as long as he lived. He had solved a problem—but it was not the one he thought he had solved. This we know now, by hindsight.

Yet clearly it is in science that we are most conscious of the problems we try to solve. So it should not be inappropriate to use problems (though we need not assume that it is in any sense aware of its problems): from the amoeba to Einstein is just one step.

XXI

But Compton tells us that the amoeba's actions are not rational,[5] while we may assume that Einstein's actions are. So there should be some difference, after all.

I admit that there is a difference: even though their methods of almost random or cloud-like trial and error movements are fundamentally not very different,[6,3] there is a great difference in their attitudes towards error. Einstein, unlike the amoeba, consciously tried his best, whenever a new solution occurred to him, to fault it and detect an error in it: he approached his own solutions *critically*.

I believe that this consciously critical attitude towards his own ideas is the one realy important difference between the method of Einstein and that of the amoeba. It made it possible for Einstein to reject, quickly, hundreds of hypotheses as inadequate before examining one or another hypothesis more carefully, if it appeared to be able to stand up to more serious criticism.

As the physicist John Archibald Wheeler said recently, 'Our whole problem is to make the mistakes as fast as possible.'[7] This problem of Wheeler's is solved by consciously adopting the critical attitude. This, I believe, is the highest form so far of the rational attitude, or of rationality.

The scientist's trials and errors consist of hypotheses. He formulates them in words, and often in writing. He can then try to find flaws in any one of these hypotheses, by criticizing it, and by testing it experimentally, helped by his fellow scientists who will be delighted if they can find a flaw in it. If the hypothesis does not stand up to these criticisms and to these tests at least as well as its competitors,[8] it will be eliminated.

It is different with primitive man, and with the amoeba. Here there is no critical attitude, and so it happens more often than not that natural selection eliminates a mistaken hypothesis or expectation by eliminating those organisms which hold it, or believe in it. So we can say that the critical or rational method consists in letting our hypotheses die in our stead: it is a case of exosomatic evolution.

XXII

Here I may perhaps turn to a question which has given me much trouble although in the end I arrived at a very simple solution.

The question is: Can we show that plastic controls exist? Are there inorganic physical systems in nature which may be taken as examples or as physical models of plastic controls?

It seems that this question was implicitly answered in the negative by many physicists who, like Descartes or Compton, operate with master-switch models, and by many philosophers who, like Hume or Schlick, deny that anything intermediate between complete determinism and pure chance can exist. Admittedly, cyberneticists and computer engineers have more recently succeeded in constructing computers made of hardware but incorporating highly plastic controls; for example, computers with built-in mechanism for chance-like trials, checked or evaluated by feed-back (in the manner of an automatic pilot or a self-homing device) and eliminated if erroneous. But these systems, although incorporating what I have called plastic controls, consist essentially of complex relays of master-switches. What I was seeking, however, was a simple physical model of Peircean indeterminism; a purely physical system resembling a very cloudy cloud in heat motion, controlled by some other cloudy clouds—though by somewhat less cloudy ones.

If we return to our old arrangement of clouds and clocks, with a cloud on the left and a clock on the right, then we could say that what we are looking for is something intermediate, like an organism or like our cloud of gnats, but not alive: a pure physical system, controlled plastically and 'softly', as it were.

Let us assume that the cloud to be controlled is a gas. Then we can put on the extreme left an uncontrolled gas which will soon diffuse and so cease to constitute a physical *system*. We put on the extreme right an iron cylinder filled with gas: this is our example of a 'hard' control, a 'cast-iron' control. In between, but far to the left, are many more or less 'softly' controlled systems, such as our cluster of gnats, and huge balls of particles, such as a gas kept together by gravity, somewhat like the sun. (We do not mind if the control is far from perfect, and many particles escape.) The planets may perhaps be said to be cast-iron controlled in their movements—comparatively speaking, of course, for even the planetary system is a cloud, and so are all the milky ways, star clusters, and clusters of clusters. But are there, apart from organic systems and those huge systems of particles, examples of any 'softly' controlled small physical systems?

I think there are, and I propose to put in the middle of our diagram a child's balloon or, perhaps better, a soap bubble; and this indeed, turns out to be a very primitive and in many respects an excellent example or model of a Peircean system and of a 'soft' kind of plastic control.

The soap bubble consists of two subsystems which are both clouds and which control each other: without the air, the soapy film would collapse, and we should have only a drop of soapy water. Without the soapy film, the air would be uncontrolled: it would diffuse, ceasing to exist as a system. Thus the control is mutual; it is plastic, and of a feed-back character. Yet it is possible to make a distinction between the controlled system (the air) and the controlling system (the film): the enclosed air is not only more cloudy than the enclosing film, but it also ceases to be a physical (self-interacting) system if the film is removed. As against this, the film, after removal of the air, will form a droplet which, though of a different shape, may still be said to be a physical system.

Comparing the bubble with a 'hardware' system like a precision clock or a computer, we should of course say (in accordance with Peirce's point of view) that even these hardware systems are clouds controlled by clouds. But these 'hard' systems are built with the purpose of minimizing, so far as it is possible, the cloud-like effects of molecular heat motions and fluctuations: though they are clouds, the controlling mechanisms are designed to suppress, or compensate for, all cloud-like effects as far as possible. This holds even for computers with mechanisms simulating chance-like trial-and-error mechanisms.

Our soap bubble is different in this respect and, it seems, more similar to an organism: the molecular effects are not eliminated but contribute essentially to the working of the system which is enclosed by a skin—a permeable wall[9] that leaves the system 'open', and able to 'react' to environmental influences in a manner which is built, as it were, into its 'organization': the soap bubble, when struck by a heat ray, absorbs the heat (much like a hot-house), and so the enclosed air will expand, keeping the bubble floating.

As in all uses of similarity or analogy we should, however, look out for limitations; and here we might point out that, at least in some organisms, molecular fluctuations are apparently amplified and so used to release trial-and-error movements. At any rate, amplifiers seem to play important roles in all organisms (which in this respect resemble some computers with their master-switches and cascades of amplifiers and relays). Yet there are no amplifiers in the soap bubble.

However this may be, our bubble shows that natural physical cloud-like systems which are plastically and softly controlled by other cloud-like systems do exist. (Incidentally, the film of the bubble need not, of course, be derived from organic matter, though it will have to contain large molecules.)

XXIII

The evolutionary theory here proposed yields an immediate solution to our second main problem—the classical Cartesian body-mind problem. It does so (without saying what 'mind' or 'consciousness' is) by saying something about the evolution, and thereby about the functions, of mind or consciousness.

We must assume that consciousness grows from small beginnings; perhaps its first form is a vague feeling of irritation, experienced when the organism has a problem to solve such as getting away from an irritant substance. However this may be, consciousness will assume evolutionary significance—and increasing significance—when it begins to *anticipate* possible ways of reacting: possible trial-and-error movements, and their possible outcomes.

We can say now that conscious states, or sequences of conscious states, may function as systems of control, of error-elimination: the elimination, as a rule, of (incipient) behaviour, that is (incipient) movement. Consciousness, from this point of view, appears as just one of many interacting kinds of control; and if we remember the control systems incorporated for example in books—theories, systems of law, and all that constitutes the 'universe of meanings'—then consciousness can hardly be said to be the highest control system in the hierarchy. For it is to a considerable extent controlled by these exosomatic linguistic systems—even though they may be said to be *produced* by consciousness. Consciousness in turn is, we may conjecture, *produced* by physical states; yet it controls them to a considerable extent. Just as a legal or social system is produced by us, yet controls us, and is in no reasonable sense 'identical' to or 'parallel' with us, but *interacts* with us, so states of consciousness (the 'mind') control the body, and *interact* with it.

Thus there is a whole set of analogous relationships. As our exosomatic world of meanings is related to consciousness, so consciousness is related to the behaviour of the acting individual organism. And the behaviour of the individual organism is similarly related to its body, to the individual organism taken as a physiological system. The later is similarly related to the evolutionary sequence of organisms—the *phylum* of which it forms the latest spearhead, as it were: as the individual organism is thrown up experimentally as a probe by the *phylum* and yet largely controls the fate of the *phylum*, so the behaviour of the organism is thrown up experimentally as a probe by the physiological system and yet controls, largely, the fate of this system. Our conscious states are similarly related to our behaviour. They anticipate our behaviour, working out, by trial and error, its likely consequences; thus they not only control but they try out, *deliberate*.

We now see that this theory offers us an almost trivial answer to Descartes's problem. Without saying *what 'the mind' is*, it leads immediately to the conclusion that our *mental states control (some of) our physical movements*, and that there is some give-and-take, some feed-back, and so some *interaction*, between mental activity and the other functions of the organism.[10]

The control will again be of the 'plastic' kind; in fact all of us—especially those who play a musical instrument such as the piano or the violin—know that the body does not always do what we want it to do; and that we have to learn, from our ill-success, how to modify our aims, making allowances for those limitations which beset our control: though we are free, to some considerable extent, there are always conditions—physical or otherwise—which set limits to what we can do. (Of course, before giving in, we are free to try to transcend these limits.)

Thus, like Descartes, I propose the adoption of a dualistic outlook, though I do *not* of course recommend talking of *two kinds of interacting substances*. But I think it is helpful and legitimate to distinguish *two kinds of interacting states* (or events), physico-chemical and mental ones. Moreover, I suggest that if we distinguish only these two kinds of states we still take too narrow a view of our world: at the very least we should also distinguish those artifacts which are products of organisms, and especially the products of our minds, and which can interact with our minds and thus with the state of our physical environment. Although these artifacts are often 'mere bits of matter', 'mere tools' perhaps, they are even on the animal level sometimes consummate works of art; and on the human level, the products of our minds are often very much more than 'bits of matter'—marked bits of paper, say; for these bits of paper may represent states of a discussion, states of the growth of knowledge, which may transcend (sometimes with serious consequences) the grasp of most or even all of the minds that helped to produce them. Thus we have to be not merely dualists, but pluralists; and we have to recognize that the great changes which we have brought about, often unconsciously, in our physical universe show that abstract rules and abstract ideas, some of which are perhaps only partially grasped by human minds, may move mountains.

XXIV

As an afterthought, I should like to add one last point.

It would be a mistake to think that, because of natural selection, evolution can only lead to what may be called 'utilitarian' results: to adaptations which are useful in helping us to survive.

Just as, in a system with plastic controls, the controlling and controlled subsystems interact, so our tentative solutions interact with our *problems* and also with our *aims*. This means that our aims can change and that *the choice of an aim may become a problem*; different aims may compete, and new aims may be invented and controlled by the method of trial and error-elimination.

Admittedly, if a new aim clashes with the aim of surviving, then this new aim may be eliminated by natural selection. It is well known that many mutations are lethal and thus suicidal; and there are many examples of suicidal aims. Others are perhaps neutral with respect to survival.

Many aims that at first are subsidiary to survival may later become autonomous, and even opposed to survival; for example, the ambition to excel in courage, to climb Mount Everest, to discover a new continent, or to be the first on the Moon; or the ambition to discover some new truth.

Other aims may from the very beginning be autonomous departures, independent of the aim to survive. Artistic aims are perhaps of this kind, or some religious aims, and to those who cherish them they may become much more important than survival.

All this is part of the superabundance of life—the almost excessive abundance of trials and errors upon which the method of trial and error-elimination depends.[11]

It is perhaps not uninteresting to see that artists, like scientists, actually use this trial-and-error method. A painter may put down, tentatively, a speck of colour, and step back for a critical assessment of its effect[12] in order to alter it if it does not solve the problem he wants to solve. And it may happen that an unexpected or accidental effect of his tentative trial—a colour speck or brush stroke—may change his problem, or create a new subproblem, or a new aim: the evolution of artistic aims and of artistic standards (which, like the rules of logic, may become exosomatic systems of control) proceeds also by the trial-and-error method.

We may perhaps here look back for a moment to the problem of physical determinism, and to our example of the deaf physicist who had never experienced music but would be able to 'compose' a Mozart opera or a Beethoven symphony, simply by studying Mozart's or Beethoven's bodies and their environments as physical systems, and predicting where their pens would put down black marks on lined paper. I presented these as unacceptable consequences of physical determinism. Mozart and Beethoven are, partly, controlled by their 'taste', their system of musical evaluation. Yet this system is not cast iron but rather plastic. It responds to new ideas, and it can be modified by new trials and errors— perhaps even by an accidental mistake, an unintended discord.

In conclusion, let me sum up the situation.

We have seen that it is unsatisfactory to look upon the world as a closed physical system—whether a strictly deterministic system or a system in which whatever is not strictly determined is simply due to chance: on such a view of the world human creativeness and human freedom can only be illusions. The attempt to make use of quantum-theoretical indeterminacy is also unsatisfactory, because it leads to chance rather than freedom, and to snap-decisions rather than deliberate decisions.

I have therefore offered here a different view of the world—one in which the physical world is an open system. This is compatible with the view of the evolution of life as a process of trial and error-elimination; and it allows us to understand rationally, though far from fully, the emergence of biological novelty and the growth of human knowledge and human freedom.

I have tried to outline an evolutionary theory which takes account of all this and which offers solutions to Compton's and Descartes's problems. It is, I am afraid, a theory which manages to be too humdrum *and* too speculative at the same time; and even though I think that testable consequences can be derived from it, I am far from suggesting that my proposed solution is what philosophers have been looking for. But I feel that Compton might have said that it presents, in spite of its faults, a possible answer to his problem—and one which might lead to further advance.

NOTES

1. The idea of 'telescoping' (though not this term which I owe to Alan Musgrave) may perhaps be found in Chapter vi of Charles Darwin's *The Origin of Species*, 1859 (I am quoting from the Mentor Book edition, p. 180; italics mine): '...every highly developed organism has passed through many changes; and...each modified structure tends to be inherited, so that each modification will not...be quite lost. ...*Hence the structure of each part* [of the organism]...*is the sum* of many inherited changes, through which the species has passed. ...' See also E. Baldwin in the book *Perspectives in Biochemistry*, pp. 99 ff., and the literature there quoted.

2. The emergence of a new problem-situation could be described as a change or a differentiation of the 'ecological niche', or the significant environment, of the organism. The fact that any change in the organism or its habits or its habitat produces new problems accounts for the incredible wealth of the (always tentative) solutions.

3. The method of trial and error-elimination does not operate with completely chance-like or random trials (as has been sometimes suggested), even though the trials

may look pretty random; there must be at least an 'aftereffect' (in the sense of my *The Logic of Scientific Discovery*, pp. 162 ff.). For the organism is constantly learning from its mistakes, that is, it establishes controls which suppress or eliminate, or at least reduce the frequency of, certain possible trials (which were perhaps actual ones in its evolutionary past).

4. This is now sometimes called the 'Baldwin Effect'; see for example, G. G. Simpson, 'The Baldwin Effect', *Evolution*, **7**, 1953, pp. 110 ff., and C. H. Waddington, the same volume, pp. 118 ff. (see especially p. 124), and pp. 386 f. See also J. Mark Baldwin, *Development and Evolution*, 1902, pp. 174 ff. and H. S. Jennings, *The Behaviour of the Lower Organisms*, 1906, pp. 321 ff.

5. See The *Freedom of Man*, p. 91, and *The Human Meaning of Science*, p. 73.

6. Cp. H. S. Jennings, *op. cit.*, pp. 334 f., 349 f. A beautiful example of a problem-solving fish is described by K. Z. Lorenz, *King Solomon's Ring*, 1952, pp. 37 f.

7. John A. Wheeler, *American Scientist*, **44**, 1956, p. 360.

8. That we can only choose the 'best' of a set of competing hypotheses—the 'best' in the light of a critical discussion devoted to the search for truth—means that we choose the one which appears, in the light of the discussion, to come 'nearest to the truth'; see my *Conjectures and Refutations*, Chapter 10. See also *The Freedom of Man*, pp. vii f., and especially p. 74 (on the principle of conservation of energy).

9. Permeable walls or membranes seem to be characteristic of all biological systems. (This may be connected with the phenomenon of biological individuation.) For the pre-history of the idea that membranes and bubbles are primitive organisms, see C. H. Kahn, *Anaximander*, 1960, pp. 111 ff.

10. As hinted in several places, I conjecture that the acceptance of an '*interaction*' of mental and physical states offers the only satisfactory solution of Descartes's problem; I wish to add here that I think that we have good reason to assume that there exist mental states, or conscious states (for example in dreams) in which the consciousness of the ego (or of one's spatio-temporal position and identity) is very weak, or absent. It seems therefore reasonable to assume that full consciousness of the ego is a late development, and that it is a mistake to formulate the body–mind problem in such a way that this form of consciousness (or conscious 'will') is treated as if it were the only one.

11. Cp. for example my *Conjectures and Refutations*, especially p. 312.

12. See, for example, Ernst H. Gombrich, *Meditations on a Hobby Horse*, 1963, especially p. 10; and the same author's *Art and Illusion*, 1960, 1962 (see the Index under 'trial and error').

Learning, Development, and Culture
Edited by H. C. Plotkin
© 1982, John Wiley & Sons Ltd.

CHAPTER 7

Kant's doctrine of the a priori in the light of contemporary biology[1]

Konrad Lorenz*

For Kant, the categories of space, time, causality, etc., are givens established a priori, determining the form of all of our experience, and indeed making experience possible. For Kant, the validity of these primary principles of reason is absolute. This validity is fundamentally independent of the laws of the real nature which lies behind appearances. This validity is not to be thought of as arising from these laws. The a priori categories and forms of intuition cannot be related to the laws inherent in the 'thing-in-itself' by abstraction or any other means. The only thing we can assert about the thing-in-itself, according to Kant, is the reality of its existence. The relationship which exists between it and the form in which it affects our senses and appears in our world of experience is, for Kant, alogical (to somewhat overstate it). For Kant, the thing-in-itself is on principle unknowable, because the form of its appearance is determined by the purely ideal forms and categories of intuition, so that its appearance has no connection with its essence. This is the viewpoint of Kantian 'trans-cendental' or 'critical' idealism, restated in a condensed version.

Kant's orientation has been transformed very liberally by various natural philosophers. In particular, the ever more urgent questionings of the theory of evolution have led to conceptions of the a priori which are perhaps not so far

* Reprinted by permission of the author and the Society For General Systems Research. Originally published in *General Systems*, 1962, **VII**, 23–35. Copyright © 1962 by Society For General Systems Research.

removed from those of Kant himself as from those of the Kantian philosopher tied to the exact terms of Kant's definition of his concepts.

The biologist convinced of the fact of the great creative events of evolution asks of Kant these questions: Is not human reason with all its categories and forms of intuition something that has organically evolved in a continuous cause-effect relationship with the laws of the immediate nature, just as has the human brain? Would not the laws of reason necessary for a priori thought be entirely different it they had undergone an entirely different historical mode of origin, and if consequently we had been equipped with an entirely different kind of central nervous system? Is it at all probable that the laws of our cognitive apparatus should be disconnected with those of the real external world? Can an organ that has evolved in the process of a continuous coping with the laws of nature have remained so uninfluenced that the theory of appearances can be pursued independently of the existence of the thing-in-itself, as if the two were totally independent of each other? In answering these questions the biologist takes a sharply circumscribed point of view. The exposition of this point of view is the subject of the present paper. We are not just concerned with special discussions of space, time and causality. The latter are for our study simply examples of the Kantian theory of the a priori, and are treated incidentally to our comparison of the views of the a priori taken by transcendental idealism and the biologist.

It is the duty of the natural scientist to attempt a natural explanation before he contents himself with drawing upon factors extraneous to nature. This is an important duty for the psychologist who has to cope with the fact that something like Kant's priori forms of thought do exist. One familiar with the innate modes of reaction of subhuman organisms can readily hypothesize that the a priori is due to hereditary differentiations of the central nervous system which have become characteristic of the species, producing hereditary dispositions to think in certain forms. One must realize that this conception of the 'a priori' as an organ means the destruction of the concept: something that has evolved in evolutionary adaptation to the laws of the natural external world has evolved a posteriori in a certain sense, even if in a way entirely different from that of abstraction or deduction from previous experience. The functional similarities which have led many researchers to Lamarckian views about the origin of hereditary modes of reaction from previous 'species experience' today are recognized as completely misleading.

The essential character of the natural sciences of today signifies such an abandonment of transcendental idealism that a rift has developed between the scientist and the Kantian philosopher. The rift is caused by the fundamental change of the concepts of the thing-in-itself and the transcendental, a change which results from the redefinition of the concept of the a priori. If the 'a priori' apparatus of possible experience with all its forms of intuition and categories is not something immutably determined by factors extraneous to nature but rather something that mirrors the natural laws in contact with which it has evolved in the closest reciprocal interaction, then the boundaries of the transcendental begin to shift. Many aspects of the thing-in-itself which completely escape being experienced by our present-day apparatus of thought and perception may lie within the boundaries of possible experience in the near future, geologically speaking. Many of those aspects which today are within the sphere of the imminent may have still been beyond these boundaries in the recent past of mankind. It is obvious that the question of the extent to which the absolutely existent can be experienced by one *particular* organism has not the slightest influence on the fundamental question. However, such consideration alters something in the definition which we have to make of the thing-in-itself behind the phenomena. For Kant (who in all his speculations took into consideration only mature civilized man, representing an immutable system created by God) no obstacle presented itself to defining the thing-in-itself as basically uncognizable. In his static way of looking at it, he could include the limit of possible experience in the definition of the thing-in-itself. This limit would be the same for man and amoeba—infinitely far from the thing-in-itself. In view of the indubitable fact of evolution this is no longer tenable. Even if we recognize that the absolutely existent will never be completely knowable (even for the highest imaginable living beings there will be a limit set by the necessity of categorical forms of thought), the boundary separating the experienceable from the transcendental must vary for each individual type of organism. The location of the boundary has to be investigated separately for each type of organism. It would mean an unjustifiable anthropomorphism to include the purely accidental present-day location of this boundary for the human species in the definition of the thing-in-itself. If, in spite of the indubitable evolutionary modifiability of our apparatus of experience one nevertheless wanted to continue to define the thing-in-itself as that which is uncognizable for this very apparatus, the definition of the absolute would thereby be held to be relative, obviously an absurdity. Rather, every natural science urgently needs a concept of the absolutely real which is as little anthropomorphic and as independent as possible of the accidental, present-day location of the limits of the humanly experienceable. The absolutely actual can in no way be a matter of the degree to which it is reflected in the brain of a human, or any other temporary form. On the other hand, it is the object of a most important branch of comparative science to investigate the type of this reflection, and to find out the extent to which it is in the form of crudely simplifying symbols which are only superficially analogous or to what extent it reproduces details, i.e., how far its exactness goes. By this investigation of prehuman forms of knowledge we hope to gain clues to the mode of functioning and historical origin of our own knowledge, and in this manner to push ahead the critique of knowledge further than was possible without such comparisons.

I assert that nearly all natural scientists of today, at least all biologists, consciously or unconsciously assume in their daily work a real relationship between the thing-in-itself and the phenomena of our subjective experience, but a relationship that is by no means a 'purely' ideal one in the Kantian sense. I even would like to assert that Kant himself assumed this in all the results of his own empirical research. In our opinion, the real relationship between the thing-in-itself and the specific a priori form of its appearance has been determined by the fact that the form of appearance has developed as an adaptation to the laws of the thing-in-itself in the coping negotiation with these continuously present laws during the evolutionary history of mankind, lasting hundreds of millenia. This adaptation has provided our thought with an innate structuralization which corresponds to a considerable degree to the reality of the external world. 'Adaptation' is a word already loaded with meaning and easily misunderstood. It should not, in the present condition, denote more than that our forms of intuition and categories 'fit' to that which really exists in the manner in which our foot fits the floor or the fin of the fish suits the water. The a priori which determines the forms of appearance of the real things of our world is, in short, an organ, or more precisely the functioning of an organ. We come closer to understanding the a priori if we confront it with the questions asked of everything organic: 'What for', 'where from', and 'why'. These questions are, first, how does it preserve the species; second, what is its genealogical origin; third, what natural causes make it possible? We are convinced that the a priori is based on central nervous systems which are entirely as real as the things of the external world whose phenomenal form they determine for us. This central nervous apparatus does not prescribe the laws of nature any more than the hoof of the horse prescribes the form of the ground. Just as the hoof of the horse, this central nervous apparatus stumbles over unforeseen changes in its task. But just as the hoof of the horse is adapted to the ground of the steppe which it copes with, so our central nervous apparatus for organizing the image of the world is adapted to the real world with which man has to cope. Just like any organ, this apparatus has attained its expedient species-preserving form through this coping of real with the real during its genealogical evolution, lasting many eons.

Our view of the origin of the 'a priori' (an origin which in a certain sense is 'a posteriori') answers very fittingly Kant's question as to whether the forms of perception of space and time, which we do not derive from experience (as Kant, contrary to Hume, emphasizes quite correctly) but which are a priori in our representation 'were not mere chimeras of the brain made by us to which no object corresponds, at least not adequately.'[2] If we conceive our intellect as the function of an organ (and there is no valid argument against this) our obvious answer to the question why its form of function is adapted to the real world is simply the following: Our categories and forms of perception, fixed prior to individual experience, are adapted to the external world for exactly the same reasons as the hoof of the horse is already adapted to the ground of the steppe before the horse is born and the fin of the fish is adapted to the water before the fish hatches. No sensible person believes that in any of these cases the form of the organ 'prescribes' its properties to the object. To everyone it is self-evident that water possesses its properties independently of whether the fins of the fish are biologically adapted to these properties or not. Quite evidently some properties of the thing-in-itself which is at the bottom of the phenomenon 'water' have led to the specific form of adaptation of the fins which have been evolved independently of one another by fishes, reptiles, birds, mammals, cephalopods, snails, crayfish, arrow worms, etc. It is obviously the properties of water that have prescribed to these different organisms the corresponding form and function of their organ of locomotion. But when reckoning in regard to structure and mode of function of his own brain the transcendental philosopher assumes something fundamentally different. In paragraph 11 of the Prolegomena Kant says: 'If anyone were to have the slightest doubt that both (the forms of intuition of space and time) are not determinations of the thing-in-itself but mere determinations of their relation to sensibility, I should like to know how it could be found possible to know a priori and thus prior to all acquaintance with things, namely before they are given to us, what their intuition must be like, which is the case here with space and time.'[3] This question clarifies two very important facts. First, it shows that Kant, no more than Hume, thought of the possibility of a formal adaptation between thought and reality other than through abstracting from previous experience. Second, it shows that he assumed the impossibility of any different form of origin. Furthermore, it shows the great and fundamentally new discovery of Kant, i.e., that human thought and perception have certain functional structures prior to every individual experience.

Most certainly Hume was wrong when he wanted to derive all that is a priori from that which the senses supply to experience, just as wrong as Wundt or Helmholtz who simply explain it as an abstraction from preceding experience. Adaptation of the a priori to the real world has no more originated from 'experience' than has adaptation of the fin of the fish to the properties of water. Just as the form of the fin is given a priori, prior to any individual coping of the young fish with the water, and just as it is this form that makes possible this coping: so is it also the case with our forms of perception and categories in their relationship to our coping with the real external world by means of experience. For animals there are specific limitations to the forms of experience which are possible. We believe we can demonstrate the closest functional and probably genetic relationship between these animal a priori's and our human a priori.

Contrary to Hume, we believe as did Kant in the possibility of a 'pure' science of the innate forms of human thought independent of all experience. This 'pure' science, however, would be able to convey only a very one-sided understanding of the essence of a priori forms of thought because it neglects the organic nature of these structures and does not pose the basic biological question concerning their species-preserving meaning. Bluntly speaking, it is just as if someone wanted to write a 'pure' theory on the characteristics of a modern photographic camera, a Leica for example, without taking into consideration that this is an apparatus for photographing the external world, and without consulting the pictures the camera produces which enable one to understand its function and the essential meaning of its existence. As far as the produced pictures (just as experiences) are concerned, the Leica is entirely a priori. It exists prior to and independently of every picture; indeed, it determines the form of the pictures, nay, makes them possible in the first place. Now I assert: To separate 'pure Leicology' from the theory of the pictures it produces is just as meaningless as to separate the theory of the a priori from the theory of the external world, of phenomenology from the theory of the thing-in-itself. All the lawfulnesses of our intellect which we find to be there a priori are not freaks of nature. We live off them! And we can get insight into their essential meaning only if we take into consideration their function. Just as the Leica could not originate without the activity of photography, carried out long before the Leica was constructed, just as the completed Leica with all its incredibly well-conceived and 'fitting' constructional details has not dropped from the heavens, so neither has our infinitely more wonderful 'pure reason'. This, too, has arrived at its relative perfection from out of its activity, from its negotiation with the thing-in-itself.

Although for the transcendental idealist the relationship between the thing-in-itself and its appearance is extraneous to nature and alogical, it is entirely real for us. It is certain that not only does the thing-in-itself 'affect' our receptors, but also vice versa, our effectors on their part 'affect' absolute reality. The word 'actually' comes from the verb 'to act'. (Wirklichkeit kommt von Wirker!) What appears in our world is by no means only our experience one-sidedly influenced by real external things as they work on us as through the lenses of the ideal possibilities of experience. What we witness as experience is always a coping of the real in us with the real outside of us. Therefore the relationship between the events in and outside of us is not alogical and does not basically prohibit drawing conclusions about the lawfulness of the external world from the lawfulness of the internal events. Rather, this relationship is the one which exists between image and object, between a simplified model and the real thing. It is the relationship of an analogy of greater or less remoteness. The degree of this analogy is fundamentally open to comparative investigation. That is, it is possible to make statements as to whether agreement between appearance and actuality is more exact or less exact in comparing one human being to another, or one living organism to another.

On these premises also depends the self-evident fact that there are more and less correct judgments about the external world. The relationship between the world of phenomena and things-in-themselves is thus not fixed once-and-for-all by ideal laws of form which are extraneous to nature and in principle inaccessible to investigation. Neither do the judgments made on the basis of these 'necessities of thought' have an independent and absolute validity. Rather, all our forms of intuition and categories are thoroughly natural. Like every other organ, they are evolutionary developed receptacles for the reception and retro-active utilization of those lawful consequences of the thing-in-itself with which we have to cope if we want to remain alive and preserve our species. The special form of these organic receptacles has the properties of the thing-in-itself a relationship grown entirely out of real natural connections. The organic receptacles are adapted to these properties in a manner that has a practical biological sufficiency, but which is by no means absolute nor even so precise that one could say their form equals that of the thing-in-itself. Even if we as natural scientists are in a certain sense naïve realists, we still do not take the appearance for the thing-in-itself nor the experienced reality for the absolutely existent. Thus we are not surprised to find the laws of 'pure reason' entangled in the most serious contradictions not only with one another, but also with the empirical facts whenever research demands greater precision. This happens particularly where physics and chemistry enter the nuclear phase. There not only does the intuition-form of space-perception break down, but also the categories of causality, or substantiality, and in a certain sense even quantity (even though quantity otherwise appears to have the most unconditional validity except for the intuition-form of time-perception). 'Necessary for thought' in no way means 'absolutely valid' in view of these empirical facts, highly essential in nuclear physics, quantum mechanics and wave theory.

The realization that all laws of 'pure reason' are based on highly physical or mechanical structures of the human central nervous system which have developed through many eons like any other organ, on the one hand shakes our confidence in the laws of pure reason and on the other hand substantially raises our confidence in them. Kant's statement that the laws of pure reason have absolute validity, nay, that every imaginable rational being, even if it were an angel, must obey the same laws of thought, appears as an anthropocentric presumption. Surely the 'keyboard' provided by the forms of intuition and categories—Kant himself calls it that—is something definitely located on the physicostructural side of the psychophysical unity of the human organism. The forms of intuition and categories relate to the 'freedom' of the mind (if there is such a thing) as physical structures are usually related to the possible degrees of freedom of the psychic, namely by both supporting and restraining at the same time. But surely these clumsy categorical boxes into which we have to pack our external world 'in order to be able to spell them as experiences' (Kant) can claim no autonomous and absolute validity whatsoever. This is certain for us the moment we conceive them as evolutionary adaptations—and I would indeed like to know what scientific argument could be brought against this conception. At the same time, however, the nature of their adaptation shows that the categorical forms of intuition and categories have proved themselves as working hypotheses in the coping of our species with the absolute reality of the environment (in spite of their validity being only approximate and relative). This is clarified by the paradoxical fact that the laws of 'pure reason' which break down at every step in modern theoretical science, nonetheless have stood (and still stand) the test in the practical biological matters of the struggle for the preservation of the species.

The 'dots' produced by the coarse 'screens' used in the reproductions of photographs in our daily papers are satisfactory representations when looked at superficially, but cannot stand closer inspection with a magnifying glass. So, too, the reproductions of the world by our forms of intuition and categories break down as soon as they are required to give a somewhat closer representation of their objects, as is the case in wave mechanics and nuclear physics. All the knowledge an individual can wrest from the empirical reality of the 'physical world-picture' is essentially only a working hypothesis. And as far as their species-preserving function goes, all those innate structures of the mind which we call 'a priori' are likewise only working hypotheses. Nothing is absolute except that which hides in and behind the phenomena. Nothing that our brain can think has absolute a priori validity in the true sense of the word, not even mathematics with all its laws. The laws of mathematics are but an organ for the quantification of external things, and what is more, an organ exceedingly important for man's life, without which he never could play his role in dominating the earth, and which thus has amply proved itself biologically, as have all the other 'necessary' structures of thought. Of course, 'pure' mathematics is not only possible, it is, as a theory of the internal laws of this miraculous organ of quantification, of an importance that can hardly be overestimated. But this does not justify us in making it absolute. Counting and mathematical number affect reality in approximately the same manner as do a dredging-machine and its shovels. Regarded statistically, in a large number of individual cases each shovel dredges up roughly the same amount but actually not even two can ever have exactly the same content. The pure mathematical equation is a tautology: I state that if my dredging-machine brings in such and such a number of shovels, then such and such a number are brought in. Two shovels of my machine are absolutely equal to each other because strictly speaking it is the same shovel each time, namely the number one. But only the empty sentence always has this validity. Two shovels filled with something or other are never equal to each other, the number one applied to a real object will never find its equal in the whole universe. It is true that two plus two equals four, but two apples, rams or atoms plus two more never equal four others because no equal apples, rams or atoms exist. In this sense we arrive at the paradoxical fact that the equation two plus two equals four in its application to real units, such as apples or atoms, has a much smaller degree of approximation to reality than the equation two million plus two million equal four million because the individual dissimilarities of the counted units level out statistically in the case of a large number. Regarded as a working hypothesis or as a functional organ, the form of thought of numerical quantification is and remains one of the most miraculous apparatuses that nature has ever created; it evokes the admiration of the biologist, particularly by the incredible breadth of its sphere of application even if one does not consider its sphere of validity absolute.

It would be entirely conceivable to imagine a rational being that does not quantify by means of the mathematical number (that does not use 1, 2, 3,4, 5, the number of individuals approximately equal among themselves, such as rams, atoms, or milestones, to mark the quantity at hand) but grasps these immediately in some other way. Instead of quantifying water by the number of the filled litre vessels, one could, for example, conclude from the tension of a rubber balloon of a certain size how much water in contains. It can very well be purely coincidental, in other words brought about by purely historical causes, that our brain happens to be able to quantify extensive quantities more readily than intensive ones. It is by no means a necessity of thought and it would be entirely conceivable that the ability to quantify intensively according to the method indicated by the example of measuring the tension in the rubber balloon could be developed up to the point where it would become equally valuable and replace numerical mathematics. Indeed, the ability to estimate quantities immediately, present in man and in a number of animals, is probably due to such an intensive process of quantification. A mind quantifying in a purely intensive manner would carry out some operations more simply and immediately than our mathematics of the 'dredging-scoop' variety. For example, it might be able to calculate curves immediately, which is possible in our extensive mathematics only by means of the detour of integral and differential calculus, a detour which tides us over the limitations of the numerical steps, but still clings to them conceptually. An intellect quantifying purely by intensity would not be able to grasp that two times two equals four. Since it would have no understanding for the number one, for our empty numerical box, it would also not comprehend our postulate of the equality of two such boxes and would reply to our arrangement of an equation that it is incorrect because no equal boxes, rams or atoms exist. And in regard to its system, it would be just as correct in its statement as we would be in ours. Certainly an intensive quantification system would perform many operations more poorly, that is, in a more involved manner, than does numerical mathematics. The fact that the latter has developed so much further than the ability of intensive quantitative estimation speaks for its being the more 'practical' one. But even so it is and remains only an organ, an evolutionarily acquired, 'innate working hypothesis' which basically is only approximately adapted to the data of the thing-in-itself.

If a biologist attempts to grasp the relationship of hereditary structure to the regulated plasticity of all that is organic, he arrives at a universal law holding both for physical and intellectual structures and as valid for the plastic protoplasm and the skeletal elements of a protozoan as for the categorical forms of thought and the creative plasticity of the human mind. From its simplest beginnings in the domain of the protozoa, solid structure is just as much a condition for any higher evolution as is organic plasticity. In this sense, solid structure is just as indispensable and as consistent a property of living matter as is its plastic freedom. However, every solid structure, although indispensable as a support for the organic system, carries with it an undesired side effect: it makes for rigidness, and takes away a certain degree of freedom from the system. Every enlistment of a mechanical structure means in some sense to bind oneself. Von Uexkuell has said aptly: 'The amoeba is less of a machine than the horse,' thinking mainly about physical properties. Nietzsche has expressed poetically the same relationship between structure and plasticity in human thought: '...a thought—Now still hot liquid lava, but all lava builds a castle around itself. Every thought finally crushes itself with "laws".' This simile of a structure crystallizing out of the liquid state goes much deeper than Nietzsche sensed: It is not entirely impossible that all that becomes solid, in the intellectual-psychic as well as in the physical, is bound to be a transition from the liquid state of certain plasma parts to the solid state.

But Nietzsche's simile and Uexkuell's statement overlook something. The horse is a higher animal than the amoeba not despite, but to a large extent because of its being richer in solid differentiated structures. Organisms with as few structures as possible must remain amoebae, whether they like it or not, for without any solid structure all higher organization is inconceivable. One could symbolize organisms with a maximum of highly differentiated fixed structures as lobsters, stiffly armored creatures which could move only in certain joints with precisely allowed degrees of freedom or as railroad cars which could only move along a prescribed track having very few switching points. For every living being, increasing mental and physical differentiation is always a compromise between these two extremes, neither one representing the highest realization of the possibilities of organic creation. Always and everywhere differentiation to a higher level of mechanical structure has the dangerous tendency to fetter the mind, whose servant it was just a moment ago, and to prevent its further evolution. The hard exoskeleton of the arthropods is such an obstruction in evolution, as is also the fixed instinctual movements of many higher organisms and the industrial machinery of man.

Indeed, every system of thought that commits itself to a nonplastic 'absolute' has this same fettering effect. The moment such a system is finished, when it has disciples who believe in its perfection, it is already 'false'. Only in the state of becoming is the philosopher a human being in the most proper meaning of the word. I am reminded of the beautiful definition of man which we owe to the pragmatist and which probably is given in its clearest formulation in Gehlen's book *Der Mensch*. Man is defined as the permanently unfinished being, permanently unadapted and poor in structure, but continuously open to the world, continuously in the state of becoming.

When the human thinker, be it even the greatest, has finished his system, he has in a fundamental way taken on something of the properties of the lobster or the railroad car. However ingeniously his disciples may manipulate the prescribed and permitted degrees of freedom of his lobster-armor, his system will only be a blessing for the progress of human thought and knowledge when he finds followers who break it apart and, using new, not 'built in', degrees of freedom, turn its pieces into a new construction. If, however, a system of thought is so well joined together that for a long time no one appears who has the power and the courage to burst it asunder, it can obstruct progress for centuries: 'There lies the stone, one has to let it be, and everyone limps on his crutch of faith to devil's stone, to devil's bridge.' (Goethe, *Faust*).

And just as a system of thought created by the individual human being enslaves its creator, so also do the evolutionarily developed supra-individual forms of thought of the a priori: They, too, are held to be absolute! The machine whose species-preserving meaning was originally in quantifying real external things, the machine that was created for 'counting rams' suddenly pretends to be absolute and buzzes with an admirable absence of internal friction and contradiction, but only as long as it runs empty, counting its own shovels. If one lets a dredging-machine, an engine, a band saw, a theory, or an a priori function of thought run empty in this way, then its function proceeds *ipso facto* without noticeable friction, heat, or noise; for the parts in such a system do not, of course, contradict one another and so fit together intelligibly and in a well-tuned manner. When empty they are indeed 'absolute', but absolutely empty. Only when the system is expected to work, that is, to achieve something in relation to the external world in which the real and species-preserving meaning of its whole existence does indeed consist, then the thing starts to groan and crack: when the shovels of the dredging-machine dig into the soil, the teeth of the band saw dig into the wood, or the assumptions of the theory dig into the material of empirical facts which is to be classified, then develop the undesirable side-noises that come from the inevitable imperfection of every naturally developed system: *and no other systems exist for the natural scientist*. But these noises are just what does indeed represent the coping of the system with the real external world. In this sense they are the door through which the thing-in-itself peeps into our world of phenomena, the door through which the road to further knowledge continues to lead. They, and not the unresisting empty humming of the apparatus are 'reality'. They are, indeed, what we have to place under the magnifying glass if we want to get to know the imperfections of our apparatus of thought and experience and if we want to gain knowledge beyond these imperfections. The side-noises have to be considered methodically if the machine is to be improved. The fundamentals of pure reason are just as imperfect and down to earth as the band saw, but also just as real.

Our working hypothesis should read as follows: Everything is a working hypothesis. This holds true not only for the natural laws which we gain through individual abstraction a posteriori from the facts of our experience, but also for the laws of pure reason. The faculty of understanding does not in itself constitute an explanation of phenomena, but the fact that it projects phenomena for us in a practically usable form on to the projection-screen of our experiencing is due to its formulation of working hypotheses, developed in evolution and tested through millions of years. Santayana says: 'Faith in the intellect is the only faith that has justified itself by the fruit it has borne. But the one who clings forever to the form of faith is a Don Quixote, rattling with outmoded armor. I am a decided materialist with regard to natural philosophy, but I do not claim to know what matter is. I am waiting for the men of science to tell me that.'

Our view that all human thought is only a working hypothesis must not be interpreted as lowering the value of the knowledge secured by mankind. It is true that this knowledge is only a working hypothesis for us, it is true that we are ready at any moment to throw overboard our favorite theories when new facts demand this. But even if nothing is 'absolutely true', every new piece of knowledge, every new truth, is nevertheless a step forward in a very definite, definable direction: the absolutely existent is apprehended from a new, up to this point unknown, aspect; it is covered in a new characteristic. For us that working hypothesis is true which paves the way for the next step in knowledge or which at least does not obstruct the way. Human science must act like a scaffolding for reaching the greatest possible height, without its absolute extent being foreseeable at the start of the construction. At the moment when such a construction is committed to a permanently-set supporting pillar, the latter fits only a building of a certain form and size. Once these are reached and the building is to continue, the supporting-pillar has to be demolished and rebuilt, a process which can become the more dangerous for the entire structure, the more deeply that which is to be rebuilt is set in its foundation. Since it is a constituent property of all true science that its structure should continue to grow into the boundless, all that is mechanically systematic, all that corresponds to solid structures and scaffolding, must always be something provisional, alterable at anytime. The tendency to secure one's own building for the future by declaring it absolute leads to the opposite of the intended success: Just that 'truth' which is dogmatically believed in, sooner or later leads to a revolution in which the actual truth-content and value of the old theory are all too easily demolished and forgotten along with the obsolete obstructions to progress. The heavy cultural losses which may accompany revolutions are special cases of this phenomenon. The character of all truths as working hypotheses must always be kept in mind, in order to prevent the necessity of demolishing the established structure, and in order to preserve for the 'established' truths, that eternal value which they potentially deserve.

Our conception that a priori forms of thought and intuition have to be understood just as any other organic adaptation carries with it the fact that they are for us 'inherited working hypotheses', so to speak, whose truth-content is related to the absolutely existent in the same manner as that of ordinary working hypotheses which have proven themselves just as splendidly adequate in coping with the external world. This conception, it is true, destroys our faith in the absolute truth of any a priori thesis necessary for thought. On the other hand it gives the conviction that something actual 'adequately corresponds' to every phenomenon in our world. Even the smallest detail of the world of phenomena 'mirrored' for us by the innate working hypotheses of our forms of intuition and thought is in fact pre-formed to the phenomenon it reproduces, having a relationship corresponding to the one existing between organic structures and the external world in general (e.g., the analogy of the fin of the fish and the hoof of the horse, above). It is true that the a priori is only a box whose form unpretentiously fits that of the actuality to be portrayed. This box, however, is accessible to our investigation even if we cannot comprehend the thing-in-itself except by means of the box. But access to the laws of the box, i.e., of the instrument, makes the thing-in-itself relatively comprehensible.

Now what we are planning to do in patient empirical research work is an investigation of the 'a priori', of the 'innate' working hypotheses present in subhuman organisms. This includes species that achieve a correspondence to the properties of the thing-in-itself less detailed than that of man. With all their incredible accuracy of aim, the innate schematisms of animals are still much more simple, of coarser screen, than those of man, so that the boundaries of their achievement still fall within the measurable domain of our own receptive apparatus. Let us take as analogy the domain that can be resolved with the lens of a microscope: the fineness of the smallest structure of the object still visible with it is dependent upon the relationship between angle of aperture and focal length, the so-called 'numerical aperture'. The first diffraction spectrum which is thrown by the structural grating must still fall into the front lens in order that the grating is seen as such. If this is no longer the case, one does not see the structure; rather, the object appears with a smooth surface and, strangely enough, brown.

Now let us suppose I had only one microscope. Then I would say structures are only 'conceivable' up to that fineness, finer ones do not exist. Moreover, though I would have to admit that there are brown objects, I would have no reason to assume that this color has the slightest relationship to the visible structures. However if one also knew of less strongly resolving lens which register 'brown' for structures which are still visible as structures by our instruments, then one would be very skeptical toward our instrument's registering brown (unless one had become a megalomaniac and pronounced one's own receptive apparatus absolute, just for the reason that it was one's own property). If one is more modest, however, one will draw the right conclusion from the comparison of the limits of achievement and the fact that the various instruments register brown. The conclusion is that even the most powerful lenses have limits as to the fineness of structure resolved, just as do simpler apparatuses. In a methodically similar way one can learn much from the functional limitations which the various apparatuses for organizing the image of the universe all have. The lesson so learned provides an important critical perspective for judging the limits of achievement of the highest existing apparatus, which today cannot be investigated from the observation tower of a still higher one.

Looking at it from a physiological viewpoint, it is self-evident that our neural apparatus for organizing the image of the world is basically like a photoprint screen which cannot reproduce any finer points of the thing-in-itself than those corresponding to the numerically finite elements of the screen. Just as the grain of the photographic negative permits no image originating from unlimited enlargement, so also there are limitations in the image of the universe traced out by our sense organs and cognitive apparatus. These too permit no unlimited 'enlargement', no unlimited view of details, however self-evident and real the image may appear at superficial inspection. Where the physical image of the universe formed by man has advanced to the atomic level, there emerge inaccuracies in the coordination between the a priori 'necessities of thought' and the empirically actual. It is as though the 'measures of all things' was simply too coarse and too approximate for these finer spheres of measurement, and would only agree in general and at a statistical-probabilistic level with that which is to be comprehended of the thing-in-itself. This is increasingly true for atomic physics, whose entirely impalpable ideas can no longer be experienced directly. For we can only 'spell-out as experience' in a directly experienceable manner (to apply Kant's own expression to this physiological fact) that which can be written on the crudely simplifying 'keyboard' of our central nervous system. But in different organisms, this keyboard can be differentiated in a more simple or more complex manner. To represent it by the analogy of the photoprint screen, the best possible picture that can be reproduced by an apparatus of a given degree of fineness corresponds to those representations encountered in cross-stitch embroideries which build round-contoured animals and flowers from small rectangular elements. The property of 'being composed of squares' does in no way belong to the represented thing-in-itself, but is due to a peculiarity of the picture apparatus, a peculiarity which can be regarded as a technically unavoidable limitation. Similar limitations accompany each apparatus for organizing the image of the world, if only because of its being composed of cellular elements (as is the case for vision). Now if one examines methodically what the cross-stitch representation permits to be stated about the form of the thing-in-itself, the conclusion is that the accuracy of the statement is dependent upon the relationship between the size of the picture and the grain of the screen. If one square is out of line with a straight-line contour in the embroidery, one knows that behind it lies an actual projection of the represented thing, but one is not sure whether it exactly fills the whole square of the screen or only the smallest part of it. This question can be decided only with the help of the next finest screen. But behind every detail which even the crudest screen reproduces there certainly lies something real, simply because otherwise the respective screen-unit would not have registered. But no tool is at our disposal to determine what lies behind the registering of the finest existent screen-unit, whether much or little of the contour of that which is to be reproduced protrudes into its domain. The fundamental indiscernibility of the last detail of the thing-in-itself remains. We are only convinced that all details which our apparatus does reproduce correspond to actual attributes of the thing-in-itself. One becomes more and more firmly convinced of this entirely real and lawful correlation between the Real and the Apparent, the more one concerns oneself with the comparison of apparatuses for organizing the image of the world of animals as different from one another as possible. The continuity of the thing-in-itself, most convincingly emerging from such comparisons, is completely incompatible with the supposition of an alogical, extrinsically determined relationship between the thing-in-itself and its appearances.

Such comparative research brings us closer to the actual world lying behind the phenomena, providing we succeed in showing that the different a priori formations of possible reaction (and thus of possible experience) of the different species make experienceable the same lawfulness of real existents and lead to its control in a species-preserving way. Such different adaptations to one and the same lawfulness strengthen our belief in its reality in the same manner as a judge's belief in the actuality of an event is strengthened by several mutually independent witnesses giving descriptions of it that are in general agreement, though not identical. Organisms that are on a much lower mental level than man struggle quite evidently with the same data that are made experienceable in our world by the forms of perception of space and time and by the category of causality; but they do it by means of quite different and much simpler achievements, which are accessible to scientific analysis. Even if the a priori human forms of perception and thought remain inaccessible to causal analysis for the time being, we as natural scientists must nevertheless desist from explaining the existence of the a priori (or in general of pure reason) by a principle extraneous to nature. We must instead regard any such explanatory attempt as a completely arbitrary and dogmatic division between the rationally comprehensible and the unknowable, a division which has done as serious damage in obstructing research, as have the prohibitions of the vitalists.

The method to be used can be explained, by analogy to the microscope, as a science of apparatuses. Basically, we can comprehend only the lower precursors of our own forms of perception and thought. Only where laws represented through these primitive organs can be identified with those represented on our own apparatus can we clarify properties of the human a priori, using the more primitive as a starting point. In this way we can draw conclusions about the continuity of the world lying behind phenomena. Such an enterprise succeeds quite well compared with the theory of the a priori forms of perception of space and the category of causality. A large number of animals do not comprehend the 'spatial' structurization of the world in the same way we do. We can, however, have an approximate idea what the 'spatial' looks like in the world-picture of such organisms because in addition to our spatial apprehension we also possess the ability to master spatial problems in their manner. Most reptiles, birds, and lower mammals do not master problems of space as we do through a simultaneous clear survey over the data. Instead, spatial problems are learned by rote. For example, a water shrew when placed into new surroundings gradually learns by rote all possible paths by slow crawling about, constantly guided by sniffing and feeling with the whiskers in such a manner as perhaps a child learns piano pieces by rote. In the laborious piecemeal sequence of limb movements first short stretches become 'known movements', followed by a smoother linking of these parts. And these movements, smoothing and steadying themselves by becoming kinesthetically ingrained, extend farther and farther and finally flow together into an inseparable whole which, running off fast and smoothly, has no longer any similarity with the original search movements. These sequences of movement, so laboriously acquired, and run-off so extraordinarily fast and smoothly, do not take the 'shortest way'. On the contrary, chance determines what spatial pattern such a path learning takes. It even happens that the winding path intersects itself, without the animal necessarily noticing how the end of the path can be brought closer by cutting off the superfluous piece.[4]

For an animal, like the water shrew, that masters its living space almost exclusively by path learning, the thesis is by no means valid that the straight line is the shortest connection between two points. If it wanted to steer in a straight line (which lies basically within its abilities) it would constantly have to approach its goal sniffing, feeling with its whiskers and using its eyes, which are not very efficient. In this process it would use up more time and energy than by going the path it knows by rote. If two points which on this path lie quite far apart are spatially close together, the animal knows it not. Even a human being can behave in this way, for example, in a strange city. It is true, however, that under such circumstance we humans succeed sooner or later in getting a spatial survey which opens up the possibility of a straight-line short cut for us. The sewer rat, which is on a much higher mental level than the shrew, likewise soon finds short cuts. The greylag goose could, as we have seen, achieve the same thing, but does not do it for religious reasons, as it were; it is prevented by that peculiar inhibition which also ties primitive people so much to habit. The biological meaning of this rigid clinging to 'tradition' is easily understandable: it will always be advisable for an organism that does not have at its disposal a spatial–temporal–causal survey over a certain situation to persist rigidly in the behaviour that has proved successful and free of danger. So-called magical thought, by no means present only in primitive people, is closely related to this phenomenon. One need only think of the well-known 'knock on wood'. The motive that 'after all, one cannot tell what is going to happen if one omits doing it' is very clear.

For the true kinesthetic creature, such as the water shrew, it is literally impossible as far as its thinking is concerned to find a short cut. Perhaps it learns one when forced by external circumstances, but again only by learning by rote, this time a new path. Otherwise there is an impenetrable wall for the water shrew between two loops of its path, even when they almost or actually touch. How many such new possibilities of solution, in principle equally simple, we humans may overlook with equal blindness in the struggle with our daily problems! This thought obtrudes itself with compelling force upon anyone who in his direct daily associations with animals has come to know their many human characteristics and at the same time the fixed limits to their achievement. Nothing can be more apt to make the scientist doubt his own God-like character, and to inculcate in him a very beneficial modesty.

From a psychological viewpoint, the water shrew's command of space is a sequence of conditioned reflexes and kinesthetically ingrained movements. It reacts to the known steering marks of its path with conditioned reflexes which are less a steering than a control to ascertain that it is still on the right path, for the kinesthetic movement known by rote is so precise and exact that the process takes place almost without optical or tactile steering, as in the case of a good piano player who need hardly look at the score or the keys. This sequence formation of conditioned reflexes and known movements is by no means only a spatial but also a spatial–temporal formation. It can be produced only in one direction. To run the course backward requires completely different trainings. To run the paths learned by rote the wrong way is just as impossible as to recite the alphabet in the wrong sequence. If one interrupts the animal running along its trained path, taking away a hurdle that has to be jumped, it becomes disoriented and tries to reconnect the chain of the ingrained links at an earlier place. Therefore it runs back searches until it becomes reoriented in the signs of its path and tries again. Just like a little girl that has been interrupted in reciting a poem.

A relationship very similar to the one we found between the disposition toward learning paths by rote and the human form of perception of space exists between the disposition toward developing conditioned reflexes (associations), and the human category of causality. The organism learns that a certain stimulus, for example, the appearance of the keeper, always precedes a biologically relevant event, let us say, feeding; it 'associates' these two events and treats the first as the signal for the occurrence of the second one by starting preparatory reactions upon the onset of the first stimulus (e.g., the salivation reflex investigated by Pavlov). This connection of an experience with the regularly followed post hoc is totally unrelated to causal thought. It should be remembered that, for example, kidney secretion, a completely unconscious process, can be trained to conditioned reflexes! The reason why post hoc was still equated with and mistaken for propter hoc is that the disposition for association and causal thought actually achieve the same thing biologically; they are, so to speak, organs for coping with the same real datum.

This datum is without any doubt the natural lawfulness contained in a major thesis of physics. The 'conditioned reflex' arises when a certain outer stimulus, which is meaningless for the organism as such, is followed several times by another, biologically meaningful one, that is, one releasing a reaction. The animal from now on behaves 'as if' the first stimulus were a sure signal preceding the biologically significant event that is to be expected. This behaviour obviously has a species-preserving meaning only if in the framework of the real a connection between the first, the 'conditioned' and the second, the 'unconditioned' stimulus, exists. A lawful temporal sequence of different events regularly occurs in nature only where a certain quantity of energy appears sequentially in different phenomenal forms through transformation of force. Thus connection in itself means 'causal connection'. The conditioned reflex 'advocates the hypothesis' that two stimuli, occurring several times in a certain sequence are phenomenal forms of the same quantity of energy. Were this supposition false and the repeated sequence conditioning the association of the stimuli only a purely accidental one, a probably never returning 'post hoc', then the development of the conditioned reaction would be a dysteleological failure of achievement on the part of a disposition which is generally and probabilistically meaningful, in the sense of being species-preserving.

Since we are today ignorant of its physiological foundations, we can examine the category of causality only through critical epistemology. In its biological function, it is an organ for comprehending the same natural lawfulness aimed at by the disposition to acquire conditioned reflexes. We cannot define the concept of cause and effect in any other way than by determining that the effect receives energy from the cause in some form or other. The essence of 'propter hoc' which alone differentiates it qualitatively from a 'uniform post hoc' lies in the fact that cause and effect are successive links in the infinite chain of phenomenal forms that energy assumes in the course of its everlasting existence.

In the case of the category of causality, the attempt to explain it as a secondary abstraction from preceding experience (in Wundt's sense) is instructive. If one attempts this, one always arrives at the definition of a 'regular post hoc', but never at that highly specific quality which lies a priori in every sensible use of 'why' and 'because' even by a little child. One cannot expect a child to have the ability to comprehend abstractly a fact which was not stated in an objective, i.e., purely physical form until 1842, by J. R. Mayer. Joule, in a lecture given in 1847 (*On Matter, Living Force and Heat*, London 1884, p. 265) declared in a surprisingly simple manner that it is 'absurd' to assume living force could be destroyed without in some way restoring something equivalent. The great physicist thus quite naïvely takes the point of view of critical epistemology. It would be a highly interesting question, from the point of view of the history of ideas, whether in his discovery of the equivalent of heat he started with the a priori 'unthinkableness' of the destruction and creation of energy, as it would appear, judging by his above remark. It does not fit into our concept of cause and effect that the a priori category of causality is actually based upon nothing but the inevitable sequence of two events and that it can happen that the event occurring later in time does not draw its energy from the preceding one, but that both are mutually independent side-chains of a branching chain of causality. The case can arise that an event regularly has two effects, of which one occurs faster than the other, thus always preceding it in experience. Thus lightning follows electrical discharge more quickly than thunder. Nevertheless, the optical phenomenon is by no means the cause of the acoustic one! Perhaps one may object here that this consideration is hairsplitting, and for many naïve people lightning still is the cause for thunder. But the hairsplitting frees us from a primitive conception and moves us one step closer to the real connection of things. Mankind today lives by the function of the innate category of causality.

We shall now examine methodologically the functionally analogous achievements of animals from the higher observation tower of human form of perception of space and category of causality; first, the disposition to kinesthetic learning by rote of paths, and then the disposition to blind association of sequential events. Is it 'true' what the water shrew 'knows' about the spatial? In the water shrew's case, learning creates an 'ordo et connectio idearum', also visible in our image of the universe: namely, the condition that places and locomotive parts are strung like a row of pearls. The water shrew's orderly scheme is entirely correct—as far as it reaches! In our perception the string of pearls is visible, too; the sequence of the links is true. Only for us there exists (and are true) an immense number of further data which the shrew lacks: for example, the possibility to short cut the loops of a path. Also from a pragmatic point of view, our perception is true to a higher degree than is the animal's image of the universe.

Something very similar results when we compare the disposition to association with our causal thought: here, too, the lower, more primitive rendering by the animal gives a connection between the events which exists also for our form of thought: the temporal relationship between cause and effect. The deeper actuality, essential to our causal thought, that energy is received from the cause by the effect is not given to purely associative thought. Here, too, then the lower form of thought corresponds a priori and adequately to the reality of a higher order, but again only as far as it reaches. Here, too, human form of thought is more true from the pragmatists's point of view; think of all it achieves that cannot be achieved by pure association! As I have said, we all live by the work of this important organ, almost as by the work of our hands.

With all the emphasis on these differences in the degree of correspondence between image of the universe and actuality we must not forget for one moment that something real is reflected even in the most primitive 'screens' of the apparatuses for organizing the image of the universe. It is important to emphasize this because we humans likewise use such apparatuses even though they may be very different. Progress in science always has a certain tendency to de-anthropomorphize our image of the universe, as Bertalanffy has correctly pointed out. From the palpable and sensible phenomenon of light, the impalpable, unvisualizable concept of wave phenomena has developed. The self-evident comprehension of causality is replaced by considerations of probability and arithmetic calculations, etc. One can actually say that among our forms of perception and categories there are 'more anthropomorphic' ones and 'less anthropomorphic' ones; or some that are more specialized and others that are more general. Doubtless a rational being lacking the sense of vision could comprehend the wave theory of light, while not comprehending specifically human perceptual experience. Looking beyond specifically human structures, as is done to the highest degree in mathematical science, must not lead to the view that the less anthropomorphic representations approach a higher degree of actuality, that is, that they approach the thing-in-itself more closely than does naïve perception. The more primitive reproduction has just as real a relationship to the absolutely existent as does the higher one. Thus the animal's apparatus for organizing the image of the universe reproduces only one detail, and in a purely associative manner, from the actuality of the transformation of energy, namely, that a certain event precedes another one in time. But one can in no way assert that the statement 'a cause precedes an effect' is less true than the statement that an effect arises from the preceding phenomenon through transformation of energy. The advance from the more simple to the more differentiated lies in the fact that additional, new definitions are added to those already existing. If in such an advance from a more primitive reproduction of the universe to a higher one certain data which are represented in the first are neglected in the second, then it is only a question of change in point of view, and not a matter of a closer approach to the absolutely existent. The most primitive reactions of the protozoa reflect an aspect of the world to which all organisms must similarly relate, just as much as do the calculations of a Homo sapiens who studies theoretical physics. But we can no more ascertain how much exists in absolute actuality in addition to the facts and relationships rendered in our image of the universe than the water shrew can ascertain that it could short cut many detours in its crooked path learning.

With regard to the absolute validity of our 'necessities of thought' we are accordingly modest: We believe only that in some details they correspond more to the actually existent than do those of the water shrew. Above all, we are conscious of the fact that we surely are just as blind in regard to as many additional things as that animal is: that we too are lacking the receptive organs for infinitely much that is actual. The forms of perception and categories are not the mind, but rather are tools the mind uses. They are innate structures that on the one hand support, but on the other hand make for rigidity like all that is solid, Kant's great conception of the idea of freedom, namely that the thinking being is responsible to the totality of the universe, suffers from the ailment of being chained to the rigidly mechanical laws of pure reason. The a priori and the preformed ways of thought are just the ones that are by no means specifically human as such. Specifically human, however, is the conscious drive not to get stuck, not to become a vehicle running on rails, but rather to maintain a youthful openness to the world, and to come closer to actuality through a constant reciprocal interaction with it.

Being biologists, we are modest regarding man's position in the totality of nature, but more demanding in regard to what the future may yet bring us in the way of knowledge. To declare man absolute, to assert that any imaginable rational being, even angels, would have to be limited to the laws of thought of Homo sapiens, appears to us to be incomprehensible arrogance. For the lost illusion of a unique lawfulness for man, we exchange the conviction that in his openness to the world he is basically capable of outgrowing his science and the a priori formulations of his thought, and of creating and realizing basically new things that have never existed before. To the extent he remains inspired by the will not to let every new thought be choked by the cover of the laws crystallizing around it, in the fashion of Nietzsche's drops of lava, this development will not so soon encounter any essential obstacle. In this lies our concept of freedom; it is the greatness, and, at least on our planet the provisional uniqueness of our human brain that, in spite of all its gigantic differentiation and structurization, it is an organ whose function possesses a proteus-like changeability, a lava-like capacity to rise against the functional restrictions imposed on it by its own structure, to the point where it achieves a flexibility even greater than that of protoplasm-lacking solid structures.

What would Kant say about all this? Would he feel that our naturalistic interpretation of human reason (for him, supernaturally given) is desecration of the most sacred? (This it is in the eyes of most neo-Kantians.) Or would he, in view of his own occasional approaches to evolutionary thought, have accepted our conception that organic nature is not something amoral and Godforsaken, but is basically 'sacred', in its creative evolutionary achievements, especially in those highest achievements, human reason and human morals? We are inclined to believe this, because we believe that science could never destroy a deity, but only the earthen feet of a man-made idol. The person who reproaches us with lacking respect for the greatness of our philosopher we counter by quoting Kant himself: 'If one starts with an idea founded but not realized and bequeathed to us by another, by continual thinking one can hope to progress further than did the ingenious man to whom one owed the spark of this light.' The discovery of the a priori is that spark we owe to Kant and it is surely not arrogance on our part to criticize the interpretation of the discovery by means of new facts (as we did in criticizing Kant with regard to the origin of the forms of perception and categories). This critique does not lower the value of the discovery any more than it lowers that of the discoverer. To anyone, following the erroneous principle 'Omni naturalia sunt turpia', who persists in seeing a desecration in our attempt to look at human reason naturalistically we counter by again quoting Kant himself: 'When we speak of the totality of nature, we must inevitably conclude that there is Divine regulation. But in each phase of nature' (since none are at first given simply in our sensory world) we have the obligation to search for underlying causes, in so far as possible, and to pursue the causal chain, so long as it hangs together, according to laws that are known to us.'

NOTES

1. Translated from: Kant's Lehre vom apriorischen im Lichte geganwärtiger Biologie. *Blätter für Deutsche Philosophie*, 1941, **15**, 94–125. This rough translation has been prepared by Charlotte Ghurye and edited by Donald T. Campbell with the assistance of Professor Lorenz and William A. Reupke. Ghurye, Lorenz, and Reupke have not had an opportunity to see the translation in its present form. While the translation is still very uneven, there is one naïveté of wording which represents a deliberate avoiding of some more sophisticated usages. The hyphenated phrase 'thing-in-itself' has been used as a translation for the Kantian phrases 'Ding an sich', 'An sich Seienden', 'An sich Bestehenden', 'An sich der Dinge', 'An sich existenden Natur', etc. This has seemed preferable here to the usual usage of leaving the phrase untranslated, or of translating it into the Greek 'noumena'. To preserve some Kantian distinctions even at the expense of awkward renditions, these equivalents have been used: Wahrnehmung = perception; Anschauung = intuition; Realität = reality; Wirklichkeit = actuality; Gegenstand = object; Ding = thing.
2. Prolegomena, First Part, Not III. The present translators have used here the translation of Kant provided by P. G. Lucas, Manchester University Press, 1953.
3. Translation of P. G. Lucas, Manchester University Press, 1953.
4. Rats and other mammals that are on a higher mental level than the water shrew notice such possibilities of a short cut immediately. I experienced a highly interesting case with a greylag goose in which the possibility of a short cut in path learning was undoubtedly noticed, but not made use of. When a gosling, this bird had acquired a path learning which led through the door of our house and up two flights of a wide staircase to my room, where the goose used to spend the night. In the morning it used to make its exit by flying through the window. When learning the path, the young greylag goose ran first of all toward a large window in the yet strange staircase, past the lowest step. Many birds, when disquieted, strive for the light, and so this goose, too, decided to leave the window and come to the landing to which I had wanted to lead it only after it had quieted down a little. This detour to the window remained once and for all an indispensable part of the path learning which the greylag goose had to go through on its way to the place where it used to sleep. This very steep detour to the

window and back gave a very mechanical effect, almost like a habitually performed ceremony, because its original motivation (anxiety and therefore shying away from the darkness) was no longer present. In the course of this goose's path learning, which took almost two years, the detour became gradually leveled off, that is, the line originally going almost as far as the window and back had now sloped down to an acute angle by which the goose deflected its course toward the window and mounted the lowest step at the extremity facing the window. This levelling off of the unnecessary would probably have led to attaining the actually shortest way in two more years and had nothing to do with insight. But a goose is, properly speaking, basically capable of finding such a simple solution by insight; though habit prevails over insight or prevents it. One evening the following happened. I had forgotten to let the goose into the house, and when I finally remembered, it was standing impatiently on the door step and rushed past me and—to my great surprise—for the first time took the shortest way and up the stairs. But already on the third step it stopped, stretched its neck, uttered the warning cry, turned around, walked the three steps down again, made the detour to the window hastily and 'formally' and then mounted the stairs calmly in the usual way. Here obviously the possibility of a solution by insight was blocked only by the existence of that learned by training!

Learning, Development, and Culture
Edited by H. C. Plotkin
© 1982, John Wiley & Sons Ltd.

CHAPTER 8

Functions and structures of adaptation

Jean Piaget*

For proposition (1) the material or dynamic elements of a structure with cyclic order we shall call A, B, C, ..., Z, and the material or energetic elements necessary for their maintenance, A', B', C', ..., Z'. We shall then have the following figure, the sign × representing the interaction of the terms of the first range with those of the second, and the sign → representing the end point of these interactions:

$$(A \times A') \rightarrow (B \times B') \rightarrow (C \times C') \times \ldots$$
$$(Z \times Z') \rightarrow (A \times A') \rightarrow \text{etc.} \tag{1}$$

In a case like this we are confronted by a closed cycle qua cycle, which expresses the permanent reconstitution of the elements A, B, C, ..., Z, A, and which is characteristic of the organism (without forming any prejudgment about the kind of frontier or absence of frontier between A and A', etc.); but each interaction $(A \times A')$, $(B \times B')$, etc., at the same time represents an opening into the environment as a source of aliment.

Now it is impossible to dissociate organization from adaptation, because an organized system is open to the environment, and its functioning therefore

* Reprinted from Chapter 4 ('Corresponding functions and partial structural isomorphisms between the organism and the subject of knowledge') of *Biology and Knowledge,* 1971, pp. 171–177, by permission of the author, Edinburgh University Press, and the University of Chicago Press. Copyright © by The University of Chicago and The University of Edinburgh.

entails exchanges with the external world, the stability of which defines the adapted character of the system. From the formal point of view, this means that in proposition (1) it is vital to distinguish between the elements A, B, $C, \ldots$, appertaining to the organism, and the elements A', B', $C', \ldots$, furnished by the environment; the cyclic form taken by the system is thus characteristic of its organization, whereas the permanence of the interactions $A \times A'$, etc., is characteristic of its adaptation.

Then again, we must distinguish between adaptation as a state, just defined, and adaptation as a process, which raises a further problem that must now be considered. The adaptation process intervenes inevitably as soon as the environment undergoes any modification, and where the life of the phenotype is concerned it is perpetually undergoing modification, at varying speeds according to its place on the evolutionary ladder.

Let us suppose, by reference to this first proposition, that the environment is modified in such a way as to replace the element (or group of elements) B' by B'', slightly differing from B'. One of two things happens: either the cycle is interrupted and the organization is destroyed through failure to adapt, or else the cycle maintains itself as before or modifies itself by substituting, for example, C_2 for C, but still without losing its cyclic form. It will then be said that an adaptation has taken place in the sense of a process:

If in

$$(A \times A') \rightarrow (B \times B') \rightarrow (C \times C') \rightarrow \ldots$$

$$(Z \times Z') \rightarrow (A \times A') \ldots$$

(prop. [1]), B' is modified into B'' and C into C_2, then, when adaptation takes place:

$$(A \times A') \times (B \times B'') \rightarrow (C_2 \times C') \rightarrow (D \times D') \rightarrow$$

$$\ldots (Z \times Z') \rightarrow (A \times A') \ldots \tag{2}$$

We must therefore try to make clear what are the conditions of such a process.

ASSIMILATION AND ACCOMMODATION

The constant functional conditions of the process are two in number—assimilation and accommodation—and their rather close solidarity must now be determined.

We might say, in a very general way, that assimilation has taken place between the new element B'' and the established organization (under proposition [1]), if this organization, while integrating B'' into its cycle, still remains the organized structure that it was. In a more general way still, it might be said that the external elements A', B', $C', \ldots$ (prop. [1]) are assimilated into the organism under discussion insofar as they are integrated into its cycle. But in the case of the new element B'', assimilation occurs if it is integrated, in its turn, into the organization's cycle without destroying it.

But if the new element does not destroy the cycle, it may modify it. In this case we shall say that there has been an accommodation in the assimilation cycle if this cycle (proposition [1]), while assimilating B'', is itself modified by this new element in such a way that, for example, one of its elements (C) is transformed by it into C_2 (proposition [2]). The accommodation is thus inseparable from the assimilation, and it might be said by reciprocation that every assimilation is accompanied by accommodation. If the assimilation of the new element B'' did not cause modification of C into C_2, this would simply mean that the previous accommodations in the cycle had been sufficient, but the assimilatory cycle would, nonetheless, have undergone accommodation.

Thus, adaptation, seen as a complement or a consequence of proposition (4), may be defined as an equilibrium between assimilation and accommodation. But two things should be noted. First of all, it is necessary to explain why we do not define adaptation simply as accommodation, as one might be tempted to do. The reason we do not is that, without assimilation, there is no adaptation in the biological sense; for example, it could be said that, metaphorically speaking, a liquid adapts its shape to that of its receptacle, but this is not a case of biological adaptation at all, for the new shape is merely an accident of the moment and will not stay the same if the water is put into something else, precisely because there has been no assimilation into any permanent organization. Therefore, adaptation presupposes an equilibrium between assimilation and accommodation and not merely an accommodation alone. If there is accommodation without lasting assimilation, the word *accommodats* may be used, meaning temporary phenotypic variations. Second, we must emphasize the indissociable nature of assimilation and accommodation, which are constitutive conditions—at once necessary and inseparable—of adaptation. In fact, in biological terms, accommodation can be nothing but the accommodation of an organized structure, and so it can only be produced, under the influence of some external factor or element, according to whether there is temporary or lasting assimilation of such element or of its extension within the structure that it modifies. This is by no means the equivalent of postulating the heredity of acquired characteristics in the Lamarckian sense of the term. It is simply a matter of affirming the fact that no exogenous variation is possible in a general conservation of the structure that varies on this point—in other words, without some assimilation of the elements involved, or of the effects produced by them, into the structure undergoing the variation.

To sum up, assimilation and accommodation are not two separate functions but the two functional poles, set in opposition to each other, of any adaptation. So it is only by abstraction that one can speak of assimilation alone as constituting a function of essential importance; but it must always be remembered that there can be no assimilation of anything into the organism or its functioning without a corresponding accommodation and without such assimilation's becoming part of an adaptation context.

This having been said, it must now be recalled that the basic functions of adaptation and assimilation, embodied in the most diverse structures, are to be found at every hierarchical level, from the genome and epigenotype up to the cognitive mechanisms of the higher orders.

2. ADAPTATION AND THE GENOME

To take the genome, or genetic system generally, first: Lamarck saw it as unconditionally pliable under the influence of environment, which was as much as to attribute to it an indefinite power of accommodation, though without assimilation into unchangeable structures as far as the (cyclic) conditions of their organization are concerned. To put it another way, the hereditary organization, as in our recent example, was compared to a liquid which assumes the shapes of all receptacles without stabilizing itself and even without any sort of historic irreversibility. In the case of mutationism, the positions are reversed, and the genetic system is supposed to have assimilation without accommodation insofar as it lives off the somatic organization but undergoes no variation as a result of this; even the effects of radiation are seen as setting off endogenous mutations, which means that they are not supposed to influence their form, and that again is a case of assimilation without accommodation, despite variation. On the other hand, phenotypic *accommodats* were certainly considered to be attempts at individual adaptation, but without the possibility of heredity. This radically antithetical situation, which, in mutationism, set phenotypic variation against stability and genotypic mutation, caused Cuénot, Caullery, and others to say that characteristics were of two kinds, one kind being adaptive and not hereditary, and the other hereditary but not adaptive. And this attitude continued among biologists for a good fifty years because of the amorphous doctrine of anti-Lamarckism or the negation of any kind of influence of the environment except by selection (this was at the cost of setting up a perpetual vicious circle: selection is based on 'useful' characteristics, but utility, for lack of any clear notion of adaptation to environment, is defined by selection) or because biologists took refuge in finalism (which, as we have seen, is a way of implying the intervention of environment).

A third solution at last appeared in the form of Waddington's synthesis; now the genetic system is seen as being adaptive in itself, in the precise sense that there is an equilibrium between assimilation and accommodation. A phenotypic variation, resulting from an interaction between the genetic pool, or genome, and the environment, is explicitly seen as a 'response' made by the genome to external stimuli. There is thus an accommodation in the very sense we have given it, an accommodation to the circumstances imposed by the environment and assimilation of the effects of this accommodation into the structures of the genome. The variation thus produced may be fixed in heredity by 'genetic assimilation' conceived as being caused by selection, but in the strict sense of a modification in the proportions of the genes by means of development and the survival of the fittest phenotypes, that is, the best responses to the environment that the genotype can make.

However, for the selection exerted on the genetic system (in the sense of a modification of the proportions inherent in the genome) to be achieved solely by the death or survival of the adult phenotypes, or by regroupings imposed on it during the development of the epigenotype, there must of necessity be both accommodation and 'genetic assimilation' within the genome itself as soon as we escape from the blind alley alternative of accommodation in the neo-Darwinian sense. Insofar as the term 'response' has any special meaning, this meaning cannot be other than that of an adaptive response; otherwise we are back again with the random variation theory. Waddington rightly shows this to be both mathematically and biologically insufficient to take account of the evolutionary processes. It is therefore of great interest for the study of the isomorphisms that we intend to single out in this chapter to note that the three aspects of adaptation, assimilation, and accommodation quickly recur in an analysis of genetic structures when it is undertaken with an open mind by one of those rare scholars who combines in his work the twin qualities of a gift for synthesis and the caution proper to an experimentalist.

3. PHENOTYPIC ADAPTATION

In the field of individual development (embryogenesis and growth), however, adaptation is recognized by most scholars apart from those who are in the process of changing their minds, as happens from time to time, in favor of preformation models and who see environmental influence during embryogenesis as merely a feeding process entirely assimilated into the genetic program without any accommodations other than quite temporary ones. On the other hand, in Waddington's conception of homeorhesis and chreods and, generally speaking, in those interpretations according to which ontogenesis determines phylogenesis just as much as the reverse, it is taken for granted that epigenesis is the result of a collaboration between the synthetic activity of the genome and the environment. This inevitably implies an equilibration of a progressive kind between assimilation and accommodation, and that means adaptation.

In those cases where development adheres to its customary channeling or normal chreods, this collaboration manifests itself in the kind of equilibrium of movement or homeorhesic equilibrium in which subsequent assimilations and correlative accommodations keep the organs under formation in their normal channels. But, starting from the functional stages, an increasing role is given to exercise in cooperation with maturation. In the case of some new or disturbing influence, a certain formation may be conducted out of its normal chreod and made to adopt another, slightly different or very different; when this happens there is phenotypic variation, harmful or adaptive according to whether the accommodation thus imposed either does not or does find a new equilibrium with the assimilating cycle. This adaptation may remain individual or may subsequently be fixed by 'genetic assimilation', which presupposes, even at this level, a distinction between two kinds of adaptation, the one individual or even merely temporary, and the other hereditary.

As for the adult phenotype, both its physiological and its morphological adaptations obey the same principle of an equilibrium between assimilation and accommodation. It must, however, be understood that such a description must remain for the moment essentially functional, despite the tentative structural analysis contained in proposition (2). In fact, proposition (2) does no more than explain 'a displacement of equilibrium' in relation to proposition (1), but, being relative to a process of cyclical order, both this displacement and, generally speaking, the equilibrium between assimilation and accommodation presuppose the existence of differentiated and more or less refined mechanisms of equilibration. These are, in fact, regulations which, even in their details, present striking isomorphisms between the organic and the cognitive domains. Moreover, physiological or morphological equilibrium between assimilation and accommodation presupposes some conservation of the past, or 'memory', and leads to various anticipations widening the field of accommodation.

Learning, Development, and Culture
Edited by H. C. Plotkin
© 1982, John Wiley & Sons Ltd.

CHAPTER 9

Organism and environment

R. C. Lewontin

Anyone who wants to make sense of the shape of scientific explanation must understand the powerful grip that certain metaphors have on our thinking. Indeed, one can easily reach the conclusion that metaphorical thinking is itself the dominant mode of theorizing about the social and natural world. It is transparent that Descartes' metaphor of the machine, described in Part V of the *Discourses*, is the meta-model on which all reductionist science depends. The world, organic as well as inorganic, is a machine, a vast clockwork mechanism, that can be understood ultimately only by taking it to bits, by studying the intrinsic properties of the bits, and then by reassembling the machine to see how each bit subserves the whole. So powerful is that metaphor, and so unconsidered by the vast majority of social and natural scientists, that we simply cannot conceive of any other way of thinking about the world. We no longer think that the universe is *like* a machine; we think it *is* a machine. It is interesting to speculate, as Turbayne (1962) has done, on what the consequence for our explanations would have been if Berkeley's language metaphor had replaced Descartes' clock. Subsumed under the grand meta-model of the clockwork world there are a number of particular metaphorical structures that appear over and over again as organizing armatures on which models of the world are built. These are sometimes consciously and explicitly asserted to be models, but with continued use in various fields of explanation they become, like Descartes' machine, part of the unquestioned substructure of our thought. Metaphors become identities and, as a consequence, come to rule our picture of the world. We then lay on nature all sorts of properties drawn from the model, forgetting that it had only an 'as if' validity to begin with.

In E. H. Gombrich's *Art and Illusion* there is a rendering by a Japanese painter of an English countryside that looks for all the world like the craggy, jagged, stunted landscape that we have come to accept as Japanese *nature*. Nature mimics art not only in landscape painting but in our 'scientific' descriptions of natural phenomena. There are two powerful metaphors that have come to permeate both biology and the social sciences, and these have passed back and forth between social and natural historical explanations until their origin is lost from sight. One is the metaphor of *unfolding*, and the other is the model of *trial and error*. The first is a *transformational* model, the other a *variational* one.

The concept of unfolding is that any historical process, whether it be the passage of an individual from fertilized egg to eventual death, or the change over time of a society or of all human culture, is a passage through predetermined stages that are immanent in the objects from their very beginning and which require only an original *déclenchement* to set their progress in motion. Indeed, the very word 'development' (like the word "evolution") originally meant an unfolding or unrolling, a meaning that it retains in photography and analytic geometry, and is more transparent in the Spanish *desarrollo* (literally, 'unrolling'). Grand theories of history like Toynbee's cycles of birth, growth, and decay of civilizations seem to be modelled directly on the supposed periods of an individual's lifetime, Shakespeare's 'seven ages of man'. The periodization of history has a hoary tradition, going back at least to the Greek Ages of Gold, Silver, Bronze, and Iron, marking humanity's progressive decay. Marx's theory of history makes explicit one basic element of transformational theories, that *the conditions of each stage are the preconditions for the next*. There are no shortcuts. The succession is ordered. The most influential theories of human psychic development are theories of unfolding, and they seem clearly to have been derived directly from notions of physical development in 19th century embryology. Both Freud and Piaget understood the passage from infant to adult as a passage through ordered stages each of which must be successfully traversed before further development can occur. These structures of psychic periods introduce explicitly a second characteristic of unfolding themes, that of *arrested development*. While each stage is a necessary condition of the next, it is not sufficient, and the entire unfolding may become blocked. In this way, major variations among individuals are interpreted not as the outcome of divergent pathways of psychic development, but as fixations at various stages of a single linear array. There are of course minor variations around the main developmental line, but the major features of human personality are to be understood in terms of the main sequence.

The linear array and arrested development make their appearance in evolutionary theory as well, in the concept of neoteny. The embryos of humans and gorillas are much more like each other morphologically than are the adults of the two species, and the gorilla resembles, in shape, the human adult. It is as if the human were a gorilla born too soon, a foetal ape with an adult existence. The implication, of course, is that if development should, by accident, become unblocked in some unfortunate infant, it would develop the receding jaw, long arms, and sagittal crest of the adult gorilla that is immanent in it.

Neoteny is a marginal notion in evolutionary theory. It enters the theory by an inversion of the causal direction that characterizes neo-Darwinism as a whole. Neoteny asserts the ontological primacy of embryology over history. That is, the historical evolution of a lineage is interpreted as the outcome of arrested development at various stages of a fundamental embryological sequence, common to all the organisms in the lineage and immanent in the lineage from its historical beginning. In this sense, it is a left-over from a pre-Darwinian, Platonic view of organisms, and, of course, simply evades the issue of how the developmental sequence came into being in the first place. Neo-Darwinism, on the contrary, takes historical contingency to be prior to embryological development. The sequence of developmental stages of an individual is the outcome of the evolution of the species, not vice versa. Ernst Haeckel's theory of recapitulation is, in this way, quintessentially Darwinian, for it asserts that each embryo goes through a succession of stages that reveal the evolutionary history of its lineage. Human embryos have rudimentary gill slits that disappear during further development because the fish and amphibia who were our ancestors had gill slits. But we have gone further than they did. Evolution has added stages to development in producing us, stages that were not immanent in the Devonian fish. Evolution is not an unfolding but an origination. In this way Darwinism made a fundamental break with embryology, dominating it by rejecting the metaphor of *desarrollo*.

In place of the transformational metaphor of unfolding, Darwinism introduced the model of trial and error as a fundamental description for historical processes. Variation arises from causes extrinsic to the system. At the same time challenges, also from extrinsic sources, impinge on the system. History then consists of confronting the challenges with the variations, until one variant succeeds and is then assimilated into the evolving units. The neo-Darwinian picture of evolution is then a three-fold process: variation, trial and error, and assimilation. More specifically, the theory of natural selection is that:

1) There is variation in morphology, physiology, and behavior among individuals within a species (The Principle of Variation);

2) The variation is in part heritable in that offspring resemble their parents more than they resemble unrelated individuals (The Principle of Heredity);

3) Some variants leave more offspring than others (The Principle of Natural Selection).

To these three mechanical principles which are necessary and sufficient for evolutionary change to occur by natural selection is added a fourth, explanatory principle:

4) The reason that some variants leave more offspring than others is that they are better able to meet challenges from the environment, either from other organisms competing for resources in short supply, or from physiological stresses (The Principle of the Struggle for Existence).

These principles explicitly incorporate the element of variation and challenge. The process of assimilation is an automatic one consequent on the heritability of variation. If some variants leave more offspring than others, and if offspring resemble their parents, then the population as a whole becomes enriched for the successful variant, and, after many generations of the process, the entire population will consist of the successful type.

While unfolding has an ancient intellectual tradition, trial and error as a model for historical processes seems to be a genuine intellectual novelty in the 19th century. That 'many are called but few are chosen' has long been assumed, but that variation is generated by a process extrinsic to the historical developments themselves, that it is 'random' with respect to the challenge from the environment, was not only a novel contribution of Darwin but was, and continues to be, a major point of contention for those who challenge the Darwinian paradigm (see, for example, the symposium *Mathematical Challenges to the Darwinian Theory of Evolution*). Yet the metaphor of trial and error introduced by Darwin has become the unquestioned model for so-called 'evolutionary' processes. 'Challenges' and 'response' mark all stages of Toynbee's historical cycles. 'Evolutionary' anthropology supposes a variation among cultures, some of which predominate because of their superior capacity in the struggle for existence (Dunnell, 1978). It is the culture as a whole that is thought to spread by physically displacing groups that are less efficient, less warlike, less entrepreneurial. This is the genocidal warfare and 'genosorption' of Wilson (1975). Sometimes it is only the ideas or cultural artifacts themselves that win out in the struggle for existence that is supposed to take place in people's heads. This is Dawkins' selection of 'memes' (1976). In like manner, 'evolutionary' epistemology views the assimilation by individuals of a world view through a process of conjectures and refutation (Popper, 1959), of trying out more or less random interpretations of the outer world, only some of which meet the demands of practice.

The contrast between transformational and variational models of change is illustrated by the difference between the theories of stellar and organic evolution. The evolution of the universe is the collection of individual life histories of stars, each of which undergoes eventually the same set of transformations from its birth as a contraction of interstellar gas, through the main sequence, to its dotage as a red giant and finally its extinction as a white dwarf. Each element in the universe undergoes the same set of transformations, generated by processes internal to each star itself. On the other hand, the variational evolution of organisms is by a selection among elements of different qualities and an enrichment of the collection for particular variants. It is only the collection that changes, not the individuals of which it is composed, and these changes are a consequence of phenomena external to the organisms themselves. It is important to note that there is nothing intrinsically more 'evolutionary' about variational evolution than about transformational evolution. 'Evolutionary' anthropology and 'evolutionary' epistemology do not represent the introduction of evolution into these fields but rather the change from one metaphor to another, a reversal of the location of change from internal factors to external ones. Yet one can never quite reject the one for the other. Rather, evolutionary epistemologies show themselves as a battle ground in which the roles of internal and external forces are being fought out. Darwinism, the challenger, meets embryology, the reigning champion, to see which metaphor will have intellectual hegemony. The irony of the situation is that unfolding and trial-and-error are bad metaphors even for embryology and organic evolution, so it is little wonder that they have failed to resolve the contradictions in the theory of cognition.

WHY DEVELOPMENT IS NOT AN UNFOLDING

The idea of the development of an organism as an unfolding is, in its modern form, the notion of the hegemony of the genes. The DNA inherited from father and mother are seen as setting a developmental program that is triggered by the fertilization of the egg and that then proceeds like a computer program being read from memory storage. It is indeed the case that some truth about development is captured in this picture. The egg of a *Drosophila* hatches into a larva which molts exactly twice, then transforms into a pupa and then develops into an adult. No known environmental manipulation will alter the number of larval instars or make a *Drosophila* pupa hatch out into a grasshopper. There are, moreover, autoregulatory feedback systems in developing embryos that buffer out the effect of environmental variations. If the developing wing of an insect is partly excised, the entire development of the organism may be held up while the lesion is repaired, so that, in the end, the adult hatches out whole. The examples of self-regulated development have seemed so striking, and so demanding of explanation, and the metaphor of development as an unfolding process so pervasive, that many of the facts of developmental biology have been put aside as unworthy of attention.

First, there is the relation between gene and environment. The compound eyes of an insect are made up of many identical cells. Different mutations of the genes are known that affect eye size. However, eye size is also a function of temperature. In some genotypes the number of cells increases with temperature, in some it decreases. There is a unique interaction between genotype and environment that determines the number of cells in the eye. Even that statement is too strong. A *Drosophila* is about 3 mm long and 1 mm wide, and it undergoes its development in the laboratory glued upright to the inside of a glass bottle in a constant temperature room. No sensible meaning of the term 'environment' would allow that the left side of a *Drosophila* is developing in a different environment than the right side, yet the number of cells in the two eyes are never the same. Small perturbations of cellular events, thermal noise at the level of the movement of molecules, influence the exact number of cell divisions in each eye. 'Developmental noise' is a source of variation that in many cases is quite as powerful as genetic and environmental variations. Development is not determined by the initial state of the organism, nor is it even determined by that initial state and the sequence of environments through which the organism passes. I am not entering here into the issue of whether chance is an ontological property of microscopic events, but only that thermal noise, whatever its ontological status, is "random" with respect to environmental causes.

Second, development is, at every stage, a contingent process. If a heat shock is given to some strains of *Drosophila* during a critical 4 hours of their development, their wings will lack some of the veins that characterize normal flies. The shock given before or after this critical period will not affect wing veins, but it may affect other characters like eye size. At each moment of development the organism may move from one developmental pathway to another, dependent upon its current state and the state of the environment. Moreover, genetically different individuals may undergo the same development in some environmental sequences, yet differ from each other in other environments. Most flies develop normal wing vein patterns at 25 °C, but only some genotypes will produce abnormal vein patterns under heat shock.

Third, development is not, in general, a linear array of stages but a branched process in which different states may be accessible from many other states. Tropical vines develop a variety of shapes of stems and leaves depending upon the location of the growing tip as the leaves are produced. There is one form while growing across the ground, another while climbing a tree, another near the top of the tree, another while descending from the branches of the tree, hanging free. The vine will shift from one of these developmental paths to another depending upon the tactile and light cues it receives at the growing point and virtually independent of any previous growth history.

The problem with trying to sum up the embryological development of an individual in any simple scheme is that the relation between genes, environment, and organism is extraordinarily diverse from one species to another, from one organ or tissue or enzyme to another, from one genotype within a species to another. Some organisms show some regulation of development some of the time. Some species develop virtually the same morphology in any non-lethal environment, while others are remarkably plastic. There is no model that is not trivially generalized, that can serve as a useful metaphor for psychic development. It all depends.

WHY ORGANIC EVOLUTION IS NOT
TRIAL-AND-ERROR ADAPTATION

It is a common vulgarization of our understanding of the process of organic evolution to characterize it as a process of trial and error problem solving. The environment poses the problems while the characteristics of organisms are regarded as their solutions. Fins are a 'solution' to the 'problem' of locomotion in a liquid medium, wings are a 'solution' to the 'problem' of flight, teeth to the 'problem' of chewing. These solutions are arrived at through natural selection of those organisms who approximate more and more closely the optimal solution. The consequence of the process is adaptation, the alteration of the species to fit the demands of the environment. Unfortunately, as a description of the actual process of organic evolution, this is both incomplete and inaccurate.

First, the process of natural selection cannot be shown to maximize or even increase the average reproductive fitness of organisms as a general rule. That is, if one writes out the equations of genetic change under natural selection, it is not the case that they are equivalent to the maximization of average reproductive fitness, total population size, population growth rate, stability of populations under fluctuating environment, or any other optimal principle. It is trivially easy to construct biologically reasonable cases in which natural selection actually decreases any of these measures of 'adaptation'. The kinematics of natural selection are simply not of a form that allows a representation by a maximizing principle, except in special cases. Thus, appeals to natural selection as an optimizer are generally incorrect, although they may on occasion be accidentally true. This apparently paradoxical result, that natural selection is differential reproduction yet does not generally lead to maximum average reproductive fitness of the population, arises from two sources. One is Mendelian segregation of genes in sexually reproducing organisms, the result of which is that parents of a particular genotype will produce offspring of many different genotypes. The other is that reproductive fitness of genotypes is itself contingent on the genetic composition of the population (so-called 'frequency-dependent fitness'), so that as the population evolves genetically it may reduce the fitnesses. While evolutionary geneticists sometimes behave as if fitnesses are usually independent of frequency and that frequency-dependent fitnesses are a sort of exceptional case of secondary interest, the reverse is the case. In sexually reproducing organisms differential fertility is a form of 'frequency-dependent' fitness, as are all forms of selection that involve selection of some proportion of the population with the largest (or smallest) value of a measurable trait. In fact, fitnesses that are intrinsic properties of genotypes in a given environment, independent of the population distribution of genotypes, are the exception.

Second, traits may be established in species as a secondary consequence of selection of quite different traits. Genetic differences of particular genes have manifold (*pleiotropic*) effects on different characteristics of organisms because of developmental connections. So, red pigment in the eyes of *Drosophila* may have been selected because of the sensitivity to certain wavelengths of visible light that it provides to the flies' visual apparatus, but the same pigments are deposited internally in the Malpighian tubules of the insect where their color is totally irrelevant to any requirement of the organism. A special and widespread form of pleiotropy is allometric growth. All dimensions of organisms do not grow at the same rate, either during the development of an individual or in comparisons of closely related species. Thus, simple change in size results in change of shape. Across all primates, for example, teeth increase in size less then proportionately with skull size, so large primates have *relatively* smaller (although *absolutely* larger) teeth than small primates. The apparently large teeth of small monkeys is then not a consequence of direct selection for teeth size, but a consequence of the small size of the body.

Third, and related to the previous consideration, is that some traits are simply alternative attributes of the primary objects of selection. Hemoglobin has been selected in vertebrates to carry oxygen from the exchange surfaces to the internal cells of the body. The absorption spectrum of the iron-containing heme molecules happens to give it a red color in visible light, so our livers are red, but redness *per se* has certainly not been selected for. Indeed some invertebrates have a copper containing respiratory pigment instead, and their blood is green!

Fourth, traits can be established in evolution because of their chromosomal, rather than their developmental or physiological, association with selected characters. The genes of all organisms are organized on chromosomes, and these chromosomes are passed on in inheritance as units with limited recombination of genes on the same chromosome. When a new favorable mutation is increased in the population by natural selection, it carries along with it other, non-selected, genes on the same chromosome as genetical 'hitch-hikers'. The linked hitch-hiking genes will appear to be favored by natural selection because their carriers have higher reproductive fitness. This is not a consequence, however, of their own properties but of their statistical association with the genes directly selected. In effect, deleterious genes can be fixed in a population because they are genetically linked to those that are selectively favored.

Fifth, because populations are finite in size, unselected or even mildly deleterious genes can be established in a species by purely random chance. Gene frequencies fluctuate from generation to generation as a result of accidents of sampling, and eventually one or another gene allele will be randomly established, much as family names go extinct or spread for reasons that are utterly at random with respect to the names themselves. A consequence is that new mutations that are mildly favorable in reproductive fitness are usually lost almost immediately. Even in an extremely large population, because of the random events in Mendelian distribution of genes into gametes, a new mutation with reproductive fitness advantage $S\%$ has a chance of only $2S\%$ of being incorporated into the population.

Sixth, it is the organism itself that determines the actual object of natural selection. If, in an experiment, one selects *Drosophila* by always breeding the next generation from large winged parents, wing size will increase. If this is done repeatedly in unrelated lines of flies, it will turn out that in some lines the number of cells has increased while in others it is cell size that has changed. What has selection been 'for'? Depending upon the initial genetic variation in the line, the organisms have converted 'selection for wing size' into 'selection for cell size' or 'selection for cell number'. So selection, *a priori*, may have been for cold resistance, but different species have, in the course of their evolution, converted this pressure into selection for fur (the polar bear), selection for body fat (the seal), or selection for enough brains and skill to wear the bear's fur and eat the seal's fat (the Eskimo).

THE INTERPENETRATION OF ORGANISM AND ENVIRONMENT

The realization that organisms convert a generalized *a priori* selection pressure into a particular 'selection for', *a posteriori*, brings us to the central problem in the metaphor of trial-and-error adaptation. It leads us, moreover, to the central contradiction in evolutionary epistemologies. If organisms adapt either in evolution or in learning, there must be something out there to which they are being fitted. The notion of adaptation is the notion of an independent and pre-existent circumstance to which an object is being adapted, as a key is ground to fit a lock, or my American electric shaver is fitted by an adapter to work on British voltage. There must be a challenge for there to be a response, a problem for there to be a solution. That is, the metaphor of adaptation begins with a world in which an organism's environment is somehow defined without reference to the organism itself, but as a given to which the organism adapts itself. This is the notion that the world is divided up into pre-existent ecological niches and that evolution consists of the progressive fitting of organisms into these niches. Environment begins as alienated from the organism, which must then bring itself into conformity with the given world. This view of environment as causally prior to, and ontologically independent of, organisms is the surfacing in evolutionary theory of the underlying Cartesian structure of our world view. The world is divided into causes and effects, the external and the internal, environments and the organisms they 'contain'. While this structure is fine for clocks, since mainsprings move the hands and not vice versa, it creates indissoluble contradictions when taken as the meta-model of the living world.

The world external to a given organism can be partitioned into *a priori* ecological niches in a non-denumerable infinity of ways. Yet only some niches are occupied by organisms. How can we know, in the absence of the organisms that already occupy them, which of the partitions of the world are niches? Unless some way exists for picking them out, the concept of niche loses all value. Moreover, quite aside from the epistemological problem of how we know an unoccupied niche when we see it, there is the ontological problem of whether such unoccupied niches have a prior existence. There are no vertebrates that lay eggs, wriggle on their abdomens, and eat grass. That is, there are no herbivorous snakes. Birds live in trees, but no flying vertebrate eats the leaves at the tops of trees either.

In fact, it is impossible to describe an environment except by reference to organisms that interact with it and define it. Organism and environment are dialectically related. There is no organism without an environment, but there is no environment without an organism. The interpenetration of organism and environment takes a number of forms, all of which need to be incorporated into any theory of how organisms evolve.

First, *organisms assemble their environments out of the bits and pieces of the world*. Indeed, an environment is nature organized by an organism. Phoebes in my garden gather bits of dead grass to make nests. It is that act which makes dead grass part of the phoebe's environment. The stones among which the grass grows are not part of the phoebe's environment, but they are part of the environment of the thrushes that use them as anvils to break snails on. Neither stones nor grass are part of the environment of the sapsucker who lives in the tree at whose base both grass and stones lie. Nor is it only behavior that determines which part of closely adjacent bits of the world belong to an organism's environment. Animals and plants are surrounded by a layer of warm air a few millimeters thick, produced by their own metabolic heat. In the case of human beings, this insulating layer is in motion, from the feet and torso up over the face and head. We do not live in the outside air, but literally in an atmospheric shell of our own manufacture. Moreover, small organisms like fleas or other ectoparasites live completely immersed in that boundary layer, provided they are small enough. Should they grow a bit larger they would suddenly find themselves only up to their knees in the warm boundary layer while their bodies and heads would emerge into the stratosphere of the outside world. It is the total morphology, physiology, and behavior of an organism that determines what bits of the world are assembled into its environment.

Second, *organisms alter their environments*. It is a fundamental feature of life that organisms both create and destroy the conditions for their own existence by physical alterations in their milieu. Small mammals burrow in the ground to make their nests, and beavers dramatically alter water levels to create the ponds on which they depend for defense and feeding. In the northeastern United States beaver activity has been the main force altering water tables and topography in forested regions since the end of the Pleistocene glaciation. Even maggots who burrow in rotting fruit increase the surface areas on which the yeasts grow that are the food of the maggots. At the same time organisms destroy the conditions that made their lives possible in the first place. They consume food, they deposit wastes. They may strangle their own offspring. White pine in New England cannot maintain itself in pure stands because the dense shade it creates prevents its own seedlings from surviving, so it gives way to shade-tolerant hardwoods. The entire phenomena of ecological succession in which fields yield to weeds, weeds to shrubs, shrubs to trees, and trees to other trees is a consequence of the alteration of soil texture, chemistry, moisture, and light created by assemblages of plant species to their own detriment. Obviously human beings are both the producers and consumers of their own environment, but they only bring to a higher pitch activities that are characteristics of all organisms.

Third, *organisms transduce physical inputs qualitatively*. The physical changes that occur in nature are not necessarily detected by organisms as changes of the same quality. A change in external temperature is not sensed by my body organisms as heat flux but as a change in the concentration of various hormones, sugars, and inorganic ions that are released and consumed when I thermoregulate. The photon energy and compression waves that reach my eyes and ears when I see and hear a rattlesnake become converted by my central nervous system into chemical flows of adrenalin and the release of stored sugar. The same sight and sound will presumably have a very different effect on another rattlesnake.

Fourth, *organisms modulate signals from the environment statistically*. Variations in environmental factors are altered in amplitude and in period by physiological and behavioral mechanisms as they are transformed into effects on organisms. In this sense, animals and plants are like analogue computers that can integrate signals over time to iron out fluctuations or that can differentiate signal sequences so that the instantaneous rate of change is what matters rather than the actual level of the factor. Fluctuations in available food supply are damped by storage devices, either directly as when a squirrel stores nuts and acorns for the winter or indirectly in storage organs like body fat, glycogen, starchy roots, etc. Indeed, direct storage of food by animals depends on the indirect storage by plants. The potato tuber may have evolved as a statistical damping device for *Solanum tuberosum*, but it has been captured by *Homo sapiens*. Temperature 'storage' occurs when plants initiate flower development only after a sufficient number of accumulated degree days above a certain temperature. These are all devices for damping the effect of environmental fluctuation. On the other hand, signal variation is also amplified. While homeotherms damp temperature fluctuations internally, poikilotherms can amplify temperature signals, as when butterflies orient their wings flat to the sun when it comes out from behind the clouds, to act as solar collectors. The central nervous system of vertebrates has a system of volume-control feedback circuits so that at low levels of light or sound there is internal amplification of small differences.

Difference detection is itself a mode of organismal transformation of the environment. The analogues of differentiation circuits enable living beings to respond to rapid rates of change in the environment rather than to the level of the environment itself. Copepods reproduce asexually for long periods provided conditions of temperature, oxygen, and food supply remain constant, but a sudden raising or lowering of any of these factors triggers sexual reproduction. This is a common response for organisms that have a facultative sexual phase.

Not only amplitude but frequency can be modulated. Some oscillatory frequencies are simply not perceived as oscillation at all, while variation of the same factor at lower frequency or higher frequency is physiologically effective. Deciduous trees do not respond to diurnal fluctuation in light by losing their leaves, but seasonal variations in light of much lower amplitude are the signal for leaf fall. Multi-voltine insects are triggered by a single seasonal change to produce several generational cycles within a slowly changing annual cycle of climate. On the other hand, periodic cicadas hatch out when it is warm enough in their fated year, but then proceed to ignore seasonal fluctuations until another 13 or 17 years have gone by.

The importance of these various forms of dialectical interaction between organism and environment is that we cannot regard evolution as the 'solution' by species of some predetermined environmental 'problems' because it is the life activities of the species themselves that determine both the problems and solutions simultaneously. Nothing better illustrates the error of the problem–solution model than the seemingly straightforward example of the horse's hoof given by Lorenz in the essay reproduced in this volume (Chapter 7). He writes that the

> central nervous apparatus does not prescribe the laws of nature any more than the hoof of the horse prescribes the form of the ground.... But just as the hoof of the horse is adapted to the ground of the steppe which it copes with, so our central nervous apparatus for organizing the image of the world is adapted to the real world with which man has to cope.

And, further,

> ... the hoof of the horse is already adapted to the ground of the steppe before the horse is born and the fin of the fish is adapted to the water before the fish hatches. No sensible person belives that in any of these cases the form of the organ 'prescribes' its properties to the subject.

Indeed, there is a real world out there, but Lorenz makes the same mistake as Ruskin who believed in the 'innocent eye'. It is a long way from the 'laws of nature' to the horse's hoof. Rabbits, kangaroos, snakes, and grasshoppers, all of whom traverse the same ground as the horse, do not have hooves. Hooves come not from the nature of the ground, but from an animal of certain size, with four legs, running, not hopping, over the ground at a certain speed and for certain periods of time. The small gracile ancestors of the horse had toes and toenails, not hooves, and they got along very well indeed. So, too, our central nervous systems are not fitted to some absolute laws of nature but to laws of nature operating within a framework created by our own sensuous activity. Our nervous system does not allow us to see the ultraviolet reflections from flowers, but a bee's central nervous system does. And bats 'see' what night hawks do not. We do not further our understanding of evolution by general appeals to 'laws of nature' to which all life must bend. Rather, we must ask how, within the general constraints of the laws of nature, organisms have constructed environments that are the conditions for their further evolution and reconstruction of nature into new environments. Organisms within their individual lifetimes and in the course of their evolution as a species do not *adapt* to environments; they *construct* them. They are not simply *objects* of the laws of nature, altering themselves to bend to the inevitable, but active *subjects* transforming nature according to its laws.

EVOLUTIONARY EPISTEMOLOGY

In casting about for a way to understand how human beings construct their knowledge of the world, evolutionary epistemologists have taken the metaphor of trial-and-error adaptation as central. Whether trial-and-error in individual ontogeny is thought to be the whole story (as for Popper), or is the force that drives the unfolding of an already immanent sequence of developmental changes (as for Piaget), or has been crystallized by natural selection into innate schemata for the species as a whole (as for Lorenz), the concept of adaptation is of the essence.

Popper's epistemology, as explicated in *Of Clouds and Clocks*, appears to originate in a double metaphorical act. An individual human being, during the course of his or her psychic development, learns about the world by a series of 'conjectures' and 'refutations', *just like* the body of science learns about reality by throwing up and then throwing out hypotheses. But science develops *just like* organic evolution in which species throw up novelties that are tested and rejected by natural selection.

For Popper, science and nature, the individual and the real world, are each alienated from the other in the same way that classical Darwinism alienated the organism from the environment. Each has its autonomous processes. The external world is in part a fixed reality with eternal laws of nature, but in part evolves by physical processes of cosmic and terrestrial evolution. Suns cool, mountains build, day follows night, and all these are independent of organisms. Living beings, on the other hand, have an autonomous process of variation, the throwing up of novelties, of 'conjectures'. Their generation has no particular connection with external nature, except, of course, that they are manifestations of universal molecular and physical forces. The autonomous variation of organisms and the autonomous states of external nature are then connected to each other by a unidirectional process in which the organism adapts to outer nature by the differential survival of variations. So, too, individual psyches generate conjectural novelties which are then refuted by the outer world.

This scheme has an advantage and a disadvantage for Popper. By assimilating the process of learning to the process of evolution, Popper turns his back on the problem of induction, a problem that lurks constantly behind the scenes in his account of scientific explanation. Philosophy has recognized two problems of epistemology: the problem of discovery and the problem of justification. Popper, in "The Logic of Scientific Discovery", ironically ignores the context of *discovery* and concentrates on justification. For scientific explanation he simply rejects the question of where ideas come from as irrelevant to understanding scientific change. It is enough that ideas appear, whatever the process. But how can he so consistently sidestep the theories of induction or of *a priori* categories, problems treated by Hume and Kant, which have always been regarded as the fundamental issues in epistemology? By asserting that the acquisition of individual knowledge is just like organic evolution in which the generation of novelties by mutation is, in fact, random with respect to the selective process. This assumption is critical in neo-Darwinism and counterposes it to Lamarckist notions that the 'problems' of the environment give rise, in a directed way, to the possible solutions. Indeed, everything that is currently known about the mutational process in organisms supports Darwin. High temperature induces mutation, but not proportionally mutations that are conducive to better survival at high temperatures. In contrast there is nothing at all except the sheer opacity of the problem of induction that would lead us to suppose that a child's hypotheses about the world are generated independently of its experiences of the world. Popper has conveniently converted a metaphysical difficulty into an ontological reality by seizing upon mutations as a metaphor for conjectures.

The disadvantage of the metaphor for Popper is that it demands a mechanism of selection. In Darwinian theory, the sorting out of 'conjectures' is accomplished by differential birth and death rates. But, of course, children do not learn by making fatal mistakes, but by sorting out hypotheses in their heads. Thus, Popper must postulate an 'argumentative function' that is the selective device. Nothing is said about the origin of that 'system of plastic control' or of how it gets its particular shape. He thus avoids the second great problem of epistemology, 'What is the *basis* of judgement?' Popper's evolutionary epistemology fails for the same reason as his account of science, because in both he avoids the real epistemological issues.

Lorenz, unlike Popper, confronts directly the question of the origin and shape of the 'argumentative function'. He takes the Kantian alternative of postulating *a priori* categories, but unlike Kant, supposes that the *ding-an-sich* is knowable and provides a mechanism by which the *a priori* schemata can be brought into conformity with the reality of the *ding-an-sich*. Natural selection, by eliminating individuals whose innate schemata do not conform as well to reality, fixes in each species innate patterns of thought and learning which make the species best adapted to the environment. Popper's problem of finding a force *like* natural selection to serve the function of refutation is thus solved by making natural selection the molder of the mind. The scheme has both an advantage and disadvantage for Lorenz. If our innate schemata are a consequence of evolution, we might expect to see a trace of our ancestry in these schemata. That is, the evolutionary continuity of life suggests some continuity and homology of mental construction between lower animals and humans, a contingency of what humans are on what their ancestors were. Moreover, to the extent that the outer world poses the same 'problems' to the grey lag goose and water-shrew as to human beings, we may expect similarities in their innate schemata. The evolutionary perspective thus allows Lorenz to learn something about human beings by studying geese. It justifies the carry-over from experimental animals to people by asserting not merely analogy but homology of behavior. On the other hand, if innate schemata are really constructed by natural selection, we must expect each species to have its own schemata reflecting its own particular evolutionary 'problems' and their 'solutions'. This means that we cannot in general carry over knowledge of one species to another since adaptation may be specific. So people are not geese after all, and the ethologist has nothing to say about human behavior. If people are like geese in some particulars but not in others, then there is nothing for it but to study people, since we cannot know, *a priori*, in which ways they will be similar to other species by virtue of general adaptation and in which way they will differ because of specific adaptation. A reminder of how difficult species comparisons can be comes from different species of passerine birds, all more closely related to each other than we are to our nearest living non-human relatives. Some species know their songs from birth, some will only sing them if coached, and some will sing any bird song they hear.

The metaphor of adaptation is both more complex and more restricted in its role in the epistemology of Piaget than it is for Popper or Lorenz. In the older psychological tradition, Piaget cannot escape from embryological notions of developmental stages through which we must pass to adulthood, and of the unfolding of stages according to an inbuilt organizational principle. Evolutionary theory in general no longer incorporates notions of progress or of unidirectional change. Evolution, at least in the modern view, is going nowhere in particular. Older ideas that evolution has led and is leading to greater complexity, greater homeostasis, greater stability, are now seen as vestiges of a 19th century progressivism that is without empirical foundation in the history of life. Piaget, however, like Freud, continues the metaphor of unfolding but embeds in it trial-and-error as a motive force. We move from Piagetian stage to Piagetian stage by a successful solution of the problems posed by the external world. There are not so much specific challenges as there are demands on our modes of conceptualization of space, time, matter, other human beings, physical, historical and social necessity.

Piaget is also the intellectual inheritor of another pre-Darwinian tradition, that of Lamarck. The metaphor of mutation implies an autonomy of the generation of conjectures from the environment to which there are potential responses. In an effort to establish a functional connection between the environment and the appearance of variation among organisms, Piaget fastens his attention on the phenomenon of 'genetic assimilation' first observed by Waddington (see Chapter 10 of this volume) and later much more extensively analyzed and illuminated by the experimental work of J. M. Rendel. Characters that do not normally vary in development within the usual range of environment can be caused to show individual variation by subjecting the embryo to an unusual environmental stress. So, a high temperature shock in *Drosophila* will cause a certain proportion of the adult flies to have abnormal wing vein patterns, while in the normal temperature range for development the wing veins are identical in all individuals. Moreover, different genotypes in the population have different probabilities of responding to the environmental stress. So, by breeding only from individuals that produce altered wing vein patterns after heat shock, the proportion of affected individuals increases each generation, as does the intensity of the effect, because more and more sensitive genotypes are being accumulated in the population. It turns out that genotypes that are highly sensitive to the environmental stress also have some probability of producing the abnormal wing vein pattern even in the absence of the stress. As a consequence, as the selection proceeds, more and more of the population shows the new wing pattern even under normal temperatures, and a population composition is finally arrived at where all individuals have the new pattern in the old environment. An environmentally induced pattern has become genetically 'assimilated' into the population. There is, of course, nothing Lamarckian about the process, which depends entirely on the fact that genotypes developmentally more sensitive to the shock also have the property that their development may be abnormal even in the absence of the shock.

There are two problems in basing a view of the origin of variation on the phenomenon of genetic assimilation. First, although the phenomenon definitely exists, it is not at all clear that it is a frequent process in evolution. Most characters of organisms show some genetic variation in most environments so that selection can work directly on that variation. Only for invariant species characters that are highly canalized in their development is environmentally induced variation so critical in revealing the underlying genetic variation. That genetic variation itself was produced of course by an autonomous mutation process. The role of environmental variation has been to reveal the variation at the phenotypic level by stressing the development beyond its usual capacity for self-regulation. Second, there is little experimental evidence to support the assimilation of *adaptive* responses. The appearance of abnormal wing vein patterns as a response to heat shock, or of extra thoracic structure in response to ether treatment of eggs in *Drosophila*, are not what one usually thinks of as *adaptation*. They are, like mutation, random with respect to the quality of the environmental challenge. The appearance of physiological heat resistance would be an adaptive response. We have no evidence that such resistance can be assimilated, although, in principle, there is no reason why it should not. Further, it is not clear under what circumstances natural selection would favor genotypes that give a certain pattern unconditionally when, after all, the pattern is advantageous only in certain conditions. Take, for example, the development of callus pads on the feet and hands. The production of such calluses is an adaptive developmental response to friction and abrasion. Since the development of such calluses is a painful process, as I learn each summer when I take up manual labor after a winter of idleness, and may even lead to infection, it would seem advantageous to be born with callus tissue. Since *Homo sapiens* walked barefoot for nearly all of its evolutionary history, we might expect assimilation to have occurred at least on the soles of our feet. But it has not to any effective extent. People who walk barefoot their entire lives on rough surfaces develop immensely thick sole calluses as compared with the tender feet of the shod. Callus formation has remained essentially a facultative response, although a slight thickening is observed even in the newborn. Unless the reproductive cost of somatic plasticity is high compared to the benefits that accrue, facultative adaptive responses are likely to remain facultative rather than being assimilated inflexibly into development. An organism should profit from history but not be burdened by it. Assimilation is one of the processes of evolution. It is not a model for the whole (see Chapter 11 for further comment on this issue).

Whatever their differences, all evolutionary epistemologists are united in their view of the relation between organism and environment. The environment is something autonomous, 'out there', that appears to the organism as a challenge or problem that must be solved. Adaptation is the process of reconstituting the organism to fit the environment. Adaptation may be based on autonomously generated novelties, as in the strict Darwinism of Lorenz and Popper, or it may be a directed pseudo-Lamarckian response as for Piaget, but it is always the organism that responds to the environment and not vice versa. Yet our understanding of the real history of organisms has shown us that the asymmetric picture is untrue. Organisms construct and reconstruct their environments, not just in their own heads as Piaget would allow, but in reality, 'out there'. That is not to say that organisms can do just anything. Their construction and reconstruction of their environments is constrained by what they already are. Thrushes may use stones to break snail shells, but they will never, as long as their remote offspring remain birds, build houses from stones or chisel inventory lists into them. The reconstruction of the environment that organisms accomplish during their evolution is a quasi-continuous process with the new environment in the neighborhood of the old one in environment space. *Natura non facit saltus* is a statement not only about the shapes of organisms but about the evolution of the environments that the organisms define. Also, of course, the reconstruction of environment must be in accordance with certain natural relationships. Human beings cannot keep the sun from cooling or the universe from expanding. There are no perpetual motion machines. But there is more than one way to skin a cat. An epistemology based solely in a process of accommodation of the individual to a fixed reality cannot cope with real invention. Piaget accepts the Gordian knot on its own terms. Alexander had superior knowledge.

The fact that there are physical and historical constraints on what organisms can do should not mislead us into making facile assertions about what is possible. Life is hierarchically organized. Molecules are arranged in organelles, organelles in cells, cells in organisms, organisms in social interactions. At each level there are constraints, but these constraints are not, in general, translated into constraints on the next higher level. This is most strikingly true when we consider social organization. Far from being limited by individual constraints, social organization is the negation of those constraints, and it is tempting to regard human social organization as having arisen historically precisely for that reason. No individual can fly by flapping her or his arms. That is a revelation of certain 'laws of nature'. But people do fly as a consequence of the existence of airplanes, pilots, radios, fuel, and airports, all of which are social products. No individual can remember more than a few facts, but printing, libraries, computers, data banks, all artifacts of social organization, negate the feebleness of our individual memories. Yet it is not 'society' that flies or reads books, but individuals. In this way, social organization and individual life interpenetrate each other. Social knowledge is both the product and the provider of individual knowledge.

There are four ways in which the problem of knowing can be framed. In the first, the question is 'How do individuals learn about the real world?' and this seems to be the problem as Popper sees it. The second is 'How do individuals form a picture of the world and what is the relation, if any, of that picture to the world of objects?' This might be called the 'Plato–Hume–Kant problem' and I take it to be the problematic of the mainstream of western epistemologic investigation since the Greeks. It is the problem to which Lorenz and Piaget address themselves. The third form of the epistemologic problematic might be called 'Marx's problem' and that is 'How is the picture of the world formed by, and how does it, in turn, form the real world?' Mainstream epistemology had previously been concerned only with the influence of the objects of thought on the subjects of thought. Marx's major break with the history of epistemology is precisely parallel to his redirection of the problematic of economics in *Capital*, where he shifts from the classical concern with the exchange process to a concern with the production process.

Finally, there is an epistemological problematic, dialectical as is Marx's, but explicitly incorporating social existence. It might be called 'Levi-Strauss's problem'. 'How does an individual's picture of the world emerge in a social context and, reciprocally, how are shared views of reality altered by individual knowledge?' It is the problem of the social construction of reality. Epistemology has classically been concerned with the way in which individual human beings seem all to come to a common universal knowledge of the outer world. The social construction problem, on the contrary, asks how at different times and in different places, reality and the knowledge of it are formed in different ways in different societies. How is it that in some societies individuals believing that they have aural, tactile, and visual knowledge of spirits can actually die at their hands? How do we come to be able to differentiate among thousands of faces of our own race, but find that all of 'them' look alike? Such a social problematic can be made formally equivalent to the usual question of how a developing individual learns about external reality, by equating social convention with that reality, but only formally. In fact, it redirects inquiry. Most, if not all, of the experiments Piaget has done with children become irrelevant, as do all the famous experiments in experimental epistemology on the blind who regain their sight. They are simply asking questions about a different kind of knowledge. The question of how we come to see 'sharp' and 'round' is different from how 'we' come to know how to make an atomic bomb, or how Giotto's contemporaries could find his paintings so life-like as to confound the senses while we find them stereotyped and wooden.

The fundamental error of evolutionary epistemologies as they now exist is their failure to understand how much of what is 'out there' is the product of what is 'in here'. Organism and environment are co-determined. Piaget is correct that wishing will not make it so. But, although desire and will are not sufficient to alter the world, they are necessary. As Marx pointed out in the second thesis on Feuerbach, 'The materialist doctrine that men are the product of circumstances and upbringing...forgets that it is men that change circumstances.' The one-sidedness of evolutionary epistemology is nowhere better displayed than in Piaget's description of maturation:

> Adolescent egocentricity is manifested by a belief in the omnipotence of reflection, as though the world should submit itself to idealistic schemes rather than to systems of reality....
>
> Equilibrium is attained when the adolescent understands that the proper function of reflection is not to contradict but to predict and interpret experience. (Piaget, 1967, pp. 63–64)

To which I can only reply: 'The philosophers have only interpreted the world in various ways; the point, however, is to change it.'

REFERENCES

Dawkins, R. (1976). *The Selfish Gene*, Oxford University Press, London.

Dunnell, R. C. (1978). Evolutionary Theory of Archeology (unpublished manuscript).

Moorhead, P. S., and Kaplan, M. M. (eds) (1967). *Mathematical Challenges to the Neo-Darwinian Interpretation of Evolution*, Weston Institution Press, Philadelphia.

Piaget, J. (1967). *Six psychological studies*, Random House, New York.

Popper, K. R. (1959). *The Logic of Scientific Discovery*, Basic Books, New York.

Turbayne, C. M. (1962). *The Myth of Metaphor*, Yale University Press, New Haven.

Wilson, E. O. (1975). *Sociobiology, The New Synthesis*, Belknap Press of the Harvard University Press, Cambridge.

Evolution, behaviour and socio-culture

Waddington observed that genetic replication is an insufficient basis for a theory of evolution. He held that it is the active and interactive nature of living things that makes life 'interesting'. As a way of emphasizing his point, Waddington referred to phenotypes as 'operators'. Recently, Hull has raised similar issues by pointing out that to replicator selection must be added the concepts of 'interactors' and 'lineages'. One of the ways by which phenotypes operate on and interact with their environments is through that special set of traits that we call behaviour. Waddington assigned active (i.e. causal) status to behaviour which, within his scheme, he called the exploitive system. In this way Waddington was the only major evolutionary theorist to ascribe such a role to behaviour. Another contribution made by Waddington was genetic assimilation. That the latter occurs is not in doubt now. Its role in evolution is, however, open to question. In his 1966 book, Williams considered this point and it is reprinted here along with his current thoughts on the matter that he asked to have added to the 1966 extract. It should be noted that genetic assimilation is raised again in the next section by Ho and Saunders where they present a quite different approach to Williams.

The kind of re-appraisal that is now occurring in evolutionary theory is exemplified by Hailman's contribution. Unconvinced by the neo-Darwinian explanation for the role of natural selection as a causal agent in a number of evolutionary phenomena, Hailman examines alternative accounts of phylogeny, speciation and adaptation. He also scrutinizes some of the evidence for the existence of selection and finds it lacking in many important respects. This is a serious challenge to neo-Darwinism. Natural selection has been at the centre of evolutionary theory ever since the Darwinian thesis was formulated. Why, then, after 120 years is it so difficult to point to evidence for its existence? Is it possible that this is a case of an essentially 'correct' theoretical construct being difficult to match with appropriate data? Or is it more likely that there is something wrong with the idea of natural selection?

There is, of course, no question that behaviour and psychological processes have evolved, including those that are essential to socio-culture. Why socio-culture evolved, how, and what the appropriate conceptual framework for analysing the biology of socio-culture is, are as much a part of a general theory of evolution as are any other issues in evolutionary biology. One approach to these problems is genetic reductionism, the central tenet of which is that evolution occurs because genes have to maintain their continuity in time. The concepts of inclusive fitness and genetic kinship have been used by radical sociobiologists to account for the evolution of social behaviour and culture. The latter are 'caused' by inclusive fitness, that is, by the action of identical alleles operating in different animals in order to maintain their existence. Baylis and Halpin call this kind of thinking into question: 'Much sociobiology commits the error of assuming that a correlation of relatedness with sociality implies a causal relationship' (Baylis, personal communication). It does not, of course, and the direction of causality that Baylis and Halpin suggest is the opposite to that of radical sociobiology: life-history phenomena (including behaviour) in sexually reproducing animals leads to (causes) certain kinds of social groupings, and the latter then show genetic relatedness. This is the opposite of arguing that genes working through inclusive fitness cause the social group and its accompanying behaviours to evolve, and is an important alternative to accepted sociobiological thinking. Baylis and Halpin also supply a framework for field behavioural studies that is, by definition, lacking in genetic reductionist approaches to social behaviour.

Hull's chapter is an analysis of socio-culture within the wider purview of evolutionary epistemology. What kinds of entities evolve? Are the characteristics of biological evolution found in cultural evolution? The sustained contrast provided by Hull between biological and cultural evolution points up analogies and disanalogies between the two which are sometimes unexpected. Above all, Hull takes a hard look at the supposed Lamarckian nature of socio-cultural evolution and he finds it wanting. Disanalogies between biological and cultural evolution there are, but they are not centred around the distinction between Darwinian and Lamarckian modes of evolution. One of the reasons why evolutionary epistemology will succeed in showing the way towards a general theory in biology is because it does not consign socio-culture to simple genetic causation. Culture is perhaps the most complex phenomenon in biology. If we are going to understand it from a biological point of view then, as Hull points out, we are going to have to use every resource available to us.

Learning, Development, and Culture
Edited by H. C. Plotkin
© 1982, John Wiley & Sons Ltd.

CHAPTER 10

Evolutionary adaptation

C. H. Waddington*

The subject of this paper is the origin of adaptation, still an issue one hundred years after Darwin, and recently characterized by George Gaylord Simpson as the 'primary problem of evolutionary biology' (Roe and Simpson, 1958).

The assemblage of life-sciences that are usually classed together as 'biology' form a group at least as complex and diversified as the whole group of the physical sciences. Within this enormous range one can discern three main foci toward which the individual sciences tend to be oriented. One of these is analytical biology—the attempt to determine the ultimate constituent units upon which the character of living things depend. Analytical biology investigates development and heredity through the analysis of genes and subgenic units and so to the macrochemical entities such as DNA, RNA, and protein of the chromosomes. The whole group of such studies plays the same role in the biological field as does atomic physics in the physical sciences.

Another major focus of interest is what may be called 'physiological biology'—the study of the mechanisms by which organisms carry on their existence. This corresponds perhaps to chemistry and engineering in the physical role.

Finally, there is what may be called 'synthetic biology', which is concerned with providing an intellectually coherent picture of the whole realm of living

* Reprinted from *The Evolution of Life*, volume one in the trilogy, *Evolution after Darwin*, Sol Tax (Ed.), 1960, pp. 381–402, by permission of The University of Chicago Press. Copyright © by The University of Chicago.

matter. In the structure of biology this fulfils the same role as cosmology does in the physical sciences; and just as in the physical realm we find that cosmology and atomic physics have very close connections with one another, so in biology the analytical and synthetic approaches to the world of the living employ very similar concepts.

In the hundred years since Darwin wrote, it has become universally accepted that the only synthetic biological theory which needs serious consideration is that of evolution. In an appraisal of evolutionary biology as it stands now in this centenary year, it is perhaps well to begin by reminding ourselves of the fundamental reasons for mankind's interest in this subject. During the century of intensive work which has been devoted to its study, so many detailed problems have emerged which have a great fascination of their own that one is sometimes inclined to be carried away by enthusiasm for these puzzles; however, they are really attractive only to those who have already taken their first steps toward this direction of study. The enormous impact of Darwin's theories on the whole intellectual life of his own day—and, indeed, on that of all later generations— arose not from details but from the relevance of the broad outline of his thinking to one of the major problems with which mankind is faced.

That problem is presented by the appearance of design in the organic world. Animals and plants in their innumerable variety present, of course, many odd, striking, and even beautiful features, which can raise feelings of surprise and delight in the observer. But over and above this, a very large number of them give the appearance of being astonishingly well tailored to fit precisely into the requirements which will be made of them by their mode of existence. Fish are admirably designed for swimming, birds for flying, horses for running, snakes for creeping, and so on, and the correspondence between what an organism will do and the way it is formed to carry out such tasks often extends into extraordinary detail.

It is clear from the oldest literatures that man has always been impressed by this correspondence. The simplest explanation—and the one almost universally accepted in prescientific times—is that this appearance reflects the activities of an intelligent Being who has designed each type of animal and plant in a way suitable for carrying out the functions assigned to it. It is the challenge presented to this explanation that constitutes the major interest of the theory of evolution. A really convincing alternative account of the origin of biological adaptation is the major demand which must be made of it.

The essential feature of an evolutionary theory is the suggestion that animals and plants, as we see them exhibiting an apparently designed adaptedness at the present day, have been brought to their present condition by a process extending through time and were not designed in their modern form. This does not, as many of Darwin's contemporaries thought it did, necessarily deny the existence of any form of intelligent designer. It means only that any designing activity there may be has operated through a process extending over long periods of time and has not brought suddenly into being each of the biological forms as we now see them. The question of theism or atheism, which played such a large part in the public discussions of Darwin's day, is, we now recognize, not critically answered by the acceptance or rejection of an evolutionary hypothesis but must be settled—if it ever can be—in some other way. We need not, therefore, be further concerned with it in this discussion.

Evolutionary theories had, of course, been put forward some time before Darwin wrote *Origin of Species*. The most famous of these earlier discussions is that associated with the name of Lamarck. It has suffered a most surprising fate. Lamarck is the only major figure in the history of biology whose name has become, to all intents and purposes, a term of abuse. Most scientists' contributions are fated to be outgrown, but very few authors have written works which, two centuries later, are still rejected with an indignation so intense that the sceptic may suspect something akin to an uneasy conscience. In point of fact, Lamarck has, I think, been somewhat unfairly judged.

Lamarck's theory involved two main parts, and each of these has encountered some essentially spurious difficulties in gaining acceptance. The first part supposed that the initial step toward an evolutionary advance involves something which Lamarck characterised as an act of will. Clearly, in this form the postulate applies only to animals and not to plants. Lamarck was, I take it, suggesting that the organism's own behaviour is involved in determining the nature of the environmental situation in which it will develop and to which its offspring will become adapted. In this form his theory could perhaps be generalized to cover the plant kingdom also if one accepts a wide enough definition of the concept of behaviour. However, let us leave that on one side: Lamarck himself was concerned primarily with animal evolution.

Now a concept such as an act of will was for a long time very unfashionable in the scientific study of biology. It is only relatively recently that biologists have shown any confidence in tackling the problems presented by the study of animal behaviour. Most students of behaviour still avoid such terms as 'act of will', but the concept of a choice between alternative modes of behaviour or conditions of life is by now quite respectable, and one must make allowances for the terminology used by someone writing in the eighteenth century.

If a certain sympathy is shown in interpreting Lamarck's words, the second phase of his theory also appears less unacceptable than it is usually considered to be. This is the well-known hypothesis of the inheritance of acquired characters. Conventionally at the present time this is interpreted as though Lamarck used the word 'inheritance' as we should now use it, that is to say, to mean transmission of a character from a pair of parents to their offspring in the next or immediately subsequent generation. But, at the time Lamarck wrote, no distinction had yet been made between heredity over one or two generations, as we study it in genetical experiments, and heredity over much longer periods of time, as we encounter it in evolution. Nor was there any discrimination between the genetics of individuals and what we now call 'population genetics'. Lamarck's theory could quite well be interpreted to mean not that an individual organism which acquires a character during its lifetime will tend to transmit this to its immediate offspring, but that, if members of a population of animals undergoing evolution in nature acquire a character during their lifetime, this character will tend to appear more frequently in members of a derived population many generations later. In this form it is not so easy to reject his view. In fact, in a later part of this lecture I shall produce some evidence in favour of it.

Lamarck's words were, however, not interpreted in the way that I have suggested. His postulated 'act of will' was rejected as something vitalistic and non-scientific. His doctrine of the inheritance of acquired characters was interpreted in terms of individual genetics and not population genetics. Even with this interpretation it has frequently been accepted by comparative anatomists and naturalists as providing the simplest explanation for the occurrences which they can observe in the natural world. However, practically all experimentalists have rejected it. I need not summarise the well-known experiments which have failed to demonstrate an effect of environmental conditions on the hereditary qualities which are passed on from parent to offspring.

In quite recent years the situation has changed somewhat. We have now obtained abundant evidence of the induction of hereditary changes—in the form of gene mutations, chromosome aberrations, etc.—by external agents such as ionising radiation and highly reactive chemicals. But these changes are non-directional; and induced mutagenesis as we normally encounter it in the laboratory does not provide any mechanism by which relatively normal environments could induce hereditary changes which would improve the adaptation of the offspring to the inducing conditions. Directional hereditary changes have, indeed, also been induced, but, so far, only in very simple systems such as bacteria, and by the use of highly specific inducing agents—for instance, the transforming principles. A more general mechanism of biological alteration, which does not depend on such exceptional inducing agents, is the induction of the synthesis of specific enzymes related to particular substrates. The changes produced in enzyme induction are for the most part not hereditarily transmissible, but it seems in principle not inconceivable that under suitable conditions actual gene mutations could be induced by some such mechanism.

Finally, one should notice some recent evidence which has been produced to support the hypothesis that variations of the normal environment may in some cases induce hereditarily transmissible changes. This evidence relates largely to plants, and most of it has emanated from Russia and is regarded with considerable scepticism in other countries, where attempts to repeat the experiments have been rather uniformly unsuccessful. Nevertheless, evidence of a not entirely dissimilar character has begun to appear in Western countries also—for instance, in the studies of Durrant (1958) on the hereditary transmission of the effects of manurial treatment of flax, the work of Highkin (1958) on the effects of alternating temperature on peas, and a few others. It is not clear in any of these cases that the hereditary effects produced, if any, are of a kind that improves the adaptation of the organism to the inducing conditions. The field of work is clearly one of great inherent interest, but it remains true that the vast majority of changes in the environment do not directly produce any hereditary modifications in the organisms subjected to them, and we are certainly very far from being able to provide a general explanation of evolutionary adaptations in terms of the type of effects which have just been mentioned.

The development of evolutionary theory in the last hundred years has in fact proceeded along quite other lines. Darwin's major contribution was, of course, the suggestion that evolution can be explained by the natural selection of random variations. Natural selection, which was at first considered as though it were a hypothesis that was in need of experimental or observational confirmation, turns out on closer inspection to be a tautology, a statement of an inevitable although previously unrecognized relation. It states that the fittest individuals in a population (defined as those which leave most offspring) will leave most offspring. Once the statement is made, its truth is apparent. This fact in no way reduces the magnitude of Darwin's achievement; only after it was clearly formulated, could biologists realise the enormous power of the principle as a weapon of explanation. However, his theory required a second component—namely, a process by which random hereditary variation would be produced. This he was unable himself to provide, since the phenomena of biological heredity were in his day very little understood. With the rise of Mendelism, the lacuna was made good. Heredity depends on chromosomal genes, and these are found in fact to behave as the theory requires, altering occasionally at unpredictable times and in ways which produce a large, and, it is usually stated, 'random' variety of characters in the offspring bearing the altered genes. On these two foundations—natural selection operating on variation which arises from the random mutation of Mendelian genes—the present-day neo-Darwinist or 'synthetic' theory of evolution has been built up.

This theory has brought very great advances in our understanding of the genetic situation in populations as they exist in nature, of the ways these genetic systems may change, and of the differences between local races or between closely related species. The question discussed in this paper is the adequacy of its treatment of the major problem of the 'appearance of design', or biological adaptation. In dealing with this problem, neo-Mendelian theory relies essentially on the hypothesis that genes mutate at random; that is to say, if one waits long enough, an appropriate gene mutation will occur which will modify the phenotypic appearance of the organism in any conceivable way that may be required. It is pointed out that, however rare such a mutation may be, the mechanism of natural selection is eminently efficient at engendering states of high improbability, so that, from rare and entirely chance occurrences, an appearance of precisely calculated design may be produced.

This explanation is a very powerful one. It could, in fact, explain anything. And there is no denying that the processes which it invokes—random gene mutation and natural selection—actually take place. I should not dream of denying it—as far as it goes—but I wish to argue that it does not go far enough. It involves certain drastic simplifications which are liable to lead us to a false picture of how the evolutionary process works, whereas, if we take into account certain factors which have been omitted from the conventional picture, we shall not only be closer to the situation as it exists in nature but will find ourselves with a more convincing explanation of how the appearance of design comes about.

Let us consider some examples of the type of biological adaptedness which we are trying to understand. In many cases in which we speak of an animal as being adapted, the adaptation is comparatively trivial and its precise character is not critical. As an example, one may take the phenomenon of industrial melanism in Lepidoptera, which is one of the best-studied examples of natural selection in the field. In industrial areas of Great Britain several species of moths which a century ago most commonly appeared in fairly light-coloured forms have in recent years shown increasing numbers of dark melanic varieties; in several instances these have now become by far the most common type in regions contaminated by industrial fumes. A typical region where this replacement of light by dark forms has occurred has earned the nickname 'The Black Country'. It was natural to suppose that the blackening of the moth is connected with the darkening of the general vegetation by contamination with industrial smoke.

One of the earliest investigatiors to examine the subject in some detail was Heslop-Harrison (1920). He held somewhat Lamarckian views about the origin of the melanic form and, indeed, claimed at one time to show that it could be induced by feeding larvae on leaves which had been contaminated by various metallic salts. This claim has not found general acceptance in later years. However, Heslop-Harrison also made a further and more important contribution to the subject. He demonstrated that natural selection operates differentially on dark and light forms of the moth *Oporabia autumnata*, the melanics being favoured in regions with a dark background whereas the light forms were favoured in the presence of light-coloured vegetation. He was able to show this with particular clearness by studying a wood in which one section had been separated in about 1800 by the cutting of a wide gap, later grown up with heather. A considerable number of years later, in 1885, the southern section of the wood was planted with light-coloured birch trees, while in the northern portion nearly all the trees were dark pines. By 1907 the population of moths in the two sections of the wood showed a quite different proportion of dark to light forms. In the birch part of the wood only 15 per cent were melanics; in the pine section about 96 per cent were dark. Moreover, Heslop-Harrison showed that in the dark pinewood section, where by far the majority of the moths were melanics, the majority of the wings found isolated on the ground—representing remnants left after the insect's body had been eaten by a predator—were actually light. Thus it was clear that the pale-coloured forms were at a disadvantage in the dark wood.

A similar situation has been re-examined in a much more thorough form quite recently by Kettlewell (1955). He found that the predation is in this case, at least to a large extent, carried out by birds, and he has been able to demonstrate very clearly the reality of the natural selective advantage enjoyed by an insect which blends reasonably well with its background. We have here, then, a well-studied example of an evolutionary process in which a species acquires a characteristic—namely, melanism—which can be considered to adapt it to its surroundings. However, in this example the adaptive character is of the very simplest kind. It is a mere darkening of the wings, and it does not seem at all likely that the precise pattern in which the blackening is laid down can have any great importance. The effective change probably involves nothing more elaborate than a markedly increased production of the melanic pigment. It is perhaps satisfying enough in such a case to attribute the appearance of the relevant new hereditary variation simply to a random gene mutation.

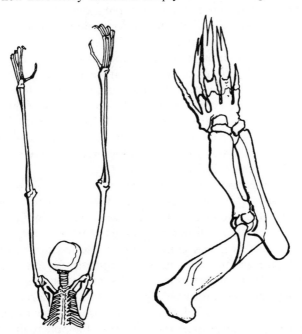

Figure 1 The skeleton forelimbs of a gibbon (*left*) and of a pangolin

But the adaptations which have tempted man to think of design are rather more far-reaching. For instance, Figure 1 shows the skeleton forelimbs of a gibbon and a pangolin. The former uses its arms for climbing in trees, the latter for digging in hard soil. The limb bones are very precisely modeled in relation to the functions they will carry out, and the difference between them involves something more than a simple over-all change comparable to the blackening of a moth's wing. A mere lengthening of the pangolin's arm would not turn it into that of a gibbon. We are dealing here with a precise set of carefully co-ordinated changes involving several different bones of the limb and the shoulder girdle. Now we know that during the lifetime of any single individual the use of the limb muscles in a particular way will increase the size and strength of those muscles, and if the operations take place early enough, they have some effects on the associated bony structures, these effects being of a co-ordinated kind, such as those which distinguish the two forelimbs illustrated. In conventional neo-Mendelian theory, these effects of the use of an organ, exerted during the organism's own lifetime, are dismissed as irrelevant to the evolutionary process. They are 'acquired characters' and are not genetically inherited. Insofar as the individual exhibits them, his phenotype is likely to deceive us as to the characters which he will pass on to his offspring. The acquired characters act, the neo-Mendelian theory asserts, merely as genetic 'noise', in the information-theory sense of that term. We have to find the explanation for such evolutionary changes in random gene mutations, to whose occurrence the physiological processes which lead to the formation of adaptive ontogenetic changes are completely irrelevant.

However, that explanation leaves us with two major points on which we may feel some lack of satisfaction. One is that we have no specific explanation for the co-ordinated nature of the changes as they affect the different bones or other subunits in the system. Can we do no better than fall back on the very general explanation in terms of the efficiency of natural selection in engendering highly improbable states? Since we see similar co-ordinated changes being produced by physiological adaptation within a lifetime, this highly abstract principle seems a little inadequate.

Second, we are bound, both for practical reasons and on the basis of fundamental theory, to regard all forms, functions and activities of an organism as the joint product of its hereditary constitution and its environmental circumstances; the exclusion of acquired characters from all parts in the evolutionary process does less than justice to the incontrovertible fact that they exhibit some of the hereditary potentialities of the organism. All characters of all organisms are, after all, to some extent acquired characters, in the sense that the environment has played some role during their development. Similarly, all characters of all organisms are to some extent hereditary, in the sense that they are expressions of some of the potentialities with which the organism is endowed by its genetic constitution.

This point is one which has only recently forced itself firmly into the attention of geneticists, perhaps largely through current interest in characters to whose variation hereditary differences contribute only a small fraction, such as the milk yield of cattle. It is still not always kept in mind in all contexts in which it is relevant, and in the earlier days of genetics it was very frequently ignored. To take a relevant example from the very early years of this century, Baldwin and Lloyd Morgan pointed out that a capacity for carrying out adaptive changes during their lifetimes might enable organisms to survive in environments in which they would otherwise be inviable and that they could in this way exist until a suitable hereditary variation occurred which could be seized upon by natural selection and enable a genuine-evolutionary adaptation to take place. They did not point out that there was any hereditary variation in the capacity for forming such ontogenetic adaptations. Mayr, writing in 1958, actually describes their view as 'the hypothesis that a non-genetic plasticity of the phenotype facilitates reconstruction of the genotype.' But a plasticity of the phenotype *cannot* be 'non-genetic'; it *must* have a genetic basis, since it must be an expression of genetically transmitted potentialities. It is conceivable, of course, that in any given population there will be no genetic variation in the determinants of this plasticity, but our experience of natural populations shows that this is a very unlikely state of affairs. When wild populations have been investigated, they have, I think, always exhibited some genetic variation in respect of any character that has been studied.

There is actually no need to rely on purely a priori arguments in this respect. Experiments have recently been made in which *Drosophila* populations were searched for the presence of genetic variation in the capacity to respond by ontogenetic alterations to the stimuli produced by various abnormal environments, and the effectiveness of selection on this genetic variation was studied. Both the characters involved and the environmental stimuli applied were of rather diverse kinds in the different experiments in the series, but in all cases genetic variation in capacity to response, utilisable by selection, was revealed.

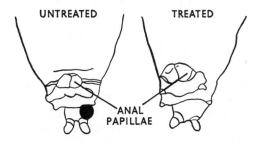

Figure 2 Outline drawings of the anal papillae of 'Oregon K' *Drosophila* larvae representing extreme variants in size, the larger from a selected strain grown on a medium with 7 per cent salt added, the smaller from an unselected strain grown on normal medium with no added salt

Perhaps the simplest of these experiments was actually the last to be performed (Waddington, 1959). It attempted to bring about the adaptation of a population of *Drosophila* to a high concentration of sodium chloride in the medium in which the larvae live. The larvae possess anal papillae on either side of the anus (Figure 2), and these are known to play some part in regulating the osmotic pressure of the body fluids (Gloor and Chen, 1950). The size of the papillae can be measured most accurately just after pupation when the hardening of the puparial skin prevents distortion by the muscular movements of the body. Three stocks were employed. One was a wild-type 'Oregon K'; the other two, sp^2 bs^2 and al b c sp^2, each contained the gene speck in which the anal area is pigmented in the pupa, making it somewhat easier to see the anal papillae. From the Oregon wild-type stock two selected lines were set up, known as 'Oregon L' and 'Oregon E', while for each of the other two stocks one selected line was maintained. These selected lines were carried on by growing the larvae of each generation on normal *Drosophila* medium to which various concentrations of sodium chloride had been added, the concentrations being adjusted so that only 20–30 per cent of the eggs laid on the medium survived to the adult condition. No artificial selection was made, the selection pressure being entirely the natural selection exerted by the stringent medium.

After 21 generations of selection in this way, the survival of the various strains on different concentrations of salt was tested and the mean size of the anal papillae estimated by measurements on 20 individuals from each culture at each concentrations of salt (Figure 3). The selected stocks became somewhat more tolerant of high salt concentration, though the difference was not very great. However, there is no doubt that some genetic variability exists in the capacity of the animals to adapt themselves to the environmental stress and that this genetic variability has been utilisable by the natural selection employed.

A number of further deductions can be made from Figure 3. In the first place, it is clear that the size of the anal papillae tends to increase with increasing concentration of salt in the medium, although the effect is rather slight until the concentration reaches a high level. For any one stock the curve relating size of papillae to the salt concentration gives a picture of a physiological function which we might call its 'adaptability'. By a comparison of the selected stocks with the corresponding unselected ones, it is clear that two things happen to these curves of adaptability. In the first place, their steepness increases and to some extent their general shape changes; that is to say, the selection favours, as might be expected, those genotypes which endow the individual with a relatively high capacity to carry out an ontogenetic adaptation to the stress of high salt content. Second, the general level of the curves is raised. One might refer to this general level as the 'level of adaptation to high salt content'; we can say, therefore, that the level of adaptation has been increased. A third and perhaps most important point is that the anal papillae in the selected races remain larger, even at low salt content, than the papillae of the unselected

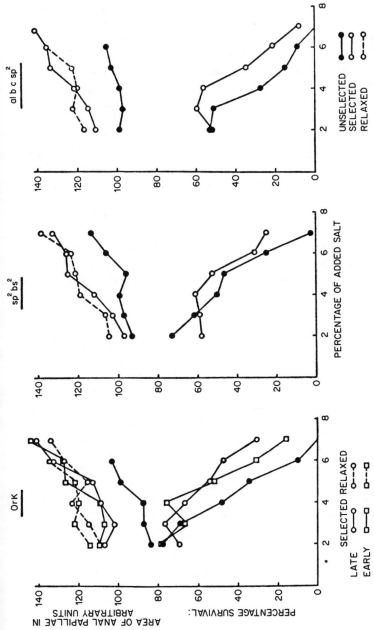

Figure 3 Selected and unselected strains in three stocks of *D. melanogaster*, in relation to the salt content of the larval medium. *Above*, the size of the anal papillae at various concentrations, in units derived from micrometer measurements. *Below*, the percentage of adults appearing from a given number of eggs. For the wild-type stock, two selected strains were prepared, one selected also for early emergence and the other for late. The papillae of the selected stocks were measured both in larvae derived from parents grown in the selection-medium (7 per cent added salt) and in 'relaxed' lines in which there had been one generation on normal medium between the end of the selection and the setting-out of larvae on the various concentrations

strains at the same concentration. The adaptation to high salt content which has been produced by 21 generations of selection is not immediately reversible by 1 or 2 generations in the normal medium. In the botanical terminology employed by Turesson (1930), the ecotype which has been produced in relation to high salt concentration is to some extent an ecogenotype. The character of the adapted strain depends, of course, on its genotype, as all characters of all strains do, but the point to notice is that the genetic difference between the selected and unselected strains is expressed also in the normal low salt medium. We have obtained a result which is effectively the same as would have resulted from the direct inheritance of acquired characters but which has been produced, not by the mechanisms which are usually thought of in connection with Lamarck's hypothesis, but by a population-genetical mechanism which involves selection.

The failure of the selected strains when grown in normal medium to revert completely to the condition of the unselected strains must depend on a certain inflexibility of their developmental processes. Although their adaptability becomes higher, as we have seen, it is not large enough to allow the anal organs to regress completely on the low salt medium. Such lack of flexibility in the developmental system has been referred to as 'canalisation' (Waddington, 1940, 1942).

It is sometimes useful to discuss development in terms of a diagram in which the course of normal development is represented as the bottom of a valley, the sides of which symbolise the opposition that the system presents to any stresses which attempt to deflect development from its normal course. A cross-section of the valley represents, in fact, the curve that we have defined as the adaptability of the system, with the minor modification that the scale on which the stress is represented is reversed as between the two sides of the valley, so that it measures divergencies from the normal—below it on one side or above it on

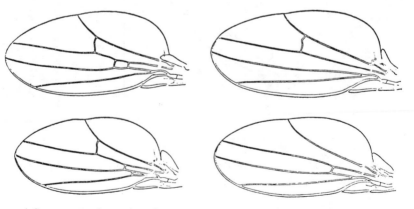

Figure 4 Some types of venation phenocopies induced by a heat stock to the 18-hr pupa in *D. melanogaster* (Bateman, 1956)

the other. The surface which in this way symbolizes the developmental potentialities of the genotype has been called the 'epigenetic landscape'.

This diagrammatic form of representation is particularly appropriate for discussing certain points which emerge from some other *Drosophila* experiments. In these, quite abnormal environmental stresses were applied to the developing system, and artificial selection was made for certain categories of response. Although both the stresses and the selection were artificial, these experiments reveal a type of process which might well go on in natural populations under the influence of natural stresses and natural selection.

In the first experiment (Waddington, 1953; Bateman, 1956), heat shock was applied to pupae of an age which was known to be suitable for producing a number of phenocopies affecting the cross-veins. In point of fact, several different phenocopies appeared, involving absence of one or another of the cross-veins or in some cases increase in venation (Figure 4). If selection was exercised for any specific one of these types of phenocopy, strains could be rapidly built up which responded to the standard stress by a high frequency of this particular developmental abnormality. Moreover, after fairly intensive selection it was possible to produce strains in which the particular modification which had been selected for appeared in high frequency even in the absence of the stress. We had again carried out the process, which I have called 'genetic assimilation', by which selection produces genotypes which modify development in the same manner as did the original environmental stress.

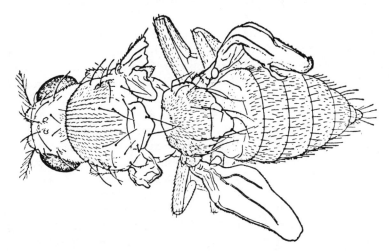

Figure 5 The bithorax phenotype as developed after ether treatment of the egg. The main wings have been removed to show more clearly the transformed metathorax. The individual depicted is actually from the 'assimilated' stock and developed *without* ether treatment (Waddington, 1956; reproduced by permission of the Society for the Study of Evolution)

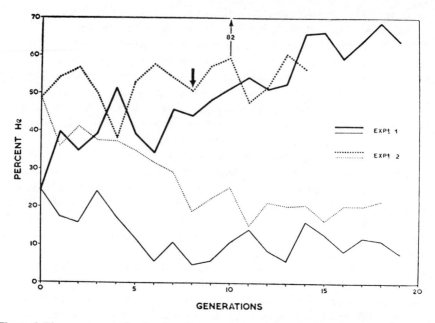

Figure 6 The progress of selection for or against bithorax-like response to ether treatment. Two experiments are shown, starting from two wild-type populations which reacted with rather different frequencies (Waddington, 1956; reproduced by permission of the Society for the Study of Evolution)

An attempt was also made to produce the genetic assimilation of a very remarkable phenotypic modification which, if it appeared in nature, would probably be considered of macro-evolutionary importance (Waddington, 1956, 1957a). If the eggs of a normal wild-type *Drosophila* stock are treated with ether vapour soon after laying, a certain proportion of them develop a bithorax phenotype (Figure 5; cf. Gloor, 1947). If one exerts artificial selection for the capacity to respond to this peculiar environmental stress, one can increase the frequency of the response—or, by selecting against it, decrease it. Again, after something over 20 generations of selection, it was possible to produce an assimilated bithorax stock in which the phenotype is developed in high frequency even in the absence of any ether-vapour treatment (Figure 6).

It seems profitable to discuss these last two experiments in terms of the canalisation model mentioned above (cf. Waddington, 1957b). We can picture the development of the cross-vein region (or of the thorax) proceeding under normal circumstances along a certain valley leading to the normal adult condition (Figure 7). The slope of the sides of the valley towards the bottom means that the system is to some extent resistant to stresses which might tend to produce an abnormal end result. The fact that the system responds by phenocopy formation to certain stresses applied at definite times can be

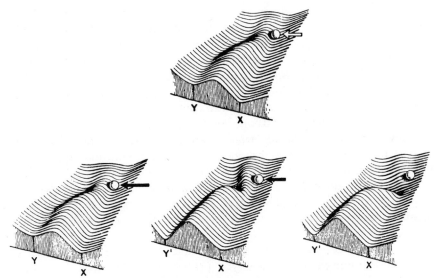

Figure 7 Modification of the epigenetic landscape by selection. The upper drawing shows the situation in the unselected foundation stock; a developmental modification Y will occur only if an environmental stress (*white arrow*) forces the developing system to cross a threshold or col. Of the lower figures, that on the left shows the Baldwin–Lloyd Morgan hypotheses—that a new gene mutation (*black arrow*) appears which substitutes for the environmental stress, everything else remaining unaltered. The two lower right figures show stages in the selection of genotypes in which threshold is lowered (requiring only a 'small' gene mutation or, eventually, a single specifiable mutation) and the course of the developmental modification is made more definite and directed to the optimal end-result, Y (Waddington, 1975b)

represented by drawing a side valley, reached over a col, at that time in development. The particular configuration of the surface drawn at the top of Figure 7 represents the developmental potentialities of one specific genotype. In any large population the genetic variation in the frequency with which the response occurs will correspond to variations in the height of the col above the main valley floor. Similarly, variation in the type of phenocopy produced (an absence of the posterior or the anterior cross-vein, etc.) will be represented by variations in the course of the side valley. Selection, we have seen, has been able to utilise both types of variation. In the assimilated stocks we have selected and combined low-col genes until we have reached a condition in which the col is non-existent and the floor of the upper part of the main valley leads off into what was originally the side branch. In the selection of one particular phenocopy rather than another, we have selected genotypes in which one particular type of developmental modification is particularly favoured; that is, we have made the course of the side valley more definite and have led it to our chosen end point.

We may ask ourselves where this genetic variability has come from. Was it perhaps created during the course of the experiment? There is rather good reason to believe that this was definitely not the case in the work involving the cross-veinless phenocopies. For instance, cross-veinless types occur spontaneously in some wild stocks; that is to say, genes which tend to lower the height of the col which defends the side valley are present in sufficiently high frequency for an occasional individual to contain sufficient of them to abolish the col even before selection starts, although the frequency of such combinations is so low that natural selection would scarcely be able to utilise them in the absence of the reinforcement produced by the environmental stress. Again, when selection for environmental response was made in highly inbred stocks, no effect was produced, indicating that new mutations were not occurring frequently enough to be effective (Figure 8). This experiment also shows definitely that no direct Lamarckian inheritance of the acquired character is occurring in this system.

In the bithorax experiments, however, and also in another experiment involving the dumpy-wing phenotype (Bateman, 1956), there is a strong suggestion that genes acting in the direction of selection turned up during the course of the experiments. Since the experiments involved some hundreds of thousands of flies, the occurrence of such mutations is not so unexpected that we have to attribute it to the environmental stress itself. The mutations

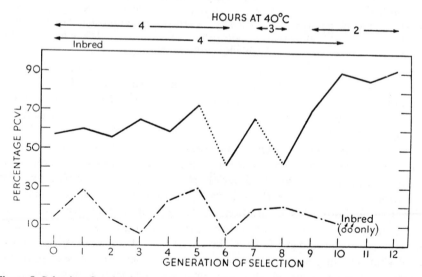

Figure 8 Selection for the frequency of formation of a broken posterior cross-vein in response to a temperature shock. *Above*, a wild-type stock, subjected for five generations to a 4-hour treatment, but later to treatments of only 3 and 2 hours; *below*, an inbred stock, subjected to 4-hour treatments throughout the experiment (Bateman, 1956)

presumably occurred in the normal manner, that is, 'at random'. But although the change in the chromosomal nucleoprotein may well have been quite undirected, the phenotypic effects of the genes were certainly influenced by the selection which had been practised on the stock. The new 'bithorax-like' gene has a strong tendency to produce bithorax phenotypes (actually by a maternal effect, but that is irrelevant to the present discussion) when in the genetic background of the selected stock but only a very weak tendency to do so in a normal, unselected, wild-type background. A similar consideration applies to the 'dumpy-like' gene. Selection, if you like, by reducing the height of the col and making the side valley more definite, has produced genotypes whose developmental potentialities are such that the course of development is easily diverted to the production of the particular adult condition that has been selected for. We have, as it were, set the developmental machine on a hair trigger. Quite a number of gene mutations, which are random at the level of nucleoprotein structure, are likely to produce this preset phenotype, and are therefore by no means random in their developmental effects.

The particular importance of this conclusion concerns the evolutionary origin of *co-ordinated* effects on the subunits of a structure, of the kind which were illustrated in the forelimbs of the gibbon and pangolin. The adult form of any animal is the result of the interaction between its genotype and the environmental stimuli and stresses to which the developing system has been subjected. If one thinks of the stresses produced by a life dependent on digging for food, it is clear that the stimuli may be very complex. When only a single stress is involved and the response of the developing system shows a certain approximation to an all or none character, as in the temperature-shock or ether-treatment experiments, one can represent the system by a diagram involving a single col or even a sharply defined threshold. When one considers the more complex stresses which arise in real life, such a representation becomes more difficult and also more artificial. But the essential point is that the complex stresses give rise to developmental responses which are co-ordinated. If in a wild population these responses are of adaptive value, natural selection will occur and will increase not only the intensity of the response but also its co-ordination. It will build up genotypes whose developmental potentialities include a high capacity for producing a well organised and harmonious adaptive phenotype. This capacity may then be released by quite a variety of random changes in the nucleoproteins of the chromosomes.

In this way, by taking into account the possibility of selection for both capacity to respond and type of response to environmental stresses, we can once again find justification for attributing the 'appearance of design', or co-ordinated adaptations, to the epigenetic processes which we know to have co-ordinated effects; and we can reduce our dependence on the abstract principle that natural selection can engender states of high improbability. We have, in fact, found evidence for the existence of a 'feedback' between the conditions of the environment and the phenotypic effects of gene mutations. The 'feedback' circuit is the simple one, as follows: (1) environmental stresses produce developmental modifications; (2) the same stresses produce a natural selective pressure which tends to accumulate genotypes which respond to the stresses with co-ordinated adaptive modifications from the unstressed course of development; (3) genes newly arising by mutation will operate in an epigenetic system in which the production of such co-ordinated adaptive modifications has been made easy (Waddington, 1957b).

Before concluding, I should like to return to the earlier point that the stresses to which an animal will be subjected depend at least in part on its own behaviour. Nearly all animals live in surroundings which offer them a much greater variety of habitats than they are willing to occupy. Naturalists, of course, are very familiar with the fact that closely related species often show markedly different preferences for particular types of habitat; even within species, different races may exhibit relatively specific patterns of behaviour. These obviously play a considerable evolutionary role in connection with reproductive isolation (e.g., on *Drosophila*, Knight, Robertson, and Waddington, 1956; Koref and Waddington, 1958; Spieth, 1958). They may also affect more general choice of living conditions (e.g., Waddington, Woolf, and Perry, 1954), but this field is still very incompletely explored. For instance, it is clear that cryptic coloration is of very little use to an animal unless its behaviour is such that it makes use of the possibilities of concealment which are offered to it, but we know little about the genetic correlations, if any, between the production of cryptic coloration and the appropriate types of behaviour, although Kettlewell (1956) has shown that melanic moths do in fact tend to settle on the darker areas of trees more frequently than would be expected by chance. It is clear, however, that here again selection will be operating not on the isolated components— behaviour on the one side and developmental and physiological response on the other—but on an interlocking system in which behaviour and other aspects of function mutually influence one another.

The result of this discussion it to suggest that we have perhaps been tempted to oversimplify our account of the mechanism by which evolution is brought about. This mechanism—the evolutionary system, as it may be called—has often been envisaged as consisting of no more than a set of genotypes which are influenced, on the one hand, by a completely independent and random process of mutation and, on the other, by processes of natural selection which again are in no way determined by the nature of the genotypes submitted to them. Perhaps such a simplification was justified when it was a question of establishing the relevance of Mendelian genetics to evolutionary theory, but it can only lead to an impoverishment of our ideas if we are not willing to go further, now that it has served its turn.

In point of fact, it would seem that we must consider the evolutionary system to involve at least four major subsystems (Figure 9). One is the 'genetic system',

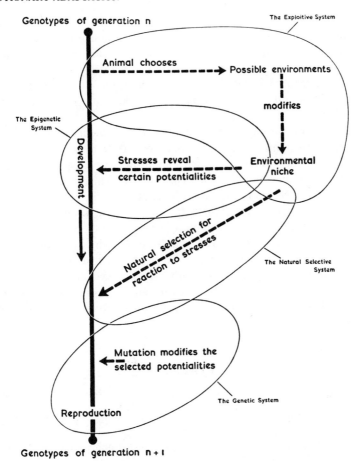

Figure 9 The logical structure of the evolutionary system. Changes in gene frequency between successive generations involve the operation of four subsystems: the exploitive, the epigenetic, the natural selective, and the genetic (Waddington, 1959)

the whole chromosomal-genic mechanism of hereditary transmission; the second is natural selection; a third, which might be called the 'exploitive system', comprises the set of processes by which animals choose and often modify one particular habitat out of the range of environmental possibilities open to them; and the fourth is the 'epigenetic system'—that is, the sequence of causal processes which bring about the development of the fertilised zygote into the adult capable of reproduction. These four component systems are not isolated entities, each sufficient in its own right and merely colliding with one another when impinging on the evolving creature. It is inadequate to think of natural selection and variation as being no more essentially connected with one another than would be a heap of pebbles and the gravel-sorter onto which it is thrown.

On the contrary, we have to think in terms of circular and not merely unidirectional causal sequences. At any particular moment in the evolutionary history of an organism, the state of each of the four main subsystems has been partially determined by the action of each of the other subsystems. The intensity of natural selective forces is dependent on the condition of the exploitive system, on the flexibilities and stabilities which have been built into the epigenetic system, and so on.

Very much remains to be done in working out the theory of evolution from this more inclusive point of view. But one general point is already clear. We can now see that the system by which evolution is brought about has itself some degree of organisation, in the sense that its subsystems are mutually interacting, and, in fact, mutually inter-dependent. In the recent past we have been working with a theory in which the obvious organisation of the living world had to be engendered *ab initio* out of non-organised basic components— 'random' mutation, on the one hand, and an essentially unconnected natural selection on the other. We had to rely on a Maxwell demon, and persuade ourselves not merely that natural selection could show some of the properties of such a useful *deus ex machina* but that it had them so fully developed that we needed nothing further. This was a rather uncomfortable position, and we can now escape from it.

REFERENCES

Bateman, G. (1956). Studies on Genetic Assimilation. *Proc. Roy. Phys. Soc. Edinburgh*, **25**, 1–6.

Durrant, A. (1958). Environmentally Induced Inherited Changes in Flax. *Proc. Xth. International Congress in Genetics*. **I**, 71.

Gloor, H. (1947). Phaenokopic Versuche mit Aetter an Drosophila. *Rev. suisse zool.*, **LIV**, 637.

Gloor, H., and Chen, P. S. (1950). Ueber ein Analorgan bei Drosophila Larven. *Rev. suisse zool.*, **LVII**, 570.

Heslop-Harrison J. W. (1920). Genetical Studies in Moths. *J. Genet.*, **IX**, 195.

Highkin, H. R. (1958). Transmission of Phenotypic Variability in a Pure Line. *Proc. Xth. International Congress in Genetics*, **II**, 120.

Kettlewell, H. B. D. (1955). Selection Experiments in Industrial Melanism in the Lepidoptera. *Heredity*, **IX**, 323.

Kettlewell, H. B. D. (1956). Investigations on the Evolution of Melanism in Lepidoptera. *Proc. Roy. Soc. Lond.*, *B.*, **CXLV**, 297.

Knight, G. R., Robertson, A., and Waddington, C. H. (1956). Selection for Sexual Isolation within a Species. *Evolution*, **X**, 14.

Koref, S. S., and Waddington, C. H. (1958). The origin of sexual isolation between different lines within a species. *Evolution*, **12**, 485–493.

Mayr, E. (1958). Behaviour and Systematics. In Roe A. and Simpson G. G. (Eds), *Behaviour and Evolution*, Yale University Press, New Haven. p. 341.

Roe, A. and Simpson, G. G. (Eds) (1958). *Behavior and Evolution*, Yale University Press, New Haven.

Spieth, H. T. (1958). Behaviour and Isolating Mechanisms. In Roe A. and Simpson, G. G. (Eds), *Behaviour and Evolution*, Yale University Press, New Haven. p. 363.

Turesson, G. (1930). The Selective Effect of the Climate upon Plant Species. *Hereditas*, **XIV**, 99.

Waddington, C. H. (1940). *Organisers and Genes*, Cambridge University Press, London.

Waddington, C. H. (1942). The Canalisation of Development and the Inheritance of Acquired Characters. *Nature*, **CL**, 563.

Waddington, C. H. (1953). The Genetic Assimilation of an Acquired Character, *Evolution*, **VII**, 118.

Waddington, C. H. (1956). Genetic Assimilation of the Bithorax Phenotype. *Evolution*, **X**, 1.

Waddington, C. H. (1957a). The Genetic Basis of the Assimilated Bithorax Stock. *J. Genet.*, **LV**, 241.

Waddington, C. H. (1957b). *The Strategy of the Genes*, Allen and Unwin, London; Macmillan, New York.

Waddington, C. H. (1959). Evolutionary systems: animal and human. *Nature*, **183**, 1634–1638.

Waddington, C. H., Woolf, B., and Perry, M. M. (1954). Environment Selection by *Drosophila* Mutants. *Evolution*, **VIII**, 89.

CHAPTER 11

A comment on genetic assimilation

G. C. Williams*

The most prominent recent challenge to the adequacy of natural selection for morphogenetic phenomena is that propounded by Waddington (1956 *et seq.*), who argued that natural selection must be supplemented by another process, which he calls *genetic assimilation*. His conviction that natural selection is not enough is apparent from his statement that the theory of genetic assimilation 'goes some way—though by no means the whole way—towards filling the major gap in Darwin's theory of evolution' (1958, p. 18); and from his statement that with genetic assimilation 'we can reduce our dependence on the abstract principle that natural selection can engender states of high improbability' (1959, p. 398).

It is easy, on superficial acquaintance, to overestimate Waddington's departure from current tradition and even to regard it as Lamarckian. It is also easy to make the opposite mistake and regard his conclusions as entirely compatible with the traditional model of natural selection. I will therefore discuss Waddington's views of adaptive evolution in some detail, so that I can point out exactly where I find them unacceptable.

The phenomenon of genetic assimilation is a real one, and throws important light on the nature of the genetic control of development. The best experimental

* Reprinted from Chapter 3 of *Adaptation and Natural Selection: A Critique of Current Evolutionary Thought* (1966) (copyright © 1966 by Princeton University Press), pp. 71–83, with the permission of the author. Reprinted by permission of Princeton University Press.

demonstration of the phenomenon is Waddington's work on the assimilation of the *bithorax* phenotype. He subjected some fruit-fly eggs to ether vapor in sublethal doses. Most of the survivors gave rise to normal flies, but a few developed into an abnormal type, called bithorax. These abnormal flies were selected as the parents of the next generation and the ether treatment repeated on their eggs. This treatment with ether and selection of bithorax was continued for many generations. The incidence of bithorax in this selected line increased steadily. The most significant observation was that after a number of generations, some eggs in the selected line produced the bithorax condition even without exposure to the ether. Within thirty generations of the original selection, Waddington produced a stock in which a large proportion of bithorax flies appeared every generation, even without the ether treatment. Bithorax was at first an individually acquired character, developed as a result of an environmental influence on development. At the end of the experiment it had become, in the selected line, a hereditary character. All relevant experimental controls, such as replications and parallel lines in which bithorax was selected against, were performed. Other characters were assimilated in other experiments. There can be no doubt about the reliability of these observations.

Waddington's interpretation of the initial appearance of bithorax may be summarized as follows. First of all, there is a certain specificity in the original stimulus. Specific environmental stresses on development, for instance ether, tend to produce specific abnormalities, such as bithorax. Secondly, any strongly abnormal environmental factor, such as a near-lethal dose of ether, will greatly increase the variability of development. A normal fruit-fly genotype is the result of selection for the reliable and precise production of a certain normal phenotype in the particular range of environmental conditions usually encountered by the species. This genotype is not designed to produce the normal phenotype in an environment that contains a high concentration of ether fumes. Hence, a general increase in variability may be expected in such abnormal environments. Thirdly, there is much unexpressed genotypic variability in the original population. There are a number of genes present, at different loci and in different individuals, that have some tendency to produce the bithorax phenotype. These variations, like normal environmental variations, have their effects suppressed by the normal self-regulatory developmental processes, which Waddington calls *canalization*. However, this genetic variation can become expressed as a result of the ether treatment. The specificities of this treatment, plus the augmentation of variability (decrease of canalization) by the ether, result in the production of a weakly developed bithorax condition in those individuals that have the strongest genetic tendencies in that direction. The continued selection of such individuals results in a rapid increase in the concentration of genes that favor the production of bithorax. Eventually, such genes become so numerous in each individual that they can, by their combined effect, match or exceed the bithorax-producing effect of the ether on a normal genotype. When the stock has been changed to this extent, the ether becomes unnecessary.

This explanation is not in any way Lamarckian. Selection of chance differences between individuals was the evolutionary force that produced the bithorax stock from the normal stock. The environment, however, played a role that is not recognized in the traditional model of natural selection. The ether did not, in the Lamarckian sense, produce the genetic variation that was selected by the experimenter, but it certainly did produce the expression of that variation. Without this expression, there could be no selection and no production of a genetically bithorax stock.

On the basis of such experimental results, Waddington envisioned a role for genetic assimilation in evolution, and he argued that this process provides a mechanism whereby populations can respond very rapidly to changed conditions. On the ordinary view, selection would act on genetic variation in preexisting characters when the environment changed, or, if the necessary character did not yet exist, it would have to wait for new mutations to fill the deficiency. In the experiment described there was no preexisting character of bithorax, nor, probably, were there any important mutations during the period of selection. Yet a major evolutionary change took place with extreme rapidity by genetic assimilation.

The experiment is of great importance for its demonstration of a previously unsuspected store of latent genetic variability, but I question its value as a model of adaptive evolution. One source of difficulty is in Waddington's tendency to think of the development of bithorax, after an ether treatment, as a response to a stimulus. The term 'response' usually connotes an adaptive adjustment of some sort, and would not be used for disruptive effects. It would be normal usage to say that some Frenchmen responded to the Terror by conforming to the Jacobin demands and that others responded by fleeing the country. It would not be normal usage to say that some responded by losing their heads. Decapitation was the result, not of a response, but of a failure to respond soon enough or in an effective manner. Similarly we may say that some of the flies responded adequately to the ether and produced a normal phenotype in spite of the difficulty presented by the treatment. Others showed an inadequate response. They were able to survive in the protected confines of the culture bottle but could only produce a grossly imperfect phenotype, bithorax. By favorably selecting the bithorax condition, Waddington produced an extreme but simple kind of degenerative evolution. He was selecting for specific kinds of inadequacies in the mechanisms of developmental canalization. I would suspect that there is less genetic information in the bithorax stock, which was produced by selection, than there was in the original stock.

Waddington apparently sees no need to distinguish between response to environmental stimuli and susceptibility to environmental interference. It is my belief that these classes of phenomena are utter opposites and that no more fundamental distinction can be made. Here in brief is my dispute with Waddington.

It is possible to confuse responses and susceptibilities because both conform to a pattern of cause–effect relationships involving organisms and their environment. It is important that they not be confused because a response shows the unique biological property of adaptive organization, and susceptibility results from the absence or deficiency of this property. For a response to occur, there must be sensory mechanisms that perceive particular aspects of the environmental situation and activate effectors that efficiently prevent the same, or other, correlated environmental factors from producing a certain undesirable effect. Susceptibility results from the environmental factors getting through and producing an effect in spite of any responses that may be activated.

The distinction is important enough to warrant an illustrative hypothetical example. Suppose we were to attach to each of two experimental animals—a man and a large reptile—a pair of physiological monitoring devices, one that records the moistness of the skin and another that records heartbeat. Next we put the two organisms in a room where the temperature oscillates slowly between 20° and 40°C. We would find that a physiological measurement records, for both organisms, a history of temperature fluctuations, but that a different physiological variable makes the record in each case. For the reptile we could establish a simple mathematical relationship between temperature and heartbeat, but we would find no record of variation in skin moisture. In the man we would find that skin moisture gives a reliable indication of environmental temperature, at least within much of the studied range, but that little could be learned about temperature from heart rate. The explanation for the difference illustrates the present point. Temperature fluctuations get through to the reptile and produce a direct effect. The temperature of the heart and the rest of the body follow that of the environment and, other things being equal, heart rate is a function of heart temperature for purely physical reasons. By contrast, the temperature fluctuations do not get through to the man. They are perceived by sensors that activate special effectors (sweat glands) to a degree adaptively appropriate to both the ambient temperature and the activity of the organism. The sweat glands and other mechanisms of temperature regulation prevent the environmental changes from having an effect on heartbeat.

The reptilian variation in heartbeat, and the human variation in skin moisture, are both *effects* of a certain *cause*, but a biologist should regard them as examples of very different kinds of cause–effect relationships. Waddington fails to make this distinction, and uses the evolutionary origin of a susceptibility to illustrate the origin of a response.

It might be argued that the evolutionary relevance of the bithorax experiment in no way depends on the supposition that bithorax is adaptive or should be called a response. The great majority of phenotypic abnormalities that would result from the ether or other extreme treatments would be expected to be nonadaptive. We likewise believe that the majority of mutations are harmful, but this does not prevent us from believing in mutation as the basic source of variation in evolutionary change. This argument would be valid if genetic assimilation were thought to operate only on very slight changes. The theory of the 'hopeful monster' of the early mutationist school has presumably been discredited, and I feel that the arguments against hopeful monsters are equally valid whether the monstrosities are genetic or epigenetic in origin. On the other hand one might say that the bithorax experiment is merely an extreme example of the generally acknowledged principle that environmental changes can alter the expression of genes. The experiment would be considered a macroscopic model of a process that, on a microscopic scale, would be of evolutionary importance. This would seem to violate the spirit of Waddington's proposal, because he believes genetic assimilation to be of primary importance in providing for the rapid development of really novel adaptations.

There are any number of individually acquired characters that are obviously adaptations, and not merely disruptions of development like bithorax. Might not some of these be genetically assimilated and play an important role in evolution? The best examples are inferential rather than experimental and comprise what are called pseudoexogenous adaptations. For example, wherever the human skin is subjected to frequent friction it becomes thicker and tougher and forms a callus. The sole of the foot is the region most subject to friction, and, appropriately, it develops the most pronounced callus layers. This seems like a simple example of an adaptive individual response, but it happens that the thickening of the soles relative to the rest of the skin is a process that starts *in utero*, before any possible frictional stimulus. It would seem that what is normally, for the rest of the body, an individual response, has become a genetically fixed adaptation of the foot. This certainly has the look of a response that has become, in part, genetically assimilated.

Somewhere in man's ancestry there may have been a protoamphibian that occasionally came out on land and pushed itself along with its fin lobes. Such animals might have responded by a minor thickening of the part of the skin that came in contact with the ground, just as our skins thicken wherever they are subjected to friction. At this earliest stage we are dealing with what is entirely an acquired character. Among those that acquired the character, not all would be genetically identical in their ability to develop calloused 'soles'. If terrestrial locomotion became an important capacity, and if the development of calluses on the feet were an important component of this capacity, there would be selection in favor of those individuals best able to develop this character. In the selected line, those genes that promote the sole thickening would become more and more concentrated, and ultimately there would be individuals that would develop the response purely on the basis of these genetic tendencies, and without any assistance from what had been the necessary stimulus. An individually acquired adaptation of the fishes would have become an obligate adaptation of the tetrapods. This adaptation, with genetic variation in its development, would have arisen at the same time as the ecological demand to which it was related, but not before. There was no preexisting character of sole thickening in the fishes, and no need to wait for the appearance of new mutations to give the character a start. The parallel with the bithorax experiment is obvious.

It seems to me that the sort of process pictured here must have occurred many times, but I would question its importance as an explanation of adaptive evolution. To explain adaptation by starting with a facultative response and ending with an obligate response is to beg the question entirely. The process starts with a germ plasm that says: 'Thicken the sole if it is mechanically stimulated; do not thicken it if this stimulus is absent', and ends with one that says: 'Thicken the soles.' I fail to see how anyone could regard this as the origin of an evolutionary adaptation. It represents merely a degeneration of a part of an original adaptation. If the origin of the sole thickening as a fixed response is hard to explain, surely its origin as a facultative response is much more so. It must, as a general rule, take more information to specify a facultative adaptation than a fixed one.

Thus at the most general theoretical level, all of Waddington's examples of genetic assimilation would be cases of degeneration, not adaptive evolution. This need not mean that all facultative responses represent higher levels of adaptation than all fixed responses. The confinement of the obligate calluses to particular parts of the body, and the specific patterns that they take must require a considerable amount of genetic information. Nevertheless, as a general class, facultative adaptations represent more difficult evolutionary attainments than obligate adaptations. To use the facultative as an axiom in explaining the obligate is to turn the whole problem upside down. Warburton (1955) expressed this objection in a forceful manner when he said that to acquire an adaptation in Waddington's sense is like 'being sewed into one's winter underwear.' Underwood (1954) has also expressed opinions similar to mine on the relation between facultative and obligate responses. A formal theory of the optimization of morphogenetic responses in varying environments is provided by Kimura (1960).

It must be understood that calling a character fixed or obligate does not imply that it is inevitable or invariable. All vital functions are susceptible to environmental interference, given sufficiently great stresses. Likewise there is great variation in the range of possible adjustment in facultative responses. In general the adaptive adjustments would be most apparent in the ecologically normal range of stimuli. Susceptibility to interference would be most common and most marked for uncommon or abnormally severe stresses.

The origin of a fixed adaptation is simple. The population merely needs to have or to acquire some genetic variation in the right general direction. The origin of a facultative response is a problem of much greater magnitude. Such an adaptation implies the possession of instructions for two or more alternative somatic states or at least for adaptively controlled variability of expression. It also implies sensing and control mechanisms whereby the nature of the response can be adaptively adjusted to the ecological environment. A facultative response would require much more delicate genotypic adjustments than a comparable fixed response. As an example from man, I would imagine that the obligate difference in skin color between a light and a dark race could be easily evolved on the basis of a wide variety of possible gene differences, and that such racial divergence could take place rapidly on the basis of whatever genes happen to be available. By contrast, the capacity, found in all races, to adjust the melanin content of the skin in response to variations in solar irradiation is an adaptation that must have taken a much longer time to evolve, and must require the carrying of a much larger burden of genetic information.

Waddington gives very little attention to the origin of the facultative responses with which he starts his arguments. He summarized his attitude in one discussion (1958, p. 17) by postulating that natural selection 'would, in fact, build in to the developmental system a tendency to be easily modified in directions which are useful in dealing with environmental stresses and to be more difficult to divert into useless or harmful paths.' It would appear that he finds the theory of natural selection entirely adequate to explain facultative adaptations, but feels that this theory has a 'major gap' in its application to fixed adaptations.

The principle of the economy of information, discussed in connection with the genetic code in Chapter 3 of this volume, may be useful in predicting whether an adaptation will be found to be obligate or facultative. Whenever a given character would be more or less universally adaptive in a population, it can be expected to be obligate. Only when adaptive adjustment to uncertain conditions would be important would one expect facultative control. Since the obligate is more economical of information, it can always be expected in situations in which a facultative response would not be significantly more effective. This principle is relevant to the current controversy between the nativists and the empiricists on the use of sensory experience for environmental interpretations. It would be expected that whenever a certain physiological state, for instance the parallel orientation of the optical axes of the eyes when focused on an object, *always* indicates a certain environmental state, such as the great distance of the object, the response, here the interpretation of distance, will be instinctive. Similarly in any animal, man included, for which fear of the edges of precipices would be universally adaptive, we can expect such fear to be instinctive, rather than learned. Complex systems of behavior, such as the more elaborate reproductive patterns, will usually be a blend of learned and instinctive elements. There are things that have to be learned, such as the individual characteristics of a particular mate or the location of a nest site. All elements that can be instinctive, however, will be instinctive. Instinct costs less than learned behavior, in the currency of genetic information.

REFERENCES

Kimura, Motoo (1960). Optimum mutation rate and degree of dominance as determined by the principle of minimum genetic load. *J. Genet.*, **57**, 21–34.

Underwood, Garth (1954). Categories of adaptation. *Evolution*, **8**, 365–377.

Waddington, C. H. (1956). Genetic assimilation of the *Bithorax* phenotype. *Evolution*, **10**, 1–13.

Waddington, C. H. (1957). *The Strategy of the Genes*, Allen and Unwin, London.

Waddington, C. H. (1958). Theories of evolution. In S. A. Barnett (Ed.), *A Century of Darwin*, Heinemann, London. pp. 1–18.

Waddington, C. H. (1959). Evolutionary adaptation. *Perspectives Biol. Med.*, **2**, 379–401.

Waddington, C. H. (1961). *The Nature of Life*, Allen and Unwin, London.

Waddington, C. H. (1962). *New Patterns in Genetics and Development*, Columbia University Press.

Warburton, Frederick E. (1955). Feedback in development and its evolutionary significance. *Am. Naturalist*, **89**, 129–140.

POSTSCRIPT WRITTEN IN 1981

I took too limited a view of facultative adaptation when I wrote the foregoing comments. I failed to recognize that a developing organism can get different kinds and degrees of guidance from its environment. Perhaps the following gives an improved perspective.

Poetic tradition provides the Continental army at Boston with two distinct defensive strategies. One would be used if the British approached from the sea, the other if they came by land. This crucial information was flashed by a coded signal from a widely visible church tower. Though extremely simple, this signal decided which of the elaborate plans would be put into effect, and which entirely abandoned.

There must be many biological analogies. A thermal signal determines whether a turtle develops into a male or a female. A nutritional signal decides whether a female bee becomes a worker or a queen. The plans activated or abandoned are complex, although the signal may be a simple matter of whether some environmental factor lies above or below a certain threshold. It was this sort of effect on development that I had in mind when I wrote 'Adaptation and Natural Selection' and my reasoning was valid for this sort of phenomenon. If bees someday lose their eusocial coloniality and genetically assimilate the queen phenotype, this would mean a loss of plans for making workers and an example of degenerative evolution. The same would be true if turtles genetically assimilate the female plan and lose the male by becoming parthenogenetic.

There are other environmental effects on development that do not conform at all to this picture of a simple signal deciding among elaborate alternatives. Sometimes a substantial component of the developmental plan may be taken from the environment. The existence of essential nutrients such as vitamins, which an animal requires but does not know how to make, could be cited as examples. Instructions for making vitamins are in the environment, in other organisms that the animal uses as food. If an instructional theory of antibody formation is correct, a developing vertebrate is instructed by environmental antigens on what sort of molecular structures it should impose on its antibodies.

The best examples of the use of complex environmental information may be in behavior development. A Columbia River salmon is born ignorant of geography. It learns all it needs to know about the river system on its way downstream. Genetic assimilation here would mean developing a DNA-coded map, and I assume that this would require more genetic information than the learning mechanism. This would be a positive change, not degenerative, because it would be based on an increase of genetic information used in the development of homing behavior.

Of course it is unlikely that all environmental contributions to development will fall neatly into the categories of simple signal or of elaborate instruction. A given character may depend for its development on several kinds of signals and of prepackaged information received from the environment. It is still important to recognize that production of complex phenotypes, such as male or female reproductive systems, can sometimes be triggered by simple signals, even though other characters may have a more elaborate environmental dependence. It is even more important to realize that the environment can not only provide both simple signals and complex plans, but can also disrupt. I would still claim that the ether used in Waddington's experiments functioned neither as signal nor instruction. It was a toxin that prevented the normal developmental plan from producing a normal phenotype.

CHAPTER 12

Evolution and behavior: an iconoclastic view

Jack P. Hailman

Parapsychologist J. B. Rhine emphasized in his retirement lecture at Duke University in the early 1960's that most of his studies concerned only the *effects* of extra-sensory perception because the basic phenomenon had already been so well established in fact. Most biologists disagree, yet take a curiously similar stance with respect to natural selection. I challenge this stance that natural selection is empirically well established as the principal mechanism of evolutionary processes, especially those concerning behavior.

In order to reason clearly about evolutionary phenomena it is desirable to separate cleanly several topics that are often inexorably interwoven. Lewis (1980: 554–555) emphasizes that 'In the *Origin of Species*, Darwin gives us two major theories of evolution: the kinematic theory of descent with modification and the dynamic theory of natural selection ... yet for 120 years most biologists have failed to recognize the descent theory explicitly.' Lewontin (1978: 213) notes that already at the time of the *Origin* 'it was widely (if not universally) held that species had evolved from one another' so that Darwin's contribution was to provide the notion of natural selection not only as the means of phylogeny but more importantly 'to solve both the problem of the origin of diversity and the problem of the origin of adaptation at one stroke.' In sum, we have one causal agent or mechanism (natural selection) that ostensibly explains three evolutionary phenomena: phylogeny, specification, and adaptation.

Many behaviorists hold three truths to be self-evident. First, that behavioral patterns of contemporary animals originated from similar (usually simpler) patterns of ancient ancestors and were altered over geological time through the action of natural selection. Second, that one ancestral species may give rise to multiple descendent species which selection endows with specific behavioral reproductive isolating mechanisms to prevent hybridization with the others. And third, that behavioral patterns are adapted to the environmental problems faced by the animals that perform them and are perpetuated over successive generations by stabilizing selection, so that each such pattern has a discrete and identifiable function. I propose that none of these three propositions is self evident and in fact each may be false.

Throughout this essay the attempt will be to shake off the mental cobwebs of complacency by forcing the reader to scrutinize assumptions concerning evolutionary processes and mechanisms, especially as they relate to behavior. It is necessary first to formulate the three major phenomena of adaptation, phylogeny, and speciation in terms of measurable variables, offering in the process what might be a new criterion for adaptation. I then question natural selection as the principal mechanism of these phenomena by reviewing traditional conceptions and some of their alternatives, and conclude this section with an analysis of the types of empirical evidence usually marshalled in support of selection. Upon this base I proceed to manifestly behavioral questions, first by considering how behavior differs from morphology in ways relevant to evolutionary questions, and then by considering some examples of behavioral phenomena. The essay concludes with a general discussion of the roles of selection in evolutionary phenomena.

THE THREE MAJOR EVOLUTIONARY PHENOMENA

In order to make clear sense of organic evolution it is desirable to begin with two tasks. The first is to distinguish between a process, such as speciation, and its result, such as the diversity of species. The second is to formulate the process–result phenomena in operational terms. Lewis (1980) emphasized that the process of phylogeny (descent with modification) is itself a biological theory, apart from the theory of natural selection as its causal agent or mechanism. Therefore, it is necessary to define the evolutionary phenomena of phylogeny, adaptation, and speciation without reference to their presumed mechanisms so that we understand clearly what it is that natural selection is supposed to explain.

Phylogeny

With the realization that fossils were remains of once-living organisms, it was natural to compare their anatomy with that of contemporary species. The outcome of this endeavor led to an extraordinary result: although most fossil organisms were obviously similar to contemporary species they almost always differed from them in multiple ways. In other words, species formerly inhabiting the earth were virtually all extinct and had been replaced by similar, but not identical, species. The most parsimonious hypothesis that could explain this result is that of phylogeny, or descent with modification. (I use 'phylogeny' to refer to the history of a population of organisms, reserving 'evolution' for the more general term that embraces speciation and adaptation as well.)

Virtually the only competing idea to account for the existence of fossils involved a tortuous reinterpretation of views current at the dawn of Western civilization. Primitive man, in his egocentric view of the world, often supposed that animals and plants were placed upon the earth for his use and enjoyment. This view, originating in the Indian subcontinent or Asia Minor, spread westward and was incorporated in the creation stories of *Genesis* (e.g. 'And out of the ground made the Lord God to grow every tree that is pleasant to the sight, and good for food' II: 9). Many persons must have noticed that not all plants and animals were either pleasant or useful, but before the discovery of fossils there was no really compelling reason to question a one-time creation of immutable species. Fossils, however, presented a real quandary, so that in order to maintain the older view one had to suppose either that fossils were not in fact remains of extinct species (but rather were a sort of artefact), or else that there was a one-time disaster (such as a great flood) that destroyed all life and a subsequent second creation of contemporary species.

The phylogeny theory made an important and specific prediction. Namely, if fossils were temporally ordered one should see a succession of types that could be ordered according to their anatomical modifications with descent. The analysis of sedimentary layering, and later the use of radioactive-decay dating and other means, led to massive evidence conforming to the prediction. Adherents to older views then had to strain their explanations considerably: either the artefacts had to be placed in the rocks by a particularly manevolent agent bent on confusing man, or else one had to postulate multiple disasters and multiple special creations. And if one took the latter view, it was also necessary to include the stipulation that each newly created species had to differ from the one it replaced only slightly, so that over many extinctions and new creations a gradual set of changes occurred that mimicked modification with continuous descent.

The competition between a highly predictive theory such as phylogeny and a weak alternative that continually requires new and ever more ludicrous suppositions (yet itself delivers no testable predictions) is no contest. Today, the theory of phylogeny is virtually universally accepted (as it was nearly so already in Darwin's time), its only vocal critics being some American fundamental Protestants who manage to profess literal belief in two creation stories of *Genesis* that conflict with one another (for an anecdote on the two creation stories, see Hailman, 1982).

We have, in sum, a result (similarity among different forms that lived at different times) and a well-tested hypothesis for the process that leads to that result (descent with modification). In any particular case, of course, it remains a hypothesis to be tested that some given species is descended with change from some particular earlier species. What remains is to find the mechanism or mechanisms whereby animals are modified by descent.

Adaptation

Unquestionably the most difficult and confused of the three major evolutionary phenomena is the subject of adaptation. The assumption that animals are well adapted to their environments has been attacked in recent years (e.g. Lewontin, 1978; Gould and Lewontin, 1979), but the target has been more the assumptions of how natural selection works than the underlying notion of adaptation. Indeed, much of the confusion in discussions of adaptation seems to stem from inadequate definition of the phenomenon being discussed (e.g. Williams, 1966; Lewontin, 1978; Rosen, 1978; Gould and Lewontin, 1979; Reed, 1981). Most authors deftly avoid explicit definition of the term adaptation, even when writing a book (e.g. Williams, 1966) or an influential essay (e.g. Lewontin, 1978) with that world in the title. As a result, the actual meaning of adaptation continually and subtly shifts from passage to passage in such discussions, probably without the author even being aware.

Multiple problems surround attempts to define adaptation. First, there is an inherent ambiguity in the word itself, which can mean either a product of evolution (wings are an adaptation for flying) or the process whereby the product is attained. This linguistic ambiguity is related to the second problem: absence of logical separation between postulated processes and the observable results they bring about. In fact, in the case of adaptation, there is the derived third problem of separating processes that create adaptive traits originally from those that perpetuate them. The fourth problem is the failure to separate the evolutionary processes of adaptation from their causal mechanism (i.e. natural selection). Lastly, there is in existing discussions almost a total lack of operational definitions of any of the notions concerning adaptation. I shall try to unravel this tangle.

The pervading notion of adaptation that seems to underlie most discussions relates to some 'suitable' fit between the organism and its environment. Lewontin (1978: 216–217) put it thus: 'Evolutionary biologists assume that each aspect of an organism's morphology, physiology and behavior has been molded by natural selection as a solution to a problem posed by the environment.' Similar passages are found in Williams (1966, e.g. p. 9). This 'fit' between animal and environmental has given rise to peculiar and inconsistent uses of the word 'fitness' as an expression of how well the animal is adapted to its environment (see criticisms by Hailman, 1980, as an example).

The fitness, or lock-and-key, view of adaptation entails at least two of the problems mentioned above. First, this view almost always incorporates the separate notion of natural selection as the agent bringing about the observed fit, and it is precisely that unnecessary link that we need to break in order to consider the attendant problems logically. Even if we were to view adaptation simply as a fit between the organism as key and its environment as lock—without any implication as to how this fit came about or is perpetuated—a second problem would still exist. Namely, there are no clearly implied operational criteria for assessing whether or not something is in fact such an adaptation: the presence or absence of 'fit' is a subjective judgement. I take Bridgman's (e.g. 1927, 1938) view that science must be based on measurable variables to be our most fundamental working rule, and unfortunately operationalism is noticeably scarce in studies of both evolution and behavior (but see Hailman, in press, for an attempt to formulate the problems of behavioral control and ontogeny in a thoroughly operational framework).

There is a way out of this quandry about adaptation—one that many authors note in passing without realizing its potential as an operationally defining criterion. Lewontin (1978: 228) very nearly made this point with an illustration showing similarities among a whale, seal, penguin, fish, and sea snake, but the caption (probably not written by the author) unnecessarily incorporates natural selection as the causal agent: 'Reality of adaptation is demonstrated by the indisputable fact that unrelated groups of animals do respond to similar selective pressures with similar adaptation.' Put simply, if unrelated animals inhabiting one environment show similar characteristics while their relatives inhabiting another environment show different characteristics (Hailman, 1965, 1976a), we should look for some cause of this correlation.

It is the *character–environment correlation* that is measurable and hence what I propose as the operational criterion for adaptation. Such correlations are by no means restricted to morphological characteristics or to the sea as the environment. Cliff-nesting gulls and terns, for example, share many behavioral characteristics that are not found in their surface-nesting relatives (e.g. E. Cullen, 1957; J. M. Cullen and Ashmole, 1963; Hailman, 1965).

The criterion of character–environment correlation embodies the intuitive notion of fit between animal and environment while providing a way of testing for its occurrence without the subjective assessment of fit. If we are to analyze the causes of such character–environment correlations we must be careful to avoid incorporating the assumption that natural selection has brought about the correlations, for that is a separate issue to be tested separately. Therefore, the use of the word 'adaptation' to mean character–environment correlation exclusive of its causal agent might engender confusion, but the longer phrase is so awkward that the possible confusion is worth risking.

It might appear, then, that the phenomenon of adaptation reduces to a special case of phylogeny: modifications with descent occur such as to produce the observed character–environment correlations. However, this statement fails to recognize that the correlations persist generation after generation, and hence must be perpetuated in some way. In short, the student of evolution in faced with an almost paradoxical problem: what causes traits to change within a line of descent over the vastness of geological time (the process of phylogeny), and what causes adaptive traits to remain the same within a line of descent over shorter periods of time (the process of perpetuation)? The usual answer to both questions is 'natural selection', in the forms directing selection and stabilizing selection, respectively, but this is the assumption we wish to avoid in the definition of the evolutionary phenomena so that it may be answered separately.

In sum, we have a well established result (adaptations, in the sense of character–environment correlations) that arose during phylogeny and are maintained by some process of perpetuation. That a given character is adapted in this sense, of course, is still a hypothesis to be tested by comparative evidence in each individual case. What remains is to find the mechanisms whereby adapted traits are evolved and then perpetuated from generation to generation.

Speciation

The possibility that one ancestral species might give rise to two or more descendent species is related to the process of phylogeny so closely that many authors have not seen speciation as a separate phenomenon. Darwin's *Origin of Species* really concerned phylogeny: how a given ancestral species was sufficiently altered through geological time that its later descendent is recognized as a different species. When biologists of this century became more keenly aware of the furcation of species, interest focused on the causal mechanisms that brought about and perpetuated the split (e.g. Mayr, 1942), with natural selection playing the key role.

The reality of speciation is well attested by the fossil record, but the related hypothesis of merging of ancestors to form new species has only scattered empirical support. (Such speciation through merging may occur via polyploid hybridization in some plants.) Furthermore, the phenomenon of speciation opens yet another possibility, namely that all living forms are evolutionarily derived from a common ancestor. This possibility has grown ever more likely with the realization that living matter is all based on very special chemical relationships, the finding of prokaryote fossils in Precambrian rocks, and the creation of organic molecules in the laboratory under conditions similar to those prevailing on earth billions of years ago. The hypothesis of monophyletic life, however, is not crucial to any further points in this essay and hence need not be labored.

If the descendent species occupy geographic ranges without overlap (allopatry), the problem of speciation is simply a special case of phylogeny. The original population becomes divided geographically and the two (or more) parts become differently modified by descent. However, if the descendent species overlap geographically (sympatry), there is a new phenomenon to contend with (in sexually reproducing organisms, which are the vast majority). Were males and females to mate at random with the opposite sex of their own and other species, then closely related species would frequently hybridize and all sorts of intermediate animals would occur. Such intermediate animals are in fact extremely rare in nature, so the special evolutionary problem of speciation is how the species are kept from interbreeding.

It should also be noted that divorcing the phenomenon of speciation from its reputed mechanisms involving selection does not affect accompanying evolutionary phenomena. For example, homology—the similarity of characters in contemporaneous species due to their derivation from a common ancestor (Hailman, 1976b)—accompanies speciation regardless of the mechanisms producing and perpetuating the furcation.

In sum, we once again have a well-established result (the diversity of similar species at a given time) and a process that brings about that result (the splitting of an ancestral species in such a way that the descendent parts do not hybridize). Just as with phylogeny and adaptation, the hypothesis of speciation in particular cases requires empirical verification for the conclusion that two or more given concurrent species evolved from a particular pre-existing species. What remains is to find the mechanism or mechanisms whereby the furcation of species insures that they do not remerge to obliterate the separation.

Were ancestors adapted?

One simple question immediately arises: namely did there exist the same sort of character–environment correlations in evolutionary ancestors that we observe in contemporary animals? If such correlations did not formerly exist, then it would appear that today we see the latest stage in a long process by which the correlations have been perfected. The apparent stability of animal characteristics from generation to generation might be illusory, with the actual continuing change transpiring so slowly as to go undetected (i.e. there is no problem of perpetuation of adaptations). On the other hand, if character–environment correlations also occur in ancestral species, then the perpetuation of adapted characters could be real and evolutionary change over geological time could be due to changes in the environment.

The final answer to this particular question is not available, but it appears from the existing evidence that the second, rather than the first, possibility is the case. That is, in so far as we can tell there did exist character–environment correlations in ancestral species, even when the environments and the species were quite different from those of today. Fossils of long-extinct forms having characters similar to those of modern species are found correlated with similar environments. For example, ichthyosaur and plesiosaur fossils are found associated with other oceanic rather than with terrestrial species, and these reptiles had many similarities with whales, seals, penguins, fishes, and sea snakes of today. Finally, environmental changes seem to accompany the most rapid alterations of animals in the fossil record. If we accept the character–environment correlation for fossil species, then intergenerational perpetuation of characters during periods of stable environments is a real phenomenon and its cause can be divorced logically from that producing evolutionary change: the two might or might not be similar.

THE MECHANISMS OF EVOLUTIONARY PHENOMENA

The immense attractiveness of Darwin's notion of natural selection is that it provides a possible mechanism or causal agent for all three of the major evolutionary phenomena, as shown in Table 1. This view that selection is the pervasive mechanism of evolutionary phenomena may be called the pan-selectionist view. Although there have been repeated attacks on the pan-selectionist view, the bulk of modern evolutionary literature consists of interpreting examples of phylogeny, adaptation, and speciation in terms of individual selection—rather than trying to disprove predictions generated from selection theory.

In his much-cited essay on 'strong inference', Platt (1964) emphasized the importance of testing by critical experiment those predictions that separate alternative theories. The problem of applying his advice to mechanisms of evolutionary phenomena has been two-fold: the phenomena have tended to be defined so as to include the mechanism of selection (so that to reject selection one had to reject the whole evolutionary phenomenon), and there have been few theoretical alternatives to selection articulated. In the previous section I showed that the evolutionary phenomena can be defined without reference to

Table 1 The types of pan-selectionist mechanisms proposed as causal agents for the three major evolutionary phenomena

Evolutionary phenomenon	Result	Process	Pan-selectionist mechanism
phylogeny	similarity among non-contemporary species	modification with descent	directing selection
adaptation	character–environment correlations	perpetuation of adapted traits*	stabilizing selection
speciation	diversity of contemporary species	furcation and reproductive isolation*	reinforcing selection

* Also involves modification with descent.

their causal agents, and in this section I shall show that there exist alternatives to directing, stabilizing, and reinforcing selection as the mechanisms of phylogeny, adaptation, and speciation.

Traditional selectionist views

The traditional view—if we may call anything with so short a history 'traditonal'—of the relationship between the mechanisms of adaptation and phylogeny has been ably summarized by many authors, perhaps most notably in the *magnum opus* by Ernst Mayr (1963). This traditional view is based ultimately upon observations of two empirically established generalizations emphasized by Darwin and Wallace (1859): first, that offspring tend to resemble their parents, and second, that more offspring are brought into the world than will live to reproduce. The first notion is, of course, an ancient observation: '... great whales, and every living creature that moveth ... after their kind, and every winged fowl after his kind' (*Genesis*, I: 21). The second notion, based on Malthus, stands as one of the great quantitative discoveries in biology. The truths of parent-offspring similarity and offspring-mortality are unchallenged, but what Darwin, Wallace, Mayr and others have done with these truths is to interpret them in a joint hypothesis about the mechanisms of phylogeny and adaptation. The same two truths are also consistent with alternative hypotheses, as we shall see further below.

The first generalization—offspring tend to resemble their parents—has been greatly expanded by the discipline of genetics, the details of which are unnecessary to an initial analysis of the mechanistic implications for phylogeny and adaptation. Depending upon which part of the phrase receives emphasis, two different interpretations can be drawn. If one emphasizes the resemblance, then the problem of perpetuating adaptations from generation to generation is simply the problem of the mechanisms of inheritance. However, resemblance is not synonymous with identity, and the 'tendency' toward resemblance redundantly emphasizes the less-than-perfect correlation between parent and offspring. We know today what Darwin and Wallace could not know: that mutation and (in sexually reproducing species) recombination are principal sources of genetic variation mitigating the parent–offspring correlation. Both men, however, recognized that variation did appear from somewhere, and they proposed that such variation in combination with differential offspring-mortality is non-random and more specifically variant-dependent, so that some variants live to reproduce themselves and others do not. This straightforward theory-building was subsequently united with genetics beginning with R. A. Fisher's (1930) great book.

The traditional selectionist view therefore attributes both modification with descent and perpetuation of characters to such natural selection. New variants that are 'better' than former types lead to higher survival and reproductive rates, until the population of animals reaches some sort of equilibrium with its new environment. This equilibrium is the point at which the characters that have evolved are so well suited to the environment that any new variations arising are less likely to succeed: all selection becomes 'stabilizing' selection. Only when the environment changes will new selective forces come into play and begin shaping the population toward a new end. Thus the traditional selectionist view attributes phylogeny and adaptation to the same cause, namely differential survival and reproductive rates based on phenotypic characteristics.

The extension of these traditional selectionist views to the furcation of species is an ecological and ethological modern extension (e.g. Dobzhansky, 1951; Mayr, 1963). New species are seen to arise during geographic isolation among parts of the ancestral species' population. Because different selection pressures occur among the isolated populations, they evolve along different lines (modification with descent). Later, when they disperse to greater areas, two (or more) of these newly differentiated populations may come into contact with one another, and at this point reinforcing selection can occur in either of two forms.

In the ecological form the similarity between the sympatric species in some character (such as size) provides strongest competition on those animals in each population that are most similar to animals of the other population. Variants that are dissimilar therefore have the competitive advantage and selection acts to make the species diverge, resulting in (say) a large and a small species.

In the ethological form the similarity between the sympatric species leads to confusion in mate-selection so that some males pair with females of the other species and *vice versa*. Animals that make such pairing mistakes leave fewer ultimate descendants because of factors such as infertility, reduced viability of hybrid offspring, sterility of hybrid offspring, or competitive disadvantage of hybrid offspring. Selection thus favors courtship signals that cannot be confused with those of the other species and the two populations diverge (evolve reproductive isolating mechanisms).

In sum, the traditional pan-selectionist view has natural selection as the mechanism for phylogeny, adaptation, and speciation (Table 1). This view is not some 'straw man' erected here for purposes of argument, but is the view of evolution taught to students by almost all textbooks of biology.

Wright's 'shifting balance' view

Sewell Wright (1980) justifiably complained that his own subtle formulations of natural selection have been greatly distorted by the pens of others. Genetic drift, the so-called Sewell Wright effect, was but a spin-off of his notion of 'fitness peaks' in local animal populations (see Wright, 1968, and subsequent volumes in that series). Wright's overall view is within the framework of selectionist theory, but he does not see a population as moving readily from its present state to some slightly fitter state.

Wright begins by emphasizing that individuals as a whole survive and reproduce, the phenotypic characteristics of animals being shaped by the entire genome of the animal. Dawkins (1976), Wilson (1975), and other contemporary writers have done much intellectual mischief in promoting the impression that for each phenotypic character there is a gene or gene-complex that produces it. As Wright emphasizes, the genetic facts are quite contrary to such a view: epistasis (one character being influenced by multiple interacting genes) and pleiotropism (one gene affecting multiple characters) are well established general phenomena rather than modifying curiosities. Indeed, the crucial point of difference in mathematical formulations of the genetical basis of evolution lies in the unit of selection: traditional selectionists following R. A. Fisher (1930) assign the gene as this unit whereas Wright gives that place to the organism and even the population.

Wright therefore argues that there is no such thing as a 'selfish gene', but only selfish animals. Given that the genome as a balanced whole produces an individual animal, any disturbance (mutation, recombination) in that genome is likely to upset the balance. Thus local animal populations are well adapted only in the sense that they have reached a fitness peak or genome-balance from which any departures are more likely to create a less fit animal than a more fit one. How then does evolution ever proceed if each geographically local population is more or less trapped in its own particular fitness peak? Wright argues that since local populations are only partially isolated, the influx of new genetic combinations greatly magnifies the variation on which natural selection can act, and hence makes possible the appearance of a genome more fit than those characterizing either contributing population. The new, superior gene combinations then spread among the local, only partially isolated populations, the entire process being called the shifting balance theory of natural selection (see Wright, 1932, for one of the most easily comprehended statements of his mathematically oriented theory).

Wright's formulations admit to an 'intergroup selection' among local populations with different fitness peaks, but he makes a sharp distinction between this notion and the kind of 'group selection' championed by Wynne-Edwards (1962) and the 'sociobiologist' tradition that grew from his views. Wright (1980: 840–841) considers altruist genomes that cause an animal to contribute to the advantage of the group at its own expense to be 'extremely fragile' in contrast with his robust genomes characterizing local populations. Wright does, however, see a place for kin selection (Hamilton, 1963), at least in the evolution of sterile worker castes of social insects.

Wright's shifting balance selectionist theory generates expectations that differ from those derived from traditional selectionist views. Traditional views lead to the expectation that species are about as fit as possible, given sufficient time has occurred for selection to work fully. Wright's view, by contrast, emphasizes relative adaptive peaks, hence generating the expectation that most populations are not fully adapted in the fitness sense. Unfortunately, it is difficult to translate this difference in expectations to testable terms under the operational conception of adaptation as character–environment correlations. Wright's theory also leads to the prediction that local populations of the same species—even in habitats that are as similar as geographicaliy different areas ever are—differ phenotypically. Traditional selectionist theory predicts uniformity among local populations of the same species in the same environment. The empirical evidence may favor Wright in this difference, although much remains to be learned about local populations within a species.

Waddington's epigenetic views

C. H. Waddington (1974) has also voiced complaints that the traditional selectionist viewpoint following Fisher–Haldane genetical models should be replaced with more realistic formulations. (Waddington includes Wright as holding similar view, but it is not clear to me that he has fully understood how Wright's views differ.) As an embryologist Waddington focuses attack on the assumption that phenotypes of animals are well correlated with their genotypes, a view implicit in almost all evolutionary formulations that are either derived from or relate to models of population genetics. He points out that when a phenotypically uniform population of 'wild type' individuals is investigated genetically it is found to be heterogeneous genotypically. Or, in Waddington's words (1974: 36), 'The individuals that are phenotypically almost identical . . . contain wildly different genotypes.'

Waddington looks upon phenotypes as being 'homeorhetically' buffered against vagaries of genotype. That is, the developmental processes are regulated so as to achieve similar phenotypic endpoints regardless of the genotype (obviously within certain bounds). He emphasizes (1974: 41) that one may change both genes and environment 'and nothing happens' with respect to the phenotype. Therefore, whatever the role played by selection, it has been to create especially robust developmental systems. In one sense, Waddington's point is similar to Wright's emphasis upon the entire genome as the unit of selection, but in another sense the same point speaks against the genetically based variation that supposedly provides the basis for selection to operate.

Another major point in Waddington's thinking is what he has called 'genetic assimilation' (e.g. Waddington, 1961). This is a process that appears to result in Lamarckian-like acquisition of acquired characteristics, and may be illustrated with an example. A blacksmith develops calluses from working, but the capacity to develop calluses is itself polygenically based. Suppose that those successful blacksmith families carrying such genes tend to intermarry. Because of the polygenic basis for the development of calluses certain offspring may be endowed with more of these genes than either parent (who may have different combinations of the callus-capacity genes). The son of such a marriage might then develop calluses at some much lowered work threshold, say before he even goes into the trade as an apprentice. It thus appears that the acquired calluses of the father have been passed genetically to the son. How common such 'genetic assimilation' really is, no one can be certain without further research, but the phenomenon underscores the importance of the entire developmental system as the evolutionary unit.

Paterson's speciation-dispersal hypothesis

The traditional selectionist views a population of animals living in some habitat, and then adapting to that habitat by natural selection. But there is an 'opposite' way to achieve character–environment correlation, the point of which can be shown by an extreme statement of the hypothesis. Suppose there were somewhere a manufacturing place for new species, and as these species were made, each according to its separate blueprint, they were dispersed everywhere. Then in some places a given species would be 'adapted' and hence survive to reproduce its kind, whereas in other places it would not be suited to the environment and so either leave or die out. If indeed the population dies out, we have a sort of group-selection occurring, but no selection at all is involved if the animals simply leave those environments to which they are not suited. The end result of this process is the character–environment correlation we seek to explain.

A version of the foregoing hypothesis—which we may for lack of an established term call simply the 'speciation-dispersal' hypothesis—is defended by H. E. H. Paterson, Director of George Evelyn Hutchinson Laboratory of the University of the Witwatersrand. Paterson (1978, 1980, 1981, pers. comm.) believes that new species evolve from very small, geographically isolated populations (but not from just one manufacturing plant as in my extreme statement). He proposes that during this initial phase in isolation the species' characteristics are genetically fixed, and thereafter in the species' expansion–dispersal phases these characteristics do not markedly change. (Genetic fixation can occur in many ways, the commonest of which is that close inbreeding leads, by random events, to homozygosity in the population, hence eliminating alternative alleles from the gene pool.)

In Paterson's version fixation is guided by selection so the population is adapted in a traditional sense to the immediate area in which it first originates. However, such selection is not logically necessary, and a new, distinct population of animals can arise purely by genetic drift, random fixation, and other genetic mechanisms without being adapted to the immediate environment. The ultimate survival of the new species, however, rests upon its dispersing into suitable habitats. This hypothesis is certainly consistent not only with the fact of character–environment correlation, but also the widespread tendency of animals—especially newly invading or artificially introduced species—to disperse into all sorts of new habitats (usually without becoming established).

It follows from Paterson's speciation-dispersal hypothesis that reinforcing selection for reproductive isolating mechanisms (or other species-distinctive characters) is impossible. Either the potential species are sufficiently different when coming into geographic contact that they have no problem in mate-recognition and hence breed true, or else they hybridize and obliterate the difference between them. (An intermediate possibility is that the two species continually produce some stable rate of hybridization.) Furthermore, if the two new species are sufficiently different in their ecological requirements, they will occur sympatrically; but if they are too close, then one will either drive the other out (no selection) or drive the other to extinction through competition (a form of group selection). In no case, however, will reinforcing selection alter either species in response to the presence of the other.

What is selection?

In the foregoing subsections I have tried to present not only the traditional pan-selectionist views but also some alternatives that have sprung from dissatisfaction with those views. To the latter might be added a number of criticisms of traditional selectionist interpretations of characters as adaptations (e.g. Lewontin, 1978; Gould and Lewontin, 1979). Before one can seek critical testing of selectionist hypotheses, however, it is necessary to face the question of what one is willing to term 'selection'. I will consider three problems of defining selection: the genetic, the relative, and the replacement problems.

Probably the vast majority of writers on evolutionary topics define natural selection in some way that involves genetics, such as this definition from the glossary of Wilson (1975: 589): 'The differential contribution of offspring to the next generation by individuals of different genetic types but belonging to the same population.' There are many problems with such definitions, but the focus here is on the genetic types. By defining selection in terms of the genetics of populations, testing for the occurrence or absence of selection is clearly put out of the reach of any biologist who is not working in population genetics. Wilson claims that 'this is the basic mechanism proposed by Charles Darwin', but that is untrue, since Darwin said only that variants forming the substrate for selection must somehow be heritable.

If we return to the original proponents of selection (Darwin and Wallace, 1858) for guidance, we need not complicate the definition of selection with reference to genetic mechanisms. Instead, we need only show that there is phenotypic variation in a population, that offspring tend to resemble their parents, and that some of these phenotypic variants make a greater contribution to successive generations than do others.

The second problem in conceptions of selection relates to how one goes about measuring populations in order to establish the Darwin–Wallace phenomenon. Beginning with Fisher (1930) most workers have explicitly or implicitly assigned coefficients of contribution to phenotypes (or their supposed genotypic bases), whether or not their views are formulated mathematically. Put another way, researchers have almost always looked for a shift in the *proportion* of phenotypes composing a population.

The problem with defining selection in terms of changes in the *relative* numbers of each phenotype in the population is easily demonstrated. Suppose a population consists of 1000 animals of phenotype *A* and 10 animals of phenotype *B*. In the next generation suppose there are still 1000 *A*'s but now 50 *B*'s. In successive generations suppose the number of *A* phenotypes remains constant but the number of *B*'s continually increases. It is a matter of choice whether one wishes to recognize this situation as involving selection. By the criterion of relative phenotypic frequencies it is true that selection is taking place; but in a more important sense, the increase in *B*'s is at no expense to the number of *A*'s, so that it is not meaningful to say that *B* is replacing *A* in the population. Darwin and Wallace would have rejected relative numbers of phenotypes as demonstrating selection, as evidenced by the principal example used by both men: the constancy of breeding bird populations in the face of annual production of huge numbers of offspring. Yet many empirical studies purporting to test for and even demonstrate natural selection are based simply on the relative numbers of phenotypes in temporally spaced samples from the population, with no evidence that the population size has remained constant.

The final problem of defining selection relates to the replacement phenomenon. Suppose one population of animals declines or even goes extinct before the arrival of a second population. The second population then expands its range, occupying the place formerly held in the environment by the now extinct population. This situation is not hypothetical: apparently just that happened when the red squirrel (*Sciurus vulgaris*) declined in England and the gray squirrel (*S. carolinensis*) introduced from North America subsequently occupied its place (Shorten, 1954). The gray squirrel does not seem to have had any causal effect on the population of the red squirrel, a fact we can deduce only because the red squirrel declined in numbers prior to the gray squirrel's occupying the same area. However, if these changes in populations had occurred simultaneously, it would tempting to infer that the gray squirrel was the cause of the red squirrel's decline. If these two similar rodents were in fact color morphs of the same species, such a situation would be interpreted by most authors as an example of natural selection.

We do not know enough about population dynamics of animals to judge how large a problem the replacement phenomenon really is. It may sound far-fetched to assert that animal populations rise and fall, even go extinct, without relation to ecological competitors, but that view is part of the argument by Andrewartha and Birch (1954). Examples that were brought to my attention while on leave in Hawaii concern introduced bird species that become established, expand explosively, then decline and sometimes go extinct—a phenomenon that has occurred time and again, although given little attention by biologists. A recent case is the songbird *Leiothryx lutea*, which Peterson (1961) called abundant but Shallenberger (1978: 81) later said 'has been declining . . . and is now very scarce.' Pyle (1979), in reporting the 1978 Christmas bird count, said 'This was one of the more abundant species on the Honolulu count through 1967, then dropped to 18 in '68, and to zero in '69. Since then, it has been found on only four counts, and only one or two birds each time.' It would be instructive now to follow the fate of another introduced songbird, the spotted munia or ricebird (*Lonchura punctulata*). Its population had built to 172 birds sampled by the 1973 Christmas count and to 665 the following year. In 1978 the population was still high (702 birds), but the following year dropped by half (336 birds). The data concerning such species have been tabulated over the years in the local journal '*Elapaio*' but never thoroughly analyzed to my knowledge.

I think that any conception of natural selection must face the potential replacement problem: that animal numbers change for no easily identified reason, and certainly not due to competition with 'superior' phenotypes. Thus if one population becomes numerous simultaneously with the independent decline of another, this will appear to be a causal relationship. If the two groups in question are morphs or different phenotypes of the same species, the phenomenon will resemble individual selection; if they be different species, it will resemble group selection.

I am in the unfortunate position of having no firm solution to the replacement problem in defining selection. The problem points up the need for some evidence of causal relationship in the replacement of one type by another—if our conception of selection is to stay intuitively close to the intentions of Darwin and Wallace. Indeed, if we fail to demand demonstration of causal relationship in replacement phenomena, the notion of selection is a simple tautology (that which survives, survives), bereft of scientific interest.

Although the foregoing shows that it is difficult to formulate satisfactory criteria for the notion of selection, some attempt is necessary if we are to decide whether or not selection is operating. *First*, the unit of selection—individuals, local populations, whole species—must be specified. *Second*, there must exist phenotypic differences among the units. *Third*, the phenotypic differences must be transmitted to the successive generation of the unit. This criterion means that offspring must resemble their parents to a greater degree than they do other parents (when the unit is individuals), or that the F_1 generation must resemble the P generation of the same population more than it resembles the P generation of other populations (when the unit is a populational one: local populations or entire species). The mechanisms for transmission may range from classical genetics to inheritance via cultural tradition, but it must yield the intergenerational correlation. *Fourth*, there must be differential change with time in the numbers of individuals of differing phenotypes. This differential change can be due to differences in rates of reproductive output or of survival (or its inverse, mortality). *Fifth*, and last, the differential reproductive or survival rates must be shown to be due to the phenotypic differences among the units (i.e. there must be an identifiable 'selection pressure' or agent operating differentially among the units, even if this agent be quite complex).

It is good evidence for the combination of the fourth and fifth points that makes an argument for the operation of selection convincing because their conjunction is so difficult to demonstrate. Perhaps the most cogent case is the sort of argument used by both Darwin and Wallace as part of their hypothetical examples of songbird populations. When the total number of individuals remains constant but there is a shift in the relative proportions (and hence absolute numbers) of different phenotypes with time, then one phenotype is truly replacing the other and the change is unlikely to be due to the fortuitous replacement discussed above.

EMPIRICAL EVIDENCE FOR SELECTION

The point of this essay is to stimulate thinking and dialogue through logical analysis of evolutionary notions rather than to attempt a review of data. Nevertheless, there are some points to be made concerning empirical evidence relating to the hypotheses of natural selection as the causal agents in evolutionary phenomena.

If selection is truly a testable hypothesis rather than an empty tautology it should be possible to identify predictions from the hypothesis that are capable of empirical falsification. Such tests will be stronger if some alternative to selection predicts different results. Therefore, in each case of reputed stabilizing, reinforcing, and directing selection considered below, I have tried to see if an alternative to selection fits the results just as closely.

Stabilizing selection

Fretwell (1972:201, Figure 64) attempted to test directly the stabilizing selection hypothesis applied to the size of field sparrows (*Spizella pusilla*). He measured wing lengths (a standard index of size; the units are unlabeled in his graph but are certainly millimeters), both before and after a hard winter. He reasoned that if the average wing-length represented the best adapted size, overwinter mortality should be larger in proportion to the distance from that mean.

A principal alternative to Fretwell's formulation of stabilizing selection is that predicted by Paterson's views discussed previously: because species do not change after the initial fixation of genes in small populations, this alternative predicts no differential mortality by phenotype. Waddington's formulations suggest that it is not some individual phenotypic character than is under selection, but entire developmental systems, and Wright's views pretty much coincide on this point. Therefore, all of the alternatives predict no differential mortality according to size.

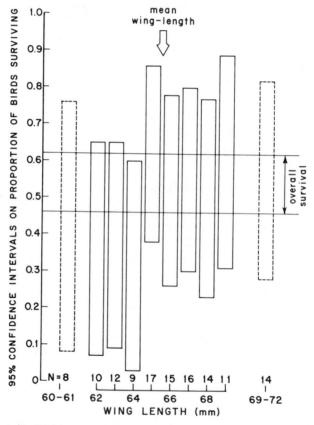

Figure 1 Survival of field sparrows according to size class. Stabilizing selection predicts greatest survival at the mean size with monotonically decreasing survival in proportion to the distance above or below the mean size. In this case, the overall average survival is included within the 95% confidence interval of every size class and the data are nothing like the form predicted by stabilizing selection. See text for further analysis. (Calculated from the original data in Fretwell, 1972: 201, Figure 64)

Fretwell (1972) originally concluded that there was no differential survival according to size, but after being challenged he analyzed the data more thoroughly and 'found tentative evidence for the stabilizing selection hypothesis I was hoping to reject' (Fretwell, 1977:1029). I have calculated the 95% confidence intervals on the proportions of birds surviving in each size class and plotted these data as Figure 1.

The overall survival rate of birds in Fretwell's population was 48%, a figure that is included within the confidence limits of every size class. Furthermore, the 95% confidence interval for the overall proportion of survivors is itself included wholly within the intervals of every size class excepting 64 mm, which nearly includes the entire interval. (Size classes 60 and 61 are combined to provide a sufficient sample to determine confidence limits, as are classes 69 through 72, as indicated in the figure.)

Another way to consider such data is in terms of the parameters of the overall distribution. If stabilizing selection is at work, the population mean should remain the same while the dispersion decreases due to greater selection in proportion to the distance from the mean value. I have calculated the population mean as 65.46 mm (median 66, mode 65), and the mean of the survivors is very nearly the same, as predicted: 65.89 mm (median 66, mode 65). However, the standard deviation is also virtually identical in the two cases: 2.56 and 2.49 mm. Put simply, there is no demonstrable evidence for stabilizing selection in the data.

The data of Figure 1 show that if there is real differential survival according to size it lies in the smaller birds dying more readily than the larger ones, and the split is not at the mean but at a size class lower than the mean. One possible interpretation of this kind of difference in survival (if it be real) is that smaller birds are younger, hence less experienced and so less adept at surviving the hardships of winter (predation, starvation, etc.).

Fretwell (1977: 1210) states that 'In Fretwell (1969a), I show an even clearer case, previously overlooked, of stabilizing selection in juncos (*Junco hyemalis*).' However, these data are in fact less convincing. Fretwell (1969: 20, Figure 8) shows eight size-classes having positive recovery values, which according to the text (p. 19) represent only nine birds; in other words, seven of the eight classes are represented only by a single recovered bird each and the remaining class has two birds. The sample size is not sufficient to calculate confidence intervals on the proportion of surviving birds, and from the figure presented it looks again simply as if smaller (younger?) birds die more readily, if there be any differential mortality at all.

The point of this example is not to single out one study or investigator for particular scrutiny, but rather in part to demonstrate how easily an honest researcher can be convinced of stabilizing selection by his peers, even when his stated predilection was not to find it and even when the data were not convincing. One wonders how many biologists persist in interpreting their data in terms of stabilizing selection when the data in fact show no such thing.

There are, of course, ways to rationalize this finding without abandoning pan-selectionist views. For example, one might suggest that the data are too few for a critical test, that character variance is such that it is not distributed symmetrically about the mean, or that directing selection is in the process of changing the phenotypic structure of the population so that the hypothesis of stabilizing selection is not even applicable. It is not a satisfactory procedure in science, however, merely to erect *ad hoc* interpretations when data do not conform to expectation. It is incumbent upon the interpreter to seek new critical tests of such interpretations if we are to have empirically substantiated bases for acceptance of selectionist interpretations.

Reinforcing selection

A critical test for reinforcing selection was identified by Vaurie (1951) in his study of Asian rock nuthatches (*Sitta*), and subsequently developed as a general principle by Brown and Wilson (1956). The idea is to find two related species that are highly similar and have only partially overlapping ranges. Then in the area of overlap (sympatry), where reinforcing selection can operate, their characters should diverge from one another: the phenomenon known as character divergence or character displacement. The prediction from alternative views, such as those of Paterson discussed previously, is that no divergent effect peculiar to the area of sympatry should occur.

Figure 2 shows Vaurie's data for the bill length of an eastern and western species of nuthatch whose ranges overlap. It can be seen that in the allopatric areas (far west and far east) the two species do indeed have similar

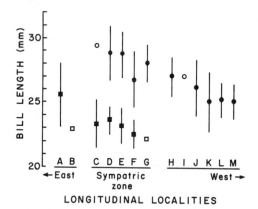

Figure 2 Geographical variation in bill size of *Sitta neumayer* (squares) and *S. tephronota* (circles). Reinforcing selection predicts similar sizes in the allopatric zones of the east and west, and then abrupt divergence in the sympatric zone. Instead, the bill size varies clinally with longitude, becoming gradually smaller toward the west in each species independent of the other. (Redrawn from Vaurie, 1951)

bill lengths, and that in the sympatric zone their bills are different in length. The case for a special divergent effect in the sympatric area, however, is weak. It is difficult to tell much about geographic variation in allopatry of the eastern species because only one sample exists with sufficient data for dispersion estimates of size, but the western species clearly shows a clinal variation in allopatry. It appears from the data that the most parsimonious interpretation is that there exists a similar clinal variation in both species, each becoming increasingly smaller as one moves westward within its range, with no indication that the presence of the other species is having any effect on this variation.

As in the case of reputed demonstrations of stabilizing selection that fail to deliver the expected results, there are ways to rationalize the nuthatch results in order to maintain a pan-selectionist interpretation. For example, one could as always focus on the inadequacy of the data, pointing out that if there were a large sample size at locality B in Figure 2 it might show a long bill length for the eastern species; then its much shortened length in the sympatric zone would show the influence of the western species, even if no reciprocal influence can be demonstrated. Or, one might erect a scenario concerning the relative abundances of the two species in the area of overlap along these lines: the eastern species will be more abundant in localities C and D, so force the western species to long bill lengths, whereas the western species will be more abundant at localities F and G, forcing the eastern species to have shorter bill lengths—the more abundant species always keeping closest to the apparently most favorable bill length of about 26 mm. It is not satisfactory, however, simply to make *ad hoc* dismissals of failures to find expected results; if the viability of selectionist hypotheses is to be credible, it is necessary to pursue the new, more complicated interpretations and show empirically that they correctly predict the situation in nature.

Note added to final manuscript. In an important paper Grant (1975) has made a thorough reanalysis of the rock nuthatch variation, including extensive new data. His Figure 5 (p. 249) 'makes it clear that *neumayer*, if anything, has converged in bill length in sympatry toward the *tephronota* condition.' Similarly, he finds no clear evidence for character divergence in bill width, eye-stripe length, eye-stripe width, wing length, or tarsus length. 'Weight data are consistent with an hypothesis of mutual divergence in body size but not sufficient to assess it' (p. 261). The paper should be consulted for details of evidence that some local divergence in eye-stripe size may occur in south and west Iran.

Directing selection

It is no accident that textbooks tout the example of industrial melanism as the principal empirical study demonstrating directing selection. Through the careful work of H. B. D. Kettlewell (e.g. 1955a, 1955b, 1956, 1957a, 1957b,

1957c, 1958a, 1958b, 1959, 1961) a tremendous body of fact has accumulated concerning dark and light moths, especially of the species *Biston betularia*. Industrialization in Great Britain killed the light-colored lichens on trees and deposited soot which blackened the trunks. Collections of moths of many species in unpolluted areas are dominated by light-colored individuals, whereas similar collections in polluted areas show a preponderance of dark moths—so that the character–environment correlation is unquestioned. Because this massive alteration of the environment took place in historical times the phylogenetic process has been more accessible to study than perhaps in any other case so far analyzed.

Ford (1971: 293) stated that 'Over a hundred species have been affected in Britain alone as well as large numbers in other countries also; events which constitute the most striking evolutionary change ever actually witnessed in any organism, plant, or animal.' This statement is misleading, however. The first black specimen in collections was caught at Manchester in 1848 and by 1895 about 98% of the captures were of black individuals. Hence the evolution was essentially complete more than a half-century before it was subjected to analytical scrutiny and therefore was not witnessed by evolutionary biologists as it occurred.

Kettlewell's experimental results may be sketched as follows. Moths of the light and black forms were experimentally released in an area free of pollution where birds were observed to take 164 black ones but only 26 light moths. Release and recapture of marked individuals showed that light moths had a much higher probability of being retaken (12,5 vs 6.3%). In an industrially polluted area this trend was reversed (13.1 vs 27.5% in one year and 25.0 vs 52.3% in the next). There is some evidence for other differences between light and black moths, particularly greater physiological viability of the black ones. Kettlewell found some evidence that the moths move around a bit once alighting upon a tree trunk, the dark ones settling on darker patches and the light ones on lighter patches. Melanism in *Biston betularia* is due to a dominant allele at a single locus, and this genetic pattern prevails among the other known species showing industrial melanism.

A parsimonious interpretation of these facts follows straightforward selectionist notions. Prior to industrial pollution *Biston betularia* was principally light in color; any black moths arising by mutation were preyed upon heavily. Following the blackening of substrates by soot, black individuals survived predation more frequently because of their concealing coloration, and hence eventually replaced the lighter colored individuals. Thus evolution occurred due to mutation and subsequent individual selection in a changed environment.

There is some reason to believe that the case of industrial melanism may not be very typical of evolutionary phenomena. As pointed out by Waddington and many other authors, most adaptive characters are highly buffered against genetic and environmental change. Melanism in *Biston betularia* and most other moths showing industrial melanism is due to a dominant allele, and if one accepts Fisher's (1930) analysis, dominance should evolve to protect a genome from unadaptive change. Traditional selectionist views therefore suggest that melanism has always conferred some advantage to its possessor, prior to any industrial pollution, and as noted above there is some evidence for this. Typical or not, the case of industrial melanism stands as an apparently convincing example of directing selection.

Suppose we play devil's advocate in scrutinizing this best known case of evolutionary change by asking the two key questions. First, is the empirical case for individual selection as the mechanism of change really secured by the evidence? And second, are the same facts consistent with any alternative view about the mechanism of phylogenetic change?

To begin, we may ask whether *Biston betularia* consists of one freely interbreeding, polymorphic population or two essentially isolated populations of different colors. So far as I can determine from the published record there are no data available on mating frequencies. Taking the case of Manchester as having 98% melanistic moths, if the animals are mating without respect to color 0.98^2 or 96% of the matings should be of the black–black type and $0.02^2 = 0.04\%$ of the light–light type. Therefore, slightly less than 4% of matings should be of the mixed light–dark type, and this is a sufficiently small number that it renders distinction between the two possibilities difficult to test.

In the absence of critical data, let us ask what the possible interpretations are under the assumption that *B. betularia* consists of two reproductively isolated populations. The selectionist interpretation has the light population being reduced by predation at the expense of the black population. Paterson's alternative hypothesis would have the black population arising from some small group in a specific locality and dispersing into areas of the light population's range. Directing selection in the sense of one incipient species replacing another might still occur, but let us pause before considering that possibility to examine the evidence concerning dispersal. Kettlewell (1958a) provides massive evidence for the dispersal of black moths, wrested from analysis of more than 20 000 specimens taken in more than 80 localities in the British Isles. In some unpolluted areas melanistic moths were appearing in increasing numbers which cannot be accounted for satisfactorily by mutation rates or by predator pressures (which in any case should be *removing* the black moths).

The data on dispersal of black moths into previously uninhabited areas suggests that the same thing could have happened at Manchester in the middle of the last century. Therefore, we are faced with two possible interpretations: either the black moths replaced the light moths at Manchester due to selection, or else the black moths simply became numerous without effect on the light moth population. In other words, the crucial data stressed by Darwin and

Wallace are missing: constancy of the total population. The Manchester data merely provide ratios of the two phenotypes in collections made in the last century without any evidence that the black moth was *replacing* the light one. The selectionist interpretation is not secured by the data and a viable alternative hypothesis exists.

To be totally iconoclastic, I should also point out that even if the total population of moths were proven constant over the period of change in Manchester, some residual doubt concerning selection might still occur. As pointed out previously in discussing the meaning of 'selection' it is possible that one population can decline simultaneously with the rise of another population without there being any causal connection between the two changes. The ideal study would have to demonstrate not only that the total population of moths remains constant, but that the change in frequencies of black and light morphs is due to differential values of the same selection pressure. Kettlewell's results only suggest this process in moths, in that they combine two separate pieces of information: there is differential survival by morph in release–recapture studies on the one hand, and differential predation by birds in experiments on the other hand. Although it may be parsimonious to infer that the first result is due to the second one, this link is not actually secured by empirical evidence.

Note added to the final manuscript.   Although the title of an article by Bishop and Cock (1975) emphasizes the apparent increase in light forms with cleaner air, the evidence for such reverse selection is quite limited and their stress is quite different: 'it is prudent to emphasize the unknowns in what may at first seem to be an attractively clear-cut example of evolution in action' (p. 90). Dark and light moths have always coexisted, even in totally pollution-free and heavily polluted environments, which might be due to some advantage of heterozygotes but has other interpretations (above). They note that chemical changes in the environment may be influencing color directly or indirectly, which fact again has both genetic-selectionist interpretations and an alternative in chemically induced developmental influences on color. Three species carefully sampled do not show covariance in color frequencies as expected if avian predation were the sole selection pressure. In fact, one species has a density of 'as many as 50 000 to 100 000 moths per square kilometer per night' (p. 96), raising the question of whether avian predation could possibly have a selective influence. Bishop and Cook also note that 'in nature melanic moths remain common in areas where theoretically the birds should have exterminated them' (pp. 97–98). Finally, they emphasize the importance of migration among areas (see discussion above). In sum, as the industrial melanism phenomenon is investigated ever more carefully, it continues to raise critical new questions and to suggest new interpretations rather than supplying firmer evidence for the traditional selectionist interpretation.

Perspective

One or a few cases of failure to substantiate predictions surely cannot constitute general rejection of selectionist theory. I tried to pick examples where selectionist predictions were straightforward and the results were accepted at least by the authors as conforming to prediction, and then to show that these same results were consistent with some alternative to selection. It is understandably difficult to find straightforward examples of critical studies that test directing selection because of the need to catch evolutionary change in progress, but if stabilizing and reinforcing selection be real our textbooks should be full of examples similar to those analyzed above. That such is not the case suggests either that these forms of selection are rare to absent, or else that biologists have not been seeking critical tests of the selection hypotheses.

It will probably have occurred to the reader that I have ignored two entire bodies of evidence showing the efficacy of selection. First there is the long history of animal breeding, artificial selection having been used by both Darwin and Wallace as an analogy for natural selection. Second, there is huge literature on selection experiments in the laboratory. I certainly do not imply through omission that these two massive literatures fail to demonstrate the reality of effects due to selection, for quite the opposite is true. However, showing that selection *can* have an effect on a captive or laboratory population and showing that the mechanism of evolutionary phenomena in naturally occurring population *is* selection are totally different matters. Artificial selection and selection experiments strengthen our willingness to put forth a theory of natural selection as the mechanism of evolution, but that theory must be tested in its own right.

The major lesson to be drawn appears to be a simple one. Compared with the theories of modification by descent, character–environment correlations, and furcation of species—all of which are attested by massive empirical evidence—the theory of natural selection, especially in its classic forms, is weakly supported. This conclusion does not mean that selectionist interpretations are necessarily wrong, but it does mean that they should be tested with greater rigor and completeness if they are to be fully convincing.

SOME DIFFERENCES BETWEEN BEHAVIOR AND MORPHOLOGY

To this point I have purposely concentrated upon classical issues in evolution as they relate to morphological traits so as not to confuse issues too early with the special considerations that must be paid behavioral phenomena. Some authors have asserted that behavior is 'just like' morphology in so far as evolutionary study goes, but I assert that there are at least three important differences.

Variation

In order to test directly the application of selectionist models to any phenotypic character one has to assess the variation in that character. Phenotypic behavioral traits, however, have a source of variation that does not occur in morphological traits, a point that can be illustrated by a straightforward example.

Suppose the morphological trait of interest is the forearm-length of orangutans. One can place a ruler next to a captive animal's forearm or next to the radius bone of a museum specimen to obtain a measurement. Different investigators will record slightly different lengths, and even the same investigator repeatedly measuring the same bone will generate a distribution of measurements. In some cases of morphology action required by the measurer will exacerbate his or her measuring variation, as when a curved feather is flattened upon a rule, but even here the feather remains physically the same. The recorded variation in morphology defines the precision of measurement, which must be taken into account when comparing traits of different individuals. Obviously, it will not do to study reputed differences among individual orangutans if those differences are smaller than the precision of measurement.

If we now consider the brachiating behavior of the orangutan we find an additional source of variation to contend with. Suppose first that one measures the distance of extension of the arm as part of the brachiation motor pattern, as from a motion picture clip. Repeated measurement from the same film clip yields the same kind of variation as found when measuring a bone with a ruler, and again, different investigators will also measure differently. However, the next time the same animal brachiates, it will do so differently, even under highly standardized conditions. A bone is a physical entity but a behavioral pattern is a concept: a behavioral pattern is ultimately a collection of observations or measurements.

The lack of correspondence in measuring morphology and behavior widens when the characters being measured are more complicated. Morphologists often use indices to express aspects of animals that are more abstract than simple linear measurements: e.g. the ratio of length to width of an irregular shape such as a bird's wing to characterize its shape. Even simple abstractions of behavioral patterns have a nearly limitless choice of such expressions based on temporal and sequential combinations of motor elements. Therefore, while most ways of characterizing an abstract morphological trait such as the shape of a wing will yield tolerably comparable results, ways of characterizing an abstract behavioral trait such as an aggressive display are so numerous that the results of different investigators may be wildly incomparable. These definitional problems are often exacerbated in the behavioral literature, where workers stray far from operational descriptions when they incorporate functional aspects, as in erecting entities such as 'altruistic behavior'.

At the very least, then, measurement of even simple traits entails an additional source of variation in behavior. In no meaningful sense is variation in behavior 'just like' that in morphology.

Inheritance

Earlier in this essay I accepted as empirical fact the tendency of offspring to resemble their parents to some non-random degree, implying that parents somehow transmit traits to their offspring. The degree to which this inheritance is genetic has been well studied in many cases of morphology but not so well in behavior. Studies of this sort fall into two major classes: precise and quantitative genetic analysis.

Simple traits that are influenced by only a few genetic loci are not often of great evolutionary interest, even though the inheritance can be traced precisely. For example, those monofactorial traits of human morphology used as illustrations in genetics classes (hair on the penultimate segment of the index finger, attached earlobes, blue eyes, PCT-tasting) are hardly the kinds of traits evolutionists view as importantly adapted. It is likely that most important traits, especially of vertebrates, are multifactorial, such as milk production in cows which is estimated to be influenced by some 10 000 loci (E. L. Jensen, pers. comm.). Minor color morphs in the head-striping of the white-throated sparrow (*Zonotrichia albicollis*) are associated with behavioral differences in aggression (Ficken *et al.*, 1978), the difference in morphs being due to replacement of a whole chromosome in the karyotype (Thorneycroft, 1966); the number of included loci affecting aggressive behavior could therefore be quite large.

In considering the genetics of evolutionarily important morphological and behavioral traits, we are therefore usually considering quantitative treatment of polygenic systems. One analytical tool of quantitative genetics is analysis of variance, in which the total phenotypic variance of the population is the sum of genetic (s_g) and environmental (s_e) variance and twice their covariance. Analysis of a given trait through breeding experiments can yields its heritability (h^2) or degree of genetic determination, where $h^2 = s_g/(s_g + s_e)$. For a given environment, this index tells a breeder how easily he can enhance a trait through artificial selection. Heritability varies from zero (no genetically attributable variance in the population) to unity (all variance attributable to genetic variance), and typical values for economically important traits in domestic animals often run about $h^2 = 0.2$, with some higher and many lower values. The point of this brief foray into breeding experiments is that even under well studied and stable conditions, most of the phenotypic variance among individuals of a population cannot be attributed to genetics. As noted previously,

Waddington (1974) also emphasizes this point, stressing the 'wildly different' genotypes underlying the wild-type phenotype in naturally occurring populations of *Drosophila.*

The implications of this point must be carefully drawn. Population analysis does not say anything direct about the roles of genes and environment in individual inheritance. However, at the population level, any finite h^2 means that it is possible to select for the trait, and hence natural selection in populations of wild animals could operate with at least some effectiveness. On the other hand, usual h^2 values emphasize that most variability in traits within a population is not attributable to genetic bases, and furthermore it is possible to have high parent–offspring correlations in traits while having low genetic heritability in the same population. The logical endpoint of this reasoning is, of course, that parents must 'transmit' traits to their offspring by some means additional to usual genetics. For both morphological and behavioral traits extragenetic 'inheritance' may consist of similar environmental influences of development: habitat, diet, and other factors shared by parent and offspring.

In addition to 'inheritance' via environmental similarity, behavior has a kind of transmission of traits not directly found in morphology: namely, traditions and culture. For animals that can and do learn—certainly the case in most higher vertebrates—those species having parental contact with the young possess an important capacity for transmitting behavioral traits in addition to genetic inheritance. Indeed, recognition of this fact has been the basis for a multiple-level view of evolution in which, for example, the culture is conceived as a population of trait-influencing units (memes) in analogy with the gene pool as a population of genes (Plotkin and Odling-Smee, 1981).

Evolutionary record

Yet a third way in which behavior differs from morphology is simply that there can be no fossils of behavior. Of course some morphological structures, physiological traits, and other attributes of life also cannot fossilize. It is further true that a few behavioral patterns can leave indirect evidence in the fossil record: dinosaur footprints leave some record of locomotion, fossil termite nests some record of nest-building, and so on. On the whole, though, there is virtually no record of phylogenetic change in behavior over geological time so that our guesses about what transpired are extrapolations from comparative or other evidence.

INTERPRETATION OF BEHAVIOR

It is now possible to consider what the foregoing issues mean in interpreting evolutionary aspects of behavior. I have tried to show that evolution—formulated as operationally stated theories of phylogeny, adaptation, and speciation—is empirically well supported, whereas the theory of natural selection as the causal agent of these phenomena is poorly supported. Furthermore, there exist alternatives to pan-selectionist views that are consistent with available evidence. Lastly, even if traditional selectionist views be correct for morphological characters, there are important differences between these and behavioral characters relevant to evolution. So I take several examples of behavior to show how the foregoing considerations influence possible interpretations of the evolutionary causes producing the observed results.

Colonial nesting habits

One of the most straightforward of behavioral studies that seems to demonstrate stabilizing selection is I. J. Patterson's (1965) careful analysis of colonial nesting in the black-headed gull (*Larus ridibundus*). Many seabirds nest in colonies, which is to say that they clump nesting in both space and time. Under selectionist views one would expect some advantage to this habit, such as protection from nest predation, so that the colonial habit would be perpetuated by stabilizing selection.

It is difficult to formulate a clear prediction of classical stabilizing selection at work on the spatial variable because variation could be conceived as 'one sided'. That is, the optimal nesting place might be at the center of the colony, and obviously not all birds can occupy that spot. Patterson did show that of 1703 eggs laid by pairs within colony areas, 157 produced fledged young, whereas no young were produced from 358 eggs laid by birds nesting in isolated areas near the colonies.

It is easier to formulate predictions for the temporal variable, as any pair can nest either before or after the mean time of nesting of the colony. Patterson measured time of nesting and success by breaking the season into temporal blocks of five days the first year and three days the second. He provides graphs (in his Figure 3) of percentage of total pairs beginning laying in each block for both years, and matching graphs of the percentages of eggs reared. The general similarity between the distribution of nesting times and the distribution of egg success within each year is evident.

The way in which the data are presented, however, does not provide the comparison needed to test for stabilizing selection. I have taken the data of the second year for calculations, as it is apparently free from the renesting attempts included in the first year's data and also provides finer temporal discrimination (3-day rather than 5-day blocks); there is some loss of precision from the original data, as numbers must be taken from graphs. First I calculated the number of nests in each temporal block by multiplying the percentages by the stated total sample of 208 nests. I then calculated the number of young reared by taking (from the graph) the percentage of eggs reared and multiplying this in each temporal block by the number of eggs laid (given as exact figures

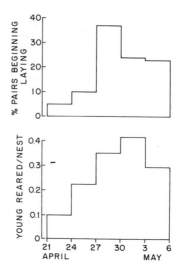

Figure 3 Time of laying the first egg (above) and average number of young reared per nest (below) in the above temporal groups of black-headed gulls. The results are consistent with predictions from stabilizing selection in that production of young is greatest for birds nesting near the mean date. To secure selection, it must be further shown that variations in nesting time are heritable. (Upper graph redrawn from Patterson, 1965; lower graph calculated from his data as explained in text)

printed on the graph). Finally, I divided this second product by the first one in order to find the number of young *per nest* produced within each temporal block, and the results are shown in my figure 3.

The most number of young produced per nest falls in the block between 30 April and 3 May (lower graph) whereas the peak nesting time was in the previous block (upper graph in figure 3). Nevertheless, given some leeway for random variation and more leeway for year-to-year variation in the timing of the best conditions for nesting, the results are consistent with expectations generated by the hypothesis of stabilizing selection. There are also some technical problems that could be raised about the data, but let us ask simply why these results fail to secure an interpretation of stabilizing selection.

What Patterson's results show is that there exists a best time to nest in terms of producing reared young (lower graph) and that the gulls tend to zero-in on that best time (upper graph), with some variation. We do not know certainly to what extent the gulls are choosing the time and place of nesting independently and to what extent they are influenced in these matters by the other gulls of the colony. In a tropical gull species, with a very extended nesting season, there is local synchrony of nesting (Hailman, 1964) which suggests that social factors do play a role. In any case, one could compile comparative evidence to show that gulls in the south temperate region also tend to nest around a given time in their spring (even though that be half a year's difference from Patterson's gulls). In other words, there is a demonstrable character–environment correlation in nesting behavior, so that these and other results secure the interpretation that the timing of nesting is a behavioral adaptation.

However, our task is not to see if the behavior is adaptive; rather, it is to see if the adaptive behavior is being perpetuated by stabilizing selection. The example is a good one because the data are about as convincing as one could expect in behavioral studies and the missing piece of evidence that would secure stabilizing selection is not necessarily obvious. The missing evidence is, of course, proof that variation in the timing of nesting is heritable. There is, so far as I can find, no evidence whatever that offspring tend to nest at the same time as did their parents. We do know that younger adult gulls (and other birds) frequently attempt nesting at inappropriate times or places and have lower nesting success than experienced birds. But we do not know that offspring coming from the peak time of nesting themselves nest closer to the peak than offspring coming from early or late nests.

The data are just as consistent with alternative views as they are with the hypothesis of stabilizing selection. If species' characteristics are essentially fixed after initial speciation, as in H. E. H. Paterson's view, then gulls might well be adapted to respond appropriately to environmental or social stimuli without the phenotypic variance in timing being the result of genotypic differences among individuals. There might (or might not) have been selection initially involved in the evolution of this behavioral trait, but once evolved it is not subject to individual selection. Nothing in the data serve to discourage such an alternative interpretation.

Honey bee dancing

As is well known, A. M. Wenner (e.g. 1971) challenged Karl von Frisch's functional interpretation of the waggle dance of the honey bee (*Apis mellifera*) which is reputed to communicate the direction and distance of food sources to other workers. In defending von Frisch's interpretation Lindauer (1971: 89) stated that '...each morphological structure and behaviour act is associated with a special function. On this basis alone, it would seem unlikely that information contained in the waggle dance of a honey bee is not transmitted to her nest mates.'

The point of mentioning this controversy is not to review it in detail, but rather merely to show how traditional selectionist bias influences the interpretation of behavior. Lindauer takes as fact that each behavioral act has a special function—a generalization that is hardly established even within the framework of traditional thinking, where characters are more often viewed as being the best compromises between conflicting selection pressures and hence unassignable to a specific 'special function'. From this unsupported assertion, he then concludes that communication most likely takes place. As this second issue is not an evolutionary issue, it is more readily testable. Hence study should proceed first by establishing whether or not communication in fact takes place, and then (only if it does) to ask the evolutionary question of whether the communication has been selected to have this reputed function. The empirical evidence is complicated and there are several derivative epistemological issues as well (see Hailman, 1977a), but the point here is a straightforward one: prejudgement concerning evolutionary phenomena biases thinking away from empirical tests and substitutes for data a nexus of conceptual notions. This sort of mental pitfall cannot lead to clear interpretation of behavior.

The enthusiasm for pan-selectionism among ethologists is not restricted to extreme cases. As Rowell (1979: 20) points out, 'It is the nature of our discipline to try to suggest adaptive significance to the observed differences.' For example, J. L. Brown (1975: 267) states that 'The goal in this type of study is to find out how the behavior benefits the individual animal and, consequently, how natural selection might have acted to bring about its evolution.' In other words, the question of adaptation is not *whether* some kind of behavior benefits the individual, but rather *how* it does so because individual selection has already been implicitly assumed. Indeed, Rowell's iconoclastic paper represents a rare voice among behaviorists. She analyzes many cases of phenotypic variation in social behavior of primates, and although her only alternative to individual selection appears to be 'genetic or cultural drift', she fails to find even a *prima facie* case for stabilizing or directing selection. If proposing selective functions for behavior, argues Rowell, 'is to be more than an entertaining parlor game, we must formulate such explanations as hypotheses which can be tested and potentially disproved by further observations.'

Eggshell removal in gulls

Parents of many species perform acts that support the survival of their offspring. Such cases provide opportunities to test for the efficacy of stabilizing selection in perpetuating these parental acts, and one such act is the removal of the eggshell after the hatching of a young bird. Tinbergen *et al.* (1962), who studied this behavior in the black-headed gull, noted several possible functions of eggshell-removal: avoidance of injury to the young from sharp edges of the shell, parasitic infection from organisms in the organic matter of the shell, interference with parental brooding of the young, and so on. For one reason or another all such possibilities were deemed unlikely except for predator-protection. After hatching the white insides of the eggshell might be more readily visible to predators, especially crows flying overhead, than is the greenish-splotched outside of the egg.

In order to test the anti-predator function of eggshell-removal, Tinbergen *et al.* performed a number of admirable experiments which yielded clearcut results. They first established in a series of tests that artificially painting eggs to camouflage them was not sufficient because predators found them as readily as white hens' eggs or gulls' eggs painted white. They then laid out gulls' eggs with and without an eggshell, but found no difference in the predation-rate, which failure they relate to various unnatural aspects of the experiment. They therefore repeated the experiment with more concealment of the eggs using grass straws and found that eggs with an eggshell nearby were taken at a statistically significant greater rate than were eggs without shells. Finally, in a massive experiment they showed that the closer the eggshell to the concealed egg, the greater the probability of egg predation. It would appear from these results, secured by careful investigators who were intimately familiar with their animals, that eggshell-removal functions as an anti-predator device being maintained by stabilizing selection: birds failing to remove the eggshell have low probabilities of bringing off viable young, and hence cannot pass on any genes or traditions for 'non-removal'.

Let me once again play iconoclast and see if there could be any chink in the armor of evidence. One could, as in the case of the timing of nesting discussed previously, argue that variation in the behavior has not been demonstrated to be heritable—but there is in this case a prior problem: "The Black-headed Gull invariably removes the egg shell" (Tinbergen *et al.*, 1962). In other words, we cannot (even in theory) measure the heritability of presence or absence of eggshell-removal because the behavior is a universal trait in this species. This is the very reason that Tinbergen *et al.* had to lay out their own experimental eggs and nests: there was no natural variation to observe. In order to test for stabilizing selection one would have to identify some variable aspect in eggshell-removal, show that such variation is heritable, and then look at the differential production of offspring according to different phenotypes of the parents.

The demonstration by Tinbergen *et al.* of the usefulness of eggshell removal to the survival of the young does not bear on alternatives to natural selection, which are just as consistent with the known facts. Paterson's view easily allows for useful, universal traits of species, so the kind of evidence available does not discriminate among alternative hypotheses concerning the perpetuation of adaptive behavior.

Courtship display

One of the truly pervasive assumptions in the ethological literature is that one function of specialized courtship signals is prevention of hybridization. Writers on communicative topics use terms such as the 'species information' in courtship signals, and many studies of pairs of phylogenetically related species concentrate on enumerating the differences between the two, especially in terms of courtship signals. One of the rare humorous remarks I have heard given by the chairman of a paper-session occurred some years ago at the annual meeting of the American Ornithologists' Union. After hearing a paper in which the author showed careful and massive evidence for a huge number of differences in behavior and morphology between species of goldfinches (*Spinus*), the chairman said afterward 'where's the problem?' The search for ethological isolating mechanisms and differences that ameliorate ecological competition is so ingrained in field biologists that they come to assume that differences among species are the result of specific selection for such differences. Until the criticisms were raised by Paterson (1978, 1979, 1981) no one seems seriously to have questioned this assumption.

Paterson (pers. comm.) pointed out to me that I recognized the problems with the evidence for ethological isolating mechanisms without drawing the obvious conclusion that the concept in general was faulty. In considering optical signals involved in courtship, I had said that prevention of hybridization was an explanation that 'has been employed uncritically and overworked. Many closely related species whose breeding ranges overlap have highly similar signals, yet rarely interbreed' (Hailman, 1977b: 280). I was arguing against interspecific explanations for the evolution of characteristics of signals when the signals 'have not been analyzed with respect to the species' own needs and environment' (p. 306). Paterson, however, goes further to say that signals, like other characters, are established at the time of speciation in small populations, so that courtship signals act simply to bring the mates together. When a new species contacts another, similar species either (a) the two will fail to interbreed because their signals are different, or (b) they will interbreed—but there is no subsequent selection to render the signals more species-specific.

Paterson has already presented some of the evidence on this subject (e.g. Paterson, 1978, 1980, 1981) and has a major paper in preparation, so I will provide just one more example of how the reinforcing-selectionist view leads to difficulties with the evidence. Two avian ethologists once proposed that the courtship acts and coloration of dabbling ducks were structured by reinforcing selection for species' specificity. I tried to show the absurdity of this belief applied to the wood duck (*Aix sponsa*) and to provide an alternative explanation of its strikingly colorful plumage (Hailman, 1959). The species has no congeners within its range, and does not remotely resemble any kind of duck that has been known ever to exist. It is therefore necessary to propose the existence of some now-extinct species in order to account for the wood duck's courtship plumage by reinforcing selection! As absurd as such an *ad hoc* postulate may seem, it is still being promoted (see audience discussion at the end of Hailman, 1979).

The only really straightforward way to separate the traditional reinforcing-selection hypothesis from Paterson's alternative is in situations that should lead to character divergence (character displacement). Demonstrating that two species enhance their differences in sympatric areas, in response to the presence of the other, would be strong evidence. I have reviewed the display plumage and to some extent studies of the courtship acts of North American birds, and have thus far been unable to find an even good suggestive case of character divergence. In sum, the notion that courtship behavior and coloration are evolved for species' distinctiveness through reinforcing selection remains a hypothesis without empirical support.

Food preparation

Having found problems with interpreting behavioral evolution in terms of stabilizing and reinforcing selection, we should conclude with considering the role of selection in promoting evolutionary change. The problem here, however, is large because characters are thought to evolve slowly through selection acting on small variants, and hence the chances of finding a suitable system for analysis are slim. However, there is a case in which the phenotypic structure of a population changed rapidly over a period of years and was followed closely.

Because the reader will probably be familiar with this example, it needs to be laid out in an unfamiliar way. Namely, instead of providing initially all the facts about the identification of individuals and their behavior, we look instead only at those characteristics of a population usually measured in studying an evolutionary change: the relative frequency of phenotypes and how they change over time. In 1952 all the behavioral phenotypes in the population were of type A, but the following year one individual of the new type B was detected. Within ten years, 90% of the individuals in the population in all age classes except two were of the new type B. If we knew no more than these facts, which are the kind usually encountered, it would be easy to say that phenotype B arose by mutation in 1953 and quickly replaced phenotype A by directing selection. (Furthermore, in another population of the same species, geographically isolated from the population in which phenotype B arose, this behavioral trait has never been observed.)

Of course we do know more than these facts. We know that on Koshima Island the primatologist Kawamura observed the Japanese macaque (*Macaca fuscata*) named Imo brush sand from a sweet potato and then dip the vegetable into a nearby brook. And we know that Masao Kawai (1965) followed the spread of this phenotypic trait through the population of positively identified individuals for the next decade. From Imo, her mother Eda learned the trait in the initial year when Imo was between one and two years old, as did a male which was a year older than Imo. In 1954 a male of Imo's age picked up the trait, and in 1955 Imo's younger brother (or half-brother) and two other young individuals (two and four years old) learned it. By 1958 (after 5 years) about 80% of the 2-to-7-year olds were practising sweet-potato washing, but only about 18% of the adults, and all these females. Within 10 years only infants less than a year old and the old adults (those more than 12 years of age) were not showing the phenotypic trait; in all other age classes the incidence was between 90 and 100%.

This familiar example, recounted initially in an unusual way, serves as a reminder of several points. First, documenting a change in the relative frequency of phenotypes—or in this case even the absolute frequency—is not sufficient to invoke a cause of natural selection. Second, totally new phenotypes can arise in a population without either genetic mutation or recombination. Third, the inheritance of a behavioral trait need not be via the genes, but can be due to cultural factors—in this case, transmission from offspring to mother and among the juveniles within their subculture. Fourth, the spread of a phenotypic character in a population does not have to be due to selection, but rather can be via 'phenotypic conversion' with individual animals changing from phenotype A to phenotype B. Lastly, the perpetuation of the character, once it has become nearly universal in the population, need not be due to stabilizing selection of any sort. Indeed, the washing of sweet potatoes may have no assignable 'function' in any sense of the word, and in any case cannot be attributed to natural selection.

CONCLUSIONS

A frequent question asked by persons who read the manuscript of this essay or discussed evolutionary issues with me was: 'but what do *you* think is correct?' There are three kinds of answers.

The first kind of answer is that my opinion is irrelevant. My tasks have been to separate evolutionary theories from one another, especially the principal evolutionary phenomena from their presumed mechanisms of natural selection; to formulate the theories in operational form so that they are testable; to present not only pan-selectionist views but also some alternatives that exist; to evaluate the empirical evidence concerning mechanisms; to show the complications that behavioral evolution entails; and finally to see how this whole endeavor alters our interpretation of behavioral phenomena. Those important things have been done, my opinions as to what are correct simply do not matter to anyone else.

But they do matter, apparently—or else no one would have asked the question. So my second kind of answer is that I am agnostic; I really do not know what is correct because the available empirical evidence seems sparse and open to multiple interpretation. My purpose has been to lay the groundwork for better empirical tests, and I certainly would not have bothered to do that if I had felt the available evidence sufficiently indicated the opinions we should hold concerning the mechanisms of evolutionary phenomena.

The third kind of answer is the reluctant kind: 'if you must press me, read on.'

Apology

Several critics of the manuscript suggested the importance of pointing out that many relevant topics have been omitted from consideration. One is historical documentation of earlier attempts to grapple with evolutionary mechanisms, leading to conceptions such as 'saltation' and so on. Clearly there is insufficient space to do this and I can only state explicitly that I lay no claim to originality of specific concepts in this essay.

More importantly, however, I have not had space to deal with three highly relevant topics, namely alternative modes of speciation (including sympatric speciation proposals), the problems attendant specifically to Darwinian sexual selection, and the implications of coevolutionary phenomena in general. Among the last are the coevolution of flowers and their pollinators, models and their (Müllerian or Batesian) mimics, social signals and their receiving sensory filters, predator and prey, and parasite and host. Perhaps critical scrutiny of these phenomena will show them immune to alternative explanation and thus provide the solid evidence for traditional individual selection that I have been unable to find in the foregoing analyses. The discussion that follows is perforce based solely on the issues actually dealt with in the foregoing essay.

Where does selection operate?

To begin the speculation observe that if selection is occurring today, the easiest place to detect it should be in the perpetuation of adaptive characters by stabilizing selection. Here, within one animal generation or within a single breeding season of some species, it should be possible to document differential mortality or reproduction according to heritable variation in phenotype. Yet the empirical evidence for stabilizing selection seems especially unconvincing and open to alternative interpretation. This assessment does not mean that the original evolutionary development of adaptive characters failed to involve selection. But it does mean that once evolved these characters seem to be perpetuated from generation to generation in the absence of stabilizing selection.

It seems to me that there are at least three overlapping possibilities for the perpetuation of adaptive chatacters without selection: (a) characters are genetically fixed in a rigid system that counters mutation and recombination with allelic dominance and other straightforward genetic mechanisms; (b) the genome dictates an extraordinarily robust developmental system that guarantees a phenotypic endpoint regardless of most genetic changes and environmental influences; or (c) the environment directs development toward some consistent phenotypic endpoint regardless of the genetic base, an included case being perpetuation of behavior by cultural tradition. The first possibility follows the views of Paterson and Wright to some extent; the second is largely a cross between the views of Waddington and Wright, and is consistent with the first; and the third is simply a generalization of behavioral evidence on ontogeny and traditions, which to some extent conflicts with the first two possibilities.

The second easiest place that we should be able to detect natural selection is the character divergence (displacement) expected from reinforcing selection for species' distinctiveness. There are many species-pairs with only partially overlapping geographic ranges, providing thousands (perhaps tens of thousands) of systems for empirical study. Yet I have thus far been unable to find a truly convincing case of character divergence. This fact leads me to the tentative conclusion that reinforcing selection, like stabilizing selection, cannot be playing a major role in evolution.

If two species are too similar ecologically to survive the competition in the same habitat, it must be that one either leaves or goes extinct. The second possibility actually involves a form of group selection, for if one species goes extinct due to competition with an ecologically similar species we have the necessary and sufficient causes for selection: heritable phenotypic differences and differential mortality based on those differences. Unless we can find convincing examples of one species driving another to extinction before our very eyes, so to speak, this kind of group selection is difficult to establish with any confidence. I can think of no easy way to test the hypothesis of competitive extinction with after-the-fact empirical evidence.

Similarly, if two species are so closely related that hybridization is a possibility, then either their already evolved courtship is sufficient to render mating mistakes unlikely, or else the two species do actually interbreed. If they do so, then we expect to find either some consistent rate of hybridization or total loss of species identity due to interbreeding. Apparently stable rates of hybridization do occur in nature (e.g. in *Vermivora* warblers, where the two principal hybrid types have been given the names of Lawrence's and Brewster's warblers). Pan-selectionists explain such situations with the assumption that reinforcing selection has not yet had time to evolve the species' distinctiveness that is sure to come, but the alternative view seems more parsimonious to me at this juncture.

In sum, it appears that selection plays only a minor role in the perpetuation of adaptive characters and in the enhancement of species-distinctive characters through reinforcement. Therefore, if selection is operating at all, it has its major role in the initial evolution of characters.

How do characters evolve?

There are two, not necessarily exclusive, possibilities for the evolution of phenotypic characteristics. The first follows traditional arguments in having individual selection continuously moulding species according to their environments, whereas the second sees major changes occurring at the time of speciation, species thereafter remaining essentially constant. There seem to be at least three ways in which these two views might be distinguished by empirical evidence: direct observation of change, the distribution of extinction rates, and changes through the fossil record.

Direct observation of evolutionary change is, of course, a difficult matter. Pan-selectionists view animals as well adapted to their environments, so that only when some rapid environmental change occurs—as in industrial pollution—should it be possible to detect directing selection. As discussed earlier, the evidence that industrial melanism is due to individual selection is not now convincing and seems to be in the process of becoming less so. The alternative—that black moths represent an incipient species that spread into industrial and other areas without affecting the pre-existing light moths—remains viable until further crucial evidence on population dynamics is available. At present, then, the evidence does not discriminate hypotheses as to how characters evolve.

Lewontin (1978: 215–216) has considered the data compiled by Leigh Van Valen on extinction rates as a test of directing selection. The null hypothesis is that the probability of going extinct is independent of how long a taxon has already survived; such cases will plot as straight lines on semi-logarithmic survivorship curves. The idea is that if directing selection were continuously adapting populations to their constant environments, the curves from the fossil record should show concavity; the longer a taxon has survived, the higher its probability of surviving still longer. This expectation is not met by Van Valen's data on genera of marine invertebrates, the curves being closer to straight lines than to concave shapes.

Van Valen's interpretation is that the environment is continuously changing and at random times the adaptation of a population fails to keep pace so that extinction occurs. Lewontin is critical of the idea of directing selection but does not show clearly that there is an alternative explanation of the random extinctions. That alternative is simply the second hypothesis under consideration in this section: namely, that once having evolved the species do not change. Therefore, due to either changes in the environment or the evolution of new competitive species, extinction occurs randomly in time. We are left, then, with an individual-selectionist interpretation (Van Valen's 'Red Queen' hypothesis of adaptation 'tracking' environmental changes) or its alternative of constant species being randomly eliminated, and I see no way that the extinction data alone can ever resolve the choice. Lewontin has argued against Van Valen's interpretation on other grounds, and in any case that interpretation seems less parsimonious than random extinction of constant species.

The third approach toward separating continual adaptation from change via speciation lies in the nature of change revealed by the fossil record. If directing selection occurs, one should be able to observe gradual changes within species over geological time. Although the fossil record at first appears to demonstrate such changes, there are two major difficulties of interpretation. For example, Kennett's data (Rhodes, 1974: 48) show continuous and gradual changes in shape over time in the foraminiferan *Textularia*. The first difficulty of interpretation is in how many species are involved. Kennett recognizes one from the lowest stratum and two subspecies of another in the upper strata of this Miocene–Pliocene series. We have no criteria for determining genetically separate species in fossils, so guesses are made on the basis of morphology—a procedure that confounds the very issue we wish to resolve. The other problem is that even if we are working within one species for an entire series, there is no way of knowing whether selection is altering the population over time or alternatively that the growth form changes with predominating environmental conditions. That is, we cannot show that the variation is heritable. These two

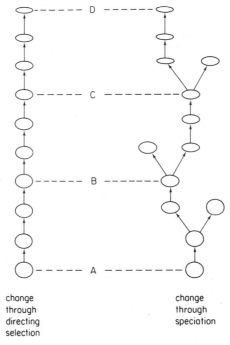

change
through
directing
selection

change
through
speciation

Figure 4 Two extreme views on evolutionary change. In traditionally viewed change through directing selection (left) one line of descent is gradually modified as natural selection favors new variants arising by mutation and recombination. In the alternative view (right), furcation of species provides the new types, which may outlive the unmodified ancestral line. Sampling of fossils at times A, B, C, and D provides an indistinguishable record in the two cases. These two possibilities are not mutually exclusive; both processes could be occurring simultaneously

problems apply throughout the fossil record to all such examples of gradual changes and I see no way to choose between the two alternative interpretations of such changes.

We are therefore left with two possible hypotheses of how characters evolve, as shown diagrammatically in Figure 4. There seems to be no critical evidence available for distinguishing which is correct, and in any case both kinds of processes could be operating in evolution. If the second and newer hypothesis of change by speciation has applicability, it raises further questions about the role of selection in creating new species.

Selection in speciation

Regardless of which hypothesis of phylogenetic change applies (Figure 4), one must consider the possible role of selection in the speciation process. I will not consider the case of sympatric speciation, which Fisher (1930) demonstrated as a possibility, but for which little empirical evidence exists. Instead, inquiry will be directed toward the role of selection in creating new species from reproductively isolated populations of some pre-existing species.

There is general agreement among population geneticists that rates of evolutionary change should be more rapid in smaller populations than larger ones. This agreement is due to the fact that at least two random processes can have large effects in small populations: random mortality regardless of phenotype and hence its underlying genotype (i.e. genetic drift), and random loss of alternative alleles (i.e. genetic fixation). The question of selection therefore becomes one of whether the appearance of new and different species can be explained fully by random processes in small populations, or whether it is necessary to invoke selection as structuring the incipient new species. Paterson endorses the role of natural selection in this creative phase of evolution, the species once having evolved thereafter remaining constant. Traditional selectionists also endorse selection in this initial phase, although they see it as continuing to change the species thereafter. Therefore, the question of individual selection in speciation is not an issue in distinguishing between the hypotheses diagrammed in Figure 4. However, it should be pointed out that this mutually acceptable selectionist view of the creation of new species is itself a separate theory in need of empirical test, with random genetic events in small populations being the alternative possible mechanism for creating new species.

Selection in adaptation

If evolutionary change occurs through directing selection (as diagrammed on the left side of Figure 4), the appearance of character–environment correlations could be attributed solely (although not necessarily) to selection at the individual level. However, if evolutionary change occurs solely through speciation (as in the right side of Figure 4), character–environment correlations cannot be due to individual selection because species characters remain constant after initial speciation. Either possibility for evolutionary change could occur with selection at the species level operating to create the character–environment correlations of adaptation.

The first question is therefore whether individual selection is adequate to explain adaptations under the hypothesis of change through directing selection. There is clearly growing dissatisfaction with this view (e.g. Lewontin, 1978; Gould and Lewontin, 1979). If selection at the individual level were as great an adapting force as is required, we would see it operating also in stabilizing selection and in reinforcing selection. Yet this is precisely where support for individual selection is weakest. I believe this means that whichever view of evolutionary change (Figure 4) applies, we must consider the strong possibility that group selection is playing an important role in evolution.

The notion of group selection has a tortuous history that cannot be reviewed here. Clearly the concept is not a unitary one and therefore cannot be discussed without explicit reference to the unit of selection. Wright's (e.g. 1980) formulation of evolutionary change is one of a malleable species being modified by descent (left side of Figure 4), yet rests on intergroup selection among small, partially isolated populations within one species. This view, given our current understanding of evolutionary processes, seems the most likely mechanism of adaptational change through directing selection. Whether or not there exists an additional adaptive pressure manifest in selection at the species level remains an open question.

If we turn to change through speciation (right side of Figure 4), where intraspecific selection cannot by definition be operating, our only choice is between selection at the species level and no selection whatever. For traditional pan-selectionists this is a choice between the devil and the deep blue sea, yet we must face up to it if adaptation is to be explained under the hypothesis of change through speciation. First, however, let us consider an apparent way out of this choice.

Suppose that character–environment correlations come about because animals choose the habitats for which they are best suited. A pan-selectionist might argue that animals choosing other habitats will die without leaving offspring, and hence this situation constitutes selection at the individual level. This could indeed be intraspecific selection, but the subtle fallacy of this argument lies in the fact that if such habitat-choice is based on genetic variation so that selection can operate, one has abandoned the defining assumption of invariant species. In other words, one is no longer considering the process diagrammed on the right side of Figure 4, but instead proposing some new view intermediate between the two extreme possibilities. Indeed, such an intermediate view might prove correct and should be entertained, but we must not confuse it with the mechanism for adaptation under the extreme view of change through creation of new, invariant species.

If species really are immune to intraspecific selection because any relevant variation in phenotypic characters is not transmitted to offspring, character–environment correlations could still be due to animals choosing the habitat for which they are best suited. This interpretation requires either selection or random genetic processes to create at the time of speciation a behavioral predilection for a particular habitat—namely the one that matches the morphological, physiological, and behavioral characters that dictate the suitable habitat for the animal. So long as animals can find such suitable habitat, the species thrives; when the environment no longer offers this habitat, the species goes extinct. The result is indeed a character–environment correlation, but the requirements of such fine-tuned habitat choice to match other characters of the animal seems an unreasonable requirement.

A closely related and more realistic formulation is that the new species disperses widely into many habitats. In some habitats the animals thrive and in others they die without leaving offspring. So long as variations in the choice of habitat are not transmittable to offspring, no intraspecific selection can occur, yet the end result is the character–environment correlations we seek to explain.

The final possibility left to change through speciation (right side of Figure 4) is that adaptation is due to interspecific selection. As before, habitat-choice need not be finely tuned, and in any case its variations are not heritable. In this case, interspecific competition is responsible for the differential survival of two species in the same habitat. Because the animals of each species transmit their characteristics to their offspring and we have differential survival based on that heritable difference, the result is interspecific selection.

In trying to find critical cases for separating these various possibilities, I keep returning to the impressions made on me by seeing first-hand Darwin's finches (Geospizidae) and the Hawaiian honeycreepers (Drepanididae). We find sparrow-like, grosbeak-like, woodpecker-like, and warbler-like finches in the Galapagos and sparrow-like, grosbeak-like, woodpecker-like, and even parrot-like honeycreepers in the Hawaiian Islands. In each case one ancestral stock evolved environmentally correlated characters through species-radiation over a much greater range of types than ever found within one group of birds on continents. The presence of competitive species on continents must therefore inhibit such radiation within one group, implying that selection at some level must be a reality.

Furthermore, an additional fact about such island avifaunas suggests the kind of selection operating. If the lack of competitors promotes survival of variant phenotypes within a species, one expects to see a single species becoming highly variable. Yet on Cocos Island there is but one species of geospizid finch that seems to be no more variable than any given species in the Galapagos Archipelago. Only when a group of islands allows for the geographic isolation promoting speciation do we find an ancestral type producing variants that occupy the places normally filled by species of other groups on continents. I have been unable to think of an alternative explanation to this one: speciation alone produces the phenotypic variation on which competitive selection works, so it must be that this selection is at the species level.

In sum, whichever view (Figure 4) is correct to account for evolutionary change, the evolution of adaptations (character–environment correlations) seems likely to involve selection above the individual level. Directing selection might operate through intergroup selection within a species, but either kind of adaptational process could involve interspecific selection.

Thesis and antithesis

We have had the 'modern synthesis' of Huxley (1943) and the 'new synthesis' of Wilson (1975), and the time may have come that we should avoid further syntheses and concentrate on the task of articulating and testing the theses and antitheses. In the foregoing sections I have tried to show through speculative reasoning where the primary uncertainties about selection occur.

The evidence seems to be such that in the 'worst case scenario' we can have all the phenomena of evolution without natural selection operating at any level. Briefly assembled from different aspects of the foregoing discussion, one no-selection possibility goes as follows. A small population of animals becomes geographically separated from the parent species, and while in isolation is transformed by random mortality (genetic drift) and random loss of alleles (genetic fixation). This new species then disperses widely, becoming established in some habitats but not in others. Any phenotypic variation, including habitat-choice, is not heritable so that intraspecific selection is impossible. Eventually, environmental changes destroy all suitable habitats and the species goes extinct. This process of creation and extinction of new species goes on incessantly, leaving us with marked correlations between environments and the characters of animals that successfully inhabit them (adaptation), modifications of related animals through geological time (phylogeny), and a great diversity of non-interbreeding populations (speciation).

Conservative estimates state that there are at least a thousand extinct species for every one alive today. Are two billion speciation events since the Precambrian sufficient to account for evolution without selection? Clearly, no one knows. If the 'worst case scenario' needs selection to drive evolution there remain many possibilities to choose from: interindividual selection in the formation of new species and possibly their continuing change, intergroup selection within species to exacerbate that change, and interspecific selection to solidify character–environmental correlations. Perhaps even stabilizing and reinforcing selection at the individual level still have a role somewhere. The various possibilities are becoming clearer and more sharply defined; we must now concentrate on devising ways to test for their existence and importance. Only one conclusion seems truly firm: whatever final view of evolutionary processes emerges, it is not likely to be facile Darwinian pan-selectionism.

SUMMARY

I have tried to wrest positive advances in understanding from the growing disenchantment with classical Darwinian pan-selectionist views of evolution. The three major evolutionary phenomena—phylogeny, adaptation, and speciation—are theories separate and apart from the theory of natural selection as the mechanism (causal agent) of these phenomena. Phylogeny is modification with descent yielding similar species replacing their ancestors in the fossil record. Speciation is the furcation of species yielding a diversity of contemporary, non-interbreeding populations. Adaptation has traditionally proven difficult to formulate operationally, here defined as correlations between environments and the characters of animals inhabiting those environments, produced and perpetuated by processes that require further specification. All three phenomena are well documented.

The traditional theory of natural selection provides a mechanism for all three evolutionary phenomena. Phylogeny is due to differential survival and reproduction of individuals within a species, the heritable variations in phenotype arising through mutation and recombination. Adaptation comes about initially through such directing selection, and is then perpetuated in a well-adapted population through stabilizing selection, which trims new heritable variants arising. Finally, differences among similar species that both reduce competition and promote species-identification of mates are enhanced by reinforcing selection following geographic contact between populations that diverged during allopatric separation.

Alternatives to classical pan-selectionism are many and varied. Sewell Wright emphasizes the importance of the whole genome as the adaptive unit; the need for small, semi-isolated subpopulations to generate sufficient genetic variation; and the possibility that selection is at the intergroup level within the species. C. H. Waddington emphasizes the great degree to which developmental systems are buffered against both genetic change and environmentally induced change that might otherwise alter the resulting phenotype. H. E. H. Paterson emphasizes the importance of the speciation event in providing new phenotypes in evolution, with any variants in species once solidified being essentially non-heritable.

Selection should not be defined in terms of genetics since selection requires only that phenotypic variation among parents be transmitted to their offspring, which could be via non-genetic inheritance as (for example) in behavioral traditions. Furthermore, a change in phenotypic ratios within a population is not even *prima facia* evidence for selection unless it is also shown that the overall population size remains constant (that is, one phenotype is truly replacing the other). Finally, the possibility is considered that one phenotypic population increases simultaneously with the decline of another without any causal connection between the two.

Five tentative criteria are proposed for cases of suspected selection. (1) The unit of selection—individuals, local populations, entire species—must be explicit. (2) There must exist phenotypic differences among the alternative units. (3) The differences must be transmittable to the successive generation of the unit, either by genetic or extragenetic means. (4) There must be a differential change with time in the numbers of individuals of differing phenotypes. And (5), the changes must be shown to be due to the transmittable phenotypic differences among the units. Perhaps the most convincing case for selection can be made when the total population of individuals remains constant but the phenotypic frequencies of transmittable traits changes so that one form is truly replacing the other.

Examination of examples adduced as evidence for classical selection reveals multiple problems. Stabilizing selection should be easily demonstrable, yet has weak empirical support. Reinforcing selection should leave an abundant record of character divergence, yet the best case proves faulty. Directing selection might be occurring in the phenomenon of industrial melanism, but even here the critical evidence to distinguish this interpretation from alternatives is lacking. The long history of artificial selection and the literature on laboratory selection experiments certainly demonstrate conclusively that individual selection can change populations, but these results cannot constitute a test of whether or not selection has been the mechanism of evolutionary processes in nature.

Behavior is not 'just like' morphology in relation to evolution. Unlike a bone or feather that remain the same physical entities through repeated measurement, a behavioral pattern is an abstract conception of many occurrences, each of which is different. Furthermore, behavior can be transmitted to offspring by cultural tradition, whereas extra-genetic inheritance of morphology is severely limited. Finally, behavior itself does not fossilize, and the record of its results in footprints, nests, and the like is scanty.

Examination of evolutionary interpretations of exemplary behavioral studies shows that although behavior is useful to its possessors' survival and reproduction, a selective advantage cannot be established until the missing evidence for heritability of phenotypic differences is forthcoming. The enthusiasm for pan-selectionism has even led some behaviorists to the unwarranted belief that each behavioral act has a special selective function. Contrary to frequent statements in the ethological literature, there is virtually no evidence that courtship signals are selected for species distinctiveness. Some ethologists have even proposed hypothetical, extinct species from which existing species were selected to diverge. Finally, real changes in phenotypic ratios of behavior in a single, stable population have been followed carefully, but these are due to the spread of traditions rather than selection based on heritable variation.

In the 'worst case scenario' all the phenomena of evolution can be generated without recourse to the mechanism of selection operating at any point or at any level. We need to take this 'worst case scenario' as the null hypothesis and devise ways of testing whether and to what extent interindividual, intergroup, and interspecific selection play a role in phylogeny, adaptation, and speciation,

ACKNOWLEDGMENTS

I think it useful to note explicitly that expression of my gratitude to others in no way necessarily implies their endorsement of any view put forth in this essay. One colleague found the alternatives to selection 'wildly improbable'—a sentiment that helpfully strengthened my resolve to be a cogent, if reluctant, devil's advocate. To many colleagues and students over the years I am grateful for discussions that contributed to my thinking about evolutionary problems. Five colleagues improved the original manuscript immensely through their detailed critical comments: Jeffrey R. Baylis, Millicent S. Ficken, Robert G. Jaeger, Robert L. Jeanne, and Charles T. Snowdon; I wish only that there had been space enough and time to deal with many of the issues they raised. For criticisms of the second draft I am grateful to editor H. C. Plotkin and my colleagues John T. Emlen and Karen Steudel. Special thanks go to Hugh E. H. Paterson, who in 1979 in a tiny room at the University of Hawaii participated in a no-audience, half-day, non-stop debate with me over evolutionary matters. I thought at the time that it ended in a draw; now I am not so certain.

REFERENCES

Andrewartha, H. G., and Birch, L. C. (1954). *The Distribution and Abundance of Animals*, University of Chicago Press, Chicago.

Bishop, J. A., and Cook, L. M. (1975). Moths, melanism and clean air. *Sci. Amer.*, **232(1)**, 90–99.

Bridgman, P. W. (1927). *The Logic of Modern Physics*, MacMillan, New York.

Bridgman, P. W. (1938). *The Intelligent Individual and Society*, MacMillan, New York.

Brown, J. L. (1975). *The Evolution of Behavior*, W. W. Norton, New York.

Brown, W. L., and Wilson, E. O. (1956). Character displacement. *Syst. Zool.*, **5**, 49–64.

Cullen, E. (1957). Adaptations in the kittiwake to cliff-nesting. *Ibis*, **99**, 275–302.

Cullen, J. M., and Ashmole, N. P. (1963). The black noddy *Anous tenuirostris* on Ascension Island, II. Behaviour. *Ibis*, **103b**, 423–446.

Darwin, C., and Wallace, A. (1858). On the tendency of species to form varieties: and on the perpetuation of varieties and species by natural means of selection. *J. Linn. Soc. Lond.*, **3**, 45–62.

Dawkins, R. (1976). *The Selfish Gene*, Oxford University Press, New York.

Dobzhansky, T. (1951). *Genetics and the Origin of Species*, 3rd ed. Columbia University Press, New York.

Ficken, R. W., Ficken, M. S., and Hailman, J. P. (1978). Differential aggression in genetically different morphs of the white-throated sparrow (*Zonotrichia albicollis*). *Z. Tierpsychol.*, **46**, 43–57.

Fisher, R. A. (1930). *The Genetical Theory of Natural Selection*, Clarendon Press, Oxford.

Ford, E. B. (1971). *Ecological Genetics*, 3rd ed. Chapman and Hall, London.

Fretwell, S. D. (1969). Dominance behavior and winter habitat distribution in juncos (*Junco hyemalis*). *Bird-Banding*, **40**, 1–25.

Fretwell, S. D. (1972). *Populations in a Seasonal Environment*, Princeton University Press, Princeton, N. J.

Fretwell, S. D. (1977). Stabilizing selection in field sparrows—a retraction. *Amer. Natur.*, **111**, 1209–1210.

Gould, S. J., and Lewontin, R. (1979). The spandrels of San Marco and the Panglossian paradigm: a critique of the adaptationist programme. *Proc. Royal Soc. Lond., B, Biol.*, **205**, 581–598.

Grant, P. R. (1975). The classical case of character displacement. *Evol. Biol.*, **8**, 237–337.

Hailman, J. P. (1959). Why is the male wood duck strikingly colorful? *Amer. Natur.*, **93**, 383–384.

Hailman, J. P. (1964). Breeding synchrony in the equatorial swallow-tailed gull. *Amer. Natur.*, **98**, 79–83.

Hailman, J. P. (1965). Cliff-nesting adaptations of the Galapagos swallow-tailed gull. *Wilson Bull.*, **77**, 346–362.

Hailman, J. P. (1976a). Uses of the comparative study of behavior. Chapter 2 in R. B. Masterton, W. Hodos, and H. Jerison (Eds), *Evolution, Brain, and Behavior: Persistent Problems*, Erlbaum, Hillsdale, N. J. pp. 13–22.

Hailman, J. P. (1976b). Homology: logic, information and efficiency. Chapter 14 in R. B. Masterton, W. Hodos, and H. Jerison (Eds), *Evolution, Brain, and Behavior: Persistent Problesms*, Erlbaum, Hillsdale, N. J. pp. 181–198.

Hailman, J. P. (1977a). Bee dancing and evolutionary epistemology *Amer. Natur.*, **111**, 187–189.

Hailman, J. P. (1977b). *Optical Signals: Animal Communication and Light*, Indiana University Press, Bloomington and London.

Hailman, J. P. (1979). Environmental light and conspicuous colors. Chapter 7 in E. H. Burtt (Ed.), *The Behavioral Significance of Color*, Garland STPM Press, New York and London, pp. 289–354.

Hailman, J. P. (1980). Fitness, function, fidelity, fornication, and feminine philandering. *Behav. Brain Sci.*, **3**, 189.

Hailman, J. P. (In press). Ontogeny: toward a general theoretical framework for ethology. In P. P. G. Bateson and P. Klopfer (Eds), *Perspectives in Ethology*, Vol. 6. Plenum, New York.

Hailman, J. P. (1982). Creation stories, *BioScience*, **32**, 129–130.

Hamilton, W. D. (1963). The evolution of altruistic behaviour. *Amer. Natur.*, **97**, 354–356.

Huxley, J. (1943). *Evolution: the Modern Synthesis*, Harper and Brothers, New York and London.

Kawai, M. (1965). Newly acquired pre-cultural behavior of the natural troop of Japanese monkeys on Koshima Islet. *Primates*, **6(1)**, 1–30.

Kettlewell, H. B. D. (1955a) Recognition of appropriate backgrounds by the pale and black phase of Lepidoptera. *Nature*, **175**, 934.

Kettlewell, H. B. D. (1955b). Selection experiments on industrial melanism in the Lepidoptera. *Heredity*, **9**, 323–342.

Kettlewell, H. B. D. (1956). Further selection experiments on industrial melanism in the Lepidoptera. *Heredity*, **10**, 287–301.

Kettlewell, H. B. D. (1957a). Problems in industrial melanism. *Entomologist*, **90**, 98–105.

Kettlewell, H. B. D. (1957b). The contribution of industrial melanism in the Lepidoptera to our knowledge of evolution. *Advan. Sci.*, **52**, 245–252.

Kettlewell, H. B. D. (1957c). Industrial melanism in moths and its contribution to our knowledge of evolution. Proc. Roy. Inst. Great Britain, **36**, 1–14.

Kettlewell, H. B. D. (1958a). A survey of the frequencies of *Biston betularia* (L.) (Lep.) and its melanic forms in Great Britain. *Heredity*, **12**, 51–72.

Kettlewell, H. B. D. (1958b). Industrial melanism in the Lepidoptera and its contribution to our knowledge of evolution. *Proc. X Int. Congr. Entomol.*, 1956, **2**, 831–841.

Kettlewell, H. B. D. (1959). New aspects of the genetic control of industrial melanism in the Lepidoptera. *Nature*, **183**, 918–921.

Kettlewell, H. B. D. (1961). The phenomenon of industrial melanism in the Lepidoptera. Ann. Rev. Entomol., **6**, 245–262.

Lewis, R. W. (1980). Evolution: a system of theories. *Perspectives Biol. Med.*, **23**, 551–572.

Lewontin, R. C. (1978). Adaptation. *Sci. Amer.*, **239**(3), 213–230 (pagination not continuous).

Lindauer, M. (1971). The functional significance of the honeybee waggle dance. *Amer. Natur.*, **105**, 89–96.

Mayr, E. (1942). *Systematics and the Origin of Species*, Columbia University Press, New York.

Mayr, E. (1963). *Animal Species and Evolution*, Harvard University Press, Cambridge, Mass.

Paterson, H. E. H. (1978). More evidence against speciation by reinforcement. *S. Afr. J. Sci.*, **74**, 369–371.

Paterson, H. E. H. (1980). A comment on 'mate recognition systems'. *Evolution*, **34**, 330–331.

Paterson, H. E. H. (1981). The continuing search for the unknown and unknowable: a critique of contemporary ideas on speciation. *S. Afr. J. Sci.*, **77**, 113–119.

Patterson, I. J. (1965). Timing and spacing of broods in the black-headed gull *Larus ridibundus*. *Ibis*, **107**, 433–459.

Peterson, R. T. (1961). *A Field Guide to Western Birds*, Houghton Mifflin, Boston.

Platt, J. R. (1964). Strong inference. *Science*, **146**, 347–353.

Plotkin, H. C. and Odling-Smee, F. J. (1981). A multiple-level model of evolution and its implications for sociobiology. *Behav. Brain Sci.*, **4**, 225–268.

Pyle, R. L. (1979). 1978 Honolulu Christmas bird count. '*Elepaio*, **39**, 95–99.

Reed, E. S. (1981). The lawfulness of natural selection. *Amer. Natur.*, **118**, 61–71.

Rhodes, F. H. T. (1974). *Evolution*, Golden Press, New York.

Rosen, D. (1978). Darwin's demon. *Syst. Zool.*, **27**, 370–373.

Rowell, T. W. (1979). How would we know if social organization were *not* adaptive? In I. Bernstein and E. O. Smith (Eds), *Primate Ecology and Human Origins*, Garland STPM Press, New York.

Shallenberger, R. G. (1978). *Hawaii's Birds*, 2nd ed. Hawaii Audubon Society, Honolulu.

Shorten, M. (1954). *Squirrels*, Collins, London.

Thorneycroft, H. B. (1966). Chromosomal polymorphism in the white-throated sparrow, *Zonotrichia albicollis*. *Science*, **154**, 1571–1572.

Tinbergen, N., Broekhuysen, G. J., Feekes, F., Houghton, J. C. W., Kruuk, H., and Szulc, E. (1962). Egg shell removal by the black-headed gull, *Larus ridibundus* L.: a behaviour component of camouflage. *Behaviour*, **19**, 74–118.

Vaurie, C. (1951). Adaptive differences between two sympatric species of nuthatches (*Sitta*). *Proc. X Inter. Ornithol. Congr.*, 1950, Uppsala. pp. 163–166.

Waddington, C. H. (1961). Genetic assimilation. *Advan. Genet.*, **12**, 257–293.

Waddington, C. H. (1974). A catastrophe theory of evolution. *Ann. N. Y. Acad. Sci.*, **231**, 32–42.

Wenner, A. M. (1971). *The Bee Language Controversy*, Educational Programs Improvement, Boulder, Colorado.

Williams, G. C. (1966). *Adaptation and Natural Selection*, Princeton University Press, Princeton, N. J.

Wilson, E. O. (1975). *Sociobiology: The New Synthesis*, Harvard University Press, Cambridge, Mass.

Wright, (1932). The roles of mutation, inbreeding, crossbreeding and selection in evolution. *Proc. 6th Intern. Congr. Genet.*, **1**, 356–366.

Wright, S. (1968). *Evolution and the Genetics of Populations, Vol. 1. Genetic and Biometric Foundations*, University of Chicago Press, Chicago.

Wright, S. (1980). Genic and organismic selection. *Evolution*, **34**, 825–843.

Wynne-Edwards, V. C. (1962). *Animal Dispersion in Relation to Social Behaviour*, Oliver and Boyd, Edinburgh.

Learning, Development, and Culture
Edited by H. C. Plotkin
© 1982, John Wiley & Sons Ltd.

CHAPTER 13

Behavioural antecedents of sociality

Jeffrey R. Baylis and Zuleyma Tang Halpin

It is argued that sociality presupposes communication, and hence contact between individuals. This limits the possible behavioural antecedents of sociality to only three times in the life history of most sexually reproducing organisms: 1. Aggregations; 2. Gamete exchange; 3. Parturition or egg hatching (sib groups and parent/neonate groups). Gamete exchange and parent/neonate associations are argued to be the most likely sources for the evolution of sociality because both are potentially ubiquitous sources of proximity in sexually reproducing organisms and involve pre-existing communication systems. Examples of social systems derived from the above sources are discussed in terms of the social signals used and the role of life history patterns in the evolution of sociality.

INTRODUCTION

A major difficulty in the study of sociality is that it is an attribute than can only be defined by describing the behaviour and interactions of individual organisms. That is, since the concept of 'sociality' does not provide an objective physical attribute to measure, it can be defined only in behavioural terms. The description of behaviour is basic to, and always a first step in, ethological investigations. In particular, if one wishes to examine the adaptive function of a behaviour pattern, or the mechanisms by which it is expressed, the behaviour in question must first be described in a manner that does not prejudice either function or origin. This approach, which is basic to the field of ethology, has yet to be applied to the study of animal sociality.

At least three approaches may be used to study the evolution of animal sociality:

(1) The study of the adaptive function(s) of group living.
(2) The study of the mechanisms by which behaviour patterns are expressed and transmitted.
(3) The study of the previous evolutionary history and origins of the social group.

To date, most studies have emphasized function and mechanisms, while largely ignoring the evolutionary history and possible behavioural antecedent origins of social species.

In the present paper we propose a system of classifying animal sociality based solely on the description of the distribution of individuals in space and time. We then propose a restricted set of possible origins of animal social groupings, and argue that these origins can be used to distinguish between alternative paths to sociality. Finally, we argue that such a consideration of behavioural antecedents is essential to the proper testing of hypotheses about adaptive functions and mechanisms by which animal societies evolve.

There has been a trend in recent years for biologists to describe the evolution of social behaviour in terms of simple population genetics models. This is largely the result of Hamilton's (1964a, b, 1972) influential papers on the genetic theory of inclusive fitness which can be used to explain the evolution of sterile worker castes among the social Hymenoptera. Wilson (1975), Trivers (1971, 1972) and others have followed suit emphasizing various aspects of 'altruism' as a common theme in the evolution of social behaviour. While these 'selfish gene' (Dawkins, 1976) models have proved to be convincing and powerful within their original framework and have had great explanatory power in interpreting functional consequences, they have had little or no predictive power concerning the evolution of specific behaviour patterns. As a result, they have been of little practical use to the ethologist interested in studying the social behaviour of individual organisms within a society rather than the hypothetical behavioural genetics of a population. To the population geneticist it is not the origin of a behavioural act that matters, but its total effect on allelic fitness. That is, population genetics focuses on the *process* that maintains a trait in a population. On the other hand, when an ethologist examines the evolution of a behavioural trait, he is interested not only in function, but also in the *origin* of the behaviour and in the *modifications* which it may have undergone as part of its evolutionary history.

A consideration of origins is essential if one is to adequately test hypotheses about the maintenance of traits in a population (Hailman, 1977). However, the question of origin must be dealt with in a slightly different conceptual framework from that of population genetics, and preferably one that is less dependent upon a single hypothetical mechanism. The present paper attempts to develop such an alternative framework that we believe is of value in studying the evolution of specific behaviour patterns and the interindividual social structure within an animal society.

Our viewpoint is based on the Darwinian principle of evolutionary continuity. Sociality does not emerge full blown when natural selection favours it; rather it starts from some pre-existing condition that, by modification through natural selection and descent, becomes the origin of the social system. Therefore, if we are to understand fully the forms of modern animal societies, we should attempt to identify these probable origins from a viewpoint that does not prejudice mechanism or function.

Our scheme is based upon the question, 'What behaviour patterns shown by solitary organisms might have served as an origin for the evolution of sociality?' It is our assertion that the number of available behavioural categories is small, and that our scheme makes clear predictions about the origins of social signals likely to be used within societies and about the categories of individuals that are likely to typify the social group.

The cases we wish to consider are those that might have given rise to 'cooperative societies'. We agree with Wilson (1971, p. 6) that 'Reciprocal communication of a cooperative nature is the essential intuitive criterion of a society.' Since the essence of a society is communication, only by studying the origins of social signals can we test hypotheses about mechanisms, origins, and adaptive function within a society, and then truly judge if the social grouping is indeed 'cooperative'.

We define three possible social states, very loosely patterned on Wilson (1971):

Solitary; no persistent interaction with conspecific individuals except for the immediate requirements of gamete release in sexual species, and the immediate results of reproduction.

Demisocial; an individual spending a portion of its life cycle, beyond that required for reproduction, in interactive proximity with one or more conspecifics.

Social; permanent groups of conspecifics, with reproduction normally occurring within such groups. The group contains more than one generation, and the group exhibits properties of continuity beyond the lifespan of individual members.

A 'group' is defined as two or more individuals.

'Interactive' is defined as mutual influence on one another's behaviour. For example, a group may result from mutual attraction between conspecifics rather than from attraction to an exogenous environmental factor.

Doubtless the above definition of social will leave many people dissatisfied. The difficulty arises as a result of the discrepancy in meaning given to the words 'social' and 'society' when used in common parlance and when used by entomologists. Any definition of sociality that is applicable to the vertebrates as well as to the social insects must emphasize the shared attributes instead of the dissimilarities between the two cases. Our definition does this by emphasizing the continuity and persistence of the group, rather than the presence of a sterile caste and parental care, as the essential features.

A second reason for using the above definition of social is that it does not define sociality in terms of parental care. We submit that parental care is only one of several possible origins of sociality, and it is by no means a logical necessity that only those species that show parental care can exhibit properties we would care to call cooperatively social (e.g. Brown, 1974). If cooperative parental care is part of the *definition* of sociality, it can hardly be surprising that all 'eusocial' species appear to have originated through modification of parental care behaviour (Wilson, 1975). While we would be fairly comfortable with this as a conclusion, it is hardly satisfactory to have it true by definition.

We coined the term 'demisocial' with extreme reluctance. However, all the reasonable prefixes for 'social' seem to have been previously used by entomologists concerned with defining social states in terms of degree of parental behaviour (Wilson, 1971). Since in our scheme, to define degree of sociality based on parental care would beg the question, we felt it better to coin a new word and avoid confusion with existing terms that have a precise meaning. The demisocial state encompasses an extremely large category of species where individuals temporarily cluster in groups as a result of mutual interaction and attraction, yet do not live permanently in groups.

We seek the evolutionary origins of sociality in the types of behaviour that bring individuals of solitary species into close proximity during their normal life history. To do this, we have treated living organisms as Brownian particles that can reproduce. Our Brownian particles can come into proximity by chance or due to environmental factors external to the particles; we call such groupings *aggregations*. If the particles reproduce sexually, males and females will be attracted into close proximity for mating or *gamete transfer*. Finally, when actual reproduction occurs, *parturition* will produce a group consisting of a parent and one or more offspring. We consider these to be the three basic sources of proximity in solitary organisms.

Note that our solitary Brownian particles are not assumed to have any direct mutual attraction, except for the minimum requirements of reproduction. However, chance assemblages of individuals may produce selection that will favour individuals who remain in such groups longer, or who are attracted to conspecifics independently of other environmental factors (Allee, 1940; Hamilton, 1971; Wilson, 1975; Brown, 1975). The effect of such selection will favour the evolution of demisocial species.

In the following section we examine each of the above sources of proximity. We attempt to characterize the attributes of the demisocial groupings that can be expected to be derived from each. We then discuss the ways in which true social groups might evolve from such demisocial groups, and the properties we might expect them to exhibit.

THE ANTECEDENTS

Aggregations

This category corresponds to the 'Coincidental' group of Brown (1975), and the 'Kinetic' and 'Tropistic' aggregations of Klopfer and Hailman (1967). Aggregations result when individuals are brought into proximity by chance or by some environmental circumstance other than mutual attraction. The individuals involved often appear to take no more notice of each other than they would of any other class of objects in their immediate environment. A resource that is both scarce and patchy can produce such a gathering. Likewise, predation can bring individuals of prey species into close proximity. The functional advantages of such groupings may be various (Allee, 1940; Springer, 1957; Hamilton, 1971; Murton et al., 1971; Henry, 1972; Brown, 1975; Wilson, 1975).

Although aggregations may be composed of individuals of many species, most such groupings can be expected to be either monospecific or to have one species which predominates. This is because an individual organism will most resemble others of its own species in terms of physiological needs, distribution and habits.

Aggregations form as a result of individuals responding to environmental conditions rather than to conspecifics. However, the presence of conspecifics may provide an excellent cue to the location of suitable habitats or resources (i.e. 'conspecific cuing', Kiester 1979). Thus, the presence of conspecifics has been shown to be a settling stimulus for sodium-limited puddling butterflies (Arms et al., 1974). Such groups, formed as a result of attraction to conspecifics, are interactive and hence can be considered demisocial.

Two social taxa may have originated from a demisocial state derived from an aggregation. The Isoptera, as noted by Wilson (1975), lack the haplodiploid sex determination system invoked to explain the high incidence of sociality among the Hymenoptera, and thus demand another explanation for their obviously social condition. The termites require protozoan symbionts to digest cellulose. They moult repeatedly and grow through a series of gradual metamorphoses into the adult form. With each moult, the foregut and hindgut are shed and the protozoan symbionts necessary for survival are lost. The only available source of reinfestation is the ingestion of fresh faeces of another termite with an intact gut (Wilson, 1971, 1975).

It is possible that this condition was instrumental in shaping the evolutionary history of the taxon; only by living in a group could an individual be assured of reinfection after a moult. Cellulose is generally found in large patches, and hence there was probably little individual competition for food among ancestral termite group members. Such a group, which may have been the first step toward sociality in the termites, would have to be classed as a demisocial association. However, a more likely initial step may have involved parental care (see below).

A second society that may have arisen from aggregations is represented by an early step in the parasocial scheme for the evolution of some of the social bees (Michener, 1958) and wasps (West-Eberhard, 1978). In many species of bees and wasps, groups of females utilize a communal nest cavity with one entrance, in which each female constructs and tends her own brood cells. The initial aggregation may be the result of a scarcity of suitable nest sites. The individual advantage is that while only one nest cavity and entrance need be constructed, it can then be guarded by many females, thus lowering the probability of predation while any one individual is away from the nest. The next step in the evolution of sociality is the quasisocial state where females cooperate in constructing and provisioning brood cells, and all reproduce.

The stage that derives from an aggregation is the first step where females nest independently within the same large cavity; the actual last step to sociality may best be considered a parent/neonate situation (see below). Thus, the parasocial scheme suggests that two sources of proximity have been important in the evolution of sociality in some of the Hymenoptera. This is in contrast to Wheeler's (1923, 1928) 'subsocial' scheme, which derives insect sociality entirely through parent/neonate association. Although the parasocial sequence cannot be said to represent an origin of sociality directly derived from aggregations, it is easily one of the strongest cases for the evolution of sociality from such a source. It also raises some interesting issues concerning the founding of colonies in social species (see Discussion).

Recent evidence suggests that the dictynid spider *Mallos gregalis* may have evolved social groups from aggregations. This species is commonly found living in large permanent groups consisting of hundreds of individuals of both sexes and various ages (Burgess, 1978; Jackson, 1978). There is no evidence of parental care and it is not clear whether any of the group behaviours shown by this species involve true cooperation (Jackson, 1979). Jackson (1978) reviewed the natural history of the family Dictynidae and suggested three stages in the evolution of their social behaviour. Most species in the family are solitary and show typical territorial behaviour with individual web defence. Communal and territorial species are intermediate and may have originated from aggregations; each individual spider constructs and defends an individual web but the webs are interconnected to one another by interstitial threads. Lastly, there are species such as *M. gregalis* that are communal and non-territorial.

Of the three major life history phenomena that bring animals into proximity, we might expect the aggregation of individuals to be the most general in all phyla of animals. The individuals concerned need have only sufficient mobility to aggregate. Thus, if mere proximity were the only factor involved, we would expect this to be the most common origin of sociality. However, there is scant evidence that sociality has ever evolved exclusively from such a source, although many demisocial phenomena may be traced to this origin. The lack of a pre-existing signal system is the clearest obstacle to further social evolution from this stage. Signal patterns between group members must evolve largely on an *ad hoc* basis from locomotory and orientation movements that would promote group cohesion and coordination of activities. Because of the opportunistic nature of the gatherings it is not easy to specify the classes of individuals we would expect to comprise such demisocial groups. However, we would expect similarity of needs to dictate group composition; individuals of a single species and of a similar age, sex, size, etc. would tend to be found together, so that group composition would tend to be uniform. Any tendency for an aggregation to lead to sociality would probably be superseded by one of the following potential sources, which is more likely to provide the advantage of a pre-existing signal system.

Gamete transfer

Among most sexually reproducing organisms, mating requires close proximity. In species with internal fertilization, copulation usually demands some form of cooperation, and in species with external fertilization, a reasonable amount of synchrony is necessary. In both cases, successful fertilization is dependent upon some sort of communication, and hence a signal system.

Many species have elaborate courtship with days, weeks, or even years of interaction before the first egg is fertilized. This type of courtship usually involves what has come to be called a 'pair bond'. Because of the cooperative nature of the association, and the intense selection for a signal system, we consider such 'long-term' courtship to be a viable substrate for the evolution of more elaborate social behaviour.

If the species requires resources such as a prepared oviposition site or other special needs for reproduction, selection may favour the pair remaining together and cooperating to sequester and defend the necessary resources. A scarcity of mates in populations that live at low density could produce the same phenomenon. Thus, we would have the evolution of a prolonged association between the reproductive pair and the evolution of a pair bond. If the association becomes permanent, persisting beyond that period required for reproduction alone, and is expanded to include other members, then the evolution of sociality is possible. Such extension of the pair bond is usually associated only with intensive parental care, and hence overlaps the next category.

Among the fishes, there are species where long-term pair bonds exist without parental care, and in at least two families of tropical marine fishes gamete transfer seems to have given rise to sociality. The best documented case is the cleaner wrasse, *Labroides dimidiatus* (Robertson, 1972). This species lives in small territorial groups typically composed of one male and five females, and the individuals are all protogynous hermaphodites. The dominant individual within the group is the male, and all subordinate group members are female. If the male is removed, the most dominant female changes sex and is a functional male within days. Among the females there appears to be some role different-iation based on degree of dominance, and the range of size in the females suggests that more than one generation is involved. Eggs and larvae are pelagic, so parental care is ruled out, and it is doubtful that the group is composed of related individuals. A similar social system is shown by the anthiid, *Anthias squamipinnis*, another protogynous coral reef fish (Shapiro, 1979). This latter species lives in sedentary bisexual groups where the number of females greatly exceeds the number of males, and sex is behaviourally determined. Again, eggs and larvae are pelagic, and there is no parental care.

Demisocial and social groupings derived from this source will be composed of individuals of both sexes. The groups will be closed or semi-closed, with admission to the group dependent upon the sex of the applicant, current group size, and group composition. All individuals would be physiologically able to reproduce at some point in their life cycle. Individual recognition of group members would be likely.

The social signals used between group members will be derived largely from signals and activities associated with courtship and reproduction. This would be revealed by comparative studies of solitary and demisocial congeners. A characteristic of the signal system may be the use of courtship or sexual signals in contexts other than immediate gamete release, although the signals may still occur in their original context as well.

We expect gamete transfer to be a possible source for the evolution of sociality in all sexually reproducing organisms. However, as a necessary first step there has to be selection for a prolonged association between the sexes. Since intensive parental care is the likely source for such selection, it is neither feasible nor desirable to separate parental care from the gamete transfer origin, especially in cases in which there is joint parental care.

Parturition (or egg hatch)

The moment of birth (or hatching) may result in a parent(s)/neonate(s) association. If birth is multiple, or eggs are deposited in a clutch and hatch synchronously, a sib group may result. Since their characteristics will differ markedly, we will consider these two kinds of groups which may form as a result of parturition as two separate cases.

Sib groups

Whenever multiple, synchronous births occur and there is no parental care, or when several eggs are deposited in the same place and hatch synchronously, the potential for a sibling based social system exists. However, since there is no obvious pre-existing signal system, such a group would be at a disadvantage in competition with social groupings derived from sources where a signal system already exists. In spite of not having a pre-existing signal system, the potential for such sib groupings among vertebrates and invertebrates is very high.

Sib groups are a well-developed phenomenon in many insects. Many species show more or less elaborate demisocial behaviour as larvae, even though they may be solitary as adults. The best documented and most familiar examples to North Americans are the tent caterpillars (*Malacosoma* spp). The degree of organization is quite sophisticated and communication is well documented (Fitzgerald, 1976; Wellington, 1957). Some degree of role specialization is apparent, although no morphological caste differences appear to be present. A proportion of individuals in many colonies fail to eclose, and hence do not reproduce. The parents show no social behaviour beyond that required for mating.

The available evidence suggests that the colonies are composed of sib groups, although some colonies probably result from the fusion of sib groups from separate egg masses (J. R. Baylis and R. L. Jeanne, pers. obs.). Females lay eggs totalling a few hundred in each mass. The eggs are the only overwintering population, so there is no chance of direct parental care. The larvae spin a tent of silk which acts as a refuge from predation and desiccation. Silk threads form chemical trails leading from the tent to feeding areas on the tree or bush sheltering the colony, and thus are analogous to the pheromone based foraging trails of ants (Fitzgerald, 1976; Wellington, 1957).

Although not noted for their complex social behaviour, some reptiles show a degree of cooperative movements in groups when young. Hatchling green iguanas (*Iguana iguana*) show such complex interactions. There is evidence that synchronous hatching, probably triggered by sounds, occurs between adjacent nests. The young emerge synchronously, move together in a group, and frequently remain in groups for some time. This is a clear example of demisocial behaviour derived from a sib group origin (Burghardt *et al.*, 1977).

The social spiders of the Eresidae and Theridiidae exemplify another social system that might have been derived from sib aggregations, although a strong case can also be made for the derivation of this society from parental care (Kullman, 1972). These spiders build webs used for capturing prey. In the primitive state, females inhabit solitary webs where they build an egg cocoon. The female usually dies before the emergence of the spiderlings who, upon hatching, feed on the corpse of the mother. The young do not disperse immediately, but remain in the web as a group. They may jointly attack and feed communally on prey that are trapped in the web, but are too large for individual spiderlings to subdue and digest.

In general, it appears that sib derived demisocial systems do exist. However, there is no evidence that a social species has emerged by this route. It would be difficult to identify such a system in most cases, as any substantial overlap of generations would lead to confusion with the next category, parental care.

A society based on a sib group origin would be composed of cohorts of sibs. The group need not be closed; the key factor will be the stage of development of the individuals composing the group relative to the applicant. As long as the applicant is at a similar stage of development, the group may be open (e.g. see reference above to fusion of sib groups in tent caterpillars). However, in most cases it will be more likely that the members of such groups will have come from the same egg clutch; consequently any tendency to develop castes would have to be based on individual genetic or cytoplasmic differences, since all members of the group would most likely have developed in the same environment.

Signals would be derived largely from behaviour patterns peculiar to larvae or young, since generational overlap would occur late in the evolution of such a social system. Thus, the majority of social signals would appear to be derived *ad hoc* from action patterns characteristic of the young.

The most likely candidates for the evolution of such a social system may be found among taxa that are characterized by laying batches of eggs that hatch synchronously. The young must be precocial and capable of independent movement and foraging upon hatching. Thus, most of the spiders and insects would be candidates for the evolution of such a system, as would be many fishes, reptiles and amphibians. In species that show parental care, sib groupings and parent/neonate groupings may occur simultaneously and it may not be possible to distinguish the sib group origin from the parent/neonate origin.

Parent/neonate groups

Parent/neonate associations can be considered an antecedent of sociality because, in many species, the parent/neonate association is extended into a prolonged period of parental care. This period of parental care often involves much mutual interaction, and favours the evolution of signal systems of varying degrees of elaboration. As numerous authors have observed, parental behaviour appears to be the precursor of most of the elaborate social systems studied to date (Wheeler, 1923; Evans, 1958; Markl, 1971; Wilson, 1975).

Parental care is an important component of all insect and mammalian societies. Social hymenopteran insects and termites show parental care, and many of the behavioural signals used in communication between adults within a colony appear to have been derived from parent/young signals. For example, trophallaxis is probably derived from parental care activities, as is food sharing in some vertebrate social systems. The African lion, the only social felid, has the most intensive parental care of any cat although it does not share food. Parental care is intensive among the social canids, and food sharing is well developed. Many of the signals used among adult social canids are derived from the parent/young signal system (Kleiman and Eisenberg, 1973). Most primates, generally considered among the most social of the vertebrates, also have extended parental care.

Because of the link with reproduction, especially in species with external fertilization, intensive parental care may subsequently favour the extension of the gamete transfer association into the parental phase, so that parental care becomes a joint activity of both parents as occurs in some fishes. This allows for increased role specialization and increases the potential signal diversity available to the social system. We would expect to see joint parental care in species which have a brief interval between copulation and parturition, or in which copulation overlaps the egg-laying period, as in many birds. We would expect joint parental care to be far less common in mammals, due to their relatively long gestation period.

Although the vast majority of social species show some degree of parental care, the reverse is not the case. Indeed, whole taxa where species typically show behavioural parental care are devoid of any known social species. This could be a matter of definition. The traditional definition of sociality, derived from insect societies, demands cooperative parental care (Wilson, 1971). However, even our 'relaxed' definition adds only a handful of social species to the list. We believe that there are three attributes of parental care which can strongly facilitate the evolution of sociality. These correlate with the intensity and duration of parental care.

1. Viability of offspring at birth (or hatching). The young of different parental species vary widely in their ability to independently regulate their physiological processes and obtain needed resources. It is this varying degree of offspring independence that we are calling viability. Reduced viability at birth can be expected to correlate with increased parental care, and hence proximity.

A wide range of factors can affect offspring viability at birth. These include the ability of the offspring to regulate temperature, oxygen levels, and other physical factors as well as the ability of the young to resist or avoid predators or disease. Trophic dependence of the young on the parent is also an important factor.

2. Vagility of offspring. The ability of the offspring to move freely through their environment should be inversely correlated with the degree of parental care. This factor may tend to covary with the viability of the offspring, but often will not. For example, marsupial mammals give birth to offspring of low viability, but high vagility. Because they spend much of their period of parental care in the mother's pouch, their vagility is actually equal to that of the mother, and their effective vagility is as high as that of any precocial ungulate or

gallinacious bird. Vagility is a very important aspect of the system, as low vagility ties the offspring for some period of time to a specific site or area. Since the offspring are tied to a specific site, suitable habitat can become an important factor in offspring survival. All of these factors can directly or indirectly favour site constancy and/or territorial behaviour by the parent (Baylis, 1981). As with any resource, once the young become fixed in space, they are defendable. Such spatial fixity also means that environmental modification by the parent to create an optimum habitat is possible.

3. Environmental modification. Environmental modification can involve direct action by the parent, such as nest construction. It may also involve indirect effects, such as an artifact or long term environmental modification that can be left by the parent as a 'bequest' to the young. Web construction by some of the presocial spiders is an example of the latter. These effects are of importance, because they can lead to tenancy on a specific site for several generations (Kullman, 1972; Evans, 1973, 1977; Kleiman and Eisenberg, 1973).

The most important single step in the evolution of sociality from parent/neonate proximity is an overlap of generations, which permits parents to interact with offspring and allows for the evolution of parental care. This provides continuity of the group over time. Two complementary mechanisms are available for producing additional overlap of generations. The young may delay maturation, thus remaining with the parents during a prolonged juvenile stage while they are not reproductively mature, and during which they may overlap with subsequent broods. A second mechanism is to delay dispersal that normally occurs at the time of reproductive maturity. This results in adults, who may or may not breed, remaining in the group and overlapping subsequent broods produced by the original parents. In any such groups derived via parental care, we would expect that many of the social signals used in interactions between group members will be neotenic; that is, they will consist of signals that were originally used between offspring and parents, but that are now used between adults as well. If joint parental care occurs, sexual signals may also be used outside their normal context of gamete transfer.

Thus, groups that show the combined characteristics of low viability of individual young at birth, low vagility of young at birth, and environmental modification should be the taxa predisposed to the evolution of sociality through antecedent parental behaviour.

DISCUSSION

The present argument characterizes animal societies by the distribution of individuals in space. If cooperative sociality is to evolve, individuals must remain in proximity. Three potential sources for initial proximity in otherwise solitary organisms have been identified:

1. Aggregations
2. Gamete Transfer (Mating)
3. Parturition
   (a) Sib groups
   (b) Parent/neonate groups.

Each antecedent condition describes a pathway to a demisocial state, and can be used to predict the properties of demisocial groups. Our behavioural antecedents do not depend on any assumptions about the type of selection involved or upon the kinship of individuals composing the social group. They are based solely on the life history patterns of sexually reproducing organisms. Our assumptions are that evolution through natural selection is opportunistic, and that it proceeds in a continuous fashion so that one of the important variables influencing the final form of sociality is the antecedent condition from which it arose. Parental care is relatively rare in animals, although it is derived from our most universal antecedent condition; yet parental care appears to have been the origin of the majority of social species. This observation has been made before by many authors (Wheeler, 1923; Evans, 1958; Markl, 1971; Kullman, 1972; Wilson, 1975), but has lacked force because alternative origins for sociality have remained unspecified. The one partial exception to this is Michener's (1958) scheme for the evolution of sociality discussed above. A problem is that as long as parental care of a cooperative nature is considered to be one of the defining characteristics of sociality, any origin other than parental care becomes logically difficult. One measure of the utility of the present scheme is that under our relaxed definition of sociality, at least two social species do seem to have emerged via mating proximity (*Labroides dimidiatus* and *Anthias squamipinnis*).

The present model is a descriptive classification rather than a hypothesis, but it can be used to generate hypotheses and make predictions. One hypothesis, which might be called the 'null hypothesis of sociobiology', is that animal societies will tend to be derived from those individuals that are most likely to come into close proximity and remain in proximity during some portion of their life cycle. Such a hypothesis does not require an explanation based on inclusive fitness, but follows directly from our assumption that organisms behave like Brownian particles. The obvious first place to test this hypothesis is precisely where the genetic model has been tested; in the social insects, specifically the Hymenoptera.

The Hymenoptera are a large, diverse group with both social and solitary members. Parthenogenesis is common in the group, and a haplo-diploid method of sex determination appears to be universal (Wilson, 1971). There are two major groups within the Hymenoptera: the Apocrita, which are characterized by legless larvae of great helplessness, and the Symphyta, whose larvae are legged and free living. All examples of hymenopteran eusociality are confined to the Apocrita. Within the Apocrita, there are solitary, wholly parasitic species at one extreme, and eusocial species at the other; larvae of low viability and low vagility characterize both of these extremes.

The apparent success of the genetic model for the evolution of social behaviour in the Hymenoptera has virtually excluded other types of evolutionary models from this literature, even when they make similar predictions. The following argument parallels one proposed by Evans (1958) to describe the evolution of sociality in wasps. We believe this type of model should be re-examined.

Assume a small wasp, parasitizing a large host. The wasp larva is small and helpless, but is living inside a host that contains all its requirements; one host is sufficient, or more than sufficient, for larval development. Suppose that due to competition, or a change in the size of the host species, or changing ecological conditions, the wasp starts parasitizing small hosts, and one host is no longer sufficient for complete development. The larvae are still helpless and have low vagility, a state they evolved as internal parasites; therefore, females that somehow provision each larva with several prey items will be favoured. Wilson and Farish (1973) describe a primitive, ant-like wasp that is at just such a stage.

Within the above scheme, the parasitic habit of primitive wasps is seen as having produced 'helpless' larvae. By switching to multiple smaller prey, the female must provision, thus favoring site attachment and nest construction. If a female is still in the process of provisioning when the egg hatches, direct parental care and generational overlap becomes possible.

The group composition of a society derived from such a wasp parent/neonate association would be an extended family. All of the social Hymenoptera are thought to have arisen from ancestors exhibiting female nest building and parental care, as described above. No example of pair formation is to be found in the entire taxon, including the parasitic and solitary species. Thus, only female helpers are to be expected in social wasps, as only the females showed ancestral site attachment and provisioning behaviour. Therefore, a simple consideration of antecedent conditions predicts two key features of hymenopteran sociality; in spite of haplo-diploidy being universal to the taxon, sociality is confined to the Apocrita because they have larvae of great helplessness. Furthermore, helpers would be expected to be exclusively female because female care is ancestral. Inclusive fitness may be resorted to as an explanation of why the workers are sterile in hymenopteran societies, but haplo-diploidy is suspect as an explanation for the predisposition to sociality.

Sociality among the termites may also have derived from parental care. Newly hatched termites must be infested with cellulose digesting symbionts. Selection would have favored females that remained with the eggs until they hatched to provide fresh faeces or that even fed the young, to insure infestation. Delayed maturation and the overlap of several generations could then produce a substrate for a more complex society. All modern termites exhibit pair bonding and, as our consideration of origins would predict, sterile termite workers are composed of both sexes. The modern woodroaches are the nearest surviving relatives of the termites, and have similar symbionts and cellulose ingesting habits (Wilson, 1971). If they are truly similar to ancestral termites, we predict that they will exhibit parental care and perhaps pair bonding.

All mammals show some degree of parental behaviour, yet few species have achieved any degree of cooperative sociality. A consideration of neonate development in different taxa may help to explain why sociality has emerged more often in some taxa than in others. Kleiman and Eisenberg (1973) noted that the canids have lower viability and vagility at birth than do the felids, and felt this was a key factor in explaining the multiple independent emergence of sociality in the Canidae, and its having emerged only once in the Felidae. They also pointed out that joint parental care by the male and female is not a characteristic of felids as a taxon, and argued that this antecedent condition explained the mother/daughters helper system in the African lion. Joint parental care *is* characteristic of the canids as a taxon, and social species typically include males and females as helpers.

The classification of antecedents is useful in another context dealing with animal societies; this is the question of how new colonies are founded. Colonies are often founded by constituents and mechanisms that are very different from those that maintain a mature colony (Wilson, 1971). Our scheme can be used to describe both colony founding and maintenance, with no overt implication of evolutionary derivation. It may be used to produce evolutionary arguments, but its basis is purely descriptive. Other schemes, such as Wheeler's subsocial and Michener's parasocial routes to sociality, become muddy and blurred when confronted with the issue of group founding versus mature group composition and function (see Wilson, 1971. Chapter 5).

For example, hymenopteran and isopteran societies appear to be very similar, parent/neonate based societies when mature colonies are compared. However, new termite colonies are founded by a male and female pair who locate a new colony site and excavate a nest cavity before copulation; thus, colony founding is actually part of courtship, not parental care, and the new colony must be said to derive from a gamete transfer origin (Nutting, 1969). But hymenopteran colonies are typically founded by a lone female reproductive, by female sibs either in a swarm or fertile sibs returning to the vicinity of eclosion (R. L. Jeanne, pers. comm.; Evans, 1973). Thus, when classified by colony foundation, the situation is diverse and differences are emphasized. Similar diversity may emerge in colony foundation in vertebrate societies when such information becomes available.

Genetic models for the evolution of sociality are powerful and potentially very useful. However, they must be tested against competing frameworks and in studies where the original data are gathered to test the specific hypotheses. The only critical study we know of at present did not find the sex ratio bias in *Polistes fuscatus* which had been predicted by genetic theory (Noonan, 1978). An early comparative attempt by other workers (Trivers and Hare, 1976) contained methodological flaws (Alexander and Sherman, 1977). There is an increasing tendency in the literature to view relatedness within animal societies as evidence that kin selection or inclusive fitness is operating. As we hope to have demonstrated, this is neither a proof nor a test of the theory (Platt, 1964). Indeed, any model that derives sociality from parental care or even low dispersal rates would make similar predictions. We must be able to predict the actual form of the behaviour and the structure of the society if we are to test competing hypotheses by behavioural observation. Unfortunately, current genetic models predict the *functional interpretation* of a behaviour (i.e. 'altruistic'), not its origins or form.

We have argued that parental care is the most likely origin for social behaviour in animals. This is to be expected from propinquity alone. While any mobile organism is expected to occur in chance aggregations, aggregations must always depend on such factors as the population density and the external environment. By their nature, such contacts are random and fleeting. Gamete exchange is an origin potentially common to all sexually reproducing organisms, and probably has been influential in the evolution of sociality in at least two species. However, parturition must be considered the only origin that is common to all living organisms and provides a host of pathways for prolonging proximity. Reproduction is a fundamental property of life, and it is an event that produces two or more syntopic organisms. Parental care is the most likely route for evolution to follow from parturition to sociality whenever the 'parent' is clearly more independent than the 'offspring'.

We have assumed only that it is possible for selection to favour the evolution of sociality; we have not assumed the nature of the selective advantage or the mode by which it operates. The adaptive aspects of sociality and the mechanisms by which natural selection operates are hypotheses to be tested. They must be tested in a framework that admits other possible hypotheses. Our classification provides a framework free of mechanism, and shows that by chance alone and by the nature of reproduction in living organisms, we should expect social groups to be composed of close kin.

The present scheme was developed to classify social systems into types based on antecedent conditions. The specification of these origins allows us to make predictions about which taxa are likely to evolve sociality because of their life history patterns. We can make general predictions about the probable derivation of the social signals they show, and about the categories of individuals we would expect to compose the derived society. These abilities are viewed as being more valuable to the working ethologist than the prediction that, '...animals should behave so as to maximize their inclusive fitness' (Barash, 1977, p. 63).

ACKNOWLEDGEMENTS

We thank Roy L. Caldwell for asking us why there are no social marsupials. William Z. Lidicker and our fellow members of Zoology 268 at the University of California, Berkeley, provided helpful and stimulating discussions at a very early stage. Jack Hailman, Robert L. Jeanne, Ivan Chase, and Katherine C. Noonan critically read the manuscript and offered valuable suggestions. Peter B. Stacey and James H. Hunt read portions of the manuscript and provided helpful suggestions. The University of Missouri-St. Louis provided financial assistance and travel funds for Z. T. H. The Graduate School of the University of Wisconsin-Madison provided summer support for J. R. B.

REFERENCES

Alexander, R. D., and Sherman, P. W. (1977). Local mate competition and parental investment in social insects. *Science*, **196**, 494–500.

Allee, W. C. (1940). Concerning the origin of sociality in animals. *Scientia*, **67**, 154–160.

Arms, K., Feeny, P., and Lederhause, R. C. (1974). Sodium: stimulus for puddling behavior by tiger swallowtail butterflies, *Papilio glaucus*. *Science*, **185**, 372–374.

Barash, D. P. (1977). *Sociobiology and Behavior*, Elsevier, New York.

Baylis, J. R. (1981). The evolution of parental care in fishes, with reference to Darwin's rule of male sexual selection. *Environ. Biol. Fishes*, **6**(2), in press.

Brown, J. L. (1974). Alternate routes to sociality in jays—with a theory for the evolution of altruism and communal breeding. *Amer. Zool.*, **14**, 63–80.

Brown, J. L. (1975). *The Evolution of Behavior*, W. W. Norton Co., New York.

Burgess, J. W. (1978). Social behavior in group-living spider species. *Symp. Zool. Soc. Lond.*, **42**, 69–78.

Burghardt, G. M., Greene, H. W., and Rand, A. S. (1977). Social behavior in hatchling green iguanas: life at a reptile rookery. *Science*, **195**, 689–691.

Dawkins, R. (1976), *The Selfish Gene*, Oxford University Press, Oxford.

Evans, H. E. (1958). The evolution of social life in wasps. *Proceedings of the Tenth International Congress of Entomology, Montreal, 1956*, **2**, 449–457.

Evans, H. E. (1958). Burrow sharing and nest transfer in the digger wasp *Philanthus gibbosus* (Fabricius). *Anim. Behav.*, **21**, 302–307.

Evans, H. E. (1977). Extrinsic versus intrinsic factors in the evolution of insect sociality. *Bioscience*, **27**, 613–617.

Fitzgerald, T. D. (1976). Trail marking by larvae of the eastern tent caterpillar. *Science*, **194**, 961–963.

Hailman, J. P. (1977). *Optical Signals*, Indiana University Press, Bloomington.

Hamilton, W. D. (1964a). The genetical theory of social behavior. I. *J. Theor. Biol.*, **7**, 1–16.

Hamilton, W. D. (1964b). The genetical theory of social behavior. II. *J. Theor. Biol.*, **7**, 17–32.

Hamilton, W. D. (1971). Geometry for the selfish herd. *J. Theor. Biol.*, **31**, 295–311.

Hamilton, W. D. (1972). Altruism and related phenomena mainly in the social insects. *Ann. Rev. Ecol. Syst.*, **3**, 193–232.

Henry, C. S. (1972). Eggs and repagula of *Ululodes* and *Ascaloptynx* (Neuroptera: Ascalaphidae): a comparative study. *Psyche*, **79**, 1–22.

Jackson, R. R. (1978). Comparative studies of *Dictyna* and *Mallos* (Araneae, Dictynidae): I. Social organization and web characteristics. *Rev. Anachnol.*, **1**, 133–164.

Jackson, R. R. (1979). Predatory behavior of the social spider *Mallos gregalis*: Is it cooperative? *Insectes Sociaux*, **26**, 300–312.

Kiester, A. R. (1979). Conspecifics as cues: A mechanism for habitat selection in the Panamanian grass anole (*Anolis auratus*). *Behav. Ecol. Sociobiol.*, **5**, 323–330.

Kleiman, D. G., and Eisenberg, J. F. (1973). Comparison of canid and felid social systems from an evolutionary perspective. *Anim. Behav.*, **21**, 637–659.

Klopfer, P. H., and Hailman, J. P. (1967). *An Introduction to Animal Behavior.*, Prentice-Hall, Englewood Cliffs, New Jersey.

Kullman, E. J. (1972). Evolution of social behavior in spiders (Araneae; Eresidae and Theridiidae). *Amer. Zool.*, **12**, 419–426.

Markl, H. (1971). Vom Eigennutz des Uneigennutzigen. *Naturw. Rdsch.*, **24**, 281–289.

Michener, C. D. (1958). The evolution of social behavior in bees. *Proceedings of the Tenth International Congress of Entomology, Montreal, 1956*, **2**, 441–447.

Murton, R. K., Isaacson, A. J., and Westwood, N. J. (1971). The significance of gregarious feeding behaviour and adrenal stress in a population of woodpigeons *Columbia palumbus. J. Zool. Lond.*, **165**, 53–84.

Noonan, K. M. (1978). Sex ratio of parental investment in colonies of the social wasp *Polistes fuscatus. Science*, **199**, 1354–1356.

Nutting, W. L. (1969). Flight and colony founding. In K. Krishna and F. M. Weesner (Eds), *Biology of Termites*, Academic Press, New York. pp. 233–282.

Platt, J. R. (1964). Strong inference. *Science*, **146**, 347–353.

Robertson, D. R. (1972). Social control of sex reversal in a coral-reef fish. *Science*, **177**, 1007–1009.

Shapiro, D. Y. (1979). Social behavior, group structure and the control of sex reversal in hermaphroditic fish. *Advances in the Study of Behavior*, **10**, 43–102.

Springer, S. (1957). Some observations on the behavior of schools of fishes in the Gulf of Mexico and adjacent waters. *Ecology*, **38**, 166–171.

Trivers, R. L. (1971). The evolution of reciprocal altruism. *Quart. Rev. Biol.*, **46**, 35–57.

Trivers, R. L. (1972). Parental investment and sexual selection. In B. Campbell (Ed.), *Sexual Selection and the Descent of Man 1871–1971*, Aldine Publishing Company, Chicago, pp. 136–179.

Trivers, R. L., and Hare, H. (1976). Haplodiploidy and the evolution of the social insects. *Science*, **191**, 249–263.

Wellington, W. G. (1957). Individual differences as a factor in population dynamics: the development of a problem. *Can. J. Zool.*, **35**, 293–323.

West-Eberhard, M. J. (1978). Polygny and the evolution of social behavior in wasps. *Jour. Kansas Entomol. Soc.*, **51**, 832–856.

Wheeler, W. M. (1923). *Social Life Among the Insects*, Harcourt Brace, New York.

Wheeler, W. M. (1928). *The Social Insects. Their Origin and Evolution*, Harcourt Brace, New York.

Wilson, E. O. (1971). *The Insect Societies*, Belknap Press of Harvard University Press, Cambridge.

Wilson, E. O. (1975). *Sociobiology: The New Synthesis*, Belknap Press of Harvard University Press, Cambridge.

Wilson, E. O., and Farish, D. J. (1973). Predatory behaviour in the ant-like wasp *Methocha stygia* (Say) (Hymenoptera: Tiphiidae). *Anim. Behav.*, **21**, 292–295.

Learning, Development, and Culture
Edited by H. C. Plotkin
© 1982, John Wiley & Sons Ltd.

CHAPTER 14

The naked meme

David L. Hull

INTRODUCTION

As Campbell (1965, 1974, 1975, 1979) amply documents, the apparent similarities between biological and sociocultural evolution have intrigued scientists and philosophers alike from before Darwin to the present. In its most ambitious form, the program which Campbell terms 'evolutionary epistemology' seeks not only to extend a theory of biological evolution to include social and cultural traits but also in the process to supply an epistemic justification for our knowledge of the external world. Some authors even propose an evolutionary ethics, as if a system of human ethics could be based on evolutionary theory. More than this, those evolutionary epistemologists with the maximum ambitions propose to accomplish their task with a minimum of resources. They are gene selectionists, biologists who think that the general features of the evolutionary process can be explained entirely in terms of genes.

A common objection to evolutionary epistemology is that it is not 'epistemology'. Throughout the history of philosophy, epistemological systems have included a great deal of empirical content. They were as much psychology as epistemology. However, I agree with the critics that a purely descriptive epistemology is 'epistemology' in name only. I do not take this admission to count in the least against Campbell's research program. To the contrary, I find a scientific theory of sociocultural evolution a vastly more significant goal than an evolutionary epistemology. A theory of sociocultural evolution, like any scientific theory, is more than merely descriptive, but any necessity it may have is nomic, not epistemic. My use of the appellation 'evolutionary epistemology' in this paper should not be taken as an endorsement of any epistemological views whatsoever. If evolutionary epistemology were a genuine epistemological theory, I would not be in the least interested in it.

Certain advocates of evolutionary epistemology seem to propose a literal extension of a theory of biological evolution to cover sociocultural phenomena. I happen to think that much more about the behavioral traits and social organization of *Homo sapiens* is going to be explicable in strictly biological terms than most of us would like, in particular those traits most closely connected to reproduction. I disagree with those authors who seem to think that such an extension of evolutionary theory is *a priori* impossible. However, I also think that no strictly biological theory is going to explain everything about human sociocultural development, in particular it is not going to explain very much about changes in the *content* of human conceptual systems. It is not going to explain the rise of the sonnet in Elizabethan England or the transition from deterministic to relativistic physics in this century.

In part, my reservations about the extension of a theory of biological evolution to cover totally sociocultural development stems from the nature of current theories of biological evolution. A major discontent with these theories as strictly biological theories is that they do not imply anything about particular species *qua* particular species, in particular *Homo sapiens*. If evolutionary theory cannot predict whether the brains of human beings are going to increase or decrease in size or whether we are going to lose our little toe, so the critics reason, then it is no theory at all. But these are not the sorts of predictions that evolutionary theory is designed to make. No one complains that celestial mechanics cannot predict things about Mars *qua* Mars. Celestial mechanics cannot predict very much about the physical makeup of Mars, whether it is solid, liquid, or a bit of both. In order for predictions to be made about particular heavenly bodies on the basis of celestial mechanics, these bodies must fit one or more reference classes. Because planets revolve around stars in elliptical orbits and Mars is a planet, its path should be elliptical.

Evolutionary theory as a strictly biological theory does not imply anything about particular species. One reason why people think that it should is that particular species have long been a paradigm example of natural kinds, and natural kinds are the sorts of things about which scientific theories are supposed to allow predictions. However, I shall argue in this paper that the reason that no predictions can be made about particular species on the basis of evolutionary theory is that particular species are not natural kinds but historical entities (particulars) and particulars are not the sort of thing that function in scientific laws. Instead, they are the things about which predictions can be made once they have been included in an appropriate reference class. The appropriate reference classes in biological evolution are such things as peripheral isolates, polytypic species, and species invading unoccupied adaptive zones. To the extent that *Homo sapiens* (or any other species) fits one of these reference classes, predictions can be made about it.

Gould (1977) has termed the attempts by biologists to provide evolutionary explanations for particular adaptations in particular lineages 'just-so stories'. In spite of how derogatory the phrase sounds, Gould cannot intend to condemn such activities wholesale because he has spent much of his own professional career telling such stories. The point of Gould's objection is that evolutionary narratives deal with highly contingent particulars. More than one plausible story can be told for any sequence of events, and it is unlikely that we will ever have sufficient evidence to decide between these various alternatives. As fascinating as these stories are, we should not put very much weight on any one of them.

No strictly biological theory of evolution is going to explain very much about the content of human conceptual systems because these particularities are not the sort of thing evolutionary theory is designed to explain. It can set limits to how quickly a new allele can spread through a population of a particular size, structure, etc., it can set out possible mechanisms for the maintenance of genetic polymorphisms, it might even explain the prevalence of sexual reproduction, but it cannot predict the complex series of genetic changes which result through time in a particular species. If it cannot make such predictions about the genetic makeup of biological populations, it certainly will not be able to explain comparable changes in societies or conceptual systems. These observations no more detract from the power or importance of evolutionary theory as a strictly biological theory than the observation that no physicist can predict the physical makeup of Pluto a million years from now on the basis of celestial mechanics detracts from celestial mechanics.

However, most advocates of evolutionary epistemology do not propose a literal extension of a theory of biological evolution to cover sociocultural phenomena. Rather they propose either to reason analogically from biological evolution to social and cultural evolution or to present a general analysis of evolution through selection processes which applies equally to biological, social, and conceptual evolution. I prefer the second way of putting the research program of evolutionary epistemology. Such a theory cannot be couched in terms of genes, gene pools, biological species and the like, because these terms are too restrictive. They apply literally only to biological evolution. Instead more general terms must be provided. In this paper I propose to use the terminology devised by Dawkins in his highly controversial *The Selfish Gene* (1976). Dawkins' key notion is 'replicator'. Although Dawkins steadfastly maintains that genes are the primary replicators in biological evolution, he is willing to accept any entity with the appropriate characteristics as a replicator — any entity which can pass on its structure largely intact (Hull, 1980). The physical details of replication are irrelevant. For example, in genetic replication, each replicate receives only half the material in the ancestor molecule, but it receives all, or nearly all, its structure.

Dawkins (1976) coins the term 'meme' to refer to the units of sociocultural evolution (see also Semon, 1904). Genes are one sort of replicator; memes another sort. Once again, the particular mechanisms involved in memetic replication are not important. Memes can exist in brains, books, computers, and a wide variety of physical vehicles of knowledge (Campbell, 1979). Mental telepathy notwithstanding, memes cannot be transferred directly from one brain to another. Some sort of physical intermediary is necessary. Regardless of all these contingencies, from the point of view of memetic evolution, all that matters is that the messages contained in the structure of these physical vehicles be transmitted largely intact. Central to the notion of a 'message' is the distinction between the structure of a physical object which follows necessarily from its physical makeup and that which does not. In order to replicate, molecules of DNA must uncoil, split down the middle, fill in the appropriate nucleotides, and so on. This sequence of events is as lawful as any other chemical reaction. However, there is something about the structure of a particular molecule of DNA which depends on the sequences of selection processes which gave rise to it—the order of bases along its backbone. From the point of view of their physical makeup, any base can follow any base. Thus, the actual order of bases can function as a message.

Dawkins, views have been controversial, not so much because he maintains that replication is central to selection processes or that replication in biological evolution is concentrated at the lowest levels of biological organization, chiefly at the level of the genetic material, but because he maintains that the evolutionary process can be understood entirely in terms of replication (but see Wimsatt, 1980). For Dawkins, genes are the primary focus of selection. Organisms are merely machines designed by genes to aid in their own transmission. The only 'good' that matters in biological evolution is the 'good' of individual genes. This is why he entitled his book *The Selfish Gene*. To some extent, the wide denunciation of Dawkins' gene selectionist views by evolutionary biologists is puzzling. With the rarest of exception, current expositions of population genetics are set out entirely in terms of the transmission of genes—pious allusions to the role of the phenotype notwithstanding (Michod, 1981). Dawkins' offense is that he proclaimed openly and without apology a view of the evolutionary process that other biologists express only with some embarrassment. Biologists would like to account for the role of the phenotype in their theories, but the task is too difficult. The organism/environment interface is too variable and messy. Dawkins, to the contrary, delights in terming organisms 'gene machines'.

As justified as Dawkins might be for using a strictly gene-selectionist version of evolutionary theory as the analog for his exposition given the current state of evolutionary biology, the results are no less deficient. The ultimate purpose of organisms may well be to function as survival machines for their constituent genes, but excluding reference to organisms in our formulations of evolutionary theory results in the omission of the causal mechanism responsible for replication being differential. In order for evolution to occur, not only must replicators replicate themselves, but also they must do so differentially. Entities more inclusive than genes function in this process along with genes. No theory of biological evolution which ignores the relations which result in replication being differential can possibly be adequate (Wright, 1980; Hull, 1980). If a purely gene selectionist version of evolutionary theory is not adequate for explaining ordinary biological traits like blood type and eye color, then the attempt to extend this overly parsimonious theory to include social and cultural evolution is sure to fail. Comparable observations hold for a general analysis of selection processes as such. Reference to replication alone, whether genetic or memetic, is not going to be sufficient. If any theory of evolutionary epistemology is going to have any hope of success, it must make full use of all the resources available to it at the biological level (Plotkin and Odling–Smee, 1981).

One also should not expect more of a theory of sociocultural evolution than one does of a theory of biological evolution. Anyone who expects a theory of sociocultural evolution to predict changes in the makeup of particular societies or the content of particular conceptual systems is going to be disappointed. After being shuttled back and forth between New York and Lawrence, Kansas, the editorship of the journal *Systematic Zoology* moved to the West Coast. No theory of the development of scientific communities is going to be able to predict that. However, it might have something to say about the connections between successful research programs and the editorship of the relevant outlets for publication. In Darwin's day, saltative versions of evolutionary theory were popular. According to these views, the origin of new taxa is abrupt, not gradual as Darwin contended. More moderate saltative views have recently arisen in evolutionary biology (Eldredge and Gould, 1972). No theory of conceptual development is going to be able to predict the rise and fall of particular views. Instead, predictions can be made only to the extent that a particular event fits one of the appropriate reference classes of sociocultural evolution. Considerable disagreement currently exists over the appropriate reference classes for theories of biological evolution. Are varieties incipient species or are the only precursors to new species peripheral isolates? Biologists are still struggling to come up with just the right combination of evolutionary units. The task has hardly begun for sociocultural evolution.

One source of the difficulty in producing an evolutionary analysis of sociocultural evolution is the existence of considerable disagreement among present-day biologists over the nature of strictly biological evolution. Is evolution primarily gradual, primarily saltative, or a little bit of both? Does selection occur exclusively at the level of the genetic material, or can more inclusive entities also be selected? Do all mutations have some selective value or are most neutral? Do species evolve or do they, once formed, remain largely unchanged? Can species themselves be selected? Even the existence of Lamarckian evolution, an idea once thought dead, has once again raised its head. Might not inheritance in immunological systems be Lamarckian? And the list goes on.

The multiplicity of opinion among evolutionary biologists makes the comparison of biological evolution with other forms of evolution quite difficult, but evolutionary epistemologists are in no position to complain of these difficulties. If scientific theories evolve in anything like the way that biological species do, variation is essential. As Ackermann (1976: 58) remarks, 'We might expect scientific theories in an extended evolutionary metaphor to embrace a variety of interpretations in order to incorporate a rational hedge against the vagaries of an uncertain future.' Evolutionary epistemologists are hardly in the position to complain that evolution theory has one of the characteristics that they claim all theories must have. The most that one can do under the circumstances is to show that the variety of alternatives that present themselves with respect to biological evolution are mirrored in other forms of evolution. In general, I find that many of the objections raised against attempts to present an evolutionary analysis of social groups and conceptual systems, if valid, would count just as much against evolutionary theory as a strictly biological theory.

As the numerous responses to Campbell (1975) collected in Wispé and Thompson (1976) amply document, the three main criticisms of evolutionary epistemology are:

(1) that biological species are classes, while social groups and conceptual systems are not,
(2) that biological evolution is Darwinian, while sociocultural evolution is to some extent Lamarckian, and
(3) that sociocultural evolution has a significant intentional element, while biological evolution does not.

In this paper I argue that all three of the preceding objections are not especially well taken. (1) Neither social groups nor conceptual systems can be treated as classes, but contrary to a tradition that stretches back for centuries, biological species also cannot be treated as classes, at least not if they are the things which evolve through natural selection. Instead, social groups, conceptual systems, and biological species must be interpreted as the same sort of thing—historical entities.

(2) As common as the claim is that sociocultural evolution is Lamarckian, I am not sure how seriously to take it. Social learning is possible. Culture would be impossible without it. But social learning is not an instance of the inheritance of acquired characteristics. On a literal reading, it is not an instance of inheritance; on a metaphorical interpretation, the things being transmitted are

not characteristics but the analogs to genes. The only sense in which sociocultural evolution is 'Lamarckian' is in the grossest caricature of this notion—that it is intentional. Just as giraffes grow longer necks by 'striving' to reach the leaves at the tops of trees, cultural change is to some extent a function of the conscious striving of the people in that culture.

(3) The implications of intentionality for sociocultural evolution depend on how biological and sociocultural evolution are to be distinguished. If they are distinguished by means of the phenomena investigated, the effects of intentionality cut across biological and sociocultural evolution. The changes brought about by plant and animal breeders are just as intentional as those produced by social planners, probably more so. If the presence of intentional behavior itself is used to distinguish between biological and sociocultural evolution, then artificial selection cannot count as part of evolutionary theory as a biological theory, even though it modifies strictly biological traits, such as gene frequencies. On this construal, biological and sociocultural evolution differ but as I shall argue not to the extent that one might think.

SPECIES AS HISTORICAL ENTITIES

The species question has had the longest and stormiest career of any dispute in biology. Even today considerable disagreement exists over the nature of biological species and the roles they play in evolution. According to most evolutionists, species are the things that evolve, the things that change indefinitely through time. According to an increasingly popular view, however, species are incapable of evolving. Once formed they stay fairly much the same. Significant change occurs only at speciation. The things which evolve are the lineages formed by successions of species (Eldredge and Gould, 1972; Stanley, 1979). But regardless of whether one thinks that species or sequences of species evolve, the question remains, what sort of thing are species? The usual answer given to this question is that they are a special sort of class—natural kinds. On more serious consideration, however, both philosophers and biologists are becoming convinced that species, if they play any of the roles usually attributed to them in evolution, cannot possibly be natural kins. Instead they must be construed as spatiotemporally localized individuals—historical entities (for further discussion, see Ghiselin, 1974; Hull, 1974, 1976, 1978a, 1980, 1981; Griffiths, 1976; Mayr, 1978; Patterson, 1978; Rosenberg, 1980; Toulmin, 1972; Wiley, 1979, 1981; Sober, 1980, 1982; Williams, 1981; Eldredge and Cracraft, 1980; for objections see Smart, 1963, 1968; Cohen, 1973, 1974; Kitts and Kitts, 1979; Caplan, 1980, 1981).

As long as biologists treated species as classes and organisms as individuals, no great effort was needed to distinguish between them. However, now that a significant number of philosophers and biologists maintain that species themselves are at least quasi-individuals, the distinction warrants more careful examination. The relevance of this discussion to the topic at hand—sociocultural evolution—is the need to discover appropriate analogs to organisms and species for sociocultural phenomena. Unless we are clear about the nature of the entities that function in biological evolution, we are liable to draw inappropriate comparisons between biological and sociocultural evolution. In fact, this is precisely what has happened, for example, in a dispute between Toulmin (1972) and Cohen (1973).

In his *Human Understanding*, Toulmin proposes to exploit Mayr's (1963) notion of a biological population to aid him in accounting for the evolution of intellectual professions and their disciplines, that is, the evolution of such social groups as the Darwinians and such conceptual systems as Darwinism. Because of his own animosity toward the 'cult of systematicity', Toulmin (1972:128) emphasizes the variability and flexibility of populations:

> Rather than treating the content of a natural science as a tight and coherent logical systems, we shall therefore have to consider it as a conceptual aggregate, or 'population', within which there are—at most—localized pockets of logical systematicity.

Cohen (1973: 48–9) objects:

> But a rational discipline is not merely not a biological species: it is not a species at all—at any rate as Toulmin conceives it. It does not consist of a set of individual members that are similar to one another in all relevant respects and may be said to instantiate it. The individual animal at present on my hearthrug instantiates the species *felis domestica*, but the concept of mass cannot be said to 'instantiate' modern physics: it merely has an essential role or function therein. The relation between a concept and the rational discipline to which it belongs is, roughly, that of part to whole, not that of member to species or member to population. (See also Losee, 1977.)

In this section I argue that Cohen is right about conceptual systems but definitely wrong about biological species. In no way can biological species be treated as classes with members. Toulmin is closer to the mark, but biological populations are not mere 'aggregates' either. They are more highly organized than aggregates but not quite as well as organized as organisms. Crucial to our understanding of the evolutionary process is the nature of the sort of organization present in the entities which are supposed to change indefinitely through time. In this section, I deal with biological evolution. In the next, I extend these considerations to sociocultural evolution, in particular to conceptual evolution.

According to present-day biologists, ontogenetic development is a teleonomic process. Although Pittendrigh (1958) coined the term, Mayr (1961, 1974) has developed the notion of teleonomy most fully. According to Mayr (1976:389), 'A teleonomic process or behavior is one that owes its goal directedness to the operation of a program.' A program in turn is 'coded or pre-arranged information that controls a process (or behavior) leading it toward a given end' (Mayr 1976:393—see Chapter 2 of this volume). Mayr (1976:695) further distinguishes between closed and open programs, 'A genetic program that does not allow appreciable modifications during the process of translation into the phenotype I call a *closed program*—closed because nothing can be inserted in it through experience... A genetic program that allows for additional input during the lifespan of its owner I call an *open program*.' Some programs verge on being totally closed, but no program could be totally open and count as a program, any more than a totally open system could actually be a system. In both cases, considerable closure is required.

Ontogenetic development results from a three-way interaction between the genome, the developing phenome, and the environment. As everyone is well aware, the terminological difficulties inherent in any attempt to talk clearly and sensibly about this three-way relation are all but insuperable. Natural languages are not designed to express these complex interrelations. Nevertheless, a gesture must be made. Although both genes and environments are necessary for the development of any phenotypic trait, the roles they play vary. A particular range of environments is always necessary for ontogenetic development, sometimes quite narrow, sometimes exceedingly broad, but in ordinary phenotypic development, the environment provides little in the way of 'instruction'. Most of the structure of the resulting organism comes from the structure of its genome. Depending on the trait under investigation, the guidance provided by the genome can vary from merely constraining the reaction (the reaction norm is extremely broad) to dictating one structure and one structure only (the reaction norm is narrow).

Organisms are systems, in certain respect homeostatic systems, in certain respects homeorhetic. The causal feedback loops controlled by the genes sometimes lead organisms to remain in the same state in the face of considerable, though not unlimited, variation in the environment. Other feedback loops result in the organism progressing through its life cycle. In fact, Bonner (1965, 1974) individuates organisms on the basis of genetically programmed life cycles. Although these life cycles can be extremely variable, there is some point in emphasizing this feature of ontogenetic development. Organisms have beginnings and endings in time (frequently quite abrupt). Not all developmental paths are equally open to an organism. Although particular ranges of environments are necessary for development, sometimes even particular sequences of environments, it is primarily an organism's genome which guides its development.

In spite of the difficulties in discussing the organization of particular organisms, at least everyone agrees that organisms are individuals and not classes. No one claims that the cells which make up an organism are part of that organism *because* they have the same genetic makeup. The cells which go to make up a single organism tend to be genetically quite similar, usually identical, but that is not why they belong to the same organism. Different organisms frequently possess cells with exactly the same genetic constitution (clones), and single organisms can be made up of genetically quite diverse cells (gynandomorphs); see also Brown (1981). A single organism is not a class of cells grouped together because of some essential or possibly statistical similarity. They are integrated wholes.

These observations are not based on common conceptions, although in this case they happen to coincide with them, but because the only way that organisms can play the role that they do in evolution is to be construed in this way. In order for selection to take place, certain entities must come into existence, reproduce themselves, and pass away. In this process, certain entities are more successful than others. Whether one believes that this process itself produces speciation or that it serves only to fine tune a species to its environment, it plays a central role in all present-day versions of evolutionary theory. Organisms are not the only entities which perform this function, nor is this process of adaptation through natural selection the only process involved in biological evolution, but it is an important process, and organisms are clearly one of its chief foci (Grant, 1963; Mayr, 1963; Jacob, 1977).

The situation with respect to phylogeny is complicated by disagreements over the ontological status of species: are they classes or individuals? If species are interpreted in the traditional way as classes or even as aggregates, then they cannot possibly be directively organized systems. If species are not systems at all, then they cannot possibly be directively organized systems. However, if species are organized systems of some sort, then it is at least possible for them to be homeostatic and/or homeorhetic systems. If they are systems, then the disanalogy Cohen (1973) points out between biological species and conceptual systems no longer applies. Both are really the same sort of thing after all. Just as the relation between a 'concept and the rational discipline to which it belongs is, roughly, that of part to whole' (Cohen, 1973:49), the relation between an organism and its species is also roughly part to whole.

It certainly must be admitted that Cohen has two thousand years of philosophy on his side. From Aristotle to the present, most philosophers (not to mention biologists) have viewed biological species as akin to what modern philosophers call classes or natural kinds. Although philosophers differ to some extent over the precise character of natural kinds, most agree that they have four fundamental properties. They are eternal, immutable, discrete, and important. Although natural kinds are 'eternal', this does not mean that every natural kind has to be exemplified at all times (though for Aristotle they had to be). For example, just as all gold might cease to exist for a while, all pterodactyls might die off. Natural kinds are 'eternal' in the sense that, if individuals with the appropriate characteristics ever come into existence again, they must be placed in the original natural kind, not a new one.

Natural kinds are also 'immutable'. By this philosophers do not mean particular individuals cannot change their natural kinds; only that these kinds themselves cannot change. For example, a wire triangle might be reshaped into a rectangle, but triangularity cannot evolve into rectangularity. Similarly, a sample of lead might be transmuted into a sample of gold, but leadness cannot be transmuted into goldness. Whether or not these individuals are to be considered the same individuals before and after these transitions varies from author to author.

Until recently, philosophers maintained that natural kinds are 'discrete'. By this they meant that all natural kinds must be defined in terms of a set of characteristics which are severally necessary and jointly sufficient for membership. The traits must 'universally covary'. All plane triangles are three-sided plane closed figures, and all three-sided plane closed figures are triangles. Similarly, all atoms of gold have atomic number 79, and every atom with atomic number 79 is an atom of gold. In recent years, certain philosophers have been willing to countenance 'cluster concepts', natural kinds defined by traits which covary only statistically. For them, the boundaries between natural kinds in character space are 'fuzzy'.

Although philosophers tend to agree that natural kinds are important (Sober, 1980), the criteria which they suggest for distinguishing between natural kinds and the myriads of classes which fertile imaginations can dream up vary considerably. The criterion which I think is the most promising for science is appearance in a law of nature. In the context of science at least, those classes which function in scientific laws are important and properly termed natural kinds. The problem then becomes that of distinguishing between laws of nature and other sorts of generalizations. But the distinction which is relevant here is between natural kinds and the individuals that instantiate them, e.g. planets and Mars. The term 'planet' appears in certain laws of celestial mechanics, while particular planets such as Mars actually function in these processes.

The point to notice is that classes are not the sort of thing that can evolve. Evolution is essentially a spatiotemporal process. Everything which functions in the evolutionary process or results from it must share in this spatiotemporal character. For instance, genes can be classed together in a variety of ways: similar structure, similar effect, and common descent. Mutations which produce chlorophyl deficiency all have the same effect, but in maize alone mutations in at least 180 different loci have this same effect. With respect to effect, they are all the 'same' gene. On all other criteria, they are 'different' genes. The question is the criterion for 'sameness' which is relevant to the evolutionary process.

The answer to this question is as straightforward as it is counterintuitive.

Both the entities which function in the evolutionary process and the entities which result from it are necessarily spatiotemporal entities and must be ordered in spatiotemporal sequences. Otherwise selection cannot produce the sort of cumulative change necessary for adaptation. Biologists consistently insist on distinctions which make their science look 'historical'. Certain genes have the same structure; others have the same structure because they are replicates of common ancestral genes. They are identical by descent. Certain organisms have the same structure; others have the same structure because they are descended from common ancestors. Once again, descent is what matters. Certain exemplifications of a trait are observationally indistinguishable. From a wide variety of perspectives, they are the 'same' trait. However, they may not be evolutionary homologous. Physicists draw precisely these same distinctions. Mars remains Mars through time because of continuity in development. It also happens to remain largely unchanged, but individual planets, atoms, and lead balls are individuated by means of spatiotemporal location and continuity through time. The only reason that biology looks peculiarly historical is that biologists propose to treat biological species, entities which in the past have been viewed as natural kinds, as historical entities. If species were natural kinds *and* historical, then biology would be peculiar. But once one conceptualizes species as individuals, then biology ceases to be so peculiarly historical.

In an early attempt to apply set theory to biological classification, Gregg (1950:426) decries certain unfortunate modes of expression used by biologists who should know better. For example, biologists insist on claiming that species have geographic ranges and that borderlines exist between species. But, as Gregg rightly points out, if species are classes, then such claims are literally nonsense. 'Classes are *abstract, non-spatiotemporal* entities.' One possible conclusion is that biologists do not know what they are talking about. Species really do not have ranges and borders. Another more likely conclusion is that biologists know very well what they are talking about, and they are not talking about abstract, non-spatiotemporal entities. One cannot have it both ways. If one wants to use set theory to characterize the relations between organisms and their species, species can have none of the spatiotemporal characteristics necessary for them to evolve. One biological species can no more give rise to another, then triangularity can give rise to rectangularity. Conversely, if one insists that species, whatever else they might be, are the things which evolve, then they cannot be classes of the sort which function in set theory. For species as well as organisms, origin is essence.

In the preceding pages I have argued that species are spatiotemporally localized entities of some sort, but I have yet to describe this sort at sufficient length. Biological populations are extremely peculiar. They are not just classes described by some sort of abstract similarity. Species of sexually reproducing organisms form networks: sexual organisms must mate to reproduce, and these offspring in turn must do the same. Strictly asexual organisms do not form such networks. At most they form connected trees. Problems arise when we turn from spatiotemporal continuity to cohesiveness. Populations are not just aggregates of similar organisms. They exhibit some sort of internal cohesiveness. The three most likely candidates for the cause of this apparent cohesiveness are gene flow, the unity of the genotype, and the nature of the selection process itself.

One of the basic tenets of the synthetic theory of evolution is that gene flow among the organisms comprising a biological species promotes the cohesiveness of its gene pool. Any statistical differences which begin to build up in one part of a species are neutralized by gene flow. The larger and more dispersed a species happens to be, the more extensive the gene flow must be. Whether or not gene flow alone is adequate to sustain the cohesiveness of gene pools is still a moot question (Mayr, 1963; Endler, 1977). However, it is reasonably clear that gene flow is not adequate to make species homeostatic or homeorhetic systems. Species may have these characteristics, but not because of gene flow alone. The most that one can say is that a species' gene pool *constrains* the evolutionary development of that species *locally* but not *globally* (Richards, 1981). Perhaps any gene pool can be converted into any other gene pool, given enough generations and both the right mutations and the right selection pressures, but not in the space of a single generation.

Gene flow is a characteristic of population structure. Mayr (1963, 1975) suggests a characteristic of individual genotypes to explain the cohesiveness of gene pools—the unity of the genotype. According to Mayr, each species is characterized by its own basic genotype which allows only so much variation without ceasing to be functional. Hence, speciation can occur only through genetic revolution, possibly the alteration of a single regulatory gene. On this view, species are relatively static systems. Once they are formed, they remain relatively unchanged until they go extinct. Although the unity of the genotype can explain why species are static systems, it does nothing toward justifying the claim that they are homeostatic systems. To do that, feedback loops must be discovered that are adequate to maintain species in roughly the same state in the face of environmental fluctuations. The functioning of particular genotypes is what makes organisms homeostatic and homeorhetic systems, but so far no one has shown how the unity of the genotype can lead to species themselves being teleonomic systems. In addition, the evidence for and against the very existence of the unitary nature of genotypes is still highly equivocal. However, the unity of the genotype, if it is applicable at all, is as applicable to asexual organisms as to sexual.

Finally, a few authors have suggested that selection itself organizes species into teleonomic systems. Of all the reproductive links possible in a species, only the tiniest percentage are ever realized. At the level of single organisms, the tree of life is pruned vigorously. Perhaps *selection* can provide the relations necessary for phylogenetic development to be in some sense programmed.

According to Bajema (1971:2), natural selection is the 'feedback mechanism which favors the production of DNA codes—"programs"—which enables the species to adapt to the environment. It is via natural selection that information about the environment is transmitted to the gene pool of a population. This is accomplished by differential reproduction of different genotypes changing the frequency of genes in populations.' Popper (1975:74) agrees, 'The elimination of error, or badly adapted trial instructions, is also called "natural selection": it is a kind of "negative feedback"' (see also Boorse, 1976:83). However, the claim that natural selection is itself an example of negative feedback is definitely a minority view. Woodfield (1976:199) presents the majority view as follows:

> Finally, the biological statement commits a further error in calling natural selection a feedback process. Strictly speaking, evolution is not a process which consists of a system's being influenced by the consequences of its previous behaviour. This is merely an analogy which derives from our regarding a species as a unitary system which persists over time, and which 'responds' to ecological pressures in such a way as to issue changes in its own composition as 'output'. In reality, there is no single continuing entity which does things and is influenced by what it does, when a species changes its characteristics over time. Only the organisms which make up the species do things. What actually happens is that individuals of one generation reproduce differentially, and the consequences of this, when aggregated, determine the composition of the next generation ... Species-survival (when it occurs) is not a goal, therefore, but a *de facto* result of the evolutionary process. Species are neither goal-directed systems nor feedback-controlled systems. Indeed, to be accurate, they are not systems at all.

Contrary to superficial appearances, species are systems. However, it is quite another question whether they are goal-directed systems. On a frequency interpretation of goal-directedness, one would have to conclude that if species are goal-directed, their goal is extinction because that is the near universal outcome of evolution. Of course, on this same interpretation, the goal of organisms is death even more frequently than it is reproduction. On a feedback analysis of goal-directedness, however, these conclusions do not follow. The problem is to specify the sense in which selection involves feedback loops. In the cybernetic diagram supplied by Bajema (1971:3), variation in the environment affects the organism–environment interaction which produces differential reproduction, which changes the composition of the gene pool (see Figure 1). At this point, the environment enters in again, this time in the production of mutations. The altered gene pool produces organisms in interaction with the environment, and so on round the flow chart again.

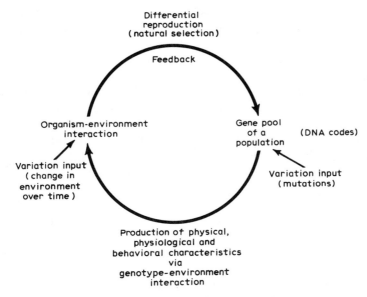

At first glance, Bajema's diagram looks very much like the representation
of a causal feedback loop, but on closer inspection, problems arise. In
ontogenetic development, each pass through a feedback loop acts on the same
perduring entity. Perhaps the structure of the organism changes through time,
perhaps the functioning of its genetic code changes through time, but the
structure of its genome remains the same. Organisms cannot change indefinitely
through time. If Eldredge and Gould (1972) are right, species also cannot
change through time but not because a species as a system has some sort of
species-level program. Rather the limits to its evolutionary development are
fixed by the genotypes of its constituent organisms. Organisms have life cycles
guided by their genetic constitutions. On the Eldredge and Gould model, species
cannot evolve, but not because they have programmed life cycles. Similarly, if
phyletic evolution can occur, one species changing gradually through time into
another, then evolution even at the species level is constrained but not
programmed, because the genetic programs themselves change through time
and nothing directs this change in any sort of a programmed way. Each loop
in Bajema's diagram feeds into a 'new' system, not the same old system as in
genuine examples of feedback.

On the traditional view, species are not homeostatic systems integrated by
numerous closed causal loops because they are not systems at all but 'classes'.
On the new view, species are chunks of the genealogical nexus. Continuity
through time is guaranteed by gene transmission in the ancestor–descendant

relation. Cohesion at any one time is promoted by gene flow and the unity of the genotype. However, it seems very unlikely that feedback loops actually function at the level of entire species to integrate organisms into homeostatic systems—static perhaps but not homeostatic. If selection processes are instances of negative feedback, someone has yet to explain exactly how this is possible. Evolutionary change seems to be totally dependent on environmental changes and totally reactive to them. It is neither programmed nor prescient. Natural selection is extremely effective but not very efficient. The waste at every level is so tremendous that it would stagger even the Pentagon. The God who devised this system is hardly the Protestant God of waste not/want not.

CONCEPTUAL SYSTEMS AS HISTORICAL ENTITIES

Toulmin (1972:356) maintains that the criteria of identity-through-change for biological species are essentially the same as those for scientific disciplines. Cohen (1973:49–50) disagrees:

> Darwin shed an immense flood of light on the identity-through-change of a biological species by pointing out how the forces of natural selection operated to preserve most similarities between the members of a population, while at the same time causing some new similarities to replace old ones. The identity or continuity of the species consisted not in any identity or continuity of the individual members, whose life-spans might well be quite short—but in the broad spectrum of mutual similarities that the members of one generation shared with those of the immediately preceding generations. But in the identity-through-change of a scientific discipline is nothing remotely like this.

The point of the preceding section was to show that Cohen is mistaken about biological species. The identity or continuity of species is not to be found in any 'broad spectrum of similarities' but in the ancestor–descendant relation. In this section I attempt to extend a similar analysis to conceptual systems. Even though the sort of variation characteristic of biological species has been studied extensively and described at great length, most people find it very difficult to comprehend. Mayr's 'population thinking' does not come easily. In the case of natural kinds, we try to find at least one trait which all and only the members of that natural kind have. If we fail, we are unhappy. The same can be said for historical entities. We desperately try to find one element which persists throughout its duration. I think that some natural kinds can be defined in terms of necessary and sufficient conditions, and there may be historical entities that do not undergo total transformation during their existence. But in neither case do I think we can demand in advance that these requirements be met.

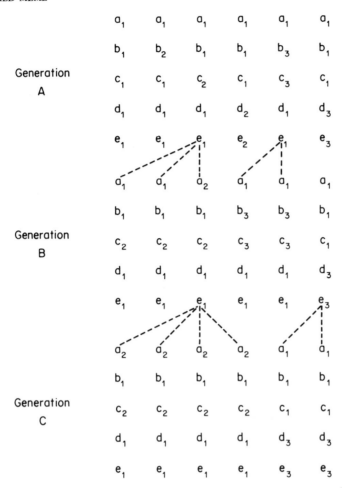

Figure 2 On one interpretation, three generations of a biological population are shown. Each column represents the genome of a particular organism. Dashed lines indicate which organisms gave rise to which. For sake of simplicity, only a sexual reproduction is depicted. On a second interpretation, three generations of a scientific theory are shown. Each column represents a version of this particular theory. Dashed lines indicate which version of a theory gave rise to which subsequent versions. In moving from generation A to generation B, b_2, d_2, and e_2 are lost and a_2 is introduced. In moving from generation B to generation C, b_3 and c_3 are lost, while the frequency of a_2 is increased dramatically

If thinking of biological species appropriately is so difficult, one can imagine how difficult it is to extend this mode of conceptualization to conceptual systems themselves. For example, in Figure 2, each column represents an organism with its particular genetic makeup. Successive rows represent successive generations of this same population. The dotted lines represent descent. Figure 2 can also be used to portray conceptual change. The columns represent different versions of the same conceptual system and successive rows successive generations. We are all used to treating concepts as types and their individual exemplifications as tokens. For example, the inheritance of acquired characteristics might be viewed as a single 'unit idea'. Slightly different versions of this idea can be found exemplified in the conceptual systems of particular biologists from Lamarck and Darwin to early Mayr (Zirkle, 1946). It matters not at all whether these various tokens are related by descent, that is, whether Mayr came to accept the inheritance of acquired characteristics by reading Darwin, Lamarck, or someone else, or whether this person in turn might have taken the notion from some earlier biologist.

Numerous philosophers have argued that the temporal dimension to conceptual development must be paid greater attention. Several have even suggested an evolutionary analysis of conceptual development. However, no one has worked out this suggestion in sufficient detail. In particular, no one has seen the implications of an evolutionary analysis of conceptual development for the nature of concepts themselves. Whether conceptual systems are termed paradigms (Kuhn, 1962), disciplinary matrices (Kuhn, 1970), research programmes (Lakatos, 1970), intellectual disciplines (Toulmin, 1972), theories (McMullin, 1976), or research traditions (Laudan, 1977), they must be organized into trees and networks, not similarity classes (see also Hull, 1975 and Burian, 1977). Evolutionary theory is not a type with numerous tokens, but a 'population' of different 'versions'. The columns in Figure 2 connected by dotted lines happen to be similar to each other, but they are versions of the 'same' conceptual system not because they are similar to each other but because of their origins. Two columns could be identical in assertive content and belong to two different, possibly even competing, conceputal systems. Conversely, two quite different columns could be part of the same conceptual lineage.

In response to Lakatos' insistence that every research programme have a 'hard core', Richards (1981: 65) remarks:

> Evolving conceptual systems may undergo fundamental modifications, changes more basic than simple adjustment of peripheral principles. A system will be regarded as forsaken only when historical continuity has been broken and the problem situation vacated.

'But,' one might justifiably ask, 'Why adopt such a counterintuitive way of structuring conceptual development? Nothing but confusion can result from treating two formulations that contradict each other as versions of the "same" theory.' One can certainly group individual propositions and even entire conceptual systems into kinds on the basis of shared assertive content. There may even be reasons for doing so. However, these kinds are not the kinds relevant to evolutionary development. If conceptual systems evolve in anything like the way that species do, then they must be treated as historical entities related by descent and not as timeless sets of similar ideas.

Numerous questions must be answered if an evolutionary analysis of conceptual development is to be more than a suggestive metaphor. Memes are bound up in memetic systems. Are both individual memes and memetic systems historical entities, or just the systems? What sorts of relations 'bind' memes together in memetic systems? How are we to individuate memes and memetic systems at any one time as well as through time? How can we tell whether we have one meme or several? In this section I provide tentative answers to these questions. Some of these answers will appear somewhat less than satisfactory. Part of this dissatisfaction will surely have some foundation. However, I suspect that much of it will stem from an inappropriate choice of standards. On the analysis I provide, the boundaries between memetic systems are not always sharp. They could not be and at the same have memetic systems be the things which are evolving. The only concepts that can grow are those that blur (Hull, forthcoming). Hence, the discontent which arises because of absence of absolute, sharp boundaries is misplaced. In order to set the stage for my discussion of memetic evolution, I must return for a moment to the biological analog.

The genetic material can be subdivided into units in many different ways— according to the needs of Mendelian genetics, molecular biology, or evolutionary theory. Mendelian genes are the physical entities whose transmission and recombination explain Mendelian patterns of inheritance. Mendelian genes come in a variety of kinds—dominant, recessive, epistatic, and so on. At the molecular level, biologists distinguish between codons, mutons, cistrons, operons, regulatory genes, and so on. Finally, from an evolutionary perspective, a gene is any replicator that lasts long enough through enough replications to serve as a unit of selection (Dawkins 1976:30). Literally speaking, genes are not conserved, only their messages. As Williams (1966:25—see Chapter 3 of this volume) puts it. 'In evolutionary theory, a gene could be defined as any hereditary information for which there is favorable or unfavorable selection bias equal to several or many times its rate of endogenous change.'

Right now no simple relation exists between Mendelian, molecular, and evolutionary genes (Hull, 1973). Eventually, these different gene concepts may become welded into a single, interrelated set of definitions as the theories of which they are part coalesce—which is not quite to say that Mendelian genetics and evolutionary theory will be reduced to molecular biology. For now, however, they must be treated separately. Molecular genes are individuated along structural and functional lines. They do not have any significant historical dimension. Both Mendelian and evolutionary genes are historical entities. They form lineages. A Mendelian gene is held to be 'dominant' because of its behavior in past crosses. Eventually, the historical dimension to Mendelian genetics may be eliminated as we come to understand the relevant biochemistry more fully. However, the historical dimension to evolutionary phenomena is uneliminable.

Evolutionary genes are not historical entities just because of current ignorance: they are necessarily historical. The only way that selection processes can result in differential replication is by genes being organized into lineages. The identity that counts in evolution is identity through descent.

If memes are like genes, then they must exist in numerous 'memotypes'—versions of the same memetic system. These versions compete with each other, becoming more prevalent or less prevalent. In addition, different memetic systems must also exist. They too compete with each other. There is both intra- and inter-memetic competition. Generations must also be distinguishable. Later versions of the same system are integrated into lineages via descent. Some similarity must exist in versions from generation to generation, but it is secondary to descent. For example, in Darwin's day, many different versions of evolutionary theory were popular. Some were Darwinian; some were not. Darwin's version of evolutionary theory had to compete not only with special creation but also with other Darwinian versions of evolution as well as with non-Darwinian versions. Gould (1977), for instance, groups 19th century evolutionists into eight categories according to the alternatives they chose on three sets of beliefs—the direction of evolution (steady-state versus directional change), mode of change (environmentally or internally induced), and tempo of change (punctuational or gradual). Several of these combinations were not especially popular (e.g. steady-state, internal gradualism), but at least one important evolutionist held each of these combinations.

Gould selected only three variables to group 19th century versions of evolutionary theory. The classification could be expanded by adding a dozen or more variables, such as the role of sexual selection, geographical isolation, hybridism, and so on. All of these variables concern assertive content. Which of these many combinations are to be considered Darwinian? Which evolutionary but not Darwinian? And which are really not evolutionary at all? Gould (1977:3) is forthright in declaring that his discussion should not be taken literally as history:

> Some will be offended at what might seem to be a claim of patrimony. A modern directionalist may well reject an 'ancestor' like Buckland, claiming with invincible logic either that he never heard of the man, or that he chooses not to be ranked with the author of 'Geology and mineralogy considered with reference to natural theology' (Buckland, 1836). But I am not making a claim of homology via chains of physical descent like pedigrees of kinship. Pedigrees of ideas can be 'homologous'—indoctrination of child by parent, or student by teacher, for example. But the chains of which I speak are forged of analogous links. Basic ideas, like idealized geometric figures, are few in number. They are eternally available for consumption, and the sequential list of their consumers is no pedigree, but the convergence of independent minds to one of a very limited set of basic attitudes.

For a truly evolutionary analysis of conceptual development, sequential lists of people who happened to hold the same basic idea will not do. The specification of chains of physical descent are required. Analogies won't do; only homologies. For example, the combination of variables which I mentioned earlier as being relatively rare in Darwin's day was the combination actually set out by Lamarck in his *Philosophie zoologique* (1809). According to Lamarck, very simple organisms are generated spontaneously from inorganic matter at the bases of several 'trees of life'. The trees themselves are invariant. Inherent in all organisms is a tendency to increased complexity. It is this internal tendency which impels organisms through successive generations up their particular tree. Lamarck also thought that, as organisms confront new environments, new needs are produced. These needs give rise to new habits which in turn produce heritable changes in the organism. This particular sequence of events does not cause evolutionary change but merely determines which branch particular sequences of organisms take in their respective trees of life. The end result is the transmutation of species.

In many respects Lamarck's ideas were not especially controversial in his day. Biologists both before Lamarck and after believed in spontaneous generation, the adaptability of organisms during their lifetimes, and the inheritance of these adaptations. Darwin can be included on this list. Although Darwin did not publicly advocate spontaneous generation—this was one battle he chose not to fight—his theory presupposes some naturalistic explanation for the first origins of life back in the midst of time (de Beer, 1960, 4:160). The only views especially peculiar to Lamarck were his belief in a tendency to increased complexity, the role of needs in eliciting new characters, and the adequacy of these processes to transmute one species into another. Although Lamarck was far from clear about what he meant by 'needs' and 'habits', he did not mean that organisms can *will* hereditary changes. After all, he thought that his theory applied as readily to plants as to animals. The common translation of *besoins* as 'needs' is due to parodies of Lamarck's views popularized by his opponents such as Cuvier.

When Darwin and his contemporaries rejected Lamarckian nonsense about 'volition' in plants (Darwin, 1859:3; Darwin, F., 1899, 1:542) and the 'wish of parents' (de Beer, 1960, 1:227), they were not rejecting Lamarck's views but parodies of Lamarck. The same can be said for the 'necessary progression' implied by Lamarck's system (Darwin, F., 1899, 2:198). No one at the time, Darwin included, seemed sufficiently interested in what Lamarck actually said to read his work with sufficient care. If they had, they would have discovered that organisms progress up trees, but these trees themselves are comprised of eternal, immutable natural kinds. For Darwin, most species had gone extinct and once extinct cannot come into existence again (Darwin, F., 1899, 2:134). Lamarck thought that permanent extinction is impossible. If all organisms of a particular sort were to die, they would soon be replaced by others moving up the Great Escalator of Being. Organisms progressed through successive generations; species themselves did not (Simpson, 1964; Hodge, 1971; Mayr, 1976; Burkhardt, 1977).

Similar observations can be made with respect to Darwin and everyone else involved in the dispute over species. Even though Darwin repeatedly explained that by 'chance variation', he did not mean that variations were in the least 'uncaused', his critics declined to listen. The preceding examples of what particular scientists did or did not actually say are not motivated by petulant antiquarianism. Rather, they serve to raise the question of which views must be considered as operative in the course of science. The rational reconstructions produced by philosophers (and some historians) wander from one extreme to the other. Sometimes they include in their rational reconstructions what the scientist actually said, sometimes what he was interpreted as saying, and sometimes what he should have said but didn't (Lakatos, 1971).

For anyone interested in an evolutionary analysis of conceptual development, only one choice is possible. The claims that scientists should have made but did not, as long as no one thought that these were the claims being made, are clearly irrelevant. No matter how much it shocks my historical sensibilities, the claims which a scientist makes are equally irrelevant if no one interpreted him in the way he intended. If the set of views termed 'Lamarckian' was widely believed to include the efficacy of volitions and necessary progress, then these are the views that must be included in the Lamarckian conceptual system. The only other alternative is simply to ignore Lamarck. Since no one seems to have understood Lamarck as saying what he actually said, then we can ignore Lamarck and concentrate on pseudo-Lamarck. For example, Weismann's famous experiment in which he cut off the tails of mice for several generations with no effect may have counted against pseudo-Lamarck. It counted no more against genuine-Lamarck then did the circumcision of Jewish males for generations with no greater effect because in neither cases were needs demonstrated.

The force of the preceding observations can be seen by returning to Gould's (1977) classification. Charles Lyell is listed twice, once as early Lyell (steady-state, environmentally induced gradualism) and once as late Lyell (directional, environmentally induced gradualism). Scientists change their minds on issues throughout their careers. During his early years, Darwin thought that the chief mechanism for the evolution of species was probably the direct influence of the environment, but he changed his mind on this score long before he published the *Origin* in 1859. Early on he also thought that geographic isolation was necessary for speciation, but eventually decided otherwise. Later, when Moritz Wagner published a theory of speciation by means of geographic isolation, Darwin attacked him fiercely (Sulloway, 1969; Kottler, 1978).

To make matters worse, Darwin's views at any one time are not always clear or mutually consistent; e.g. Gould places part of Darwin with early Lyell and part with later Lyell. How can scientific theories come in incompatible parts?

To put yet another turn to the screw, very few of Darwin's contemporaries agreed with him totally even on essentials, and this includes such staunch Darwinians as Huxley and Gray. Huxley thought that evolution was largely saltative, while Gray maintained that it was in some sense directed and progressive. If Huxley and Gray do not count as Darwinians, who does? If their views are not part of Darwinism, what ideas are? Such questions arise for the Darwinians as an actual social group of interacting individuals and for Darwinism as a conceptual system as it developed in the English speaking world. The situation becomes even more complicated when we turn to the Darwinians at large and the Darwinism which swept across Europe like the flood. As the authors in Glick (1974) amply document, the Darwinians were a highly diverse and scattered group of people, and 'Darwinism' meant many things to many people.

If we follow conceptual development as it actually occurs, the story gets extremely complicated, so complicated that at times it is difficult to make any sense out of it at all, almost as complicated as species. However, if we succumb to the temptation to treat ideas as types with numerous tokens, then conceptual systems cannot possibly evolve. For example, Lovejoy (1936) traces the idea of the Great Chain of Being through the years. Many critics have complained that some of his tokens were not sufficiently similar to each other to be counted tokens of the same type, and Lovejoy (1936:1–23) acknowledges the difficulties invloved with discerning unit ideas. For example, the term 'Christianity' is the name of a 'very mixed collection of ideas' (Lovejoy, 1936:6). The problem to which Lovejoy and his critics refer is real, possibly unsolvable. When are two 'unit ideas' similar enough to count as tokens of the same type? When do two conceptual systems have enough unit ideas in common to count as tokens of the same type? The traditional way of viewing concepts has its own problems.

My objection to Lovejoy's story is that too often he gives no evidence that the ideas that he is grouping together actually are related in any way besides abstract similarity in assertive content. It is one thing to argue that Patrick Matthew and Darwin thought of the 'same' idea—natural selection. It is quite another to show that Darwin got his idea from Matthew. But, one might respond, this is all a matter of priority. Perhaps scientists engage in demeaning priority disputes, but that is just an embarrassing weakness of less than perfect scientists. An idea is equally important and true regardless of who thought of it first. Historians might be interested in how much de Vries' reading of Mendel affected his own formulation of 'Mendel's' laws (Kottler, 1979; Campbell, 1980), but the results of these investigations are irrelevant to the issue of whether Mendel's laws as he stated them are tokens of the same type as the laws enunciated by de Vries. From the point of view of evolutionary epistemology, nothing could be further from the truth. The 'types' which are operative in conceptual development are not abstract similarity classes, but historically connected lineages. If the content of Mendel's paper did not materially influence the views set out by its so-called 'rediscoverers', then the content of Mendel's paper does not belong in the conceptual system usually termed 'Mendelian genetics'.

All sorts of considerations enter into how we treat past science which, on a little reflection, are irrelevant. For example, scientists are frequently chastized for not being sufficiently humble. Humility is a Christian, not a scientific virtue. I have seen no evidence that humble scientists produce better science than their more arrogant colleagues. Similarly, I think we all feel some sympathy for unappreciated precursors—scientists who set out ideas early on similar to ideas which later became widely acclaimed, but were ignored or disdained in their own day. However, I think such sympathy is misplaced if it leads us to include scientists in a lineage where they do not belong. With one minor exception, the history of Mendelian genetics would have been the same had Mendel never existed (Olby, 1979; Brannigan, 1979). The one exception is that in the absence of Mendel as a patron saint, a priority dispute between the so-called 'rediscoverers' would have been all but unavoidable. Since Mendel had anticipated everyone, the issue was alteady settled. Strangely, the same line of reasoning was not applied to Darwin and his clearest precursor—Matthew. When historians insist that de Vries, Correns, and Tschermak are 'rediscoverers' of Mendel's laws, not discoverers, I think they are succumbing to the precursoritis against which they rail so loudly. The historically relevant issue is not how similar the ideas happen to be, but where they came from. In conceptual development, unappreciated precursors do not count.

If a genuine evolutionary analysis is to be provided for scientific development, as Kuhn (1970:172) proposes, then I think that particular versions of scientific theories must be identified with particular scientists at some stage in their development and organized into lineages by means of their being held successively by the same scientist. Scientists serve as 'central subjects' for the individuation of simple conceptual systems (Hull, 1975). Similarly, I think more general, amorphous conceptual systems such as Darwinism can be individuated only by connecting them with actual scientific communities defined by their social connections.

In the postscript (1970:175) to his *The Structure of Scientific Revolutions* (1962), Kuhn distinguished between two senses of 'paradigm'. In one sense, paradigms are disciplinary matrices, the 'entire constellation of beliefs, values, techniques, and so on shared by the members of a given community.' In a second sense, they are exemplars, 'one sort of element in that constellation, the concrete puzzle-solutions which, employed as models or examples, can replace explicit rules as a basis for the solution of the remaining puzzles of normal science.' Kuhn (1970:176) goes on to claim that a 'paradigm is what the members of a scientific community share, *and*, conversely, a scientific community consists of men who share a paradigm.'

I approve heartily of Kuhn's suggestion but disagree with his later development. In the first place, if scientific communities are individuated on the basis of their social connections (e.g. reading and commenting on early drafts of papers, citing positively, voting in favor of medals and honors), then not all scientists in the same community share the same paradigm. For example, Henslow was sociologically an important Darwinian, e.g. he was the first scientist Darwin sought out on his return from his voyage, and he was in the chair at the famous Darwin—Wilberforce debate. Yet he never accepted even the rudiments of Darwin's theory. Conversely, many anti-Darwinians (e.g. Mivart) held views indistinguishable from Darwin's closest allies. If one defines scientific communities in terms of agreement, then one guarantees that the members of scientific communities will all share a common paradigm, but these 'communities' play no role in science. In the absence of a requirement of actual social interconnection, scientists from all ages and places must be included in the same scientific community if they happened to hold sufficiently similar views. Such a criterion also groups supporters with archenemies. Scientific communities and disciplinary matrices are interconnected in complex ways, but their boundaries do not everywhere coincide. But this is exactly what one should expect if such communities and conceptual systems are analogous to evolving species. Natural kinds may have sharp boundaries; historical entities rarely do (Hull, 1975).

One way to individuate scientific communities and conceptual systems is by a method analogous to the one used by taxonomists to individuate biological species. Pick an organism, any organism, and invent a name. Any other organisms with the appropriate relations to this type specimen belong in the same species with it. The appropriate relations are gene transmission and gene exchange, not similarity. The type specimen is in no sense 'typical'. It is merely one node in the genealogical nexus. Scientific communities can be individuated in the same way. Pick a scientist, any scientist, and trace out his scientific connections. If he belongs to a community, the contours of that community will materialize. Any scientist who actually belongs in a community can serve as the 'type specimen' or 'exemplar' of that community. He need not be the most important member of that community, nor even the scientist after whom the community is named. Hooker would do as well as Darwin as a type specimen for the Darwinians. Mendel, to the contrary, could not serve as a type specimen for the Mendelians. Regardless of what one thinks about the similarity of his views to those of such men as Bateson, Mendel was not sociologically a Mendelian.

Treating conceptual systems as historical entities is not quite so straightforward. The temptation is to group similar ideas together and to limit the relevant relations to purely inferential connections, preferably deductive. According to Lovejoy (1936:14–15), a unit idea is a 'single specific proposition or "principle" expressly enunciated by the most influential European philosophers, together with some further propositions which are, or have been supposed to be, its corollaries.' In addition, these unit ideas have a 'natural logical affinity for certain other principles.' When Kuhn (1977:477) turns to expanding on his notion of an exemplar, he does so in the context of similarity relations. His particular examples are ducks, swans, and geese! Instead of an exemplar being one node in a nexus, it is a representative of a similarity class. However, if examplars are going to aid in the individuation of conceptual systems as historical entities, they must be treated as being genuinely *concrete*.

In order for two ideas (or memes) to be part of the same conceptual system in the simplest case, they must both reside in the same physical vehicle, for example in a human brain. To the extent that such physical vehicles are organized into more inclusive systems, such as scientific communities, conceptual systems can be expanded. For example, Darwin's insistence that natural selection is the chief mechanism for evolutionary change was part of his own conceptional system from at least 1838 until his death. Because Darwin was a Darwinian, this idea belongs in Darwinism even if no other Darwinian agreed with Darwin. As it turned out, a few Darwinians did share Darwin's views on natural selection. Hence, on these grounds, the principle of natural selection deserves at least a minor place in Darwinism.

The opponents of particular research programs also play a role in the individuation of these programs. They typically latch onto what they take to be the weakest tenets and criticize them vocally. Their very criticism makes these tenets more important. If the advocates of this position can be led to defend these tenets, they become even more important. Natural selection is an important element in Darwinism, not so much because all Darwinians accepted it as adequate to produce evolutionary change (most did not), but because they were forced to defend it against their common enemies. Examples of the important role that criticism plays in elevating the importance of particular elements in a conceptual system are legion, from the reading of heads in phrenology to the discontinuous nature of traits in Mendelian genetics.

As necessary as co-existence is in the individuation of conceptual systems, it can be treated as sufficient only at the price of trivializing the notion. Brains are filled with a hodgepodge of ideas. For some, the only connection they have is that they happen to exist in the same physical vehicle. Something more than this is required. The specification of this something more is far from easy. Deduction is too strong. Certain views, once extracted from their exemplifications and converted into propositions, can be deductively related; e.g. the so-called 'deductive core' of Darwin's theory. Sometimes the scientists themselves are aware of these connections; sometimes not. Only the former can count as part of a conceptual system. Unnoticed deductions play no role.

Similar observations apply to contradictions. Many scientific theories as they were set out by particular scientists contain contradictions. According to well-known principles of deductive logic, contradictions imply any proposition whatsoever. Hence, all these scientific theories are one, even of one is a theory of celestial mechanics and another a theory of inheritance. On the view I am urging, contradictions do no harm as long as the scientists involved did not actually exploit them,

Deduction is much too strong a connection for integrating concepts into conceptual systems. Most of Darwin's views could not and still cannot be deductively connected. Many of the ideas which scientists hold in some sense 'support' each other even though the inferential relations between them fail to fit any current logical reconstructions. This fact may well explain Toulmin's (1972) antipathy to the 'cult of systematicity'. As inadequate as current formal systems of inference are in capturing the sorts of relations which actually exist between the elements of conceptual systems as historical entities, evolutionary epistemologists cannot afford to dismiss 'systematicity' and leave it at that. The most pressing task awaiting those workers who think that science must be given a genuine temporal dimension (whether evolutionary or otherwise) is an explication of the sort of support one idea can give another when simple inferential relations do not exist between them—i.e. the vast majority of ideas in any conceptual system (Laudan, 1977).

In this section, I cannot pretend that I have done more than hint at the outlines of what an adequate treatment of conceptual systems, both individual and collective, looks like. The scope of the undertaking strikes me as staggering. But more than this, if one accepts the evolutionary perspective, attempts to discuss science (or any other sort of conceptual activity) become much more difficult, so difficult as to produce total paralysis. It is not enough that two scientists express similar ideas. One must also discover if these scientists actually communicated with each other, read each other works, read someone else who had read their works, etc.

Treating conceptual systems as historical entities also has its advantages. It explains the animosity that professional historians have for 'precursoritis' and the sense in which Western thought is 'western'. But more importantly, it resolves the major disanalogy which Campbell sees between biological and conceptual evolution—cross-lineage borrowing (see also Childe, 1951; Ginsburg, 1961; Waddington, 1961; and Campbell, 1965). According to Campbell (1979:41):

> While holding to this basic paradigm, there is not a one-to-one analogy to biological evolution. For example, there is no counterpart to bisexuality. Cross-lineage borrowing, precluded in biological evolution, becomes an important selective and reproductive process in social evolution.

As is so often the case, the situation in biology is not as simple as commonly believed. Most sexual species consist of only two sexes, but some have a dozen or so mating types. Conceptual evolution has as many 'mating types' as operative scientists. Contrary to popular belief, not all inter-specific hybrids are sterile. Species are distinguished in sexual organisms, not by the total absence of gene exchange but by its rarity (Simpson, 1964; Wiley, 1981). The production of an occasional hybrid does not seriously affect the integrity of the species involved, but if gene exchange becomes too common, two species which were previously distinct merge into a single species. If cross-lineage borrowing becomes too common, it is converted into within-lineage borrowing. The splitting of one species into two (speciation) is a relatively rare event in evolution. Most species go terminally extinct. The merging of two species into one (introgression) is even rarer.

Similar observations can be made for social groups. Sometimes a single group splits into two (sometimes because of conceptual disagreements; sometimes not). Sometimes two groups can merge into one. Again, the merging of two groups does not guarantee the total elimination of disagreements. Cooperation is more important than agreement in the formation and maintenance of social groups. It is possible for two groups to have exactly the same members, but the distinctness of these groups tends usually to be a convenient fiction, e.g. when a corporation consists of no one save the members of a nuclear family. The merging of social groups entails the expansion of the social relations which formerly existed only within the two groups to include a sufficient number of the members of both groups (Hull, forthcoming).

Parallel distinctions in conceptual evolution are a bit more difficult to make. At the turn of the century, the biometricians and the Mendelians were different scientific communities. They shared few members, and disagreed vehemently on several points. Their conceptual systems also were quite different. The first was primarily a theory of evolutionary development, built on a poorly specified 'blending' theory of inheritance. The second was primarily a theory of hereditary transmission which appeared to imply quite a different sort of evolution. After a protracted period of nasty squabbling, the two conceptual systems were 'synthesized' into one. In the process, the two communities were not merged. Old animosities died slowly. Instead a new community grew up to promote the emerging synthetic theory of evolution. As in the case of biological species, cross-lineage borrowing in conceptual evolution becomes within-lineage borrowing if it becomes too prevalent. The only difference between biological and conceptual evolution is the greater frequency with which introgression occurs in conceptual evolution. What is it about conceptual systems which makes them so prone to merger?

If conceptual evolution is to be viewed from an evolutionary perspective, fundamental alterations must be made in how we conceive of 'memes' and 'memetic systems', several of them strongly counterintuitive. For example, two systems with precisely the same assertive content must be viewed as two different systems if they are not interrelated in the same conceptual lineage, just as the eyes of cuttlefish and vertebrate eyes are different structures. The inheritance of acquired characteristics, defined in terms of similarity in assertive content, is no more a natural kind in conceptual evolution as eyes, defined in terms of structure and function, are in biological evolution. Although it disappoints the romantic streak in all of us, from an evolutionary perspective genuinely unappreciated precursors do not count. Genius flickers on and off in the dark of conceptual history. No matter how pretty the light, the only messages that matter are those that are received.

INDIVIDUAL LEARNING AND CHANCE VARIATION

Psychologists typically distinguish between two sorts of learning—individual and social. This distinction depends on two different sorts of 'structure' which exist in an organism's environment. An organism's environment includes both animate and inanimate elements. Sometimes the role which other organisms play in individual learning does not differ materially from that played by the inanimate environment. An organism can learn that touching glowing coals and a bristling porcupine hurts. Organisms can also learn vicariously, i.e. by observing another organism interact with its environment. In the cases mentioned thus far, an organism's memetic system is being shaped by regularities in its interactions with regularities in its environment, but these regularities are not themselves memetic systems. In the most important sort of social learning, memes encoded in one entity are transmitted to another entity. It is this latter sort of learning which makes culture and social life possible.

The distinction between individual and social learning hinges on the difference mentioned earlier between lawful regularities and the peculiar sort of regularity termed 'messages' or 'information'. For example, in DNA molecules a nucleotide containing guanine typically bonds with a nucleotide containing cytosine. The bonding properties of these molecules make other sorts of bonding extremely difficult. The linear order of bases in the molecule, however, is not constrained by the nature of the molecules themselves. Any base can follow any base. The actual sequence results from a retention of the results of a long series of past interactions. Given the relevant lawful regularities and the contingencies at a particular time, guanine was laid down next to cytosine. Given these same lawful regularities and a different set of contingencies later on, another nucleotide containing cytosine is laid down. The result is the codon GCC which codes for alanine.

In the absence of the preceding distinction, social learning degenerates to simple individual learning. In one instance, an organism reacts to regularities in its environment (e.g. water putting out fire). In the other instance, it reacts to regularities in another organism's behavior which are systematically related to other regularities (e.g. a lioness teaches her cubs how to hunt). It makes little difference whether this difference is marked by the distinction between individual and social learning or between first and second order individual learning, but the distinction is crucial. Without it, either all regularities become memes or else memetic regularities become regularities like any other. The nature of representation is at issue. As Lewis Caroll aptly remarked, a country cannot serve as its own map. Sooner or later, representations must culminate in something which is not a representation. Metaphors are parasitic on literal meanings. In individual learning, symbolic structure arises from non-symbolic structure. In social learning, symbolic structure is transmitted from one physical vehicle to another.

Several authors have attempted to draw parallels between biological evolution and individual learning; others between biological evolution and social learning. The three processes take place on different time scales. Biological evolution can occur only through successive biological generations. Individual learning always has as its upper boundary the life cycle of the organism. Once an organism is dead, that behavioral lineage ceases. The 'generations' operative in individual learning are repeated trials. Social learning bridges the gap between the two. Some social learning can take place within the limits of a biological generation, but it can also bridge these generations. One problem with establishing appropriate analyses of biological evolution and learning is the latter is literally *part* of the former. Not only is an organism learning via memetic selection, but also the results of this process enter into genetic selection. Learning is part of an organism's ontogenetic development, and ontogenetic development is part of phylogenetic development. In this section I deal primarily with individual learning, the sort that can take place only within the confines of an organism's life cycle. In the next selection, I turn to social learning.

Blute (in prep) will present the most detailed discussion so far of individual learning as a selection process. On her analysis, organisms are analogous to acts, adapted organisms to competent acts, and natural selection to reinforcement and punishment. Correlations exist between the frequency with which an organism emits a behavior and variations in its immediate environment. Behaviors which are emitted in close proximity to certain sorts of environmental variables (such as food) increase in frequency; others emitted in close proximity to other sorts of environmental variables (e.g. red hot coals) decrease in frequency. According to Blute, an organism learning about its environment is analogous to a species evolving. A change in the frequency of an emitted behavior in the history of a particular organism is analogous to a change in the frequency of a particular trait or allele in the history of a particular species. The rapidity with which a pigeon pecks a key is comparable to the rapidity with which a species becomes melanic. However, individual learning differs from species evolving in three ways: (1) learning is at least partially 'programmed' while evolution is not, (2) learning is cumulative in a way that evolution is not, and (3) learning can go on only so long while evolution proceeds indefinitely through time. Each of these apparent differences will be treated in turn.

Early behaviorists were strict environmentalists. All behaviors were held to be equally likely, regardless of the evolutionary history of the organism. Genes are irrelevant. Instincts are figments of the imagination. Although behaviorists still disdain the sorts of instincts which, say, the Freudians hypothesize, they now allow a role for genes in learning. Although an environmental factor may trigger a particular behavioral sequence, the environment does not provide the structure for this particular emission of this complex behavior; the genotype of the organism does. But plenty of behavior remains for which genes hardly warrant a mention. These behaviors are shaped by interactions between the organism and its environments. These are the sorts of behaviors to which Blute's analysis is intended to apply.

As species evolve, certain genes are transformed, others acquired, and others lost altogether. At times biological evolution is cumulative. The total inform- ation content of the gene pool is increased. Initially in evolution this sort of cumulation must have been extremely prevalent. There is no evidence that it still is. Genes are as likely to be lost from a gene pool as gained. Lineages have at most temporary 'memories'. The role of memory in individual learning is still a matter of some dispute. No one wishes to deny, I hope, that organisms have long-term memory. Initially, at least, learning is a matter of accumulation. Each organism is born with a variety of behavioral predispositions. It rapidly accumulates more. Neurophysiologists currently do not know whether ideas, once coded in whatever corresponds physiologically to long-term memory, are ever completely lost or whether they simply cannot be retrieved.

Many behaviorists are opposed to any talk of brain physiology. For their purposes organisms must be treated as black boxes. The physiological mech- anisms which mediate acts and reinforcement are of no interest. All that matters are variations in the relative frequencies of acts and reinforcers. This particular position should look suspiciously familiar. It is the same strategy employed by population geneticists. Perhaps learning as changes in statistical frequencies of acts can be made analogous to evolving as changes in statistical frequencies of genes, but neither would be the less deficient for that. Just as the mechanisms which are responsible for differential perpetuation in biological evolution are too important to ignore, so too is the physiology of learning. If one admits the relevance of neurophysiology to learning, as Blute does, then at least a potential disanalogy crops up. If learning is always a matter of accumulation with no loss, then learning differs in this respect from biological evolution. However, this differences does not make much of a difference. Information in a particular organism's ontogenetic development can be effectively lost. Even though a meme once acquired may remain permanently in the memory banks of an organism, it may not be retrievable. Whether a meme no longer resides in an organism's brain or whether it cannot be retrieved makes no difference to the actual behavior of the organism.

Blute is well aware that individual learning is part of the ontogenetic development of an organism. In fact, her (1981:1401) major criticism of Langton's (1980) Darwinian behavioral theory of sociocultural evolution is that he does not distinguish consistently between individual and social learning. 'In the former case, a behavior is repeated or a rule is repeatedly applied *in the life history of a single individual* under the pressure of differential reinforcement. In the latter, a behavior or a rule is transmitted *from individual to individual in a social group*, presumably under the pressure of sociocultural selection.' An organism's ontogenetic development differs from a species' phylogenetic development in that the former is at least partially programmed and has a finite duration while the latter does not. Phylogenetic development is at most locally constrained and can go on indefinitely. (On the Eldredge and Gould model, a single species can no more evolve than a single organism can. Species lineages are the things which evolve.)

While individual learning is going on, it may well be amenable to Blute's selective retention model, but the analogy can be made complete only by moving to the level of social learning. As Blute (1981:1401) remarks, 'The point however is that when transmission by observation or by verbally or otherwise encoded instruction occurs, we do not have to await such a new repeated origin in *each* individual. If we did, obviously culture and social life as we know it would not exist.' Newton and Leibnitz had to invent calculus before they could use it. All we have to do today is learn it. Before moving to our main concern—social learning—one further point about individual learning must be discussed—the sense in which it is random.

In connection with the well-worn example of Simmelweis and purpural fever, Blute (1981:1401) argues that while 'Simmelweis himself acquired handwashing by random variation and differential reinforcement, his students almost certainly did not. They acquired it by observation or instruction, and had it maintained by differential reinforcement. The medical community, as a whole, of the hospital and eventually beyond it, acquired it by socicoultural "descent" from its ancestral origin in Langton.' In part, all Blute is doing is pointing out a difference between individual and social learning. In social learning, we learn from other organisms. But in what sense was Simmelweis' original discovery 'random'? The answer is straightforward enough. Prior to any reinforcement, the emission of a behavior cannot be explained by reinforcement. The first time a pigeon pecks a key and receives food is 'random' with respect to reinforcement. It is in no way 'uncaused'. Both genetic and physiological explanations can be given for any behavior. Some concern regularities. For example, certain strains of mice run in circles in the absence of any sort of reinforcement regimen. Others have to be conditioned to act in this way. But much of an animal's behavior is 'random' in a stronger sense. Certainly it is caused, totally caused, but these causes are so idiosyncratic and variable that such causal connections are liable to occur only once in the history of the universe.

Darwin was attempting to make a parallel point when he termed the variations operative in biological evolution 'chance'. No aspect of Darwin's theory of evolution caused more consternation and confusion than his claim that variations are 'chance'. By this he did not mean that they were uncaused but that they were not planned by some outside agent such as God or directed by some internal program the way that ontogenetic development is. He also did not think that very much of evolutionary change was 'Lamarckian'. In general, there is no correlation between the variations an organism might need and those it might get. Darwin's contemporaries were shocked enough by his claim that species evolve. They were even more put off by Darwin's conviction that this change was not in the least 'teleological'. It was strictly naturalistic. Needless to say, Darwin's contemporaries who were led to accept evolution tended to adopt a progressive form of evolution, and needless to say, its crowning glory, its ultimate goal was *Homo sapiens*. In this connection, present-day evolutionists side with Darwin (Simpson, 1964; Williams, 1966; Mayr, 1976).

Simmelweis' discovery of the connection between dirty hands and purpural fever is one of the paradigm examples of scientific method (Hempel, 1966). Terming it 'random' may seem like a defiant rejection of analyses of science as rational inquiry. I do not think it is. No aspect of Campbell's (1974) theory of sociocultural evolution has caused more consternation and confusion than his claim that individual variations in sociocultural evolution are 'blind'. Richards (1977:495) responds that the 'contemporary scientist, unlike his forebearers, is not troubled by the idea that nature is blind. But he may have some hesitation in admitting his own blindness.' Thagard (1980:190) registers the same objection. 'It is ironic that the great merit of Darwin's theory— removing intentional design from the account of natural development—is precisely the great flaw in evolutionary epistemology.' However, I am not sure that either Blute or Campbell wishes to deny the role of intentionality in individual learning.

In response to Richards' sharp but nevertheless sympathetic criticisms, Campbell (1977) ticks off the characteristics which he thinks individual variations in sociocultural evolution do not have. They boil down to one: they are not 'prescient'. But I doubt that any responsible authors think that they are. On the basis of our current knowledge and understanding of how the world is, we can make predictions about the future. In certain areas of science, these predictions are very reliable, but no scientist claims clairvoyance. Predicting the future is not the same thing as witnessing it in advance. Obviously the real source of Campbell's choice of terminology must lie elsewhere. In biological evolution, the future development of a lineage is locally constrained by its gene pool. However, a specification of these constraints says little about the long term prospects of distant generations, and it surely does not explain the mutations which happen to arise. To a large extent, scientific investigation is guided by and constrained by the state of knowledge at the time. Knorr (1977) argues that these constraints are extremely localized and idiosyncratic. But if some genuinely novel idea crops up, it is genuinely novel only to the extent that it goes beyond what we currently know. Richards (1977) and Thagard (1980) emphasize how reasonable and intelligent scientific investigation is. Campbell (1977:503) responds that 'innovation, however small, is not explained by the *restraints* or *guidance* provided by previous conceptualizations' (italics added).

On one interpretation, as Richards (1977:498) notes, Campbell is merely emphasizing a pair of tautologies. A scientist cannot discover what he already knows, and he cannot already know the future development of science without making the future the present. Everyone now agrees that no strict logic of discovery exists, no set of rules which, if applied automatically, guarantee results. Various strategies do exist for improving one's chances, but that is all. One of these strategies is simple trial and error. Certainly neither Blute nor Campbell want to claim that scientists *always* flail about blindly. Science is as goal-directed a process as exists, but it must be carried on in the absence of fore-knowledge of the goal. The goal may not even exist. Much of scientific activity is programmed, most of the rest is at least locally constrained, while only a small percentage of a scientist's activity takes place at the cutting edge of science. Campbell is arguing that at times of greatest innovation, scientific investigation does not differ materially from simple trial-and-error learning. Trial and error is not all there is to science by a long shot, but in the attempt to go from some knowledge to more knowledge, it is indispensable. Science is a social activity. It is the clearest example possible of social learning. But at times of greatest innovation, it converges on individual, trial-and-error learning.

Rescher (1977:153) argues that blind trial-and-error search is adequate for biological evolution but inadequate for scientific development because in the latter case there are '*just too many* imaginable hypotheses to be gone through.' Feyerabend (1975) recommends the proliferation of hypotheses, the more the merrier. Rescher disagrees. According to Rescher (1977:157), cognitive evolution is not a 'blind groping amongst *all conceivable* alternatives, but a carefully guided search among the *really promising* alternatives.' This he takes to be a 'crucial disanalogy between biological and cognitive evolution.' Rescher is surely right about cognitive development. Scientists have too much sense to follow Feyerabend's advice and generate hypotheses endlessly, no matter how hairbrained or improbable. Occasionally a view that appears insane, given the conceptual system of the day, turns out to be correct, but not often enough for scientists to risk their careers by always selecting the most unlikely hypotheses to examine. It is this feature of science which leads the general public to view scientists as 'close-minded'.

Although Rescher is right about cognitive development, he is wrong about biological evolution. Biological evolution does not result from selection of all possible gene combinations. There are more possible combinations of genes in *Homo sapiens* alone than there are atoms in the universe. Selection takes place only among the actual combinations which appear, a tiny minority of the possible combinations. Although much of this narrowing is the result of happenstance, some of it is not. If Mayr (1963, 1976) is right, genes tend to assort in pre-tested blocks. Although the ultimate source of variation in biological evolution is mutation, in the vast majority of cases, selection operates on recombinations of the same genes which existed in the immediately preceding gene pool. The same can be said for conceptual evolution. Most conceptual evolution does not occur via innovations but by means of the recombinations of the same old ideas, not by novel ideas but by novel combinations of familiar ideas.

The real difference between biological and sociocultural evolution is the different roles which intentions play in each. I find it hard to deny that organisms in addition to human beings are conscious and strive to fulfil goals. An antelope strives as mightily to elude a lion as the lion strives to catch it. However, with the possible and thus far marginal exception of *Homo sapiens*, organisms do not strive to produce mutated progeny. But scientists do strive to accomplish the analogous state of affairs in conceptual evolution—they strive to produce conceptual innovations. Most scientists who strive to solve particular problems fail. (The sociological data on this score is depressing, close to immobilizing.) On occasion, a scientist striving to solve one problem happens to solve quite a different problem. But striving is not irrelevant. A scientist striving to solve a problem is more likely to solve it than another scientist who is not. However, I see no need for evolutionary epistemologists to deny the role of striving in either biological or conceptual evolution (see later discussion).

The chief difference which I see between biological and sociocultural evolution is that genes play two roles in biological evolution (autocatalysis and heterocatalysis), while memes perform only one (autocatalysis). Genes not only produce other genes, they also produce organisms of which they are part. These organisms are an important focus for one of the two relations necessary for evolution through selection. All organisms are gene machines. Some organisms are also meme machines. Memes can be seen as replicating themselves, but the sense in which memes produce 'meme machines' to act as their proxies in memetic competition is not clear. To put the point differently, the genotype/phenotype interface, which is so important in biological evolution, is not all that apparent in memetic evolution. Single memes are part of memotypes, but this relation is comparable to genes and genotypes. Memes can exist only as part of physical vehicles of knowledge such as computers and people. Perhaps memes function in the production of computers, but they do not function significantly in the production of people. The difficulty of distinguishing between 'genotype and phenotype' in sociocultural evolution is the topic of the next section.

SOCIAL LEARNING AND LAMARCKIAN INHERITANCE

Nearly everyone who writes on sociocultural evolution agrees on at least one thing—biological evolution is not in any way Lamarckian while sociocultural evolution to some extent is (Waddington, 1961; Maynard Smith, 1961). Certain authors think that this disanalogy totally invalidates evolutionary epistemology (Cohen, 1973; Losee, 1977; Thagard, 1980). Others think that it does not (Popper, 1972; Toulmin, 1972; Rescher, 1977; Campbell, 1979; Richards, 1981). The idea that sociocultural evolution is Lamarckian is so familiar that no one bothers to say very much about what they mean by this appellation. For myself I have been unable to devise an interpretation of this claim which is both coherent and in any significant sense 'Lamarckian'. The point is not that these authors have failed to set out a view of sociocultural evolution that adheres to the views which Lamarck actually held about biological evolution (Kroeber, 1960). That would be asking too much. Rather, in this section I argue that sociocultural evolution is 'Lamarckian' only in the most caricatured sense of this much-abused term.

What most authors seem to have in mind when they claim that sociocultural evolution is Lamarckian is that in social learning acquired characteristics are inherited. In biological contexts, the inheritance of acquired characteristics involves both a particular mechanism and a particular correlation between environmental causes and phenotypic effect. Changes in an organism's environment produce changes in its phenome. The organism acquires a characteristic which it did not formerly have. This alteration in the phenome produces a change in the genome. These altered genes are then transmitted to the organism's progeny, resulting in this acquired characteristic appearing once again in the next generation. This acquired characteristic is not just *transmitted*; it is *inherited*. Of equal importance, a correlation must exist between the nature of the environmental factor which altered the phenome to begin with and the nature of the ensuing alteration. For example, growing a shade plant in the sun might cause it to have smaller leaves. This change results in the hereditary material being altered in such a way that the progeny of this plant have smaller leaves. If this process is kept up in successive generations, a species of broad-leafed plant can be converted quite rapidly into a species of narrow-leafed plant. The reason that the immunological phenomena reported by Gorczynski and Steele (1980) have caused such a stir is that they fulfil all the requirements for the inheritance of acquired characteristics.

As long as biologists thought that modifications in the phenotype of an organism could be transmitted to the hereditary material, there was some reason to expect that organisms, through successive generations, might get and be able to pass on the variations they might need. Not only would an organism be able to adjust to changes in its environment, but also it would be able to produce offspring even better able to adjust to these same changes. Heritable variations would be preserved by the very conditions that produced them. The converse inference is not nearly so well-founded. If one discovers what appears to be a Lamarckian correlation, it does not follow that a Lamarckian mechanism is producing it. All sorts of other mechanisms can have this same result, e.g. the process called somewhat misleadingly 'pre-adaptation'. Because natural populations include so much genetic heterogeneity, they sometimes posses in very low frequencies genes which prove to be advantageous in new environments.

In the past the term 'Lamarckian' has been applied too readily to natural phenomena. On everyone's view, the causal chains which eventuate in mutations pass through the phenome. For example, a rise in the temperature of an organism might lead to a mutation in the gonads of this organism. If this mechanism counts as Lamarckian, then of course all hereditary variations are 'Lamarckian'. Another possibility is changes in the phenotype of an organism being transmitted to the phenotypes of its progeny without touching the genetic material. For example, a mother can transmit syphilis to her unborn child. Such transmission is congenital, not hereditary, and for this reason is no more an example of the inheritance of acquired characteristics than is the transmission of fleas. In order for acquired characteristics to be literally *inherited*, the genetic material cannot be bypassed. Thus, three questions must be answered with respect to sociocultural evolution: (i) are the mechanisms Lamarckian, (ii) are the correlations between causes and effects Lamarckian, and (iii) are the Lamarckian correlations the result of Lamarckian mechanisms? In the remainder of this section I argue that Lamarckian correlations do exist in sociocultural evolution, but they are not produced by mechanisms which can be termed 'Lamarckian' in any but the most caricatured sense of this term.

In order for sociocultural evolution to be Lamarckian in a literal sense, the ideas which we acquire by interacting with our environment must somehow become programmed into our genes. Sociobiologists argue that certain behavioral predispositions are innate. However, they do not think that these behavioral predispositions were programmed into the genetic material by Lamarckian means. To the contrary, the sociobiologists are strict Darwinians. Those organisms that tended to behave in certain ways survived to pass on these dispositions to their offspring. No one thinks that sociocultural evolution is *literally* Lamarckian. To the contrary, the transmission that is supposed to be Lamarckian is of the memes that are *not* passed on in the genetic material. Instead it is social learning that is supposedly Lamarckian, and it is Lamarckian only in the context of the meme-transmission metaphor.

In order for sociocultural evolution to be Lamarckian in a metaphorical sense, conceptual genotypes must be distinguishable from conceptual phenotypes and the two must be related in appropriate ways. Julian Huxley (1960:225) argues that 'in culture you can't distinguish ontogeny from phylogeny: you can't separate them as you can in a higher organism, just as you can't separate germ plasm from soma in culture. The two are one.' I disagree. In culture, individual learning is analogous to ontogeny and social learning to phylogeny. The genotype–phenotype distinction is trickier. One might be tempted to suggest that the axioms of a deductive system are analogous to genes and the theorems to phenotypic traits. But axioms and theorems are equally memes. If anything, they are related as genes are to their genomes. Another possibility is to treat ideas (memes in people's heads) as analogous to genes and the outward manifestations of these memes as analogous to the phenome. For a consistent metaphor, however, two sorts of manifestations must be distinguished: those that retain the structure of the initiating ideas and those that result from this structure but do not retain it. Examples of the first sort are the written and spoken word. They are as much memes as those transcribed in brains. Not until memes become translated into non-memetic action do we reach the phenotypic level. The conceptual phenotype is the *application* of theorems (Wimsatt, 1981: 96).

The only way that an organism can learn about its environment is by interacting with it. In doing so, it can be said to 'acquire new characteristics'. An organism's sense organs are part of its phenome. Hence, changes in the phenome are producing changes in the 'genome'. More than this, Lamarckian correlations seems to result. To the extent that perception is viridical, correlations exist between the character of the environment producing the perception and the resulting memes. Hence, it would seem that Lamarckian mechanisms are producing Lamarckian correlations. As Medawar (1977:14) describes the situation:

> Human beings owe their biological supremacy to the possession of a form of inheritance quite unlike that of other animals: exogenetic or exosomatic heredity. In this form of heredity information is transmitted from one generation to the next through nongenetic channels—by word of mouth, by example, and by other forms of indoctrination; in general, by the entire apparatus of culture....
>
> Apart from being mediated through nongenetic channels, cultural inheritance is categorically distinguished from biological inheritance by being Lamarckian in character; that is to say, by the fact that what is learned in one generation may become part of the inheritance of the next. This differentiates our characteristically human heredity absolutely from ordinary biological heredity....

I agree with everything that Medawar says save his claim that this system is 'Lamarckian'. It is made to look Lamarckian by mixing literal and metaphorical usages. From the literal perspective, ideas might well count as acquired characteristics. If they were transmitted genetically, then acquired characteristics could be inherited. However, the distinguishing feature of social learning is that knowledge is *not* passed from person to person *genetically*. In the context of the metaphor of sociocultural evolution, ideas are analogous to *genes*, not *characteristics*. If social learning is an example of anything, it is an example of the inheritance of acquired memes.

Several authors have noted that sociocultural evolution looks more like contagion than evolution through selection (Cavalli-Sforza, 1971; Cloak, 1975; Shrader, 1980). The infection metaphor seems appropriate, once again, only from the point of view of the literal transmission of genes in contrast to the metaphorical transmission of memes. The issue is not merely one of terminology, but of providing a consistent story that does not mix literal with metaphorical usage. In the only sense in which memes are characteristics, they are not inherited; and in the only sense in which they are inherited, they are not characteristics. Sociocultural evolution is not *literally* Lamarckian for exactly the same reason that it is not *literally* Darwinian. In neither cases do ideas and the like produce the organisms of which they are part. At the metaphorical level, a distinction can be made between conceptual genotypes and phenotypes, but these entities are not related in the ways necessary for social learning to be Lamarckian. Lamarckian correlations exist in sociocultural evolution. Conceptual variants can be preserved by the very considerations that produced them, but not because of Lamarckian mechanisms. At the metaphorical level, however, a consistent story can be told for sociocultural evolution being Darwinian.

For some reason, those authors who comment on sociocultural evolution are strongly wedded to the term 'Lamarckian', even though sociocultural evolution has little in common with anything Lamarck ever said, and even though it cannot be characterized consistently as an instance of acquired characteristics being inherited. These authors can, of course, use any terms they choose, just so long as they do not allow the usual connotations of these terms to color their discussion. In the case of sociocultural evolution being 'Lamarckian', inappropriate connotations intrude time and again. As Campbell (1979:41) remarks, social evolution 'involves the social inheritance of learned behavior, or taught behavior or socially acquired adaptations', but he rightly objects to social evolution being termed 'Lamarckian' on this account. 'This is a distracting usage for those of us for whom Lamarckianism also connotes selfconscious purposiveness and insightful knowledge on the part of the organism as to what it needs, which we deny is essential.'

According to the terminology devised by Toulmin (1972:337), mutation and selection are 'uncoupled' in biological evolution, 'coupled' in sociocultural evolution. In scientific development, for example, 'novel variants entering the relevant pool are already pre-selected for characteristics bearing on the requirements for selective perpetuation', while in biological evolution, the 'factors responsible for the selective perpetuation of variants are entirely unrelated to those responsible for the original generation of these variants.' Toulmin is apt in his description of this distinction, but he (1972:339) then goes on to remark that if mutation and selection were in fact coupled in biological evolution, gemetes would have 'some clairvoyant capacity to mutate, preferentially, in directions pre-adapted to the novel ecological demands which the resulting adult organisms are going to encounter at some later time.' Critics such as Cohen (1973:47) and Losee (1977:350) are quick to agree. Gametes have no 'clairvoyant capacity'.

But something is desperately wrong. The coupling of variation and selection in sociocultural evolution has no more to do with clairvoyance than it does in biological evolution. Although scientists can anticipate the future, they are no more clairvoyant than are gametes. Nor does Lamarckian inheritance imply clairvoyance. Even if biological evolution were Lamarkian, it would be neither programmed nor prescient. It would be less wasteful and take place much more rapidly, but it would be just as reactive to changes in the environment as Darwinian evolution. The trouble with terming sociocultural evolution 'Lamarckian' is that it obscures the really important difference between biological and sociocultural evolution—the role of intentionality. In sociocultural evolution, Lamarckian correlations exist between the environmental causes and the conceptual effects, but the mechanism responsible for these correlations is not in the least Lamarckian. Rather, it is the conscious striving of intentional agents. Such phenomena can be termed 'Lamarckian' in only the most caricatured sense of this term—the sense in which giraffes increase the length of their necks through the generations by striving to reach the leaves at the tops of tall trees.

INTENTIONALITY AND THE DIRECTION OF EVOLUTION

The characteristic which commentators have in mind when they claim that sociocultural evolution, especially conceptual development in science, is 'Lamarckian' is that at least sometimes people notice problems and try to solve them. In his criticisms of Toulmin's (1972) analysis of conceptual change, Cohen (1973:47) remarks that 'conceptual variation and intellectual selection are coupled. Conceptual variants are for the most part purposively thought up in order to solve the intellectual problems that beset a discipline.' Toulmin (1972:323) also admits that contemporary Darwinian biologists emphasize the lack of coupling between mutation and selection in order to discourage providentialist or Lamarckian interpretations of organic evolution. Skagested (1979:95) characterizes Peirce as maintaining that science 'progresses in a Lamarckian fashion, through purposive efforts at modifying old theories to make them fit new observations.' Similarly, Thagard (1980:189) notes, 'Scien-

tists strive to come up with theories which will survive the selection process.'
Finally, in his discussion of coupled evolution, Losee (1977:350) remarks:

> ...there is a connection between the factors responsible for the
> generation of variants and the factors responsible for the selection of
> variants. Conceptual variants are not 'mutations' that arise in a
> spontaneous, random manner. Scientists invent conceptual variants to
> solve specific disciplinary problems. Thus, it is the judgements of
> scientists about disciplinary problems that are responsible both for the
> generation and for the selection of concepts.

Two questions arise at this juncture: what does it mean to say that certain
acts are intentional and what difference does the intentional character of certain
sorts of sociocultural evolution make to this development? Julian Huxley
(1960:213), echoing the sentiments of his illustrious grandfather, states that in
sociocultural evolution, there is a 'changeover from a teleonomic to a strictly
teleological mechanism.' In a nice turn of phrase, Rescher (1977:133) contrasts
natural selection with 'rational selection' (see also Campbell 1965:31). According to Rescher, 'Rational selection is a process of fundamentally the same *sort*
as natural selection—both are simply devices for elimination from transmission.
But their actual workings differ, since elimination by rational selection is
not telically blind and bio-physical, but rather preferential/teleological and
overtly rational.'

Elster (1979:1) agrees with the distinction which Rescher makes between
sociocultural and biological evolution but thinks that it poses an unbridgeable
gulf between the two:

> ...in spite of certain superficial analogies between the social and the
> biological science, there are fundamental differences that make it
> unlikely that either can have much to learn from the other. The
> difference, essentially, lies in the distinction between the *intentional*
> explanations used in the social sciences and the *functionalist* expla-
> nations that are specific to biology.

Elster is not claiming merely that social theories are irreducible to biological
theories—a claim that is controversial enough in its own right—but that neither
can even learn much from the other. If Elster is right, then the sociobiological
research program, both in its literal and its analogical versions, is doomed from
the start.

Biology can be distinguished from the social sciences in a variety of ways.
One way is in terms of the phenomena investigated. The social sciences deal
with behavior and social organization; biology is limited to studying all other

characteristics of plants and animals. It is usually this sense which reductionists such as Wilson (1974) have in mind when they propose to reduce the social sciences to biology. Phenomena which in the past social scientists explained in terms of social theories, sociobiologists propose to explain in strictly biological terms. Just as organisms can be selected for the shape of their sex organs, they can be selected for the structure of their courtship behavior. Both phenomena are equally biological if the information for these characteristics is transmitted genetically. A behavioral trait is properly in the domain of the social sciences only to the extent that genes are irrelevant to its transmission.

Elster's conclusion about the gulf which exists between the biological and social sciences stems from his distinguishing between them, not in terms of differences in the phenomena studied, but in terms of the role of intentionality. Any situation in which intentions function is the proper subject matter of the social sciences even though the phenomena affected are non-social. For example, on Elster's characterization, the behavior of plant and animal breeders is part of the subject matter of the social sciences; evolution by natural selection is not. Elster's claim that, contrary to the functionalist school in sociology, societies do not form functional systems stems from his requirement that actual feedback loops be present in any genuine functional system. In order for a function to maintain an institution or behavioral pattern, a causal feedback loop must be shown passing through the relevant social group (Elster 1979:28). According to Elster, functionalists in sociology rarely, if ever, actually demonstrate the existence of such a causal feedback loop. Biologists do. Hence, functional explanations are the province of biology and not the social sciences.

Although no one has provided a definition of 'functional system' which accommodates the variety of entities which people tend to treat as functional systems, I do not think that Elster's requirement is overly restrictive. However, I think that at least sometimes it can be met by social groups in their production of conceptual systems. In previous sections of this paper, I have argued that species are historical entities, individuals, or particulars, not spatiotemporally unrestricted classes. Although the arguments in favor of treating species as individuals are, I believe, conclusive, more precise characterizations of species as individuals are more problematic. If species are individuals, then it is at least possible that they are teleonomic systems, either homeostatic or homeorhetic. To be either they must possess some 'species program'. No evolutionist is currently claiming that species are homeorhetic systems, as if the course of their development were somehow programmed. A growing number of evolutionary biologists are claiming that species are static systems, possibly homeostatic systems (Eldredge and Gould, 1972). However, no mechanism has been suggested for the production of such homeostasis. Thus, functional explanations of species development are as questionable as traditional functional explanations in sociology.

In previous sections of this paper, I have also argued that both scientific communities (like the Darwinians) and conceptual systems (like Darwinism) are historical entities. As historical entities, they are at least candidates for functional systems. Whether they are or not depends on the fulfilment of several additional requirements, including the presence of the necessary feedback loops. Elsewhere I (Hull, 1978b) have argued that scientific development has the characteristics it does because of the presence of appropriate causal feedback loops. Two processes are involved: one is the striving of individual scientists to get their solutions to scientific problems accepted as *their* solutions by their fellow-scientists; the second is the mutual checking of results which goes on in science. To some extent individual scientists are aware that they are striving for recognition, but much of the time they are not. They really are attempting to discover what the world we live in is like. The degree to which the functions are latent or manifest is not very important. What is important is that the crucial form of recognition in science is *use*. The best thing that a scientist can do for another scientist is to use his work, perhaps with an appropriate citation, perhaps not. Scientists actually check each other's findings very rarely, and the checking that does go on is a function of the bearing of other scientists' work on their own. Nothing motivates a scientist to check another scientist's work like that work threatening his own.

Several points need to be emphasized about the preceding characterization. First, it involves no 'hidden hand'. The causal feedback loops I am suggesting are there to be seen if one only cares to look. Second, it is an empirical claim about how science operates. It can be checked by observational data. For example, if the social prohibitions against lying and stealing are actually responsible for the relatively high degree of honesty found among scientists in their mutual relations, then lying and stealing should be equally rare (or common) and should by punished with equal severity. However, if my explanation is right, stealing should be much more common than lying and should be punished less severely. Stealing harms only the person from whom the idea is stolen, while lying hurts everyone who uses the false claim. This is why the announcement that Sir Cyril Burt used the data gathered by two assistants, frequently without giving credit, caused so much less of a commotion than the revelation that he may have fabricated both the assistants and his later data.

Finally, I have not shown that either research groups or the conceptual systems which they generate are themselves functional systems. I have argued that causal feedback loops are present in the generation, use, and testing of scientific hypotheses, but the presence of such loops is only a necessary condition for a system being functional or teleonomic; it is not sufficient. In addition, such systems would have to exhibit system-level programs to guide their functioning either homeostatically or homeorhetically. I think that it is absolutely central to scientific conceptual systems that they not be homeostatic. The whole point of the scientific process is that built into it is a mechanism which can lead scientists to change their minds, to modify their conceptual systems—even in their essentials. At least sometimes the causal loops built into the scientific process lead to the modification of the 'program' being developed. I think that both scientific communities and conceptual systems can change *all* of their elements while remaining the 'same' system just so long as they do so gradually and maintain their cohesiveness in the process. For example, particular versions of a scientific theory come and go. In the process the larger 'theory' of which they are part 'evolves'. Thus, versions may well be selected but the larger theories are the things that evolve. If they are analogous to anything, it is to evolving species.

Of course, if species themselves can be selected, as some evolutionists argue, then the analogy has to be reworked. Because the processes that result in evolutionary development do not seem to respect the levels of the commonsense hierarchy of genes, cells, organs, organisms, kinship groups, etc., but wander from one level to another, I have suggested elsewhere (Hull, 1980), that evolutionary theory be couched in terms defined in terms of these processes. The terms I have suggested are replicators, interactors, and lineages. Replicators are the entities that pass on their structure largely intact, interactors are those entities that bias replication because of their relative success in coping with their environments. Interactors are the entities that exhibit adaptations. As a result of the interplay of these two processes, certain other entities, lineages, change indefinitely through time. Replication, interaction, and evolution are conceptually distinct processes. In nature, one and the same entity can function both as a replicator and as an interactor, but anything that has what it takes to function in either of the first two processes cannot function as a lineage in the third. Although the adoption of these more general terms makes the comparison of biological, social, and conceptual evolution much simpler, I have retained the more familiar terminology in this paper.

Another equally important feature of scientific change is that it is not directed or homeorhetic. (Exactly how deeply the teleological worldview of previous ages has infected our language can be seen by the paucity of words in English for change which do not connote progress of some sort.) The appearance of homeorhesis in science, of scientific theories zeroing in on the truth, does not stem from the working out of a program that already contains this information. Rather it stems from the apparent existence of certain eternal, immutable regularities in nature. To the extent that such regularities exist, all organisms must be adapted to them at all times, but numerous contingencies also exist. Organisms come in various sizes. For most organisms gravity is an important feature in their environment. For extremely small organisms, surface tension is much more important. These tiny organisms do not 'defy' the law of gravity anymore than evolution 'defies' the basic principles of thermodynamics. They are simply so small that other forces overwhelm gravity.

Nothing is so obvious about the environments to which organisms must be adapted as that they vary. As fast as a species adapts to its environment, this environment is liable to move out from under it. Species are forever chasing a changing environment. The long-standing goal of science is to discern in this flux some unchanging regularities. It is these regularities that scientists attempt to capture in their theories. Thus far, they have been extremely successful in fulfilling this goal. Scientific theories are constantly being changed, not because these regularities themselves are changing (so scientists believe) but because our understanding of them is changing. Science is surely not a matter of simple accretion. It is difficult to believe that anyone ever thought that it was. But it is a sequence of successive approximations punctuated by periodic revolutions in which the basic axioms of science are reworked. The scientific theories accepted at any one time in a scientific community *constrain* conceptual development *locally*, but nothing exists to *direct* the *global* development of science. In functional systems a changeless program influences the state of the system in a changing environment, sometimes to remain the same, sometimes to change along a partially determined path. In scientific development it is the putative existence of eternal, immutable regularities in nature—in the environment itself—that accounts for scientists being able to produce ever more adequate theories. Such regularities may not exist. If they do, scientific theories have something to approximate. However, as I argue later, the *paths* to these goals are highly variable. Science is surely a goal-directed activity, but the *shape* of conceptual evolution is not determined.

If science is analogous to anything, it is analogous to artificial selection, not natural selection. Just as the breeder consciously selects the organisms that he breeds in order to produce desired changes in his stock, the scientist chooses conceptual variants in order to improve his scientific theories. Both processes involve conscious, intentional choices even though many of the results in both cases may be unanticipated. Before turning at last to the mystery of mysteries— intentionality—a few minor misunderstandings must be removed.

Darwin viewed the relation between artificial and natural selection quite differently from present-day evolutionists. He thought that the two processes were different in kind. He also thought that the existence and effects of artificial selection were much less problematic than the existence and effects of natural selection. That is why he was able to reason analogically from the partially understood mechanisms and known effects of artificial selection to his hypo-thetical mechanism and probable effects of natural selection (Young, 1971; Ruse, 1973, 1975). Present-day evolutionists, to the contrary, treat artificial selection as a special case of natural selection. The sort of change which population geneticists produce in their population cages is 'natural selection, no matter how "artificial" the experimental environments may be' (Dobzhan-sky, *et al.*, 1977:121).

Dobzhansky's irritation with the convention of terming any effects produced by human beings 'unnatural' or 'artificial', while the effects of the behavior of all other species are considered perfectly 'natural', is easy to understand. On this usage, the domestication of certain aphids by ants is natural; the domestication of sheep by human beings is unnatural. The dams which beavers build are natural and enrich the local environment; the dams which human beings build are unnatural and degrade the environment. But this is really not what Elster his in mind. Rather the appropriate contrast between artificial and natural selection is in terms of agency, the contrast which Nagel (1977:303) details in the following quotations:

> For a breeder deliberately selects the animals he will mate, on the basis of what he knows of the likelihood that the traits for which he is breeding well appear in the *next* or other *future* generations of the mated animals. But natural selection has no eye to the future; and if any zygotes are eliminated by natural selection, it is because they are not adapted to this *present* environment.

This is precisely the distinction which Elster (1979:3) has in mind when he contrasts the puny gradient-climbing action of natural selection which is only locally maximizing and the global maximization possible in cases of human action. The center of gravity in the state of our understanding and what counts as understanding have shifted dramatically since Darwin's day. In Darwin's day the role that the human agent played in artificial selection was found much less problematic than the role of natural selection. Although many commentators still succeed in misunderstanding the nature of natural selection, it is relatively unproblematic. 'Natural selection' denotes a particular sort of situation—replication being biased by entities interacting with their environments in varying degree of success. Similarly, 'free will' does not denote a thing, a magic spark that enters into certain causal situations, but a particular sort of causal situation.

Today explanations in terms of natural selection are much less problematic than explanations in terms of human intentions. When Elster (1979:87) turns to an explication of human agency, he does so in terms of different sorts of 'machines'—those that are globally maximizing and those that are only locally maximizing. A system is locally maximizing if it can react only to immediate conditions, globally maximizing 'if it can say No to a favourable mutation in order to be able to say Yes to an even more favourable one later on.' Although Elster (1979:10–7) thinks that animals other than human beings may be capable to some limited extent of behaving in a globally maximizing way, only human beings have the generalized capacity for global maximization. This capacity does not stem from prescience, foreknowledge, clairvoyance and the like but in our coming to understand the laws of nature. Early breeders had some success in the production of new varieties based solely on certain perceived empirical correlations. White, blue-eyed male cats are always deaf. Today, given our increased knowledge of the mechanisms of heredity, breeders can do much more. They can even produce a few generations of organisms which they know will not have the desired characters in order to increase the likelihood that these characters will crop up in later generations.

Because we understand how nature works, we can anticipate the future, but how about the process of discovering these very laws of nature, how about the anticipation of the future development of science? Can people use their generalized capacity for global maximization in going from some knowledge of the world in which we live to more knowledge of it? For example, can global maximization help in going from Newton's laws to Einstein's laws? As ultimately mistaken as Newton's laws turned out to be, the partial understanding which they provided was some help in the development of even better understanding, but these are not the laws at issue here. Because we understand the mechanisms of heredity in biparental organisms like human beings and the details about the formation of eye pigment in human beings, we can predict with high certainty that the offspring of two blue-eyed parents will have blue eyes.

But where are the comparable laws governing the scientific enterprise itself? Certainly science is an intentional activity. If the presence of intentions makes a phenomenon the proper subject matter of social science, whatever regularities that might exist to enable human beings to utilize their global maximizing capacities in the study of the scientific process itself will necessarily be social. One goal of evolutionary epistemologists is the discovery of these laws of they exist. If they do not, then the globally maximizing capacities of human beings will be of no help in understanding these globally maximizing capacities. If they do exist and are of the right sort, then a scientific theory of scientific development is possible. When they become known, then Elster's argument will apply as much to science as to any other process. Once we understand the putative social laws that govern the scientific process, then we can use the knowledge of these laws to help discover other laws. Many, probably most, philosophers contend that no such laws exist, but even those of us searching for such laws cannot claim that their outlines are very clear at the moment, let alone throughout the history of science. Hence, our globally maximizing capacity has not been of much help throughout the history of science. As intentional as science surely is, so far it has not departed markedly from the gradient—climbing characteristic of natural selection that Elster denigrates, and it will not until we know much more about the nature of science.

Intuitively the preceding argument seems fundamentally mistaken. Scientific development seems so clearly progressive. Scientists seem to zero in on the truth while species chase their fleeting environments. In the first place, strictly biological evolution itself looks extremely progressive. Time and again commentators have suggested criteria for this apparent 'direction' to biological evolution—increased number of organisms, increased number of species, increased complexity of organisms, increased adaptability, and so on—and in every case these criteria must have been realized initially in evolution, at least until the Cambrian. Thereafter, however, their application becomes extremely problematic. No matter the criterion used, it will be seen to apply in certain lineages throughout their existence, for other lineages for a while, and for other lineages not at all. For example, early on, Sahlins and Service (1960:13) argued that 'Life inevitably diversifies.' However, more recently, several evolutionists have argued that 'there is no intrinsic trend towards increasing (or decreasing) diversity. Ecological roles are, in a sense, "preset" by nature of environments and the topological limits to species packing; they are filled soon after the Cambrian explosion. Thereafter, inhabitants change continually, but the roles remain' (Gould, 1977:19). Life may inevitably diversify but not for the past 400 million years!

If biological evolution looks so progressive even though natural selection is capable only of gradient-climbing, one should proceed very cautiously from the apparent progressive nature of scientific development to the presence of globally maximizing processes. I think scientific development has been progressive in a sense in which biological evolution can never be, but I also think that it is not as progressive as it appears. All historical reconstructions make the events under investigation look more progressive and directional than they actually are because such reconstructions depend on current records. Past histories of all sorts are reconstructed on the basis of the records which have survived to the present, whether these records be fossils or clay tablets. These records are far from an unbiased sampling of past entities and events. The most extensive record of extinct species can be found in the makeup (both genetic and ontogenetic) of extant species. Hence, we are able to reconstruct those lineages which succeeded in reaching to the present in much greater detail than those that did not. As much as historians rail against 'presentism', we are forced to reason from the present to the past, and whether we like it or not, successfully surviving in some form to the present will inevitably bias the story that the historian tells.

Given what we know about the evolutionary process, we know that it usually eventuates in extinction. We do not know nearly as much about the scientific process, but one thing that is painfully apparent is that the usual outcome of the scientific enterprise is failure. The literature on this subject is overwhelming. Most experiments are inconclusive, most scientific publications go entirely unnoticed, and on and on. Then why does science look so progressive? Why do scientists seem to zero in so ineluctably on the truth? Part of the answer is that scientists rarely try to publish their failures. Even though mutual checking of the work of fellow scientists is central to science, negative results are rarely important enough to publish. Botched experiments and false leads are systematically excluded from the official records of science. The histories of science, especially those written by scientists, exaggerate the progressive nature of science still further by ignoring the research that went nowhere and by concentrating only on the successes. Sometimes being wrong is important in science and calls for some attention, but one must be wrong in important ways.

Professional historians of science are currently recommending that greater attention be paid to the entire picture, to the non-entities as well as to the geniuses. These historians are surely right. Any philosophy of science that can account for success but not failure is as inadequate as any theory of biological evolution that can explain persistence but not extinction. Any logic of discovery that is true to its subject matter must depict methodologies that usually result in failure. Such histories of science do have a couple of problems. One of them is that documentation of pedestrian science is extremely difficult to come by. We have the published letters, biographies, and bibliographies of scientists famous in their own day or soon thereafter. Only an occasional accident produces a comparable wealth of information for non-entities. Another problem is that such histories tend to be extremely boring. They contain useful data for anyone studying science, but they defy anyone to read them from cover to cover.

If one is a realist, which I am, then science should be progressive in a way and to a degree that biological evolution is not. However, this difference in the degree to which science is more globally maximizing than biological evolution. Science is as rational and as intentional an activity as exists, but scientific theories would be just as progressive whether the mechanisms involved were nearer the locally maximizing end of the spectrum. Scientists do not leap from total ignorance to final theories. They work their way painfully from theory to theory. They may well be coming closer and closer to an ever-more accurate portrayal of the regularities which characterize the empirical world, but the actual paths taken are highly contingent. Early theories of the universe placed the earth in its center. Such theories were possible because the earth's orbit is very close to circular. If it had been extremely elliptical, early astronomers would have been hard pressed to begin with a geocentric system. They might well have been forced to go directly to a heliocentric system or some totally different system. The first step might have been so large in such circumstances that astronomy, instead of being one of the first sciences to develop, might have been among the last. Similarly, given the ambient temperatures on the earth, Boyle's law is a good first approximation to the behavior of enclosed gases. If the ambient temperatures here on Earth had been much hotter or much colder, physicists would have had to have started somewhere else. Scientists may all have common goals, but from this it does not follow that they will take the same paths to these common goals. In the past, historians have emphasized the common factors which led Darwin and Wallace to come up with the 'same' theory, but differences in the paths that these two men took are equally striking; e.g. Wallace does not rely on the analogy between artificial and natural selection the way that Darwin does (McKinney, 1972).

CONCLUSION

In a review of Margaret Mead's *Continuities in Culture* (1964), Bronowski (1977) ponders the absence of any genuine theories of sociocultural evolution. Why don't we have a better understanding of the mechanisms of social change? His answer is that 'we have not been able to pin down the units with which it works—which it shuffles and regroups, and whose mutations make the raw material for new culture' (see also Bronowski, 1961). One negative effect which the analogy between biological and sociocultural evolution has had is a tendency to misconstrue the units of sociocultural evolution. Because species have traditionally been viewed as classes, the temptation has been to treat the things that evolve in social and conceptual evolution as classes. But according to more recent analyses, species are exactly the same sort of thing as social groups— historical entities. The task of reworking our understanding of conceptual systems as historical entities has only begun. Now that we have a clearer conception of the nature of the units of sociocultural evolution, we are in a better position to develop a genuine theory of sociocultural evolution.

One consequence of interpreting conceptual systems as historical entities is that on this view the continuity of *social* groups plays a much more important role in the individuation of *conceptual* systems. As long as concepts like the gene or propositions like Mendel's laws are interpreted as classes, as types with similar tokens, no attention need be paid in defining these classes to who held which views, who learned what from whom, who opposed whom, and so on. If Confucius happened to assert something similar in content to Mendel's first law, his pronouncement counts as much as an instance of this proposition as the formulations of de Vries and Bateson. It is this way of viewing conceptual development which produces the histories of ideas that present-day historians find so ahistorical. If conceptual systems and their elements are interpreted as historical entities, actual transmission is essential, either directly from agent to agent in conversation or more indirectly through such means as the printed page. On the view being advocated by evolutionary epistemologists, conceptual evolution cannot be studied in isolation from social development. Conceptual evolution in the absence of social evolution leaves memes as naked as the apes who are their chief authors.

ACKNOWLEDGEMENTS

This paper was written in part under a grant from the John Simon Guggenheim Memorial Foundation. I owe a note of thanks to the following people for reading and commenting on an early draft—Marion Blute, Rob

Boyd, Carla Kary, Henry Plotkin, Robert Richards, David Roos, Aaron Snyder, Paul Thagard, and to the members of the Department of Philosophy, the University of Alabama-Birmingham as well as to the conferees at the ERISS conference at Casenovia, NY.

REFERENCES

Ackermann, R. J. (1976). *The Philosophy of Karl Popper*, University of Massachusetts Press, Amherst.

Bajema, C. J. (Ed.). (1971). *Natural Selection in Human Populations*, John Wiley and Sons, New York.

Blute, M. (1981). Learning, social learning, and sociocultural evolution: a comment on John Langton's 'Darwinism and the behavioral theory of sociocultural evolution'. *Amer. J. Sociol.*, **86**, 1401–1406.

Bonner, J. T. (1965). *Size and Cycle*, Princeton University Press, Princeton.

Bonner, J. T. (1974). *On Development*, Harvard University Press, Cambridge.

Boorse, C. (1976). Wright on function. *Phil Rev.*, **85**, 70–86.

Brannigan, A. (1979). The reification of Mendel. *Soc. Stud. Sci.*, **9**, 423–454.

Bronowski, J. (1961). Introduction to M. Banton (Ed.), *Darwinism and the Study of Society*, Tavistock, London. pp. ix–xx.

Bronowski, J. (1977). *A Sense of the Future*, MIT Press, Cambridge.

Brown, D. D. (1981). 'Gene expression in eukaryotes'. *Science*, **211**, 667–674.

Buckland, W. E. (1836). *Geology and Minerology Considered with Reference to Natural Theology*, W. Pickering, London.

Burian R. (1977). More than a marriage of convenience: on the inextricability of history and philosophy of science. *Phil. Sci.*, **44**, 1–42.

Burkhardt, R. W. (1977). *The Spirit of System: Lamarck and Evolutionary Biology*, Harvard University Press, Cambridge.

Campbell, D. T. (1965). Variation and selective retention in sociocultural evolution. In H. R. Barringer, G. I. Blanksten, and R. W. Mack (Eds), *Change in Developing Areas*, Shenkman, Cambridge. pp. 19–49.

Campbell, D. T. (1974). Evolutionary epistemology. In P. A. Schilpp (Ed.), *The Philosophy of Karl R. Popper*, Vol. 1, Open Court, LaSalle, IL. pp. 413–463.

Campbell, D. T. (1975). On the conflict between biological and social evolution and between psychology and moral tradition. *Amer. Psychol.*, **30**, 1103–1126.

Campbell, D. T. (1977). The natural selection model of conceptual evolution. *Phil. Sci.*, **44**, 502–507.

Campbell, D. T. (1979). Comments on the sociobiology of ethics and moralizing. *Behav. Sci.*, **24**, 37–45.

Campbell, M. (1980). Did de Vries discover the law of segregation independently? *Annals Sci.*, **37**, 639–655.

Caplan, A. (1980). Have species become déclassé? In P. D. Asquith and R. N. Giere (Eds), *PSR 1980*, Vol. 1. Phil. of Sci. Assoc., Ann Arbor, MI. pp. 71–82.

Caplan, A. (1981). Back to class; a note on the ontology of species. *Phil. Sci.*, **48**, 130–140.

Cavalli-Sforza, L. L. (1971). Similarities and dissimilarities of sociocultural and biological evolution. In F. R. Hodson, D. G. Kendall, and P. Tautu (Eds), *Mathematics in the Archaeological and Historical Sciences*, University Press, Edinburgh. pp. 535–554.

Childe, V. G. (1951). *Social Evolution*, Watts, London.

Cloak, F. T. (1975). Is a cultural ethology possible? *Human Eth.*, **3**, 161–182.

Cohen, L. J. (1973). Is the progress of science evolutionary? *Brit. J. Phil. Sci.*, **24**, 41–61.

Cohen, L. J. (1974). Professor Hull and the evolution of species. *Brit. J. Phil. Sci.*, **25**, 334–336.

Darwin, C. (1859). *On the Origin of Species, a Facsimile of the First Edition* (1966), Harvard University Press, Cambridge.

Darwin, F. (Ed.). (1899). *The Life and Letters of Charles Darwin*, Appleton, New York.

Dawkins, R. (1976). *The Selfish Gene*, Oxford, New York.

de Beer, G. (1960). Darwin's notebooks on transmutation of species. *Bull. Brit. Mus. (Nat. Hist.)*, **2**, 1–183.

Dobzhansky, Th., Ayala, F., Stebbins, G., and Valentine, J. W. (1977). *Evolution*, Freeman, San Francisco.

Eldredge, N., and Cracraft, J. (1980). *Phylogenetic Patterns and the Evolutionary Process*, Columbia, New York.

Eldredge, N., and Gould, S. J. (1972). Punctuated equilibria: an alternative to phyletic gradualism. In T. J. M. Schopf (Ed.), *Models in Paleobiology*, Freeman, San Francisco. pp. 82–115.

Elster, J. (1979). *Ulysses and the Sirens: Studies in Rationality and Irrationality*, Columbia, New York.

Endler, J. (1977). *Geographic Variation, Speciation, and Clines*, Princeton University Press, Princeton.

Feyerabend, P. (1975). *Against Method: Outline of an anarchist theory of knowledge*, New Left Books, London.

Ghiselin, M. (1974). A radical solution to the species problem. *Syst. Zool.*, **23**, 536–544.

Ginsberg, M. (1961). Social evolution. In M. Banton (Ed.), *Darwinism and the Study of Society*, Quadrangle Books, Chicago. pp. 95–127.

Glick, T. G. (Ed.). (1974). *The Comparative Reception of Darwinism*, University of Texas Press, Austin.

Gorczynski, R. M., and Steele, E. J. (1980). Inheritance of acquired immunological tolerance to foreign histocompatibility antigens in mice. *Proc. Natl. Acad. Sci.*, **77**, 2871–2875.

Gould, S. J. (1977). Eternal metaphors of palaeontology. In A. Hallam (Ed.), *Patterns of Evolution as Illustrated by the Fossil Record*, Elsevier, New York. pp. 1–26.

Grant, V. (1963). *The Origin of Adaptation*, Columbia, New York.

Gregg, J. R. (1950). Taxonomy, language, and reality. *Am. Nat.*, **55**, 421–433.

Griffiths, G. C. D. (1976). The future of Linnaean nomenclature. *Syst. Zool.*, **25**, 168–173.

Hempel, C. G. (1966). *Aspects of Scientific Explanation*, Columbia, New York.

Hodge, M. J. S. (1971). Lamarck's science of living bodies. *Brit. J. Hist. Sci.*, **5**, 323–352.

Hull, D. L. (1973). Reduction in genetics—biology or philosophy? *Phil. Sci.*, **39**, 491–499.

Hull, D. L. (1974). Are the 'members' of biological species 'similar' to each other? *Brit. J. Phil. Sci.*, **25**, 332–334.

Hull, D. L. (1975). Central subjects and historical narratives. *Hist. Theory*, **14**, 253–274.

Hull, D. L. (1976). Are species really individuals? *Syst. Zool.*, **25**, 174–191.

Hull, D. L. (1978a). A matter of individuality. *Phil. Sci.*, **45**, 335–360.

Hull, D. L. (1978b). Altruism in science: a sociobiological model of cooperative behavior among scientists. *Animal Behav.*, **26**, 685–697.

Hull, D. L. (1980). Individuality and selection. *Ann. Rev. Ecol. Syst.*, **11**, 311–332.

Hull, D. L. (1981). Discussion: Kitts and Kitts and Caplan. *Phil. Sci.*, **48**, 141–152.

Hull, D. L. (1982). Cladistic Theory: Hypotheses that Blur and Grow. In T. Duncan and T. Steussy (Eds), *Cladistic Perspectives on the Reconstruction of Evolutionary History*, Columbia University Press, New York. In press.

Huxley, J. S. (1960). Discussion of social and cultural evolution. In S. Tax and C. Callender (Eds), *Issues in Evolution Vol 3*, University of Chicago Press, Chicago. pp. 207-243.

Jacob, F. (1977). Evolution and tinkering. *Science*, **196**, 1161-1166.

Kitts, D. B., and Kitts, D. J. (1979). Biological species as natural kinds. *Phil. Sci.*, **46**, 613-622.

Knorr, K. D. (1977). Producing and reproducing knowledge: descriptive or constructive? *Soc. Sci. Inform.*, **16**, 669-696.

Kottler, M. J. (1978). Charles Darwin's biological species concept and theory of geographic speciation: the transmutation notebooks. *Annals Sci.*, **35**, 275-298.

Kottler, M. J. (1979). Hugo de Vries and the rediscovery of Mendel's laws. *Annals Sci.*, **36**, 517-538.

Kroeber, A. L. (1960). Evolution, history, and culture. In S. Tax (Ed.), *Evolution After Darwin*, Vol. II, University of Chicago Press, Chicago. pp. 1-16.

Kuhn, T. (1962). *The Structure of Scientific Revolutions*, University of Chicago Press, Chicago.

Kuhn, T. (1970). Postscript—1969. In *The Structure of Scientific Revolutions*, 2nd ed. University of Chicago Press, Chicago. pp. 174-210.

Kuhn, T. (1977). Second thoughts on paradigms. In F. Suppe (Ed.), *The Structure of Scientific Theory*, University of Illinois Press, Urabana, IL.

Lakatos, I. (1970). Falsification and the methodology of scientific research programs. In I. Lakatos and A. Musgrove (Eds), *Criticism and the Growth of Knowledge*, University of Cambridge Press, Cambridge. pp. 91-196.

Lakatos, I. (1971). History of science and its rational reconstruction. In R. Buck and R. S. Cohen (Eds), *Boston Studies in the Philosophy of Science*, D. Reidel, Dordrecht. pp. 91-136.

Lamarck, J. B. (1809). *Philosophie zoologique* (Trans. H. Elliot, 1963), Hafner, New York.

Langton, J. (1980). Darwinism and the behavioral theory of sociocultural evolution: an analysis. *Amer. J. of Sociol.*, **85**, 288-309.

Laudan, L. (1977). *Progress and Its Problems: Towards a Theory of Scientific Growth*, University of California Press, Berkeley.

Losee, J. (1977). Limitations of an evolutionist philosophy of science. *Stud. Hist. Sci.*, **8**, 349-352.

Lovejoy, A. O. (1936). *The Great Chain of Being*, Harvard University Press, Cambridge.

Maynard Smith, J. (1961). Evolution and history. In M. Banton (Ed.), *Darwinism and the Study of Society*, Tavistock, London. pp. 83-93.

Mayr, E. (1961). Cause and effect in biology. *Science*, **134**, 1501-1506.

Mayr, E. (1963). *Animal Species and Evolution*, Harvard University Press, Cambridge.

Mayr, E. (1974). Teleological and teleonomic: a new analysis. In R. S. Cohen and M. W. Wartofsky (Eds), *Methodological and Historical Essays in the Natural and Social Sciences*, Reidel, Dordrecht-Holland. pp. 91-117.

Mayr, E. (1975). The Unit of the Genotype. *Biol. Zentralblatt*, **94**, 377-388.

Mayr, E. (1976). *Evolution and the Diversity of Life*, Harvard University Press, Cambridge.

Mayr, E. (1978). Evolution. *Sci. Amer.*, **239**, 46-55.

McKinney, H. L. (1972). *Wallace and Natural Selection*, Yale University Press, New Haven.

McMullin, E. (1976). The fertility of theory and the unit of appraisal in science. In R. S. Cohen, P. K. Feyerabend, and M. W. Wartofsky (Eds), *Essays in Memory of Imre Lakatos*, Dordrecht-Holland. pp. 395-432.

Mead, M. (1964). *Continuities in Cultural Evolution*, Yale University Press, New Haven.

Medawar, P. B. (1977). Unnatural science. *The New York Review of Books*, Feb. 3, pp. 13–18.

Michod, R. E. (1981). Positive heuristics in evolutionary biology. *Brit. J. Phil. Sci.*, **32**, 1–36.

Nagel, E. (1977). *Teleology Revisited and Other Essays in the Philosophy and History of Science*, Columbia University Press, New York.

Olby, R. (1979). Mendel No Mendelian? *Hist. Sci.*, **17**, 53–72.

Patterson, C. (1978). Verifiability in systematics. *Syst. Zool.*, **27**, 218–221.

Pittendrigh, C. S. (1958). Adaptation, natural selection, and behavior. In A. Roe and G. G. Simpson (Eds), *Behavior and Evolution*, Yale University Press, New Haven. pp. 390–416.

Plotkin, H. C., and Odling-Smee, F. J. (1981). A multi-level model of evolution and its implication for sociobiology. *Behav. Brain Sci.*, **4**, 225–268.

Popper, K. R. (1972). *Objective Knowledge*, Oxford University Press, London.

Popper, K. R. (1975). The rationality of scientific revolutions. In R. Harré (Ed.), *Problems of Scientific Revolution*, Clarendon, Oxford. pp. 72–101.

Rescher, N. (1977). *Methodological Pragmatism*, Blackwell, London.

Richards, R. J. (1977). The natural selection model of conceptual evolution. *Phil. Sci.*, **44**, 494–501.

Richards, R. J. (1981). Natural selection and other models in the historiography of science. In M. Brewer and B. Collins (Eds), *Scientific Inquiry and the Social Sciences*, Josey-Bass, San Francisco. pp. 37–76.

Rosenberg, A. (1980). *Sociobiology and the Preemption of Social Science*, Hopkins, Baltimore.

Ruse, M. (1973). The value of analogical models in science. *Dialogue*, **12**, 246–253.

Ruse, M. (1975). Charles Darwin and artificial selection. *J. Hist. Biol.*, **36**, 339–350.

Sahlins, M. D., and Service, E. R. (1960). *Evolution and Culture*, University of Michigan Press, Ann Arbor, MI.

Semon, R. (1904). *Die Mneme als erhaltendes Prinzip im Wechsel des organishchen Geschehens*, Engelmann, Leipzig.

Shrader, D. (1980). The evolutionary development of science. *Rev. Meta.*, **34**, 273–296.

Simpson, G. G. (1964). *This View of Life*, Harcourt, Brace and World, New York.

Skagested, P. (1979). C. S. Peirce on biological evolution and scientific progress. *Synthese*, **41**, 85–114.

Smart, J. J. C. (1963). *Philosophy and Scientific Realism*, Routledge and Kegan Paul, London.

Smart, J. J. C. (1968). *Between Science and Philosophy*, Random House, New York.

Sober, E. (1980). Evolution, population thinking, and essentialism. *Phil. Sci.*, **47**, 350–383.

Sober, E. (1982). Evolutionary theory and the ontological status of properties. *Phil. Stud.*, In press.

Stanley, S. M. (1979). *Macroevolution, Pattern and Process*, Freeman, San Francisco.

Sulloway, F. J. (1969). Geographic isolation in Darwin's thinking: the vicissitudes of a crucial idea. *Stud. Hist. Biol.*, **3**, 23–65.

Thagard, P. (1980). Against evolutionary epistemology. In P. D. Asquith and R. N. Giere (Eds), *PSA 1980*, Vol. 1. pp. 187–196.

Toulmin, S. (1972). *Human Understanding*, Princeton University Press, Princeton.

Waddington, C. H. (1961). 'The human evolutionary system'. In M. Banton (Ed.), *Darwinism and the Study of Society*, Tavistock, London. pp. 63–81.

Wiley, E. O. (1979). The annotated Linnaean hierarchy, with comments on natural taxa and competing systems. *Syst. Zool.*, **28**, 308–337.

Wiley, E. O. (1981). *Phylogenetics, the Theory and Practice of Phylogenetic Systematics*, Wiley, New York.

Williams, G. C. (1966). *Adaptation and Natural Selection*, Princeton University Press, Princeton.

Williams, M. B. (1981). Similarities and differences between evolutionary theories and the theories of physics. In P. D. Asquith and R. N. Giere (Eds), *PSA 1980*, Vol. 2.

Wilson, E. O. (1974). *Sociobiology: The New Synthesis*, Harvard University Press, Cambridge.

Wimsatt, W. (1980). Reductionist research strategies and their biases in the units of selection controversy. In T. Nickles (Ed.), *Scientific Discovery*, Vol. 12, Reidel, Dordrecht-Holland. pp. 213–259.

Wimsatt, W. (1981). Units of selection and the structure of the multilevel genome. In P. Asquith and R. Giere (Eds), *PSA 1980*, Vol. 2.

Wispé, L. G., and Thompson, J. N. (1976). The war between the words: biological versus social evolution and some related issues. *Amer. Psychol.*, **31**, 341–384.

Woodfield, A. (1976). *Teleology*, Cambridge University Press, Cambridge.

Wright, S. (1980). Genic and organismic selection. *Evol.*, **34**, 825–843.

Young, R. M. (1971). Darwin's metaphor: does nature select? *Monist*, **55**, 442–503.

Zirkle, C. (1946). The early history of the idea of the inheritance of acquired characteristics and of pangenesis. *Trans. Am. Phil. Soc.*, **35**, 91–151.

Zuckerman, H. (1977). Deviant behavior and social control in science. In E. Sagarin (Ed.), *Deviance and Social Change*, Sage, Beverly Hills.

Evolution, development, and learning

There are several distinctly different reasons for the current disaffection with neo-Darwinism. One of these is the virtual exclusion of the phenotype from evolutionary theory. Now, however, there is a growing recognition of the need to bring the phenotype firmly into the structure of the theory. It is not only that selection always operates on the phenotype and not the genotype, and that the phenotype is an operator, an active component of the evolutionary process and not a mere repository or passive vehicle for the transmission of genetically coded information. It is that in selection so acting, there is the further severe complication that the way in which the phenotype is formed becomes as central to evolution as the genes that constitute the genotype. If development is not all of biology, it certainly encompasses a great deal of it.

Wolpert and Stein write of the need to understand the development of pattern formation and of its especial importance to the relationship between ontogeny and evolution. If identical cells differently arranged in space can lead to different phenotypic characters, or indeed different species, then the development of pattern formation is no less, and arguably more, important than cellular differentiation. Ho and Saunders present the case for epigenesis as *the* central issue in evolution. Their chapter provides the link between this section and previous sections in the book in that they attempt to show the implications of an epigenetic approach to an understanding of behaviour and socio-culture; and also in the orientation of their argument being in the tradition of Paul Weiss, Waddington, and Piaget for whom interactions between levels in a hierarchically organized system during development are the engine that drives evolution. According to this view the accepted paradigm of neo-Darwinism, selection acting upon alternative alleles, is quite simply wrong.

There is a vast and growing literature of developmental studies of behaviour. Unfortunately, there has not been an accompanying expansion of theory to give any coherence to the great mass of data that is being generated. Partly this reflects the more general neglect of epigenetic theory in biology at large. It also, however, can be accounted for in part by a peculiar aversion to theory that experimental psychologists seem to have. One result of the lack of theoretical context is the inability to distinguish between significant and trivial data that, Kuhn notes, marks the undiscerning empiricism of preparadigmatic science. The two reprinted pieces, those by Gottlieb and Bateson, represent the small theoretical current that is running amongst biologists who study the development of behaviour. Gottlieb distinguishes between different kinds of functions that behaviour may have during development. He also contrasts the older viewpoint of a uni-directional structure-function relationship with the newer approach that stresses bidirectional structure-function relationships. The latter continues the theme raised by Ho and Saunders in their chapter of the relative importance of 'downward' as opposed to 'upward' causation in a hierarchical organization where the lowest level is generally held to be genetic and the highest is socio-culture. Bateson returns us to Waddington and Piaget. Exactly what kind of epigenetic theory should we espouse? A multiple, continuous but essentially simple and linear interactionism between the developing phenotype and its environment; or a more complex, homeorhetically controlled process whereby the interactions occur within constrained, self-correcting developmental pathways?

The final two chapters are, at least in part, concerned with the same issues. What is the relationship between development and learning; and given the failure of general process learning theory to provide a truly general theory of learning, what kind of theory of learning should we be developing? Johnston and Plotkin and Odling-Smee agree that the answer to the second question is 'whatever the specific theory, it must be very different from what we have had before.' Johnston offers an ecological approach to learning while the final chapter attempts to show some of the implications of viewing learning as just one of a hierarchy of knowledge-gaining processes. On the other hand, Johnston argues for learning as being a special case of a more general process of development, whereas Plotking and Odling-Smee present the view that though learning and development may have a special relationship to one another, they are different processes feeding information into different sites of information store. Whatever the final answers to questions such as these, there now seems little doubt that development and learning are crucial to the establishment of conceptual links between genetical and cultural evolution.

CHAPTER 15

Evolution and development

L. Wolpert and W. D. Stein

INTRODUCTION

What we want to understand is the relation between developmental processes and evolution. How do changes in development lead to novelty in cell type, pattern, and form? What constraints does development put on evolutionary change? Are all imaginable animals possible?

One must first distinguish between genotype and phenotype. Development is the phenotypic expression of the genotype, and the genotype is the genetic constitution of the zygote which controls development. While phenotype is usually thought of as the adult animal, the culmination of development, in fact it must be thought of as including all the developmental stages through which the organism passes. It is the whole of its life history. Evolution acts by selecting the fitter phenotypes and by choosing the corresponding genotype for survival. A change in phenotype in evolution can only occur by a change in genotype. Thus the relationship between genotype and phenotype is fundamental for the understanding of evolution and this relationship is development.

It is convenient to distinguish three main processes that are involved in development: cell differentiation, pattern formation, and changes in form. Cell differentiation or cytodifferentiation is the process whereby the recognizable histological cell types of the body arise: that is the development of muscle, cartilage, red blood cells, adrenal cells, liver cells, and so on. There are about 200 cell types in vertebrates. Each such cell is characterized by a spectrum of particular macromolecules, for example, haemoglobin is peculiar to red blood cells. The problem in cell differentiation is how the synthesis of these macromolecules is specified in these particular cells and especially how this may be controlled at the level of specific gene activation (Davidson and Britten, 1979; Brown, 1981). Pattern formation, by contrast, is the process whereby the spatial pattern of this cellular differentiation is specified (Wolpert, 1971). Different patterns may involve the same classes of cell differentiation. The spatial patterns of the arm and leg are different, but the cell types are the same—muscle, cartilage, and so on. In fact the skeleto-muscular system as a whole can be viewed as the spatial variation of just a few cell types. It will be argued below that pattern formation can be viewed as the assigning to cells of special states relating to position, and that there are many more such states than histological cell types. The third process, change in form, is concerned with the effect of the forces that bring about the changes in shape of the embryo. Such changes in form are particularly evident during gastrulation of sea urchins (Gustafson and Wolpert, 1967) and in the folding of the neural plate to form a neural tube (Karfunkel, 1974) and are brought about by contractile forces. The specification of which cells in the embryo generate these forces may be considered to be part of pattern formation.

In the evolution of vertebrates the histological cell types have probably not changed much either in quality or quantity. There are no cell types that we have that are not present in the chimpanzee, and vice versa. The difference between man and chimpanzee may be attributed to pattern formation.

In broader terms one can consider the evolution from bacteria to man in terms of the number of genes in their respective genomes. Reasonable estimates give 1000 for the bacterium *Escherichia coli*, 2000 for the nematode worm, 5000 for the fruit fly, and perhaps 50 000 for man. The bacterium and the worm have the same order of magnitude of genetic complexity, the fruit fly an order of magnitude greater, and man only an order of magnitude more. This strongly suggests that the real evolutionary triumph was making *E. coli*, that is making the cell, and that evolution of more complex multicellular systems required only a modest increase in the order of magnitude of the genetic information. It is remarkable that the nematode, with at least 10 cell types and complex behaviour patterns, only requires twice as many genes as *E. coli*, and man only 50 times more. One may then ask how many genes are required to characterize new cell types and how many genes are thus available for other developmental processes. If it is assumed that there are 10 cell types in the nematodes this means that on average 100 genes (or new proteins) are needed to specify each cell type and its positions in the developing organism. However, this plausible estimate does not accord well with studies on RNA complexity in guinea pig tissues (Craig et al., 1980) where liver seems to differ from mammary gland tissue by about 10 000 transcripts. Even with liver being made up of say 20 cell types, this gives 500 genes per cell type, which seems rather high. If, on the other hand, one takes for man an additional 100 genes/new cell type then this requires 20 000 genes, which is about the right order of magnitude.

The main lesson to be learned from this is that basic cellular activity requiring some 1000 genes is more complex than the process of development requiring 100 genes for each new cell type. Development may thus be much more simple than appears at first sight, relying as it does on cell complexity.

It is worth remembering that it may be much simpler to specify the construction of the end organism by developmental processes than to specify the final form. In Origami, a simple set of instructions to fold and unfold leads to surprisingly complex forms. The instructions do not describe these forms. Thus the genome provides a generative programme not a descriptive one. There are no genes describing the arm, only genes involved in specifying the processes for making it.

We can now return to the point that cell types are few in number, but their patterns of distribution are immensely varied. The reason for this is clear. It is far more difficult to generate new functional proteins that would characterise a new cell-type than to generate new plans for rearranging existing cell types. The reason for this is that most mutations affecting the amino acid sequence of a protein render it functionless, whereas changes in spatial distribution may alter function and fitness in a much less dramatic way. This latter process allows progressive change whereas this is more difficult with proteins. We thus will concentrate far more on pattern formation than on cell differentiation, for it is changes in pattern formation that characterize much of evolution.

CHANGES IN FORM

Changes in form during early development are mainly brought about by contractile forces. For example, gastrulation in the sea urchin can be accounted for by contractile forces in a small group of cells at the vegetal pole (Gustafson and Wolpert, 1967). At one stage in this process, the cells put out long processes which attach to the wall of the blastocoel and their contraction draws the future gut inwards. Other processes involved in changes in form may involve cell movement and cell division. But the basic cellular processes have probably not changed their nature during evolution of multicellular organisms. Differences in form result not from the differences in these cellular activities, but from their spatial and temporal organization.

PATTERN FORMATION

One approach to understanding pattern formation is in terms of positional information (Wolpert, 1971). This suggests that pattern formation may be thought of as a two-step process. First the cells are assigned positions as in a coordinate system, and the cells then interpret their positional values by appropriate cell differentiation. The interpretation will depend on the genetic constitution of the cell and its developmental history. Since the specification of position can be thought of as involving a graded quantity, the concept of positional information is an extension of classical gradient theories. It is also a particular formulation of the field concept: a field is defined as that set of cells all of which have their position specified with respect to a single coordinate system.

A mechanism involving positional information has several important implications. The observed pattern arises from cell interpretation, and so the only cell-to-cell interactions required are, in principle, those necessary to specify position. It also follows that the same set of positional values can be used to generate quite different patterns. This means that there could be a universal coordinate system which is used again and again, both within the same embryo as well as in other embryos. The main change in evolution would thus be in interpretation. Evidence for this comes from genetic mosaics of pattern mutants. The classical example is the homeotic mutant of the fruit fly *spineless aristapedia*, which results in a leg replacing the antenna. In genetic mosaics the cells behave according to their position and genotype. Thus, if the cells at the tip are wild type they form distal antennal structures, whereas if they carry the *aristapedia* mutant then they form distal leg structures. It is as if the positional values along the leg and antenna are the same but they interpret it differently because they have different developmental histories. For antenna to form, the wild type aristapedia gene must presumably be activated, this activation resulting from the cell's position along the main body axis. Most pattern mutants behave in this way, which suggests that the coordinate system in all insect imaginal discs is the same.

An extreme view would be to assume that there was a universal mechanism for specifying positional information. If this were the case then it would be most unlikely that such a system would alter significantly in evolution. For, like the genetic code itself, a change here would change every system using positional information. This would almost certainly have a deleterious effect. What will change will be the interpretation in specific cells. Differences in positional value can make cells nonequivalent even though they differentiate into a similar cell type. The principle of nonequivalence says that cells of the same differentiation class may have intrinsically different internal states, such as positional value (Lewis and Wolpert, 1976). This can be illustrated by amphibian limb regeneration. If the limb of a newt is cut off it will regenerate a normal limb. The nature of the regenerate is determined by the level of the cut: if cut at the humerus then structures distal to this cut will regenerate whereas if at the wrist, only a wrist and hand will regenerate. Thus the nature of the regenerate must depend on some intrinsic difference in the cells at the cut surface even though there are the same cell types at all levels, i.e. muscle, cartilage, dermis, etc. It must not be thought that regeneration is an attempt to replace missing parts. In fact, it depends only on the cells at the cut surface. So, if the hand is sutured to the belly so that a circulation is established, and a cut then made at mid-humerus, one can ask what will regenerate from the two surfaces, the proximal one and the distal one. In fact both regenerate the same distal structures, even though for the distal surface this means, for example, another radius and ulna are formed. Again, the growth of different cartilaginous elements in the limb is strikingly varied even though they are made of the same cell types (Summerbell, 1976). Thus cells are to be characterized not merely by their histological type, but perhaps also by their positional value which can affect, for example, their surface properties or growth characteristics.

CHICK LIMB DEVELOPMENT

The development of the chick wing can be used to illustrate some of the concepts of development and evolution (Wolpert, 1978). The wing of the chick develops from a paddlelike bud. It starts off as a small bulge that appears about two days after the egg is laid and at a time when the main axial structures such as the somites have already been laid down. The pattern of cartilage, muscle, and tendons takes shape within a loose network of mesenchymal cells encased in a sheet of ectodermal cells that will become skin. After 10 days in the incubator, the basic pattern of the limb bones—humerus, radius and ulna, wrist and digits—is well established in the form of cartilage (most of which will later turn into bone). Here we will only consider the antero-posterior axis and the proximo-distal axis as defining a Cartesian positional field. Position is assumed to be specified in a region about 350 μm wide at the tip of the limb bud, the progress zone. This region is specified by the overlying apical ectodermal ridge. All the cells in the progress zone are dividing, and it is only when the cells have left the progress zone that overt cell differentiation into, for example, cartilage, starts. From this time development is largely autonomous. The mechanism we have suggested for specifying position along the proximo-distal axis is based on the cells measuring the time they spend in the progress zone, possibly by counting cell divisions. Since all the cells in the progress zone are dividing, cells are continually leaving, and those that remain in longest will have divided most while in the zone, and will thus have the most distal positional values. There are about 7 cell cycles during the laying down of the wing. Each element, that is humerus, wrist, and so on, is initially about the same length, and about the size of the amount of material leaving the progress zone in 1 cell cycle. The progress zone itself is specified by the overlying apical ectodermal ridge, and if the ridge is removed, the progress zone is abolished and the limb is truncated. The earlier it is removed, the more truncated the limb. Necrosis of the apical ridge appears to play an important role in limb reduction in evolution, which always occurs in a distal to proximal sequence.

The length of the cartilaginous elements will be determined by the length of the element as specified by its positional values when it leaves the progress zone, and its growth programme, which is also linked to these positional values. The wrist elements and the ulna are about the same size when they leave the progress zone but their later growth is quite different. The wrist grows hardly at all up to 15 days of incubation, while the ulna grows a great deal (Summerbell, 1976). This is a good example of nonequivalence of cartilage.

The growth of the cartilage elements depends on cell division, cell enlargement and secretion of an extracellular matrix. During early stages, the latter two are particularly important. Lager stages of growth are due to the epiphyseal growth plate in which cells divide, undergo enlargement, and are then replaced by bone. Kember's (1978) studies on cell kinetics in the growth plates of the rat have shown that the difference in growth rate of different growth plates is due not to differences in the rate of division of the individual cells but to the number of cells that are proliferating. The size of the proliferative zone appears to be an intrinsic property of each growth plate. This makes it possible to begin to consider allometric relations in cellular terms.

Growth of the cartilaginous elements after they have left the progress zone will be autonomous. It is as if the positional values have programmed growth. There is substantial evidence for such autonomy (Summerbell and Lewis, 1975). Grafting a young wing bud progress zone in place of an older one results in a limb in which elements are repeated in tandem—humerus, radius and ulna, humerus, radius and ulna, wrist, hand. In such limbs the length of the elements always corresponds to that of the donor embryo. Similarly in limb bud grafts between axolotls of different sizes, the limb size is always of donor length.

We must now return to a consideration of the antero-posterior axis. Position along the antero-posterior axis may be specified by a graded signal from the polarizing region, which is at the posterior margin of the limb (Tickle, 1980). It has properties similar to those of the classical organizer. In our model it is the source of a diffusible morphogen whose concentration specifies positional values along the antero-posterior axis. The digits *2 3* and *4*—which provide good markers—form at successively higher concentrations. When an additional polarizing region is grafted to the anterior margin of an early limb bud the pattern of digits is *4 3 2 2 3 4* indicating a mirror-image gradient. The signal from the polarizing region can be attenuated by using a decreasing number of cells—about 120 are required for digit *4*, but only 20 for digit *2* (Tickle, 1980). Grafting experiments between species show that the signal is the same for wing and leg and for human, mouse, and turtle.

In this model the signal from the polarizing region is assumed both to specify the digits and their character. It is important to consider an alternative model in which all the cartilaginous elements in the limb are specified as a basic repeating pattern and only then do they acquire particular characteristics by virtue of the action of the polarizing region. The basic pattern of the limb can be viewed as a succession of sections, each composed of an increasing number of elements. First the humerus, then two elements in the forearm, then three to four in the wrist, and, finally, five in the hand. It is quite amazing the extent to which this basic pattern has been conserved in evolution.

THE PATTERN OF MUSCLES AND TENDONS

Recent work has shown that the muscle cells of the limb have a different lineage from the other cells in the early limb bud (reviewed McLachlan and Wolpert, 1980). They migrate into the limb bud from the adjacent somites well before limb bud formation. They do not enter the progress zone. We have suggested that the pattern of muscles is determined by the presumptive muscle connective tissue. The muscle cells are assumed to have a higher affinity for these cells, thus accumulating in such regions. This can account for the early accumulation of muscle cells in dorsal and ventral masses. These masses undergo a series of subdivisions which result in the formation of discrete muscles. This, we suggest, reflects changes in the pattern of the presumptive muscle connective tissues with time. Thus, perhaps, the pattern of muscles is determined by the muscle connective tissue. This process is analogous to that whereby the pattern of sea-urchin mesenchyme cells is determined by the ectoderm. In these terms, all muscle cells in the limb are equivalent.

There is good evidence that the pattern of the muscle and tendons uses the same positional field as described above for the cartilaginous elements, and that once the pattern is specified, later development is largely autonomous. There is little interaction between muscle, tendon, and cartilage at early stages. Tendons, for example, will initially develop in the absence of the muscle, or cartilaginous element on which they normally insert, and can be made to make quite inappropriate connections. However, at later stages the growth of muscle is coordinated with that of the cartilaginous elements. It appears that their growth is dependent on the growth of the elements on which they insert, tension on the muscles providing the stimulus to growth. Thus, if the growth of the cartilage is inhibited, the muscle too is shorter.

INTERACTIONS AND INDUCTION

It is important to realize that all the interactions between cells and tissues in development are not instructive but selective. The polarizing region in limb development does not instruct the limb to form digits but selects the appropriate response from the repertoire of cell behaviour, so that digits form. Thus, in evolution, what largely changes is not the nature of the signals that enable cells to communicate with each other, but the cellular response to such signals. Thus the signal could be a small molecule such as cyclic AMP, or calcium, but the response to such a signal can be very varied: differentiation, cell aggregation, contraction, division. A further example comes from induction. Induction is the process whereby one tissue influences the development of another tissue. The classic examples are the induction of the nervous system by the underlying mesoderm, and the induction of the lens by the eye cup. There are many examples of the mesoderm inducing the overlying ectoderm (see the review by Kratochwil, 1972). If the 5 day chick corneal epithelium is combined with dermis from a feather-forming region, then feathers develop from the epithelium. Again, if the mesenchyme of the dental papilla of the mouse is combined with epithelium from the foot of a 14 day mouse embryo, the epithelium forms an enamel organ. These are examples of what Saxen (1972) has called directive embryonic induction.

Directive embryonic induction can be best understood in terms of the transfer of positional information. In essence, the idea is that positional information is initially specified in a two-dimensional cell sheet, the mesoderm in vertebrates, and that when this mesoderm comes to underlie the ectoderm, positional information in the ectoderm is specified by transfer of positional values from mesoderm to ectoderm. If the ectoderm acquires its positional field from the underlying mesoderm, the structures formed will reflect the interpretation of these positional values. In these terms, the positional field would be the same in different species and only the interpretation would change. This is just what is found by transplantation between species (see the review by Holtfreter and Hamburger, 1955). The larval newt has a pair of balancers on the ventro-lateral part of the head, whereas the toad tadpole has no balancers but a pair of suckers in a ventral position. The larval newt has teeth, whereas the tadpole has horny denticles. Reciprocal transplants of embryonic ectoderm between these orders have shown that structures appropriate to the grafted ectoderm form in the correct position. Thus when belly ectoderm from the toad is grafted to the head region of the newt embryo, suckers and a horny mouth develop. The ectoderm acquires its positional value and interprets it in the appropriate manner.

EVOLUTION OF THE LIMB

Non-equivalence enriches the repertoire of evolution, letting small parts of the body change independently of the rest. But through all the changes, certain topological features remain remarkably constant. As Darwin (1872) puts it, 'What can be more curious than that the hand of a man, formed for grasping, that of a mole for digging, the leg of the horse, the paddle of the porpoise, and the wing of the bat, should all be constructed on the same pattern, and should include similar bones, in the same relative positions?' What changes in developmental mechanisms can bring about these evolutionary changes?

The major changes in evolution have involved changes in relative proportion of the individual cartilaginous elements. Loss of elements can however occur and this always involves the loss of the most distal elements (Lande, 1978).

There is no case where proximal elements, such as humerus, are lost, yet distal elements remain. This loss of distal elements is probably due to the death of the cells of the apical ectodermal ridge. Thus the level of truncation due to death of the ridge will depend upon the time at which it dies. It is reasonable to assume that there are genes controlling the development of the ridge and the time at which it dies. It does not seem unreasonable to think that in the case of polyphalangy—extra elements in the digits—the ridge has persisted for an even longer time. Thus changes in the timing of ridge death can give a range of limbs from polyphalangy to the complete absence of the limb.

Along the antero-posterior axis there is great variation in the number of elements in both the wrist and hand, whereas the number of elements in the forearm never changes. One can lose digits either from the anterior or posterior margins of both forelimb and hindlimb. This may be due to the change in response to the signal from the polarizing region. For example, there are only three digits in the chick wing. However, another digit (digit 5) starts to develop adjacent to digit 4 but is abortive. In the foot, however, this digit does develop.

A major feature in the change in form of the limb elements is the change in size. This will depend on the rate of growth and for how long growth continues. Each of these is a possible candidate for evolutionary change. Each element has its own intrinsic growth programme and this characterizes its rate of growth and when it will stop growing. Since the major growth takes place in the growth plate, it is here that we must look for growth control. The two most important factors are the size of the proliferative zone and when it disappears. We can now try to relate this to allometric relationships.

There is usually a well-defined relationship between the growth of any organ and the overall growth of the body—an allometric relationship. When plotted on log/log scales, a straight line is often obtained and the slope is characteristic of the organ. Different slopes reflect different growth rates for the organs considered. One can change the relative proportions of two elements by changing their intrinsic growth rate or by changing the overall time for which they grow. If Kember is correct, then changing the intrinsic growth rate of long bone elements involves changing the size of the proliferative zone of the growth plate. One can also see that if elements have different intrinsic growth rates and the time for which all the elements grow is extended, there will be major changes in the overall relative proportions. The point to emphasize is that these changes can be quite dramatic. Thus, the enormous antlers of the Irish Elk arise simply from extension of the growing period (Gould, 1980). There need be no change in the growth programme of the individual elements. This could bring about major changes in the form of the limb relatively simply. However, this mechanism is quite inadequate to deal with the whole range of changes in form of the limb elements which clearly require changes in the intrinsic growth rate and hence, presumably, the number of cells in the proliferative zone of the growth plate.

There must also be mechanisms which change in quite a detailed way the form of the individual elements. Elements become thicker in particular regions, fuse with each other, and have localized changes in shape. In the fibula of the chick for example, the distal part of the early cartilage elements breaks off and fuses with the end of the adjacent tibia. A very dramatic example is the panda's thumb (Gould, 1980). This sixth finger in fact is constructed from a bone, the radial sesamoid, normally a small component of the wrist. Such changes are compatible with the idea that positional value makes different cartilaginous elements non-equivalent. It is thus possible to change locally their cellular properties.

It is probably not useful to overemphasize the importance of heterochrony in explaining these changes in evolution. Heterochrony is the change in timing of development and involves both the rate at which growth occurs and when it starts and stops (Alberch et al., 1979). What it fails to do is to emphasize spatial organization: that is where and in what direction growth occurs. Moreover, as we have seen, alteration in growth rate, probably at the cellular level, reflects a spatial difference in the size of the proliferative zone.

One can now consider the particular case of the evolution of one-toed horses from three-toed horses (Robb, 1937). The central digit is the longest of the three toes and the two lateral digits are slightly shorter. As the horse goes up on to its toes in evolution, the three digits can still touch the ground because the two lateral digits are slightly posterior. The growth of the digits is probably linear with time (because of the nature of the growth plate) and the central digit grows faster than the lateral ones. A plot of the length of the central digit against the lateral ones shows that it grows 1.4 times faster. Thus as the animal grows longer, and thus bigger, the side digits will no longer be able to contact the ground. This is what happened in the evolution of the three-toed horses and can completely be accounted for by a smaller proliferative zone in the growth plates of the lateral digits. If the size of the proliferative zone of these digits is further reduced, however, one-toed horses will result, with the lateral digits reduced to splints. Thus the last change is not heterochrony but involves the localized change in the growth programme of the lateral digits.

DEVELOPMENTAL CONSTRAINTS

One can understand the problem relating to evolutionary constraints by considering how one would, with a limitless population of mice, and as much time as required, design a selection programme so that feathered flying mice evolved. One realizes at once that selection, and thus evolution, can only operate on existing variability. Even if we knew the detailed cellular mechanisms underlying the development of feather and hair, it might be very difficult to design an appropriate selection programme, unless there was appropriate variation in the relevant cellular processes. The essential point is that one requires variability in order to select. One cannot select for two humeri if one never finds them nor any intermediates. However, because of the pleiotropic effect of many genes, it may be possible to select for some other character to which the development of the humerus may be linked, to reach a situation in which two humeri will eventually develop. Similar consideration applies to evolving feathers from hairs. We can thus see how developmental processes constrain what can evolve.

Another aspect of this constraining process is illustrated by differentiation. It would be very difficult for liver cells to evolve in the limb. Why should this be so? This can be understood by recognizing that in the embryological development of limb mesenchyme and liver there are a number of decision events which cause the lineages to diverge more and more. One could represent their development by binary trees. Thus to convert from one to the other would involve a large change in a number of switches which are extremely unlikely to occur by random mutation. Changing an additional switch cannot convert limb mesenchyme to liver.

DEVELOPMENT AS A PROGRAMME

We wish to view development in terms of a generative programme contained within the fertilized egg's DNA. The information content within the DNA is what specifies the processes for making the organism. The three-dimensional structure of a protein (for example, an enzyme) is uniquely determined by its linear sequence of the amino-acids, which, in turn, is uniquely specified by the linear sequence of nucleotides in the DNA. In this sense, the genetic information for the structure of the protein can be thought of as being programmed by the DNA. This view is contrary to that of Stent (see Bonner, 1982) who wishes to strictly reserve the term programme for situations where there is a clear isomorphism between the programme and the outcome of the programme. In his view, the DNA contains the programme for the amino-acid sequence of the enzyme but the folding up of the chain is not in the programme but is something else. We feel however that this is too restrictive a concept, and misses the most interesting part of the programme concept. The structure of the protein, hence its enzymic activity, is completely specified by the DNA, and, what is more, the structure will be altered by a change in the DNA. Of course, specifying the structure of proteins does not lead obviously to hands or eyes. But as we have tried to point out above, the development and evolution of such structures can be seen to be understandable in cellular terms. Changes in cellular parameters, such as the change in distribution of cells in a proliferative zone, can have profound morphological effects. While we remain ignorant of the molecular basis of such cellular changes we are confident that they will result from changes in protein structure and concentration and these will only come from changes in the DNA. That is the epistemology of evolution.

ACKNOWLEDGEMENT

One of us (W.D.S.) is indebted to a Grant from The Royal Society–Israel Academy Visiting Research Professorships Scheme.

REFERENCES

Alberch, P., Gould, S. J., Oster, G. F., and Wake, D. B. (1979). Size and shape in ontogeny and phylogeny. *Palaeobiology*, **5**, 296–317.

Bonner, J. T. (Ed.) (1982). *Evolution and development*, Springer-Verlag, Heidelberg.

Brown, D. D. (1981). Gene expression in eukaryotes. *Science*, **211**, 667–674.

Craig, R. K., Bathurst, I. C. and Herries, D. B. (1980). Posttranscriptional regulation of gene expression in gained pig tissues. *Nature*, **288**, 618–619.

Darwin, C. (1872). *Origin of species*, 6th edition, Murray, London.

Davidson, E. H., and Britten, R. J. (1979). Regulation of gene expression: possible role of repetitive sequences. *Science*, **204**, 1052–1059.

Gould, S. J. (1980). *The Panda's Thumb*, Norton, New York. pp. 19–26.

Gustafson, T., and Wolpert, L. (1967). Cellular movement and contact in sea urchin morphogenesis. *Biol. Rev.*, **42**, 442–498.

Holtfreter, J., and Hamburger, V. (1955). Amphibians. In B. N. Willier, P. A. Weiss, and V. Hamburger (Eds), *Analysis of Development*, Saunders, Philadelphia. pp. 230–296.

Karfunkel, P. (1974). The mechanisms of neural tube formation. *International Review of Cytology*, **38**, 245–271.

Kember, N. F. (1978). Cell kinetics and the control of growth of long bones. Cell Tissue Kinetics, **11**, 477–485.

Kratochwil, K. (1972). Tissue interaction during embryonic development. General properties. In D. Tarin (Ed.), *Induction Tissue Interaction and Carcinogenesis*, Academic Press, London. pp. 1–47.

Lande, R. (1978). Evolutionary mechanisms of limb loss in tetrapods. *Evolution*, **32**, 79–92.

Lewis, J. H., and Wolpert, L. (1976). The principle of non-equivalence in development. *J. Theoret. Biol.*, **62**, 479–490.

McClachlan, J. and Wolpert, L. (1980). The spatial pattern of muscle development in the limb. In D. R. Goldspink (Ed.). *The Development and Specialization of Muscle*, Cambridge University Press, Cambridge. pp. 1–17.

Robb, R. C. (1937). A study of mutation in evolution. IV. Ontogeny of the equine foot. *J. Genetics*, **34**, 477–486.

Saxen, L. (1972). Directive versus permissive induction: a working hypothesis. In J. W. Lash and M. M. Burger, (Eds), *Cell and Tissue Interactions*, Raven Press, New York. pp. 1–9.

Summerbell, D. (1976). A descriptive study of the rate of elongation and differentiation of the skeleton of the developing chick wing. *J. Embryol. exp. Morph.*, **35**, 241–260.

Summerbell, D., and Lewis, J. H. (1975). Time, place and positional value in the chick limb bud. *J. Embryol. exp. Morph.*, **33**, 621–643.

Tickle, C. (1980). The polarizing region in limb development. In M. H. Johnson (Ed.), *Development in Mammals 4*, Elsevier-North Holland, Amsterdam.

Wolpert, L. (1971). Positional information and pattern formation. *Curr. Top. Devel. Biol.*, **6**, 183–224.

Wolpert, L. (1978). Pattern formation in biological development. *Sci. Amer.*, October, **239**, 154–164.

CHAPTER 16

The epigenetic approach to the evolution of organisms—with notes on its relevance to social and cultural evolution

Mae-Wan Ho and Peter T. Saunders

The enormous successes of the analytical and reductionist approach of genetics, especially of molecular genetics within the past twenty or so years, have helped to create a curious impression of organisms. It has become customary to see them as collections of genes, and to regard development as the unfolding of different 'genetic programmes' each encoded in the specific base sequences of DNA in the zygote nucleus. This picture fits neatly within the neo-Darwinian theory of evolution. Alterations in development occur as the result of random mutations and natural selection allows the fittest mutants to survive and reproduce. Environmental changes give rise to new selective forces and evolution is thereby guaranteed. There are no organisms, only genes which mutate and compete in a changing environment. The 'selfish-gene' concept—widely criticized and condemned, sometimes even by neo-Darwinians themselves—is nonetheless the inevitable, logical conclusion to neo-Darwinism (see Ho and Saunders, 1981b).

To those who refuse to lose sight of the organism, there is little to be gained from the explanatory power of the gene. An organism is not just a collection of accidental genetic mutations, nor is its development an incidental and inconsequential unfolding of a preformed genetic programme. On the contrary, it can be understood only in terms of systemic principles and relationships which transcend the properties of individual genes. Moreover, organisms develop and evolve *because* they are open to the environment. The environment enters into development not as mere disturbances to be overcome, but as necessary *formative* influences.

The fallacy of neo-Darwinism (and of sociobiological theory which is based on it) is one of the arbitrary closure of a rich interconnected system of the organism and its physical, biological, social and cultural environment at the level of the genes. The central dogma of a linear one-way causation from genes to organism, and thence to behavior, society and culture, bears little resemblance to the complex nexus of interrelationships which actually exist, enabling causation to move both 'upwards' and 'downwards' through the hierarchy. Epigenesis mediates between the biological and social levels serving to integrate the two into a structural and functional whole. The epigenetic approach, rather than the genetic approach of neo-Darwinism, is the proper basis for an evolutionary epistemology.

THE EPIGENETIC VERSUS THE GENETIC APPROACH

To avoid later misunderstandings, we should explain what we mean by the 'epigenetic' approach which we propose as an alternative to the 'genetic' approach of neo-Darwinism. The epigenetic approach is predicated on the assumption that the process of development has a primary and deterministic influence on evolution. Consequently, the study of the 'epigenetic system' is essential for the understanding of evolution. Our definition is consistent with Waddington's (1957) usage of the term 'epigenesis' to mean simply embryological development, but the idea is put into sharper focus if we bear in mind that epigenesis is the antithesis of preformation. The distinction between the two was well summarised by Weiss (1939, quoted by Løvtrup, 1974, whose abridgement of Weiss' remarks we follow here):

> [Preformation implies] . . . essentially that there is preformation of parts in the organism from its very first beginning . . . and that development consists of nothing but a gradual conversion of latent into manifest differences without attending increase of complexity or emergence of new properties.
>
> Epigenesis . . . presumes that developing systems start from a rather primitive, homogeneous, chaotic or, at least, lowly organized condition into which increasing complication and real . . . diversification come in progressively as development proceeds; . . . the later parts of the organism are not as such pre-existing in the germ but are gradually established by a process of *individualization.*

The genetic approach sees development as resulting from and therefore secondary to the natural selection of random mutations. In this regard, it is essentially performationist: development is the working out of what is already determined in the genes; consequently, a study of the process itself can contribute little or nothing to the understanding of evolution. In order to predict what would happen at any stage in the evolution of an organism', Ruse (1973) prescribes that we must try to determine what would be the most advantageous modification. Surely the most effective way to make predictions about evolution is first to try to discover what sort of changes a given epigenetic system is capable of producing, and only then to ask which are likely to be selected.

The basic difference in approach cuts across many discipline boundaries. In developmental biology the minority who adopt the epigenetic approach (represented by workers such as Needham (1950), Goldschmidt (1938), Waddington (1957), and, more recently Løvtrup (1974) and Goodwin (1976)) insist that organisms are unintelligible except in terms of laws and mechanisms of development. How is it that from the relative homogeneity of the zygote the complex adult structures are generated? By what mechanisms are the interactions between genes and cytoplasm, organism and environment, orchestrated to produce and reproduce a more or less constant end result? How do adaptations arise during development? What principles and constraints govern changes in development? How may these changes subsequently become inherited? These are some of the fundamental questions which engage their attention. In contrast, the genetic approach adopted by the vast majority today aims at identifying (if not merely postulating) genes controlling characters. The organism is thus 'explained' as a composite of so many characters controlled by so many genes, activated differentially when and where appropriate.

A similar divide occurs in ethology. In the classical Lorenzian view, the development of behaviour consists of a largely autonomous sequence of maturation of central neural mechanisms controlling the animal's behavioural repertoire. The environment, insofar as it enters in development, does so in the form of specific stimuli serving to release preformed patterns of behaviour from central inhibition. A strict dichotomy is thereby maintained between the 'innate' and 'acquired' components of behaviour (Lorenz, 1965, 1977). This fits easily within the genetic framework in the form of genes controlling behaviour in a more or less straightforward and mechanical manner. Much of the theorizing in sociobiology is based on just such an assumption, despite numerous apologies to the contrary.

In opposition to the theory of Lorenz, comparative psychologists such as Schneirla (1956) and Lehrman (1953, 1965) have shown that the 'innate' and 'acquired' interact in a complex way during development. And this applies to much of so-called instinctive behaviour. It becomes clear that a full understanding of behaviour must come from detailed studies of how different levels of behavioural organization arise in development through the interrelationships of intrinsic and extrinsic factors influencing growth and differentiation. Many present-day ethologists (for example Bateson (1976)—see chapter 18 of this book—Hinde (1970) and Gottlieb (1976)) share this emphasis on development.

Despite these attempts to formulate a theory of behaviour based on detailed observations of developmental processes, the genetic approach has come to predominate once more within the 'new science' of sociobiology. This should come as no surprise, as sociobiology is but the elaboration of neo-Darwinian principles as applied to social behavior.

The genetic approach is as vital to neo-Darwinism as the epigenetic approach is anathema. The reason for this is not difficult to discern. Maynard Smith and Holliday (1979) point out that the gift of Weismann to evolutionary (i.e. neo-Darwinian) theory is that the mode of development is irrelevant because there is no feedback channel between the soma—the product of development— and the genes. There is a fundamental flaw in this argument—even if Weismann is correct—as we shall show later. But the corollary is that if Weismann is wrong, then development can no longer be safely ignored and neo-Darwinian theory becomes grossly inadequate if not downright misleading. Hence, a dogmatic adherence to Weismannism is necessary to justify a view of evolution as little more than a change in gene frequencies in populations: developmental studies have essentially nothing to say about evolution (see Wilson (1975), Williams (1981) and Dawkins (1976), for example).

An apparent departure from the sociobiologist's position is Lumsden and Wilson's (1981) recent attempt to 'trace development all the way from genes through mind to culture' (in two easy leaps) by way of 'epigenetic rules'. Apart from their frequent confusion between 'rules' and 'processes', the authors are far from clear as to what constitute epigenetic rules. Certainly, in their formal and mathematical treatment, these rules turn out to be little more than genetic predispositions towards adopting alternative forms of behaviour. Similarly, 'epigenesis' refers not to the development of brain or mind—the cognitive and preferential emotive filters are assumed to be largely preformed—but to the 'development' of behaviour, taking the brain-mind as genetically given. It will be clear from the remainder of this chapter that we do not find their model convincing. And when Lumsden and Wilson write of 'epigenesis' they mean something quite different from what is usually intended.

Sociobiologists and their opponents debate endlessly over the extent to which behaviour is genetically determined, but in our view that is not the real issue at stake. Epigenesis can be variable and still be considered 'ultimately determined by the genes'. Learning enters into behaviour, yet the ability to learn could still be genetically constrained. Culture, as almost everyone admits, cannot be totally divorced from genetic considerations. It thus seems sufficient that 'genetic biases' in behaviour exist for natural selection to act (Lumsden and Wilson, 1981). So in a roundabout way, we are back squarely within the genetic paradigm. Organisms, consciousness, society and culture become so much epiphenomenon to the 'fundamental' process of competition between selfish genes.

The inherent fallacy of the genetic paradigm is that the 'gene'—a construct within population genetics theory—corresponds to nothing in molecular terms (see Ho and Saunders, 1981b). But even *that* is not the real issue. Opponents of sociobiology and of the genetic paradigm are right to emphasize development, but they have failed to work out the full implications of the epigenetic approach that they themselves advocate. We shall attempt to do this here. But we stress that little of what we say is really new; indeed some of the ideas are almost two hundred years old, and have been rediscovered many times since. Our task is to restate old and fundamental problems in a contemporary setting, and to examine to what extent present-day knowledge can contribute to their solution.

HIERARCHIES AND LEVELS

Almost everyone today accepts that complex systems are hierarchically organized, and many authors have discussed this in different contexts (for example, Whyte et al., 1969; Tobach, 1978; Ho and Saunders, 1979; Plotkin and Odling-Smee, 1981; Rose, 1981).

A hierarchical system consists of distinct levels in its structural and functional organization, such that there are level-specific organizing relationships which cannot be derived from the lower levels. An obvious example is a musical composition: a description of the frequencies and wave functions of individual notes contributes nothing to the musical form, the perception as much as the composition of which involves higher order integrative and organizing relationships. It is therefore quite misleading to talk of *translation* or *mapping* between levels (Rose, 1981). If this were possible, there could be no objection to working at only the lowest level, since this would be the simplest and most fundamental. It is this which justifies the reduction of organismic, social and cultural phenomena to the genes—witness Lumsden and Wilson's (1981) project of 'gene-culture translation'. The mere proliferation of levels is powerless to counteract the sociobiological thesis that everything can ultimately be explained in terms of the genes.

A truly non-reductionist view is to take full account of the essential untranslatability between levels (c.f. Sinha, 1981) and to study phenomena at their appropriate levels. We hasten to add that we are not prescribing some sort of mystical holism. Untranslatability does not imply independence: music would be impossible without noise, just as real organisms cannot exist apart from the appropriate chemistry and heredity. What we must look for between levels is not translation but *relation*, and to realize that causation does not necessarily go 'upwards' through a hierarchy (c.f. Rose, 1981). Indeed, we shall show that 'downward' causation is possible and is of great significance in evolution.

The concept of levels is usually taken to be a descriptive device (see Whyte et al., 1969; Blauberg et al., 1977) determined only by the particular point of view of the investigator. Here we shall argue for the ontological existence of levels, especially of the epigenetic level within the whole social and biological realm of being. It is the existence of the epigenetic level which guarantees continuity between human sociology and biology.

EPIGENESIS: ADAPTABILITY AND DEVELOPMENTAL INTEGRATION

As development proceeds, new kinds of cells and tissues, new organs and structures come into being in an orderly and apparently autonomous manner, so much so that some biologists may easily be misled into thinking of development (conceptually at least) as an essentially closed system. This is but an illusion created by the relative constancy of the environment within which development normally takes place: witness the range of deviations which can be produced in all organisms when the environment is disturbed or altered in some way. However, not all changes in the environment result in corresponding changes in the organism. It is a mistake to think that development is infinitely plastic to external influences (a position often wrongly attributed to those who argue against genetic determinism). On the contrary, one of the most significant characteristics of development is its ability to regulate *against* disturbances so as to produce a more or less constant end-result. The epigenetic system thus exhibits the paradoxical property responsible for both stability and change. This property is *adaptability*—a *necessary* part of normal development: necessary in a mechanical sense because the organism is open to the environment and in a teleological sense because of the need to function effectively. The development of the vertebrate skeleton is a clear illustration of this.

During the lifetime of an individual, each bone is continually remodelled by the joint action of bone-building and bone-destroying cells, thus allowing for growth and for changes in proportion well into adult life. The detailed orientation of the trabeculae inside each bone, as well as its surface moulding, are laid down in accordance with the direction of the mechanical forces of stress and strain to which each bone is subject. At all times, the various parts of the skeleton are correctly aligned in relation to each other and to the muscular elements; and the joints between bones are appropriately fashioned for the particular articulations involved. In other words, the skeleton is a 'direct adaptation' to the mechanical forces acting on its parts, which modify them, making the system mechanically efficient as a whole. There is no doubt that adaptability is necessary during normal development, and that epigenetic processes are involved in integrating external forces and internal structures into an organized and functional whole.

THE EPIGENETIC LANDSCAPE

There is nothing inherently mystical about the epigenetic system. Elsewhere (Ho and Saunders, 1979) we have pointed out that many of its general properties are precisely what one would expect from the nature of the underlying physiochemical processes. Waddington (1957) proposed the concept of the 'epigenetic landscape' to represent the totality of the biochemical and cellular interactions during development. These interactions result in a dynamic system characterised by a set of equilibrium pathways (represented in the 'landscape' as valleys separated by hills or thresholds). Under normal conditions, the topography of the landscape is such that development is *canalised* or buffered against disturbances. Thus, many genetic mutations or environmental fluctuations will not affect the end-result of the development appreciably. However, under conditions of large disturbances—genetic or environmental—the topography can become altered so that alternative pathways of development are traversed, leading to very different end-results.

The most significant aspect of the idea of the epigenetic landscape is that the alternative pathways of development are in principle predictable, and that this in turn has important deterministic influences on evolution, as we shall show.

For Waddington (1957), the epigenetic system is an integration of gene functions at a level of organization above individual genes (see also Polikoff, 1981). That it is something more than an abstract concept is demonstrated by the following evidence.

THE ONTOLOGICAL SIGNIFICANCE OF THE EPIGENETIC LEVEL OF ORGANIZATION

(a) The decoupling of genic from organismic evolution

The existence of the epigenetic landscape is fully consistent with the effective decoupling of genic from organismic evolution. This post-diction is borne out by a host of recent observations pointing to the lack of correlation between changes in structural genes and in the biology of the organisms concerned (see Ho and Saunders, 1979, and references therein). 'Neutral' mutations (Kimura, 1968) are to be expected given the systemic constraints of the epigenetic level of organization (Ho and Saunders, 1981a). (In the same way, we can predict 'neutral' environmental effects which leave the epigenetic system essentially unchanged.)

(b) Phenocopies

If the epigenetic system is not a simple additive outcome of individual gene action, then it must be a characteristic of the population or species of organisms (Ho and Saunders, 1979). Proof for this assertion is provided by the phenomenon of phenocopies (Goldschmidt, 1940) in which morphogenetic mutations are mimicked or copied by normal wild-type strains on treatment with environmental agents (Ho *et al.*, 1981). Phenocopies are found in all groups of organisms. Within a given species, the same kinds of phenocopies are found in all varieties or strains, indicating that different genotypes *per se* are irrelevant to the existence of alternative developmental pathways. The equivalence of genic and environmental effects brings home most forcefully the existence of systemic relationships which ultimately determine the kinds of variations available to evolution. In other words, the variations are by no means random.

In an attempt to explain phenocopies within the accepted framework, some neo-Darwinians, including Goldschmidt (1938) and Waddington (1957), postulated the existence of 'modifier genes' which, as the name implies, modify the expression and penetrance of the phenocopy response. (Note, however, the tacit acceptance of an underlying *structure* which is being modified.) This appears to be supported by the observations that different strains exhibit greater or lesser sensitivity to agents inducing phenocopies (Goldschmidt and Piternick, 1957). Our own investigations indicate that such an interpretation may be an oversimplification, however (see below).

(c) Patterns of morphological evolution

In the last century there was considerable interest in the implications that the study of morphology can have for our understanding of evolution. The neo-Darwinian synthesis deflected attention away from such issues, and only recently have some authors returned to them, and attempted to study them in a modern context (for example, Gould, 1977; Riedl, 1977; Alberch, 1980; Saunders and Ho, 1981; Nelson and Platnick, 1981). Relatively little of the vast amount of data available has been re-examined, but already it is enough to demonstrate the inadequacy of the purely genetic analysis. We shall mention here only two relevant phenomena: parallelism and conservatism.

Parallelism is the evolution of similar characters in different lineages of presumed common ancestry. It is of such frequent occurrence that Brundin (1968) argues it should be considered as the rule, rather than the exception. The most striking and familiar example is the existence in Australia of marsupials which very closely resemble placental wolves, cats, squirrels, ground hogs, anteaters, moles and mice (Simpson and Beck, 1965). It is exceedingly difficult to provide a convincing explanation for parallelism within the neo-Darwinist paradigm, because it requires in some cases long sequences of nearly identical mutations and selective forces. On the epigenetic approach, however, parallelism is just what one would expect: the relatively small number of alternative developmental pathways that are available makes it entirely likely that two similar organisms, faced with roughly similar environmental challenges, will evolve in much the same way.

Another common evolutionary phenomenon is conservatism. Each major taxonomic group has representatives which have remained unchanged since they first appeared in the fossil record, sometimes hundreds of millions of years ago. Among the most familiar examples are the so-called 'living fossils', such as the horse-shoe crab, the opossum and the crocodile. The standard neo-Darwinist explanation is that these organisms have failed to evolve because their environments, to which they are presumably optimally adapted, have remained unchanged. This may sound plausible enough, but we know that these organisms have, during this time, undergone as many allelic substitutions in their genes as the fastest evolving species (Kimura and Ohta, 1974). This is as clear a demonstration as one could want of the fallacy of equating genetic with phenotypic variation.

Actually we do not have to go to such spectacular organisms as the living fossils to see the problems posed by conservatism. With few exceptions, natural populations are genetically exceedingly diverse. Sexual reproduction results in an immensely large number of new recombinants in each generation. Yet the populations remain phenotypically very much the same, generation after generation. This can only be understood in terms of an integration, well above the level of the genes, maintaining the coherence of the developmental system as a whole.

(d) The 'incompleteness' of the fossil record

Darwinian natural selection requires that the variations selected are very small. Yet, continuous series of intermediates are almost never seen either in extant species or in the fossil record. Debate over the size of the variations subject to natural selection has continued unabated since Darwin's days. Whereas Darwin could easily appeal to the incompleteness of the fossil record to 'explain' the abrupt origins of every major group of organisms, recent improvements in stratigraphic analysis render this explanation increasingly untenable (see Williamson, 1981). Instead of gradual phyletic transition of forms, the emerging picture is one of 'punctuated equilibria' (Eldredge and Gould, (1972) in which long periods of stasis involving little or no change are interrupted by bursts of rapid speciation during which major morphological changes take place. This agrees with the proposal of Schindewolf (1936) and Goldschmidt (1940) that macroevolutionary changes are due to large alterations in development. Large alterations are possible only within an integrated epigenetic system. Goldschmidt (1940) and, more recently, Løvtrup (1974) postulate 'systemic mutations' or 'macromutations' to account for the origin of these large variations. We see no reason—given the existence of the epigenetic system—why these variations could not have arisen from major environmental challenges instead (Ho and Saunders, 1979). Such changes could take place rapidly, as a high proportion of the population could initially be involved, without specific mutations in specific genes.

The existence of the epigenetic system gives rise naturally to definite evolutionary consequences which have no explanation within the neo-Darwinian paradigm. The effective decoupling of organismic from genic evolution throws into sharp relief the inadequacies of a purely genetic theory. The epigenetic system determines the kinds of evolutionary changes *accessible* to evolution, without regard to specific alleles at individual loci. If we are to understand evolution, the epigenetic system itself must become the object of our enquiry.

The genetic approach is therefore grossly inadequate, even if we accept that Weismann was correct. In the next section, we shall examine the Weismannist assumption in some detail.

FORM AND FUNCTION

We have seen that the environment enters in an essential way into development. Here we shall argue that there is a deep connection between the environment and evolution by the very nature of epigenetic processes themselves.

The central problem which is unique to biology among natural sciences is adaptation—the exquisite fit between form and function. Lamarck (1809) was among the first to state this problem and to offer an explanation for it. His thesis was that the fit between form and function is by no means accidental: it is the outcome of organism–environmental interactions whereby function itself becomes defined. Hence it is the nature of these interactions which account for the origin of the adaptive variation—before natural selection could be said to act. Darwinism, and, in particular, neo-Darwinism with its Weismannist assumption precludes any explanation of adaptation in terms of organism—environmental interactions. The insistence on *random* variations and natural selection creates a paradox of adaptation which remains unsolved today.

Within neo-Darwinian theory, the environment can only take on the role of 'selector' of natural selection. The vital part it plays as 'interactor' in epigenetic processes whereby variations are generated is either totally ignored, or if not, it is supposed (ironically by Waddington, 1957, himself) that the 'interactive' and 'selective' effects can be neatly separated.

Such a separation is important because (on account of Weismann's barrier) only the selective effects are considered to be of evolutionary consequence; the interactive effects give rise to transient phenotypes that fall by the evolutionary wayside. However, the interactive effects are inextricably confounded with the selective effects. Significantly, Darwin himself was well aware of this difficulty (Vorzimmer, 1972). Natural selection acts on phenotypic variations which are the product of development. If environmental interactions produced large variations, then the role of natural selection is correspondingly diminished. It was at least partly to preserve for natural selection the *creative* role in evolution that Darwin insisted on the insensibly fine gradiations of the variations involved (Ho and Saunders, 1981a).

Once it is admitted that the environment exerts an interactive *formative* influence on organisms, the separation of development from evolution is no longer warranted. On the epigenetic view of evolution, new forms and adaptations originate from novel organism–environmental interactions which become *internalized* in the course of time. In this respect, the analogy between evolution and cognitive processes (Goodwin, 1976; Pringle, 1951; Piaget, 1979) is complete.

Many attempts have been made to explain the internalisation of adaptive characters. The problem is one of heredity: how it is that adaptive characters often appear 'genetically determined' in sense that they anticipate the environmental stimulus to which they are an adaptation?

The solution provided by Waddington (one which he insisted is within the neo-Darwinian paradigm (c.f. Polikoff, 1981)) goes as follows. A population of organisms meets with a new environment and responds developmentally in a novel fashion; in other words, a phenocopy appears. As the population is genetically heterogeneous for modifier alleles, individuals will respond to varying degrees. If the response is adaptive, there will be selection of modifier alleles resulting in *canalisation*: a deepening of the initial response and then a regulation, so that the same degree of response occurs within a range of intensity of the environmental stimulus. At a later stage, there is *genetic assimilation*, so that the response now takes place in the *absence* of the stimulus (see Chapters 10 and 11 of this book).

Canalisation was supposed to occur as the result of the selection for modifier genes. Genetic assimilation could be the end-point of the selection for modifier genes, or it could be due to a single (major) gene mutation which fixes the response genetically, as it were. Genetic assimilation of various phenocopies has been demonstrated in laboratory populations of *Drosophila* (Waddington, 1956, 1975; Bateman, 1959). Analysis of the assimilated lines indicated that, as a rule, changes in many genes spread over all chromosomes are involved, suggesting that assimilation is more likely to be the result of a selection for modifier genes. Based on this, a plausible model could be constructed in which the accumulation of modifiers lowers the threshold for the phenotypic response (through the modification of the epigenetic landscape) to such an extent that it now takes place spontaneously.

The modifier gene model presupposes that the population is heterogeneous with respect to modifier alleles and that canalisation (and genetic assimilation) would only take place when there is selection for the phenocopy, either naturally or artificially. We have recently demonstrated that canalisation could take place in both massbred and inbred lines *without* artificial selection. Moreover as we predicted earlier (Ho and Saunders, 1979) cumulative cytoplasmic modifications (inherited through the female line) appear to be involved in canalisation (Ho *et al.*, 1981).

These findings indicate that, Weismann's barrier notwithstanding, a direct channel exists whereby environmental influences can be passed on from one generation to another (c.f. Cohen, 1980). Cytoplasmic inheritance of cellular organelles is well-known and widely accepted (Grun, 1976). Less well known are a class of lingering modifications—first discovered by Jollos (1921) in *Paramecium* and subsequently found in all classes of animals and plants—in which environmentally induced modifications are inherited for a varying number of generations after the environmental stimulus has been removed (Jinks, 1964; Martin, 1956). If genetic assimilation is essentially the same process as canalisation, then it is possible that cumulative cytoplasmic modifications could play a role in the eventual genetic fixation of the canalised phenotype. In a purely speculative vein, we shall put forward a testable hypothesis concerning genetic assimilation.

If we suppose that environmentally induced modification of the cytoplasm causes an incompatibility to arise between the cytoplasm and the nuclear genes, then genetic assimilation may simply represent a state at which compatibility becomes re-established.

Nuclear-cytoplasmic compatibility characterises all stable species in nature. Its importance to normal development is revealed in interspecific crosses (Moore, 1955) in which incompatibility causes the cessation of development early in embryogenesis. There are two ways in which compatibility can become re-established when disturbed by environmental conditions: by direct 'instruction' from cytoplasm to nucleus when the accumulation of cytoplasmic modification reaches a critical threshold value, or by indirect 'selection' involving nuclear–cytoplasmic interactions whereby the incompatible recombinant genotypes become eliminated—in effect, a kind of organic selection (Baldwin, 1896).

Whatever the precise mechanism of genetic assimilation, it provides for the internalisation of novel developmental responses directly attuned to the environment, resulting not only in evolutionary change, but adaptive evolutionary change.

An insistence on mechanism characterises all those who adopt an epigenetic approach, be it in the nature of epigenetic organization, organism–environmental interactions, canalisation and genetic assimilation. This is in direct contrast to the neo-Darwinian genetic approach. To say that adaptation occurs solely by the natural selection of random mutations is merely to indulge in teleology, as any character is in principle explicable by an appeal to real or imagined selective advantage (see Huxley, 1942). To account for any biological character, and perforce for 'high' level processes such as social behaviour and learning, it is not sufficient to argue that they offer an over-riding advantage for survival, especially since such arguments are almost always hypothetical and not supported by data. A non-teleological theory to explain the origin of behavioural patterns, for example, must show how the behaviour is made *possible* by neural and non-neural mechanisms, extrinsic factors and any independent principles which may govern the interactions and integration of the elements involved.

It is often taken for granted by both sociobiologists and their critics that so far as accounting for biological evolution is concerned, neo-Darwinism is unassailable. Behaviour, social organization and culture may in turn be explained by various extrapolations from neo-Darwinist biology. We have dwelt at some length on the inadequacies of neo-Darwinism even within biology, and have proposed an alternative epigenetic framework which in our view offers a much more satisfactory explanation of biological evolution. In the following sections, we shall attempt to demonstrate that the epigenetic system is the proper interface between the social and biological levels of organization and that this has significant evolutionary implications on evolution at all levels. Of necessity, our treatment will be brief and exploratory, conscious as we are of venturing into areas far beyond our own competence. We hope this might provoke others with appropriate expertise in those areas to examine the issues from the epigenetic point of view.

FORM AND BEHAVIOUR

Behaviour is inseparable from the execution of functions to which biological form, in turn, is fitted. A necessary relationship therefore exists between form and behaviour. In his last works, Piaget (1979) returned to the study of biology in order to consider the evolutionary problem which he regarded as insoluble within the neo-Darwinian framework: how is it that the form of an organ is invariably accompanied by the behavioural repertoire appropriate to its use? It stretches credulity to imagine, for example, that the woodpecker first got a long beak from some random mutations followed by other random mutations that made it go in search of grubs in the bark of trees. The only explanation for this coincidence of form and behaviour in the execution of function is that the two must have evolved together through organism–environmental interactions.

Now the important point about such interactions is that they almost never involve the organism in a purely passive role. As many evolutionists remind us, organisms actively choose their environment so as to give themselves the greatest chance of survival. This is brought about by various means ranging from avoidance reactions in unicellular organisms to the purposive or directed exploratory behaviour of higher organisms. Thus, as Lamarck (1809) had originally envisaged, a change in habit is the efficient and mechanical cause of the change in form, which in turn accounts for the fit between form and function. We may now add that if it is true that organisms generally behave so as to maximize their prospects for survival, it follows that the resulting modification of form will most likely be adaptive. Behaviour therefore plays a central role in the evolution of adaptations which has yet to be fully analysed.

Piaget was at pains to dissociate himself from Lamarckism, mostly on account of popular misconceptions of what Lamarckism is all about. His emphasis on organism–environmental interactions and the mechanisms which he suggested for the genetic assimilation of adaptive behaviour are distinctly Lamarckian, however. Piaget's 'constructivist' approach to developmental psychology is most inspiring, but is flawed by insufficient attention to internal epigenetic organization on the one hand and external socio-cultural influences on the other (Sinha, 1980).

CULTURAL EVOLUTION

Durham (1978), in an illuminating paper, argues that as what was apparently selected in the evolution of human beings was 'an unusual capacity for modifying and extending phenotypes on the basis of learning and experience', 'it makes no sense to view the evolution of human attributes, including social behaviour, solely in terms of the natural selection models of sociobiology.' Culture enables us to alter and build onto aspects of morphology, physiology and behaviour *without any corresponding change in the genotype*. But this is all to be expected on the basis of the epigenetic potential for change which we have elaborated in this paper. Consequently, cultural evolution acting via the epigenetic system bears at least the same kind of untranslatability with respect to genotype evolution as does biological evolution.

Having argued for an effective decoupling between cultural and genotype evolution, Durham then goes on to postulate the 'cultural selection' of phenotypes which 'maximise personal inclusive fitness'—a parallel and analogous process 'complementing' the natural selection of genes. (Irresistible indeed is the Darwinian paradigm of ruthless competition.) But cultural selection, or more appropriately, the selection of culture can never be in terms of the number descendants left by an individual plus his or her relatives once it is admitted that cultural phenotypes may have no genetic basis at all. Moreover, cultural phenotypes spread predominantly by *imitation* and not by reproduction. This point has been made by many others whose views concerning evolution are not necessarily consonant with ours (for example, Waddington, 1960; Campbell, 1965; Ginsberg, 1961). Witness the spread of the habit of stealing cream from bottled milk among blue tits, or the large academic following of the 'great men' in any field. Personal reproductive success and hence any selective processes that depend on genotypes is irrelevant to the reproduction of cultural phenotypes. The success of cultural phenotypes cannot be assessed in terms of biological reproductive success but only in terms (if one so wishes) of the rapidity with which they are imitated. This in turn depends on a whole complex of sociopolitical and economic as well as cultural and psychological factors. The suggestion that culture, too, evolves by the natural selection of disembodied unit-ideas or 'memes'—in direct analogy to the natural selection of genes (Dawkins, 1976) is simply yet another instance of the indiscriminate use of the competitive paradigm which pervades nearly all evolutionary thought today. The natural selection of 'memes' suffers from the same kind of atomistic fallacy that characterises the natural selection of genes. A culture is no more a collection of unit-ideas than an organism is a collection of genes. It is a dynamic system of interdependent and interacting beliefs and conventions held by an aggregate of individuals in a particular socio-political and economic context. (Those of our colleagues who claim that the popularity of Darwinism and neo-Darwinism is just a perfect example of the propagation of a successful meme would do well to be reminded that Darwinism is part and parcel of the Victorian era of market economy and its philosophy of inexorable progress embodied in the rise of the bourgeoisie. Its subsequent success depends in no small measure on there being powerful professors of neo-Darwinism and population genetics. Fortunately, human critical reason can rise above even selfish memes.)

A cultural system forms a level of integration above individual beings who partake of the culture. Consequently, its evolution is subject to systemic constraints and dynamics which transcend individual psychology. It is for this reason that Durkheim (1938) argued for the explanation of 'social facts' in terms of other social facts. But the kind of social determinism that he and, more recently, Sahlins (1977) prescribe misses the epigenetic interconnection between the social and the biological.

The idea of *cultural selection*, as distinct from the selection of culture, is of great theoretical and practical interest; but here too, it is necessary to free ourselves from the competitive paradigm inherent in the term 'selection'. An important point made by Wahlsten (1981) as regards adaptation through cultural transmission is that it can take place rapidly and without selective deaths. (Compare this to the cytoplasmic transmission of somatic and behavioural responses described earlier, which is independent of natural selection.) This is certainly the case in the eradication of malaria with the spread of the use of drugs, insecticides, and the application of knowledge concerning the ecology of the parasite and its mosquito vector. There is more to the idea of cultural selection, however. Culture can have profound directive influences on our phenotypes (through variable epigenesis and learning), which may in turn affect our biological makeup through processes such as canalisation and genetic assimilation. In this connection, we draw attention to the idea that autodomestication—a process whereby humans create and control the environment for their own development in much the same way as they do for domestic animals and plants—may have played a major role in the evolution of our social and biological human attributes (see Leonovich, 1981). This is possible precisely because the social context is an integral part of the process of development. Social communication, and in particular, the adult–child communication necessary to the development of cognitive functions occurs within, and is dependent on a social frame of reference which supplies both meaning and value to the discourse (Sinha, 1980). Social evolution therefore necessarily influences biological evolution through redefining the parameters for individual development. Epigenesis mediates between human culture and biology and at the same time integrates them into an organized and evolving whole.

CONCLUSION

In this chapter we have argued for the epigenetic approach as an alternative to neo-Darwinism. The epigenetic system is governed by principles and dynamics which effectively decouples it from the genes. Its existence gives rise to definite evolutionary consequences which are unintelligible within Darwinian theory. Epigenesis is the interactive interface between the social and biological levels of organization, and as such occupies a key position in the integration and evolution of both. The epigenetic system itself should be the object of our enquiry if we are to understand evolution. Its dynamical properties have important deterministic influences on evolution and provide a far richer and more appropriate basis for evolutionary epistemology than the currently fashionable 'natural selection of random errors' or 'ruthless competition' between selfish genes.

REFERENCES

Alberch, P. (1980). Ontogenesis and morphological diversification. *Amer. Zool.*, **20**, 653–667.

Baldwin, J. M. (1896). A new factor in evolution. *Am. Nat.*, **30**, 441–451, 536–553.

Bateman, K. G. (1959). The genetic assimilation of four venation phenocopies. *J. Genet.*, **56**, 443–474.

Bateson, P. P. G. (1976). Rules and reciprocity in behavioural development. In P. P. G. Bateson and R. A. Hinde (Eds), *Growing Points in Ethology*, Cambridge University Press, Cambridge. pp. 401–421.

Blauberg, I. V., Sadovsky, V. N., and Yudin, E. G. (1977). *Systems Theory*, Progress Publishers, Moscow.

Brundin, L. (1968). Application of phylogenetic principles in systematics and evolutionary theory. In T. Ørvig (Ed.) *Current Problems of Lower Vertebrate Phylogeny*, Interscience, New York. pp. 473–495.

Campbell, D. T. (1965). Variation and selective and retention in socio-cultural evolution. In H. R. Barringer, G. I. Blanksten, and R. W. Mack (Eds), *Social Change in Developing Areas: A Reinterpretation of Evolutionary Theory*, Schenkman, Cambridge, Mass, pp. 19–48.

Cohen, J. (1980). Maternal constraints on development. In D. R. Newth and M. Balls (Eds), *Maternal Effects in Development*, Cambridge University Press, Cambridge. pp. 1–28.

Dawkins, R. (1976). *The Selfish Gene*, Oxford University Press, Oxford.

Durham, W. H. (1978). Towards a coevolutionary theory of human biology and culture. In A. L. Caplan (Ed.), *The Sociobiological Debate*, Harper and Row, New York. pp. 428–448.

Durkheim, E. (1938). *The Rules of Sociological Method*, The Free Press, New York.

Eldredge, N., and Gould, S. J. (1972). Punctuated equilibria: an alternative to phyletic gradualism. In T. J. M. Schopf (Ed.), *Models in Paleobiology*, Freeman, San Francisco, pp. 82–115.

Ginsberg, M. (1961). Social evolution. In M. Banton (Ed.), *Darwinism and the Study of Society*, Quadrangle Books, Chicago. pp. 95–127.

Goldschmidt, R. B. (1938). *Physiological Genetics*, McGraw-Hill, New York.

Goldschmidt, R. B. (1940). *The Material Basis of Evolution*, Yale University Press, New Haven.

Goldschmidt, R. B., and Piternick, L. K. (1957). The genetic background of chemically induced phenocopies in *Drosophila*. *J. Exp. Zool.*, **135**, 127–202.

Goodwin, B. C. (1976). *Analytical Physiology of Cells and Developing Organisms*, Academic Press, London.

Gottlieb, G. (1976). Early development of species-specific auditory perception in birds. In G. Gottlieb (Ed.), *Neural and Behavioural Specificity*, Academic Press, New York. pp. 237–280.

Gould, S. J. (1977). *Ontogeny and Phylogeny*, Belknap Press, Cambridge, Mass.

Grun, P. (1976). *Cytoplasmic Genetics and Evolution*, Columbia University Press, New York.

Hinde, R. A. (1970). *Animal Behaviour, A Synthesis of Ethology and Comparative Psychology*, McGraw-Hill, New York.

Ho, M. W., and Muir, A. (1981). Alternatives to biological reductionism—a report on a recent conference. *Scientia*, **115**, 701–706.

Ho, M. W., and Saunders, P. T. (1979). Beyond neo-Darwinism: an epigenetic approach to evolution. *J. theor. Biol.*, **78**, 673–591.

Ho, M. W., and Saunders, P. T. (1981a). Adaptation and natural selection: mechanism and teleology. In C. M. Barker, L. Birke, A. D. Muir, and S. P. R. Rose (Eds), *Towards a Liberatory Biology*, Allison and Busby, London. pp. 87–104.

Ho, M. W., and Saunders, P. T. (1981b). What is the unit of natural selection? *Evol. Theory*, **5**, 169–172.

Ho, M. W., Tucker, C., Keeley, D., and Saunders, P. T. (1981). Epigenetics and evolution—theory and experiment. In *Proc. 3rd Int. Conf. Evol. Biol.*, Brno, Czechoslovak Academy of Science, Prague (in press).

Huxley, J. (1942). *Evolution the Modern Synthesis*, George Allen and Unwin, London.

Jinks, J. L. (1964). *Extrachromosomal Inheritance*, Prentice Hall, New Jersey.

Jollos, V. (1921). Experimentelle Protistenstudien. 1. Untersuchungen über Variabilität and Vererbung bei Infusorien. *Arch. Protistenk.*, **43**, 1–222.

Kimura, M. (1968). Evolutionary rate at the molecular level. *Nature* (Lond.), **217**, 624–626.

Kimura, M., and Ohta, T. (1974). On some principles governing molecular evolution. *Proc. Nat. Acad. Sci. USA*, **71**, 2848–2852.

Lamarck, J. B. (1809). *Philosophie Zoologique*, Paris.

Lehrman, D. S. (1953). A critique of Konrad Lorenz's theory of instinctive behaviour. *Quart. Rev. Biol.*, **28**, 337–363.

Lehrman, D. S. (1965). On the organization of maternal behaviour and the problem of instinct. In P. P. Grassé (Ed.), *L'instinct dans le Comportement des Animaux et l'homme*, Mason, Paris. pp. 475–520.

Leonovich, V. V. (1981). The process of domestication from the evolutionary point of view. In *Proc. 3rd Int. Conf. on Evol. Biol.*, Brno, Czechoslovak Academy of Science, Prague (in press).

Lorenz, K. (1965). The objectivistic theory of instinct. In P. P. Grassé (Ed.), *L'instinct dans le Comportement des Animaux et l'homme*, Mason, Paris. 51–76.

Lorenz, K. (1977). *Behind the Mirror*, Methuen, London.

Løvtrup, S. (1974). *Epigenetics*, Wiley, London.
Lumsden, C. J. and Wilson, E. O. (1981). *Genes, Mind, and Culture*, Harvard University Press, Cambridge, Mass.
Martin, C. P. (1956). *Phychology, Evolution and Sex*, Charles C. Thomas, Springfield, Ill.
Maynard-Smith, J., and Holliday, R. (1979). Preface to J. Maynard Smith and R. Holliday (Eds), *The Evolution of Adaptation by Natural Selection*, The Royal Society, London. pp. v–vii.
Moore, J. A. (1955). Abnormal combinations of nuclear and cytoplasmic systems in frogs and toads. *Adv. Genet.*, **7**, 132–182.
Needham, J. (1950). *Biochemistry and Morphogenesis*, Cambridge University Press, Cambridge.
Nelson, G. J., and Platnick, N. I. (1981). *Systematics and Biogeography: Cladistics and Vicariance*, Columbia University Press, New York.
Piaget, J. (1979). *Behaviour and Evolution*, Routledge and Kegan Paul, London.
Plotkin, H. C., and Odling-Smee, F. J. (1981). A multiple-level model of evolution and its implications for sociobiology. *Behavioral and Brain Science*, **4**, 225–268.
Polikoff, D. (1981). C. H. Waddington and modern evolutionary theory. *Evol. Theory*, **5**, 143–168.
Pringle, J. W. S. (1951). On the parallel between learning and evolution. *Behaviour*, **3**, 174–214.
Riedl, R. (1977). *Order in living systems: a systems analysis of evolution* (trans. R. P. S. Jefferies), Wiley, London.
Rose, S. (1981). From causations to translations: a dialectical solution to a reductionist enigma. In M. Barker, L. Birke, A. Muir, and S. Rose (Eds), *Towards a Liberatory Biology*, Allison and Busby, London. pp. 11–26.
Ruse, M. (1973). *The Philosophy of Biology*, Hutchinson, London.
Sahlins, M. (1977). *The Use and Abuse of Biology*, Tavistock, London.
Saunders, P. T., and Ho, M. W. (1981). On the increase in complexity in evolution II. The relativity of complexity and the principle of minimum increase. *J. theor. Biol.*, **90**, 515–530.
Schindewolf, O. H. (1936). *Paläontologie, Entwicklungslehre, und Genetik*, Bornträger, Berlin.
Schneirla, T. C. (1956). Interrelationships of the 'innate' and the 'acquired' in instinctive behaviour. In P. P. Grassé (Ed.), *L'instinct dans le Comportement des Animaux et l'homme*, Mason, Paris. pp. 387–452.
Simpson, G. G., and Beck, W. S. (1965). *Life*, 2nd ed. Harcourt Brace and World, New York.
Sinha, C. (1980). What's in a cup? Origins in social negotiation of functional concepts. Cited in Ho and Muir, 1981.
Sinha, C. (1981). Negotiating boundaries: psychology, biology and society. In M. Barker, L. Birke, A. Muir, and S. Rose (Eds), *Towards a Liberatory Biology*, Allison and Busby, London. pp. 27–40.
Tobach, E. (1978). The methodology of sociobiology from the viewpoint of a comparative psychologist. In A. L. Caplan (Ed.), *The Sociobiological Debate*, Harper and Row, New York. pp. 411–423.
Vorzimmer, P. J. (1972). *Charles Darwin: The Years of Controversy*, University of London Press, London.
Waddington, C. H. (1956). Genetic assimilation of the bithorax phenotype. *Evol.*, **10**, 1–13.
Waddington, C. H. (1957). *The Strategy of the Genes*, George Allen and Unwin, London.
Waddington, C. H. (1960). *The Ethical Animal*, George Allen and Unwin, London.

Waddington, C. H. (1975). *The Evolution of an Evolutionist*, Edinburgh University Press, Edinburgh.

Wahlsten, D. (1981). Indeterminacy is inherent in an inadequate model of evolution, not in nature. *Behav. Brain Sci.*, **4**, 255–257.

Weiss, P. (1939). *Principles of Development*, Holt, New York.

Whyte, L. L., Wilson, A. G., and Wilson, D. (1969). *Hierarchical Structures*, Elsevier, New York.

Williams, G. C. (1981). A defence of monolithic sociobiology and genetic mysticism. *Behav. Brain Sci.*, **4**, 257.

Williamson, P. G. (1981). Palaeontological documentation of speciation in Cenozoic molluscs from Turkana Basin. *Nature* (Lond.), **293**, 437–443.

Wilson, E. O. (1975). *Sociobiology: The New Synthesis*, Harvard University Press, Cambridge, Mass.

Learning, Development, and Culture
Edited by H. C. Plotkin
© 1982, John Wiley & Sons Ltd.

CHAPTER 17

Conceptions of prenatal development: behavioral embryology

Gilbert Gottlieb*

In the last 15 years there has been a resurgence of interest in the prenatal development of behavior on the part of psychologists (e.g. Kuo, 1967; Schneirla, 1965), physiologists (reviewed by Provine, 1976), and anatomists (e.g., Humphrey, 1964). This area was a flourishing arena of research from 1885 (the year of publication of Preyer's monumental work, *Specielle Physiologie des Embryo*) on up to the early 1940's, at which time a decline set in. Although this decline in the area coincided with the inactivity of three of its leading investigators (Coghill, Carmichael, and Kuo), it is probable that a paucity of theoretical questions also contributed to it. Namely, almost all of the research on the prenatal development of behavior conducted in the first half of this century centered on the question of whether the sequential development of early behavior goes from undifferentiated total patterns to individuated reflexes or whether it is built up from simple reflexes that become integrated into larger patterns only as a secondary development. Coghill (1929), Hooker (1952), and other workers championed the first view, and Windle (1944), among others, argued for the second view.

While the development of behavior in some species does seem to fit one or the other of these views, the behavior of still other species (guinea pig: Carmichael, 1934; chick: Kuo, 1939) does not fit either view in that local reflexes

* Reprinted by permission of the author and the American Psychological Association. Originally published in *Psychological Review*, 1976, **83**, 215–234. Copyright © 1976 by the American Psychological Association.

and total patterns are observed to exist side by side in the same animal at the same time in development. Given the overwhelming importance of the Coghill–Windle controversy, it is perhaps not surprising that as the futility of the quest for a single general principle became clear, and for the lack of other theoretical questions of significance, research on prenatal behavioral development ground to a virtual halt and remained at a low ebb for several decades. In the 1960's, however, new workers began to enter the field, and in the ensuing period new theoretical issues have surfaced and the area has once again become rather active.

The purpose of the present article is to describe some of the most recent progress in the field and, in particular, to describe in a systematic fashion the various ways in which prenatal experience can affect the development of behavior in the neonate as well as in the embryo and fetus. Traditional conceptions of learning have not been very useful in describing the contributions of experience to the species-typical development of behavior, so it is necessary to begin to formulate these contributions in a somewhat different way. It is not that embryos, fetuses, and neonates are not capable of some forms of learning—they are. It is rather that the notions of conditioning, habituation, sensitization, and so on seem to have little utility in explaining the species-typical (i.e., the usual) course of behavioral development, even when such behavior is manifestly some consequence of experience. The distinction to be noted is that while conventional learning tasks can provide significant information on the behavioral capacities of animals at given points in development (e.g., Rubel and Rosenthal, 1975), they do not account for the development of these capacities. This point will become clearer in the course of this article as the different contributions of experience to behavioral development are described.

As indicated above, it has long been appreciated that behavior does not begin at birth. All species that have been studied—invertebrate as well as vertebrate—begin to show muscular activity and sensitivity to sensory stimulation in the embryonic or fetal stages of development (Gottlieb, 1973). In some species at least, activity precedes reactivity: motor (muscular) movements are present before reflexes are evident. Thus, the early motility in embryos of these species can be said to be truly spontaneous or autogenous (defined as movements that are not dependent on sensory stimulation for their initiation or maintenance). The sensory and perceptual systems also begin to function early in prenatal development, even in cases where they are presumably not yet 'hooked-up' to the motor system. I will discuss the motor, sensory, and perceptual aspects of embryonic behavior in greater detail, but first I would like to describe the modern conception of prenatal behavior development, especially the way in which the relations between structure, function, and behavior are viewed by most current workers in behavioral embryology. (Although I shall emphasize prenatal development in this article, the theoretical conceptions are also applicable to postnatal neurobehavioral development.)

THEORETICAL CONCEPTIONS

From its inception in modern times by Preyer (1885), the comparative study of the development of behavior in the larvae, embryos, or fetuses of various species—the field that we now call behavioral embryology—has always been linked to a study of (or at least speculation about) the maturation of the nervous system.[1] In the early days, unique neuroanatomical correlates were sought for each particular stage of embryonic behavior, and more recently, the neurophysiological and neurochemical correlates peculiar to different behavioral stages have been sought as well. Thus, in this particular field, inquiry has been interdisciplinary from the outset, with knowledge of the various disciplines occasionally residing with a single investigator, as in the case of Preyer, or, more frequently, two investigators, as in the sometime collaboration of Coghill and Herrick (e.g., Herrick and Coghill, 1915).

The traditional neuroanatomical and neurophysiological emphasis of behavioral embryology has worked well as far as empirical advance is concerned, but it has entailed certain conceptual limitations that are just now giving way. Many of the early workers in behavioral embryology were highly trained and very gifted anatomists and physiologists who specialized in the nervous system generally and neurogenesis in particular. This eventuality influenced the way in which the relationship between neural maturation and behavioral development was conceived by some of these workers. Namely, they tended to view behavior as a mere epiphenomenon or passive by-product of neural maturation, the idea being that structure determines function and not the reverse.[2] At any particular stage of embryonic development, there can be no doubt that structure *does* determine function; and in the obvious sense in which that is true, the neurobehavioral study of embryos is not different from the neurobehavioral study of adult organisms, and many of the procedures are also the same (ablation, lesioning, chemical blocking, electrical stimulation, recording). However, the study of a system (whether neural or behavioral) at a single stage or time period does not come to grips with the problem of development. Developmental analysis necessarily involves the further step of (a) determining the possible contribution of earlier functional events to present structure–function relationships or (b) determining the possible contribution of present functional events to the future development of the structure(s) and function(s) in question. Function is here construed very broadly to include the spontaneous or evoked electrical activity of nerve cells and their processes, impulse conduction, neurochemical and hormonal secretion attendant upon neuroelectric activity, the use or exercise of muscles and sense organs, and the behavior of the embryonic organism itself. The contribution of such functions to development could take any of three forms. It could be of a *determinative* or *inductive* nature, channeling development in one direction rather than another. It could be of a *facilitative* (temporal or quantitative) nature, merely influencing thresholds or the rate at which structural maturation or behavioral development occurs. Or, third, it could be of a *maintenance* nature, merely serving to maintain the integrity of already completely formed neural or behavioral systems.

The notions of facilitation and induction are assumed to be operative in immature systems, so it must be shown that incompletely mature systems are indeed capable of function—otherwise, experience could not play a role during the normal (typical) maturation of organs, muscle groups, or neural assemblies. To cite just a few diverse examples of function in immature systems, B. A. Meyerson's and H. E. Persson's (1974) work on somesthetic development in sheep fetuses indicates that sensory system is functional prior to complete physiological maturity at the cortical level; thus, experience could possibly have facilitative or inductive consequences during the maturation process in that case. Also, when the auditory system first begins to function in birds and mammals, it is possible to elicit electrophysiological responses to low frequencies only, the capability for responding to higher frequencies always maturing later in development (Gottlieb, 1971a; Konishi, 1973; Saunders, Coles, and Gates, 1973). Since the initial sensitivity of the functional part of the auditory system always improves with age, experience could be involved in improving the sensitivity of the physiologically active components of the system, and it could also influence the rate of development of the system as a whole. On the motor side, Woodward, Hoffer, and Lapham (1969) have been able to record electrical activity from Purkinje cells in the process of migration in the newborn rat's cerebellum. At the time of the recordings, the cell bodies and their dendrites were still undergoing growth and differentiation, so spontaneous function could play a role in these basic neuroanatomical processes. In all of these cases which I have cited, it is not known whether function actually plays an active role in the maturation process—we only know from these cases that function does occur in immature neural systems and therefore *could* influence the maturation process.

The recent findings of Hubel and Wiesel, Hirsch and Spinelli, Blakemore and Cooper, and others (reviewed by Daniels and Pettigrew, 1976) on the susceptibility of particular sensory cells in the visual cortex of the developing kitten to the influence of visual stimulation is a strong reason to consider function as a usual feature of normal development. Whereas these kitten experiments reveal function→function relationships (i.e., sensory stimulation affects the physiological activity of developing nerve cells), a concrete example of a developing function→structure relationship is demonstrated in other studies in which sensory stimulation or thyroid hormone administration leads to an increased number of spines on the dendrites of neurons (Schapiro and Vukovich, 1970). Although few such studies have yet been conducted prenatally, there is good reason to believe the same effects would be operative. For example, in a study by Sara and Lazarus (1974), in which pituitary growth hormone was administered prenatally to rats, the treated fetuses showed an increased number of cortical neurons and an enhanced maze-learning ability in adulthood. Since cortical neurons cease proliferation before birth in rats as well as in man and many other mammals, the achievement of these enhanced structural effects is limited to function occurring in the prenatal period. (Learning ability can of course be enhanced by postnatal as well as prenatal functions—it is the particular structural counterpart alluded to above that is limited to the prenatal period. While cortical neurons can not be produced by postnatal experience, other behaviorally significant neural changes can be. The latter build on to the axonal, dendritic, synaptic, etc. processes of the neurons already present.)

Perhaps it should be pointed out that it in no way undermines or downgrades the *genetic* contribution to neural maturation to hold open the possibility that spontaneous or evoked function (or behavior) may play a role in the normal course or development. After all, natural selection works on the phenotype, the phenotype has a certain ontogenetic background, and it makes no difference to natural selection whether function was involved in the ontogenetic development of the phenotype or not, just as long as the attribute in question has a genetic basis. In fact, genes are inextricably involved in *any* conception of the development of behavior, whether function is believed to play a role or not.

To summarize, the older and newer conceptions of early neurobehavioral development can be depicted as follows:

Older View: Unidirectional Structure–Function Relationship
Genes→ Structural Maturation→ Function

Newer View: Bidirectional Structure–Function Relationship
Genes⇆ Structural Maturation⇆ Function

In the older view, genes give rise to neural maturation processes that form a structure, which, when fully mature, begins to function in an essentially nonreciprocal way. In the more modern view, genes give rise to structural maturation processes that are susceptible to (in some cases, possibly dependent upon) the influence of function before complete maturity is attained. At the anatomical level, the term *maturation* refers to the early phase of development during which neural cells are proliferating and migrating, and to the later phase in which the nerve cells' axonal and dendritic processes grow and differentiate. It is particularly with respect to the latter that the effects of function are most readily observed. In the newer point of view, function would be considered a normal part of the late phases of neural maturation.[3] In the past, it has not been usual to consider neural activity, sensory stimulation, feedback from motor movement, etc. as normal features of neuroembryological development. The incorporation of function as a factor in the late stages of neuroembryological development does not disregard or underrate the powerful nonfunctional contributions to neural maturation (e.g., sprouting, neurotrophic factors); it only widens the traditional purview. The elegant tissue culture studies of Crain, Bornstein, and associates have shown the remarkable degree to which fetal rodent cerebral cortex can differentiate anatomically and electrophysiologically even when electrical activity has been deliberately suppressed by a blocking agent (Crain, Bornstein, and Peterson, 1968; Model, Bornstein, Crain and Pappas, 1971). This is reminiscent of Carmichael's (1926) classical study showing that amphibians become capable of swimming even when prior muscular movement has been prevented. I have elsewhere noted (Gottlieb, 1971a, pp. 109–110) that we might expect imperfections in the final functional development of explanted neural cells deprived of normal activity and/or input. That expectation has recently been supported by Leiman, Seil, and Kelly (1975), who found incomplete electrophysiological development in such preparations. Whether the failure of explanted cortical cells to achieve complete electrophysiological and anatomical differentiation is a consequence of functional deprivation or other factors has not yet been clarified. Amphibians deprived of previous motor exercise swim, but they do not do so as well as their normally reared peers (Fromme, 1941).

It is probable that during development, genes are activated and deactivated by chemical events associated with neural maturation processes; thus, in the diagram above, there is an arrow going back to genes from structural maturation to depict the probable bidirectionality of that relationship as well as of the structure–function relationship. Although the switching on and off of the activity of the specific genes by hormones during development has not yet been demonstrated in the nervous system per se, it has been shown in other systems (e.g., O'Malley and Means, 1974). Therefore, it does not seem unreasonable to expect the same sort of mechanism to hold for neural maturation as well. Such a mechanism is clearly implied in the notion that thyroid hormone regulates the timing of neural maturation (Hamburgh, 1969). For example, excess thyroxine accelerates the rate of development of synapses in the cerebellum of young rats, and it also is associated with a premature termination of the cellular proliferation phase in that region, resulting in a reduction in the number of synapses in the mature cerebellum (Nicholson and Altman, 1972). Interestingly, either reduced or excessive thyroxine in the neonatal period in rats is associated with behavioral deficiencies in adulthood (Eayrs, 1968). This poorer performance may not reflect merely an endocrine disturbance as such, but also a disruption of timing in the early maturation of the brain (e.g. Stone and Greenough, 1975). Thus, the probable bidirectionality between the activity of genes, neural structures, and functions can be highly significant for behavior well beyond the early period of development in which the formative reciprocal interactions took place.[4]

PREYER–TRACY HYPOTHESIS OF AUTOGENOUS MOTILITY: MOTOR PRIMACY THEORY

The seeds of one of the first important generalizations about embryonic behavior were planted by Preyer when he pointed out, in 1885, that the chick embryo is motile before it is able to react to exteroceptive sensory stimulation. Forty years later, Tracy (1926), observed that the embryos of certain fish develop up to and through the swimming phase before they are reactive to exteroceptive sensory stimulation. This hypothesis of motor primacy—that the early movements of embryos are autogenous (i.e., nonreflexive)—has been proven recently in one of the more elegant experiments in behavioral embryology, performed by Hamburger and his associates (Hamburger, Wenger,

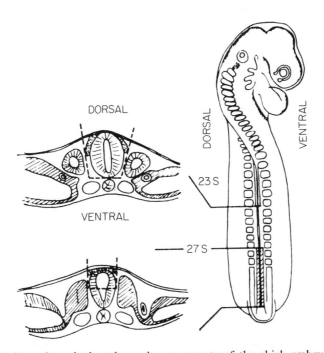

Figure 1 To determine whether the early movements of the chick embryo are truly spontaneous (without the necessity for sensory initiation or maintenance), chick embryos were deafferented at the leg level at around 40 hours of development. The microsurgery involved (a) removing the dorsal (sensory) side of the spinal cord at the leg level (below the level of 27S in the diagram) and (b) creating a complete gap at the thoracic level (between 23S and 27S) to prevent impulses from higher levels from reaching the lower limb segments. The non-deafferented control group merely had the latter operation, so that the sensory innervation of their legs was intact. (From 'Motility in the Chick Embryo in the Absence of Sensory Input' by V. Hamburger, E. Wenger, and R. Oppenheim, *Journal of Experimental Zoology*, 1966, **162**, 133–160. Reproduced by permission of Alan R. Liss, Inc)

and Oppenheim, 1966). To show that the chick embryo is, in fact, capable of instigating and maintaining its motility in the absence of sensory stimulation, Hamburger *et al.* surgically removed the dorsal part of the spinal cord in chick embryos at around 40 hours of embryonic development, thus depriving the embryos of the possibility of receiving sensory input to their legs. Figure 1 illustrates the nature of the surgical operation.

Figure 2 shows the behavioral results: the percentage of motility of the legs in each group at various ages. As indicated, the deafferented embryos showed

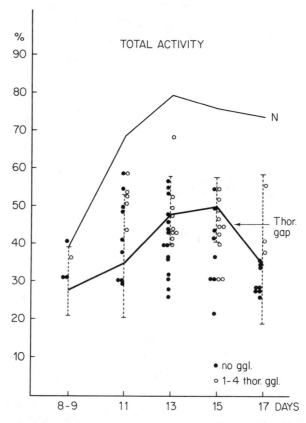

Figure 2 The motility of the deafferented and control (thoracic gap) chick embryos from 8 to 17 days of embryonic development. Each black circle represents a deafferented embryo that had no sensory ganglia intact after the operation, while the open circles represent those embryos that were incompletely deafferented (having 1–4 thoracic ganglia intact). The vertical dashed line indicates the range of activity in the thoracic-gap control group. N in the diagram shows the activity level of normal, intact embryos. (From 'Motility in the Chick Embryo in the Absence of Sensory Input' by V. Hamburger, E. Wenger, and R. Oppenheim, *Journal of Experimental Zoology*, 1966, **162**, 133–160. Reproduced by permission of Alan R. Liss, Inc)

as much motility as the control-operated embryos up until Day 17 of embryonic development, at which time degenerative processes in the spinal cord of the deafferented embryos (or perhaps the need for sensory stimulation at late embryonic stages) caused some decline of activity. (Should sensory stimulation be required for normal activity beginning in late stages, this does not detract from the conclusion that earlier motility is autogenous, as originally suggested by Preyer's motor primacy theory.) The activity of both the thoracic-gap and deafferented embryos is well below that of the normal, intact embryo, indicating that electrical activity from higher centers ordinarily contributes to the usual level of motility in the embryo's legs.

The chick embryo's autogenous motility is uncoordinated (or random), and this pattern persists to some extent even through the hatching phase. Around about 17 days of incubation, however, the embryo begins to exhibit clearly patterned motor behavior in connection with assumption of the postures that lead to hatching 3 days later. These later-appearing patterned movements are most likely triggered by sensory stimulation. In a recent study, Vince, Reader, and Tolhurst (1976) have been able to show that the appearance of the patterned movements can be accelerated by at least 2 days (the earliest they tried) by precociously administering sensory stimulation (regular loud clicks) that normally occurs later on and is known to hasten development and hatching at later stages. This finding presents very interesting problems for further analysis, both at the neurological and behavioral levels. The capacity to make the patterned movements is present several days before they usually appear, and that capacity remains latent until the 'proper' time, which implies a very high threshold for responsiveness to general stimulation and a very narrowly tuned sensory-perceptual 'trigger'. It is striking that the two behavioral systems (random and coordinated) seem to exist side by side in complete independence. Are these really two completely independent movement systems, as the current data imply, or are the later-occurring movements in any way dependent on the early autogenous ones? Or, in more obvious terms of facilitation, does the exercise of the autogenous movements early in development contribute to the increasing level of *autogenous* activity at later stages? Unfortunately, there are practical difficulties in answering these questions (see the description below on the consequences of immobilizing the embryo.)

In any event, some 90 years after Preyer first observed that chick embryos are capable of movement before they are capable of responding to sensory stimulation, we now have definite proof that these early movements are in fact of an autogenous, nonreflexive character, and that motor primacy is probably the rule at least in taxonomic groups other than mammals. In man and other primates, for example, the time gap between the onset of overt responses to sensory stimulation and the onset of possibly spontaneous movements has closed completely so that these two capabilities coincide (Gottlieb, 1971a).

In Figure 3 we can see that the quantitative trends in motility are rather

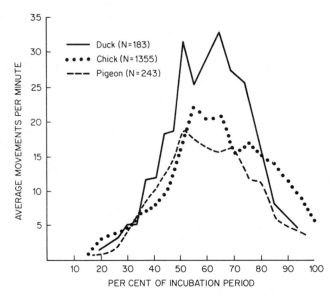

Figure 3 Motility of duck, chick, and pigeon embryos throughout their respective incubation periods. (The incubation period of the duck is 26–27 days, of the chick 20–21 days, and of the pigeon 16–17 days.) (R. W. Oppenheim made the observations on the chick and duck embryos, and M. S. Harth collected the data for the pigeon embryos.) (Slightly modified from 'Synaptogenesis in the Avian Embryo: Ultrastructure and Possible Behavioral Correlates' by R. F. Foelix and R. W. Oppenheim. In G. Gottlieb (Ed.), *Behavioral Embryology*. New York: Academic Press, 1973. Reproduced by permission of Academic Press)

similar in the embryos of three rather different avian species: duck, chicken, and pigeon. As indicated by the observations of Oppenheim and Harth, there is an initial slow rise of activity to a peak around mid-incubation, and then a decline as the time of hatching approaches.

What of the early autogenous motility of the avian embryo—does it have any consequences for subsequent structural or functional development? As yet, the only evidence we have on this point is that the motor movements of the embryo serve to keep its joints, muscles, and tendons operative: If the chick embryo is prevented from moving by a paralytic agent for as little as 1 to 2 days during its 20-day embryonic period, severe ankylosis of the joints in the legs, toes, and neck develops, some evidence of which is shown in Figure 4 from the work of Drachman and Coulombre (1962). This represents the induction of 'clubfoot' by experimental means: Clubfoot is a defect in which there is a fixation or ankylosis of the joints. The toes of the animals shown in Figure 4 were so 'fixed' that they rigidly resisted displacement.

In the literature dealing with human prenatal development, it has been suggested by Humphrey (1970) and others that lack of activity or fetal

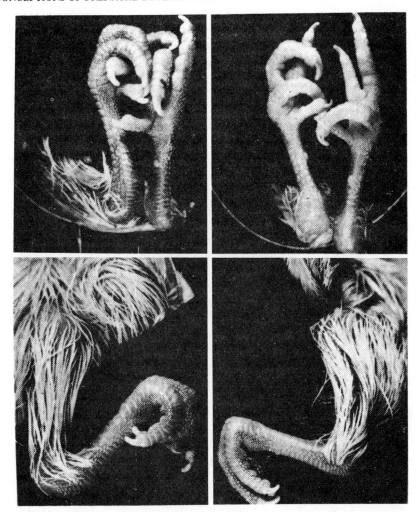

Figure 4 Variety of joint malformations in the legs and toes of chicks which had been immobilized for 1–2 days during embryonic development. (From 'Experimental Clubfoot and Arthrogryposis Multiplex Congenita' by D. B. Drachman and A. J. Coulombre, *Lancet*, 1962, **2**, 523–526. Reproduced by permission of *The Lancet*)

immobility is associated with cleft palate and ankylosis, these disorders perhaps stemming from the absence of the sheerly mechanical effects produced by the movements themselves. So it is possible that the research findings on the autogenous motility of the chick embryo may have implications for the understanding of the consequences of motor behavior in other species, whether the motor movements in the other species are autogenous or not. So far, these effects have not implicated a neural component, only nonneural skeletal deficiencies. It seems likely that after the muscle spindles have started to develop in the chick embryo, the anatomy and/or electrophysiology of the embryo's muscle receptors would be altered as a consequence of limb immobility, as is observed in young and adult cats (Eldred, Bridgman, Kano, Sasaki, and Yellin, 1967).

SENSORY FUNCTION

The principle of motor primacy is sometimes misconstrued to mean that the sensory systems are not functional during prenatal development. That is incorrect. Motor primacy means only that the motor system is capable of instigating and maintaining its own activity without sensory stimulation, or in advance of the establishment of the neural sensorimotor reflex arcs; motor primacy does not mean that the sensory systems are not functional during the prenatal period. In fact, we have considerable physiological evidence, and some behavioral evidence, of the prenatal functional capability of the sensory systems in a wide variety of species, so much so that we can be reasonably certain that we know the usual sequence or order in which the various sensory systems ordinarily become functional in a number of mammalian and avian species (Gottlieb, 1971a). A summary of that information appears in Figure 5, which shows the usual order in which the sensory systems mature: (a) cutaneous (somesthetic), (b) vestibular, (c) auditory, and (d) visual. This is true whether the systems begin to function before or after birth or hatching; this particular sequence is very general throughout the vertebrate series. In some animals (e.g., duck, chick, guinea pig, sheep, man), all of these sensory modalities become capable of functioning before hatching or birth, whereas in other species (e.g., grackle, mouse, rat, cat), the capacity for auditory and visual function does not develop until after hatching or birth.

Thus, although cutaneous (skin) sensitivity develops prenatally in all animals (including man) that have been studied thus far, some of the later-developing sensory systems become capable of functioning only after birth or hatching. Whether the later-developing systems become functional before or after birth is correlated with the precocial or altricial status of the species. In birds and mammals, for example, the onset of visual function seems to be closely related to how mature the motor system and thermoregulatory system are at hatching. In the most precocious, or precocial, species such as ducklings, chicks, quail, guinea pigs, and sheep, the capability for visual functions begins before hatching or birth; whereas in the more altricial (motorically immature, late feathering) species such as the grackle, mouse, rat, and cat, visual function develops well after hatching or birth. In Figure 6, which is taken from the work of Heaton and Harth (1974), one can see that the pigeon, which is intermediate on the avian precocial–altricial dimension, is also intermediate with respect to the onset of visual function.

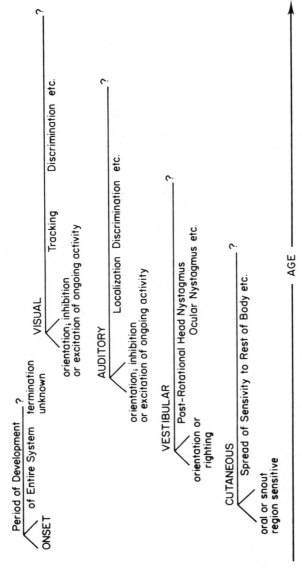

Figure 5 The order in which the sensory systems begin functioning is similar in many species: cutaneous–vestibular–auditory–visual. (From 'Ontogenesis of Sensory Function in Birds and Mammals' by Gilbert Gottlieb. In E. Tobach, L. R. Aronson, and E. Shaw (Eds), *The Biopsychology of Development*. New York: Academic Press, 1971. Reproduced by permission of Academic Press)

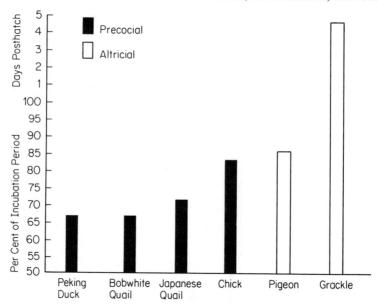

Figure 6 The onset of visual sensitivity (pupillary reflex) generally begins before hatching in precocial species of birds and late in embryonic development or even after hatching in altricial species. (While the domestic chick is classed as precocial according to its advanced locomotor ability, etc. at hatching, it more nearly resembles the semi-altricial pigeon in the relatively late maturity of its pupillary reflex.) (From 'Developing Visual Function in the Pigeon Embryo with Comparative Reference to Other Avian Species' by M. B. Heaton and M. S. Harth, *Journal of Comparative and Physiological Psychology*, 1974, **86**, 151–156. Copyright 1974 by the American Psychological Association. Reprinted by permission)

Man is a conspicuous exception to the generalization about precocial–altricial status and rate of sensory development. Although motorically immature and highly dependent on maternal care for a prolonged period after birth (thus, highly altricial), man's rate of sensory development is so accelerated that all of our sensory systems become capable of function before birth (Gottlieb, 1971a). The very early onset of sensory-perceptual function in humans undoubtedly is part and parcel of our unusually advanced cerebral and cognitive development, and may have ramifications for our social and personality development as well (cf. Cairns, 1976; Mason, 1968).

To know that the various sensory systems are capable of functioning prenatally and to know that they actually *do* function prenatally are two different things, of course, and we have regrettably little information on the significance of sensory function in the normal or usual course of embryonic development. (In a recent review of fetal sensory receptors, Bradley and Mistretta [1975] address themselves to the question of sensory stimuli in the prenatal environment. They also include a discussion of the chemical senses omitted here.)

In the next two sections I shall describe a few experiments in which the facilitative and inductive effects of prenatal sensory stimulation have been demonstrated. (An extensive empirical review of the postnatal literature on the maintenance, facilitative, and inductive effects of experience at the anatomical, physiological, and behavioral levels appears elsewhere [Gottlieb, 1976].) As the present article deals primarily with the effects of prenatal function on prenatal and postnatal behavior, I shall be describing function–function relationships rather than function–structure relationships (see Note 2).

FACILITATION (QUANTITATIVE REGULATION) OF BEHAVIORAL DEVELOPMENT

The main implication of the 'facilitation' view is that the time or age of appearance (or some other quantitative feature) of neuroanatomy, neurophysiology, or behavior such as size, threshold, amount, latency is regulated by function. In the absence of experience, the behavior (or neural feature) in question might ultimately develop, but it will appear later than it would in the presence of appropriate experience.

Among the most striking examples of facilitation are those having to do with the length of the incubation period in birds, a parameter so stable that it is usually thought to be free of such influences as the vagaries of embryonic sensory

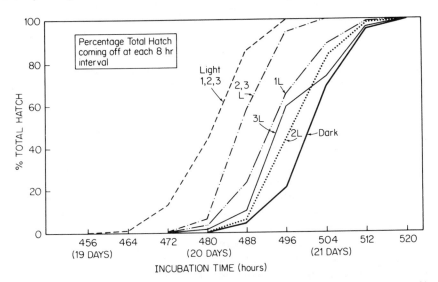

Figure 7 Chick eggs incubated under incandescent light for the first (1), second (2), and/or third week (3) of embryonic development hatch sooner than those incubated in the dark. (From 'Accelerated Growth of Embryo Chicks Under the Influence of Light' by J. K. Lauber and J. V. Shutze, *Growth*, 1964, **28**, 179–190. Reproduced by permission of Growth Publishing Co., Inc)

stimulation. Two dramatic illustrations show that the time of hatching in chicks and quail is in fact regulated by different sorts of embryonic sensory stimulation!

In an experiment with domestic chick embryos, Lauber and Schutze (1964) examined the effects of light on the length of the incubation period. The normal incubation period is 20 days. As shown in Figure 7, domestic chicken eggs exposed to light throughout the incubation period hatched much earlier than the other groups. (Heat was carefully controlled and closely monitored in these experiments so that the earlier hatching was not an effect of a slightly higher temperature in the lighted sectors of the incubator.) The interesting fact is that this facilitative effect is not directly or solely a function of *visual* stimulation because, as can be seen in Figure 7, it occurs as a consequence of light-exposure during the first week of embryonic development, a time when the visual receptors and pathways from the eyes to the brain are not yet functional. It is speculated that the effect may be some consequence of stimulating phylogenetically 'primitive' nonvisual photic receptors in the skin, muscle, or spinal cord. The probability that the effect is not mediated by the retina or the brain is further enhanced by a related experiment by Harth and Heaton (1973) in which rather immature pigeon hatchlings were found to react overtly to light when their bodies were exposed but not when only their heads were exposed with the rest of their bodies covered up.

Another experiment that indicates a quantitative regulation of hatching time by sensory stimulation comes from the work of Vince (1973) on quail embryos. The hen leads her brood from the nest very soon after hatching in nature, so some means of synchronizing the time of hatching in the multi-egg clutch is particularly important in this species. Vince found that around the time of hatching the embryos emit a low 'clicking' sound as they begin to breathe regularly—this low, repetitious sound can be transmitted between eggs quite readily if they are in contact (as they would be in the nest) but not when the eggs are not touching each other. To determine whether the clicking sound has any regulatory 'communication' value, Vince put quail eggs in an incubator so that some eggs were touching each other and others were not in contact. The results (see Figure 8) have an almost aesthetic quality, they are so uncommonly 'neat': In 9 out of 10 experiments, the eggs in contact always hatched in virtual synchrony, whereas the disparity in hatching time of the other eggs was almost always spread over many hours. It would seem that the time of hatching in quail is regulated by inter-embryonic 'clicking' that somehow mutually retards and accelerates each embryo's progress such that synchrony of hatching is achieved. (Vince [1973] has actually been able to artificially accelerate hatching in quail embryos by playing them clicking sounds of certain rates, but it is more difficult to retard hatching in such playback experiments.)

Another implication of the facilitation view holds that although certain species-specific behavioral abilities (including important perceptual capacities such as depth perception) may develop in the absence of prior experience or

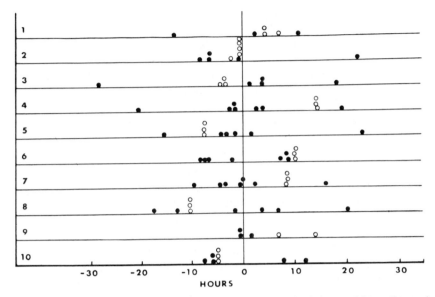

Figure 8 Inter-embryonic communication in quail. Ten experiments with quail eggs in contact (open circles) and not in contact (closed circles) in the incubator. (From 'Retardation as a Factor in the Synchronization of Hatching' by M. A. Vince, *Animal Behaviour*, 1968, **18**, 332–335. Reproduced by permission of Baillière Tindall)

function, in some cases they won't achieve their highest degree of differentiation or functioning in the absence of prior experience. Tees (1974) has precisely documented this aspect of facilitation in his study of the effects of postnatal deprivation on the development of fine depth perception in rats. Specifically, the visually deprived rats developed depth perception but not to the fine degree shown by visually experienced rats. There is as yet little direct prenatal or embryonic evidence for this proposition, but certain of my own experiments on the species-specific auditory perceptual development of young ducklings illustrate the point (Gottlieb, 1971b).

Day-old Peking ducklings (a domestic form of mallard) hatched in incubators in the laboratory and deprived of any opportunity to interact with their maternal parent can nonetheless identify the maternal call of their own species in a choice test. In such a test, the mallard maternal call is broadcast from one speaker and the maternal call of some other species is broadcast from an opposing speaker. The maternally naive ducklings unerringly walk over and stay next to the speaker emitting the maternal call of their own species. (The maternally naive young of other precocial species such as the wild wood duck, domestic chicken, and wild junglefowl also have the ability to select the maternal call of their species under these same conditions.) In investigating the basis for the Peking duckling's selective response to its species' maternal call (mallard), I wondered if some of the acoustic elements of the maternal call were perhaps present in the duckling's own vocalizations, so that hearing its own vocalizations and those of siblings played a role in facilitating the subsequent selective response to the maternal call. Since ducklings begin vocalizing as embryos when they start to breathe several days before hatching, to do the proper experiment it was necessary to devise a technique to prevent the embryos from vocalizing so they could not possibly hear their own voices.

After considerable study of the anatomy and physiology of the vocal apparatus of many ducklings, Vandenbergh and I (Gottlieb and Vandenbergh, 1968) were able to devise a simple devocalization procedure that works especially well with duck embryos. The procedure involves coating the vibratory (tympaniform) membranes of the embryo's voice box (syrinx) with a nontoxic surgical 'glue' called collodion; this prevents movement of the membranes and the embryo is made mute by this method. (They regain their voices several weeks after the experiment.)

I was now ready to examine the influence, if any, of the embryonic vocalizations in helping the duckling to detect the species' maternal call after hatching. A large number of embryos were devocalized and placed in individual auditory isolation until they hatched, at which time they were given an auditory choice test. At 24 hours after hatching, the devocalized ducklings had some

Table 1 Preference of unoperated, sham-operated, and devocal-isolated Peking ducklings in mallard versus wood duck maternal call choice test at 24 and 48 hours after hatching

Condition	Preference (N)	
	Mallard call	Wood duck call
24 hours after hatching		
Unoperated vocal-isolated	21	0
Sham-operated vocal isolated	21	0
Operated devocal-isolated	19	6
48 hours after hatching		
Operated devocal-isolated	29	0

Note: Whereas at 24 hours after hatching the sham-operated ducklings performed as well as the unoperated ducklings, the devocalized ducklings' preference for the mallard call was weaker ($p = .05$) than both the other groups. By 48 hours, however, the performance of the devocalized ducklings improved significantly ($p = .05$), and they did as well as the other groups in selecting the mallard call. (The 24- and 48-hour-old ducklings were two separate groups, each tested at only one age.) (Data from Gottlieb, 1971b) difficulty discriminating the mallard maternal call from the wood duck maternal call (see Table 1), but by 48 hours after hatching this difficulty disappeared. Thus, at the very least, the auditory deprivation introduced a temporal lag in the perfection of species-specific auditory perceptual development, a finding consonant with one aspect of the facilitation view.

Since the lag in development seemed to be rectified by 48 hours, at least with respect to the devocalized ducklings' ability to discriminate the mallard from the wood duck call, we tested other groups of muted ducklings at this later age (48 hours) in a variety of choice tests involving the mallard maternal call versus other calls (see Table 2). Just as would be predicted from that feature of the facilitation viewpoint suggesting partial but incomplete differentiation of perceptual development under the present deprivation conditions, the devocalized ducklings performed as well as normal in many but not all of the tests. At 48 hours after hatching, although the devocalized ducklings chose the mallard call over a wood duck maternal call, a pintail duck maternal call, and a duckling (sibling) brooding call, they had difficulty distinguishing the mallard from a chicken maternal call. (The latter shares some common acoustic elements with the mallard call.) To make certain that this perceptual deficiency was not attributable to the physical trauma of the embryonic surgery, a control group of embryos was allowed an opportunity to hear their own vocalizations for about 18 hours before being subjected to the devocalization operation. When these birds were tested at 48 hours after hatching, they had no difficulty in the mallad-versus-chicken maternal call test (see Table 3). Thus, it can be concluded that embryonic auditory experience contributes in a facilitative way to the differentiation of auditory perceptual development in ducklings.

More recent findings in this line of research have defined one of the perceptual

Table 2 Preference of 48-hour-old, devocal-isolated, Peking ducklings in various choice tests

Choice test calls	Preference (N)	
	Mallard call	Other call
Mallard vs. duckling (sibling)	20	1
Mallard vs. pintail duck	20	0
Mallard vs. chicken	27	15

Note: Each of the ducklings was tested only once, so the above represent three separate groups of devocalized ducklings. While the devocalized ducklings did choose the mallard over the sibling and pintail maternal calls, they did not distinguish between the mallard and chicken maternal calls as they ordinarily are able to do after hearing their own embryonic vocalizations (see Table 3). (There are about twice the usual number of ducklings in the mallard vs. chicken call test because the original published experiment [in which 12 chose the mallard and 9 chose the chicken call] was subsequently repeated and the results of the two experiments are combined here.) (Data from Gottlieb, 1971 b, with exception of previously unpublished replication of mallard vs. chicken test in which 15 devocalized ducklings chose the mallard and 6 chose the chicken call)

Table 3 Preference of 48-hour-old, devocal-isolated, Peking ducklings in mallard versus chicken call test as a consequence of a delay in the usual time of devocalization

Condition	Preference (N)	
	Mallard call	Chicken call
Embryos devocalized at usual time	27	15
Embryos devocalized 18–23 hours later than usual	17	1

Note: As the results show, 18–23 hours of exposure to their own embryonic vocalizations is sufficient to allow the birds to select the species' maternal call over the chicken call after hatching. (Data from Gottlieb, 1971 b)

deficiencies of the mute embryos and demonstrate the maintenance effects, as well as facilitation effects, of embryonic experience (Gottlieb, 1975a, b, c). The results can be briefly summarized as follows. Devocalizing duck embryos prevents them from hearing their own high-frequency vocalizations in the late stages of embryonic development, just at the time when their physiological sensitivity to these frequencies is maturing (Konishi, 1973). Behavioral tests show that these mute ducklings are then relatively insensitive to the higher frequencies in the maternal call at 24 hours after hatching. At 48 hours after hatching, this deficiency rectifies itself by intrinsic means. At 65 hours after hatching, the mute ducklings are again deficient in high-frequency sensitivity unless they have been exposed to certain of their vocalizations in the late embryonic period. Thus, the high-frequency deficiency at 24 hours is evidence for the facilitative effect of exposure to their own vocalizations in the course of normal embryonic development, and the high-frequency deficiency at 65 hours is evidence for the maintenance effects of such simulaton.[5] (Further evidence of the facilitative and maintenance effects of prenatal auditory stimulation on postnatal behavior in birds is reviewed by Impekoven [1976].)

The maintenance effect described above is particularly unusual in that the relevant experience (exposure to a certain embryonic vocalization) occurred 3 days before the behavior it maintained (perceptual sensitivity to the higher frequency components of the maternal call). (The auditory experience terminated before hatching.) Our present conceptions of development do not prepare us for such a relationship between earlier experience and later species-typical behavior. As it becomes more common to manipulate normally occurring embryonic experience and look for effects on the later development of species-typical behavior, we may discover yet other sorts of unanticipated dependencies between earlier experience and later behavior. To make genuine analytic progress in the study of early behavioral development, traditional conceptions of learning (and development) may not be helpful guides to discovery.

INDUCTIVE INFLUENCES IN BEHAVIORAL DEVELOPMENT

Inductive influences of function or experience are those that most psychologists, animal behaviorists, and neurobiologists probably find the most significant and interesting: instances in which the absence or presence of some event early in life absolutely determines whether or not a given behavioral activity, whether motoric response or perceptual preference, will manifest itself later on in development. Perhaps the most striking examples of this kind of 'irreversible' canalization of development occur most obviously in the area of the hormonal determination of sex organs, where the presence or absence of certain gonedal hormones in the prenatal or neonatal period determines whether the genitalia will be of the male or female type upon maturity. For example, it has been shown experimentally that the genital structures of genetic female guinea pig fetuses are susceptible to maculinization by testosterone propionate during a certain period in mid-gestation. With respect to later sexual *behavior*, however, these particular effects are quantitative (i.e. facilitative rather than inductive), leading to a heightened incidence of male-like mounting behavior and reduced female sexual behavior in adulthood in the female fetuses thus treated (Goy, Bridgson, and Young, 1964).

If there are few presently known instances of the facilitative effects of embryonic function on later neural maturation and behavior, there are even fewer clearcut examples of determinative, or inductive, effects known to us at the present time. Imprinting would represent an inductive phenomenon *par excellence* in those instances in which the early experience brings about a species-typical (i.e., usually occurring) later state of affairs that would not occur but for the early experience. Defined in this restrictive way, there are actually very few known examples of imprinting, the early experiential basis of song-learning in certain species of birds (e.g., bullfinches) being perhaps the best example (Nicolai, 1959). One has the impression that there may be many such examples in normal or species-typical development, but they occur within such a complex web of biopsychological constraints that we haven't yet been able to clearly grasp and appreciate them. Imprinting does not really represent a 'blank slate' model of development, although that model may be the one that most readily comes to mind in thinking about inductive influences on development.

Within the sphere of behavioral embryology, the only experiment I am aware of that seems to demonstrate an inductive influence in the restrictive manner defined above is one by Wiens (1970), involving an analysis of substrate preferences in red-legged frogs (*Rana aurora*). The usual habitat of these creatures is a shallow pond or overflow area, characterized by slender, emergent willow branches, cattails, submerged weed stems, and grasses—all essentially linear structures that cast more or less linear shadows on the muddy substrate. In the laboratory, Wiens reared red-legged larvae in one of three 'habitats' and tested them pre- and postmetamorphically for their 'habitat' preference. He reared one group in a white pan with parallel black stripes on its floor and walls, a second group in a white pan with black squares on its floor and walls, and a third group in a 'featureless' white pan. The larvae were tested for their substrate ('habitat') preference by placing them in a chamber, half of which was covered by the striped pattern and half by the black squares. Each tadpole's preference was recorded by the amount of time it spent in each half of the test chamber during a 3-minute test period. When tested premetamorphically (Stages 35–40 in Figure 9), the stripe-reared larvae showed a statistically significant preference for the striped side of the test compartment, whereas the square-reared group showed a slight but insignificant preference for the side with the square pattern. When tested postmetamorphically, the stripe-reared group continued to show a strong preference for the striped side and the square-reared group showed a slight increase in their bias toward the side with squares, but

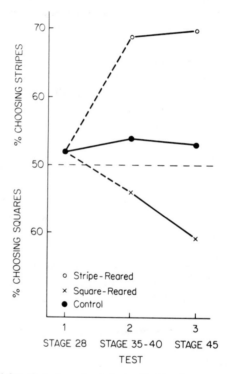

Figure 9 Red-legged frogs' choice of substrate ('habitat') pattern as a function of their larval rearing environment. The larvae were raised in a 'featureless' white pan (control condition) until they had passed Stage 28, at which time they were placed in a striped pan or one with squares on its floor and walls. Subsequently, they were given choice tests premetamorphically (Stages 35–40) and postmetamorphically (Stage 45) to determine if the rearing environment determined their substrate preference. (Data from Wiens, 1970)

this was still a statistically nonsignificant preference. As shown in Figure 9, the group reared in the featureless pan did not show a preference for either of the two substrate patterns.

Thus, the rearing environment of red-legged frog tadpoles determines their later choice of substrate pattern, and this inductive influence operates within perceptual constraints so that a preference for certain types of patterns is more readily induced than a preference for others.

Since we are inclined to think of instances of induction as indicating the height of behavioral plasticity during development and perhaps as being relegated to vertebrate species, it is noteworthy that such plasticity occurs even in invertebrate species. For example, as shown by the behavioral experiments of Jaisson (1975), if young worker ants are removed from the colony on the day of hatching, they will care for the cocoons of many different species that are offered to them. If they are exposed to cocoons of a given species during the 15 days immediately after hatching, however, they will tend only that species and treat other species of cocoons (including their own) as food. In the normal course of development, these worker ants would ordinarily be exposed to cocoons of their own species and thus tend these and devour cocoons of other species. Jaisson's experiments show that this apparently rigid, stereotyped, species-specific behavioral outcome is a consequence of a highly plastic developmental process involving induction of a positive preference for tending that species of cocoon to which the developing worker ant has been exposed during a formative period of development. Thus, developmental plasticity is not restricted to birds and mammals, or even vertebrates, but extends at least to insects. It may be that the retention of embryonic or neonatal plasticity into later stages of ontogeny is what distinguishes the behavioral development of higher from lower forms (cf. Cairns, 1976; Mason, 1968).

SUMMARY

In this brief introduction to a few selected problem areas of behavioral embryology I have tried to make the following four basic and interrelated points:

1. Function, whether spontaneous or evoked, occurs at both the neural and behavioral levels before the neural maturation or behavioral development of the system in question is complete. Therefore, it is entirely possible that function ('experience') normally participates in the neural maturation process as well as in behavioral development at early stages, both prenatally and postnatally. In addition to playing its widely acknowledged maintenance role, function may also exert a facilitative and even an inductive, or determinative, influence on early neural maturation and behavioral development.

2. Motor primacy (spontaneity of early motility) very likely holds for the behavioral development of certain of the invertebrates as well as vertebrates

such as fish, amphibians, and birds. It may not hold for the more recently evolved mammals, man and other primates in particular, in which the onset of sensory function has been accelerated to such an extent that the first overt motility and the first overt responses to sensory stimulation coincide in time. The probable facilitative (quantitative) contribution of early motility, whether spontaneous or evoked, to later motility or even to patterned movement is not known, but certainly such motility at the very least sculptures the joints and prevents muscular atrophy.

3. The sensory systems, particularly the somesthetic, vestibular, auditory, and visual, become functional in a regular order that holds for various species of mammals and birds. The contribution of early sensory function to later sensory function and perception has only begun to be investigated. Sensory systems as well as motor systems become functional while they are still anatomically, physiologically, and behaviorally immature. One of the more intriguing problems in behavioral embryology is that of determining the role of spontaneous and evoked function in the formative stages of neural maturation and behavioral development.

4. Finally, the notion that experience can play at least three rather different roles (maintenance, facilitation, induction) in the development of species-typical behavior and the nervous system is applicable to postnatal as well as prenatal development. Traditional forms of learning (habituation, conditioning, and the like) have not proven very useful in explaining the species-typical development of behavior, so it may be helpful to begin to formulate the contribution of experience to behavioral development in terms such as those that have been presented here.

REFERENCES

Bradley, R. M., and Mistretta, C. M. (1975). Fetal sensory receptors. *Physiological Reviews*, **55**, 352–382.

Cairns, R. B. (1976). Ontogeny and phylogeny of social interactions. In M. E. Hahn and E. C. Simmel (Eds.), *Communicative behavior and evolution*, Academic Press, New York.

Carmichael, L. (1926). The development of behavior in vertebrates experimentally removed from the influence of external stimulation. *Physiological Review*, **33**, 51–58.

Carmichael, L. (1934). An experimental study in the prenatal guinea-pig of the origin and development of reflexes and patterns of behavior in relation to the stimulation of specific receptor areas during the period of active fetal life. *Genetic Psychology Monographs*, **16**, 338–491.

Carmichael, L. (Ed.) (1954). *Manual of child psychology*, 2nd ed. Wiley, New York.

Coghill, G. E. (1929). *Anatomy and the problem of behavior*, Cambridge University Press, Cambridge.

Crain, S. M., Bornstein, M. B., and Peterson, E. R. (1968). Maturation of cultured embryonic CNS tissues during chronic exposure to agents which prevent bioelectric activity. *Brain Research*, **8**, 363–372.

Crowell, D. H. (1967). Infant Motor Development. In Y. Brackbill (Ed.), *Infancy and early childhood*, Free Press, New York.

Daniels, J. D., and Pettigrew, J. D. (1976). Development of neuronal responses in the visual system of cats. In G. Gottlieb (Ed.), *Development of neural and behavioral specificity*, Academic Press, New York.

Drachman, D. B., and Coulombre, A. J. (1962). Experimental clubfoot and arthrogryposis multiplex congenita, *Lancet*, **2**, 523–526.

Eayrs, J. T. (1968). Developmental relationships between brain and thyroid. In R. P. Michael (Ed.), *Endocrinology and human behavior*, Oxford University Press. London.

Eldred, E., Bridgman, C. F., Kano, M., Sasaki, Y., and Yellin, H. (1967), Changes in muscle spindle morphology and discharge with alterations in muscle status. In M. D. Yahr and D. P. Purpura (Eds). *Neurophysiological basis of normal and abnormal motor activities*, Raven Press, Hewlett, New York.

Foelix, R. F., and Oppenheim, R. W. (1973). Synaptogenesis in the avian embryo: Ultrastructure and possible behavioral correlates. In G. Gottlieb (Ed.), *Behavioral Embryology*, Academic Press, New York.

Fromme, A. (1941). An experimental study of the factors of maturation and practice in the behavioral development of the embryo of the frog, *Rana pipiens*. *Genetic Psychology Monographs*, **24**, 219–256.

Gesell, A. (1946). The ontogenesis of infant behavior. In L. Carmichael (Ed.), *Manual of child psychology*, Wiley, New York.

Gesell, A. (1954). The ontogenesis of infant behavior. In L. Carmichael (Ed.), *Manual of child psychology* 2nd ed. Wiley, New York.

Gottlieb, G. (1971a). Ontogenesis of sensory function in birds and mammals. In E. Tobach, L. R. Aronson, and E. Shaw (Eds.) *The biopsychology of development*, Academic Press, New York.

Gottlieb, G. (1971b). *Development of Species identification in birds*, University of Chicago Press, Chicago.

Gottlieb, G. (Ed.). (1973). *Behavioral Embryology*, Academic Press, New York.

Gottlieb, G. (1975a). Development of species identification in ducklings. I. Nature of perceptual deficit caused by embryonic auditory deprivation. *Journal of Comparative and Physiological Psychology*, **89**, 387–399.

Gottlieb, G. (1975b). Development of species identification in ducklings. II. Experiential prevention of perceptual deficit caused by embryonic auditory deprivation. *Journal of Comparative and Physiological Psychology*, **89**, 675–684.

Gottlieb, G. (1975c). Development of species identification in ducklings. III. Maturational rectification of perceptual deficit caused by auditory deprivation. *Journal of Comparative and Physiological Psychology*, **89**, 899–912.

Gottlieb, G. (1976). The roles of experience in the development of behavior and the nervous system. In G. Gottlieb (Ed.), *Development of neural and behavioral specificity*, Academic Press, New York.

Gottlieb, G., and Vandenbergh, J. G. (1968). Ontogeny of vocalization in duck and chick embryos. *Journal of Experimental Zoology*, **168**, 307–325.

Goy, R. W., Bridgson, W. E., and Young, W. C. (1964). Period of maximal susceptibility of the prenatal female guinea pig to masculinizing actions of testosterone propionate. *Journal of Comparative and Physiological Psychology*, **57**, 166–174.

Hamburger, V., Wenger, E., and Oppenheim, R. (1966). Motility in the chick embryo in the absence of sensory input. *Journal of Experimental Zoology*, **162**, 133–160.

Hamburgh, M. (1969). The role of thyroid and growth hormone in neurogenesis. In A.

Moscona and A. Monroy (Eds), *Current topics in developmental biology*, Vol. 4, Academic Press, New York.

Harth, M. S., and Heaton, M. B. (1973). Nonvisual photic responsiveness in newly hatched pigeons (*Columba livia*). *Science*, **180**, 753–755.

Heaton, M. B., and Harth, M. S. (1974). Developing visual function in the pigeon embryo with comparative reference to other avian species. *Journal of Comparative and Physiological Psychology*, **86**, 151–156.

Herrick, C. J., and Coghill, G. E. (1915). The development of reflex mechanisms in *Amblystoma*. *Journal of Comparative Neurology*, **25**, 65–85.

Hirsch, H. V. B., and Jacobson, M. (1975). The perfectible brain: Principles of neuronal development. In M. S. Gazzaniga and C. Blakemore (Eds), *Handbook of Psychobiology*, Academic Press, New York.

Hooker, D. (1952). *The prenatal origin of behavior*. University of Kansas Press, Lawrence, Kausas.

Humphrey, T. (1964). Some correlations between the appearance of human fetal reflexes and the development of the nervous system. In D. P. Purpura and J. P. Schadé (Eds), *Growth and maturation of brain*, Elsevier, Amsterdam.

Humphrey, T. (1970). Palatopharyngeal fusion in a human fetus and its relation to cleft palate formation. *Alabama Journal of Medical Sciences*, **7**, 398–426.

Impekoven, M. (1976). Prenatal parent–young interactions in birds and their long-term effects. In J. S. Rosenblatt, R. A. Hinde, E. Shaw, and C. G. Beer (Eds), *Advances in the study of behavior*, Vol. 7, Academic Press, New York. pp. 201–254.

Jaisson, P. (1975). L'impregnation dans l'ontogenese des comportements de soins aux cocons chez la jeune formi rousse (*Formica polyctena* Forst.). *Behavior*, **52**, 1–37.

Konishi, M. (1973). Development of auditory neuronal responses in avian embryos. *Proceedings of the National Academy of Science USA*, **70**, 1795–1798.

Kuo, Z.-Y. (1939). Studies in the physiology of the embryonic nervous system: II. Experimental evidence on the controversy over the reflex theory in development. *Journal of Comparative Neurology*, **70**, 437–459.

Kuo, Z.-Y. (1967). *The dynamics of behavior development*, Random House, New York.

Lauber, J. K., and Shutze, J. V. (1964). Accelerated growth of embryo chicks under the influence of light. *Growth*, **28**, 179–190.

Leiman, A. L., Seil, F. J., and Kelly, J. M. (1975). Maturation of electrical activity of cerebral neocortex in tissue culture. *Experimental Neurology*, **48**, 275–291.

Mason, W. A. (1968). Scope and potential of primate research. In J. H. Masserman (Ed.), *Science and psychoanalysis* (Vol. 12, *Animal and Human*), Grune and Stratton, New York.

McGraw, M. B. (1946). Maturation of behavior. In L. Carmichael (Ed.), *Manual of child psychology*, Wiley, New York.

Meyerson, B. A., and Persson, H. E. (1974). Early epigenesis of recipient functions in the neocortex. In G. Gottlieb (Ed.) *Aspects of neurogensis*, Academic Press, New York.

Model, P. G., Bornstein, M. B., Crain, S. M., and Pappas, G. D. (1971). An electron microscopic study of the development of synapses in cultured fetal mouse cerebrum continuously exposed to Xylocaine. *Journal of Cell Biology*, **49**, 362–371.

Nicholson, J. L., and Altman, J. (1972). Synaptogenesis in the rat cerebellum: Effects of hypo- and hyperthyroidism. *Science*, **176**, 530–531.

Nicolai, J. (1959). Familientradition in der Gesangsentwicklung des Gimpels (*Pyrrhula pyrrhula* L.). *Journal für Ornithologie*, **100**, 39–46.

O'Malley, B. W., and Means, A. R. (1974). Female steroid hormones and target cell nuclei. *Science*, **183**, 610–620.

Preyer, W. (1885). *Specielle Physiologie des Embryo*, Grieben, Leipzig.

Provine, R. R. (1976). Development of function in nerve nets. In J. Fentress (Ed.), *Simpler networks and behavior*, Sinauer, Sunderland, Mass.

Rubel, E. W., and Rosenthal, M. H. (1975). The ontogeny of auditory frequency generalization in the chicken, *Journal of Experimental Psychology: Animal Behavior Processes*, **1**, 287–297.

Sara, V. R., and Lazarus, L. (1974). Prenatal action of growth hormone on brain and behavior. *Nature*, **250**, 257–258.

Saunders, J. C., Coles, R. B., and Gates, G. R. (1973). The development of auditory evoked responses in the cochlea and cochlear nuclei of the chick. *Brain Research*, **63**, 59–74.

Schapiro, S., and Vukovich, K. R. (1970). Early experience effects upon cortical dendrites: A proposed model for development. *Science*, **167**, 292–294.

Schneirla, T. C. (1965). Aspects of stimulation and organization in approach/withdrawal processes underlying vertebrate behavioral development. In D. S. Lehrman, R. A. Hinde, and E. Shaw (Eds), *Advances in the study of Behavior*, Vol. 1, Academic Press, New York.

Stone, J. M., and Greenough, W. T. (1975). Excess neonatal thyroxine: Effects on learning in infants and adolescent rats. *Developmental Psychobiology*, **8**, 479–488.

Tees, R. C. (1974). Effect of visual deprivation on development of depth perception in the rat. *Journal of Comparative and Physiological Psychology*, **86**, 300–308.

Tracy, H. C. (1926). The development of motility and behavior reactions in the toadfish (*Opsanus tau*). *Journal of Comparative Neurology*, **40**, 253–369.

Vince, M. A. (1968). Retardation as a factor in the synchronization of hatching. *Animal Behaviour*, **18**, 332–335.

Vince, M. A. (1973). Some environmental effects on the activity and development of the avian embryo. In G. Gottlieb (Ed.), *Behavioral embryology*, Academic Press, New York.

Vince, M., Reader, M., and Tolhurst, B. (1976). Effects of stimulation on embryonic activity in the chick. *Journal of Comparative and Physiological Psychology*, **90**, 221–230.

Wiens, J. A. (1970). Effects on early experience on substrate pattern selection in *Rana aurora* tadpoles. *Copeia*, No. 3, 543–548.

Windle, W. F. (1944). Genesis of somatic motor function in mammalian embryos: A synthesizing article. *Physiological Zoology*, **17**, 247–260.

Woodward, D. J., Hoffer, B. J., and Lapham, L. W. (1969). Postnatal development of electrical and enzyme histochemical activity in Purkinje cells. *Experimental Neurology*, **23**, 120–139.

NOTES

1. The term *maturation* is used throughout this article to refer to neuroanatomical or neurophysiological development, or both.

2. The emphasis in this article is on behavior, so, strictly speaking, much of the ensuing discussion actually deals with function–function relations rather than structure–function relations. The latter are implied, however, even when the context is entirely functional. Namely, I assume that microscopic examination would reveal a structural correlate of a behavioral or physiological change. From the standpoint of behavioral development, however, an appreciation of function–function relationships is significant even if the structural counterpart is not identified.

3. A great number of neural cells die during neuroembryological development, so

cell death is now often added as another normal feature of neural maturation (e.g., Hirsch and Jacobson, 1975).

4. Thirty years ago, the developmental psychologist McGraw (1946) recognized that the structure–function relationship could very well be bidirectional in her study of the early motor development of the human infant. She stated: 'It seems fairly evident that certain structural changes take place prior to the onset of overt function; it seems equally evident that cessation of neurostructural development does not coincide with the onset of function. There is every reason to believe that when conditions are favorable function makes some contribution to further advancement in structural development of the nervous system. An influential factor in determining the structural development of one component may be the functioning of other structures which are interrelated' (McGraw, 1946, p. 363). As Crowell (1967) has pointed out, although McGraw did not work out a systematic theoretical position, her notions did moderate the more extreme interpretation of Gesell's (1946) 'maturational hypothesis' and thus were a step toward an appropriate resolution of the nature–nurture problem. In light of the importance of McGraw's conception and its probable correctness, it is interesting to note that McGraw's (1946) chapter was deleted from the second edition of Carmichael's *Manual of Child Psychology*, (1954), while Gesell's chapter (1946, 1954) was retained.

5. Since the high-frequency perceptual deficit is rectified at 48 hours, and the original muted ducklings failed to discriminate the mallard from the chicken maternal call at 48 hours, some other (unrectified) perceptual deficiency must still be present at 48 hours to account for the mute ducklings' deficient perceptual discrimination in the mallard-versus-chicken call test at that age (for example, insensitivity to frequency modulation and/or repetition rate differences). This problem is receiving active experimental attention.

Learning, Development, and Culture
Edited by H. C. Plotkin
© 1982, John Wiley & Sons Ltd.

CHAPTER 18

Rules and reciprocity in behavioural development

P. P. G. Bateson*

A major preoccupation in the study of behavioural development has been with what makes individuals different. Attempts to uncover sources of differences in behaviour have required an experimental approach and gave rise to techniques of great ingenuity and elegance. Ideally, any coordinated research programme ought to operate within a broad and coherent theoretical framework if the experimenting is not to become piecemeal or pedestrian. However, theories of behavioural development have not been strikingly coherent. It is possibly for this reason that much of the extensive evidence gathered on the subject appears to be fragmented into esoteric little pockets of knowledge.

As far as most experimenters are concerned, theory seems to be subservient to methodology at the moment. The characteristics of the workable theories are determined not so much by what is plausible as by what is most easily analysed. The theories offer useful if limited tactics but little in the way of an overall research strategy. It is not hard to think of reasons why this might have happened. The success of an experimental manipulation is conventionally judged in terms of whether it exerts an influence on the end state. If it does not, the experimenter is faced with the unprofitable task of proving a negative, and often the results are quickly forgotten. Inevitably this breeds a strong commitment to studying sources of positive differences in behaviour. Since the

---

* Reprinted from P. P. G. Bateson and R. A. Hinde (Eds), *Growing Points in Ethology*, 1976, pp. 401–421, by permission of the author and Cambridge University Press. Copyright © 1976 Cambridge University Press.

sources which are most easily manipulated are those external to the animal, it is hardly surprising that the principal current theories of behavioural development make a virtue of experimental convenience and place as much as possible of the control outside the animal in its environment.

It would be quite wrong to present existing ontogenetic theories as simple-minded or unsubtle. The thinking of Schneirla (1965), for example, was complex and rich. Nevertheless, in his developmental theory the underlying assumption was that, to begin with at least, the developing animal is essentially reactive, even though he postulated considerable intrinsic constraints on responsiveness. Initially, environmental conditions are held to change the young animal's behaviour, which in turn changes the animal's relation to its environment. The new stimuli from the environment produce fresh changes in behaviour and so on in chain-like fashion. This account oversimplifies a complex argument but does not misrepresent its spirit, which is to reduce to a minimum the number of postulated internal processes on which development depends. The emphasis is placed squarely on the interactions taking place between the animal and its environment. My purpose is not to discredit views which, I shall argue, have an important part to play in understanding the complex mediating role of the animal's environment in its behavioural development. Nevertheless, I believe that the relentless hunt for yet further external sources of individual variation, and the shyness of accepting substantial internal control over developmental processes, have led to a certain sterility of thinking and an incapacity to comprehend more than a small fraction of the rapidly accumulating data.

The complexity of the evidence and the lack of useful explanatory principles may, of course, be something we simply have to live with. Instead of modelling ourselves on classical physicists in search of unifying principles, we may have to treat the subject like a classical chemist and hunt for the equivalent of a Periodic table. However, the apparent conceptual difficulties presented by masses of seemingly unrelated evidence may also arise from the tight focus which experimental analysis so often requires. There may well be a case for softening the focus or, better still, changing to a lower magnification. To use a different metaphor, maybe vision outside the wood will no longer be cluttered by the tangled undergrowth of endless interactions.

Other views of behavioural development do, of course, exist. But they often consist of nothing more than vague appeals to fashionable technologies. The patterning of development is attributed, for example, to 'internal programming' without any indication being given of what the programme might be like and what precisely is being controlled. Nevertheless, the intuition lying behind such points of view may be right. Furthermore, apposite analogies may be drawn not only from machine intelligence but also from other areas of biology. Certainly, the embryologists have accepted the need to postulate considerable internal regulation of development, and the relevance of some of their concepts to the work on behavioural development has, over the years, become increasingly apparent (see for example Gesell, 1954, and Oppenheim, 1974). The first part of this chapter is devoted, therefore, to examining in some detail an idea from embryology used to explain self-stabilising developmental pathways. The second half of the chapter attempts to relate the idea about guided and buffered systems governed by rules back to the evidence on the reciprocity between the developing animal and its environment.

MODELS FOR THE CONTROL OF DEVELOPMENT

In a delightful visual aid to the biologist who has difficulty in grasping the abstractions of a purely mathematical model, Waddington (1957) represented the development of a particular part of a fertilised egg as a ball rolling down a tilted plane which is increasingly furrowed by valleys (Figure 1). He called the surface down which the ball rolls the 'epigenetic landscape'. For present purposes it is not necessary to be concerned with the embryological analogue of gravity which draws the ball downwards in the model; nor is it necessary to bother with the precise conditions that make the ball go down one valley rather than another. The essential point is that the mounting constraints on the way tissue can develop are pictured by the increasing restriction on the sideways movement of the ball as it rolls towards the front lower edge of the landscape. The landscape represents, therefore, the mechanisms that regulate

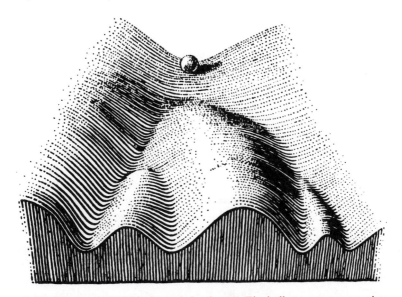

Figure 1 Waddington's (1957) epigenetic landscape. The ball represents some tissue at an early stage in ontogeny. Development is represented by the ball descending through the landscape. The mechanisms regulating development are represented by the position and shape of the valleys

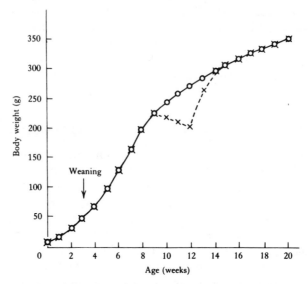

Figure 2 The gain in weight of normal rats is shown by the solid line. The dotted line shows the weights of rats which were undernourished from 9–12 weeks. (From McCance, 1962. Reproduced by permission of *The Lancet*)

development. Waddington's model is attractive to the visually minded because it provides a way of thinking about developmental pathways and the astonishing capacity of the developing system to right itself after a perturbation and return to its former track. To take a specific example from post-embryonic development, if a juvenile rat is starved during its development, its weight curve falls off while it is being deprived (Figure 2). When it is put back onto a normal diet, its weight curve rapidly picks up and rejoins the curve of the rat that has not been deprived (McCance, 1962). Similar examples of growth spurts after illness are well known in humans (e.g., Prader, Tanner, and Von Harnack, 1963). For the moment the possibility that the individuals showing the catching-up phenomenon may differ in undetected ways from normal individuals can be ignored. The prime question is how weight-gain is controlled and two individuals with quite different histories end up weighing the same.

The systems theorists in general, and von Bertalanffy (1968) in particular, have laid considerable emphasis on the self-correcting features of development, and have called the convergence of different routes on the same steady state 'equifinality'. While it is easy to become a little mystical about this (and von Bertalanffy did not always resist the temptation), Waddington's model immediately suggests a way of handling 'equifinality'. If the ball rolling down the epigenetic landscape encounters an obstacle in one of the valleys and is not

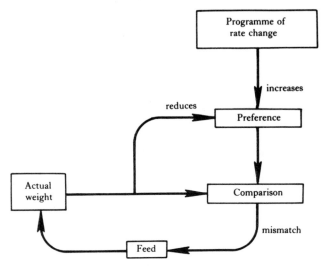

Figure 3 A model for weight control in the developing rat. The actual weight has no influence on the preference unless the discrepancy between actual and preferred weights is more than a predetermined amount

stopped dead, it would ride up round the obstacle and fall back into the valley down which it had been rolling.

Waddington's model is, of course, informal and he would have been the first to point to its limitations. Nevertheless it is not difficult to simulate with greater rigour a system which compensates for short periods of food deprivation during development. If the amount of food which the animal attempts to eat is determined by a comparison between a predetermined setting and the actual weight of the animal and if the value of the preferred weight is increased as the animal ages (see Figure 3), something very similar to the data shown in Figure 2 can be obtained. To make things more realistic the predetermined increments in the preferred value first increase and then decrease as the hypothetical animal gets older. As a consequence the weight curve of the undeprived animal is sigmoid. Furthermore, an upper limit is set on how much the model rat can eat at any one time and small periodic decrements in weight are imposed to simulate the costs of metabolism. When all this is done, the performance of the model can be readily simulated on a computer (see top line in Figure 4 and also the results of a rather similar negative feedback model proposed by Weiss and Kavanau in 1957).

It is important not to gloss over a significant feature of this model. By arranging for the preferred value of the closed feedback loop to be changed according to some predetermined plan, the system has been opened up. In the

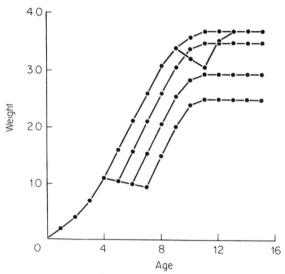

Figure 4 Results of a computer simulation of the model shown in Figure 3 showing the interaction between environmental conditions and the predetermined programme for the rate of weight gain. At Age 9 some hypothetical rats were deprived of food for 2 units of age; when allowed to feed again their weight returned to the normal value. Three other groups or rats were deprived of food at Age 4 for 1, 2 or 3 units of age. The longer the period of deprivation the greater the reduction of adult weight

simplest case the developmental process is essentially ballistic—its pathway is determined in advance and does not depend on a dynamic interaction between the system and other factors which might change during the course of development. The model can, of course, be elaborated so that the preferred weight is modifiable by environmental conditions, and I shall consider a few of the possible elaborations later. This model is not presented in the service of analysing the detailed mechanisms by which rats regulate their weight during development. In all probability such mechanisms are diffuse; possibly the change in 'preferred value' may be mediated indirectly by an increase in the size of the body; and many other factors may be involved besides those included in my model. None of this matters. At this stage the major point I wish to establish is that even rather simple models can account for different developmental routes leading to precisely the same steady state. The phenomena, which were so entrancing to an old-fashioned vitalist, do not pose inordinate conceptual problems.

I now wish to examine how the models based on the development of body tissue may be extended to the ontogeny of behaviour. I cannot claim to be the first to do this. Piaget, among others, has been concerned with the general issue of autoregulation for many years. In particular he has attempted to relate the ideas of thinkers such as Waddington and von Bertalanffy to behavioural development (Piaget, 1967)

EQUIFINALITY IN BEHAVIOURAL DEVELOPMENT

Children differ astonishingly in the age at which language development begins. Some may begin before the end of their first year and others may not utter a recognisable word until they are three or more. Furthermore, during acquisition, styles of forming word patterns may be markedly different. Despite these enormous differences it is remarkably difficult to pick out the early developers when the children are older (Nelson, 1973). Put very cautiously, behaviour at one stage of development is an exceedingly poor predictor of behaviour at another. More boldly one could argue that a child which has been initially slow to develop can demonstrate the catch-up effect seen in tissue growth and reach roughly the same steady state in one aspect of language ability as a much more precocious child.

The example from language development can be matched by many others from child development (see Dunn, 1976), but it is sufficient to demonstrate not only the advantages but also the difficulties of employing the concept of equifinality in developmental studies of behaviour. For any definitions of steady state presuppose an adequate measure of change in that state and an ability to calculate its rate; a steady state is achieved when the rate of change approaches zero. Changes in behaviour patterns pose formidable methodological problems for this kind of analysis, and so do the taxonomic and philosophical problems of specifying when two steady states are the same (which is required if the concept of equifinality is to be of any use). Even with adequate measures, how can one be sure that the absences of differences are not caused by ceiling effects on the scale of measurement? Above all, the level of description of the steady state is critically important (see Hinde and Stevenson-Hinde, 1976). In the example of language development, it is obviously untrue that the words uttered by an adult French person are the same as those made by an adult English person. If one is to talk about equifinality in language development one must be thinking about some quality of language that is more universal and more abstract than the detailed sounds people make. Finally the concept of equifinality can mislead in two distinct ways. First, it can falsely imply that a steady state can only be achieved by a goal-directed system—a steady population size could for example be achieved when births and immigration were balanced by deaths and emigration. Secondly, a steady state may not be the 'final state'; appreciation that a steady state may be followed by one or more periods of rapid change is especially important in the study of development. In any event the final state is presumably death.

Despite these very considerable practical and philosophical difficulties, achieving equifinality in behavioural development does not pose insuperable problems of principle. The parts of the model used to account for the control of weight can be readily adapted to behavioural examples. The preferred value against which the actual state is compared can be for, say, the proprioceptive feedback from a certain action or, at another level, the feedback provided by the behaviour of a parent (see for example Bowlby, 1969; Bischof, 1975). The justification for thinking in these terms is that it provides a different perspective from the more conventional interactional approach and suggests new ways of looking at the data. It makes sense of experimental studies in which a manipulation may produce obvious short-term effects on behaviour but have no apparent lasting influences (see Dunn, 1976).

Even the simple model which I have proposed so far could, with a few embellishments, lead to marked differences in the pattern of development even though the final outcome was the same. Just as two rats with different food preferences can put on weight at the same rate, so different types of action can lead to the same behavioural end-point. A feature of a system dependent for its control on feedback is that it need not be fussy about how a match between the actual value and the preferred value is achieved. It is the consequences of an action that count not the precise form and patterning of that action. Admittedly possible courses of action may be so constrained that the system is likely to do only one thing when a mismatch between the actual state and the preferred value is detected—such as an electric fire controlled by a thermostat. However, the constraints need not be so great. A remarkable illustration is given by Hoyle (1964, 1970), who found that quite different combinations of muscles in a locust's leg could contract to produce the same overall movement of the leg—the offered explanation being that movement is controlled by means of sensory feedback.

Although a considerable number of possible courses of action may be available to the animal, it may come to repeat the one it performed first, either by a process akin to 'functional validation' (Jacobson, 1969), or by conventional reinforcement when a match between the preferred and actual values is achieved. For reasons which were initially determined by chance or by local peculiarities of its environment, an animal may adopt an individually distinctive style in order to reach the same goal as other members of its species. A possible illustration of this comes from experimental work originally done by Vicari (1929) and re-analysed by Broadhurst and Jinks (1963). Vicari showed that in the early stages of learning to run through a maze, heritability of performance in the maze from one generation of mice to the next was low. However, heritability rose steadily as the mice were given more trials in the maze (see also Manning, 1976). One interpretation of these data is that, because the number of options initially open to the mice was relatively large, environmental conditions were important during the development of a solution to the task but were much less influential on the final performance, which was probably limited by such factors as speed of movement.

Different routes to the same goal may be achieved even more dramatically than in the cases already considered if the young animal is equipped with two or more alternative systems controlling development of the same pattern of behaviour. Redundancy of this kind is common enough in man-made machines when lives are at stake, as in a space capsule. Clearly redundant developmental systems could be highly adaptive for an animal, particularly if the alternative control systems were suited to different environmental conditions to which they were appropriate—the provision of special horses for particular courses. The provision of other systems protects against failure, and from time to time animals must be faced with the situation where no amount of tactical manoeuvring will enable one of their developing systems to proceed along a particular route. Such an animal is a bit like a traveller who arrives at a station only to find that the trains have been cancelled. He can still reach his destination but only by choosing a quite different method of getting there.

If contingency arrangements of this kind have been selected during evolution, Waddington's epigenetic landscape would have to be redrawn so that some valleys ran together again. It could, of course, be argued that a ball that had descended by one valley had had a different history from one that had descended by another so that even though the balls ended up in the same place, the concept of equifinality was valueless. The importance of this objection would depend on whether the different histories did indeed leave distinctive traces on the metaphorical ball. Even if they did, the objection might still not be serious since the resulting differences might be biologically trivial by comparison with the ultimate similarities.

A particularly interesting example of descriptively different developmental pathways to the same pattern of adult behaviour has been given me by Peter Marler and Mark Konishi (personal communication). Isolated white-crowned sparrows (*Zonotrichia leucophrys*) were treated in one of two ways. One group were trained during the sensitive period for song development with the typical song produced by an adult white-crowned sparrow reared in isolation (Marler, 1970). The other group were not trained. The trained group progressed rapidly from sub-song to a 'plastic' song with one theme which crystallised into the typical isolate song. The untrained birds showed a slow and variable progression from sub-song to plastic song which had several themes. Finally, however, the plastic song of the untrained birds crystallised into the typical isolate song. This may provide an example of independent developmental control mechanisms coming into operation under different environmental conditions. Much as I would like to argue for this interpretation, I am inclined to think that the experiments reveal something about the ontogeny of a single underlying mechanism regulating the development of song.

In other contexts, inputs which may be relatively non-specific are frequently required to facilitate the development of particular systems (Bateson, 1976). The inputs may be provided by external environmental conditions or by feedback from the animal's activities such as its own vocalisation (e.g. Gottlieb, 1971). Now, as Marler (1970) argues, it seems highly plausible that the white-crowned sparrow learns to produce a song by matching feedback from its own vocal output against a preferred 'template'. The development of that template may be facilitated by external input, as was the case in the trained birds; and subsequent song development would then occur smoothly. On this view, the untrained birds would have found comparison of their vocal output with their template difficult because the template was comparatively ill-formed. As a result their output would, indeed, have been variable. Later, when feedback from their own sub-song and plastic song had had the same effects on the developing template as those of external training, the untrained song sparrows would catch up the trained birds and ultimately produce a single song.

It may not yet be possible to give a clear instance where different developmental control mechanisms generate the same behavioural end-product. Nevertheless, this could well be an area where good cases will emerge once we start to look out for them.

RULES FOR CHANGING RULES

Up to this point I have implicitly set in opposition the two views of development presented by the interaction theorists on the one hand and the control theorists on the other. However, I believe that if the subject is to progress satisfactorily some synthesis must be achieved between them. I do not merely mean that a trivial compromise should be worked out whereby it is admitted that some patterns of behaviour develop totally as a consequence of interactions between the animal and its environment and others are the products of predetermined, self-correcting developmental processes.

It is already clear that, even with the highly predetermined models which I have been discussing, distinctive styles of individual development could be selected or even induced by particular environmental conditions. This implies a certain interacting relationship between the developing animal and its environment. I now want to consider the possibility that many developmental control mechanisms are themselves modifiable by the environmental conditions in which the animal grows up.

Before giving the first example it may be useful to distinguish between the *development of behaviour* and *behaviour used in development* (cf. Hinde, 1959, on evolution). The biological function of some of the behavioural mechanisms found in many developing animals, particularly higher vertebrates, seems to be the gathering of information. Their predispositions to learn the characteristics of certain things can be highly specific (see Hinde and Stevenson-Hinde, 1973). Such proclivity can be extremely important in directing the course of development. A good example is provided by the behaviour which young precocial birds normally direct towards their parents. This example also illustrates the more general point about the modifiability of control mechanisms.

When a day-old domestic chick is removed from a dark incubator where it hatched and is placed in a plain environment, it soon starts to walk about and emit piercing calls. If a visually conspicuous object, particularly something resembling the size, shape and colour of an adult hen, is presented to the chick, its behaviour changes dramatically. The disorientated movements stop and the piercing peeps are replaced by soft twittering calls. The bird orientates towards and approaches the object. It is difficult (and probably unnecessary) to avoid the anthropomorphic impression that the chick is happier. Indeed, if the chick is placed in a situation in which the presentation of the visually conspicuous object depends on the bird performing a particular act such as pressing a pedal, the bird learns with astonishing rapidity to press the pedal (Bateson and Reese, 1968, 1969). The object can evidently be used as a reward for the animal and as a means of strengthening arbitrarily selected activities. The control of the bird's behaviour can be interpreted in terms of the model shown in Figure 5. The preferred setting consists of some broad representation of visually conspicuous objects. This is matched against incoming visual input. A mismatch leads to behaviour which, in a natural situation at any rate, increases the chances of the bird encountering something more appropriate. By scanning and moving around, it is more likely to encounter its mother than if it stood stock still and, of course, the piercing calls cause the mother to emit calls herself and move towards the chick. In terms of the model, a match terminates all this and allows the chick to change its behaviour to that of approaching the stimulus achieving the match. This brings the chick underneath, or at least close to, the mother or her substitute. A match also has another effect which is crucial to

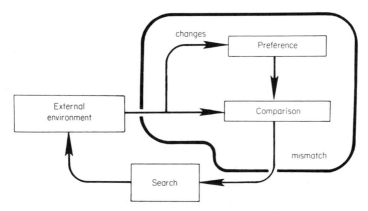

Figure 5 A model for imprinting in which the preferred value in the negative feedback loop is changed by the input from the external environment

the development of the chick's behaviour. Before a chick has seen a conspicuous object, any one of a large number of different things will be effective. However, after being exposed to one of those objects, a bird will increasingly tend to scan for that object in preference to all others. The process which restricts the bird's preferences to an object which is familiar is, of course, known as 'imprinting'. Its relevance to the argument is that, in as much as the closed-loop model for behaviour in development is justified, the model has to incorporate a self-organising principle. When a match is achieved the preferred setting is more tightly specified so as to correspond in greater detail to a representation of the particular object which achieved that match. After modification the control loop will maintain 'searching' until something resembling the familiar object is encountered.

A single rule for changing the characteristics of the control system is probably not enough to account for the developing chick's behaviour in relation to its mother (or the flashing light, moving box or whatever else is substituting for her). Since the mother in back view presents physically quite different stimuli to the young than she does in front view, it is probably necessary for the young to acquaint themselves with those different views. Considerable evidence now suggests that the young chicks do indeed prefer and work for slight novelty having learned some of the characteristics of one object (Bateson, 1973a; Jackson and Bateson, 1974; Bateson and Jaeckel, 1976). I have suggested elsewhere ways in which the chicks might narrow down their preferences to familiar objects while at the same time showing a preference for slight novelty (Bateson, 1973a, b). This mechanism coupled with a means for classifying together stimuli which have been encountered in the same temporal context (see Bateson and Chantrey, 1972; Chantrey, 1972, 1974) provides the animal with a powerful yet flexible way of developing constancies within a perceptual category such as 'mother'. It must be emphasised that such mechanisms add to but do not substantially alter the model for a self-modifying system whose eventual steady-state is determined by environmental conditions.

Another kind of modification dependent on environmental conditions is suggested by the stunting obtained if animals or humans are starved for long enough during development. The simple model which I have already used for the control of weight can be readily adapted to cope with such evidence by making the extent of the increments in preferred weight dependent on the difference between the preferred weight and the actual weight (see Figure 3). If the discrepancy is large the increment in preferred weight is less than if the discrepancy is small (see Figure 4). This one rule, which could be specified in advance, would greatly enhance the dynamic interaction with the environment. It would have one interesting consequence which would be particularly striking if the normal growth curve were sigmoid with the period of maximum growth occurring mid-way through development. The stunting effects of starvation would be particularly marked at times of rapid growth. As can be seen from

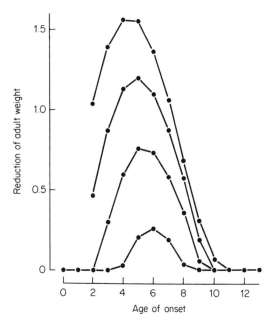

Figure 6 The reduction of adult weight of hypothetical rats deprived of food for varying amounts of time (1–4 units of age) at different ages. All units are arbitrary. The data are derived from a computer simulation of the model shown in Figure 3

Figure 6 this would give rise to periods in development when the animal was especially vulnerable to environmental disturbance. The biological advantage of a rule which allows for a change in the preferred value is that the animal does not endlessly attempt to reach a state which may never by achievable in the particular conditions in which it is developing. Deprivation of optimal conditions for one system does not necessarily imply that conditions are bad all round and normal development of the animal's other systems may still be possible. Although the animal may be handicapped, its chances of surviving and leaving offspring may not be reduced to nothing.

One behavioural example of settling for less than the best may be provided by the nest-site selection of the blue-tit (*Parus caeruleus*). Hinde (1952) found that in the spring the tits would visit a large variety of crannies many of which were obviously unsuitable. One way of interpreting their behaviour would be that, if the actual site did not match up to the characteristics of an optimal nest-site, they kept searching—to begin with at least. However, if optimal sites were unavailable or already occupied, the birds would ultimately nest in places which they had previously rejected. It would make good sense if they were equipped with a rule for gradually relaxing the conditions under which searching for a nest-site was brought to an end and nest-building began. It may seem like a glimpse of the obvious that, metaphorically speaking, a starving man is not fussy about what he eats. Nevertheless, the relevance of the blue-tit example to a discussion of development is that once the bird has selected a sub-optimal site it will, for that breeding season at least, presumably prefer it even if an optimal site should subsequently become available.

It may prove particularly profitable to examine the modification of preferred values in the context of emerging social relationships. Suppose that it is important for the maintenance of a relationship between two individuals that they both have the same general pattern of behaviour—the same activity rhythm, for example. Now in the early stages of a relationship, differences in pattern might well exist but these might reflect nothing more than the relatively unimportant peculiarities of personal history. Without cost it might be possible for one or both of them to change their preferred patterns. One simple way of doing this is shown in Figure 7. The idea is that if a pattern of behaviour is achieved by comparison with a preferred standard, that same standard could also be used for judging a companion's behaviour. What is central to this argument, A's standard could be changed by B's and vice versa. As the model is shown in Figure 7 any mismatch would immediately lead to the individuals breaking-off contact with each other. It would, therefore, be necessary to provide for a mechanism which would, in the early stages of a developing relationship,

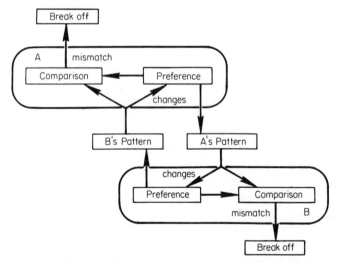

Figure 7 A model for the meshing of behaviour of two interacting animals. An animal's preferred value determines not only its own pattern of behaviour but also provides the standard by which it judges the behaviour of its partner. As the model is shown, a mismatch will lead to a break-off in the relationship. But if that is prevented, each animal's preferred value may be modified so that it resembles more closely that of its companion

over-ride or inhibit the consequence of a mismatch. For example, two individuals might be drawn together by the physical appearance of the other. During the 'honeymoon' period the relatively subtle differences of behaviour would be ignored. It would only be later, when the effects of physical appearances had started to wane that a mismatch of behaviour would become important and lead to a disruption of the relationship. But in the intervening period one or both of the individuals could have changed its pattern of behaviour so as to correspond to that of the other. Of course, the flexibility of an animal might be constrained by some social roles and facilitated by others.

An example of the behavioural meshing I have in mind could be the relationship that develops between mother and infant rhesus monkeys (*Macaca mulatta*) described by Hinde and Simpson (1975). Simpson had been able to measure independently when the mother left her infant and when the infant left its mother. In some pairs the probability that the mother would leave the infant at any particular moment after they had come together was closely related to the probability that the infant would leave the mother. Such meshing could, of course, be obtained in a variety of ways. For example, the two individuals might become highly sensitive to the immediate cues provided by their partner. However, the model proposed here makes a useful prediction. If other things are equal and if apparent plasticity of preference is not merely elasticity, then the pattern of behaviour should be maintained for some time in the absence of the particular partner with which the pattern developed.

I have only touched on a few ways in which a mechanism controlling behaviour could be modified by the social and physical environment. It is possible to think of many others and I have not even attempted a classification of such possibilities. Instead I have simply tried to draw attention to one way of thinking about the development of behaviour. The relevance of postulating rules to change rules to my general argument is that it provides a major and, I believe, fruitful point of contact between the control theorists and those who emphasise the plasticity of behaviour.

THE DEVELOPMENT AND COORDINATION OF RULES

An objection to the explanation for behavioural development which I have presented here is that is seems to be heading for an infinite regress with rules for changing the rules that change the rules and so on. Ultimately one must ask how the starting rules developed in the first place. While the issue ought not to be evaded, it need not necessarily be the immediate concern of somebody whose major research interests and competence lie at the behavioural level. If the models postulated here have some validity, the nexus of events necessary for the development of the starting rules required by the models may be largely cellular and beyond analysis at the level of the whole animal. Models of development embodying certain rules can perform a useful service in integrating evidence and offering certain predictions without ever explaining how those rules came about. But having made that disclaimer, I should not want to shovel all responsibilities for analysis of the early stages of ontogeny onto the developmental neurobiologists. Even this work may have a 'whole animal' component to it in as much as a rule governing behaviour has been selected during evolution for its adaptive outcome rather than its cellular origins. So long as the rule reliably develops in the individual, one presumes that natural selection is indifferent to how that came about. The selection may have taken place when certain environmental conditions were invariant and successful ontogeny may depend on the maintenance of those conditions. If they are changed for whatever reason (experimental, social), development may be disrupted. Knowledge of such disruption (however non-specific) is relevant to an understanding of the mechanisms involved in development (Bateson, 1976). My guess is, though, that major advances will not be made here without detailed knowledge of the cellular machinery and I prefer to focus attention on the later stages of development where behavioural evidence is likely to make most impact.

If internal mechanisms have developed, by some means or another, to control later stages of behavioural ontogeny, one would expect a considerable degree of coordination to exist between different mechanisms. For example, the rates of development of two patterns of behaviour may be independently influenced by interactions with the environment and it may be important that the development of one does not outrun the development of the other. Alternatively the order in which behaviour patterns develop may be important; for example, exploration of the environment may be disastrous if it occurs before the young animal has established some standards of what is familiar. In such cases acquisition of information must precede performance. This is particularly obvious in the development of complex motor patterns such as those used in bird song (see Marler, 1970; Marler and Mundinger, 1971). If the song is to be finely tuned to match some predetermined pattern (which may or may not be learned), feedback from the performance must be compared with the preferred value. Once a motor pattern producing the appropriate feedback has been established dependence on feedback can be reduced or even eliminated and the animal can accelerate the output rate. This is a bit like a musician learning a new part. While he has to monitor the individual sounds he is making to ensure their accuracy he must allow at least 100 msec between each note. However, in the final performance when such control is no longer needed, the gaps between notes can be greatly reduced to 50 msec or less (see Lashley, 1951).

The implication of examples such as these is that when certain conditions have been satisfied, new mechanisms of control can be brought into operation. In self-modifying systems, for instance, the conditions necessary for progressing to the next stage of development could be the levelling-off of modification—in other words the achievement of a steady state. This type of explanation would side-step an unprofitable debate about the precise chronology of developmental stages (see for example Hutt's (1973) discussion of sensitive periods). It would focus attention on the environmental conditions and on the state of the animal associated with a transition from one stage of development to the next rather than on age as such.

A great deal more can be said about the interactions between mechanisms controlling different aspects of behaviour (cf. Fentress, 1976). For the moment, I just want to add one point. Such interlocking systems, far from providing yet another way to complicate the lives of those investigating development, could be usefully harnessed for research purposes. Control mechanisms which are not directly influenced by environmental conditions may nevertheless be linked to control mechanisms that are. It may therefore be possible to gain access to the first by manipulating the second.

CONCLUSION

At the beginning of this chapter I argued that recent experimental work on the development of behaviour had been dominated by a view that admitted little in the way of internal regulation. The developing animal has been treated as though it were a billiard ball whose path is the resultant of the various external forces that acted on it. Consequently such organisation and patterning in development as has been recognised has usually been attributed to invariant features of the environment rather than to any kind of internal control.

The problem with this position is not so much that it tends to play down the development of behaviour patterns which are buffered against environmental influence but that it offers no clear strategy as to how research on the relatively labile systems should proceed. What is needed is not a comfortable compromise between two extreme theoretical view-points whereby it is admitted that some behaviour is stable and some is not. The need is for a theoretical framework that encompasses the different ways in which behaviour develops. I cannot claim to have done that but I have attempted to marry two points of view which have sometimes seemed incompatible. I have tried to show that, far from being irreconcilable, the approaches of theorists interested in interactions and those interested in control mechanisms usefully complement each other. A failure to show that some experimental manipulation of the environment has long-term effects on behaviour is not a reason for despair. It may be a useful pointer to a self-correcting feature of the underlying processes. Conversely, a developmental control mechanism whose preferred value drifts should not be dismissed as an irritating example of variability in biological material. Instead, the environmental conditions in which those drifts take place should be closely scrutinised since the modification in preferred value may have some obvious functional significance. In brief, I wish to argue that the development of behaviour very often requires internal rules for its guidance but that reciprocity between the animal and its environment is also needed in order to give those rules greater flexibility and definition.

SUMMARY

Two seemingly incompatible views of behavioural development are outlined. The dominant view in recent years has been that an adult's behaviour is the product of continuous interaction between the individual and its environment throughout ontogeny; the analytical task is seen, therefore, as uncovering the sources of individual differences by close examination of those interactions. An alternative view, much less common in studies of behavioural development, emphasises the predetermined, self-correcting features of developmental processes; this places emphasis on control systems which allow the same steady state in the adult to be reached by apparently different developmental routes. I argue that this second approach provides some valuable perspective in the study of behavioural ontogeny because it offers coherent principles by which development might be regulated. This perspective can, however, be easily reconciled with the interactionists' point of view and I go on to consider some simple ways in which it is possible to bring together the seemingly opposed positions. For example, plasticity in response to different environmental conditions may often usefully reside in those mechanisms that determine action by matching actual input values with preferred values. The main point is that if animals have rules by which their behaviour is controlled, functional reciprocity between the developing animal and its environment can be usefully achieved by equipping the animal with rules for changing the rules.

REFERENCES

Bateson, P. P. G. (1973a). Internal influences on early learning in birds. In R. A. Hinde and J. Stevenson-Hinde (Eds), *Constraints on Learning: Limitations and Predispositions*, Academic Press: London and New York, pp. 101–116.

Bateson, P. P. G. (1973b). Preference for familiarity and novelty: a model for the simultaneous development of both. *Journal of theoretical Biology*, **41**, 249–259.

Bateson, P. P. G. (1976). Specificity and the origins of behaviour. *Advances in the Study of Behavior*, **6**, 1–20.

Bateson, P. P. G., and Chantrey, D. F. (1972). Retardation of discrimination learning in monkeys and chicks previously exposed to both stimuli. *Nature, London*, **237**, 173–174.

Bateson, P. P. G., and Jaeckel, J. (1976). Chicks' preferences for familiar and novel conspicuous objects after different periods of exposure. *Animal Behaviour*, **24**, 386–390.

Bateson, P. P. G., and Reese, E. P. (1968). Reinforcing properties of conspicuous objects before imprinting has occurred. *Psychonomic Science*, **10**, 379–380.

Bateson, P. P. G., and Reese, E. P. (1969). The reinforcing properties of conspicuous stimuli in the imprinting situation. *Animal Behaviour*, **17**, 692–699.

Bertalanffy, L. von (1968). *General System Theory*, Braziller, New York.

Bischof, N. (1975). A systems approach towards the functional connections of attachment and fear. *Child Development*, **46**, 801–817.

Bowlby, J. (1969). *Attachment*, Hogarth Press, London.

Broadhurst, P. L., and Jinks, J. L. (1963). The inheritance of mammalian behavior re-examined. *Journal of Heredity*, **54**, 170–176.

Chantrey, D. F. (1972). Enhancement and retardation of discrimination learning in chicks after exposure to the discriminanda. *Journal of comparative and physiological Psychology*, **81**, 256–261.

Chantrey, D. F. (1974). Stimulus pre-exposure and discrimination learning by domestic chicks: effect of varying inter-stimulus time. *Journal of comparative and physiological Psychology*, **87**, 517–525.

Dunn, J. (1976). How far do early differences in mother–child relations affect later development. In P. P. G. Bateson and R. A. Hinde (Eds), *Growing Points in Ethology*, Cambridge University Press, Cambridge. pp. 481–496.

Fentress, J. C. (1976). Dynamic boundaries of patterned behaviour. In P. P. G. Bateson and R. A. Hinde (Eds), *Growing Points in Ethology*, Cambridge University Press, Cambridge. pp. 135–170.

Gesell, A. L. (1954). The ontogenesis of infant behavior. In L. Carmichael (Ed.), *Manual of Child Psychology*, Wiley, New York. pp. 335–373.

Gottlieb, G. (1971). *Development of Species Identification in Birds*, University of Chicago Press, Chicago.

Hinde, R. A. (1952). The behaviour of the Great Tit (*Parus major*) and some other related species. *Behaviour Supplement*, **2**, 1–201.

Hinde, R. A. (1959). Behaviour and speciation in birds and lower vertebrates. *Biological Reviews*, **34**, 85–128.

Hinde, R. A., and Simpson, M. J. A. (1975). Qualities of mother–infant relationships in monkeys. In *Parent–Infant Interaction*, Ciba Foundation Symposium, Vol. 33, Elsevier, Amsterdam, pp. 39-67.

Hinde, R. A., and Stevenson-Hinde, J., (Ed.) (1973). *Constraints on Learning: Limitations and Predisposition*, Academic Press, London and New York.

Hinde, R. A., and Stevenson-Hinde, J. (1976). Towards understanding relationships: dynamic stability. In P. P. G. Bateson and R. A. Hinde (Eds), *Growing Points in Ethology*, Cambridge University Press, Cambridge. pp. 451–480.

Hoyle, G. (1964). Exploration of neuronal mechanisms underlying behaviour in insects. In R. F. Reiss (Ed.), *Neural Theory and Modelling*, Stanford University Press, Stanford. pp. 346–376.

Hoyle, G. (1970). Cellular mechanisms underlying behaviour—neuroethology. *Advances in Insect Physiology*, **7**, 349–444.

Hutt, S. J. (1973). Constraints upon learning: some developmental considerations. In R. A. Hinde and J. Stevenson-Hinde (Eds), *Constraints on Learning: Limitations and Predispositions*, Academic Press, London and New York. pp. 457-467.

Jackson, P. S., and Bateson, P. P. G. (1974). Imprinting and exploration of slight novelty in chicks. *Nature, London*, **251**, 609–610.

Jacobson, M. (1969). Development of specific neuronal connections. *Science, Washington*, **163**, 543–547.

Lashley, K. S. (1951). The problem of serial order in behavior. In L. A. Jeffries (Ed.), *Cerebral Mechanisms in Behavior*, Wiley, New York. pp. 112–136.

Marler, P. (1970). A comparative approach to vocal learning: Song development in white-crowned sparrows. *Journal of comparative physiological Psychology Monographs*, **71**, 1–25.

Marler, P., and Mundinger, P. (1971). Vocal learning in birds. In H. Moltz (Ed.), *The Ontogeny of Vertebrate Behavior*, Academic Press, New York. pp. 389–450.

Manning, A. (1976). The place of genetics in the study of behaviour. In P. P. G. Bateson and R. A. Hinde (Eds), *Growing Points in Ethology*, Cambridge University Press, Cambridge. pp. 327–344.

McCance, R. A. (1962). Food, growth and time. *Lancet*, 2, 671–676.

Nelson, K. (1973). Structure and strategy in learning to talk. *Monographs Society for Research in Child Development*, 38.

Oppenheim, R. W. (1974). The ontogeny of behavior in the chick embryo. *Advances in the Study of Behavior*, 5, 133–172.

Piaget, J. (1967). *Biologie et Connaissance*, Gallimard, Paris.

Prader, A, Tanner, J. M., and Von Harnack G. A. (1963). Catch-up growth following illness or starvation. *Journal of Pediatrics*, 62, 646–659.

Schneirla, T. C. (1965). Aspects of stimulation and organisation in approach/withdrawal processes underlying vertebrate behavioural development. *Advances in the Study of Behavior*, 1, 1–74.

Vicari, E. M. (1929). Mode of inheritance of reaction time and degrees of learning in mice. *Journal of Experimental Zoology*, 54, 31–88.

Waddington, C. H. (1957). *The Strategy of the Genes*, Allen and Unwin, London.

Weiss, P., and Kavanau, J. L. (1957). A model of growth and growth control in mathematical terms. *Journal of General Physiology*, 41, 1–47.

Learning, Development, and Culture
Edited by H. C. Plotkin
© 1982, John Wiley & Sons Ltd.

CHAPTER 19

Learning and the evolution of developmental systems

Timothy D. Johnston

INTRODUCTION

The aim of evolutionary epistemology is, broadly speaking, to construct a theory of knowledge based on evolutionary principles (Campbell, 1974). However, in many writings its aim has been more narrowly construed as the elucidation of parallels between evolutionary and epistemological processes, especially the demonstration that both depend on the selective retention of blind variations, of which natural selection and trial-and-error learning have been offered as paradigmatic examples (Popper, 1972; Skinner, 1966; Staddon and Simmelhag, 1971; Campbell, 1960, 1974; Staddon, 1976; Glassman, 1977).

In this chapter, I want to offer an expansion of our evolutionary view of epistemological processes by considering the development of knowing agents in relation to their natural ecology, as the basis for a broader understanding of the contribution of knowledge to the adaptive relationship between the knower and its environment. This is surely an issue of central importance for an evolutionary epistemology since, ultimately, the evolution of knowing depends on the contribution that knowledge makes to an organism's ability to survive and reproduce in its natural environment.

Although the problems of behavioral development that I shall discuss in this chapter may appear remote from the concerns of epistemology, they are in fact thoroughly germane when those concerns are given an evolutionary interpretation, for at least two reasons. First, knowledge in itself is not of any evolutionary consequence. An individual benefits not from knowing about its environment, but from being able to behave knowledgeably in that environment. The evolutionary context of knowledge is ruthlessly pragmatic—it is the consequences of knowledge in action that matter, not knowledge in itself. I will interpret 'knowledgeable behavior' in this context to mean 'adaptive behavior'; although this formulation begs some interesting epistemological questions, it provides an appropriate starting point for an evolutionary inquiry. The second reason is that knowledge, like all characteristics of an organism, is a product of development. It arises as the result of complex interactions between genetic and environmental influences in the course of individual ontogeny. A necessary foundation for evolutionary epistemology must, therefore, include an account of how developmental processes give rise to the behavior that enables an animal to interact adaptively with its environment. If we neglect this problem, we are unlikely to obtain an adequate evolutionary account of the nature of knowledge.

Behavioral development has not been a major concern of evolutionary epistemologists. Most discussions have centered on problems of learning, a topic that is closer to the traditional concerns of epistemology, and one that has conventionally been rather sharply distinguished from development (see further below). However, given the developmental origins of knowledge, a good case can be made for viewing that distinction with some scepticism. A better strategy, for evolutionary purposes, might be to bring the study of learning and the study of development under a single theoretical rubric, so that we can achieve a more integrated understanding of the nature of ontogenetic change in behavior. With that understanding, it will be possible to set epistemological concerns more firmly in an evolutionary context by showing how epistemological processes contribute to the changing behavioral relationship between the animal and its environment.

THE CONCEPTS OF LEARNING AND DEVELOPMENT

Carefully drawn distinctions between related concepts play an essential role in scientific inquiry by helping to define important theoretical questions in a particular field. Sometimes, however, time-honored distinctions are preserved beyond the point where they continue to advance our understanding. I suggest that the distinction between learning and other aspects of behavioral development is one such outworn distinction that is impeding progress towards a coherent account of ontogenetic change in behavior, especially an account based on evolutionary principles. The distinction is made explicitly in two classical definitions of learning that are widely and authoritatively quoted:

> '*Learning* is a relatively permanent change in a behavioral potentiality which occurs as a result of reinforced practice . . . The inclusion of the term *practice* in the definition of learning is intended to exclude other

processes such as maturation and physiological change' (Kimble, 1967, pp. 82 and 87, original emphases).

'Learning is the process by which an activity originates or is changed through reacting to an encountered situation, provided that the characteristics of the change in activity cannot be explained on the basis of native response tendencies, maturation, or temporary states of the organism (e.g. fatigue, drugs, etc.)' (Hilgard and Bower, 1966, p. 2).

The distinction is maintained not only by reinforcement theorists, but also by Piaget (1964), a developmental theorist whose ideas have little else in common with behaviorist learning theory:

'The development of knowledge is a spontaneous process, tied to the whole process of embryogenesis... Learning presents the opposite case. In general, learning is provoked by situations—provoked by a psychological experimenter; or by a teacher, with respect to some didactic point; or by an external situation' (Piaget, 1964, p. 8).

All three definitions distinguish between two classes of developmental phenomena: those that require special circumstances such as reinforced practice (learning); and those that occur spontaneously in the normal course of events (other aspects of development, such as maturation). That distinction has been extremely important in guiding most theorizing about behavioral development in this century and it is illuminating to consider its origins and the consequences that it has had for the study of learning.

Arbitrary tasks in the study of animal learning

One of the most important concerns in the early study of animal learning was to design experimental procedures that would permit learning to be studied in the controlled and reproducible conditions of the psychological laboratory. The early work of naturalists such as Romanes (1884) and Lloyd Morgan (1896) provided a wealth of suggestive observations concerning animal learning abilities, but the limitations of an observational approach were clearly recognized by experimentalists such as Small (1900, 1901), Thorndike (1911), and Watson (1918). To Thorndike in particular must go much of the credit for establishing the study of animal learning as a major branch of experimental psychology.

Thorndike's writings, like those of many of his contemporaries, reveal a clear commitment to the view that learning and instinct are quite separate from one another. Instinct, on this view, is a provision of nature (evolution), enabling the animal to cope with the requirements of its normal, species-typical environment. Learning, on the other hand, is a different ability that permits the animal to deal with atypical or unusual circumstances by acquiring the necessary behavioral skills. In his experimental work, Thorndike sought to separate learning and instinct, so that the former could be studied in isolation, and to do this it was clearly necessary to devise problems that the animal could not solve by instinctive means. By posing unnatural problems that were biologically arbitrary in the sense that the animal would be unlikely to encounter them in its natural environment, and so have instincts available to cope with them, Thorndike believed that he would be able to study 'the association process, free from the helping hand of instinct' (Thorndike, 1911, p. 30).

It is important to recognize that the acceptance of a clear-cut dichotomy between learning and instinct provided a powerful theoretical rationale for the use of biologically arbitrary tasks for the study of learning (Timberlake, in press). The selection of such tasks by early students of learning such as Thorndike (1911), Watson (1918, 1924), and Skinner (1938) was not thoughtless or capricious—it reflected a decision to study learning rather than instinct, and an imaginative attempt to separate the two in the psychological laboratory. The use of arbitrary tasks to exclude instinctive abilities from experiments on learning implies that learning is to be treated as a *general purpose* ability, one that functions equally well in any environment that respects only a set of rather gross physiological and morphological constraints on the learner's behavior. Indeed, if the general purpose nature of learning is not assumed, the use of arbitrary tasks becomes indefensible. The issue of general versus special purpose adaptive mechanisms in learning and development will be examined in a later section.

The emphasis on arbitrary tasks as the proper objects of study for those interested in learning remains as strong today as it was at the turn of the century. In a popular recent textbook, under the heading 'The Domain of Learning,' Bugelski (1979, p. 27) writes: 'We turn now to the vast realm of stimulus and response connections that are basically unnatural or nonnatural. This is the real field of learning—we only learn what is unnatural.' Even Garcia (1981a), whose seminal work on taste-aversion learning was an important demonstration of the limitations of biologically arbitrary learning tasks (Seligman, 1970), seems wedded to their continued use in the study of animal learning:

> 'Those interested in learning should return to Pavlov's task, the search for detailed information on how new connections are made in the brain when an animal is subjected to training procedures. Those interested in unlearned adaptive behavior should search for detailed information on how that specific behavior is articulated to the niche and how that program of interaction is specifically encoded into the genes' (Garcia, 1981a, p. 156).

It would be hard to find a more forthright acceptance of the learning/instinct dichotomy as a proper basis for the study of animal learning. Garcia's statement is all the more surprising since elsewhere (Garcia, 1981b) he has strongly affirmed his long-time commitment to an ecological approach to learning.

The use of arbitrary behavior to study learning is especially important in the field of operant conditioning for, as Herrnstein (1977a) points out, the Skinnerian notion of a 'representative' response (Skinner, 1938, 1950) is really that of an arbitrary response, one that is not intimately involved with the animal's normal repertoire of behavior. Thus it is not surprising to find Skinner (1966, 1974b, 1977) embracing a particularly clear-cut version of the instinct/learning dichotomy, in his distinction between 'phylogenic' and 'ontogenic' behavior. Skinner does not insist that all behavior is learned; rather, like most learning theorists since the time of Thorndike, he recognizes two classes of behavior, that which is learned ('ontogenic behavior') and that which is inherited ('phylogenic behavior'), and has opted for the exclusive study of the former. Like Thorndike, and as urged by Garcia (1981a) in the quotation above, modern learning theorists have applied themselves to the analysis of learned rather than instinctive behavior, using biologically arbitrary tasks to isolate learning in the laboratory. The study of innate behavior, using naturalistic, species-typical tasks, is certainly important, but it is properly in the domain of ethology, not animal learning.

Sources of adaptive information in classical ethology

The distinction between learned and innate behavior also receives support from the writings of some classical ethologists, such as Lorenz (1950, 1956, 1965), Eibl-Eibesfeldt (1961, 1975, 1979), and Immelmann (1980). Lorenz's views have been particularly influential in this regard, not only because of his stature in the field, but also because of his widely-read exchange with Lehrman (1953, 1956, 1970) on the subject of instinct. The view held by Lorenz and Eibl-Eibesfeldt is that certain patterns or elements of behavior can be identified as innate whereas others are learned. Lehrman (1953, 1970) argued that the dichotomy between learned and innate behavior is inappropriate as a basis for developmental analysis, because it obscures important questions about the developmental processes that give rise to behavior. Although Lorenz and Skinner are usually portrayed as holding diametrically opposed views on the question of behavioral development, on this fundamental issue at least their positions are almost indistinguishable. Both accept the dichotomy of learned versus innate behavior, but they differ on the questions about behavioral development that they consider of greatest scientific interest. For Skinner (1938, 1974a), like other behaviorists, the important question is: How do environmental contingencies, especially contingencies of reinforcement, shape behavior in the course of individual experience? For Lorenz (1965) and the ethologists of his school, it is: What is the source of information that determines the adaptiveness of an animal's behavior?

However, as Lehrman (1953, 1970) argued at length, these concerns should be complementary, not mutually exclusive. Inquiry into the adaptiveness of behavior neither precludes nor answers questions about the development of behavior. Unfortunately, the way in which those two concerns have been articulated has made it very difficult to identify correctly the ways in which they complement each other. The commitment of learning theorists to the use of biologically arbitrary tasks means that the relevance of principles of learning to problems of adaptation is highly questionable. The application of these principles to natural examples of adaptive behavior is often purely speculative (e.g. Skinner, 1966, p. 1209), the existence of relevant environmental contingencies being assumed rather than demonstrated (Dennett, 1978). Seeking functional interpretations of learning principles, in the manner advocated by Shettleworth (1981a, b), Hinde (1981), and Hollis (1982), is not as straightforward as it may appear (Johnston, 1981), although some recent work in the study of foraging behavior (e.g. Pietrewicz and Kamil, 1977, 1979; McNamara and Houston, 1980; Kamil, 1981; Kamil, Peters and Lindstrom, in press) is very promising in this regard.

Lorenz (1956, 1965) and Eibl-Eibesfeldt (1961, 1975, 1979) defended the concept of innateness on the grounds that the adaptedness of at least some behavior cannot be explained on the basis of learning during individual development. A clear statement of their position is given by Eibl-Eibesfeldt (1961, p. 72):

'We use [the terms innate and acquired] as we feel a need to distinguish those behavior patterns which show adaptedness to specific environmental situations without the animal having experienced this situation before, from those behavior patterns which are learned by the animal by active communication with the environment during ontogeny.'

Much of the disagreement between ethologists and comparative psychologists during the 1950s and 1960s seems to have arisen because the problem of accounting for the adaptedness of behavior became confused with that of accounting for its development (Lehrman, 1970). This confusion prevented the complementarity of the two concerns from being realized, in part because of the way Lorenz uses the term 'learning'. Although he initially defined learning very broadly, to include 'all adaptive modifications of behavior' (Lorenz, 1965, p. 11), the later development of his argument employs a much narrower interpretation that would seem to include only what Lorenz calls 'higher' forms of learning, such as conditioning, observational learning, and imprinting. Although Lehrman (1953) and Schneirla (1957, 1966) emphasized the importance of considering a wider range of experiential effects in development, Lorenz (1956, 1965) rejected that proposal. He believed that one had to attribute the adaptedness of behavior either to the environment (in the case of learned behavior) or to the genetic constitution of the animal (in the case of innate behavior). Experiential effects that are not a clear source of adaptive information, even though they may make an essential contribution to the development of behavior, he repeatedly dismissed as being the province of 'experimental embryology' (see Lorenz, 1965), of very limited significance to the student of behavior.

Two dichotomies in the study of development

Throughout the debate on the issue of learned and innate behavior run two themes whose resolution is central to any evolutionary account of behavioral change. The first, which emerges most clearly from the writings of animal learning theorists, is the distinction between learning, a function of 'special' environments, and other aspects of development, which are part of 'normal' ontogeny or maturation. As I have argued, it is this distinction that has given rise to the emphasis on the use of biologically arbitrary tasks in the study of learning. The second theme, most clearly expressed in the writings of classical ethologists, has to do with identifying the source of adaptive information in behavior. If the adaptedness of some behavior can be attributed to the experience of the developing animal, then that behavior is said to be learned. Otherwise, and regardless of the necessity for other experiences that do not permit such adaptive attribution, the behavior is said to be innate; that is, the source of its adaptedness is phylogeny, not ontogeny.

Each of these themes distinguishes between the concepts of learning and development in a manner that is not at all compatible with evolutionary concerns, as those should be understood in the context of modern evolutionary theory. The theme of learning versus maturation implies that nonnatural or arbitrary situations are among those to which animals have become adapted in the course of evolution, the adaptation in question being the general purpose learning ability that they possess. However, since such situations are, by definition, not part of the natural environments in which evolution has occurred, it is inconceivable that they can figure directly in any evolutionary account of behavioral ontogeny. If learning is to be so closely identified with nonnatural situations, then it will have to be largely excluded from evolutionary considerations. From an evolutionary point of view, the distinction between learning and development cannot usefully be maintained in these terms.

One might expect that ethologists would have made distinctions that are more compatible with evolutionary theory, since the evolution and adaptedness of behavior is a primary concern of ethology (Tinbergen, 1951, 1963). Indeed, many ethologists repudiate Lorenz's distinction and argue that the subtle and complex contributions of experience to development cannot be captured in a simple distinction between learned and unlearned behavior (e.g. Hinde, 1955, 1968, 1970; Hailman, 1967, Marler, 1975, 1976, 1977). Despite Lorenz's firm commitment to an evolutionary view of behavior, the theme of phylogenetic versus ontogenetic sources of adaptive information turns out to be deeply problematical from an evolutionary point of view. The major problem has to do with the rather vaguely defined issue of whether or not behavioral adaptedness can be attributed to experiences provided by ontogeny. Such attribution is not at all the simple matter that Lorenz and others imply. We cannot simply look at the environment and decide what constitutes a source of adaptive information for a developing animal, any more than we can simply listen to a songbird and decide which aspects of the song are informative and which are not. In the latter case, the observer is not part of the communication system that includes the singer, his song, and a conspecific listener, and so his or her intuitions about informative aspects of song structure simply do not count. Similarly, the observer is not part of the developmental system that includes the animal and its natural environment, and his or her intuitions about what constitutes a source of adaptive information *for the developing animal* carry no theoretical weight at all (despite their role as a possible source of hypotheses, to be tested by experiment).

Animals evolve in a close mutual relationship with their natural environments and so 'specific information concerning the data to which the behavior is adapted' (Eibl-Eibesfeldt, 1961, p. 66) may be encoded by experiences whose adaptive relevance is not obvious to an observer who does not share in that relationship (Gottlieb, 1981). Lehrman (1956, p. 482) appreciated that point when he urged:

> 'It should not be assumed that all learning involves the practice of what the human observer regards as "the behavior", or that learning necessarily requires stimuli that are also observed by the human observer.'

The evolutionary origin of the developmental relationship between the animal and its environment is the key to an understanding of developmental processes.

THE EVOLUTION OF DEVELOPMENTAL SYSTEMS

Animals survive in their environments because they develop phenotypes, including morphological, physiological, and behavioral characters, that are adaptive in those environments. All such phenotypic characters arise as the outcome of developmental pathways whose interwining constitutes the animal's life-history (Stearns, 1976, 1977). An 'outcome' of development may be defined at any point in the life-history, not only in maturity, since juvenile characters may be adaptive in themselves, as outcomes, not just as precursors to adult characters (Oppenheim, 1980; Galef, 1981). Phenotypic outcomes, and the pathways that give rise to them, result from an interaction between the developing organism and its environment. In what follows, I will refer to those aspects of the organism that determine its response to environmental influences during development as the *epigenetic system* (following Ho and Saunders, 1979). I will refer to those aspects of the environment to which the epigenetic system responds in development as the organism's *developmental niche*.

As Lehrman (1953) pointed out, natural selection selects for outcomes, not for developmental pathways; any pathway that produces adaptive phenotypic characters at the appropriate times in development will tend to be selected for. Epigenetic systems are therefore selected on the basis of the phenotypic outcomes that they produce, but selection among epigenetic systems can only act in regard to the range of environmental conditions with which members of a population interact in the normal course of their development, namely their developmental niche. For a particular epigenetic system to be selected on the basis of the phenotypic outcomes it produces, it must give rise to an adaptive life-history, but only under the restricted range of conditions defined by the developmental niche. The ability to produce adaptive outcomes outside this range will confer no additional selective advantage.

From this evolutionary perspective, let us consider the relation between an epigenetic system and its developmental niche. There are two kinds of developmental pathways that might be part of an animal's life-history; those that produce invariant and those that produce variant phenotypic outcomes under normal conditions (i.e. within the developmental niche).

Invariant phenotypic outcomes

Consider first of all the case in which development must produce an invariant phenotypic outcome in order for adaptation to succeed, such as the species-typical song of a song sparrow (Mulligan, 1966), or the approach response of a duckling to the maternal call of its species (Gottlieb, 1971). Outcomes of this type, sometimes referred to as instinctive behavior, are species- or population-typical and their lack of individual variability may imply a lack of developmental sensitivity to environmental conditions. However there are actually two ways in which such an invariant outcome may be assured:

(1) By means of strict genetic control over development, so that the outcome of development is insensitive to the conditions under which it occurs. Such outcomes are said to be strongly canalized (Waddington, 1957) against

environmental perturbation. The development of song sparrow song appears to be canalized against variation in auditory experience early in life (Mulligan, 1966; but see Kroodsma, 1977).

(2) By means of a developmental sensitivity *only* to environmental factors that are themselves invariant within the animal's developmental niche. Although such outcomes are not canalized in Waddington's sense, they are invariant under the normal conditions of development. Gottlieb (1975, 1980a, b) has shown that the invariant approach response of two species of ducklings (*Aix sponsa* and *Anas platyrhynchos*) to the maternal calls of their respective species involves a developmental sensitivity to normally invariant auditory aspects of the prenatal developmental niche.

From the standpoint of natural selection, these two kinds of developmental pathways are adaptively equivalent; although the epigenetic systems that produce them employ different developmental mechanisms, involving either sensitivity or insensitivity to the environment, they both ensure invariant phenotypic outcomes. The first kind of system is a more general-purpose solution to the problem of producing an invariant phenotype than the second kind: It will produce an invariant outcome under a wider range of environmental conditions. However, the second kind of system is just as successful within its own developmental niche. It achieves its success by using a developmental 'rule of thumb', which may be informally stated as: 'A developmental response to environmental factor y at time t_0 produces an invariant phenotypic outcome at time t_k.' Within the developmental niche, y is invariant, and the rule works; outside the range of conditions defined by the niche, y may vary, in which case the rule will fail.

For each epigenetic system, it is possible to define a range of environmental conditions within which the system will produce an adaptive developmental outcome for the phenotypic character of interest. I will call this the *adaptive range* of the system. In the production of an invariant phenotypic outcome, a system of the first kind discussed above has a broader adaptive range than one of the second kind. However, because of the restricted range of conditions within the developmental niche (specifically, the invariance of the environmental factor y), the two systems are adaptively equivalent under normal conditions (see Figure 1). So long as the adaptive range of an epigenetic system includes the conditions of the animal's developmental niche, the rule of thumb stated above holds, and the system provides an adequate developmental solution to the problem of producing an invariant phenotype.

Rules of thumb are special-purpose, ad hoc solutions that only work under restricted conditions. But all that is required of an animal is that it solve the particular adaptive problems that it faces, not that it be able to solve some general class of problems, such as producing an invariant phenotype under

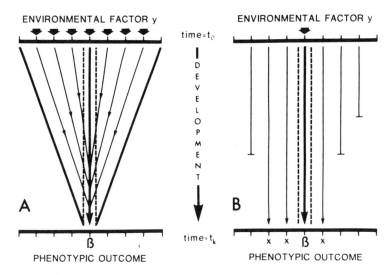

Figure 1 Production of an invariant phenotypic outcome in development. A: An epigenetic system in which production of an invariant adaptive outcome (β, is insensitive to environmental conditions such as factor y. B: An epigenetic system that responds to an environmental factor y to produce the invariant outcome only under the invariant condition of the developmental niche (dashed lines). Outside the niche, this system either produces non-adaptive phenotypic outcomes (x) different from β or fails to develop. The former system has a wider adaptive range than the latter (solid arrows on upper scale), but within the developmental niche, the two systems are adaptively equivalent

any environmental conditions. Ghiselin (1974) has pointed out that selection favors efficacious adaptive devices, those that get the job of survival and reproduction accomplished under the conditions that affect the population in question. Developmental rules of thumb are examples of such devices—they implement effective solutions within a particular developmental niche.

If we analyze such a system from a non-ecological point of view, that is, without reference to the correspondence between the system's adaptive range and the animal's developmental niche, the system will appear to operate in a rather sporadic manner, sometimes succeeding in producing an adaptive outcome and sometimes not. But set in its ecological context, the system works very well as a special-purpose adaptive solution. Organisms are not general-purpose adaptive devices, and analyzing them from a general-purpose point of view is not compatible with the evolutionary principles outlined here.

It is true that if the animal's environment (particularly factor y) were to change, the rule of thumb might then lead to a different and non-adaptive outcome (Figure 1). The system with the more general-purpose solution would be more likely to survive under changed environmental conditions, but natural selection cannot plan for such contingencies by providing genetic canalization as 'developmental insurance'.

Variable phenotypic outcomes

Consider now the situation in which the outcome of some developmental pathway must vary according to the conditions of development if adaptation is to succeed. Examples of such variable phenotypic outcomes include the feeding preferences of many species (Burghardt and Hess, 1966; Garcia, Hankins, and Rusniak, 1974; Galef, 1977), song dialects in the white-crowned sparrow (*Zonotrichia leucophys*; Marler, 1970; Marler and Tamura, 1964) and other song birds, and the dentition of some cichlid fishes (Greenwood, 1965).

The same reasoning applies here as in the case of invariant phenotypic outcomes. Natural selection favors those epigenetic systems that produce adaptive outcomes under the range of environmental conditions that characterize the animal's developmental niche. Successful systems have an adaptive range within which they can produce different phenotypic outcomes, adapted to the various environmental conditions that must be met. To the extent that this range exceeds the scope of the animal's developmental niche, the system is a relatively general-purpose device, implementing mechanisms that are relatively independent of some special set of environmental conditions. Special-purpose systems, whose adaptive ranges are closely tailored to the developmental niches of particular animals, will be equally successful at producing adaptive outcomes under normal conditions, but their adaptive operation is more readily perturbed by environmental variation outside the normal range. This may occur if normally invariant environmental factors are varied or if normally variant factors are varied outside their normal limits.

Since natural selection can select special-purpose systems as readily as general-purpose ones, we should expect to find developmental rules of thumb embodied in the production of variant as well as invariant phenotypic outcomes. Consider a situation in which, at time t_k in development, some phenotypic character β_k supports adaptation to a particular environmental variable ϕ_k. For example, ϕ_k might be a locally common source of food, and β_k the behavioral skills necessary for exploiting that source. Following Sommerhoff (1950, 1969; see Johnston and Turvey, 1980), we can define a function F relating ϕ_k and β_k so that:

$$F(\phi_k, \beta_k) = 0 \tag{1}$$

Specification of F in equation 1 defines, for each state of the environment (ϕ_k, the food source) a specific, adapted state of the phenotype (β_k, the behavioral skill). Suppose that development of the phenotypic character β takes place over an interval of the life-span, t_0–t_k, and that at t_0, a developmental response to the environment determines the eventual form of the phenotype at t_k. In order for this response to be adaptive, there must be some factor y whose value at t_0

reliably predicts the value of ϕ at t_k. That is, there must be a determinate, single-valued function of the form:

$$P(y_0) = \phi_k \qquad (2)$$

which maps y_0 on to ϕ_k. The developmental response of the epigenetic system to y_0 can be represented by another determinate, single-valued function of the form:

$$B(y_0) = \beta_k \qquad (3)$$

The nature of the function B is, of course, determined by the characteristics of the epigenetic system under analysis, and is embodied in the genetic and physiological makeup of the organism. The function P depends on the nature of the environment and it is only by virtue of P that B produces adaptive, though variable, developmental outcomes. The relations among the functions in equations 1–3 are shown in Figure 2.

In many cases of variable developmental outcomes, the function B implements a rule of thumb: 'A developmental response to factor y at time t_0 produces an adaptive (variable) phenotype β at time t_k.' The rule of thumb works because of

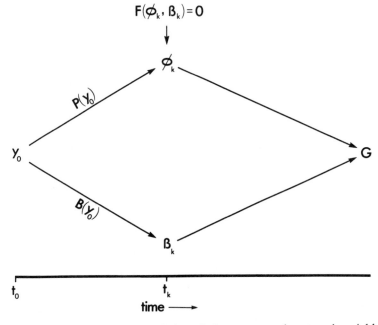

Figure 2 Graphical representation of the relations among the several variables and functions in Sommerhoff's model of adaptation. G stands for the adaptive goal (such as feeding or migrating) whose attainment depends on the developmental process under consideration. (From Johnston and Turvey (1980). Reproduced by permission of Academic Press)

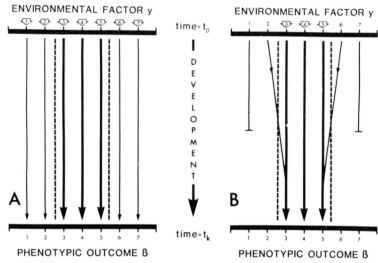

Figure 3 Production of a variant phenotypic outcome in development. In this hypothetical example, adaptation succeeds only when $\beta_k = y_0$. A: An epigenetic system that produces an adaptive outcome in the range of environmental conditions $y_0 = 1-7$, which includes the narrower range of the developmental niche (dashed lines), $y_0 = 3-5$. B: An epigenetic system that produces an adaptive outcome only within the range of the developmental niche, $y_0 = 3-5$. Outside this range, it either produces a non-adaptive outcome ($y_0 = 2$ or 6), or fails to develop ($y_0 = 1$ or 7). The former system has a wider adaptive range than the latter (arrows on upper scale), but within the developmental niche, the two systems are adaptively equivalent

the relation between y and ϕ specified in equation 2 by the function P; this relation need only hold over the limited range of conditions represented by the animal's developmental niche if the rule is to produce adaptive phenotypic outcomes over the developmental interval t_0 to t_k. The relation specified by P need not be anything more than a local ecological contingency—so long as y_0 happens to map on to ϕ_k, for whatever reason, within the animal's developmental niche, the rule of thumb $B(y_0) = \beta_k$ will produce adaptive outcomes. P does not need to be a cause and effect relation, a universal relation, or a logical entailment. It need have no validity whatever outside the conditions of the animal's developmental niche. It need only be local contingency that can serve as the basis for the developmental rule of thumb expressed in equation 3. Figure 3 shows the relation between a developmental niche and the adaptive ranges of two epigenetic systems (one with a broad and one with a narrow adaptive range) that produce variable phenotypic outcomes.

Evolution of the developmental ecosystem

Let me now draw the strands of the preceding discussion together, by way of a concept that I will call the 'developmental ecosystem'. In most ecological contexts, 'ecosystem' refers to a community of organisms interacting with their environment (Odum, 1959); examples of such community ecosystems include a hedgerow, a pond, or a tract of forest. However, problems of learning are problems of individual development, and what is needed is a concept of the ecosystem defined at the level of the individual organism and its environment. The utility of admitting such a definition of the ecosystem was noted by Evans (1956) and the concept has been elaborated by Johnston and Turvey (1980) and by MacMahon *et al.* (1981).

In order to simplify and generalize the discussion, I will use the term 'organism' (or 'animal') to refer to an individual that is typical of its species or population. Thus, the concepts defined apply at the level of the individual, but their generality is not limited by the idiosyncracies of particular (atypical) individuals. The individual organism will be understood, in this discussion, as the entire life-history of the individual, from conception to death, rather than as a single stage in the life-history. Since the focus of the discussion is on questions of development, it is essential that we work with a dynamic, life-history conception of the individual—it is the developing individual as a whole that is adapted to its environment, and the concept of the developmental ecosystem is an attempt to capture the dynamics of that adaptive relationship.

The relations among the variables and functions that define the developmental ecosystem (Figure 2) show the impossibility of making a clear separation between the animal and the environment as the source of 'adaptive information' (Lorenz, 1965). In the terms of this model, Lorenz's strategy would attribute the adaptedness of β_k (as defined by the function F) either to the variable y_0 (in which case we have an example of learning), or to the response function B (in which case we have an example of innate behavior). That strategy amounts to an attempt to write an equation defining the adaptedness of β_k as a function y_0 independently of B (in the case of learning), or as a function of B independently of y_0 (in the other case). Inspection of equations 1–3 shows this to be formally impossible.

It is a misreading of the animal–environment relationship to attempt to give *separate* accounts of the contribution of each to the development of behavior. The adaptive contribution of the animal is only defined in the context supplied by its environment, and vice versa. The minimal unit for developmental analysis must, therefore, be the ecosystem, comprising both the animal and its environment. Among the variables and functions that define the developmental ecosystem is the variable y, which Sommerhoff (1950) called the coenetic variable. The coenetic variable is a factor to which the developing system responds, so that if the value of y is changed, or exposure to it is withheld, the outcome of development (β_k) is altered. It is not specified as anything other than a component of the *ecosystem* and may be either an environmental or an organismic variable (see further below). The coenetic variable is, of course, a critical element in the adaptive analysis of development, since it is the basis for the adaptive phenotypic outcome (β_k) to which development leads (see Figure 2).

Examples of behavioral development in which the coenetic variable is an environmental variable are readily found: in many songbirds, exposure to a song model (part of the social environment) is a requirement of normal song development (Marler and Mundinger, 1971); establishment of habitat preferences in many species requires exposure to specific habitat types (e.g. Wiens, 1970; Noseworthy and Lien, 1976); the development of stellar navigation skills required for migratory orientation in indigo buntings depends on the availability of highly specific early experiences to the young bird (Emlen, 1972, 1975). Examples in which the coenetic variable is an organismic one are perhaps less familiar, but may be more important than is commonly realized. Lehrman (1953, 1956) drew attention to the role of self-stimulation in development; where self-stimulation is required for normal development, the coenetic variable y_0 is an organismic rather than an environmental factor. For example, Gottlieb (1980a, b) has shown that development of a preference for the species-typical maternal call in two species of waterfowl (the mallard, *Anas platyrhynchos*, and the wood duck, *Aix sponsa*) requires that ducklings hear, not the maternal call itself, but their own self-produced vocalizations or those of siblings during the days immediately before hatching.

A particularly interesting case may be cited in which y_0 is not clearly identifiable as either organismic or environmental in origin. Held and Hein (1963) have shown that self-produced (movement-contingent) optical stimulation is a requirement of normal visuo-motor coordination in kittens. Such stimulation (exteroceptive optic flow fields: Gibson, 1950; Lee, 1974; Warren, 1976) can only be described in *both* organismic and environmental terms, since it consists of an organism-specific transformation over an environment-specific set of texture elements.

In the analysis of development we generally aim to understand the organism's sensitivity to environmental conditions; that is, to specify some of the details of functions such as B (equation 3). In doing this, it is essential to bear in mind a point made several times in this chapter and summarized by Johnston and Turvey (1980, p. 190) as follows:

> 'The response function B has evolved in an ecosystem in which there is a *specific* relationship between y and ϕ [namely, $P(y_0) = \phi_k$] and between ϕ and β[namely, $F(\phi_k, \beta_k) = 0$]. Analysis of B cannot therefore be based on an arbitrary selection of y, ϕ, and β; selection of these variables must reflect the structure of the particular ecosystem under analysis.'

This important point may be illustrated by two examples from the field of insect development. Although these examples do not involve behavioral aspects of the phenotype, they provide particularly striking demonstrations of the evolutionary integrity of the developmental ecosystem.

My first example is the well known phenomenon of insect diapause. Diapause is a state of reduced metabolic activity and retarded development that serves as an adaptation to adverse environmental conditions. For example, many species of temperate-zone insects enter diapause with the onset of winter, and resume normal development with the return of warm weather in the spring. Although several environmental variables have been implicated in the initiation of temperate diapause, photoperiod is by far the most important of these (Danilevskii, 1965; Beck, 1968); temperature, the variable to which diapause is an adaptation, is of only secondary importance in its initiation, and acts mainly to modulate the developmental response to daylength. In this example, an adaptive relationship holds between the insect's physiological state (β_k: normal or diapause) and the environmental temperature (ϕ_k: warm or cold). However, the coenetic variable (y_0) is daylength, not temperature: the insect's developmental system is so constituted that it maps shortening photoperiod on to a state of diapause [$B(y_0) = \beta_k$].

Of particular interest is the question of the ecological circumstances that permit daylength to function as an initiator of diapause. The relation between daylength and temperature [$P(y_0) = \phi_k$] is not universal; it is an ecological contingency that characterizes certain environments and not others. There is no clear relationship between daylength and temperature near the poles or at the equator, and in some insect habitats (underground, for example) daylength is not an environmental characteristic. However, because of the nature of the earth's orbit around the sun, shortening daylength is a good indicator of an imminent period of cold weather in certain (temperate) habitats, and diapausing insects have evolved a rule of thumb, described by the function B, that exploits this local ecological contingency.

Some tropical insects do show diapause (e.g. Denlinger, 1978, 1979), although the adaptive significance of the response in this case is not so clear—it may be an adaptation to prolonged cool periods. Denlinger (1979) found that tropical flesh flies (Sarcophagidae) enter pupal diapause if they are exposed to several cool days (not cool nights) as larvae. There is no photoperiodic induction of diapause in these species, although closely related temperate species do show photoperiodically controlled diapause (Denlinger, 1979). Diapause in the tropical species appears to be a true adaptation and not a relic of an ancestral temperate diapause, since taxonomic evidence indicates a tropical origin for the group as a whole (Denlinger, 1978). This interpretation is supported by the fact that flies from generally cool areas in the tropics require a lower larval temperature to initiate diapause than do those from warmer areas (Denlinger, 1979). Daytime temperatures are typically more stable in tropical than in temperate areas, and a succession of cool days in a tropical area may be quite a reliable cue for the onset of a prolonged cool period. Tropical flesh flies appear to have exploited this local contingency, whereas their temperate relatives have exploited the contingency between photoperiod and temperature typical of temperate environments.

The second example is more complex but illustrates even more clearly the intimate relationship between the developing animal and its environment that is established in the course of evolution. Many species of the butterfly genus *Colias* are multivoltine, producing many broods in the course of a single breeding season. As the season progresses, the degree of melanization of the wings of the adult progeny changes: Those that emerge during the hottest months (June to September) have relatively pale hindwings, whereas those that emerge later, during the cooler parts of the season (October to December), have much darker wings. Watt (1969) showed that this variation in hindwing melanization is a thermoregulatory adaptation related to the energetics of flight. During warm weather, pale wings prevent the insect from becoming overheated in flight, whereas during cold weather, dark wings enable the resting animal to reach the optimal body temperature for flight more rapidly. Thus, variation in hindwing coloration (β_k) is an adaptation to changing environmental temperature (ϕ_k) over the course of the flight season.

The developmental basis of these seasonal changes in hindwing coloration in several *Colias* populations has been thoroughly analyzed by Hoffmann (1973, 1974, 1978). The results from two populations, one of *C. eurytheme* in California and one of *C. eriphyle* in Colorado, are of particular relevance to this discussion. In the California population, the degree of adult hindwing melanization is determined by the photoperiod experienced prior to the fifth larval instar, and is quite insensitive to temperature (Hoffmann, 1973). By contrast, melanization in the Colorado population shows no response to larval photoperiod, being determined solely by temperature during the pupal stage, just prior to emergence of the winged adult (Hoffmann, 1978). Thus in the California population, the coenetic variable (y_0) is photoperiod and t_0 occurs during the larval stage; in the Colorado population, y_0 is temperature and t_0 occurs towards the end of pupation. This difference in the developmental control of the same phenotypic character in two closely related species is quite striking, and Hoffmann (1978) has analyzed the environments of the two species to reveal the adaptiveness of the two epigenetic systems involved.

In the California environment, variation in photoperiod accounts for 71% of the variance in temperature over the period between larval and adult stages. By contrast, in the environment of the Colorado population, variation in photoperiod accounts for only 14% of the variance in temperature over the same period. Thus, an epigenetic system sensitive to larval photoperiod will ensure an adaptive adult phenotypic outcome in the California environment but not in the Colorado one. In Colorado, an epigenetic system that controls adult wing melanization over a much shorter period, and that responds directly to temperature rather than to photoperiod, is a more adaptive solution. The rule of thumb $[B(y_0) = \beta_k]$ relating photoperiod and melanization works in the California environment but not in the Colorado one because the relation between photoperiod and temperature $[P(y_0) = \phi_k]$ holds in the former but not in the latter. Whether the different rule of thumb employed by the Colorado population would succeed in producing adaptive adult phenotypes in California is unclear. What is clear, however, is that the epigenetic systems in these two populations are elegant adaptations to the developmental niches in which they have evolved. At least in the case of the California population the special-purpose nature of the adaptive solution is evident, since the rule of thumb only works for a limited set of circumstances, including those in which the population lives. It is not a general-purpose solution to the problem of adjusting adult hindwing melanization.

Hoffmann's (1973) data also provide an excellent illustration of the concept of an epigenetic system's adaptive range, and its relation to the developmental niche. He reared *C. eurytheme* from the California population under a wide range of larval photoperiodic regimes, from 2 to 24 hours of light per day, and measured the hindwing reflectance (inversely proportional to degree of melanization) of the adults (Figure 4). The developmental niche of *C. eurytheme* (in regard to photoperiod) is indicated in Figure 4 by the bar labelled 'ecological photoperiods', and it can be seen that within this range (10–16 hours of light per day) the epigenetic system produces an adaptive adult phenotype: steadily increasing reflectance (decreasing melanization) as a function of day length, so that light-winged adults emerge during the hotter months, following larval exposure to longer photoperiods during June and July. However, if photoperiod is extended outside the range that defines the developmental niche (i.e. less than 10 or more than 16 hours), then the response of the system changes

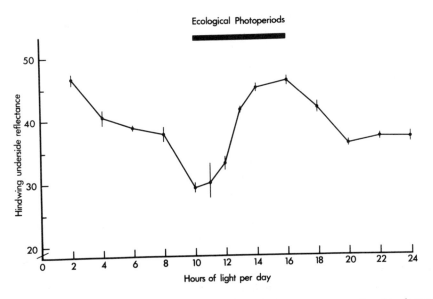

Figure 4 The dependence of adult hind wing reflectance (inversely proportional to degree of melanization) on larval photoperiod in *Colias eurytheme*. (Redrawn from Hoffman (1973). Reproduced by permission of the Society for the Study of Evolution)

PHOTOPERIOD (hours/day)

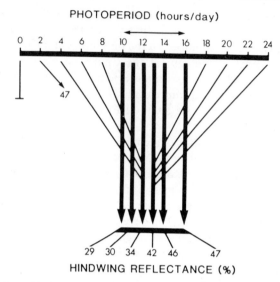

HINDWING REFLECTANCE (%)

Figure 5 Data from Hoffmann (1973) redrawn in the form previously illustrated in Figure 3. Scale of hindwing reflectance has been transformed to allow developmental pathways within the developmental niche (double-headed arrow on upper scale) to be drawn as parallel straight lines. Larvae raised in total darkness (0 hours/day photoperiod) do not survive to adulthood, because their food plants perish

markedly. Rather than continuing the adaptive trend apparent within the niche, the phenotypic outcomes converge on intermediate values in the range 37–42% for both very long and very short photoperiods. In Figure 5, I have used Hoffmann's data to construct a representation of the epigenetic system similar to that shown in Figure 3. The scale of hindwing reflectance has been transformed to allow those pathways within the developmental niche to be portrayed as parallel straight lines. The difference in the performance of the system inside and outside the developmental niche is striking.

Defining the adaptive range of this epigenetic system is difficult because we have no data to determine the nature of an adaptive response to conditions outside those of the developmental niche, for comparison with the actual response of the system. (Bear in mind that the requirement is for a degree of hindwing melanization adapted to the thermal conditions associated with very long and very short photoperiods over the interval between larval sensitivity (t_0) and adult emergence (t_k).) Hoffman (1973, p. 391) suggests that the slight darkening apparent as a response to very long photoperiods might be adaptive in high Arctic latitudes, 'where days are very long, but thermal conditions are more stringent.' Clearly, no such interpretation is available for the response to very short photoperiods, which characterize only the Arctic winter, in which no butterfly could survive. Hoffmann's suggestion is difficult to evaluate in the absence of data on the development and thermal balance of *C. eurytheme* in Arctic latitudes (where it is in any case very rare). At present it seems reasonable to view the adaptive range of the epigenetic system controlling wing melanization as limited to the range of conditions defined by its development niche (Figure 5).

These examples from insect development have been selected because they illustrate so clearly what is implied by the integrity of the developmental ecosystem. Although they are not examples of behavioral development, they illuminate the evolutionary context of development in a particularly striking manner. Their relevance to learning and behavioral development is readily demonstrated by citing a few parallel examples from the behavioral literature:

(1) Adult indigo buntings (*Passerina cyanea*) are nocturnal migrants that migrate by reference to star patterns in the vicinity of the pole star. Development of this skill depends on exposure to a rotating star field prior to the first migratory season; the axis of rotation defines geographical north when the mature birds come to select a migratory direction (Emlen, 1967, 1970, 1972). Since indigo buntings are diurnal birds, except for their migratory flights, the epigenetic system underlying development of this skill cannot provide a general solution to all problems involving the acquisition of spatial orientation skills. It is a special purpose solution to migratory orientation in a nocturnal niche.

(2) Red legged frogs (*Rana aurora*) inhabit shallow ponds with emergent vegetation that casts a striped shadow pattern on the substrate. Frogs reared as tadpoles in a striped dishes show a preference for striped over checkerboard substrates, but those reared in either unpatterned dishes, or in dishes with a checkerboard pattern do not show a preference for either striped or checkboard substrates. (Wiens, 1970). The epigenetic system involved in substrate selection provides a solution to the particular problem of selecting a striped substrate, not a solution to the general problem of selecting a familiar substrate pattern.

(3) Forty-eight-hour-old Peking ducklings (*Anas platyrhynchos*) normally prefer a recording of the maternal call of their species pulsed at the usual (species-typical) rate of about 4 notes/sec over one pulsed at either faster (6 notes/sec) or slower (2 notes/sec) rates. Surgically muted and isolated embryos do not show such a preference after hatching, but its normal development can be assured by exposing such embryos to a recording of the embryonic calls of siblings, also normally emitted at a rate of 4 notes/sec. Exposure to embryonic calls at the faster rate of 6 notes/sec does not result in a postnatal preference for either the normal maternal call (at 4 notes/sec), or for one pulsed at 6 notes/sec (Gottlieb, 1971, 1980a). The special purpose nature of the epigenetic system is again evident; it is not a general purpose 'rate preference inducer.'

The special purpose rules of thumb in these examples illustrate the integrity of the developmental ecosystem in the behavioral realm also. Epigenetic systems that implement such rules only yield to analysis in the context provided by their developmental niches, and by the environments to which adaptation is normally effected.

LEARNING AND THE EPIGENETIC SYSTEM

I have pointed out two themes in the study of behavior that have fostered a distinction between learning and other aspects of development. Students of animal learning have construed the role of learning to be that of a general purpose adaptive mechanism, and have emphasized the use of unnatural problem situations to distinguish learning from the maturation of instinctive abilities. Classical ethologists distinguished between ontogenetic and phylogenetic sources of information, the former being responsible for the learning of acquired behavior, the latter for the development of innate behavior. The evolutionary principles outlined in the preceding section provide no basis for such distinctions between learning and development and imply a shift in emphasis to a more unitary point of view of the relation between the two.

The position that learning cannot be strictly distinguished from other aspects of development has been advocated by many authors but the contrary view has had a much stronger and more pervasive influence, especially in the study of animal learning. During the 1920's, the growth of behaviorism gave rise to a strong anti-instinct movement in psychology (Kuo, 1921, 1922, 1924) that sought to attribute all developmental change in behavior to the effects of experience. Some writers, such as Carmichael (1925) and Gesell (1933), urged the importance of reconciling the concepts of learning and maturation (the developmental basis of instinct) in order to gain a deeper understanding of processes of development. For example, Gesell (1933, p. 215) wrote:

'The mechanisms of maturation rigidly conceived would lead to sterotypy of behavior, but not if there is an intimately associated mechanism for specific adaptations [learning]. These two mechanisms are not discrete, nor does environment operate on one to the exclusion of the other. They function together as a single mechanism which is constantly consolidated through the underlying processes of growth.'

The similarity of this point of view with that expressed 20 years later by Lehrman (1953) is striking. (For an even earlier expression, see Weismann, 1894.) Hinde (1955, p. 23) also emphasized 'the absolute necessity of studying [learning] in parallel with other processes involved in the development of behaviour,' but students of learning seem to have been much more sympathetic with Tolman's

(1932, p. 304) view that there is a 'pragmatically useful distinction between such responses ... as are due primarily to heredity plus mere normal maturation, and such other responses, as are due primarily to the effects of learning resulting from special environments.' The usefulness of that distinction is questionable as a basis for any evolutionary view of learning, for it is the developmental response to normal rather than 'special' (i.e. unnatural) environments that faces selection in the course of evolution.

From an evolutionary point of view, we see that the intimacy of the developmental relation between the animal and its environment (the concept of the developmental ecosystem) precludes conceptual distinctions that force a separation between the two in development. Instead, we should seek distinctions that respect the mutuality of that relation and that elucidate the processes involved in its establishment. There are a number of ways to approach this problem, each of which allows us to see development in a different light. Taken together, they provide a multi-dimensional assessment of the relations among different kinds of development, and they paint a picture that is too complex for its analysis to be based on any simple dichotomy, such as that between learning and development. Let us consider some possible approaches.

Gottlieb (1973, 1976a, b, in press) proposed three roles that experience may play in the development of species-typical behavior: (1) *maintenance*, in which experience is required for the continued manifestation of the behavior; (2) *facilitation*, in which the lack of experience delays development of the behavior; and (3) *induction*, in which the behavior does not develop at all in the absence of experience. Bateson (1976) drew attention to the various degrees of specificity in the effect that a particular determinant (coenetic variable in Sommerhoff's model) may have in development. Some determinants, such as nutrition (Leathwood, 1978), may have diffuse effects on development, affecting a wide range of unrelated neurobehavioral systems. Others, such as exposure to song in many song birds (Marler and Mundinger, 1971), have much more specific effects on only a single behavior or behavioral system.

The schemes proposed by Gottlieb and by Bateson are, in principle, orthogonal to one another, so the possibility exists of identifying maintaining, facilitative, and inductive effects with varying degrees of specificity. It would be interesting to determine whether different degrees of specificity are equally represented in the three categories, because an unequal representation might have implications about the existence of constraints on the evolution of developmental systems. For example, it seems that diffuse inductive effects might be relatively uncommon, because it is hard to envisage a situation in which it would be adaptive for a single experience to induce the development of several behaviors, unless they were the components of a single functional unit of behavioral organization (e.g. courtship or maternal behavior). On the other hand, diffuse facilitative effects of experience might be more common. If these act by altering rates of neurogenesis, synaptogenesis, or cell death, they could accelerate or retard the development of several neurobehavioral systems simultaneously, while preserving their sequence of maturation.

Throughout the lifetime of an organism there is constant adjustment of behavior to meet the adaptive demands of the environment. Some of these adjustments, such as the transition to independent feeding, or the acquisition of species-specific communication patterns, persist throughout most of the animal's life, whereas others are of much shorter duration. Among the latter are medium-term adjustments, such as those required to cope with seasonal variations in food supply, and very short-term adjustments, such as the alterations in motor coordination required for locomotion over varying slopes and substrates. Several authors have discussed the problems raised by the necessity of adapting to changes in the environment on these various time-scales (e.g. Bateson, 1963; Slobodkin, 1968; Slobodkin and Rapoport, 1974; Plotkin and Odling-Smee, 1979, 1981; Johnston and Turvey, 1980). While some of these adjustments, namely those effected over very short periods, clearly do not fall under the purview of developmental theory, those that do cover a wide range of time-scales. No clear demarcation exists between those at the short-term end of the range, such as changing patterns of search behavior in order to find hidden food in new locations (in chimpanzees; Menzel, 1978), and those at the long-term end, such as developing a life-long song dialect appropriate to the local population (in sparrows; Marler, 1970).

A fourth way in which we might characterize developmental change is by reference to the coenetic variable of development. There are several possibilities here and I will discuss only one of them. In some cases, the coenetic variable is a single physical variable, such as daylength in the example of butterfly wing coloration discussed earlier (Hoffmann, 1978). In other cases, it is composed of a relation between two such variables: Gottlieb (1980b) showed that wood ducklings (*Aix sponsa*) must be exposed at an early stage in development to the descending frequency modulation (FM) in the calls of siblings if their preference for descending FM in the notes of the species maternal call is to develop normally. Other kinds of FM were not effective in ensuring the development of this preference. In this example, the coenetic variable is defined by a relation the two simple physical variables of frequency and time.

In yet other cases, more complex relations or patterns among many simple variables may be required to define the coenetic variable. For example, Hein, Held, and Gower (1970) found that if kittens are raised in a stroboscopically illuminated environment, they fail to develop visually guided behavior. Apparently, the coenetic variable in this instance of visuo-motor development involves dynamic relations among visual contours that are disrupted by stroboscopic illumination. In the development of migratory orientation in the indigo bunting, as we have seen, the coenetic variable is best described as a rotational translation of a pattern of point light sources (Emlen, 1970, 1972). While the dynamic relation between the pattern and the axis of rotation is crucial to development, the particular pattern and axis of rotation are not.

I have described four dimensions along which examples of development might be distinguished from one another: the role of experience, the specificity of the effect, the time-scale of the change, and the complexity of the coenetic variable. At least in principle, these dimensions appear to be orthogonal (that is, position on one dimension does not constrain possible positions on the other dimensions). However, it seems likely that real epigenetic systems are subject to constraints on possible combinations among different regions of these four dimensions, constraints that may arise either from internal limitations of system design (either absolute or ancestral) or from the non-adaptiveness of certain combinations in any environment. If one were to locate examples of development in the four-dimensional space representing all possible combinations of values along these dimensions, the constraints would be apparent as unoccupied portions of the space. That approach has been used by Raup (1966) in his studies of shell coiling in gastropods, to show that actual shell forms occupy only a small portion of the space defined by three parameters that generate all possible coiled shells. Raup's studies reveal the existence of interesting constraints on the evolutionary diversification of shell form in gastropods. Figure 6 shows how this might be done for epigenetic systems, using three of the four dimensions discussed above. Understanding the nature and origin of the constraints that doubtless exist on the diversification of developmental systems is an important task for the evolutionary study of development, and it suggests some interesting questions about the relations among various kinds of development, located in different portions of the multi-dimensional space.

Those kinds of development most clearly relevant to epistemological concerns would seem to be inductive effects with a high specificity, operating over the medium- to long-term (within the individual life-span), and based on complex coenetic variables. Examples might include such things as acquiring grammatical rules of language, learning foraging strategies, and developing the ability to interact appropriately with individual members of a society (Figure 6). Examples such as these are often quite resistant to analysis in behavioral terms; the regularities involved only become apparent when they are analyzed in terms of cognitive constructs (Fodor, 1968; Hulse, Fowler, and Honig, 1978). The relation between the development of cognitive skills like these and that of the more strictly behavioral skills on which this chapter has focused is clearly of great importance to evolutionary epistemology. Presumably there is some evolutionary continuity among the different kinds of development involved, and one question for evolutionary epistemology concerns the evolutionary processes that are involved in moving from the 'behavioral' regions of the multi-dimensional space to the more 'cognitive' regions. Both internal (design) and external (selective) constraints may limit the potential of an epigenetic system to evolve along certain trajectories within the space. For example, the

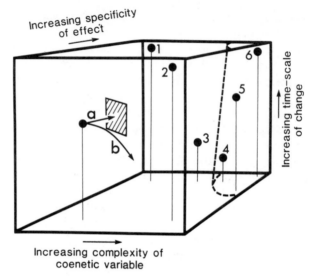

Figure 6 Three dimensions of the multi-dimensional space that describe the varieties of developmental change. Epigenetic systems controlling the development of particular kinds of behavior can be described by their positions within the space. Numbered dots show how some examples might be positioned: 1. Substrate selection by red-legged frogs (Wiens, 1970); 2. Effects of complexity of rearing conditions on behavior of rats (Rosenweig, 1966); 3. Food selection in response to dietary deficiencies (specific hungers; Rozin and Kalat, 1971); 4. Foraging strategies in relation to prey distribution (McNamara and Houston, 1980; Ollason, 1981); 5. Interactions with individual social neighbors; 6. Human language acquisition. Examples of most direct relevance for epistemology will tend to lie in the volume of the space indicated by the dashed lines. Evolutionary transitions within the space may be limited by constraints (shaded rectangle) that prevent transitions along some paths (such as *a*) but not others (such as *b*)

shaded rectangle in Figure 6 represents a constraint that might prevent a system from evolving along trajectory *a*, and force it to evolve along a different trajectory (*b*). Such constraints may mean that some portions of the space are completely inaccessible from other portions because they represent local adaptive maxima that are separated by the adaptive barrier of a design constraint (Wright, 1932; Stearns, 1977). Many discussions of the evolution of complex forms of learning out of simpler kinds of behavioral development focus primarily on their presumed adaptiveness (e.g. Lorenz, 1969; Mayr, 1974; Rozin, 1966; Sober, 1981). However, as others have argued in the case of morphological evolution (e.g. Gould, 1980; Alberch, 1980), the probable existence of constraints on evolutionary diversification raises equally important theoretical problems (see also Johnston, 1982).

The multi-dimensional view of development suggested in this final section is quite incompatible with any strict dichotomy between learning and other aspects of development. It is much more compatible with the evolutionary principles outlined earlier and may, therefore, provide a more secure foundation on which to build an evolutionary epistemology.

ACKNOWLEDGEMENTS

Preparation of this chapter was supported by Research Grant No. HD-00878 from the National Institute of Child Health and Human Development, and by funds from the North Carolina Division of Mental Health. I am grateful to Richard J. Hoffmann for permission to reproduce Figure 4.

REFERENCES

Alberch, P. (1980). Ontogenesis and morphological diversification. *Amer. Zool.*, **20**, 653–667.

Bateson, G. (1963). The role of somatic change in evolution. *Evolution*, **17**, 529–539.

Bateson, P. P. G. (1976). Specificity and the origins of behavior. *Adv. Study Behav.*, **6**, 1–20.

Beck, S. D. (1968). *Insect Photoperiodism*, Academic Press, New York.

Bugelski, B. R. (1979). *Principles of Learning and Memory*, Praeger, New York.

Burghardt, G. M., and Hess, E. H. (1966). Food imprinting in the snapping turtle *Chelydra serpentina*. *Science*, **151**, 108–109.

Campbell, D. T. (1960). Blind variation and selective retention in creative thought as in other knowledge processes. *Psychol. Rev.*, **67**, 380–400.

Campbell, D. T. (1974). Evolutionary epistemology. In P. A. Schilpp (Ed.), *The Philosophy of Karl Popper*, Volume 1, Open Court Press, LaSalle, Ill. pp. 413–463.

Carmichael, L. (1925). Heredity and environment: are they antithetical? *J. Abnorm. Soc. Psychol.*, **20**, 245–260.

Danilevskii, A. S. (1965). *Photoperiodism and Seasonal Development of Insects*, Oliver and Boyd, Edinburgh.

Denlinger, D. L. (1978). The developmental response of flesh flies (Diptera: Sarcophagidae) to tropical seasons: variation in generation time and diapause in East Africa. *Oecologia*, **35**, 105–107.

Denlinger, D. L. (1979). Pupal diapause in tropical flesh flies: environmental and endocrine regulation, metabolic rate and genetic selection. *Biol. Bull.*, **156**, 31–46.

Dennett, D. C. (1978). Skinner skinned. In *Brainstorms*, Bradford Books, Montgomery, Vt. pp. 53–70.

Eibl-Eibesfeldt, I. (1961). The interactions of unlearned behavior patterns and learning in mammals. In J. F. Delafresnaye (Ed.), *Brain Mechanisms and Learning*, Blackwell's, Oxford. pp. 53–73.

Eibl-Eibesfeldt, I. (1975). *Ethology, the Biology of Behavior*, Holt, New York.

Eibl-Eibesfeldt, I. (1979). Human ethology: concepts and implications for the sciences of man. *Behav. Brain Sci.*, **2**, 1–57.

Emlen, S. T. (1967). Migratory orientation in the indigo bunting, *Passerina cyanea*, I and II. *Auk*, **84**, 309–342 and 463–489.

Emlen, S. T. (1970). Celestial rotation: its importance in the development of migratory orientation. *Science*, **170**, 1198–1201.

Emlen, S. T. (1972). The ontogenetic development of orientation capabilities. In S. R. Galler, K. Schmidt-Koenig, G. J. Jacobs, and R. F. Belleville (Eds), *Animal*

Orientation and Navigation, N. A. S. A., Washington, D. C. (SP-262). pp. 191–201.

Emlen, S. T. (1975). The stellar-orientation system of a migratory bird. *Sci. Amer.*, **233(2)**, 102–111.

Evans, F. C. (1956). Ecosystem as the basic unit in ecology. *Science*, **123**, 1127–1128.

Fodor, J. A. (1968). *Psychological Explanation*, Random House, New York.

Galef, B. G. (1977). Mechanisms for the social transmission of acquired food preferences from adult to weanling rats. In L. M. Barker, M. R. Best, and M. Domjan (Eds), *Learning Mechanisms in Food Selection*, Baylor University Press, Waco, Tex. pp. 123–148.

Galef, B. G. (1981). The ecology of weaning: parasitism and the achievement of independence by altricial mammals. In D. J. Gubernick and P. H. Klopfer (Eds), *Parental Care*, Plenum Press, New York. pp. 211–241.

Garcia, J. (1981a). Tilting at the paper mills of academe. *Amer. Psychol.*, **36**, 149–158.

Garcia, J. (1981b). The nature of learning explanations. *Behav. Brain Sci.*, **4**, 143–144.

Garcia, J., Hankins, W. G., and Rusniak, K. W. (1974). Behavioral regulation of the milieu interne in man and rat. *Science*, **185**, 824–831.

Gesell, A. (1933). Maturation and the patterning of behavior. In C. Murchison (Ed.), *Handbook of Child Psychology*, 2nd. Ed. Russell and Russell, New York. pp. 209–235.

Ghiselin, M. T. (1974). *The Economy of Nature and the Evolution of Sex*, University of California Press, Berkeley.

Gibson, J. J. (1950). *The Perception of the Visual World*, Houghton-Mifflin, Boston.

Glassman, R. B. (1977). How can so little brain hold so much knowledge? Applicability of the principle of natural selection to mental processes. *Psychol. Rec.*, **27**, 393–415.

Gottlieb, G. (1971). *Development of Species Identification in Birds*, University of Chicago Press, Chicago.

Gottlieb, G. (1973). Introduction to behavioral embryology. In G. Gottlieb (Ed.), *Studies on the Development of Behavior and the Nervous System, Volume 1: Behavioral Embryology*, Academic Press, New York. pp. 3–45.

Gottlieb, G. (1975). Development of species identification in ducklings: I. Nature of perceptual deficit caused by embryonic auditory deprivation. *J. Comp. Physiol. Psychol.*, **89**, 387–399.

Gottlieb, (1976a). The roles of experience in the development of behavior and the nervous system. In G. Gottlieb (Ed.), *Studies on the Development of Behavior and the Nervous System, Volume 3: Neural and Behavioral Specificity*, Academic Press, New York. pp. 25–54.

Gottlieb, G. (1976b). Conceptions of prenatal development: behavioral embryology. *Psychol. Rev.*, **83**, 215–234.

Gottlieb, G. (1980a). Development of species identification in ducklings: VI. Specific embryonic experience required to maintain species-typical perception in Peking ducklings. *J. Comp. Physiol. Phychol.*, **94**, 579–587.

Gottlieb, G. (1980b). Development of species identification in ducklings: VII. Highly specific early experience fosters species-specific perception in wood ducklings. *J. Comp. Physiol. Psychol.*, **94**, 1019–1027.

Gottlieb, G. (1981). Roles of early experience in species-specific perceptual development. In R. N. Aslin, J. R. Alberts and M. R. Peterson (Eds), *Development of Perception, Volume 1*. Academic Press, New York. pp. 5–44.

Gould, S. J. (1980). The evolutionary biology of constraint. *Daedalus*, **109(2)**, 39–52.

Greenwood, P. H. (1965). Environmental effects on the pharyngeal mill of a cichild fish, *Astatoreochromis alluandi*, and their taxonomic implications. *Proc. Linn Soc. Lond.*, **176**, 1–10.

Hailman, J. P. (1967). The ontogeny of an instinct: the pecking response in chicks of the laughing gull (*Larus artricilla* L.) and related species. *Behaviour Suppl.*, **15**, 1–159.

Hein, A., Held, R., and Gower, E. (1970). Development and segmentation of visually controlled movement by selective exposure during rearing. *J. Comp. Physiol. Psychol.*, **73**, 181–187.

Held, R. and Hein, A. (1963). Movement-produced stimulation in the development of visually guided behavior. *J. Comp. Physiol. Psychol.*, **56**, 872–876.

Herrnstein, R. J. (1977a). The evolution of behaviorism. *Amer. Psychol.*, **32**, 593–603.

Herrnstein, R. J. (1977b). Doing what comes naturally: a reply to Professor Skinner. *Amer. Psychol.*, **32**, 1013–1016.

Hilgard, E. R., and Bower, G. H. (1966). *Theories of Learning*, 3rd Ed Appleton, New York.

Hinde, R. A. (1955). The modifiability of instinctive behavior. *Adv. Sci.*, **12**, 19–24.

Hinde, R. A. (1968). Dichotomies in the study of development. In J. M. Thoday and A. S. Parkes (Eds), *Genetic and Environmental Influences on Behaviour*, Plenum Press, New York. pp. 3–14.

Hinde, R. A. (1970). *Animal Behaviour*, 2nd Ed. McGraw-Hill, New York.

Hinde, R. A. (1981). Biological approaches to the study of learning: does Johnston provide a new alternative? *Behav. Brain Sci.*, **4**, 146–147.

Ho, M. W., and Saunders, P. T. (1979). Beyond neo-Darwinism—an epigenetic approach to evolution. *J. Theor. Biol.*, **78**, 573–591.

Hoffman, R. J. (1973). Environmental control of seasonal variation in the butterfly *Colias eurytheme*. I. Adaptive aspects of a photoperiodic response. *Evolution*, **27**, 387–397.

Hoffman, R. J. (1974). Environmental control of seasonal variation in the butterfly *Colias curytheme*: effects of photoperiod and temperature on pteridine pigmentation. *J. Insect Physiol.*, **20**, 1913–1924.

Hoffmann, R. J. (1978). Environmental uncertainty and evolution of physiological adaptation in *Colias* butterflies. *Amer. Nat.*, **112**, 999–1015.

Hollis, K. L. (1982). Pavlovian conditioning of signal-centered action patterns and autonomic behavior: a biological analysis of function. *Adv. Study Behav.*, **12**,

Hulse, S. H., Fowler, H., and Honig, W. K. (1978). *Cognitive Processes in Animal Behavior*, Erlbaum, Hillsdale, N. J.

Immelman, K. (1980). *Introduction to Ethology*, Plenum Press, New York.

Johnston, T. D. (1981). Contrasting approaches to a theory of learning. *Behav. Brain Sci.*, **4**, 125–173.

Johnston, T. D. (1982). Selective costs and benefits in the evolution of learning. *Adv. Study Behav.*, **12**, 65–106.

Johnston, T. D., and Turvey, M. T. (1980). A sketch of an ecological metatheory for theories of learning. In G. H. Bower (Ed.), *The Psychology of Learning and Motivation*, Volume 14, Academic Press, New York. pp. 147–205.

Kamil, A. C. (1981). Ecology and learning. *Behav. Brain Sci.*, **4**, 147–148.

Kamil, A. C., Peters, J., and Lindstrom, F. J. (in press). An ecological perspective on the study of the allocation of behavior. In M. L. Commons, R. J. Herrnstein, and H. Rachlin (Eds), *Quantitative Analyses of Behavior. II. Matching and Maximizing Accounts*, Ballinger, New York.

Kimble, G. A. (1967). The definition of learning and some useful distinctions. In G. A. Kimble (Ed.), *Foundations of Learning and Conditioning*, Appleton, New York. pp. 82–99.

Kroodsma, D. E. (1977). A re-evaluation of song development in the song sparrow. *Anim. Behav.*, **25**, 390–399.

Kuo, Z.-Y. (1921). Giving up instincts in psychology. *J. Philos.*, **18**, 645–664.

Kuo, Z.-Y. (1922). How are our instincts acquired? *Psychol. Rev.*, **29**, 344–365.

Kuo, Z.-Y. (1924). A psychology without heredity. *Psychol. Rev.*, **31**, 427–448.

Leathwood, P. (1978). Influence of early undernutrition on behavioral development and learning in rodents. In G. Gottlieb (Ed.), *Studies on the Development of Behavior and the Nervous System, Volume 4: Early Influences*, Academic Press, New York. pp. 187–209.

Lee, D. N. (1974). Visual information during locomotion. In R. B. McCleod and H. L. Pick (Eds), *Perception: Essays in Honor of J. J. Gibson*, Cornell University Press, Ithaca, New York. pp. 251–267.

Lehrman, D. S. (1953). A critique of Konrad Lorenz's theory of instinct. *Q. Rev. Biol.*, **28**, 337–363.

Lehrman, D. S. (1956). On the organization of maternal behavior and the problem of instinct. In P.-P. Grassé (Ed.), *L'Instinct dans le Comportement des Animaux et de l'Homme*, Masson, Paris. pp. 475–520.

Lehrman, D. S. (1970). Semantic and conceptual issues in the nature–nurture problem. In L. R. Aronson, E. Tobach, D. S. Lehrman, and J. S. Rosenblatt (Eds), *Development and Evolution of Behavior. Essays in Memory of T. C. Schneirla*, Freeman, San Francisco. pp. 17–52.

Lorenz, K. Z. (1950). The comparative method in studying innate behavior patterns. *Symp. Soc. Exp. Biol.*, **4**, 221–268.

Lorenz, K. Z. (1956). The objectivistic theory of instinct. In P.-P. Grassé (Ed.), *L' Instinct dans le Comportement des Animaux et de l'Homme*, Masson, Paris. pp. 51–76.

Lorenz, K. Z. (1965). *Evolution and Modification of Behavior*, University of Chicago Press, Chicago.

Lorenz, K. Z. (1969). Innate bases of learning, In K. H. Pribram (Ed.). *On the Biology of Learning*, Harcourt, Brace and World, New York, pp. 13–93

MacMahon, J. A., Schimpf, D. J., Anderson, D. C., Smith, K. G., and Bayn, R. L. (1981). An organism-centered approach to some community and ecosystem concepts. *J. Theor. Biol.*, **88**, 287–307.

McNamara, J., and Houston, A. (1980). The application of statistical decision theory to animal behaviour. *J. Theor. Biol.*, **85**, 673–690.

Marler, P. (1970). A comparative approach to vocal learning: song development in white-crowned sparrows. *J. Comp. Physiol. Psychol. Monogr.*, **71** (No. 2, Pt. 2), 1–25.

Marler, P. (1975). On strategies of behavioural development. In G. Baerends, C. Beer, and A. Manning (Eds), *Function & Evolution in Behaviour: Essays in Honour of Professor Niko Tinbergen, FRS*, Oxford University Press, Oxford. pp. 254–275.

Marler, P. (1976). Sensory templates in species-specific behavior. In J. C. Fentress (Ed.), *Simpler Networks & Behavior*, Sinauer, Sunderland, Mass. pp. 314–329.

Marler, P. (1977). Perception and innate knowledge. In W. H. Heidcamp (Ed.), *The Nature of Life*, University Park Press, Baltimore. pp. 111–139.

Marler, P. R., and Mundinger, P. (1971). Vocal learning in birds. In H. Moltz (Ed.), *The Ontogeny of Vertebrate Behavior*, Academic Press, New York. pp. 389–450.

Marler, P., and Tamura, M. (1964). Culturally transmitted patterns of vocal behavior in sparrows. *Science*, **146**, 1483–1486.

Mayr, E. (1974). Behavior programs and evolutionary strategies. *Amer. Sci.*, **62**, 650–659.

Menzel, E. W. (1978). Cognitive mapping in chimpanzees. In S. H. Hulse, H. Fowler, and W. K. Honig (Eds), *Cognitive Process in Animal Behavior*, Erlbaum, Hillsdale, N. J. pp. 375–422.

Morgan, C. L. (1896). *Habit and Instinct*, Edward Arnold, London.

Mulligan, J. A. (1966). Singing behavior and its development in the song sparrow, *Melospiza melodia*. *Univ. Calif. Publ. Zool.*, **81**, 1–76.

Noseworthy, C. M., and Lien, J. (1976). Ontogeny of nesting habitat recognition and preference in neonatal laughing gull chicks *Larus argentatus*. *Anim. Behav.*, **24**, 637–651.

Odum, E. P. (1959). *Fundamentals of Ecology*, 2nd Ed. Saunders, Philadelphia.

Ollason, J. G. (1981). Learning to forage—optimally? *Theor. Pop. Biol.*, **18**, 44–49.

Oppenheim, R. W. (1980). Metamorphosis and adaptation in the behavior of developing organisms. *Devel. Psychobiol.*, **13**, 353–356.

Piaget, J. (1964). Development and learning. In R. E. Ripple and V. N. Rockcastle (Eds), *Piaget Rediscovered*, U. S. Office of Education, Cooperative Research Project F-040. pp. 7–20.

Pietrewicz, A. T., and Kamil, A. C. (1977). Visual detection of cryptic prey by blue jays (*Cyanocitta cristata*). *Science*, **195**, 580–582.

Pietrewicz, A. T., and Kamil, A. C. (1979). Search image formation in the blue jay (*Cyanocitta cristata*). *Science*, **204**, 1332–1333.

Plotkin, H. C., and Odling-Smee, F. J. (1979). Learning, change and evolution: An enquiry into the teleonomy of learning. *Adv. Study Behav.*, **10**, 1–41.

Plotkin, H. C., and Odling-Smee, F. J. (1981). A multiple-level model of evolution and its implications for sociobiology. *Behav. Brain Sci.*, **4**, 225–268.

Popper, K. (1972). *Objective Knowledge: An Evolutionary View*, Oxford University Press, London.

Raup, D. M. (1966). Geometric analysis of shell coiling: general problems. *J. Paleont.*, **40**, 1178–1190.

Romanes, G. J. (1884). *Mental Evolution in Animals*, Appleton, New York.

Rosenzweig, M. R. (1966). Environmental complexity, cerebral change and behavior. *Amer. Psychol.*, **21**, 321–332.

Rozin, P. (1966). The evolution of intelligence and access to the cognitive unconscious. *Progr. Psychobiol. Physiol. Psychol.*, **6**, 245–280.

Rozin, P., and Kalat, J. W. (1971). Specific hungers and poison avoidance as adaptive specializations of learning. *Psychol. Rev.*, **78**, 459–486.

Schneirla, T. C. (1957). The concept of development in comparative psychology. In D. B. Harris (Ed.), *The Concept of Development: An Issue in the Study of Human Behavior*, University of Minnesota Press, Minneapolis. pp. 78–108.

Schneirla, T. C. (1966). Behavioral development and comparative psychology. *Q. Rev. Biol.*, **41**, 283–302.

Seligman, M. E. P. (1970). On the generality of the laws of learning, *Psych. Rev.* **77**, 406–418.

Shettleworth, S. J. (1981a). Function and mechanism in learning. In M. Zeiler and P. Harzem (Eds), *Advances in Analysis of Behavior, Volume 3: Biological Factors in Learning*, Wiley, New York.

Shettleworth, S. J. (1981b). An ecological theory of learning: good goal, poor strategy. *Behav. Brain. Sci.*, **4**, 160–161.

Skinner, B. F. (1938). *The Behavior of Organisms: An Experimental Analysis*, Appleton, New York.

Skinner, B. F. (1950). Are theories of learning necessary? *Psychol. Rev.*, **57**, 193–216.

Skinner, B. F. (1966). Ontogeny and phylogeny of behavior. *Science*, **153**, 1205–1213

Skinner, B. F. (1974a). *About Behaviorism*, Knopf, New York.

Skinner, B. F. (1974b). The shaping of phylogenic behavior. *Acta Neurobiol. Exp.*, **35**, 409–415.

Skinner, B. F. (1977). Herrnstein and the evolution of behaviorism *Amer. Psychol.*, **32**, 1006–1012.

Slobodkin, L. B. (1968). Toward a predictive theory of evolution. In R. C. Lewontin (Ed.), *Population Biology & Evolution*, Syracuse University Press, Syracuse, New York. pp. 187–205.

Slobodkin, L. B., and Rapoport, A. (1974). An optimum strategy of evolution. *Q. Rev. Biol.*, **49**, 181–200.

Small, W. S. (1900). An experimental study of the mental processes of the rat. *Amer. J. Psychol.*, **11**, 133–165.

Small, W. S. (1901). Experimental study of the mental processes of the rat. II. *Amer. J. Psychol.*, **12**, 206–239.

Sober, E. (1981). The evolution of rationality. *Synthese*, **46**, 95–120.

Sommerhoff, G. (1950). *Analytical Biology*, Oxford University Press, London.

Sommerhoff, G. (1969). The abstract characteristics of living systems. In F. E. Emery (Ed.), *Systems Thinking*, Penguin, Baltimore. pp. 147–202.

Staddon, J. E. R. (1976). Learning as adaptation. In W. K. Estes (Ed.), *Handbook of Learning and Cognitive Processes*, Volume 2, Erlbaum, Hillsdale, N. J. pp. 37–98.

Staddon, J. E. R., and Simmelhag, V. L. (1971). The 'superstition' experiment: A reexamination of its implications for the principles of adaptive behavior. *Psychol. Rev.*, **78**, 3–43.

Stearns, S. C. (1976). Life history tactics: A review of the ideas. *Q. Rev. Biol.*, **51**, 3–47.

Stearns, S. C. (1977). The evolution of life history traits: A critique of the theory and a review of the data. *Ann. Rev. Ecol. Syst.*, **8**, 145–171.

Thorndike, E. L. (1911). *Animal Intelligence*, Hafner, New York.

Timberlake, W. (in press). The functional organization of appetitive behavior: behavior systems and learning. In M. Zeiler and P. Harzem (Eds), *Advances in Analysis of Behavior, Volume 3: Biological Factors in Learning*, Wiley, New York.

Tinbergen, N. (1951). *The Study of Instinct*, Oxford University Press, London.

Tinbergen, N. (1963) On aims and methods of ethology. *Z. Tierpsychol.*, **20**, 410–429.

Tolman, E. C. (1932). *Purposive Behavior in Animals and Men*, Century, New York.

Waddington, C. H. (1957). *The Strategy of the Genes*, Allen and Unwin, London.

Warren, R. (1976). The perception of egomotion. *J. Exp. Psychol.: Hum. Percep. Perf.*, **2**, 448–456.

Watson, J. B. (1918). *Psychology from the Standpoint of a Behaviorist*, Lippincott, Philadelphia.

Watson, J. B. (1924). *Behaviorism*, Norton, New York.

Watt, W. B. (1969). Adaptive significance of pigment polymorphisms in *Colias* butterflies. II. Thermoregulation and photoperiodically controlled mellanin variation in *Colias eurytheme*. *Proc. Nat. Acad. Sci. U.S.A.*, **63**, 767–774.

Weismann, A. (1894). *The Effect of External Influences upon Development.* (*The Romanes Lecture*), Henry Frowde, London.

Wiens, J. A. (1970). Effects of early experience on substrate pattern selection in *Rana aurora* tadpoles. *Copeia*, **1970**, 543–548.

Wright, S. (1932). The roles of mutation, inbreeding, crossbreeding, and selection in evolution. *Proc. XI Int. Congr. Genet.*, **1**, 356–366.

CHAPTER 20

Learning in the context of a hierarchy of knowledge gaining processes

H. C. Plotkin and F. J. Odling-Smee

A. INTRODUCTION

Learning is the acquisition by an individual animal of information about some aspect of that animal's world, the storage of that information, and its integration into pre-existent behaviour patterns such that it is potentially capable of changing the behaviour of that animal in the future. Like any other form of information or knowledge gain, learning is a dynamic, dialectical process involving a changing world and a changing learner (see Chapter 1). It cannot be understood by the isolated consideration of either the one form of change or the other. Of importance also is the fact that the behavioural consequences of learning are usually, but by no means always, adaptive. Students of learning have been slow to recognize this latter point, though there has been a significant shift of ground in the last decade making that recognition now virtually universal. There continues, however, to be a general failure to realize its implications.

The initial insight regarding adaptation was owed primarily to Lorenz (1965) and Tinbergen (1951) where it formed not merely a passing observation, but part of an integrated approach to behaviour at large. That this insight should have come first from ethologists working within the paradigmatic framework of evolutionary biology is not surprising. For most of this century (see Gottlieb, 1979; Jenkins, 1979 for recent reviews) the study of learning fell within the domain of a preparadigmatic psychology where biological premises, such as the adaptiveness of phenotypic attributes, were not a part of any consistent analytical or conceptual approach.

Much has now been written about the basic tenets and assumptions of psychology and how these have affected the understanding and interpretation of behaviour in biological terms (see for example Hirsch, 1967; Hodos and Campbell, 1969; Lockard, 1971). Because of the prominence of learning in psychology, its treatment by general process theory has been especially singled out for criticism by adherents to the so-called biological boundaries approach (Seligman, 1970; Rozin and Kalat, 1971; Hinde, 1973). Such criticisms in turn have been vigorously attacked and rebutted (for example Bitterman, 1975, 1976; Revusky, 1977). It is not intended to further these exchanges here. Suffice it to say that the last two decades have not been a fruitful period for learning theory—witness the depressing re-occurrence of old arguments presented in the commentary of a recent issue of *Behavioural and Brain Sciences* in response to a provocative essay by Johnston (1981a). What is needed it seems is a new transcendent theory of learning. Such a theory must deal with whatever is general in all instances of learning (the purported province of general process theory) and whatever is diverse (the evidence of biological boundaries). It cannot confine itself to learning in some restricted taxonomic grouping, such as the vertebrates. And it must provide a framework for comparing learning across species.

In one essay we cannot cover all the ground, but we can attempt to outline the basis for such a general theory. So we will proceed as follows: first we will consider the impact of the constraints (diversity) issue on the learning literature both in terms of the failure of the biological boundary theorists to use it to effect a significant paradigm shift away from general process theory, and in terms of the failure of general process theory itself properly to incorporate this issue; second, we will provide a résumé of our own position and consider its implications both in terms of what it says about constraints (diversity) as well as what it postulates to be general to all learners (unity); third, we will present a scheme from which to view comparative studies of learning. Finally we will consider our position in the light of the adaptationist fallacy (Gould and Lewontin, 1979).

Before starting, however, it is worth pointing out that scientists who work with learning can do so in two rather different contexts. They can either perform as neuroscientists by supplying the operating characteristics of learning to the physiologist and biochemist who will then attempt to identify the neurological substrates of learning. Or they can show how learning interacts with other aspects of behaviour, and within actual ecological demands, to effect integrated behavioural change. We write this essay from the latter point of view.

B. UNITY AND DIVERSITY IN THEORIES OF LEARNING

A general theory of learning must provide an account for what is known as the 'constraints on learning'. The term constraint is inadequate because it biases thinking towards an overriding generality suggesting that what is being constrained is something general. Species-specific learning might be preferable. However, the term has become well entrenched in the literature and has meaning at least in historical terms, if in no other. So we will stick with it here.

(i) Biological boundary theory

The problem of constraints has been the most controversial issue in learning theory during the last decade. Doubts about the generality of the laws of learning, first voiced by the ethologists on conceptual rather than on empirical grounds, seemed initially to by confirmed by data from laboratory studies of learning that showed some aspects of learning to be species-typical (see Seligman and Hager, 1972; Shettleworth, 1972, 1975). These data were argued to be evidence against a general process view, although it is worth noting Hinde's (1981) assertion that biological theorists did not deny the existence of 'general principles of learning'.

One of the most powerful criticisms of general process theory came from Hinde (1973) who argued primarily on the basis of the manifest diversity of nature and the unlikelihood that learning should prove exceptional in this regard. He noted the undoubted existence of different 'forms' of learning, both within and between species, the explanation of which by general process theory was not, and still is not, immediately obvious. Nature, however, is not merely diverse. It is at once diverse and unified and no theory of any phenomenon in biology is complete unless it provides the basis for resolving this paradox. Hinde the biologist knew this, of course, and said it. But he did not say what was common to all, or even to many, learners.

Shettleworth (1972) similarly advocated a 'multiplicity of principles' but gave little indication of what these principles were. Like Hinde she too had little to say about what may be general to all learners. Seligman (1970), on the other hand, offered the notion of 'preparedness' as the unifying principle by which the diversity of learning could be accounted for, and in doing so he came closer than all the other biological boundary theorists to showing how the unity versus diversity paradox might be resolved. But preparedness, a species-specific predisposition to associate certain events rather than others, was a weak notion on three counts. First, it failed to explain the origins of these predispositions, what they might be or how they might operate. Thus it was no more than a descriptive device. Second, its determination was *ex post facto* (Johnston, 1981a) and its explanatory power entirely circular: if something could not be learned or learned only with difficulty it was called unprepared or contraprepared learning, and the latter was then defined as learning that either did not occur or did so only with difficulty. Third, it was couched exclusively in associationistic terms and thus was severely limited to conventional cases of associative learning—not a strong position from which to argue against an equally restrictive general process theory.

Certainly all of these biological boundary views revolved in a loose and informal way around the concept of adaptation. But no one developed a formal position around the explicit and powerful point made by Lorenz that 'the amazing and never-to-be-forgotten fact is that learning does, in the majority of cases, increase the survival value of the behaviour mechanisms which it modifies' (Lorenz, 1965, p. 12). Thus the biological boundary views were never firmly or consistently built on a theory of adaptation despite their appearances to the contrary. It was this failure that gave such sting to Revusky's (1977) comment that 'neo-evolutionary learning theorists aggrandize minor science, the study of the particular, at the expense of the extremely important, the study of the general' (p. 10). The theory of adaptation is not minor science. Listing instances of adaptation is.

Lacking the challenge of a coherent alternative which was based on a theory of adaptation, and confronted merely with seemingly refractory examples of obviously adaptive forms of learning, general process theory was able to shrug off the challenge posed by the biological boundaries view with no great difficulty. The reason why learning is constrained was ascribed to concepts like 'stimulus salience' (Rescorla and Wagner, 1972) or to the 'stimulus relevance principle' (Revusky, 1977). These concepts may well be powerful, if highly restricted, explanatory notions that tell us, within a framework of proximate causality, why certain limited forms of learning are constrained. But they do not explain the origin of the constraints. What they lack is explanatory power in terms of ultimate causation. Nonetheless, such notions can be, and have been, presented as a way of accounting for species differences in learning. The net result of such concepts, and of the undoubted shift in ground towards an acceptance of species-specific learning differences, is, as Johnston (1981a) points out, that there is now little to choose between general process theory and biological boundaries theory.

(ii) General process theory

General process theory can be viewed as a highly successful mini-theory. It is aimed at associative learning, as defined by the Thorndikian and Pavlovian paradigms, and does not usually pretend to be able to deal with all instances of learning (Mackintosh, 1974; Dickinson, 1980). It is also usually explicitly confined to issues of proximate causation. Despite these limitations it is likely that certain natural forms of learning, such as occur in foraging (Lea, 1981), can be at least partly accounted for by it. This much, it seems to us, cannot be disputed. But if we have accurately characterized general process theory, then it cannot be held to be a truly general theory of learning. A truly general theory must account for *all* instances of learning in any and every species of learner, and the account must be in terms of both proximate and ultimate causality. It is self-evident that general process theory does not fulfil these criteria. A general theory cannot be built around a restricted concept like associationism, nor on that data generated by conditioning and operant studies only. We would argue this at a broader level: no general theory of learning will emerge from any theoretical treatments that confine themselves to the conceptual tools of learning alone. Truly general theories of learning will only be developed from more fundamental exercises in biological theory.

In arguing against the view that associationism provides the basis for a general theory of learning, we are not attacking the notion that all learning somehow relates to environmental order. Environmental order comprises patterns in time and space that, in their description, must involve temporal and spatial intervals and other fundamental parameters such as the unidirectional flow of time. All of these feature in associationist theory. Such fundamental parameters are, however, necessary only because they reflect ecological universals. As such they must be present and must govern every instance of learning. The universality of learning is thus ultimately also to be sought in the environment, and not just in the psychological or physiological processes or mechanisms by which such aspects of environmental order are incorporated into the organization of the learner.

If general process theory is not a general theory of learning, then it cannot comment on species-specific or constrained instances of learning that fall outside of its province. Language acquisition in the human child is the classic example. The imitation of complex social behaviours in certain species of old-world monkey is another example. Song learning in certain species of song bird is a third. These can be multiplied many times over. They all make a simple point. They are all instances of learning that are not associative as defined by the Pavlovian or Thorndikian paradigms, and that are species-typical. They lead to two questions: First, is it possible to make general statements that apply to such obviously constrained and diverse instances of learning? Second, if the answer to the first question is in the affirmative, would such general statements be the same as those that are claimed to be applicable to all instances of associative learning?

We believe that answer to the first question is yes, and to the second is no. But the main point of asking these questions is to draw attention to the astonishing failure of the constraints literature to raise some very fundamental issues regarding the limits within which the debate is being conducted. Is the argument about constraints on learning or constraints on associative learning, for the two are certainly not the same thing. And if the argument has only been about constraints on associative learning, then what deep-seated assumptions and beliefs about learning and the nature of the world that is learned about are thus revealed? We need not here answer these questions. But we feel that it is time that they were brought out into the light of critical examination rather than being left buried as implicit and unspoken assumptions.

Johnston (1981a) has made a closely similar point so well, that it is worth quoting him at length:

'Lolordo's (1979) analysis is especially interesting. If his defence of associative equivalence is correct, then it is possible to identify a wide range of selective nonassociative processes, of manifest importance to learning, that it is unconvincing to dismiss as mere species-specific "contaminations" (Schwartz, 1974). If these processes have a major influence on an animal's ability to learn, as they apparently do, then our theories should reflect this fact and not view them as peripheral to "true" (i.e. associative) learning. It is, of course, quite legitimate for particular theories or investigators to focus their attention on associative rather than nonassociative phenomena, but if this is allowed to become the bias of the entire field of animal learning, then the theories that result are likely to be of rather limited explanatory scope (Rescorla and Holland, 1976).' (Johnston, 1981a, p. 128)

There is another way of putting this whole issue. The tendency to confine the debate about constraints and generality to a few selected forms of associative learning is an unhealthy symptom of the narrow vision of contemporary learning theory. If truly general 'laws' are ever to be established, then they are going to have to extend rather further than associationism.

(iii) The poverty of evidence in the face of poor theory

It is an old and often repeated lament that behavioural science at large is deficient in theory, and that what passes for theory is usually no more than a set of loosely articulating, incomplete, descriptive statements that make no strong predictions (Estes *et al.*, 1954; Koch, 1951; Madsen, 1961). This applies as much to learning as to anything else. General process theory is built on those more inclusive behavioural theories such as Hull's (1943) that preceded it. As such it forms part of the abiological tradition of psychology that has a persistent tendency to talk about an entity called 'the' organism. The implicit assumptions and explicit damage that is caused by cavalier extrapolation from single species to seemingly on entire kingdom of life have been discussed elsewhere (Lockard, 1971; Plotkin, 1979). One consequence is an overriding bias towards thinking in terms of universality and generality and the accompanying tendency to play down the importance of diversity. So when constraints on learning became an issue it was natural that the response of general process theorists should be to try to save the assumptions of the theory by 'stretching' its parameters in order to incorporate the new data. The apparent resilience of general process theory, however, really only derives from its lack of formal discipline. It is resilient because it is a bad theory. It is also worth noting that 'stretching the parameters' is the general process theory equivalent of the adaptationist fallacy (see below) and of the genetic fallacy (Ho and Saunders, 1979). Just as it is possible, but without meaning, to invent genes or 'just so' adaptational accounts of any phenomenon in biology, so it is possible, but equally meaningless, to stretch the parameters of general process theory to account for any data from any learning study.

The protagonists of the constraints, on the other hand, the biological boundary theorists whose focus is diversity, made the error of not building a theory to incorporate the constraints that they proposed and discovered. They merely made the weak claim that evidence for constraints on learning is evidence for the adapted, and to some extent species-typical, nature of learning—claims that Bitterman (1975) was able to characterize as 'loose speculation about adaptive significance' (p. 708).

And there the matter has rested. Unresolved and seemingly unresolvable. Two accounts of the same phenomenon with neither offering any intrinsic superiority over the other and the discipline unable to suggest a way of distinguishing between them. At this juncture evidence has little to contribute. Ironically, in this way, the constraints issue has made at least one valuable point. It shows how powerless data can be in the absence of strong theory.

What is needed, clearly, is a better theory. In a recent review, Shettleworth (1981) identified two approaches as being different from either general process theory or the biological boundaries view. Common to both is the attempt to develop an explanatory basis for a theory of learning that lies outside the narrow confines of learning theory itself. One approach is that of Johnston and Turvey (1980) and Johnston (1981a, b) which is built on Sommerhoff's analytical biology and ecological theory. The other is our own (Plotkin and Odling-Smee, 1979, 1981) which is based on the notion of a hierarchy of knowledge-gaining processes and which is rooted in evolutionary epistemology. In the rest of this chapter we will try to show how our position has the potential to provide the foundations for a truly general theory of learning: namely one capable of reconciling unity with diversity, and of providing a framework for the comparative study of learning in all learners. What follows is, in a sense, an attempt to marry the Johnston and Turvey approach to our own.

C. LEARNING AND A HIERARCHY OF KNOWLEDGE PROCESSES

(i) Résumé

Reference should be made to Plotkin and Odling-Smee (1979, 1981) and Odling-Smee (1982) for a more detailed account of our position. Here we will only briefly outline the salient points.

1. Following Campbell (1974—see Chapter 5 of this book), Goodwin (1976) and earlier evolutionary epistemologists, living systems are viewed as knowledge systems in the sense that the form that adaptations take reflect in part the internalization of certain aspects of the world. Thus they constitute knowledge

of the world. As noted in Chapter 1, such knowledge is only partial in that the form of an adaptation is a compromise determined by multiple factors such as allometric effects and competitive adaptive requirements. Nonetheless, adaptations constitute knowledge as defined in Chapter 1 in that they are based on a dynamic exchange of information between a living system and its environment.

2. The world is not static. For living systems it is always changing. Some change is inconstant and singular. Other change is constant but repetitive, and yet another kind is constant but non-repetitive. The form of change that an organism has to deal with is determined by that organism's longevity. For example, circadian or seasonal cycles will only be experienced as cyclic change if a creature is sufficiently long-lived. They become instances of constant directional change if only a segment of the cycle is experienced by a shorter-lived organism. There is, therefore, no absolute classification of change. The form that change takes is always relative to the organism on which it impinges.

One important source of change is the activity of the organism itself (see Bonner, 1980, for an interesting analysis of the role of activity in evolution). Such activity need not always be overt: covert manipulation of the environment, by an animal with a sufficiently complex nervous system to allow it to have internalized representations of the world, is activity as well. Furthermore activity need not merely be absolute locomotion in space, though obviously this is an important form of activity. It is any form of behaviour whose teleonomic goal is to bring about some change in the world. Thus, following Lewontin's (1978) observation that 'organisms do not experience environments passively; they create and define the environment', active organisms are constantly recreating and redefining their own environments and that of other organisms.

3. Change is the engine that drives evolution and the formation of adaptations. Different adaptations are responses to different kinds and rates of change. Thus there must be a capacity for gaining knowledge about a changing world. Since change is not single-valued in either time or space, different rates and distributions of change must become 'known' by one or, if there are limitations to that one, then by several information or knowledge gaining processes.

4. Learning is one of the knowledge gaining processes which can potentially provide organisms with knowledge about their changing worlds. However, it does not exist in isolation from other knowledge gaining processes. We have previously argued that any theory of learning must take into account at least three evolutionary or 'heuristic' levels at which knowledge gaining occurs. Similarly it must also take into account the three separate loci of information store, or 'referents', which are associated with each of these distinct knowledge gaining processes.

Within this scheme, the primary level (Level 1) is represented by the process of change which occurs in gene and allele frequencies in a reproducing population in response to a changing world. The referent, or locus of information store in this case is the population gene pool. Level 2 consists of the process of 'variable epigenesis', that is to say the flexible translation of a genotype into a phenotype. The locus of information store here is the entire phenotype. Level 3 consists of a set of processes plus their associated sites of store. The processes here include the immune system and learning amongst others. Each of these processes is organ, or organ-system specific. Our interest in this third level is, of course, restricted to learning, and to its associated locus of information store in the central nervous system. We should also briefly mention a fourth level since this too implicates learning if and when it occurs. Level 4 consists of 'cultural processes' according to which learned information is transmitted among a group of learners nongenetically. In this case the site of storage is a 'cultural pool'.

5. There is no simple identity between an individual organism and any single information store. Level 1 knowledge gaining acts on a between-organism basis, and hence any individual organism will always carry a fraction of the level 1 store within itself. On the other hand levels 2 and 3 are both within-organism knowledge gaining processes. If present these stores will be carried in their entirety by single organisms. If a fourth level is present then an individual organism will only carry a part of that store since here again the knowledge gain works on a between-animal basis.

6. In order to impose conceptual order on our model we have had to make certain assumptions. Each of these assumptions has varying degrees of plausibility. The first is that the Level 1 knowledge gaining process (the genetic) appeared earliest in the history of life, and that it also appeared earliest in any lineage which has ultimately evolved an ability to learn. The second assumption is that Level 2 and 3 in our scheme are subordinate heuristic levels that only evolved in certain populations. It is assumed that they did so as a function of those particular populations encountering rates of and types of environmental change which exceeded the capacity of the primary Level 1 genetic process to cope, by supplying the individual members of the population with adequate up to date and local knowledge about their changing worlds.

The third assumption is that the information that underlies an adaptation will be supplied by the lowest heuristic, or evolutionary level, that is able to supply it. That is to say it will be supplied by Level 1 before either Levels 2 and 3, and by Level 2 before Level 3. Put in other terms this assumption states that learning involves biological costs, both actual and potential, which are greater than those of either Level 1 or Level 2. This is identical to Williams' assertion (Williams, 1966—Chapter 11 of this book) that all behavioural elements that can be instinctive, will be. 'Instinct costs less than learned behaviour, in the currency of genetic information'. Instincts also cost less in physiological and biochemical terms (see Johnston, 1981b), and by definition are potentially subject to less error than is learned behaviour.

7. The last point is contained in the hypothesis that all knowledge gaining processes in nature, and hence all the processes which operate at each of our four heuristic levels, share a common logic, and a universal algorithm. Our belief is that this common logic is ultimately imposed on all knowledge gaining processes, relative to all biological entities, by certain ecological variables and certain properties of living systems which apply on a universal scale. Thus all knowledge gaining processes work relative to biological entities (e.g. populations, or individual organisms) which are invariably localised in space and time. Because of their localisation, such entities are only ever able to 'sample' their total environments across space and time. In addition they are invariably forced to proceed through time in only one direction. All biological entities are therefore forced to encounter their own futures on the basis of knowledge which can only be based on past samples of their environments. This makes whatever knowledge they may gain, by whatever process, and at whatever heuristic level, fundamentally uncertain. It also makes their own passage across time and space fundamentally a gamble. The point is that the nature of this gamble imposes itself upon whatever knowledge gaining process (or processes) the biological entity is relying on, and it dictates the logic of that process. This hypothesis was first proposed by Campbell (1974).

The scheme presented here goes beyond Campbell's idea of a universal knowledge gaining algorithm in only one respect. This is the recognition that each separate knowledge gaining process in nature is tied to its own separate and distinct locus of information store or referent. Given this one refinement we then follow Campbell by considering that the universal algorithm is best understood by breaking it down into three components or sub-processes. These comprise (i) the generating of variety; (ii) the selection of a limited number of those variants, and their storage; (iii) the regenerating of further variety, where this regeneration is based on a mixture of the conserved variants in store, and novel variants which are unconstrained by past selection, and which are generated either at random or on some haphazard basis. This algorithm is termed the 'generate–test–regenerate–retest heuristic', or the 'g–t–r' heuristic for short.

Learning translates into these three sub-processes of the g–t–r heuristic as follows. Both the generate and regenerate phases result in the production by the learner of both covert and overt behavioural variety. The test phase on the other hand consists of the selection by the learner itself of whatever variety has been previously generated, in the light of its interactions with its environment. Critical to the test phase are 'auto selection mechanisms' (ASMs, in contrast to the mechanisms of natural selection which apply at Level 1). These are assumed to be based on a learner's 'capacity to be reinforced' (Staddon and Simmelhag, 1971). In general, but not invariably, the ASMs select behavioural variants that are adaptive, and which therefore do permit the learner to cope successfully with critical aspects of its changing world. Finally the behavioural variants which are generated at the regenerate phase of the heuristic may differ from those which are produced by the learner at the earlier generate phase, only in being constrained by an intervening test phase and by the possible injection of novel variants. Within this scheme it is important to note that the nature of the variants that are generated by learners is expected to differ in different species relative to different learning tasks, different mixes of chance and constraint, and different prior learning and developmental experiences on the part of individual learners. The ASMs are also expected to differ across learners in much the same way.

In summary the preceding seven points describe learning as a subsidiary knowledge gaining and storing process that has greater temporal and spatial resolution than do either the genetic (Level 1) or the variable epigenetic (Level 2) processes that evolved it. Learning is not an isolated ability and cannot function independently of the other knowledge gaining processes. Collectively these various processes, plus their associated referents or information stores, therefore form a nested hierarchy as depicted in Figure 1.

(ii) The unity of learning

The preceding model comprising multiple knowledge gaining processes operating at different heuristic levels allows us to propose a basis for a theory of learning which is different from anything previously proposed. This is because, as far as learning is concerned, the model is capable of addressing both the unity and the diversity of learning simultaneously.

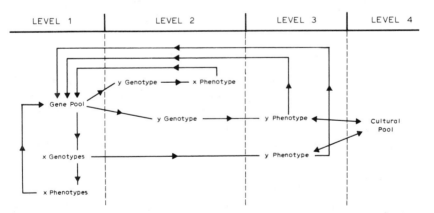

Figure 1 The nested hierarchy of knowledge gaining processes. The prefix x indicates non-information gaining units. The prefix y indicates flexible, autonomous information gaining units (Adapted from Plotkin and Odling-Smee (1979), by permission of Academic Press. Copyright © 1979 by Academic Press)

Three universals are held to be common to all learners, regardless of species, regardless of task, and regardless of the prior history of the individual learner. First there is the teleonomic nature of learning. Learning is a knowledge gaining and storing evolutionary sub-routine that is always nested under the genetic Level 1 process, and which is nearly always nested under the variable epigenetic Level 2 process as well. This means that the origins of learning should always derive from the operating limits of the Level 1 and 2 processes, and in particular from the sampling limitations of those processes relative to specified populations with specified generational turn-over times. Second, all learning occurs in accordance with the g–t–r heuristic. Consequently every kind of learning studied by either biologists or psychologists should be capable of analysis by being broken down into the three sub-processes which constitute this heuristic. Every given instance of learning should therefore conform to the generate–test–regenerate–retest–regenerate ... pattern. In addition the locus of information store, which is fed by the test phase during learning, should always be different from all other loci of information store, or referents, which occur in nature. Third, like every other knowledge gaining process learning should always be a dialectical process according to which the learner is both changed by the act of learning and simultaneously effects some change on the world that it is learning about. Unlike the other two universals we shall not pursue this third universal any further here. It requires extensive treatment in its own right. Suffice it to say that knowledge is a property of the organisation of a complex system relative to environmental order, and that neither biological organisation nor environmental order have any biological meaning in isolation from each other. This dialectical relationship is similar to the coimplicative relationship that Johnston and Turvey (1980) define between the organism and its environment.

(iii) The diversity of learning

The diversity of learning now has to be seen in the light of these universals. It must actually grow out of the unity of learning at some point. In the model just described it stems from the first universal. This is that learning is invariably nested within a hierarchy of knowledge gaining processes, having itself evolved from the underlying processes within the hierarchy. It is this feature that provides the necessary basis for accounting for learning's diversity.

Once Lorenz recognized the adaptive nature of learning, he was inevitably led down a particular road of enquiry. He realized that for learning to be adaptive, every learner must contain within itself some kind of predisposition to learn about only certain aspects of environmental order, relative to all the possible sources of information that impinge upon it. These predispositions he variously labeled 'teaching instructions', 'innate teaching mechanisms' and 'innate school marms'. The entire 1965 monograph was an attempt to locate where and how such innate mechanisms for learning operate. Lorenz was not the only theorist to understand the need to postulate the existence of such devices. Hull's (1943) postulate 3, for example, of 'a hierarchy of responses that either individually or in combination are more likely to terminate the need than would be a random selection' is another famous instance of the recognition that learning is not an infinitely open-ended phenomenon. There have also been others. Nevertheless no one else made the notion as central to their conceptual framework as did Lorenz. All he lacked was a scheme that could show, in general terms, for instance in general systems theory, the reason why these innate teaching mechanisms should exist—where do they come from?

Campbell (1974) recognized the problem at this more general level and he indicated how, in principle, it could be solved. If all knowledge processes are a part of a nested hierarchical system, then information that has been laboriously gained by a blind variation—selective retention procedure at one (more fundamental) level of the hierarchy may be fed upwards to some other (less fundamental) level where it can immediately operate as preset or predetermined criteria. He called these 'shortcut processes'. In Chapter 1 this solution was referred to as the way in which knowledge gained *a posteriori* can appear at a less fundamental level as *a priori* knowledge. Plotkin and Odling-Smee (1979, 1981), leaning heavily on both Lorenz and Campbell, then called upon this same device and referred to it as 'priming'. We merely added the logically strict framework of the sampling limitations of each level in the hierarchy and the distinction between the separate loci of information store. The advantage of priming to any learner is that it allows the learner to start its learning on the basis of its innately primed learning capacity, rather than on the basis of 'tabula rasa' learning capacity. Thus it can begin with whatever useful information may have been gained earlier at Levels 1 and 2 within the hierarchy of knowledge gaining processes, and which will have been fed up the hierarchy to Level 3 via mechanisms of inheritance and development. By this means the likelihood of successful knowledge gain occurring at Level 3 via learning is increased (hence Lorenz's observation about the adaptive nature of learning), and the time or number of learning trials needed for this gain to occur is decreased (hence the aptness of Campbell's phrase 'shortcuts').

Whatever one chooses to call these innate teaching mechanisms or priming devices, their implication for learning theory is specific. They predict that there will always be species-specific constraints on learning; that learning never begins *de novo* for any species of learner; and that no learner is ever a *tabula rasa*. It is important to realise that these are not predictions made with the benefits of hindsight. They are a consequence of placing learning within the broader context of a hierarchically organized knowledge-gaining system. If a science of learning did not yet exist but genetics and developmental biology did, and if scientists came to realize, as they inevitably would, that in some organisms these fundamental processes for generating phenotypic adaptations could not supply a sufficiently fine-grained fit of the phenotype to a rapidly changing environment, then theorists would come to predict the existence of learning in some animals, and the prediction would specify that learning is always constrained and manifests itself as species-specific diversity.

Exactly what the innate teaching mechanisms are, and how they operate, is unknown. Lorenz (1965) himself made at least five suggestions:

(1) Some aspect(s) of perceptual organization (seemingly close to what are usually called attentional factors);
(2) a spatial orientation for the discharge of motor patterns;
(3) the range of fixed motor patterns available to the learner;
(4) what the consummatory responses of the learner are; and
(5) the way in which these consummatory responses are interlocked with other behaviours and hence the way in which structural changes in behaviour can occur consequent to learning.

More recently, Pulliam and Dunford (1980) have drawn attention to the need for learners to recognize what is reinforcing (auto-selecting in the terminology of the g–t–r heuristic), and how reinforcers revise evaluations of responses, as two important points for species-specific differences. Within our own system, we would expect species-specific differences to operate at all three phases of the g–t–r heuristic. Thus, there must be some predisposition, as Hull recognized, to generate a restricted set of variants *a priori* depending upon the state of the learner at the time and the nature of the events being experienced. Auto-selection must also be constrained, and as Pulliam and Dunford argue, different selectors must alter behaviour in different and limited ways. Finally the nature of the regenerated variants and the particular mix of novelty in the regenerated responses must again be constrained.

These listings are not exhaustive. It is obvious that the possible points at which species-specific constraints operate may relate to traditional questions in learning theory. For example, is 'seeing once sufficient to believe', or must the learner 'see' many times before it reaches some statistical decision as to whether to believe, and hence to learn, or not (Rescorla, 1968)? And how do such 'seeing is believing' rules vary with the nature of the information (the cue type), the nature of the selector or reinforcer, and the nature of the animal? There are many other such examples. The nub of our argument, however, is not merely that constraints exist, but that the pattern of constraints within the same animal, between animals of the same species, and also between animals of different species, must be central to the construction of any truly general theory of learning.

D. THE COMPARATIVE PROBLEM

If this view of how learning theory must develop is correct, then a great deal more information is needed about learning in different species. Even if it is incorrect then this will still remain a requirement, since any theory claiming generality must be tested across a variety of different species if the boundaries of its generality are to be discovered. Hence the comparative study of learning is a crucial prerequisite for any general theory of learning. Furthermore the problem of reconciling the diversity of learning which is stressed by the biological boundary theorists with the unity of learning stressed by general process theorists is nowhere more evident than in the field of comparative learning studies. For these reasons the attempt will be made to apply our model to the problems which beset comparative learning. However, we do not propose to review the comparative learning literature. This has been done several times in the last decade (e.g. Bitterman, 1975; Bitterman and Woodward, 1976; Corning, Dyal and Willows, 1973a, b, 1975; Dewsbury, 1978; Warren, 1973). Instead we shall concentrate on conceptual problems. Some of these are little more than semantic quibbles, but others arise from deeper issues. They all seem to revolve around the difficulty of knowing what it is one is comparing, and what it is one ought to be comparing.

(i) Terminological confusions

If learning is to be compared across species, then it must be done within an accepted and well understood language. A far from trivial matter for the comparative analysis of learning is the number of terminological inconsistencies in the literature. There are no accepted terminological conventions, with the result that writers often use the same word to mean different things or different words to refer to the same thing. This occurs even in roughly allied approaches. Consider some of the following recent usages by biologically oriented writers. Shettleworth (1981) uses four main terms: (i) *paradigm*— this is the 'description of an experience an environment offers an animal'. This is not an adequate statement if only because the experience of an animal is not accessible. More usually, a paradigm refers to a very limited description of the environment that the observer assumes is being monitored and learned about by the animal. In experimental terms the paradigm is, as Shettleworth points out, the method. (ii) *Phenomenon*—this is the change in behaviour that results from the assumed experience. (iii) *Principle*—this is the consistent relationship between a paradigm and a phenomenon, 'a statement that certain experiences produce certain behavioural changes'. (iv) *Process* (seemingly used interchangeably with *mechanism*)—this is the entity that generates the principle. In psychological terms the process is a hypothetical construct, the mechanism presumably being its neurological substrate. Shettleworth defines her terms clearly and uses them consistently. But if one accepts the ways in which she uses these terms, then what sense is one to make of Bitterman's (1975) statement that 'The learning processes that we now are able to infer from performance in learning situations are far removed, of course, from learning mechanisms. They are at best a series of functional principles (like the S–R reinforcement principle) from which the observed phenomena of learning can be deduced and which may be expected to guide the search for mechanisms' (p. 706). Here processes and (functional) principles seem to be the same; and it is not at all clear what Bitterman means by mechanism or phenomena.

Johnston (1981a) employs two terms in a simple and effective way. *Processes*—these are events that occur. *Principles*—these are informal or formal statements about processes, and the relationships between different processes and between processes and external conditions. For Johnston, a theory uses principles to explain or predict processes. Johnston's position is elegantly simple, but quite clearly he is using the terms process and principle in entirely different ways from either Shettleworth or Bitterman. Our own writings have not helped matters. The multiple-level model that we present is based on the central notion of different processes of knowledge-gain attached to separate information stores. The processes that we refer to are changes in gene frequency in a gene pool, variable epigenesis, learning and cultural processes. Each of these processes is assigned the component subprocesses of the g–t–r heuristic. Whatever the merits of our position, we too are using terms in an idiosyncratic way.

There is the additional complication that underlying a preference for terms by any writer are his or her own conceptual preferences. Different conceptual preferences will lead to different usage of terms, and even to the abandonment of some. The paradigms are a case in point. Reference to any of the recent comparative learning reviews referred to above shows that they treat learning in terms of the experimental requirements imposed upon animals by the investigators. The associative paradigms of classical conditioning and instrumental learning are prominent, as are other well established methodologies such as habituation and different kinds of learning set. However, for Johnston and Turvey (1980) and Johnston (1981a), as well as for Plotkin and Odling-Smee (1979), the paradigms are, if not irrelevant, then certainly inadequate descriptions of anything that happens to a learner. Learning specifically, but behaviour more generally, is for Johnston and Turvey 'coimplicative' in that neither the learner not its environment can be defined separately from each other. For ourselves likewise the act of learning results in the learner's world being changed, while simultaneously the learner is changed by the act of learning. This view obviously owes much to Piaget's concepts of assimilation and accommodation (see Chapter 8 of this book) and it is certainly no accident that Piaget seldom thought the learning paradigms worth writing about. For any coimplicative or dialectical view of behaviour and learning the paradigms represent an incomplete and static account of what is actually a dynamic interaction between a changing learner and its changing environment. The net result is that while there may be virtually no disagreement regarding the definition and practical laboratory use of traditional learning paradigms, such as classical conditioning, there is a real difference of view as to the adequacy of the paradigms as descriptions or accounts of learning. Contrary to the traditional approach of making comparisons within the context of the paradigms, our view is that an analysis that is restricted to the paradigms is an inadequate vehicle for establishing similarities and differences in learning across species.

(ii) A proposed scheme

Here then is one problem. A theory of learning will be built partly on a comparative analysis. A comparative analysis requires standardized usage of terms. Terminological consistency will only be reached if there is some consensus as to what is being compared. Consensus, however, will only occur if there is agreement on what the theoretical issues are. One way to break out of this circle is to offer different schemes of learning for discussion, and to attach labels to different features of such schemes. These schemes will then compete in terms of the usually accepted criteria such as internal coherence and breadth of explanatory scope relative to data. What they do, in effect, is give us a

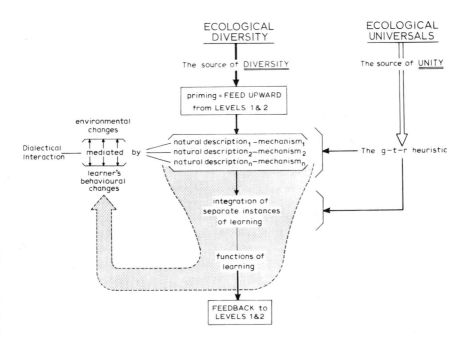

Figure 2 A scheme for the comparative analysis of learning. The ecological universals expressed in the g–t–r heuristic interact with information fed upwards from Levels 1 and 2 to result in species-specific instances and integration of learning. The thick, black arrows indicate the relationship of the learning level with the rest of the hierarchy of knowledge processes. For details see text

starting point for the elaboration of a theory. They are equivalent to Johnston and Turvey's (1980) metatheory.

Figure 2 is such a scheme. Because the word 'process' has developed an especially ambiguous status in learning theory, we have omitted it entirely. Henceforth we may refer to learning as one out of several 'knowledge gaining processes' and we may occasionally refer to the g–t–r heuristic which supports it as a 'process' also but that is all. Central to this scheme are a series of natural descriptions of behaviour each of which describes a separate instance of learning as it occurs under normal free-living conditions. Examples of such natural descriptions might be observing a conspecific, practising a motor act such as walking, sparring, stalking, foraging, or sampling the taste or smell character-istics of a food item. Each natural description will have to be underpinned by conditions and definitions which are sufficiently precise to allow some degree of certainty that learning is occurring, and it will need to be detailed rather than casual. It will therefore raise difficult technical issues that should not be underestimated. However, these issues are not crucial to the present discussion. Each natural description will also be associated with physiological mechanisms. These mechanisms are partial substrates of the natural descriptions, but they are not a direct or necessary part of a behavioural theory of learning. They obviously are a crucial part of the neuroscience of learning (see Rose (1981) for some interesting observations regarding causation and the relationship between events at the behavioural and physiological levels).

Given these natural descriptions, what is then needed is a framework capable of allowing meaningful comparisons to be made between different instances of learning, as described by the natural descriptions. In our view such a framework must refer to both sources of unity and to sources of diversity with respect to both the variety of instances of learning in any one learner, and to the variety of species of learners it must incorporate if it is to be effective. In the scheme shown the unity of learning ultimately stems from those ecological factors which are in fact universals, and which are therefore common to all learners. In one sense they are simply those particular constraints on learning which apply to all learners, and beyond that, to all knowledge gaining systems in general. They thus comprise those factors which arise from the basic spatio-temporal structure of the environment relative to organisms which are them-selves localised in environmental space and time. This is convergent evolution operating on the grand scale.

The diversity of learning, on the other hand, stems from the lower heuristic levels of the hierarchy of knowledge gaining processes within which learning itself occurs. Diversity thus stems from both level 1 (genetic) and 2 (variable epigenetic) knowledge gain. The diversity takes the form of the innate and developmental priming of each of the three phases of the g–t–r heuristic. Here we would expect the priming to be species-specific relative to Level 1 (genetic) priming, and individual learner-specific relative to Level 2 (epigenetic) priming. We would also expect it to be sensitive to all manner of diverse ecological factors which may have acted on both different species of learners, and on different individual learners during their past phylogenetic and developmental histories. The priming of each phase of the g–t–r heuristic by Levels 1 and 2 is therefore a result of divergent evolution and development, arising from divergent ecological factors.

This scheme is fully compatible with Johnston's (1981a) proposal that the comparative study of learning must be based on ecological principles. If we go beyond Johnston it is only in claiming that there are convergent as well as divergent ecological factors at work, and that some convergent factors are sufficiently general to allow the unity of learning, as well as the diversity of learning, to be discovered in the ecology of learners. The scheme is also compatible with an earlier call from Lockard (1971) for comparative psychology to be based not only on the ecological principles of convergent and divergent evolution, but also on phylogenetic relatedness, these being the warp and weft of evolutionary analysis.

An objection which is likely to be levelled at this scheme is that 'natural descriptions' of learning, however detailed, will always be insufficiently precise. In particular they may never be adequate to allow clear communication among psychologists studying learning in the laboratory. In this respect an undoubted attraction of the paradigms approach is that it is precise at least in operational terms. The trouble is that what the paradigms approach gains in precision it loses in generality. This has the unfortunate side effect of allowing any instance of learning which does not readily conform to any particular learning paradigm to escape the interest of large numbers of psychologists. For example it is likely that the relative lack of interest shown by psychologists for decades in imitation learning, which is an important starting point to Level 4 cultural knowledge gain, is because such learning does not readily fall under the rubric of any single paradigm.

A possible way out of this problem is to classify the natural descriptions of learning into 'types' of learning. To be consistent with the overall scheme one would have to base this classification on the g–t–r heuristic. One way would be to classify learning in terms of the nature of the behavioural variants generated at the generate and regenerate phases of the heuristic. Defining types of learning in terms of the behavioural variants generated would reduce to a classification of learning in terms of sub-sets of 'expectations' (covert behaviours) and of responses (overt behaviours) drawn from within the learners total repertoire of alternative possible behaviours. Thus, the modelling of a young animal's behaviour on that of its caretaker involves a particular set of covert or overt variants, whether the behaviour that is being modelled is the use of a tool or the stalking of prey: the mimetic variants are all models of action that form the basis for the imitation. The variants that are generated during observational learning are different from those that are generated during the acquisition of simple motor skills such as flying or walking where the variants will be motor programmes and different again from the vocal variants generated during language learning. Other obvious sets of variants are hypotheses, sensory template matching, and spatial and temporal correlations (associations). Less obvious sets of variants demarcating between different types of learning may be found among Campbell's (1974) ten levels of knowledge gain, many of which fall into the category of the third level process.

The advantages of such a taxonomy are twofold. First it allows all instances of learning to be classified equally readily. It would therefore provide a less restrictive basis for a comparative psychology of learning than does the present paradigms approach. Second it would classify learning primarily in terms of what animals do in their environments, rather than in terms of what experimenters do to the environments of animals. It is accepted that it may be impossible to work out a serviceable taxonomy on these lines. However, even if this proves to be the case we would still argue that a comparative science of learning needs a more liberal classification than that currently offered by the paradigms.

One other point, also indicated in Figure 2, is that the natural descriptions of learning do not apply merely to single instances of behavioural change but potentially to complex integrated changes as well. Consider, for example, the case of the human child observing an adult tying shoe-laces and coming in time with verbal and motor guidance to acquire that skill. Here a number of 'types' of learning (imitation, fine manipulative skill, the sequencing of movements, the translation of verbal instructions into overt behaviour—each comprising different sets of variants) articulate with one another to give rise to the appropriate, integrated behavioural change. Such integration is unlikely to be achieved by random combinations of learned behaviours. It must be a consequence of certain broadly pre-determined patterns of integration. The final form of such integration will itself be controlled by the operation of the g–t–r heuristic: but in this case the behavioural variants generated at the generate and regenerate phases will consist of alternative sequences of behaviours, each able to be broken down into more basic instances of learning. Similarly the auto-selection mechanisms operating at the test phase will be selecting between alternative sequences.

The final point illustrated in Figure 2 (by the cross-hatched arrow) refers to the dialectical nature of all learning. We don't propose to discuss it, but we must reference it. Learned behaviours in every learner must link back to the whole animal and contribute to a description of the proximate causes which determine the state of that animal at any moment. They are therefore partly responsible for the animal–environment interactions that occur at that moment, and thus, very likely, for setting the next learning task. Such circularity is common in epigenetic and phylogenetic systems (Waddington, 1959—

Chapter 10 of this book). The circularity, however, is less severe than it seems. As Bateson (1980) has pointed out, this kind of circularity is broken by the fact that the causal chains referred to are dynamic rather than static and occur on a time base. Earlier environmental states determine subsequent organism states, which then influence still later environmental states, and so on.

(iii) Relationship of the proposed scheme to the nested hierarchy

A basic thesis of this chapter is that learning should never be considered in isolation of the other knowledge-gaining processes. In Figure 2 the connections with the larger system shown in Figure 1 are indicated by the dark, thick arrows. In general terms, learning relates to the other levels in the hierarchy in two ways. There is first the feeding upwards of information from the more primary levels as a consequence of the way learning is nested under the genetic and epigenetic systems. This is the priming of the learning level, which includes the so-called innate teaching mechanisms. Second, there are the functions of learning that feed results, the 'fitness' or otherwise of the learning, back (downwards) into the hierarchy, since the hierarchy must in some way be responsive to the success or failure of the learning level if the integrity of the system as a whole is to be maintained. That is, every level of the hierarchy must be responsive to occurrences at all other levels if the hierarchy is to have functional efficacy.

(a) Feeding upwards from the hierarchy

We suggest that the *a priori* information that makes up the constraints is fed either from the first or second levels, or both, into two different parts of the learning scheme, as shown in Figure 2. The first part comprises the g–t–r subprocesses of each instance of learning. This means that the generated variants, the autoselection devices that operate on those variants, and the mix of chance that is injected into the regeneration of previously successful variants, will all be targets for *a priori* priming.

The second part comprises the g–t–r subprocesses that direct the integration of separate instances of learning into coherent behavioural sequences. In the case of birdsong, for example, it is known that in some species of songbird the behavioural integration may occur over a considerable period of time with perceptual and sensorimotor learning phases being separated by several months (Marler, 1981). During this period, of course, the young birds undergo significant behavioural modifications as a result of the operation of the epigenetic information gaining system. Thus birdsong provides a fine example of a complex learned behaviour, involving integration of different learning instances and types, which is nested under both genetic and epigenetic systems. The net result is learning that is both species- and individual-specific. Further evidence for the ordering and constraining of the way in which learned behaviour is integrated non-randomly comes from standard laboratory studies of second-order conditioning (Rescorla, 1980).

It is important to remember that when the second level process of variable epigenesis modifies a learning capacity, it does so in a way which itself is constrained by the operation of the first or genetic level. Thus learning may vary either on a species- or individual-specific basis, but in the latter case the variation is within species-specific limits. In either case, all constraints derive, according to the scheme shown in Figure 2, through the sub-processes of the g–t–r heuristic as it operates both on single instances of learning and the integration of these single instances into complex, integrated learning sequences.

(b) Feeding downwards into the hierarchy

We make the working assumption that most instances of learning have an adaptive function (see below for a discussion of this view and the adaptationist fallacy). However, neither the way in which natural selection acts on learning, nor the manner in which these functions relate to the natural descriptions of learning, is simple. We will treat these as separate issues and deal with the latter first.

Consider as an example the supposedly simple, 'flash-like' learning of imprinting. In fact imprinting is probably not invariably flash-like and may occur in some species over an extended period of time, during which a number of learning instances and their patterns of integration are operating. There are several competing views of how to account for imprinting, some of the most recent evidence favouring some form of perceptual learning (Eiserer, 1980); however, it is almost certainly the case that the story does not end following the initial exposure to the imprinted object, since the initial experience may then serve as a factor for reducing the likelihood of imprinting occurring to other objects. There is also the strong possibility that once imprinting has occurred the learning becomes strengthened by accompanying classical conditioning and operant learning, the chick being in close proximity to its mother during feeding, bouts of fear reduction, etc. These different instances will interact with one another, making it likely that different patterns of integration are involved. Finally, priming by the second (developmental) level is also an important determiner of when these various instances operate (see Bateson, 1978). In other words, 'simple' imprinting is a multiple-instance form of learning where both the first and second levels are priming the learners. Yet in functional terms, imprinting is relatively simple and 'presents' to natural selection only two functions for selection—the immediate welfare of the imprinted chick, and the subsequent effects on mate choice. The selection coefficients for both of these may be very high. The functional value of imprinting is not being questioned. What we are pointing out is the disparity between the complexity of the instances, integration and priming of learning underlying this particular form of behavioural change and the seeming simplicity of its functional outcome.

Furthermore, it is likely that the same functional outcomes can be achieved by different instances of learning and/or patterns of integration in different species. Thus imprinting in some species may directly involve conditioning without a perceptual learning component. Conversely, altered learning, and hence altered functions, may occur as a consequence of changes at any points in the scheme shown in Figure 2. In other words, there are many ways in which the learning of closely related species may change, and also ways in which changes in instances of learning or their integration may not be reflected in the functional outcome of the learning. So in the case of imprinting being confined to males in Mallard ducks (*Anas platyrhynchos*) whereas both male and female Chilean Teal (*Anas flavarostris*) imprint, such a difference could result from a number of possible sources, just as similarly small differences in other forms of learning between closely related species might be achieved by equally numerous ways; but the functional effects, at least in the instances just cited, appear to be simple—Mallards are sexually dimorphic, whereas Chilean Teal are not.

Thus imprinting serves a few different ends, but may come to do so through many different means. But since nature selects predominantly for ends, this suggests that similar functional requirements may result in selection for different instances and/or patterns of integration in different species. Conversely, different functions may reflect the action of preponderantly identical instances or patterns of integration—the change may be at a single but critical juncture, for example, in the way two instances articulate on one another. All of these are empirical matters and must be settled by the appropriate data in each and every case. It may seem that we are labouring a small point, but the point is not small. Knowledge of function (in the evolutionary sense) at one level of analysis is vital to the understanding of learning and to the postulation of the necessary existence of constraints in all learners; but function itself cannot be taken to bear directly upon the proximate causes of learning in the form of the instances, and the way they are integrated. This disjunction between function and proximate causation is not, of course, unique to learning (see Tinbergen, 1963). It is a disjunction that arises whenever natural selection is operating on between-animal differences, when the differences themselves are a result of within-animal selection processes.

The second problem is that whatever the functions of the many different instances of learning, how do they become selected and fixed as a species characteristic? There are two most likely answers. The first is the standard neo-Darwinian position that each and every instance of learning supplies a weighting to the overall fitness of the animal in which it appears. In the ideal case, all other things being equal, the advantage conferred by learning will be decisive and learning will be strongly selected for. But in the realistic case, all other things are seldom equal, and so the individual learning skills become merely a part of 'mean phenotypic fitness' (Williams, 1966—see Chapter 3 of this book). From this point of view it is therefore conceivable, and likely to occur with some frequency, that phenotypes with highly developed learning abilities may nonetheless have low overall fitness, and in being less reproductively competent, may jeopardize the propagation of these good learning traits. Conversely, relatively poor learners may have high mean fitness, and in this case a less impressive learning ability may be propagated with certainty in offspring. Thus the neo-Darwinian position posits overall a slow and hazardous evolution of learning forms, learning being just one of a large array of phenotypic attributes that must take their chances along with all other attributes. In any event, the consequences of learning for the phenotype are fed downwards into the gene pool, with a positive or a negative weighting attached to the alleles that are the ultimate determiners of learning, and it is only in this most indirect of ways that learning causes changes at the more fundamental levels of the hierarchy. (If the learner is a member of a species that has evolved cultural exchange of information, then the hierarchy becomes somewhat more complex and many times more dynamic: learning then feeds 'up' into the cultural pool in a much more direct way, as well as 'down' to the primary gene pool. These added complications are discussed by Plotkin and Odling-Smee, 1981).

It is important to note that the neo-Darwinian view allows for the possibility of maladaptive traits being propagated into the future provided that their effect on mean phenotypic fitness is not too drastic. Over long periods, excessively harmful traits will be selected out as they segregate into different individuals where their effects will be decisive determiners of mean fitness. However, it is possible that harmful, or at least less effective, forms of learning may in this way be observed to be present in contemporary animals, if the neo-Darwinian view is correct.

The second possible answer follows the less conventional arguments of epigenetic theorists like Ho and Saunders (1979: see also Chapter 16 of this volume). Here genetic changes are less of a factor. Central is 'the intrinsic dynamical structure of the epigenetic system itself, in its interaction with the environment' that becomes the principal source of *non-random* variations, including learning abilities. Such epigenetic theory has yet to be properly worked out, and if it is correct it places learning much closer to epigenesis (as Johnston argues in Chapter 19 of this book) than does our view. It has the advantage of making learning more rapid and less a slave to chance events and statistical effects. Epigenetic theory, however, predicts no less species-specificity than neo-Darwinian theory; indeed it arguably predicts more. Also, whatever the origins of these learning abilities, like all phenotypic attributes they must eventually become grounded in some genetic form if they are to endure. So even if Ho and Saunders are correct, learning must ultimately feed its consequences down into the genetic system—and in its origins, down into the epigenetic system as well.

E. LEARNING AND ADAPTATION

In this final section we deal with issues that have no direct bearing on learning constraints, theories of learning or comparative studies of learning. We want instead to discuss whether our position is an intrinsically weak one by its being a part of the adaptationist programme and hence by its committing the adaptationist fallacy (Gould and Lewontin, 1979). The adaptationist fallacy is the assumption that all phenotypic attributes are adaptive. According to Lewontin (1979) the fallacy is the result of adopting one of two methods— 'progressive ad hoc optimization' which involves actual data gathering and computation of the optimal model, coupled to attempts to match the two and frequently accompanied by adaptive explanations as to why a match cannot be obtained; or 'imaginative reconstruction', which is a matter of telling fanciful, and often plausible, stories. The entire adaptationist programme is fallacious because it cannot be proved false, and because it fails to consider alternative explanations for phenotypic traits. Johnston (1981a) has accused biological boundary theorists of using *ex post facto* plausible stories, and hence of falling into the trap of the adaptationist fallacy. Since we are so concerned with learning and adaption, can we be similarly condemned?

Consider our position: we are claiming that a capacity for learning is itself an adaptation that constitutes one possible response to environmental changes that occur within certain rate limits. From this it does not follow that we assume that all phenotypic traits or even that all behavioural changes due to learning are adaptive. We merely assume that learning as a process is. Our reasoning is simple: whether or not all phenotypic traits are adaptive (and it seems to us that Lewontin is correct and they are not) is not relevant to a position which is concerned with the nature of adaptations when they do occur, or with knowledge gaining processes and information stores within a multiple level hierarchical system that are responsible for the formation of these adaptations. The latter is our concern but this does not make our position a part of the 'adaptationist programme'. In other words, our chief concern is for learning as a process for generating adaptations, rather than learning itself as an adaptation. Furthermore, it is clear from our discussion of the relationship of learning to the rest of the hierarchy of knowledge gaining processes that we concede the likelihood that learners will display some maladaptive learning. Instances will arise from the slow and uncertain effects of natural selection on mean phenotypic fitness.

There are, however, three ways in which we are vulnerable to this general form of criticism. The first is 'that the entire framework (of adaptational theory) is in question' (Lewontin, 1981). The general tenor of Lewontin's criticism in this case is that current theories of adaptation in general, and ours in particular, describe too static an organic world in which being 'adapted' is more noteworthy than 'adapting'; and in which organisms are viewed merely as passive reactors rather than as active interactors and instigators of change. Lewontin's criticism here is correct. It has been indicated at several points in this chapter that learning is a dynamic and dialectical set of processes, but on their own such statements are hardly enough to meet the criticism. What is needed is a thorough analysis of learning in terms of change; and in line with the larger evolutionary epistemological framework, an analysis of learning within the wider perspective of all adaptations as part of a dialectical interaction between organism and environment. These are challenges for the future of which we are mindful.

The second way in which we are open to criticism is the belief that the constraints on learning are themselves adaptations. Learning, we argue, will be seen to vary from species to species when the appropriate analyses are performed, and the reason for this variation lies in the species-typical requirements placed on learning. Because this is a statement about the adaptive nature of an attribute, and not a statement about the nature of adaptations, we can indeed be accused of performing an *ex ante facto* analysis. Our defence is that learning has to be constrained for a specific logical reason. This is that learning cannot by directly scrutinized by natural selection except as a subsidiary information gaining and storing device that is 'playing the same game' as natural selection at level 1, and it must therefore have consequences that would more often than not be the same as those that would occur were natural selection acting directly on the consequences of learning (Plotkin and Odling-Smee, 1981). For this reason, the consequences of learning can never be completely open-ended, but must always be partially constrained and directed. Such constraint must originate from somewhere. While they could be pleiotropic or allometric or entirely accidental in origin, we are assuming until the case is otherwise proven, that the source of these constraints is prior genetic and epigenetic knowledge gain. In part, the strength of this argument depends on the ability to demonstrate that the constraints act to push learning in the direction that natural selection itself would do. For the moment, we cannot suggest how this can be demonstrated. Furthermore, even if this could be achieved, it would still not rule out allometric brain growth, developmental noise or any other alternatives as contributing influences.

Finally, even if learning evolved as a species-typical response to a specific problem of animal–environment interaction in the first instance, it is always possible that the specific learning ability that one sees in an animal 'now' can be, and has been, employed to deal with aspects of environmental change that are different from those which formed the original selection pressure for its initial evolution. In other words, there is the possibility that, contrary to our assertion made elsewhere in this chapter, learning can be generalist in the sense that it may originally evolve to deal with one form of change and then subsequently be put to use relative to other forms of change. This is at least as likely as our simplifying assertion especially since learning, though it certainly has evolved independently many times over in different lineages of learners, once evolved as an ability, may have a long and varied phylogenetic history. There is, it seems to us, only one way of answering the questions this raises—intensive comparative study.

REFERENCES

Bateson, G. (1980). *Mind and Nature*, Fontana, London.

Bateson, P. P. G. (1978). Early experience and sexual preferences. In G. B. Hutchinson (Ed.), *Biological determinants of sexual behaviour*, Wiley, Chichester, pp. 25–53.

Bitterman, M. E. (1975). The comparative analysis of learning. *Science*, **188**, 699–709.

Bitterman, M. E. (1976). Issues in the comparative psychology of learning. In R. B. Masterton, C. B. G. Campbell, M. E. Bitterman, and N. Hotton (Eds), *Evolution of Brain and Behaviour in Vertebrates*. Lawrence Erlbaum, Hillsdale, New Jersey. pp. 217–226.

Bitterman, M. E., and Woodward, W. T. (1976). Vertebrate learning: common processes. In R. B. Masterton, C. B. G. Campbell, M. E. Bitterman and N. Hotton (Eds), *Evolution of Brain and Behaviour in Vertebrates*, Lawrence Erlbaum, Hillsdale, New Jersey. pp. 169–189.

Bonner, J. T. (1980). *The evolution of culture in animals*, Princeton University Press, Princeton.

Campbell, D. T. (1974). Evolutionary epistemology. In P. A. Schilpp (Ed.), *The Philosophy of Karl Popper*, Open Court Publishing, Chicago. pp. 413–463.

Corning, W. C., Dyal, J. A., and Willows, A. O. D. (1973a). *Invertebrate learning*, Vol. 1, Plenum, New York.

Corning, W. C., Dyal, J. A., and Willows, A. O. D. (1973b). *Invertebrate learning*, Vol. 2, Plenum, New York.

Corning, W. C., Dyal, J. A., and Willows, A. O. D. (1975). *Invertebrate learning*, Vol. 3, Plenum, New York.

Dewsbury, D. A. (1978). *Comparative animal behavior*, McGraw-Hill, New York.

Dickinson, A. (1980). *Contemporary animal learning theory*, Cambridge University Press, Cambridge.

Eiserer, L. A. (1980). Development of filial attachment to static and visual features of an imprinting object. *Animal Learning and Behavior*, **8**, 159–166.

Estes, W. K., Koch, S., MacCorquodale, K., Meehl, P. E., Mueller, C. G., Schoenfeld, W. N., and Verplank, W. S. (1954). *Modern learning theory*, Appleton-Century-Croft, New York.

Goodwin, B. C. (1976). *Analytical physiology of cells and developing organisms*, Academic Press, London.

Gottlieb, G. (1979). Comparative psychology and ethology. In E. Hearst (Ed.), *The first century of experimental psychology*, Erlbaum, Hillsdale, New Jersey. pp. 147–173.

Gould, S. J., and Lewontin, R. C. (1979). The spandrels of San Marco and the Panglossian paradigm: A critique of the adaptationist programme. *Proceedings of the Royal Society, Series B*, **295**, 581–598.

Hinde, R. A. (1973). Constraints on learning. In R. A. Hinde and J. Stevenson-Hinde (Eds), *Constraints on Learning*, Academic Press, New York. pp. 1–19.

Hinde, R. A. (1981). Biological approaches to the study of learning: does Johnston provide a new alternative? *The Behavioural and Brain Sciences*, **4**, 146–147.

Hirsch, J. (1967). Behavior-genetic or experimental analysis: the challenge of sciences versus the lure of technology. *American Psychologist*, **22**, 118–130.

Ho, M. W., and Saunders, P. T. (1979). Beyond neo-Darwinianism—an epigenetic approach to evolution. *Journal of Theoretical Biology*, **78**, 573–591.

Hodos, W., and Campbell, C. (1969). Scala naturae: Why there is no theory in comparative psychology. *Psychological Review*, **76**, 337–350.

Hull, C. L. (1943). *Principles of behavior*, Appleton-Century-Croft, New York.

Jenkins, H. M. (1979). Animal learning and behavior theory. In E. Hearst (Ed.), *The first century of experimental psychology*, Lawrence Erlbaum, Hillsdale, New Jersey. pp. 177–228.

Johnston, T. D. (1981a). Contrasting approaches to a theory of learning. *The Behavioral and Brain Sciences*, **4**, 125–173.

Johnston, T. D. (1981b). Selective costs and benefits in the evolution of learning. *Advances in the Study of Behavior*, **12**, in press.

Johnston, T. D., and Turvey, M. T. (1980). A sketch of an ecological meta-theory for theories of learning. *The Psychology of Learning and Motivation*, **14**, 147–205.

Koch, S. (1951). Theoretical psychology 1950: an overview. *Psychological Review*, **58**, 147–154.

Lea, S. E. G. (1981). Correlation and contiguity in foraging behaviour. *Advances in the Analysis of Behavior*, **2**, in press.

Lewontin, R. C. (1978). Adaptation. *Scientific American*, **239**, 157–169.

Lewontin, R. C. (1979). Sociobiology as an adaptationist program. *Behavioral Science*, **24**, 5–14.

Lewontin, R. C. (1981). On constraints and adaptation. *The Behavioral and Brain Sciences*, **4**, 244–245.

Lockard, R. B. (1971). Reflections on the fall of comparative psychology. *American Psychologist*, **26**, 168–179.

Lolordo, V. M. (1979). Constraints on learning. In M. E. Bitterman, V. M. Lolordo, J. B. Overmier, and M. E. Rashotte (Eds). *Animal Learning: Survey and analysis*, Plenum, New York. pp. 473–504.

Lorenz, K. (1965). *Evolution and modification of behaviour*, University of Chicago Press, Chicago.

Mackintosh, N. J. (1974). *The psychology of animal learning*, Academic Press, London.

Madsen K. B. (1961). *Theories of motivation*, Howard Allen, Cleveland Ohio.

Marler, P. (1981). Birdsong: the acquisition of a learned motor skill. *Trends in Neuroscience*, **3**, 88–94.

Odling-Smee, F. J. (1982) Multiple levels in evolution: an approach to the nature-nurture issue via. applied epistemology. In G. Davey (Ed.), *Animal Models and Human Behaviour*. Wiley, Chichester. In Press.

Plotkin, H. C. (1979). Brain-behaviour studies and evolutionary biology. In D. A. Oakley and H. C. Plotkin (Eds), *Brain, behaviour and evolution*, Methuen, London. pp. 52–77.

Plotkin, H. C., and Odling-Smee, F. J. (1979). Learning, change and evolution: an enquiry into the teleonomy of learning. *Advances in the Study of Behaviour*, **10**, 1–41.

Plotkin, H. C., and Odling-Smee, F. J. (1981). A multiple-level model of evolution and its implications for sociobiology. *The Behavioural and Brain Sciences*, **4**, 225–268.

Pulliam, H. R., and Dunford, C. (1980). *Programmed to learn*, Columbia University Press, New York.

Rescorla, R. A. (1968). Probability of shock in the presence and absence of CS in fear conditioning. *Journal of comparative and physiological psychology*, **66**, 1–5.

Rescorla, R. A. (1980). *Pavlovian second-order conditioning: studies in associative learning*, Lawrence Erlbaum, Hillsdale, New Jersey.

Rescorla, R. A., and Holland, P. C. (1976). Some behavioral approaches to the study of learning. In M. R. Rosenzweig and E. L. Bennett (Eds), *Neural mechanisms of learning and memory*, MIT Press, Cambridge, Mass. pp. 165–192.

Rescorla, R. A., and Wagner, A. R. (1972). A theory of Pavlovian conditioning: variations in the effectiveness of reinforcement and nonreinforcement. In A. H. Black and W. F. Prokasy (Eds), *Classical Conditioning II*, Appleton-Century-Crofts, New York. pp. 64–99.

Revusky, S. (1977). Learning as a general process with an emphasis on data from feeding experiments. In N. W. Milgram, L. Krames, and T. M. Alloway (Eds), *Food Aversion Learning*, Plenum, New York. pp. 1–51.

Rose, S. P. R. (1981). From causations to translations: what biochemists can contribute to the study of behaviour. In P. P. G. Bateson and P. H. Klopfer (Eds), *Perspectives in Ethology*, Vol. 4, Plenum, New York. pp. 157–177.

Rozin, P., and Kalat, J. W. (1971). Specific hungers and poison avoidance as adaptive specializations of learning. *Psychological Review*, **78**, 459–486.

Schwartz, B. (1974). On going back to nature: a review of Seligman and Hager's Biological Boundaries of Learning. *Journal of the Experimental Analysis of Behaviour*, **21**, 183–198.

Seligman, M. E. P. (1970). On the generality of the laws of learning. *Psychological Review*, **77**, 406–418.

Seligman, M. E. P., and Hager, J. L. (1972). *Biological Boundaries of Learning*, Appleton-Century-Croft, New York.

Shettleworth, S. J. (1972). Constraints on learning. *Advances in the Study of Behaviour*, **4**, 1–68.

Shettleworth, S. J. (1975). Reinforcement and the organization of behaviour in Golden Hamsters. *Journal of Experimental Psychology: Animal Behavior Processes*, **1**, 56–87.

Shettleworth, S. J. (1981). Function and mechanism in learning. *Advances in the Analysis of Behaviour*, **3**, in press.

Staddon, J. E. R., and Simmelhag, V. L. (1971). The superstition experiment. *Psychological Review*, **78**, 3–43.

Tinbergen, N. (1951). *The Study of Instincts*, Oxford University Press, Oxford.

Tinbergen, N. (1963). On the aims and methods of ethology. *Zeitschrift fur Tierpsychologie*, **20**, 410–433.

Waddington, C. H. (1959). Evolutionary adaptation. In Sol Tax (Ed.), *The Evolution of Life*, University of Chicago Press, Chicago. pp. 381–402.

Warren, J. M. (1973). Learning in vertebrates. In D. A. Dewsbury and D. A. Rethlingshafer (Eds), *Comparative Psychology: A modern survey*, McGraw-Hill, New York. pp. 471–509.

Williams, G. C. (1966). *Adaptation and Natural Selection*, Princeton University Press, Princeton.

Author index

Ackermann, R., 90, 92, 104, 278, 323
Agassiz, J., 90, 94, 104
Alberch, P., 340, 342, 350, 358, 436–437
Alexander, R. D., 270–271
Allee, W. C., 258–259, 271
Andrewartha, H. G., 220, 251
Aristotle, 18–21, 26, 31, 33–35, 282
Arms, K., 259, 271
Asch, S. E., 87, 104
Ashby, W. R., 3, 12, 77–78, 81, 94, 104
Atkinson, R. C., 75, 104
Ayala, F. J., 21, 26, 33, 36

Bacon, F., 18, 33, 83
Bain, A., 83, 104
Bajema, C. J., 286, 323
Baldwin, E., 118
Baldwin, J. M., 81, 87, 92, 94–96, 98, 104, 119, 181, 354, 358
Bandura, A., 87, 105
Barash, D. P., 270, 271
Barr, H. J., 77, 99, 105
Bateman, K. G., 184, 185, 188, 192, 353, 358
Bateson, G., 9, 12, 434, 437, 463, 469
Bateson, P. P. G., 345, 358, 391–410, 433, 437, 464, 469
Baylis, J. R., 255–272
Beck, S. D., 427, 437
Beckner, M., 17–18, 33, 36
Bergson, H., 19, 36, 93
Berkeley, G., 151
Bertalanffy, L. von, 99, 102, 105, 140, 394, 397, 409

Bigelow, J., 38
Birch, L. C., 46, 58
Bischoff, N., 398, 409
Bishop, J. A., 228, 251
Bitterman, M. E., 444, 449, 457, 469
Blakemore, C., 366
Blauberg, I. V., 347, 358
Blum, H. F., 49, 58
Blute, M., 302–305, 323
Bok, W. J., 4, 12
Boltzmann, L., 99
Bonner, J. T., 281, 323, 341, 342, 450, 469
Boorse, C., 286, 323
Born, M., 112
Bornstein, M. B., 368
Bowlbey, J., 398, 409
Bradley, R. M., 376, 386
Braithwaite, R. D., 18, 19, 36
Brandon, R. N., 4, 12
Brannigan, A., 296, 323
Bridgman, P. W., 209, 251
Broadhurst, P. L., 398, 409
Bronowski, J., 322, 323
Brown, D. D., 282, 323, 332, 342
Brown, J. L., 236, 251, 258, 259, 271
Brown, W. L., 55, 58, 224, 251
Brundin, L., 350, 358
Buckland, W. E., 292, 323
Bugelski, B. R., 414, 437
Burgess, J. W., 260, 271
Burghardt, G. M., 263, 271, 422, 437
Burian, R., 290, 323
Burkhardt, R. W., 294, 323
Burt, C., 315

473

Cairns, R. B., 375, 385, 386
Campbell, D. T., 3, 4, 6, 8, 12, 73–107,
    142, 273, 276, 278, 299, 305–306,
    308, 311, 313, 323, 356, 358, 411,
    437, 449, 452, 455, 462, 469
Campbell, M., 295, 323
Canfield, J. V., 18, 36
Cannon, W. B., 91, 105
Čapek, M., 92–93, 98, 105
Caplan, A., 279, 323
Carmichael, L., 363, 368, 386, 390, 432,
    437
Cassirer, E., 99
Caullery, 148
Cavalli-Sforza, L. L., 311, 323
Chantrey, D. F., 402, 409
Child, A., 99, 105
Childe, V. G., 299, 323
Clarke, C. A., 42, 58
Cloak, F. T., 311, 323
Coghill, G. E., 363, 365, 386
Cohen, J., 353, 358
Cohen, L. J., 279–280, 282, 288, 308, 312,
    324
Compton, A. H., 112–113, 118
Cooper, J. F., 366
Corning, W. C., 457, 469
Craig, R. K., 332, 342
Craig, W., 24, 37
Craik, K. J. W., 85, 105
Crain, S. M., 368, 386
Crowell, D. H., 387, 390
Cuenot, L., 148
Cullen, E., 209, 251
Cullen, J. M., 209, 251
Cuvier, G., 293

Daniels, J. D., 366, 387
Danilevskii, A. S., 427, 437
Darwin, C., 4, 10, 12, 18, 22, 31f, 35, 46,
    85, 92, 95, 118, 154, 173–177, 195,
    205, 213, 218–219, 220f, 228f, 251,
    273, 277, 290, 293f, 305, 317, 324,
    338, 342, 351f
Darwin, F., 293, 324
Davidson, E. H., 332, 342
Davis, B. D., 26, 37
Dawkins, R., 154, 170, 215, 256, 271,
    275–277, 291, 324, 346, 356, 358
de Beer, G., 293, 324
Delbruck, M., 26, 33, 34, 37

Denlinger, D. L., 427, 437
Dennett, D. C., 416, 437
Descartes, R., 18, 33, 68, 113, 116, 118,
    151
de Vries, H., 295
Dewey, J., 94, 95, 105
Dewsbury, D. A., 457, 469
Dickinson, A., 446, 469
Dobzhansky, T., 4, 12, 214, 251, 317, 324
Drachman, D. B., 372, 373, 387
Driesch, H., 19, 37
Dunn, J., 397, 398, 409
Dunnell, R. C., 154, 170
Durham, W. H., 8, 12, 356, 358
Durkheim, E., 357, 358
Durrant, A., 177, 192

Eayrs, J. T., 368, 387
Eibl-Eibesfeldt, I., 415–418, 437
Einstein, A., 112–113
Eiserer, L. A., 464, 469
Eldred, E., 374, 387
Eldredge, N., 277, 279, 287, 304, 314, 324,
    351, 358
Elster, J., 313–314, 318–319, 324
Emerson, A. E., 43, 58
Emlen, S. T., 426, 431, 434, 437
Endler, J., 285, 324
Estes, W. K., 75, 105, 448, 469
Evans, F. C., 425, 438
Evans, H. E., 264–269, 271

Fentress, J. C., 407, 409
Feyerabend, P., 306, 324
Ficken, R. W., 231, 252
Fisher, R. A., 39–42, 58, 213, 215, 219,
    227, 245, 252
Fitzgerald, T. D., 263, 271
Fodor, J. A., 435, 438
Foelix, R. F., 372, 387
Ford, E. B., 42, 58, 226, 252
Fouille, A., 99
Fretwell, S. D., 221–223, 252
Freud, S., 152, 165
Fries, J., 98
Frisch von, K., 88, 105, 235
Fromme, A., 368, 387

Galef, B. G., 419, 422, 438
Galen, C., 31
Garcia, J., 414–415, 422, 438

Gehlen, 130
Gesell, A., 387, 390, 393, 409, 432, 438
Ghiselin, M. T., 4, 7, 12, 90, 106, 279, 324,
    421, 438
Ghurye, C., 142
Gibson, J. J., 426, 438
Ginsburg, M., 299, 324, 356, 359
Glassman, R. B., 411, 438
Glick, T. G., 295, 324
Gloor, H., 186, 192
Goethe, J. W., 131
Goldschmidt, R. B., 24, 345, 349–351, 359
Gombrich, E. H., 119, 152
Goodwin, B. C., 3, 12, 345, 353, 359, 449,
    469
Gorczynski, R. M., 308, 324
Gottlieb, G., 345, 359, 363–390, 400, 409,
    418–420, 426, 431, 433–434, 438,
    443, 469
Gould, J. L., 88, 106
Gould, S. J., 4, 12, 208, 218, 246, 252, 275,
    292, 294, 320, 324, 339–340, 342,
    350, 359, 436, 438, 444, 467, 469
Goy, R. W., 383, 387
Grant, P. R., 225, 252
Grant, V., 282, 324
Gray, A., 295
Greenwood, P. H., 422, 438
Gregg, J. R., 284, 324
Griffin, D. R., 79, 106
Griffiths, G. C. D., 279, 324
Grun, P., 353, 359
Gustafson, T., 332–333, 342

Haeckel, E., 153
Hailman, J. P., 4, 205–254, 256, 271, 418,
    438
Haldane, J. B. S., 38–39, 43, 46, 58
Halpin, Z. T., 255–272
Hamburgh, M., 368, 387
Hamburger, V., 369–370, 387
Hamilton, W. D., 42, 58, 215, 252, 256,
    258, 259, 271
Harth, M. S., 372, 378, 388
Harvey, W., 32
Hawkins, D., 99
Heaton, M. B., 374, 376, 388
Hebb, D. O., 87, 106
Held, R., 426, 439
Hein, A., 434, 439
Helmholtz, H., von, 98, 125

Hempel, C. B., 305, 324
Henry, C. S., 259, 271
Herrick, C. J., 365, 388
Herrnstein, R. J., 415, 439
Heslop-Harrison, J. W., 178, 192
Highkin, H. R., 177, 192
Hilgard, E. R., 413, 439
Hinde, R. A., 29, 32, 37, 87, 106, 345, 359,
    397, 400, 403, 405, 409, 416, 418,
    432, 439, 444, 445, 469
Hirsch, H. V. B., 366, 388, 390
Hirsch, J., 444, 470
Ho, M. W., 5, 11–12, 343–361, 419, 439,
    448, 466, 470
Hodge, M. J. S., 294, 324
Hodos, W., 444, 470
Hoffding, H., 97–98, 106
Hoffman, R. J., 428–430, 434, 439
Hollis, K. L., 416, 439
Holmes, S. J., 81, 106
Holtfreter, J., 338, 342
Hooker, D., 363, 388
Hooker, J. D., 297
Hoyle, G., 398, 409
Hubel, D., 366
Hull, C. L., 448, 455–466, 470
Hull, D. L., 17–18, 24, 37, 273–327
Hulse, S. H., 435, 439
Hume, D., 74–75, 95, 97, 102, 113, 124,
    125, 164
Humphrey, T., 363, 372, 388
Hutt, S. J., 407, 409
Huxley, J., 40, 55, 58, 248, 252, 309, 313,
    325, 354, 359
Huxley, T. H., 90, 106, 295

Immelman, K., 415, 439
Impekoven, M., 381, 388

Jackson, P. S., 402, 409
Jackson, R. R., 260, 272
Jacob, F., 282, 325
Jacobson, M., 398, 409
Jaisson, P., 385, 388
James, W., 85, 90, 93, 99, 106
Jeanne, R. L., 269
Jenkins, H. M., 443, 470
Jennings, H. S., 78, 106, 119
Jensen, E. L., 231
Jevons, S., 83, 85, 106
Jinks, J. L., 354, 359

Johnston, T. D., 411–442, 444–449, 452, 454, 458, 460–461, 467, 470
Jollos, V., 354, 359
Joule, J. P., 139

Kahn, C. H., 119
Kamil, A. C., 416, 439
Kant, I., 35–37, 66, 70, 93, 96–101, 121–143, 164
Karfunkel, P., 332, 342
Kawai, M., 239, 252
Kawamura, S., 239
Kellog, W. N., 79, 106
Kember, N. F., 336, 339, 342
Kennett, 244
Kepler, J., 112
Kettlewell, H. B. D., 179, 190, 192, 225–228, 252–253
Kiester, A. R., 259, 272
Kimble, G. A., 413, 439
Kimura, M., 47–58, 200, 202, 349, 351, 359
Kitts, D. B., 279, 325
Kleiman, D. G., 265–266, 272
Klopfer, P. H., 259, 272
Knight, G. R., 190, 192
Knorr, K. D., 306, 325
Koch, S., 448, 470
Kohler, W., 82, 102, 106
Konishi, M., 366, 381, 388, 399
Koref, S. S., 190, 192
Kottler, M. J., 294–295, 325
Kratochwil, K., 338, 342
Kroeber, A. L., 308, 325
Kroodsma, D. E., 420, 439
Kuhn, T. S., 90, 92, 106, 290, 296, 298, 325
Kullman, E. J., 263, 266–267, 272
Kuo, Z.-Y., 363, 388, 432, 439

Lack, D., 40, 58
Lagerspetz, K., 20–21, 37
Lakatos, I., 290, 294, 325
Lamarck, J. B., 9, 21, 92, 94, 97, 147–148, 166, 175–176, 290, 293–294, 325, 352, 355, 359
Lande, R., 338, 342
Lange, F. A., 98, 106
Langton, J., 304, 325
Lashley, K. S., 406, 409
Lauber, J. K., 377–378, 388

Laudan, L., 290, 299, 325
Lea, S. E. G., 446, 470
Leathwood, P., 433, 440
Lee, D. M., 426, 440
Lehrman, D. S., 345, 359, 415, 418, 426, 432, 440
Leibniz, G. W., 97
Leiman, A. L., 368, 388
Leonovich, V. V., 357, 359
Lewin, R., 4, 12
Lewis, J. H., 334, 342
Lewis, R. W., 205–206, 253
Lewontin, R. C., 4, 7–9, 12, 43, 49, 58, 151–170, 205, 208–209, 218, 243–244, 246, 253, 450, 467, 470
Lindauer, M., 235, 253
Lockard, R. B., 444, 448, 461, 470
Locke, J., 97
Lolordo, V. M., 448, 470
Lorenz, K., 4, 6, 13, 81, 99–101, 103, 106, 119, 121–143, 162–165, 168, 345, 359, 415–417, 425, 436, 440, 443, 446, 454, 456, 470
Losee, J., 280, 308, 312–313, 325
Lotze, R. H., 65
Lovejoy, A. O., 21, 37, 102, 106, 295, 297, 325
Løvtrup, S., 344–345, 351, 360
Lucas, P. G., 142
Lumsden, C. J., 346–347, 360
Lyell, G., 294

Mach, E., 82, 85, 93, 99, 101, 103–104, 106
MacCormac, E. R., 89, 106
Mackintosh, N. J., 446, 470
MacLeod, R. B., 18, 37
MacMahon, J. A., 425, 440
Madsen, K. B., 448, 470
Magnus, R., 99
Mainx, F., 37
Malthus, T. R., 213
Manning, A., 398, 410
Markl, H., 264, 267, 272
Marler, P., 399–400, 406, 409, 418, 422, 426, 433–434, 440, 463, 470
Martin, C. P., 354, 360
Marx, K., 152, 169
Mason, W. A., 376, 385, 388
Mather, K., 46, 58
Matthew, P., 296

Maxwell, G., 99
Mayer, J. R., 139
Maynard-Smith, J., 308, 325, 346, 360
Mayr, E., 5, 13, 17–38, 181, 192, 210,
    213–214, 253, 279–282, 285, 288,
    290, 294, 305, 307, 325, 436
McCance, R. A., 394, 410
McClachlan, J., 337
McFarland, J. D., 35–37
McGraw, M. B., 388, 390
McKinney, H. L., 322, 325
McMullin, E., 290, 325
McNamara, J., 416, 436, 440
Mead, M., 90, 106, 322, 325
Medawar, P. B., 5, 13, 310, 326
Mendel, G., 177, 295, 297
Menzel, E. W., 434, 440
Merleau-Ponty, M., 99
Merton, R. K., 91, 106
Meyerson, B. A., 366, 388
Meyerson, E., 99
Michener, C. D., 260, 267, 269, 272
Michod, R. E., 276, 326
Mill, J. S., 95, 97–98
Milne, A., 46, 58
Mirsky, A. E., 49–50, 59
Model, P. G., 368, 388
Monod, J., 21, 26, 31, 37, 90, 106
Moore, J. A., 354, 360
Moorhead, P. S., 170
Morgan, C. L., 81, 99, 181, 413, 440
Muller, H. J., 40, 59
Mulligan, J. A., 419–420, 440
Munson, R., 30, 37
Murton, R. K., 259, 272
Musgrave, A., 118

Nagel, E., 17–18, 37, 318, 326
Needham, A. E., 54, 59
Needham, J., 345, 360
Nelson, G. J., 350, 360
Nelson, K., 397, 410
Neumann, J., Von, 38
Newell, A., 86, 106
Newton, I., 34, 100
Nicholson, J. A., 44, 59
Nicholson, J. L., 368, 388
Nicolai, J., 383, 388
Nietzsche, F., 130, 141
Noonan, K. M., 270, 272
Northrop, F. S. C., 99

Noseworthy, C. W., 426, 440
Nutting, W. L., 269, 272

Odling-Smee, F. J., 443–471
Odum, E. P., 425, 441
Olby, R., 296, 326
Ollason, J. G., 436, 441
O'Malley, B. W., 368, 388
Oppenheim, R. W., 372, 393, 410, 419,
    441
Osborn, H. F., 81

Park, T., 45, 59
Paterson, H. E. H., 217–218, 222, 224,
    227, 235, 237–238, 242, 245, 249,
    253
Patterson, C., 279, 326
Patterson, I. J., 233–235, 253
Pavlov, I. P., 138, 414
Peirce, C. S., 92, 94, 106, 114, 312
Pepper, S. C., 99
Peterson, R. T., 220, 253
Petrie, H. G., 102, 106
Piaget, J., 3, 5, 9–10, 13, 99, 145–150,
    152, 163, 165–170, 353, 355–356,
    360, 396, 410, 413, 441, 458
Pietrewicz, A. T., 416, 441
Pittendrigh, C. S., 4–5, 13, 18, 25–26,
    37–38, 281, 326
Platt, J. R., 99, 212, 253, 270, 272
Plotkin, H. C., 3–13, 232, 253, 277, 326,
    347, 360, 434, 441, 443–471
Poincaré, H., 78, 83, 85, 93, 99, 101, 103,
    106
Polikoff, D., 349, 353, 360
Popper, K. R., 3, 13, 73, 75–76, 90–92,
    96–97, 100–102, 104, 106,
    109–119, 154, 163–164, 168, 170,
    286, 308, 326, 411, 441
Poulton, E. B., 81
Prader, A., 394, 410
Preyer, W., 363, 365, 369, 371, 389
Pringle, J. W. S., 81, 106, 353, 360
Provine, R. R., 363, 389
Pulliam, H. R., 456, 470
Pumphrey, R. J., 79, 106
Pyle, R. L., 220, 253

Quine, W. V., 3, 6, 13, 89, 99, 107

Raup, D. M., 435, 441

Raven, C. P., 27, 37
Reed, E. S., 208, 253
Reichenbach, H., 99
Rendel, J. M., 166
Rescher, N., 3, 13, 306, 308, 313, 326
Rescorla, R. A., 446, 448, 456, 464, 470
Restle, F., 75, 107
Reupke, W. A., 142
Revusky, S., 444, 446, 471
Rhine, J. B., 205
Rhodes, F. H. T., 244, 253
Richards, R. J., 285, 290, 305–306, 308, 326
Riedl, R., 350, 360
Robb, R. C., 340, 342
Robertson, D. R., 262, 272
Roe, A., 37, 173, 192
Romanes, G. J., 413, 441
Rose, S. P. R., 347, 360, 460, 471
Rosen, D., 208, 253
Rosenberg, A., 279, 326
Rosenbleuth, H., 25, 29, 37
Rosenzweig, M. R., 436, 441
Roux, W., 32, 37
Rowell, T. E., 236, 253
Rozin, P., 436, 441, 444, 471
Rubel, E. W., 364, 389
Ruse, M., 317, 326, 345, 360
Ruskin, J., 162
Russell, B., 81, 107

Sahlins, M., 320, 326, 357, 360
Santayana, G., 132
Sara, V. R., 367, 389
Saunders, P. T., 343–361, 366, 389
Saxen, L., 338, 342
Schapiro, S., 366, 389
Schindewolf, O. H., 351, 360
Schlick, M., 113
Schneirla, T. C., 345, 360, 363, 392, 410, 416, 441
Schrödinger, E., 112
Schwartz, B., 448, 471
Sebeok, T. A., 88, 107
Seligman, M. E. P., 414, 444–445, 471
Sellars, W. S., 99
Semon, R., 276, 326
Shallenberger, R. J., 220, 253
Shakespeare, W., 152
Shapiro, D. Y., 262, 272
Shelton, H. S., 99

Sheppard, P. M., 48, 59
Shettleworth, S. J., 416, 441, 445, 449, 457–458, 471
Shimony, A., 3, 13, 99
Shorten, M., 219, 253
Shrader, D., 311, 326
Siegfried, W. R., 272
Sigwart, C., 31–32, 37
Simmel, G., 63–71, 93, 101, 103, 107
Simon, H. A., 86, 107
Simpson, G. G., 5, 13, 21, 26, 37, 40, 59, 99, 119, 173, 294, 300, 305, 326, 350, 360
Simpson, M. J. A., 405
Sinha, C., 347, 356–357, 360
Skagestad, P., 312, 326
Skinner, B. F., 411, 414–415, 441
Slobodkin, L. B., 434, 441
Small, W. S., 413, 442
Smart, J. J. C., 279, 326
Smith, W. J., 32, 37
Sober, E., 279, 283, 326, 436, 442
Socrates, 41
Sommerhoff, G., 5, 6, 13, 37, 422–423, 425, 442, 449
Souriau, P., 84–85, 107
Southwood, T. R. E., 11, 13
Spencer, H., 85, 92, 97–98, 100
Spiegelman, S., 76, 107
Spieth, H. T., 190, 193
Spinelli, N., 366
Springer, S., 259, 272
Staddon, J. E. R., 411, 442, 452, 471
Stadler, H., 36–37
Stanley, S. M., 279, 326
Stearns, S. C., 418, 436, 442
Steele, E. J., 9, 13
Stein, W. D., 331–342
Stemmer, N., 99
Stent, 341
Stern, J. T., 4, 13
Stone, J. M., 368, 389
Sulloway, F. J., 294, 326
Summerbell, D., 335, 336, 342

Taylor, R., 22, 37
Tees, R. C., 379, 389
Teilhard de Chardin, P., 21, 37
Thagard, P., 305–306, 308, 312, 326
Thoday, J. M., 55, 59
Thorndike, E. L., 413–415, 442

Thorneycroft, H. B., 231, 253
Tickle, C., 336, 342
Timberlake, W., 414, 442
Tinbergen, N., 236–237, 253, 417,
    442–443, 465, 471
Tobach, E., 347, 360, 375
Toulmin, S. E., 3, 13, 90–92, 99, 107,
    279–280, 288, 290, 299, 308,
    311–312, 326, 432, 442
Toynbee, A. J., 152, 154
Tracy, H. C., 369, 389
Trivers, R. L., 256, 270, 272
Turbayne, C. M., 151, 170
Turesson, G., 183, 193

Uexkull, J., von, 93, 99, 130
Underwood, G., 200, 202
Ungerer, E., 36–37

Valen, L., Van, 243, 244
Vandenbergh, J. G., 380
Vaurie, C., 224, 253
Vendrely, R., 49, 59
Vicari, E. M., 398, 410
Vince, M. A., 371, 378, 379, 389
Vorzimmer, P. J., 352, 360

Waddington, C. H., 4, 9, 10, 13, 22, 23, 37,
    50, 55, 59, 99, 107, 119, 148, 149,
    166, 173, 193, 195, 203, 216, 217,
    222, 226, 232, 242, 249, 253, 254,
    299, 308, 326, 344, 345, 349, 350,
    352, 353, 356, 360, 393, 394, 397,
    399, 410, 420, 442, 462, 471
Wagner, M., 294
Wahlsten, D., 357, 361
Wallace, A. R., 91, 213, 220, 221, 228, 229
Wallraff, C. F., 98, 107
Warburton, F. E., 200, 202
Warren, J. M., 457, 471
Warren, R., 426, 442
Wartofsky, M., 99, 107
Watanabe, S., 99
Watson, J. B., 413–414, 442

Watt, W. B., 428, 442
Weismann, A., 21, 38, 294, 346, 352, 432,
    442
Weiss, P., 344, 395, 410
Wellington, W. G., 263, 272
Wenner, A. M., 235, 254
West-Eberhard, M. J., 260, 272
Wheeler, J. A., 113, 119
Wheeler, W. M., 260, 264, 267, 269, 272
Whewell, W., 90
Whitrow, G. J., 99
Whyte, L. L., 347, 361
Wiener, N., 38
Wiener, P. P., 94, 107
Wiens, J. A., 383, 384, 389, 426, 431, 436,
    442
Wiesel, T., 366
Wiley, E. O., 279, 300, 326–327
Williams, G. C., 4, 5, 7, 8, 13, 39–59,
    195–203, 208, 254, 291, 305, 327,
    346, 361, 451, 466, 471
Williams, M. B., 279, 327
Williamson, P. G., 351, 361
Wilson, E. O., 154, 170, 215, 218, 248,
    254, 256–259, 264, 265, 267–269,
    272, 314, 327, 346, 361
Wimsatt, W. C., 76, 107, 276, 310, 327
Windle, W. F., 363, 389
Wispe, L. G., 278, 327
Wolpert, L., 331–342
Woodfield, A., 286, 327
Woodward, D. J., 366, 389
Wright, S., 39, 42, 59, 214–216, 222, 242,
    246, 249, 254, 277, 327, 436, 442
Wright, W. K., 99, 107
Wundt, W., 125, 138
Wynne-Edwards, V. C., 215, 254

Yilmaz, H., 99
Young, R. M., 317, 327

Zirkle, C., 290, 327
Zuckerman, H., 327

Subject Index

accommodation, 146–150, 458
accommodats, 147–148
acquired characters, 196, 199, 216, 278
action, 65–71
action and conceptualization, 68–69
activity, 364
adaptability, 348
adaptations, 4–7, 19, 25, 26, 29, 30,
    39–59, 124–127, 133, 145–150, 157,
    159–163, 173–193, 199, 205–206,
    208–210, 248–251, 282, 353–355,
    417, 449–453
adaptation
  and energy costs, 4
  and epistemic processes, 7
  and fitness, 208
  and natural selection, 208
  and organization, 145–150
  and phylogeny, 209
  and rates of change, 11
  as information, 6, 11
  as knowledge, 4–7
  as moulding, 6
  as organization, 4, 6
  character–environment correlation, 209
  continual, 243
  creation and perpetuation, 208
  criteria for, 209
  definitions of, 208
  ecological, 52
  effectiveness of, 55–58
  facultative, 202
  directed, 5
  innate, 200–201

origins of, 173
phenotypic, 4, 149–150
processes and results, 208
pseudoexogenous, 199
role of behaviour, 355
selection in, 245–248
special status of, 7
trial-and-error, 157–159
adaptationist fallacy, 444, 448, 467–469
adaptedness of ancestors, 211–212
adaptive range, 420
adaptiveness of behaviour, 416
aggregations, 258
alleles, 8, 42, 46–47
allometric growth, 158
allopatry, 210, 225
alternatives, 41
analogy, 316, 322
  vs. homology, 293
analogical reasoning, 275, 291, 313, 317
analogs, 280
animal-environment relationship, 425
anthropomorphism, 20
a priori, 63, 121–143
  and *a posteriori*, 122
a posteriori, 124, 132
asexual organisms, 284
assimilation, 9, 146–150, 153, 458
association, 137, 139, 414
associationism, 447
associative learning, 445–448
autogenous motility, 364, 369–373
autoregulation, 396
autoregulatory feedback, 155

autoselection mechanisms, 452–469

Baldwin effect, 119
behaviour, 190, 201, 205, 355–356
    and evolution, 205–254
    and morphology, 229–232
    as cause, 10
    comparative study of, 10
    definition of, 10
    development of, 391–410
    inheritance of, 231–232
    measurement of, 230
    role in evolution, 175
    variation in, 230–231
behavioural embryology, 363–390
behavioural interpretation, 232–240
behavioural patterns, 205–206, 230
behaviourism, 205, 303, 432
biology, analytical, 173
    and behaviour, 9–11
    physiological, 173
    synthetic, 173
blind exploration, 74
blind variation, 8, 77f
body–mind problem, 119
Brownian particles, 258, 267

canalization, 5, 25, 184, 196–197, 349,
    353–355, 383, 420
categories, Kant's, 96–101, 121–143
causal explanation, 27
causality in biology, 9, 17–38, 121–143,
    192
causation, 344
    circular, 192, 462
    downward, 347
    proximate, 446
    ultimate, 17f, 446
causes and effects, 159, 198
cell differentiation, 331, 334
cell division, 336
cell enlargement, 336
chance, 158
change, 41, 288, 397, 450
    in form, 331, 333
    location of, 155
    rapid response to, 197
    time scales of, 434, 450
changing environment, 317

character divergence, 224, 239, 242
character–environment correlations,
    209–210, 245
characters, acquired or inherited, 180
choice, effects on evolution, 175
chreods, 149, 393–396
chromosomal associations, 158
classes, 278, 284
classes vs. individuals, 282
clouds and clocks, 109–119
coenetic variable, 425, 428, 433–435
coevolutionary phenomena, 241
cognitive constructs, 435
    function, 11
    in animals, 9
    mechanisms, 148
    processes, 353
colonial nesting, 233–235
colony founding, 269
communication, 255–272
comparative problem, 456–469
comparative research, 126, 135
comparisons across species, 165
computer problem solving, 86
conceptualization, 66
conditioning, 137, 364
conjectures, 164
consciousness, 20, 65–67, 115
conservatism, 350
conspecific cuing, 259
constraints, 168, 393
    on epigenesis, 435–436
    on learning, 443–449
control theorists, 400
conventionalism, 103
coordinate system, 334
courtship display, 237–239
creative processes, 7, 78
cross-lineage borrowing, 299–300
culture, 232, 346, 355, see also socio-
    culture
cultural cumulation, 89
cultural evolution, 356–358
    see also socio-cultural evolutio~
cultural pool, 451, 466
cultural tradition, 242
cybernetics, 18, 25
cytoplasmic inherit~

damping ~

Darwinism, 39, 164, *see also*
  neoDarwinism *vs.* Lamarckianism,
  278
deduction, 84
descent with modification, 207
design, in organic world, 174, 177
determinative influence, 385
determinism, 40
  vs. chance, 113
development, 3, 52, 152, 155–156, 173,
  180, 195, 343–361
  and evolution, 331–342, 343–361
  arrested, 152
  as a programme, 341
  as selective not instructive, 337
  as unfolding, 155–156
  behavioural, 391–410, 411–442
  dichotomies, 417–418
  facilitation of, 399
  intrinsic constraints, 392
  neonatal, 269
  neurobiological, 365–368
  of language, 88, 397
  perceptual, 381–382
  prenatal, 363–390
  reactive, 392
  self-correcting, 394
  self-regulated, 155
  self-stabilizing, 393
developmental constraints, 340
  ecosystem, 424–432
  interactions, 337
  niche, 419–437
  noise, 156
  outcomes, 418–424
  pathways, 8, 399, 418–437
  self-regulatory processes, 196
  'rule of thumb', 420–424
  rules, 400–405
  stages, 165
  system as evolutionary unit, 217
  systems, evolution of, 411–442
dialectical interaction, 9, 162
differential fertility, 157
  replication, 277
  reproduction, 201
Ding an sich, 68, 100–101, 121–143
directive embryonic induction, 338
disciplinary matrices, 290
dispersion, 218
distance receptors, 79

division of labour, 53–55
DNA, 27, 34, 48–49, 76, 155, 173, 276,
  301, 341, 343, *see also* genes
  amount of, 50–51
  codes, 203, 286–288
  programmes, 17–38
dualism, 68

early experience, 381
echolocation, 79
ecogenotype, 183
ecological niches, 159
  a priori partitioning, 159
  universals, 447
ecosystems, 425–426
élan vital, 19
empiricism, 3, 201
end-directedness, 17–38
Entelechie, 19
environmentalism, 303
environmental modification, 266
  order, 6, 447
  range, 196
epigenesis, 149, 348
  variable, 451
epigenetic landscape, 185, 187, 348–349,
  353, 393–394, 399
  ontological significance of, 349–352
  process, 189
  rules, 346
  system, 191, 419–437
  theory, 5, 11, 216–217, 343–361, 466
  vs. genetic approach, 344–347
epigenotype, 148
epistasis, 215
epistemology, 63–71
equifinality, 394, 397–407
equilibration, 149–150
error-elimination, 109–111, 115, 286
ethology, 10, 236, 345, 415–417, 443
ethological isolating mechanisms, 238
evidence and theory, 448–449
evolution, adaptive, 197
  and behaviour, 205–254
  and change, 8
  and development, 331–342
  and pattern formation, 333–341
  as a knowledge process, 7, 73
  causal agents, 212
  conceptual, 288–322
  constraints on, 331

evolution, adaptive (*contd.*)
    coupled–uncoupled, 311, 356
    decoupling genes, 349–352
    degenerative, 197, 202
    direction of, 312–320
    emergent, 111
    epigenetic approach, 343–361
    exosomatic, 113
    intentionality in, 307
    Lamarckian, 277–279
    levels of, 8
    mechanisms of, 212–220
    memetic, 288–322
    morphological, 350–351
    of characters, 242
    progressive, 292–294
    saltative, 277, 295
    scientific theories of, 278
    socio-cultural, 273–327
    unified theory of, 12
evolutionary anthropology, 154–155
evolutionary epistemology, 3–13, 73–107,
    154–155, 159, 163–169, 273–275,
    277–278, 295, 305, 308, 319, 322,
    341, 344, 411–412, 435, 437
evolutionary phenomena, 205–212
evolutionary record and behaviour, 232
evolutionary tendency, 53–55
evolutionary theory, 3–471
    and prediction, 274–275
exemplars, 296–298
experience, 364, 366, 377, 385–386
explanations, functional, 313–317
    intentional, 313–317
exploitive system, 191
exploratory behaviour, 355
extinction, 44–45, 320

facilitation, 371, 377–382, 386
facilitative effects, 383
    influence, 385
facultative response, 200–201
feedback loops, 285–288, 314–316
field concept, 334
final causes, 17–38
fitness, 42, 46, 157–158, 208
    frequency-dependent, 157
    mean phenotypic, 46, 466
    peaks, 214–216
food preparation, 239–240
foraging, 416, 446

form, and behaviour, 355–356
    and function, 352–355
    changes in, 331, 333
fossil record, 351
free will, 318
functional validation, 398
functions, determinative, 365–368
    facilitative, 365–368, 377
    inductive, 365–368, 377
    maintenance, 365–368
function–function relations, 389

gamete transfer, 258, 261–262
generation overlap, 266, 268
generative programmes, 333
genes, 7–8, 12, 41, 46, 173, 177, 283–288,
    291–292, 307, 367–368, *see also*
    DNA
    analogs to, 279
    as construct, 346–347
    definition of, 42
    feedback to, 346
    flow, 285–288
    hegemony of, 155
    mutation, 5, 177, 189
    numbers of, 332
    pool, 7–8, 12, 285–288, 451, 466
    selectionists, 273–277
genetic, assimilation, 149–150, 166–167,
    185–188, 195–203, 216, 353–355
    drift, 217, 248
    fallacy, 448
    fixation, 217, 248
    programmes, 27–29, 343
    system, 148–150, 190
    variation, 200
genetical hitch-hikers, 158
genome, 148–150
genome-balance, 215
genotype, 27, 41, 155, 157, 281, 287,
    308–312
    unity of, 285–287
geographic isolation, 214, 217, 294
global–local constraints, 317–321
goals, 17–38
goal-directedness, 5, 17–39, 281, 306, 317,
    397
gradualism, 4
group composition, 269
group function, 269
growth, 339

g–t–r heuristic, 452–469

habit, 81–82, 355
habitat choice, 190, 246–248, 384
habituation, 364
heredity, 173
hereditary changes, 176
heritability, 231–232, 398
heterochrony, 340
hierarchies, 347
hierarchical, level, 148
    organization, 168
    system, 109, 111
hierarchy of knowledge processes,
    443–471
histological differentiation, 54
historical entities, 274, 278, 314, 322
    and conceptual systems, 288–300
    species as, 279–288
homeorhesis, 149, 216, 281, 316
homeorhetic systems, 282, 285, 314, 394
homeostasis, 31, 281, 315
homeostatic systems, 282, 285, 314
homology, 10, 165, 211
honey bee dancing, 235–236
hopeful monsters, 199
hormones, 366–368
hybridization, 242, 299–300
hypotheses, 84, 110–113, 128, 132

idealism, 63
    critical, 121
    transcendental, 121
imitation, 74, 87, 356, 461–462
imprinting, 383, 401–402, 464
inclusive fitness, 256, 267, 268, 270
individual differences, 391
induction, 75, 84, 164, 338, 386
inductive achievements, 77
    effects, 435
    inference, 83
    influence, 383–385
industrial melanism, 178, 225–228
information, 21, 24, 27–28, 200, 201, 400
    and knowledge, 6
    genetic, 47–51
    positional, 333, 338
    propagation, 6
    state, 6
    store, 450
    theory, 18, 27

translation, 6
zygotic, 50
information-gain, 6, 443–471, see also
    knowledge gain
    algorithm of, 7
    fundamental levels of, 7
    nested hierarchy, 8, 76–92
inheritance, cultural, 240
    extragenetic, 232, 357
    of acquired characters, 175, 184
innate, forms of thought, 125
    modes of reaction, 122
    schemata, 164
    structures, 141
    structures of the mind, 128
    teaching mechanisms, 454–456
    vs. acquired, 345
    working hypotheses, 129, 133
input transduction, 161
instinct, 10, 81–82, 201, 303, 345,
    413–416, 419, 432, 451
instrumentalism, 95, 101
intention, 312–320
intentionality, 20, 278–279, 305
interactors, 316
interaction theorists, 400
intergenerational correlation, 221
internalization, 353–355
interpenetration of organism-environment,
    159–163

kin selection, 215, 270
knowledge and, activity, 9
    a posteriori, 455
    a priori, 455
    and reality, 9
    and truth, 67
    as a relationship, 6
    as dialectical interaction, 9
    evolution and, 73–107
    forms of, 76–92, 123
    in action, 412
    in biological terms, 6
    legitimation of, 3, 63–72, 73–107
    philosophy of, 3, 63–72, 92–104
    social, 168
knowledge-gain, process, 76–92, 443–471
    locus of store, 452–453
    universal algorithm, 75–78, 452–453
    in action, 412

language, 74, 87–89, 109
Lamarckianism, 9–10, 122, 175, 195, 197,
    308–312, 355
law of nature, 163, 283
learning, 11, 24, 27, 74–75, 159, 164, 346,
    354, 356, 364, 367, 381, 386,
    400–403, 411–442, 443–471
learning, and adaptation, 443–471
    and epigenesis, 432–437
    as a dialectical process, 443–471
    associative, 446–448
    biological boundaries, 414–417,
        444–456
    classification of, 461
    comparisons, 443–471
    constraints, 443–456
    costs of, 201, 451
    definitions of, 412
    ecological principles, 422–432, 461
    forms of, 416
    functions of, 463–467
    general principles, 445
    general process theory, 415–416,
        444–456
    individual, 301–307
    innate mechanisms of, 454–456
    instinct dichotomy, 413–417
    natural descriptions, 460–463
    observational, 87, 460, 462
    paradigms, 446–448, 457–459
    predispositions, 454–456
    priming, 455, 463
    social, 278, 301–320
    species-typical forms, 445–447
    taste-aversion, 414
    terminological inconsistencies, 457–459
    theories of, 81, 412, 443–471
    trial-and-error, 75, 306, 411
    unity and diversity, 444–456
    universals, 454
levels, 347
    heuristic, 450–453
    of evolution, 450–453
    translation between, 347
life cycles, 43, 52–53, 281
life history patterns, 267
lineages, 279, 291–292, 295, 316, 320
local–global maximization, 318–321

machine intelligence, 392
maintenance, 385–386

mate-selection, 214
maturation, 367, 389
macromutations, 351
mechanists, 18
meiotic drive, 43
memes, 154, 232, 273–327, 356
memory, 73, 82, 150
memotypes, 292–321
Mendelian genetics, 39, 157, 291, 296
metaphor, genes, and memes, 309–312
    in science, 151–152
    of trial-and-error, 152–155, 163
    of unfolding, 151–152
methodology vs. theory, 391
modifier genes, 350, 353
morphological complexity, 51–53
motor primacy, 369–373, 385
mutations, 42, 158, 164, 213, 333,
    343–344

naive realists, 127
nativists, 201
natural kinds, 274, 279, 282–285,
    288–290, 293
natural selection, 5, 21–26, 30–31, 39–59,
    65, 69, 75–77, 157, 165, 177, 189,
    191, 195–197, 205, 257, 267, 278,
    282, 285–288, 295, 298, 317,
    343–344, 346, 351–355, 367, 406,
    411, 419, 421–422
natural selection, definitions, 218
    of science, 91
    selector vs. interactor, 352
    vs. rational selection, 313
nature–nurture problem, 390, 411–437
neo-Darwinism, 4–5, 10, 177, 343–347,
    350–351, 357, 465–466, see also
    Darwinism
neoteny, 152–153
nested hierarchy, 76–92, 453–456
neuroembryological development, 368
neutral mutations, 349
noumena, 142
novelty, 402
nuclear-cytoplasmic compatibility, 354

objective truth, 63
objectivity, 101
ontogenesis and phylogenesis, 149
ontogenetic adaptation, 182

ontogeny, 22, 24, 52, 242, 280–281, 287,
    302–304, 392, 411–442, *see also*
    development and epigenesis
open programs, 24
optimal principle, 157
order, environmental, 6
    conserved patterns of, 6, 451–454
organism and environment, 151–170
organization and adaptation, 145–150
orthogenesis, 21–22, 40, 54
orthoplasy, 82

pair bonds, 261–262
pan-selectionist mechanisms, 212
paradigms, 290, 296–297
parallelism, 64, 350
parental care, 258, 261–262, 264–270
parturition, 258, 262
pattern formation, 331
Peircean indeterminism, 114
    system, 114
perception, 75, 135, 364
permanence and evolution, 41
phenocopy, 185–186, 349–350, 353
phenotypes, 41, 146, 308–312, 352, 367,
    418
    cultural, 356
    differential change, 221
    invariant, 419–422
    role in evolution, 4, 7, 276
    variable, 422–424
phenotypic differences, 220
    fitness, 5
    variation, 248
pheromones, 88
phylogeny, 205–207, 213–214, 248–251,
    282, 287, 302–310, 417
plastic controls, 109, 111, 113
plasticity, 40, 181, 385
pleiotropic effects, 158, 215
polygenic systems, 231
population geneticists, 303
positional information, 333, 338
post hoc ergo propter hoc, 138
pragmatism, 3, 93, 95–96, 99, 101–104
preadaptation, 45, 309
preformationism, 344–346
preparedness, 445
prescience, 8–9, 305, 312, 318
Preyer–Tracy hypothesis, 369–373

principle of, heredity, 153
    natural selection, 153
    the struggle for existence, 154
    variation, 153
problem, Levi-Strauss's, 169
    Marx's, 168
    Plato–Hume–Kant, 168
problem solving, 78–79, 109, 111
programmes, 17–38, 286–288, 316, 341
    closed and open, 27, 281
progress, 165, 316
    in evolution, 39–59
progressionism, 21–22
progressive evolution, 319–320
progressive science, 321–324
propagating selected variants, 77
proximity, sources of, 258
psychic selection, 64
punctuated equilibria, 351
purpose, 17–38

random mutations, 354
random variations, 177
rationality, 113
realism, 63, 74, 101
recapitulation, 153
reconstruction of environment, 167
red queen hypothesis, 243
reductionism, 151, 314, 343
redundancy, 399
reference classes, 274–275, 277
reflexes, 364
regulation, quantitative, 377–382
reinforcement, 398
replication, 275–277, 282
replicators, 275, 316
representations, nature of, 302
reproductive, competition, 46
    isolating mechanisms, 214, 218
    patterns, 201
research programmes and traditions, 290
responses *vs.* susceptibilities, 198
rules, change of, 405
    coordination, 405–408
    developmental, 405–408

scala naturae, 21
science, 90–92, 112
scientific community, 296–297
    discovery, 75
    hypothesis, 315–320

scientific community (*contd.*)
  laws, 283
  theory, 273–275, 294, 316–321
selection, 28, 32, 164, *see also* natural
    selection
  and phenotypes, 219
  and population genetics, 218
  and replacement, 219
  artificial, 229, 279, 314, 317–318
  coefficients, 41, 49
  directing, 210, 225–228, 239, 243, 245
  evidence for, 221–229
  group, 215, 217, 242, 246
  hypothesis or tautology, 221
  individual, 246
  intellectual, 312
  intergroup, 215
  interspecific, 246–248
  nature of, 218–221
  of concepts, 66
  organic, 82, 354
  pressure, 221
  reinforcing, 214, 218, 224, 238–239,
    242, 246
  processes, 77, 276–279, 285–288
  sexual, 241
  stabilizing, 206, 210, 214, 221–224,
    233–234, 241, 246
  theory of, 63–71
  unit of, 7, 215, 216, 220, 246
  vicarious, 79–92
selectionist views, traditional, 213–214
selective elimination, 75
  filter, 5
  retention, 76–92, 411
selfish gene concept, 343, 346
self stimulation, 426
sensitive periods, 399, 407
sensitization, 364
sensory function, 364, 374–377, 386
set theory, 284
sexual reproduction, 41
shifting balance theory, 214–216
sib groups, 260–264
signal modulation, 161
simulated prescience, 8
social behaviour, evolution of, 255–272
  origins and modification, 256
  population genetics, 256
social organization, 355
social relationships, 404

social roles, 405
social sciences, defining features, 314
social signals, 255–272
social states, definitions, 257
socially vicarious exploration, 87
sociality, antecedents of, 255–272
  evolution of, 256
  evolutionary continuity, 257
  study of, 255–272
societies, cooperative, 257
sociobiologists, 10, 267, 309, 313, 314,
    344–346, 354
socio-cultural evolution, 7, 11, 89, 90,
    273–327, *see also* cultural evolution
space, 121–143
spatial apprehension, 136
speciation, 4, 205, 206, 210–211, 246,
    248–251, 282, 285, 351
  and phylogeny, 210
  as furcation, 210
  by merging, 210
  change by, 245
  selection in, 245
speciation-dispersal hypothesis, 217–218
species, 274–278, 314–317
  historical entities, 279–288
species-typical behaviour, 364, 381, 386,
    419
species-typical environment, 413
steady state, 397
structural genes, 349
structure-function relations, 365, 367, 389
subjective utility, 64
sympatric species, 214
sympatry, 210, 224
systemic mutations, 351
systems theorists, 394

teleology, 17–38
teleomatic, 23, 29
teleonomic *vs.* teleological, 313
teleonomy, 17–38, 280–281, 285–286
template, 400
temporal sequence, 138
theories, 290
theories in science, 75
thing-in-itself, 121–143, *see also Ding an
    sich*
thought, 135
  mnemonic, 82
  visual, 82–87

time, 121–143
time scales, 434
tissue specialization, 54
transformational model, 152
transformational *vs.* variational models, 154
translation *vs.* relation, 347
transmission of differences, 220
trial-and-error, 109, 115, 153
trinism, 102
truth, and action, 64–71
    as practical results, 69
    evidence for, 64–71
    varieties of, 68

Umwelten, 101
utilitarianism, 101, 103
utilitarian nominalism, 103
utility principle, 63, 70

vagility of offspring, 265

variant behaviours, 8
variational model, 152
variations, 22, 73–92, 147, 153, 164, 196, 278
    and learning, 449–456
    blind, 77–78, 305–306, 411
    chance, 301–307
    generation of, 8, 77
    genetic, 197, 213
    phenotypic, 148, 218
    propagation of, 8
    selection of, 8, 77
viability of offspring, 265
vicarious locomotor devices, 79–81
    search process, 80
vision, 74, 79–82
vitalism, 18, 20

Weismannist assumption, 352
worlds, Popper, 102
world-views, evolution of, 67